SEEING IN SIXES

Six-image Projects from LensWork Readers

BROOKS JENSEN & MAUREEN GALLAGHER
Editors

Photography & the Creative Process

A Series by LensWork Publishing

On Being a Photographer

David Hurn/Magnum and Bill Jay

Letting Go of the Camera

Brooks Jensen

Single Exposures

Brooks Jensen

Single Exposures 2

Brooks Jensen

Single Exposures 3

Brooks Jensen

The Best of EndNotes

(LensWork #83)

Bill Jay

The Creative Life in Photography

Brooks Jensen

Looking at Images

Brooks Jensen

Seeing in SIXES

Six-image Projects from LensWork Readers

Brooks Jensen
Maureen Gallagher
Editors

LensWork Publishing
2016

Introduction

For some years now, I've had two independent ideas rolling around in opposite corners of my brain, neither of them fully developed nor coming to fruition. Recently, they bumped into each other and an exciting *LensWork* book idea was born. You now hold that book in your hands.

The two ideas are *micro-portfolios* and a *juried publication.*

Idea #1 — Small Projects

You are all familiar with the Japanese form of poetry called the *haiku* — micro-sized poems that are restricted to just 17 syllables. Are you familiar with a similar concept in fiction writing called the *six-word story*? Background: Supposedly, Ernest Hemingway (who was famous for his brief and compact writing style) was offered a wager that he couldn't write a story in just six words. "Easy," he said, and immediately offered up the following:

Baby Shoes For Sale
Never Worn

From this, an entire genre of writing was born which can be seen at a very entertaining website, www.sixwordstories.net.

I love the core idea of both the haiku and the six-word story: an art form of exceedingly compact style that challenges us as producers, and as readers engages our visual imagination. Well, if this is a good idea for written art forms, why not for photographic ones, too?

Since the beginning of photography, the multiple-image project has been a part of our medium. Most famously, the "photo-essay" was a staple of such publications as the long-defunct *Life* and *Look* magazines. Of course, here at *LensWork*, we have a 23-year history of publishing multiple-image projects. We studiously avoid the more common photographic phenomenon we refer to as "greatest hits" photography.

Yes, but …

There is a world of difference between a large *LensWork* portfolio of 12-20 images and a compact project that fits in half a dozen.

More to the point, you would be amazed how many absolutely wonderful portfolios we review and ultimately reject for *LensWork* because the project begins to repeat and/or devolve to secondary images after the first half-dozen amazing images. We've noticed this for years and it has been a frustration in our selection process. Quite simply, we see so much wonderful work that is just too short for the portfolio format of *LensWork*!

In fact, this is so common that for years I've wondered why: Is there something inherent in photography that lends itself naturally to a deeper exploration than is possible in *one image*, but fully satisfied in just a few additional ones? I've been exploring this in my personal project I call *Kokoro*—small bodies of work each encapsulating a single subject or idea. (see www.brooksjensenarts.com). I publish them as PDFs, but they could just as easily be gathered together in book form. Perhaps I will, someday.

So, what if there were (just to pick a number) a six-image presentation format for photography? Well first, there is an inherent problem in a six-image presentation: Where does one show it? This is too many images for a "greatest hits" presentation—either framed above the fireplace or published in single-image magazines; it's too short to be a book or even for publication as a portfolio in *LensWork*. To make matters worse, for *LensWork* we typically require 30-40 images in a submission so we have some editorial flexibility. Such a volume of work can be very intimidating for many photographers.

Elsewhere I've written about a similar problem with the fiction genre known as the *short story*. In essence, the format you and I now know as the short story simply didn't exist until the magazine business became ubiquitous. Without a medium for publication, there was no outlet for an author to find an audience for a short piece of fiction—so it literally didn't exist. Instead, writers wrote for the medium that could find an audience: long-form fiction which could easily be published as books. With the invention of the magazine business (roughly the mid-1800s), short fiction had a home and a new genre of writing and storytelling was popularized.

Similarly, where does the photographic project of a few images find a publication home? Simply said, without a vehicle for publication, the small, micro-project struggles to find an audience.

So, why not create a vehicle for such projects—a book of short … um … what shall we call these? I struggled for a name that defines them clearly:

- Micro-project (too brewery-sounding)
- Mini-portfolios? (too Austin Powers)
- Photo-essay? (too W. Eugene Smith)
- Short story? (too O. Henry)
- Sketches? (too Charles Dickens)
- Photographic sketch? (too Photoshop)

Perhaps a look at the content might help.

Small bodies of work tend to fall into a number of styles or categories. The most common are:

Exploring a common subject
Exploring an interesting place
Exploring an idea or concept
Personal diary, exposition
Narrative story, often over time
Extended portrait

There, of course, are numerous other possibilities, but these appear most frequently — at least in the form of submissions to *LensWork* .

I'll bet every one of you reading this has at least a few small projects of images that fit one of the above categories and would be a perfect fit for presentation of half-a-dozen images you'd like to have seen as a group.

And I should add, these are not diptychs, triptychs, or grids, i.e., multiple images intended to be seen as a visual singularity in the same field of view or picture frame.

I envisioned these small projects as a visual cousin to the haiku or six-word story — a compact expression of a single nature, possibly a story, definitely a theme, held together stylistically, and making a whole that is greater than the sum of its parts. Tight, distilled to the essentials, impactful, deeper than what is possible with a single image.

I still don't know what to call them, but I see them in the work of almost every photographer.

Which brings me to the second idea that has been rolling around in my brain …

Idea #2 — Juried Publication

In photography today, juried events are fairly common — in the form of magazine contests, gallery exhibitions, and even state fairs! We've always avoided that type of thing here, but in some sense, *LensWork* itself is "juried" — i.e., not everyone who submits work for review can be published. We do our best to bring you the best of what we see — and to some degree one subscribes to *LensWork* because of one's confidence in our editorial process. That's the nature of anthology publications.

The Book Concept

Other magazine publishers have "contests" for their publications, but as far as we know, none of them result in a book publication with all the attendant qualities of state-of-the-art printing that we use here at LensWork. We want this book to be an inspiration for the long-term — not a 30-day disposable "exhibit." These photographs (and their creators) deserve more attention than that.

Seeing in SIXES was born from a juried process. Some 1,100 photographers sent in almost 1,900 projects for consideration. We had room for just 50 of them in this book. You are literally seeing less than 3% of the work we reviewed. Actually, this saddens me a bit because there were so many projects that we simply did not have room to include that truly deserve to be seen.

We founded *LensWork* in 1993 with a huge assumption based entirely on faith and very little evidence: that there exists a tremendous number of creative photographers working in isolation and solitude whose work is rarely seen because they are not — as I like to joke — a "famous dead guy." You can find these talented and productive photographers in the occasional solo exhibit of their work, sometimes as fellow participants in a workshop or photo group, occasionally by lucky happenstance of meeting a fellow traveler. We knew with *LensWork* we would have a vehicle to bring their work to light (no pun intended) in the pages of our bimonthly publication.

Similarly, we launched *Seeing in SIXES* as a *LensWork* community book project because we had the same faith that there was work deserving to be seen in a small-portfolio presentation. Our faith turned out to be true, but completely underestimated our readers' response. Quite literally, it was a painful process to cull the entries down to only the 50 you see here. Talent and productivity in photography (and particularly in the universe of *LensWork* readers) is incredibly abundant. We are so honored to have all of you in our publishing family.

So, here are the 50 chosen projects. It is perfectly natural to wonder about our criteria for inclusion in this book. We looked for several things, not necessarily in this order: originality; consistency of style; engaging content that grabbed our attention; projects about life rather than about photography; images that complemented and supplemented one another instead of becoming repetitious; projects that engaged our imagination; projects that included compelling text that expanded the viewing experience; projects that reflected a point of view rather than a camera's view; excellence of craft both photographic and with text; projects that created their own small world within the limitation of six images only. Selections like this are, of course, a matter of personal taste. We didn't always agree as we were reviewing all the projects, but all of us did agree on the project that made it into the book — and in truth, another 100 or so we could just as enthusiastically included had there been room for them.

What an anthology! Landscapes, still life, street photography, travel photography; intimate stories, poetry, narrative, no text whatsoever; abstracts, straight and classic black and whites as well as heavily imaginative Photoshopped flights of fancy — I hesitate to use the phrase "creative cornucopia," but it does most definitely apply accurately to what you will find in these pages.

Most importantly, these are visual expressions of ***life***. For decades now, readers of *LensWork* have read my philosophy that photography should be not "about light" as is so often read in photographic literature, but rather about *life*. Cameras and light are our *tools*, but not our *subjects* — if we want our photographs to be considered art. Excellence in craft is a fundamental, but as you will see in this book, it is content *about life* that still remains king. Sometimes that "about life" is as simple as a moment of observation and reflection, sometimes it is deeply personal and revealing, sometimes it is full of questions with few, if any, answers. It is life that binds us to each other and makes our photographic expressions accessible to non-photographers. We sincerely hope this book is of keen interest to the latter.

We've specifically sequenced this book so that every turn of the page to a new project brings a surprise and another small world to explore. Sips or gulps — however you choose to enjoy this book — we have no doubt you will return to it over and over again.

Needless to say, with such abundance in our *LensWork* community we are already looking ahead to another project like this in 2017!

Brooks Jensen
Anacortes, Washington

Table of Contents

Alphabetical Index by Photographer

Cinco Hojas: The Experience of a Cuban Cigar, in Cuba

by Kent Burkhardsmeier
kjbimages.com • burkphotos@hotmail.com

Story by Kent Burkhardsmeier and Michael Sperger; photos by Kent Burkhardsmeier

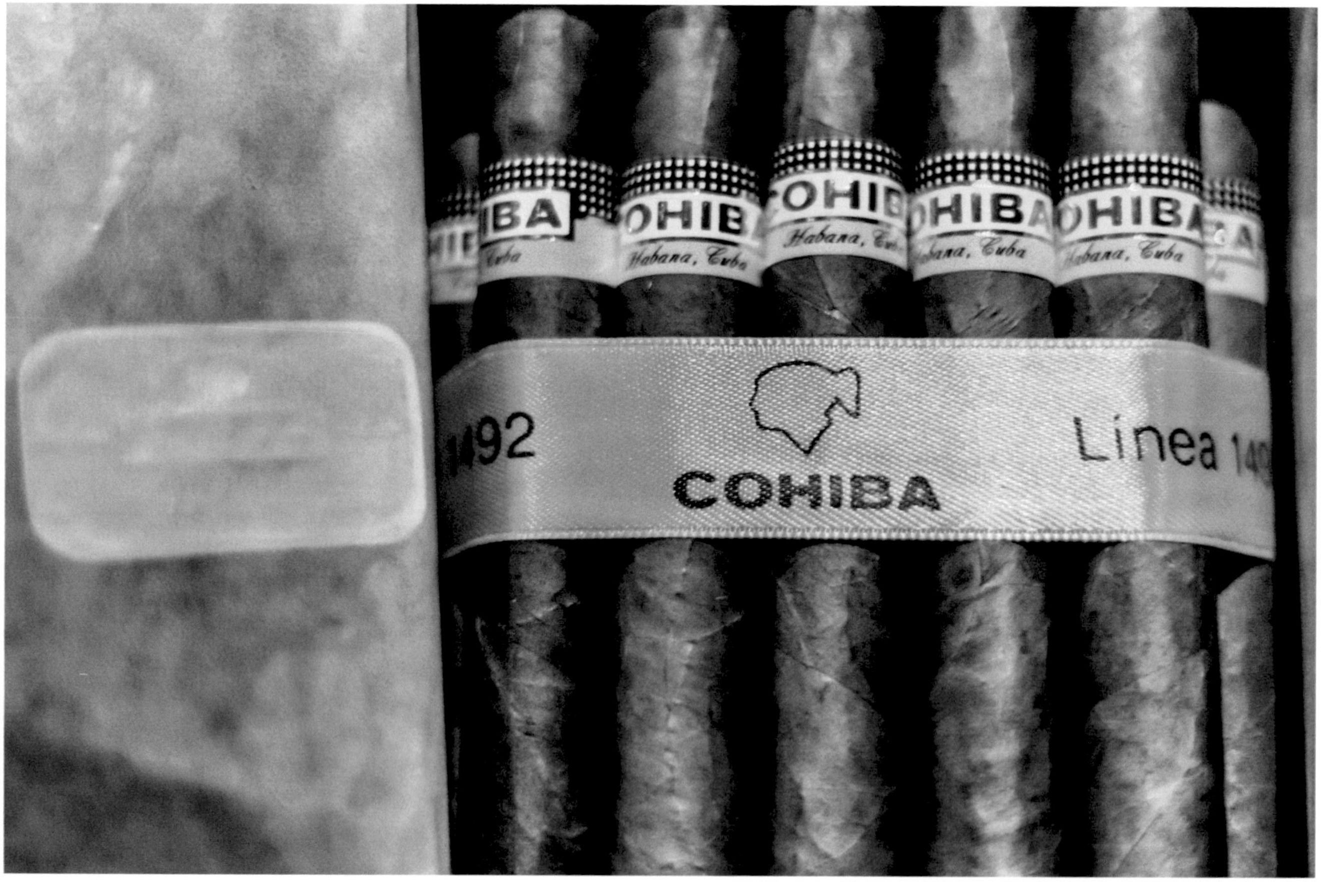

Cohiba Robustos

On a warm January evening, in a café in Santiago de Cuba, our tour guide, William, introduced us to the "real" art of cigar smoking. Cuban cigars are made from five tobacco leaves — cinco hojas de tobaco cubano. Each tobacco maker cultivates the leaves to provide a unique color, texture, flavor, aroma, air flow (draw), and burn.

William explained the origins of the top cigar labels and the significance of the various sizes of cigars. His favorite cigars are the Cohiba Robustos — handed-rolled.

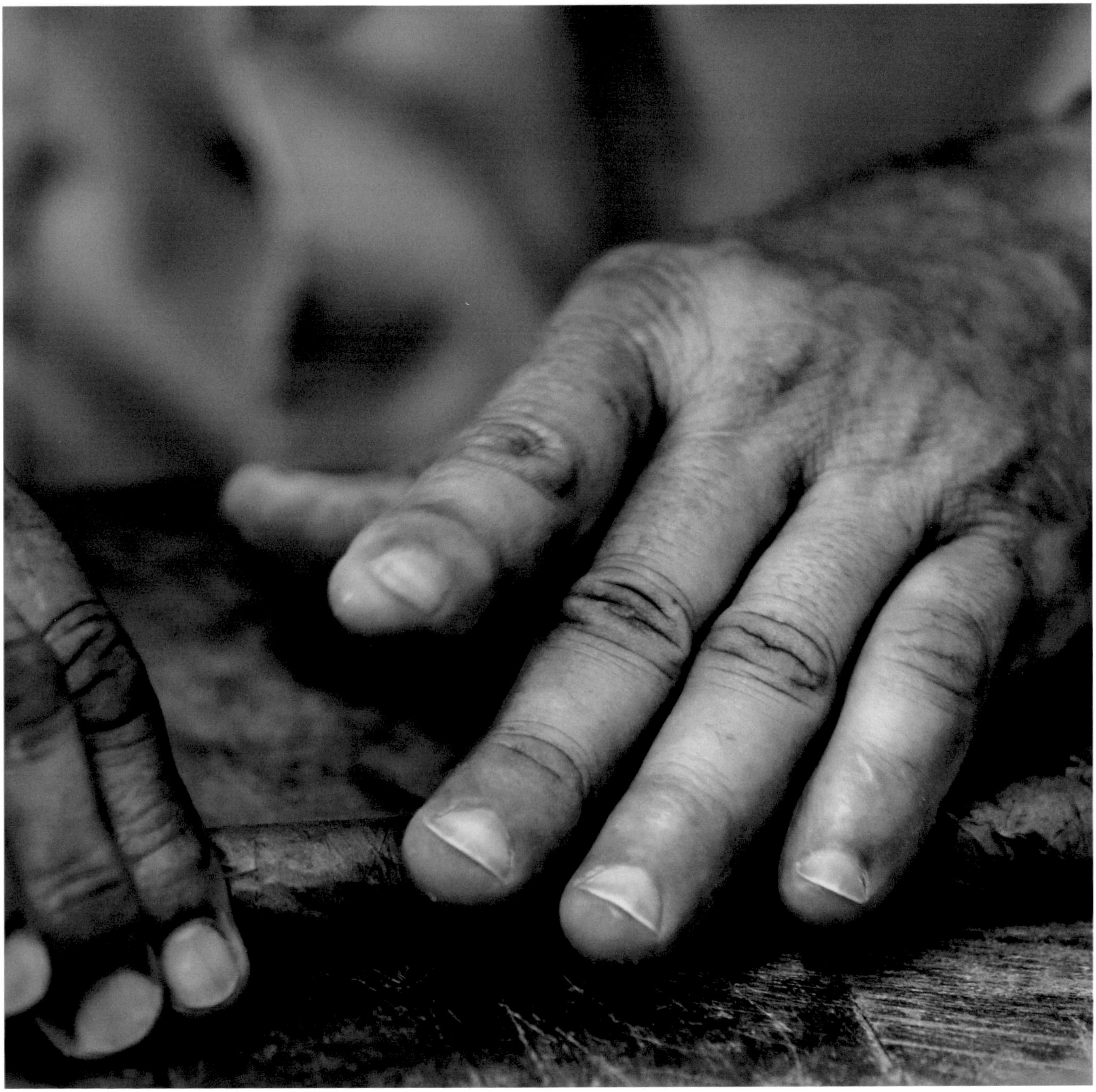

Hand Rolling a Cigar

William ordered a glass of rum (Santiago rum, claro!) and an espresso. He told us that these two drinks complemented the cigar's flavor and "enriched" the experience. Then, he gave each of us a cigar — instructing us to smell and feel them.

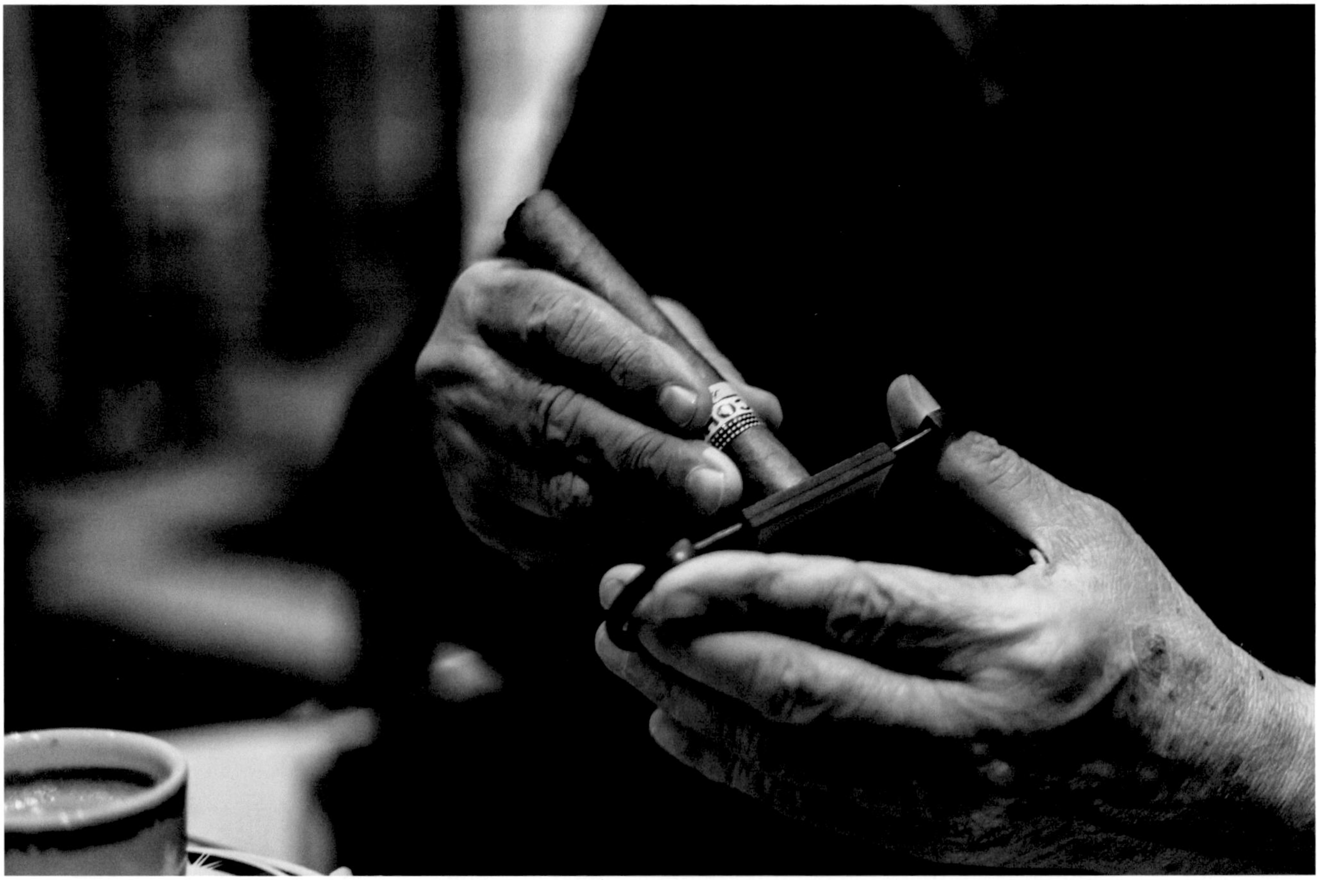

Special Cohiba Cutter

First, you need a special cutter. Not your typical cigar cutter that chops off the whole end, but one that would only cut off a fixed amount with tapered ends. This enhances the drawing of air through the cigar.

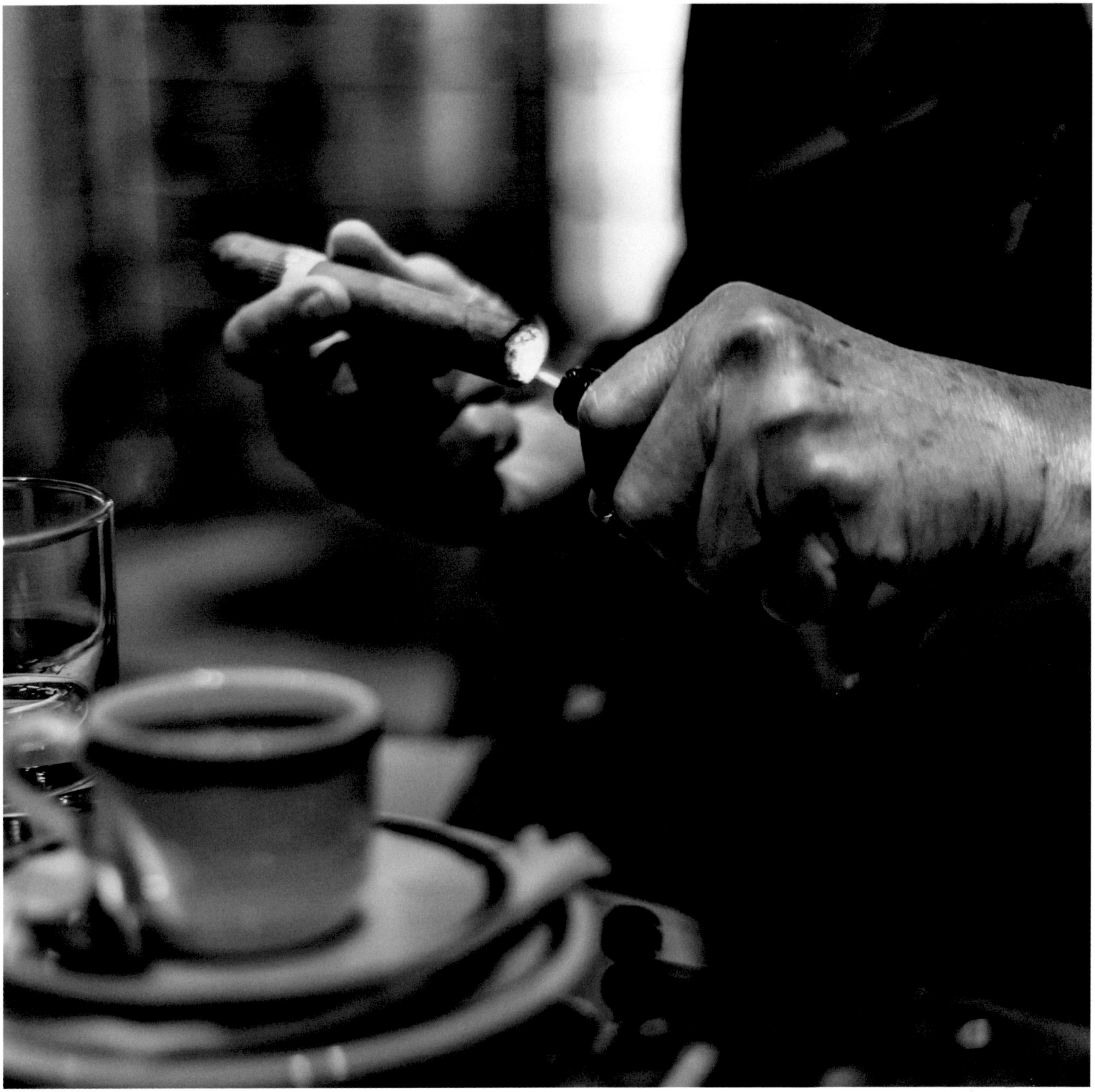

Creating an Even Burn

Next step was lighting the cigar. William emptied a pouch full of lighters. These were not your everyday lighter but mini torches. Some even threw two flames. The key, he explained, was establishing a nice even burn on the cigar before taking the first puff from it.

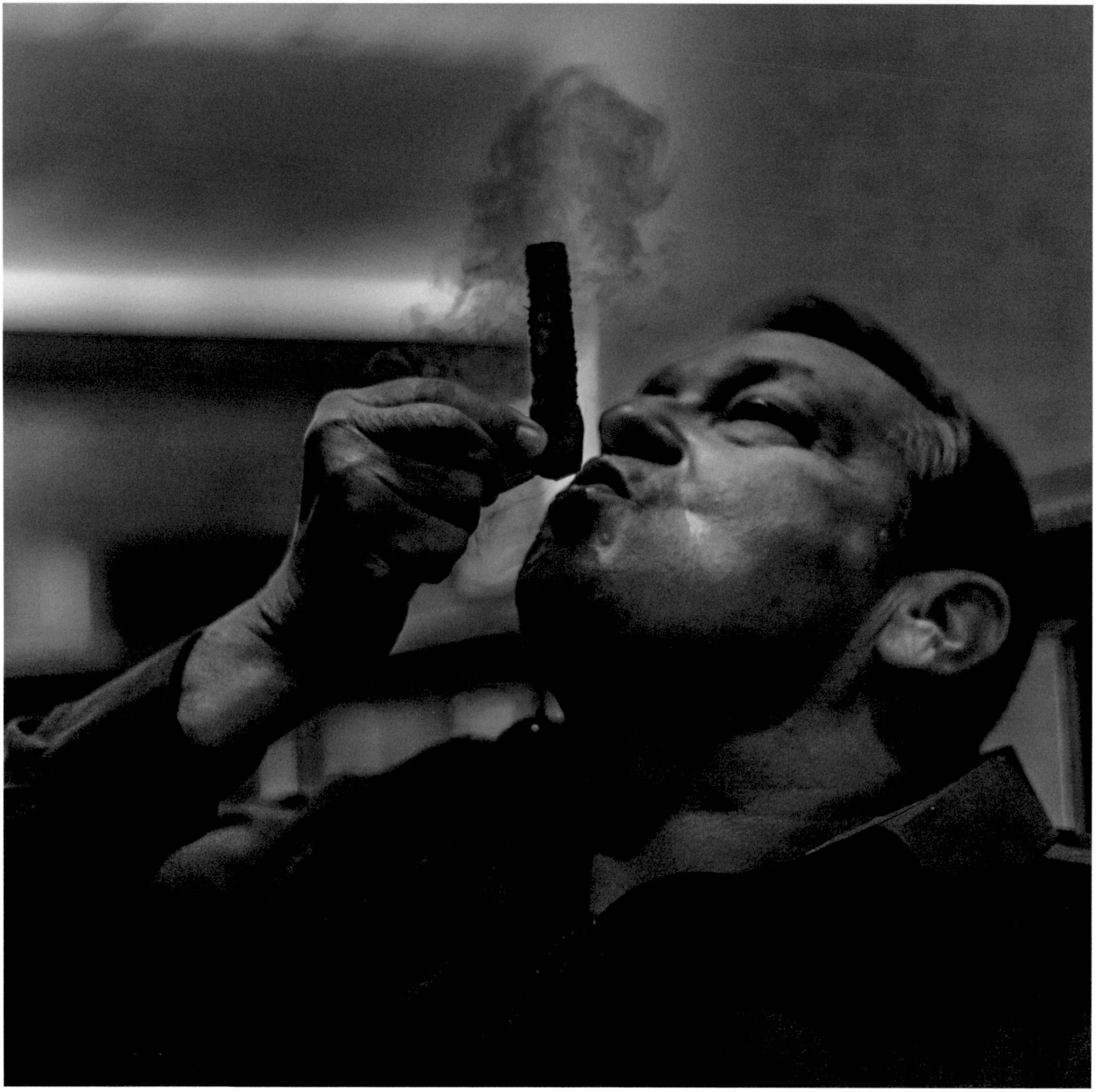

Stacked Ashes

Then, William explained how the flavor of the cigar depends on the ashes staying intact. Once they fall off, the cigar burns hotter, and the flavor becomes too strong. The key was keeping the ashes intact with the cigar for as long as possible — ideally until the cigar is finished — as he demonstrated his technique for us.

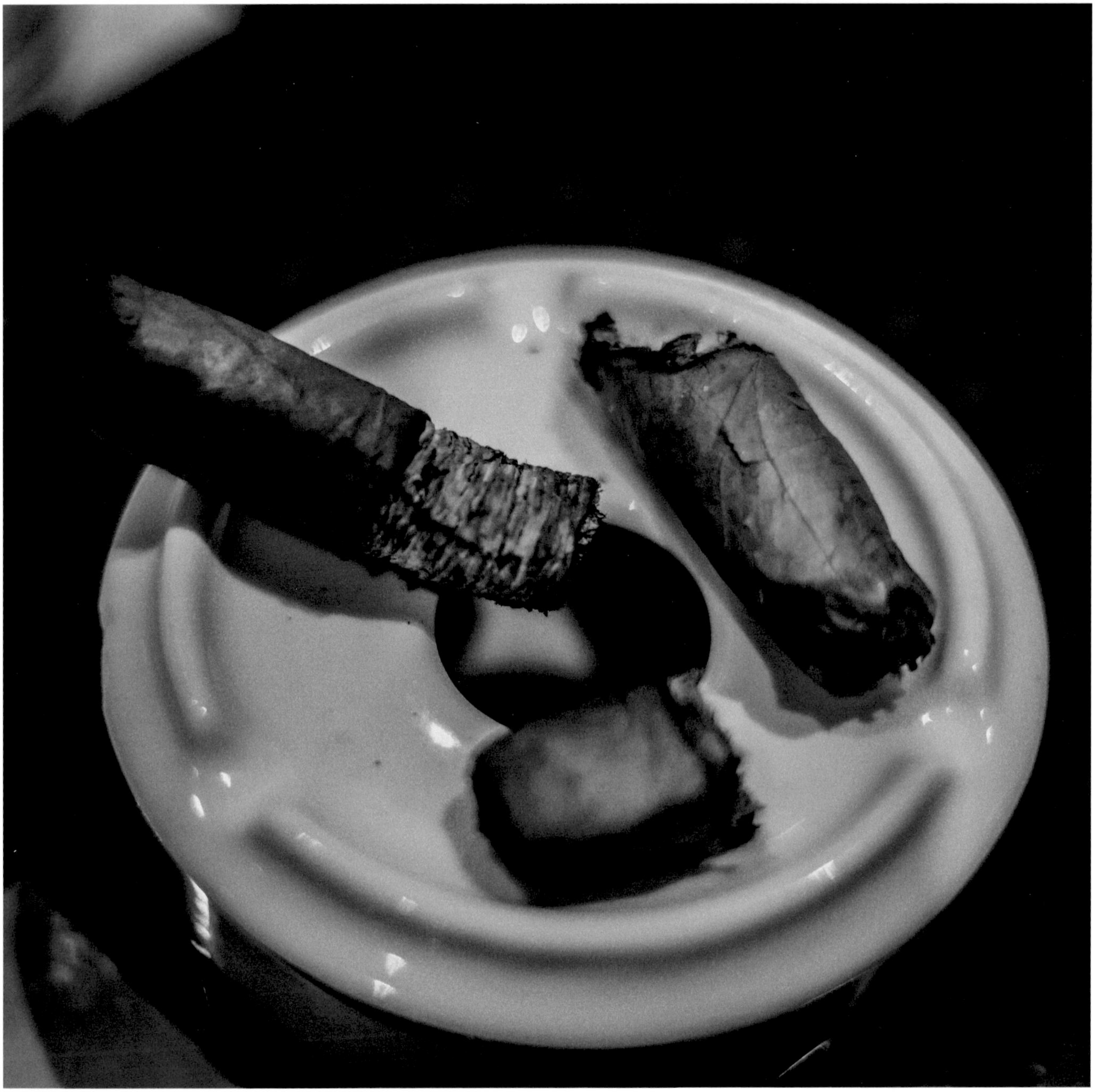

Dignity and Respect

Finally, after enjoying a proper cigar, one must show respect and appreciation by letting the cigar "die" with dignity.

"Never snuff out the cigar!" chided William. "Place it respectfully into the ash tray and let it burn itself out on its own time."

Mourning Tide

by Sharon Madden Harkness
sharonmaddenharkness.com ♦ sharon@sharonmaddenharkness.com

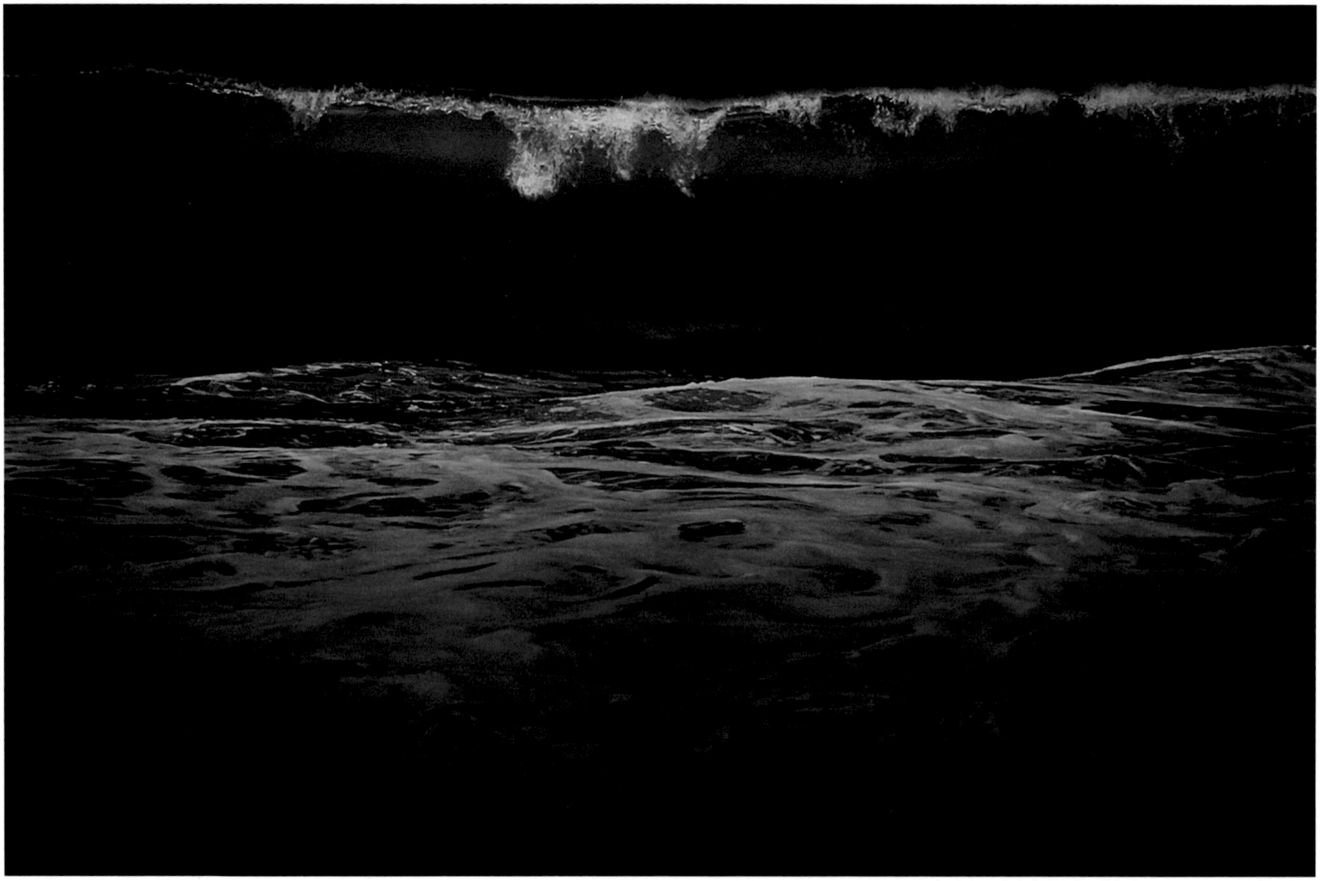

Entering grief I found
there were
no words,
only the pounding
rage
of loss.

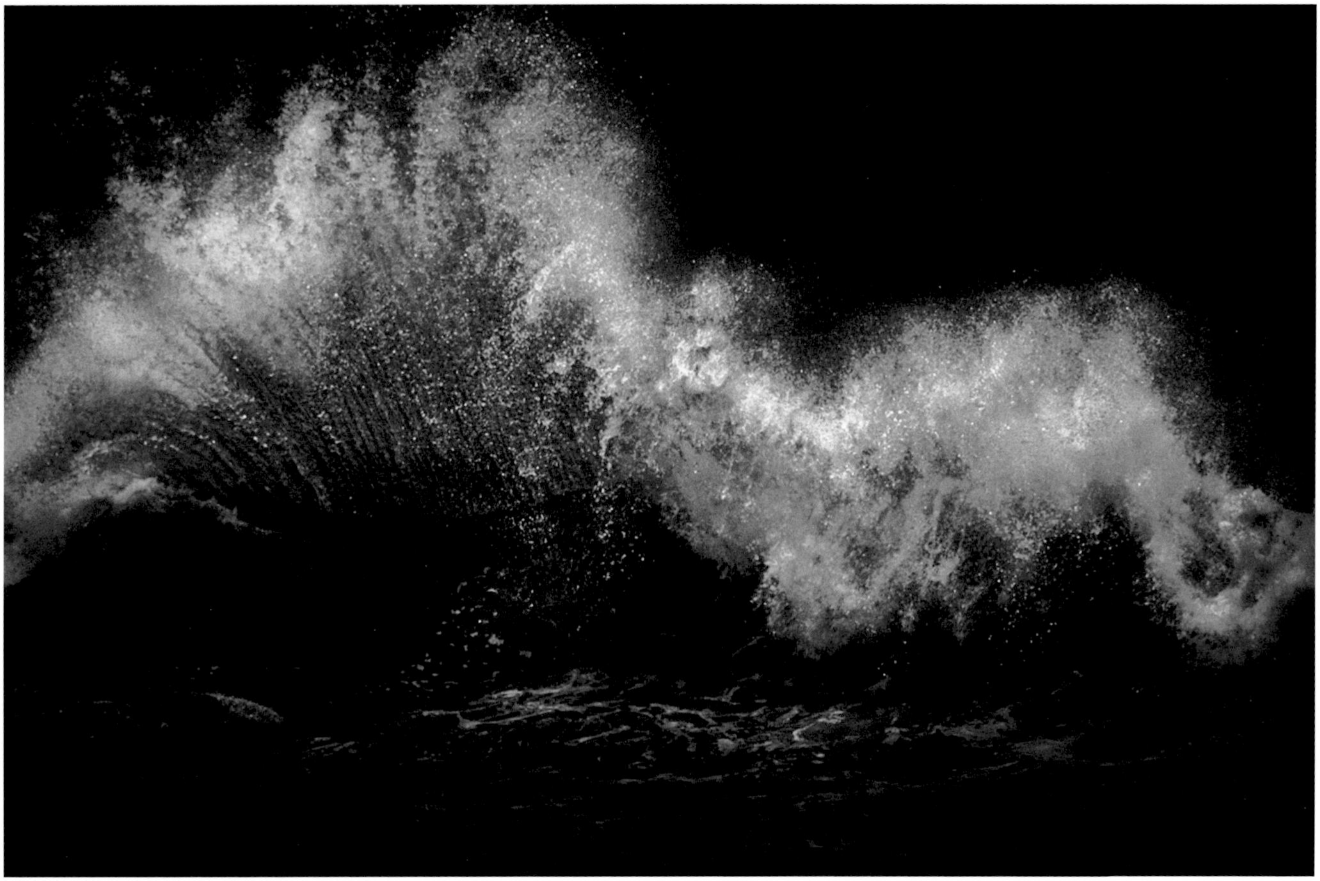

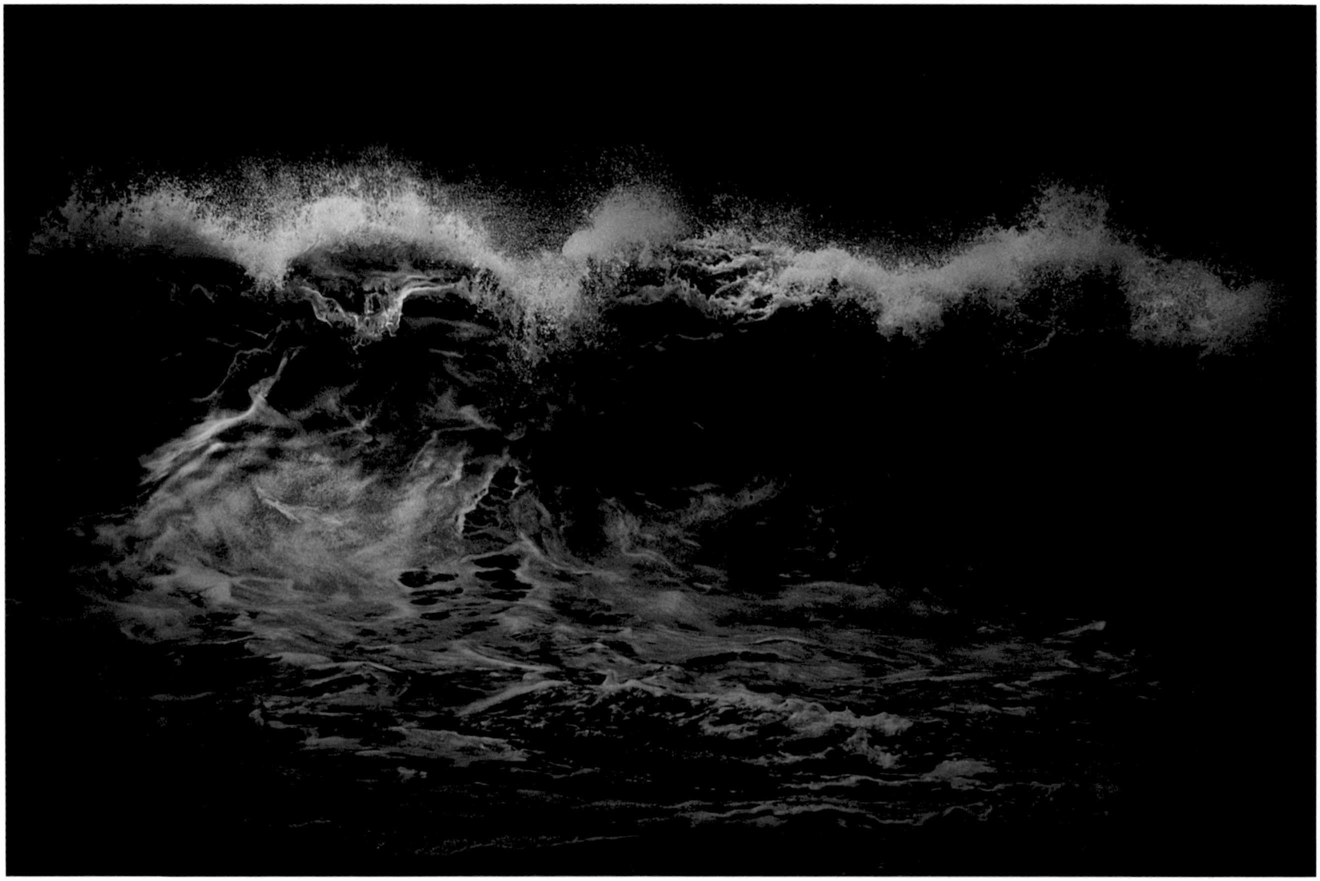

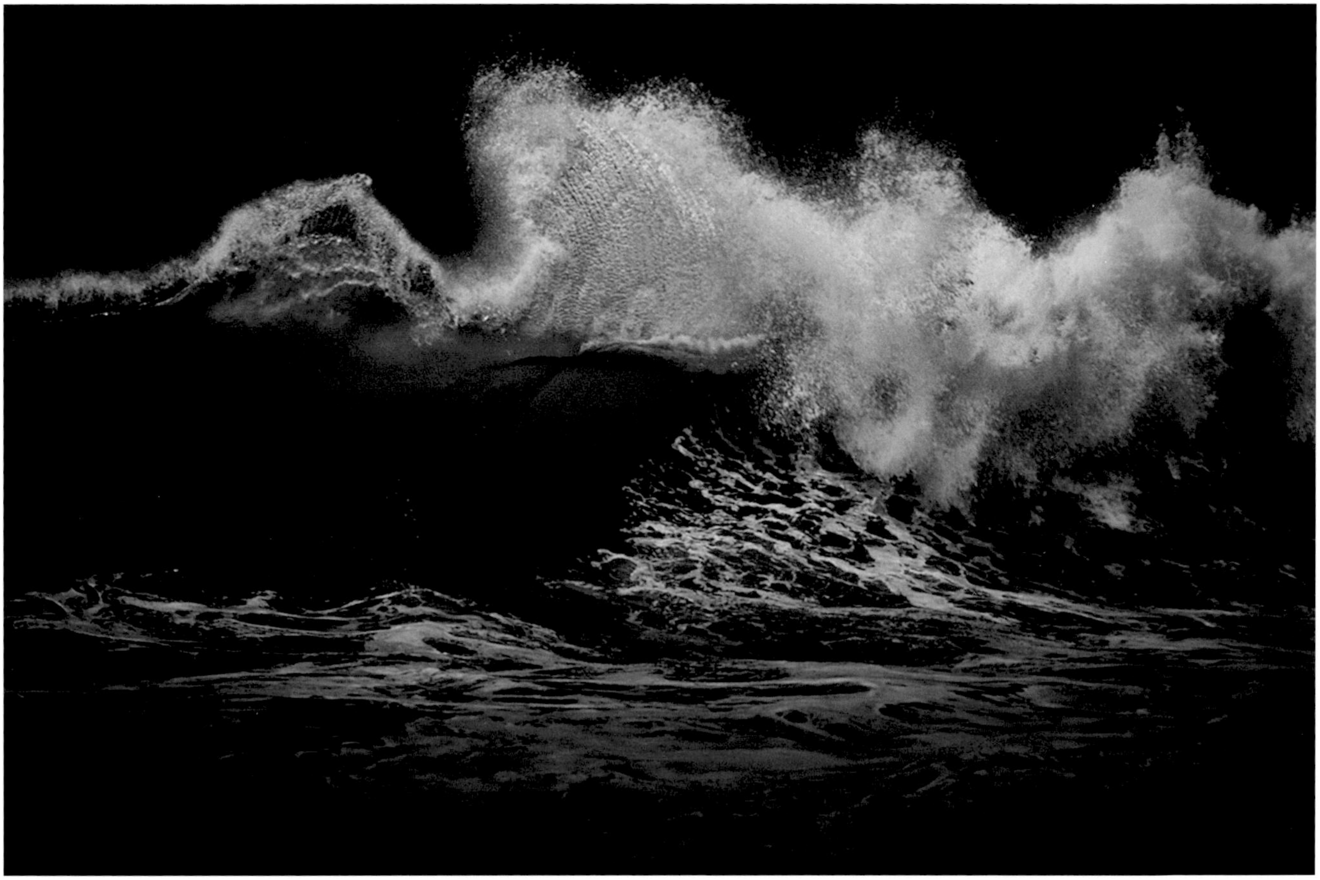

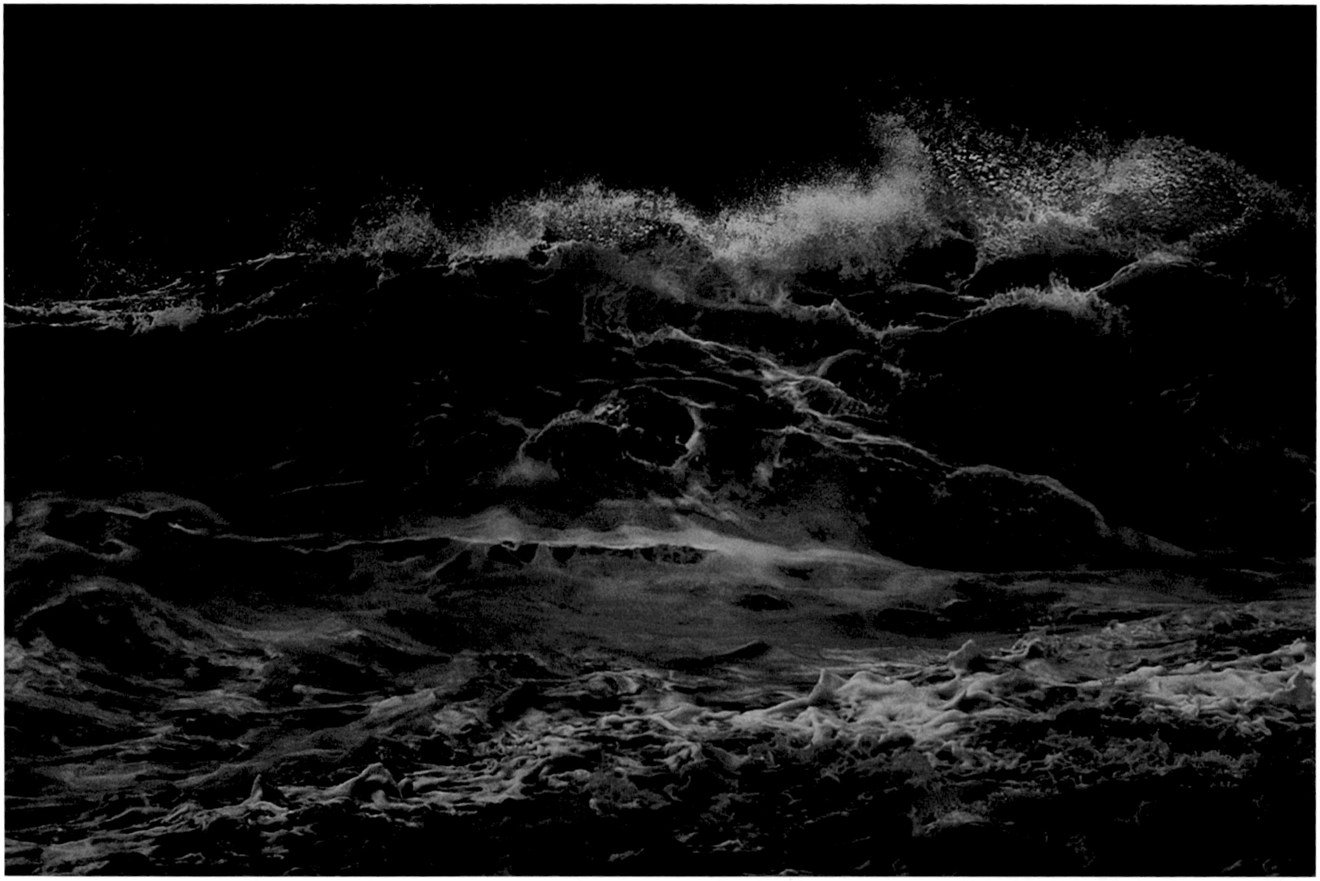

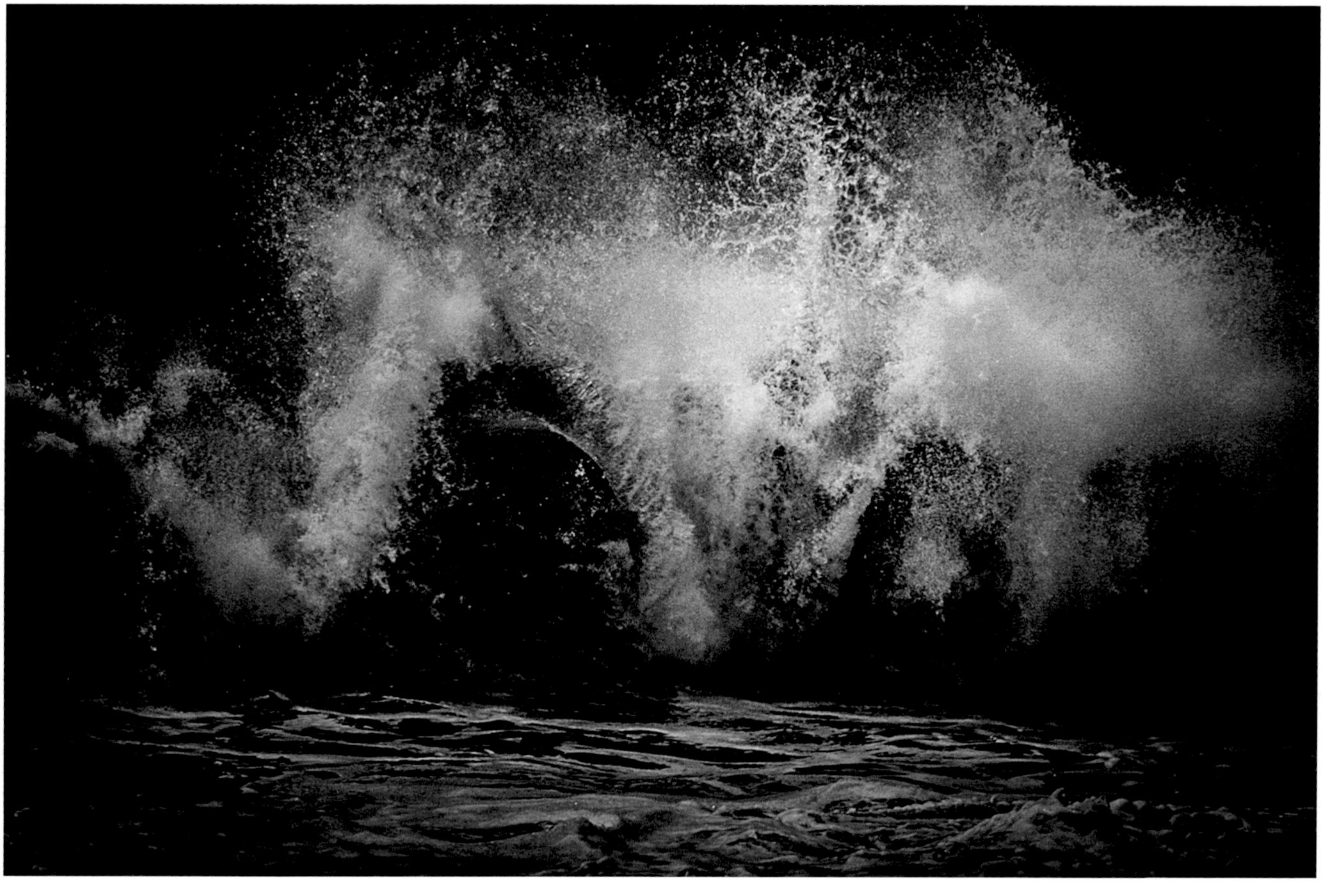

Death Valley Light: Death Valley National Park

by Jack Curran
www.jackcurranphotography.com • jack@jackcurranphotography.com

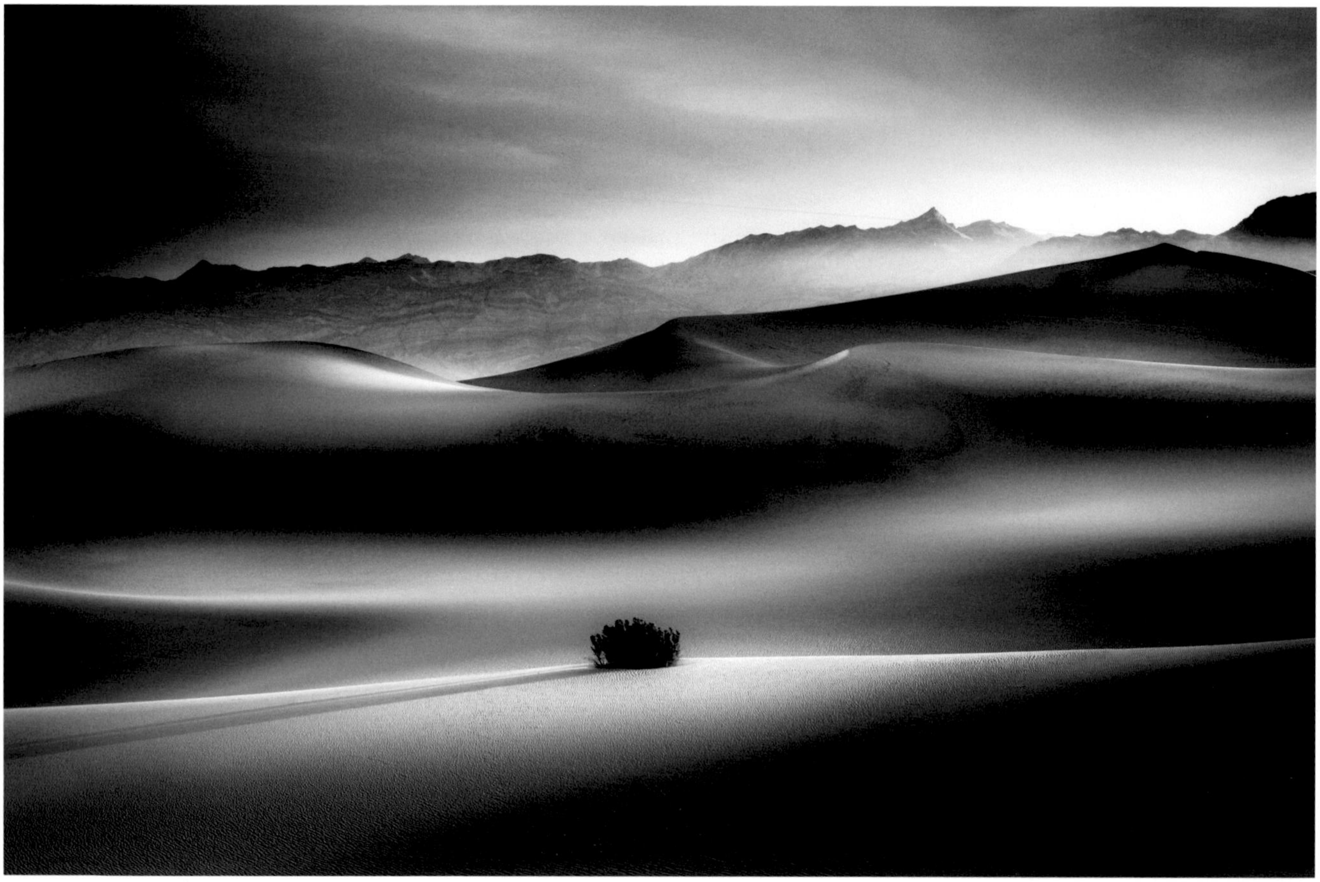

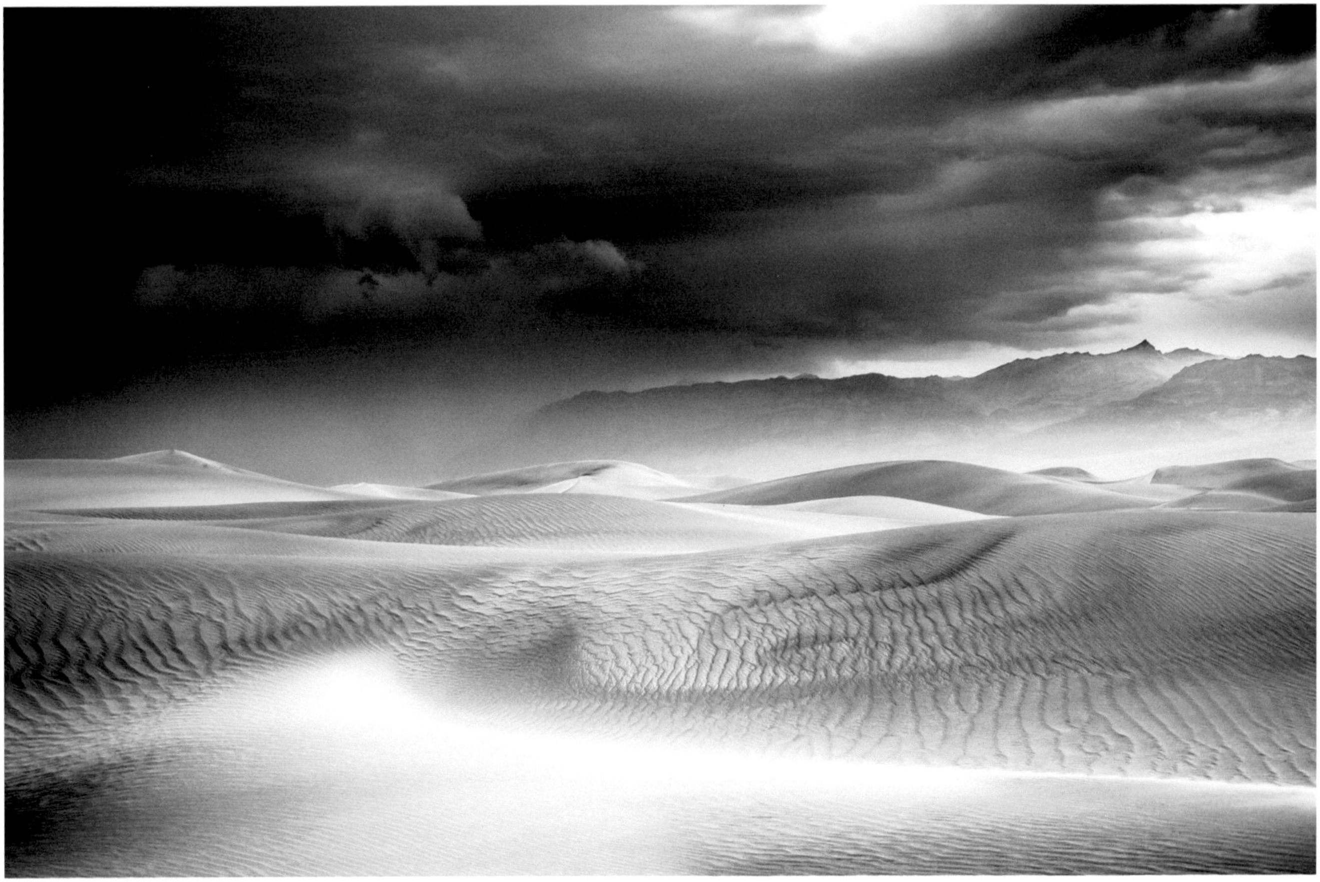

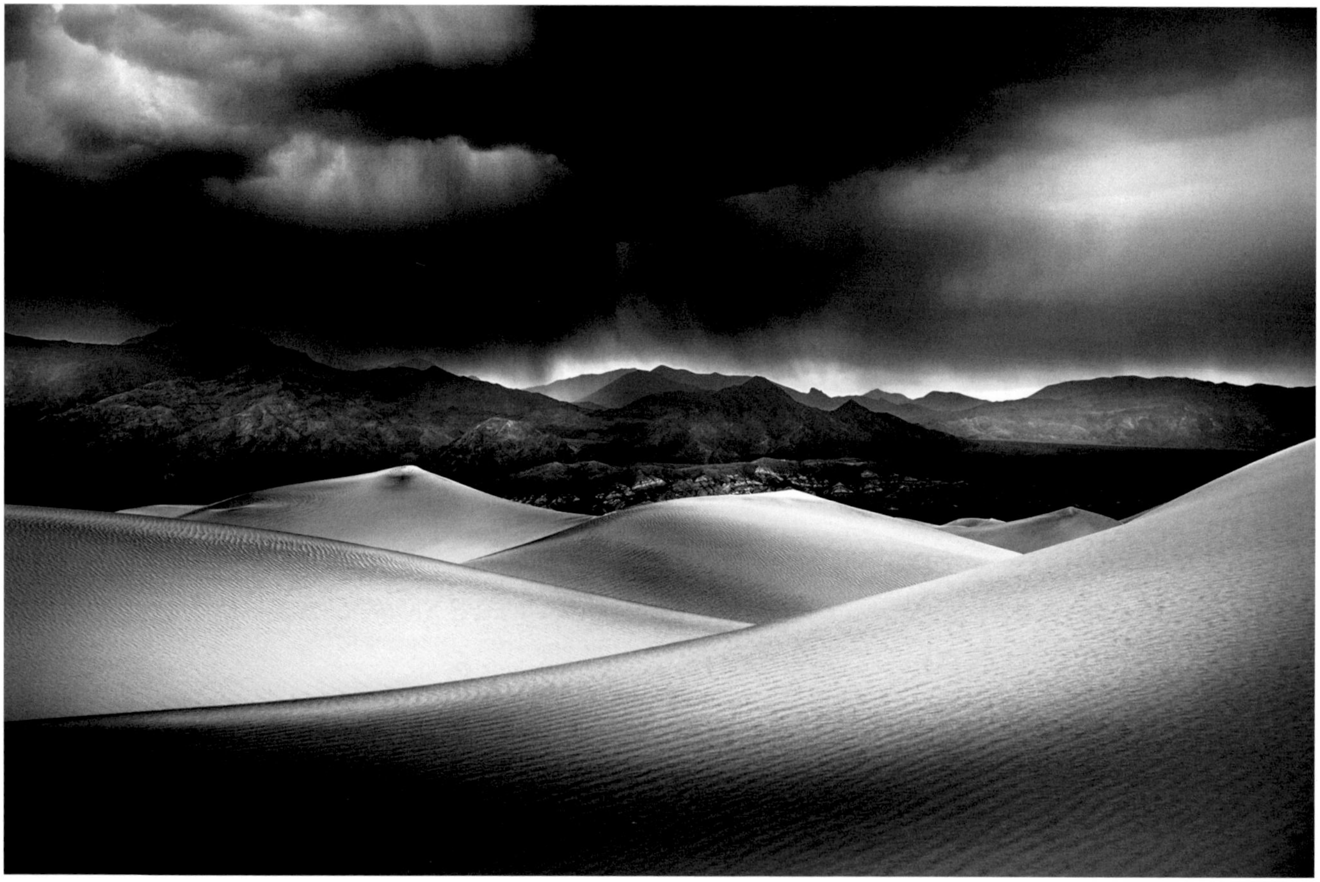

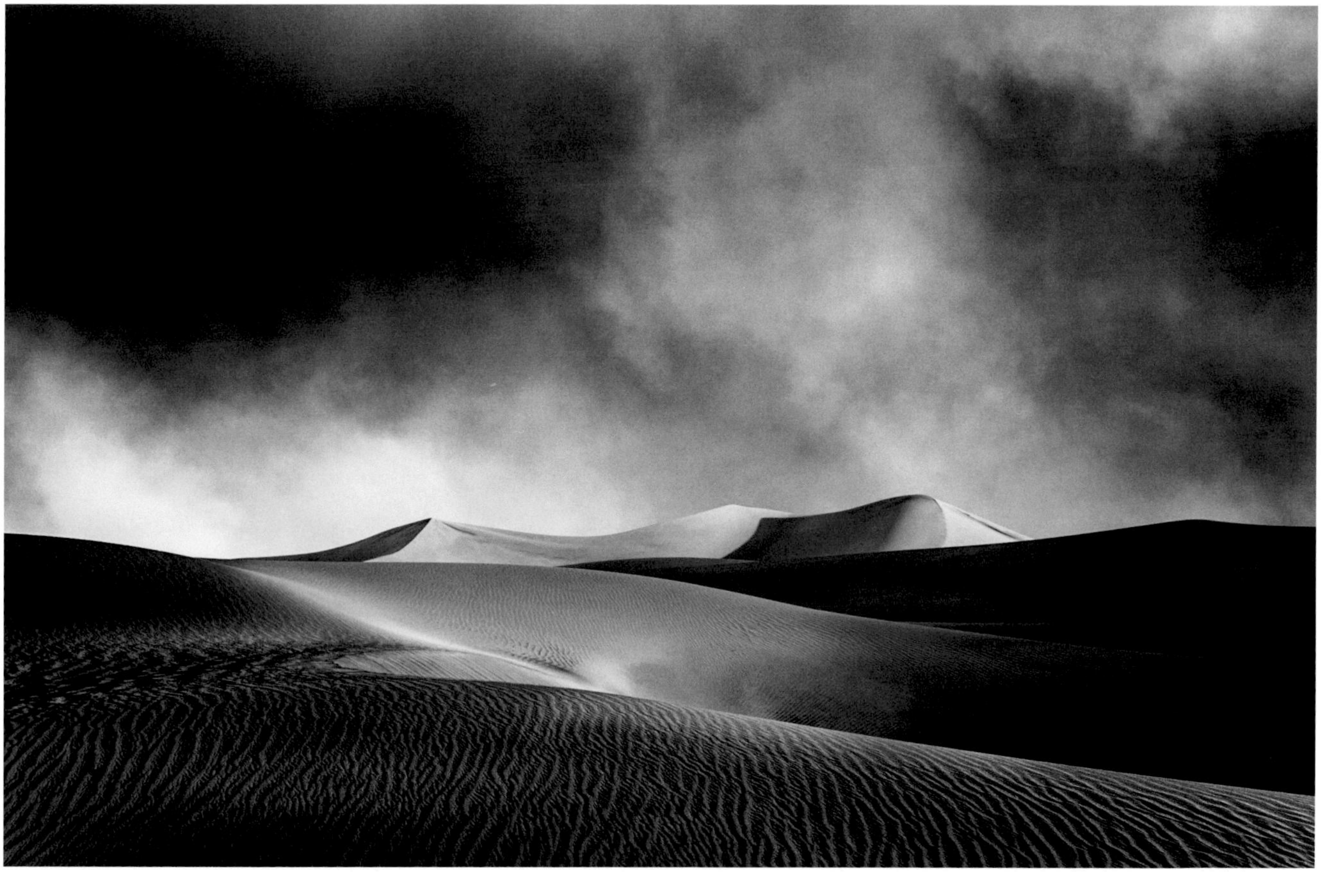

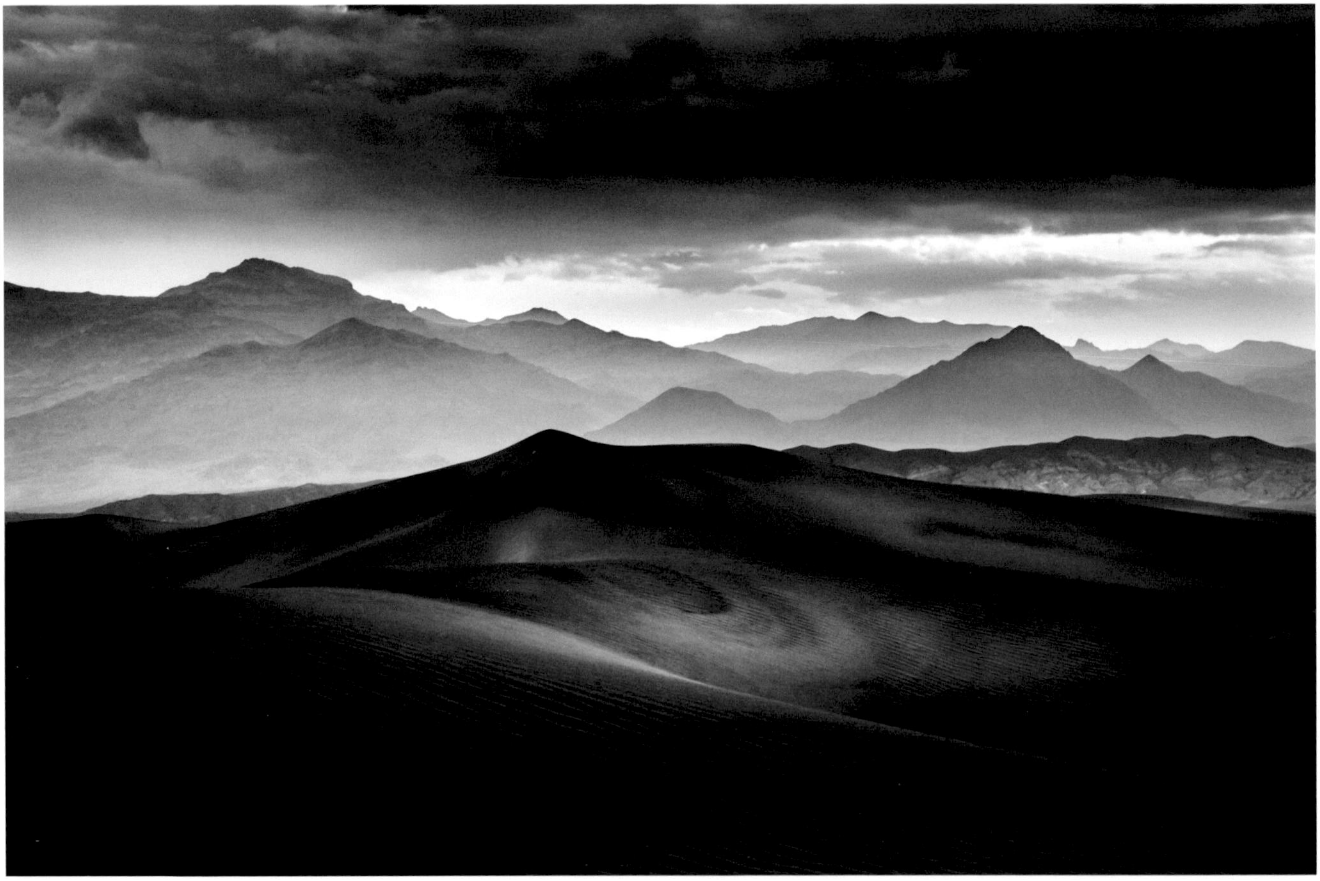

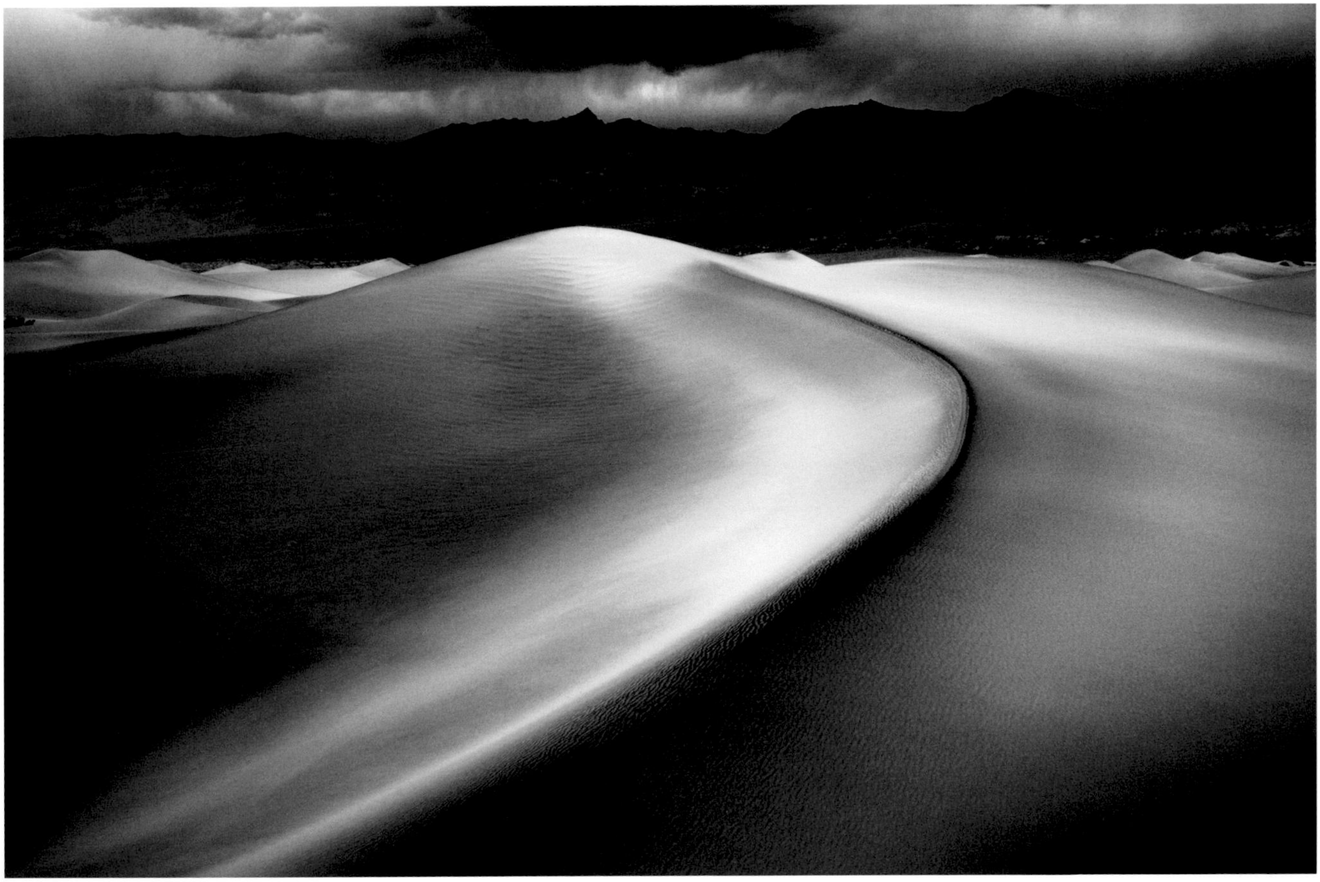

I went to Death Valley in May fully expecting to burn in the Sun and get wonderful high-contrast, highly-textured and rippled dunes photographs. What actually transpired was three days of overcast skies, extremely high winds, and the occasional thunderstorm. Of course, adapting to what Mother Nature delivers is all part of the game. During this particular visit to the park, I was so lucky to arrive at a time when the challenge of the weather also created great opportunity. I was able to focus on the quality of light to really bring out the diversity of the landscape, texture, and form.

Sundial Songs

by Robert Hansen

www.brightfamephotography.com • info@brightfamephotography.com

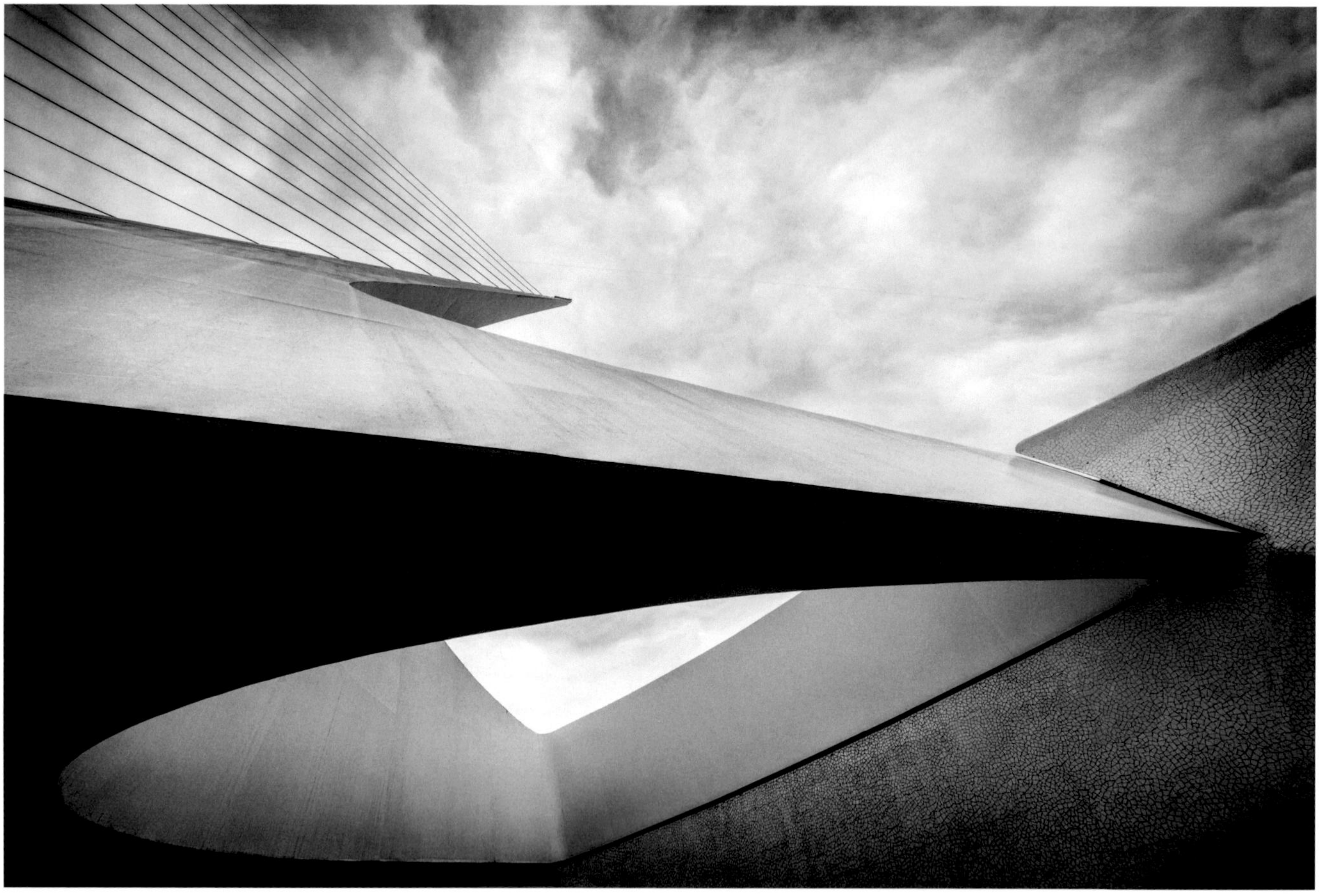

Sky Harp

I first saw the wonderful Sundial Bridge in Redding, California after a massive thunderstorm had flooded the Sacramento River and the sun was just starting to burn through the storm clouds. My first thoughts were of a harp and songs being lifted to the life in the clouds. What an incredible juxtaposition — the steel and glass of man lifting lilting songs heavenward, with the energy of the storm clouds drawing out nature's softening glow of approval. Enjoy the music.

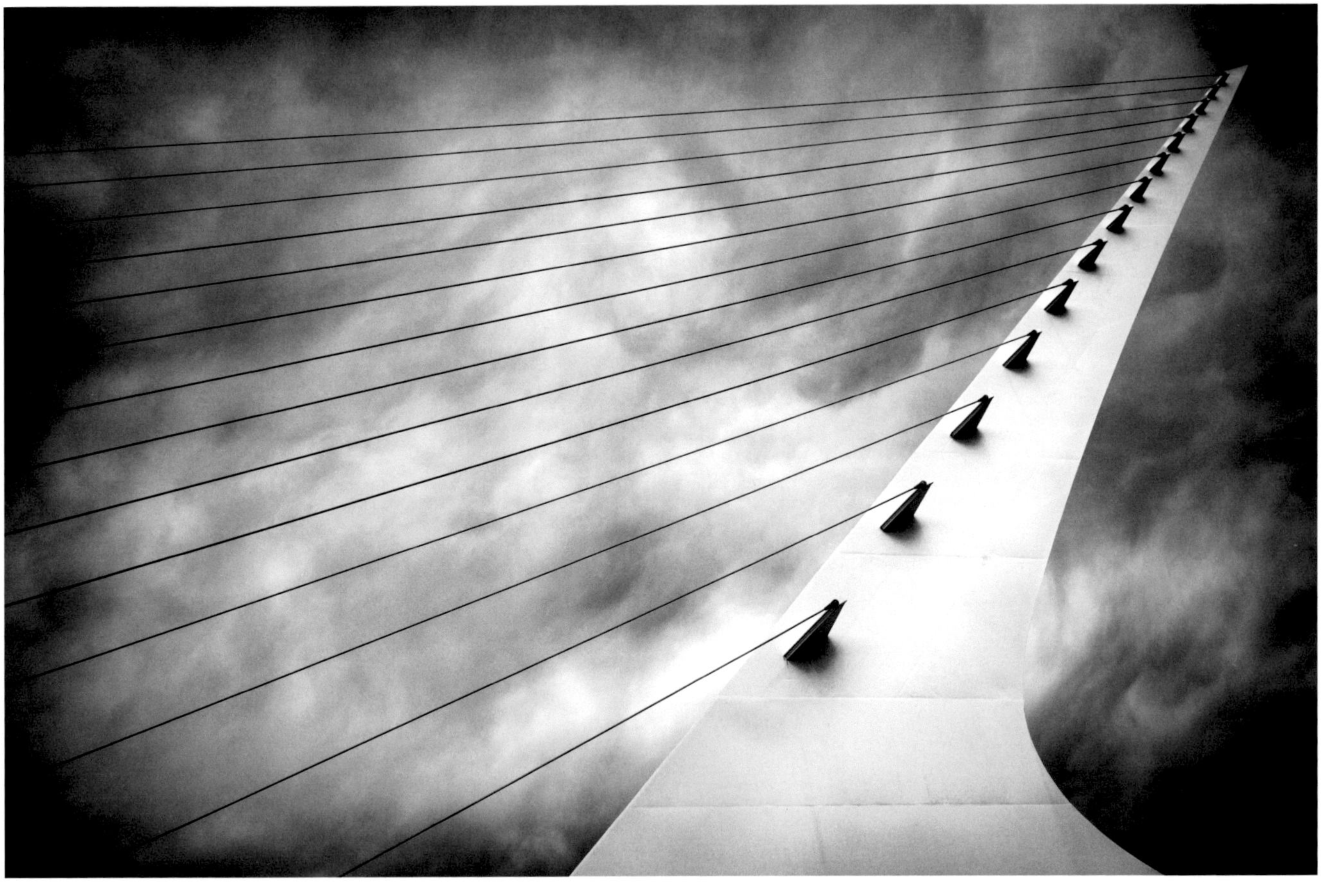

Wind Strings

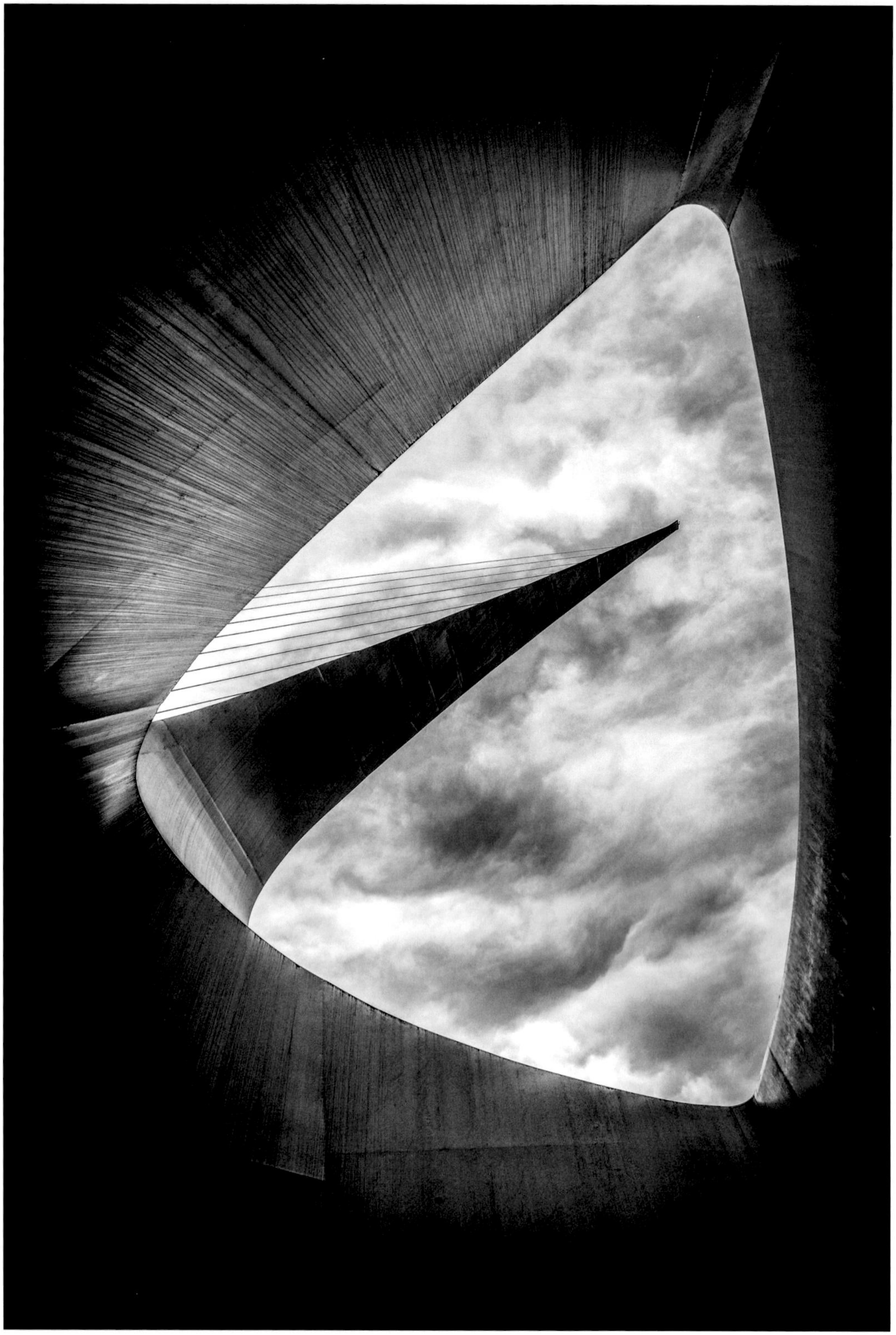

Cloud Songs

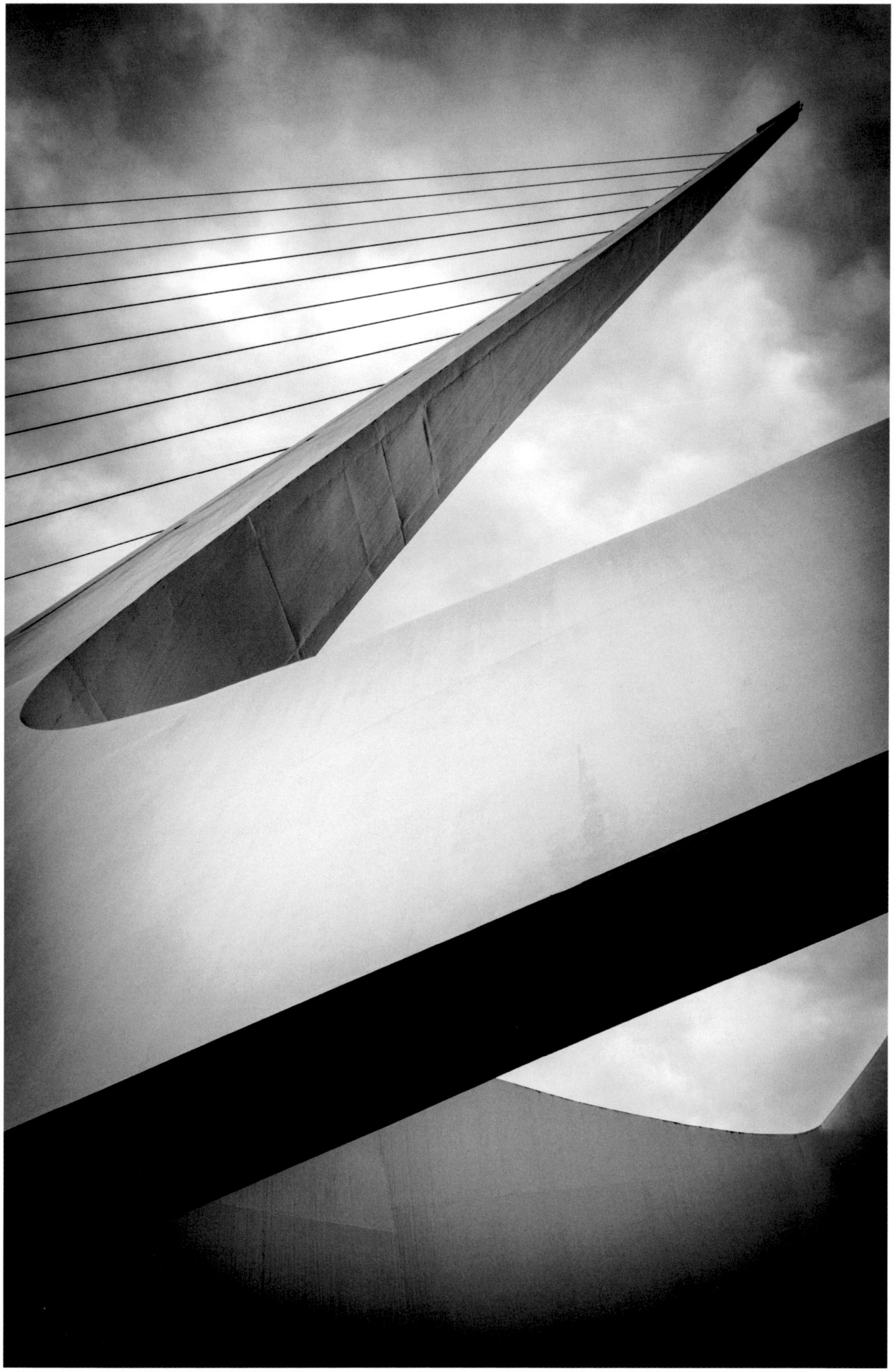

New Song

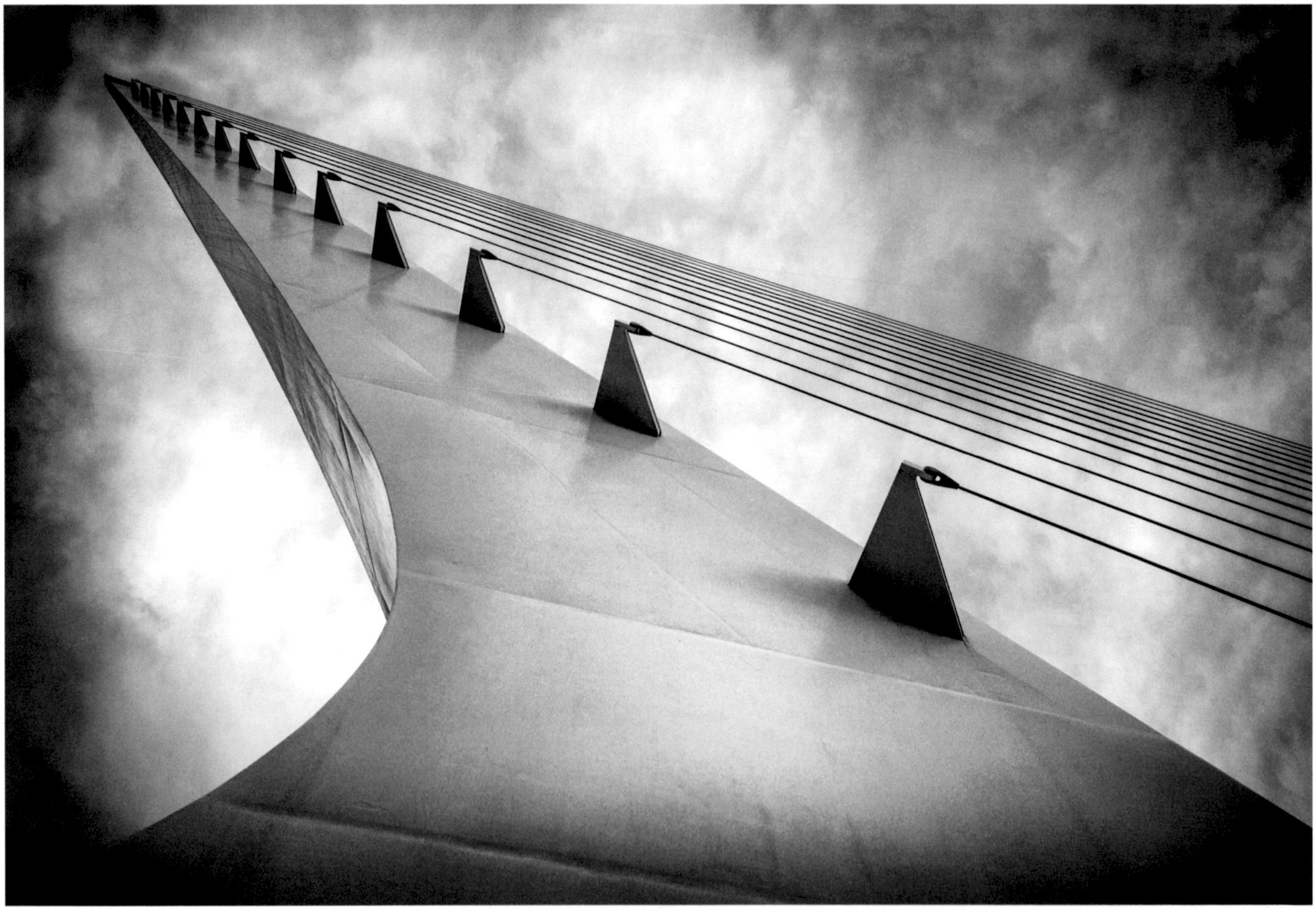

Sundial Sitar

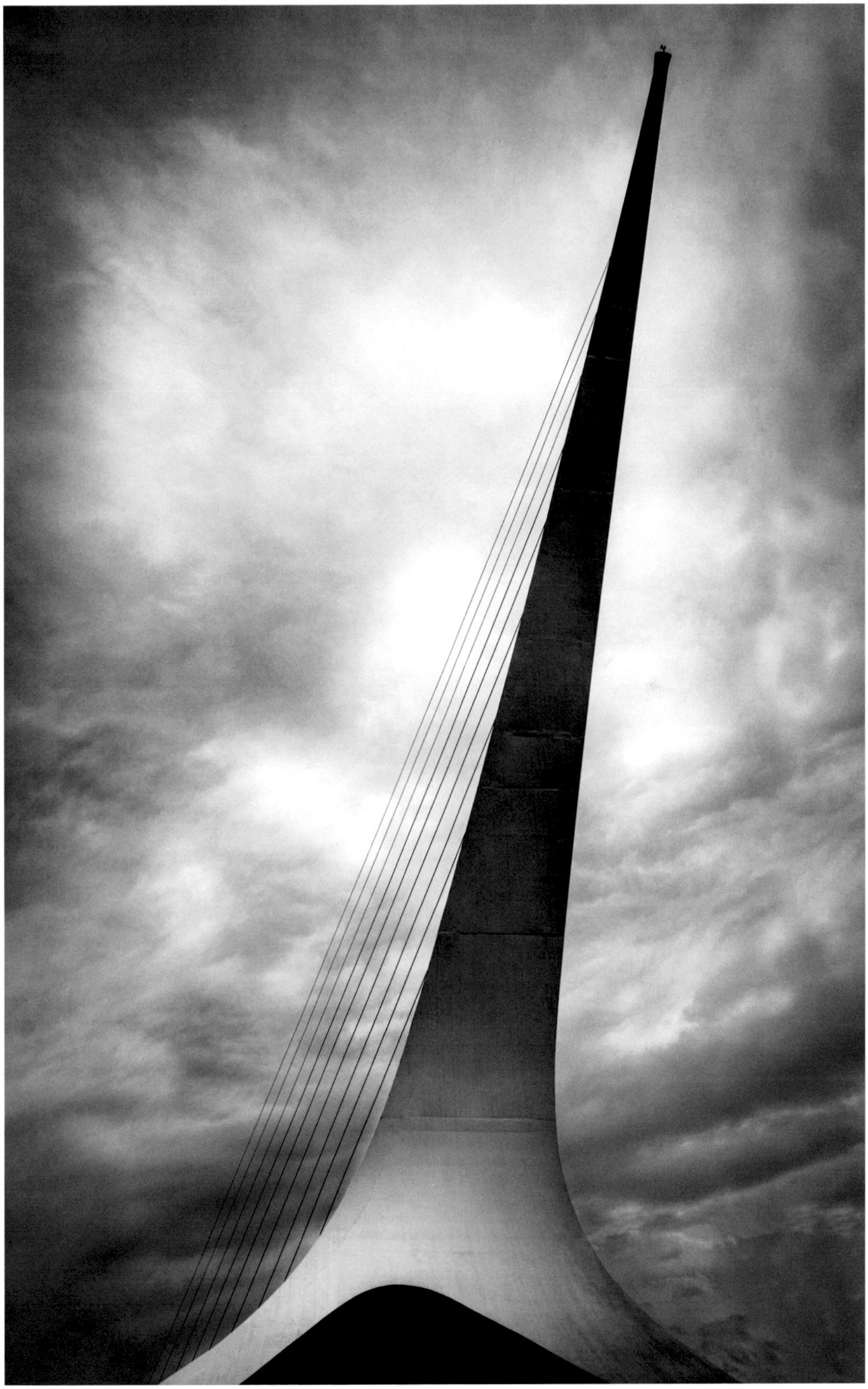

Stringed Stiletto

Night Creatures

by Stephen Allworth

www.stephenallworth.com • stephenallworth@gmail.com

Hidden in plain sight during the day, creatures emerge from the darkness to guard and protect the city throughout the night.

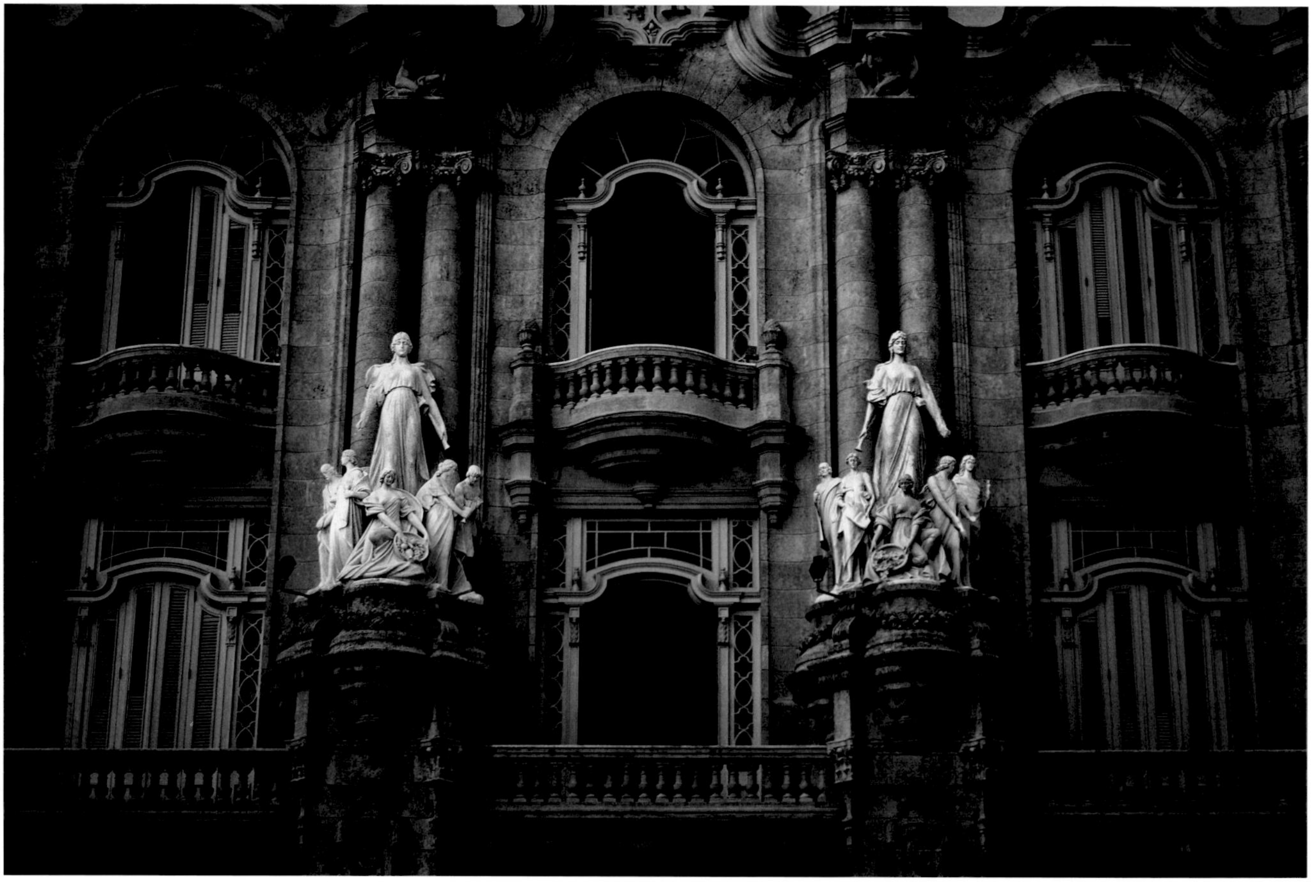

Angels protect the Opera

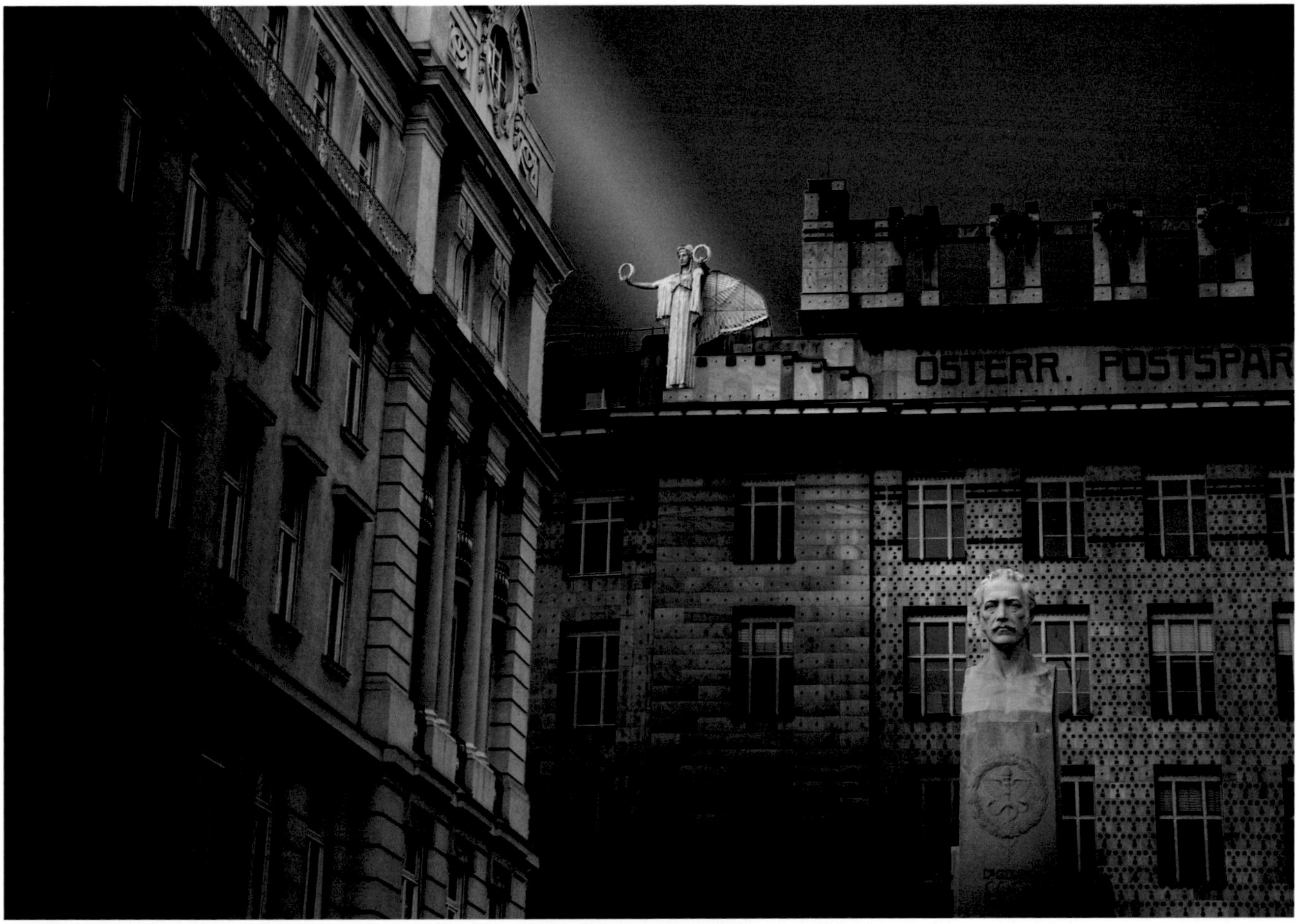

His guardian angel

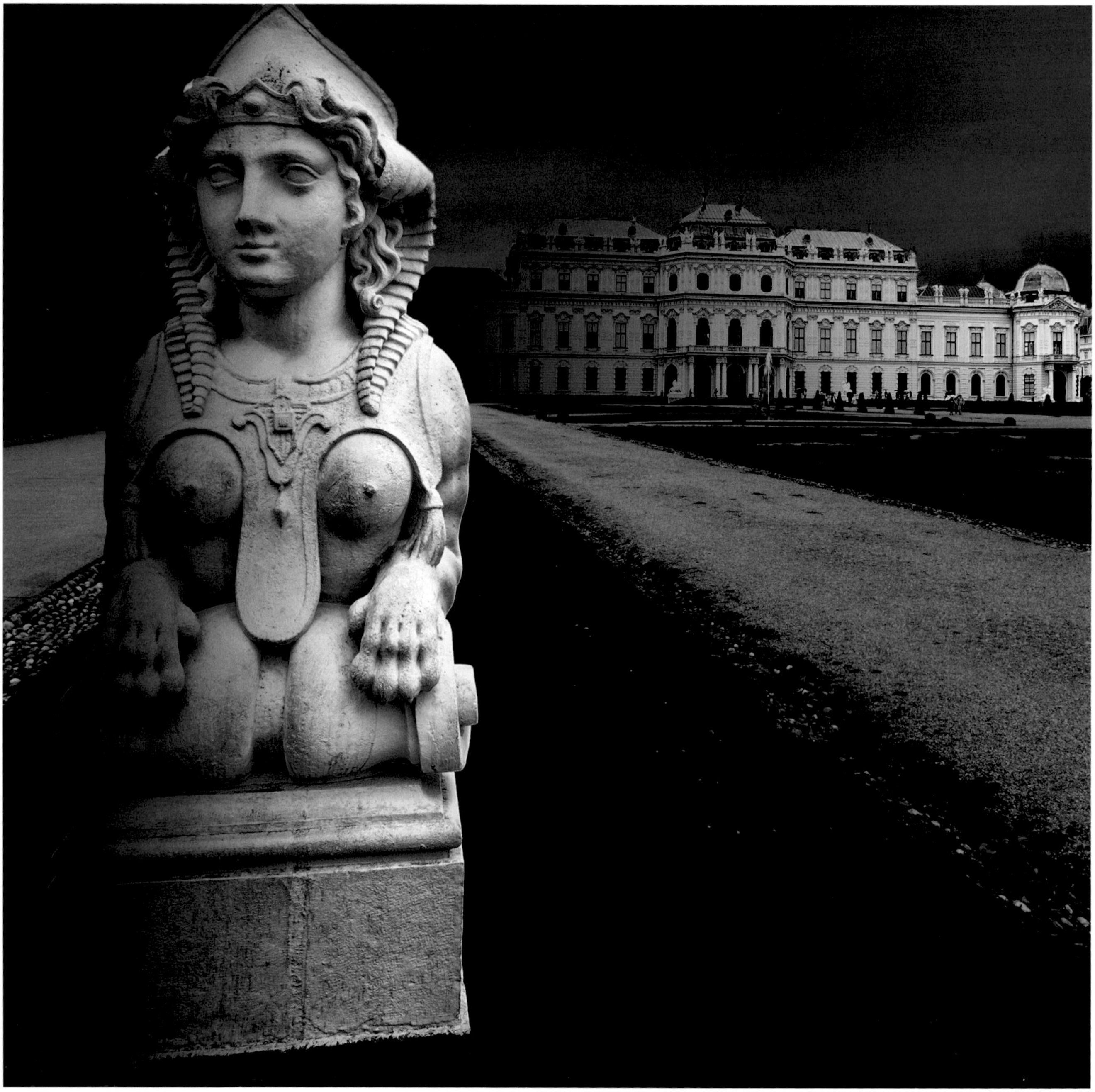

Ever vigilant, she guards the Palace by night

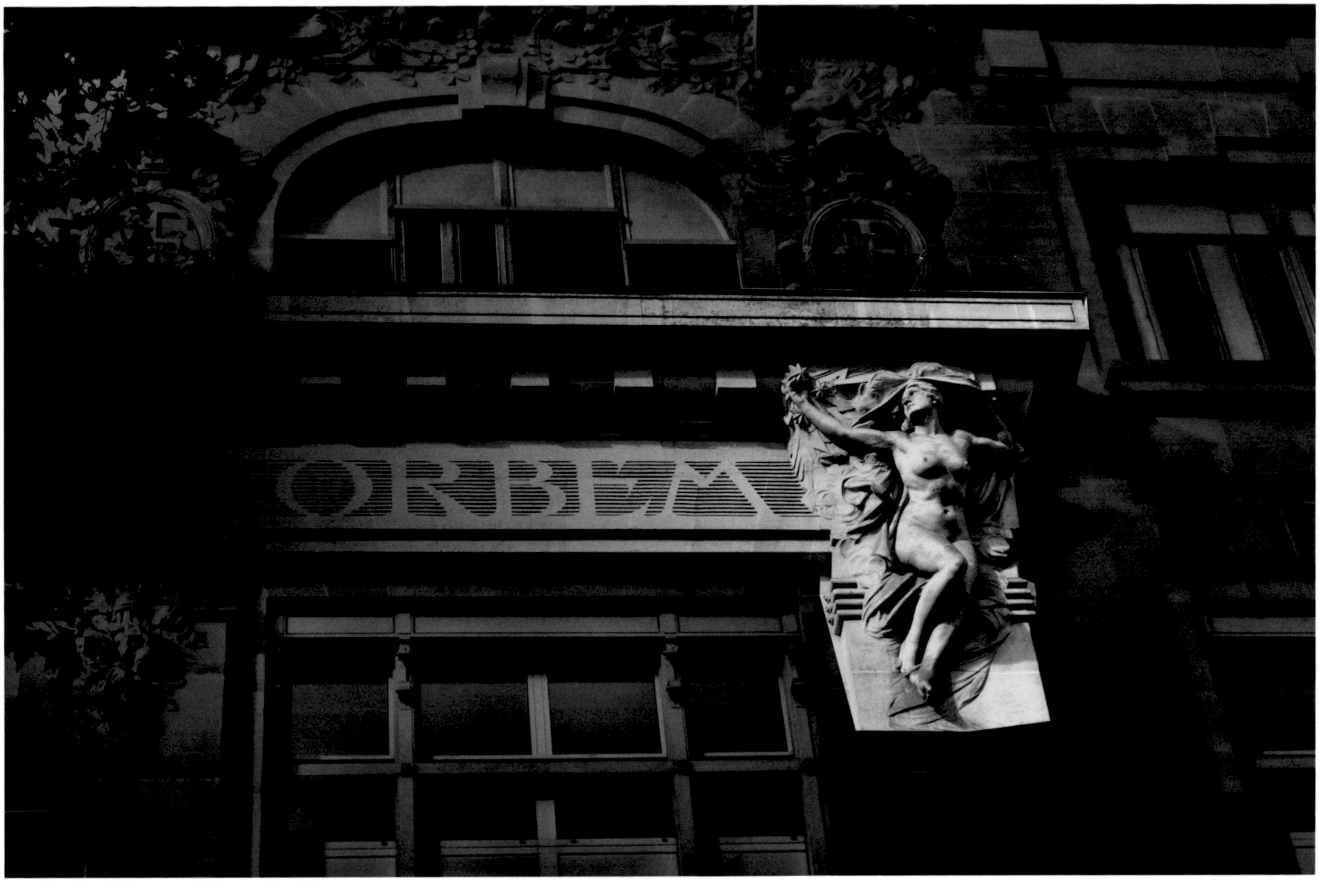

Safe in a woman's embrace, the building sleeps

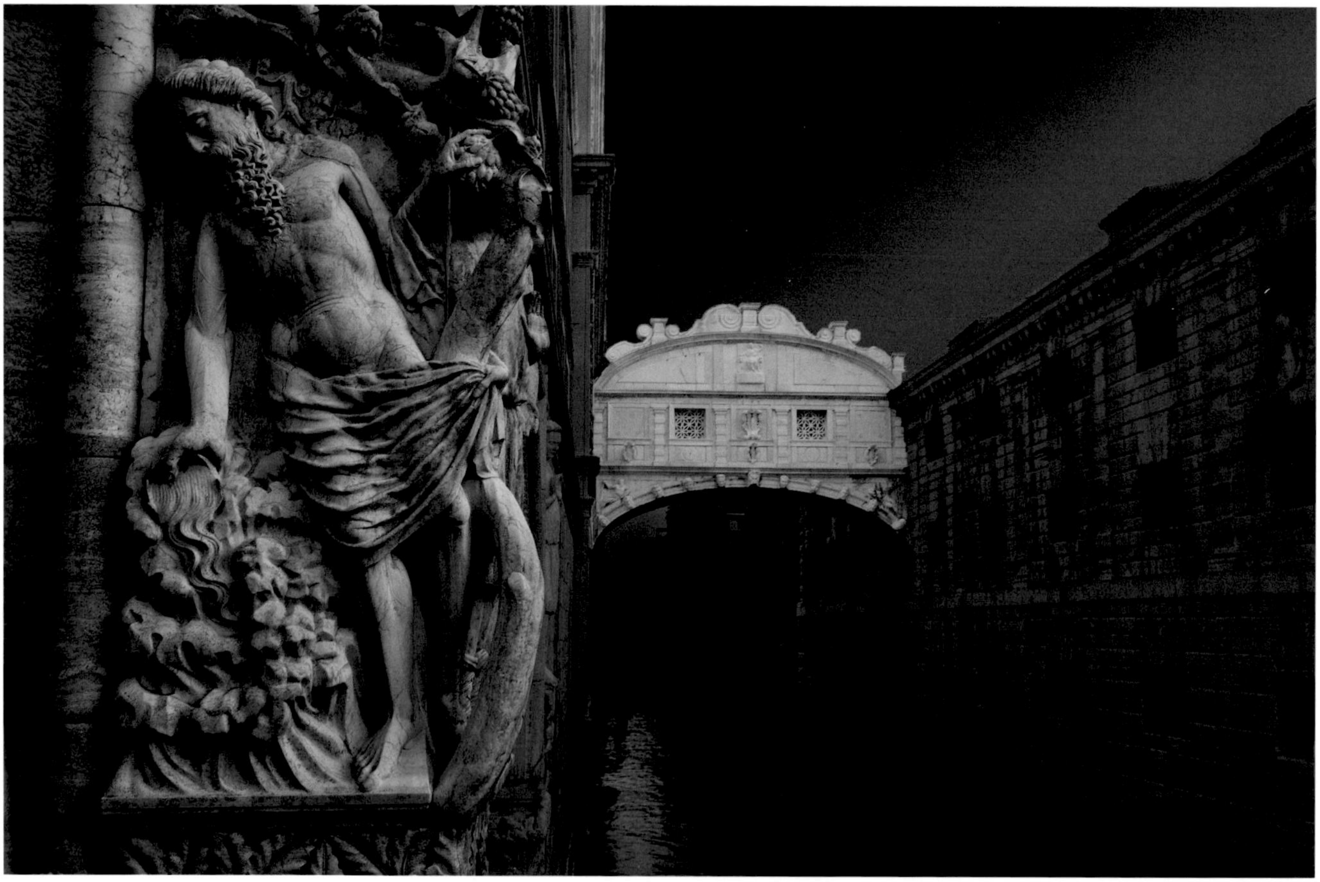

Almost invisible by day, he guards the bridge in the darkness

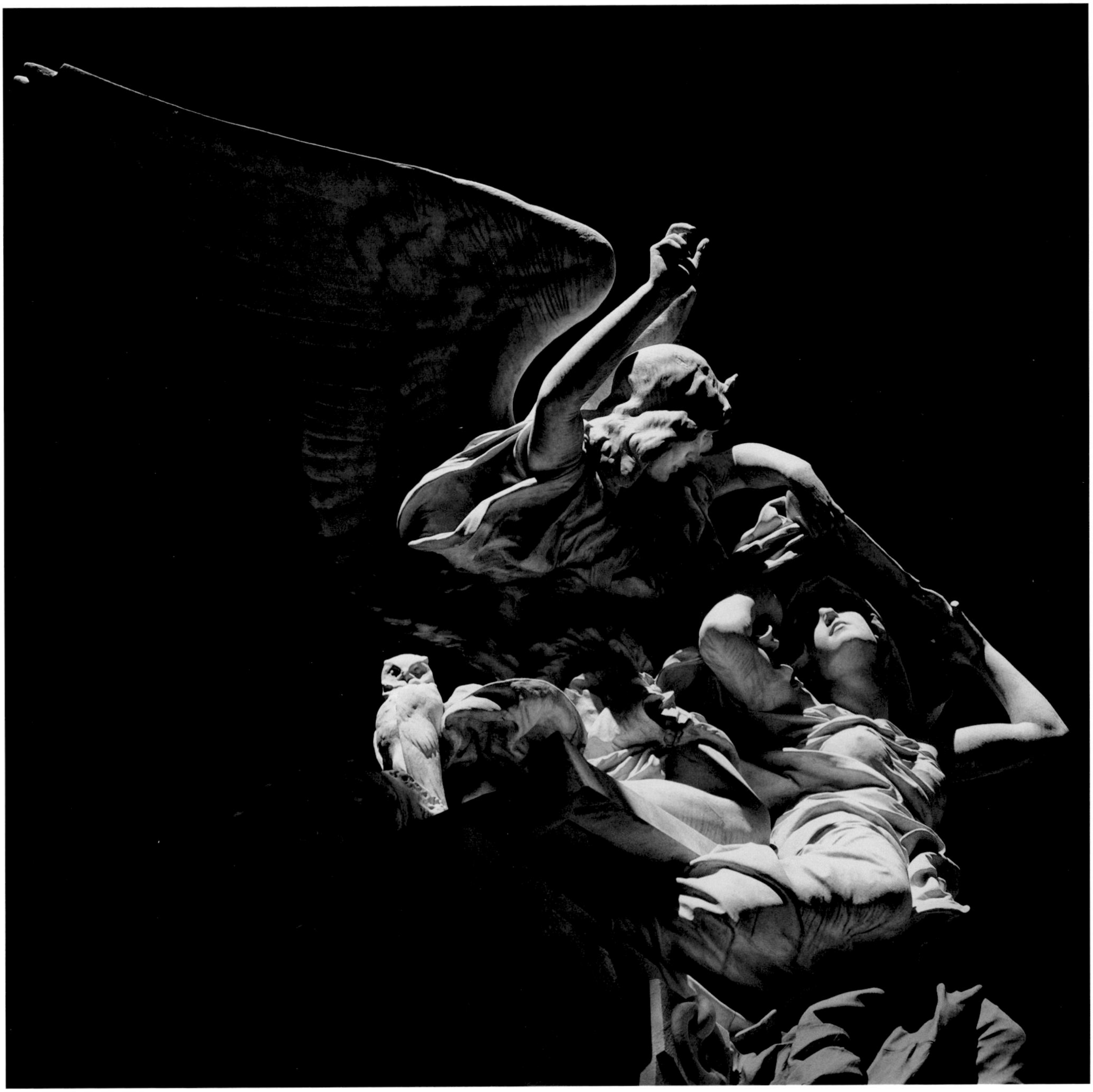

The owl keeps watch

Heroes Lived Here

by James R. Popovic

www.kpphoto.com ♦ james@kpphoto.com

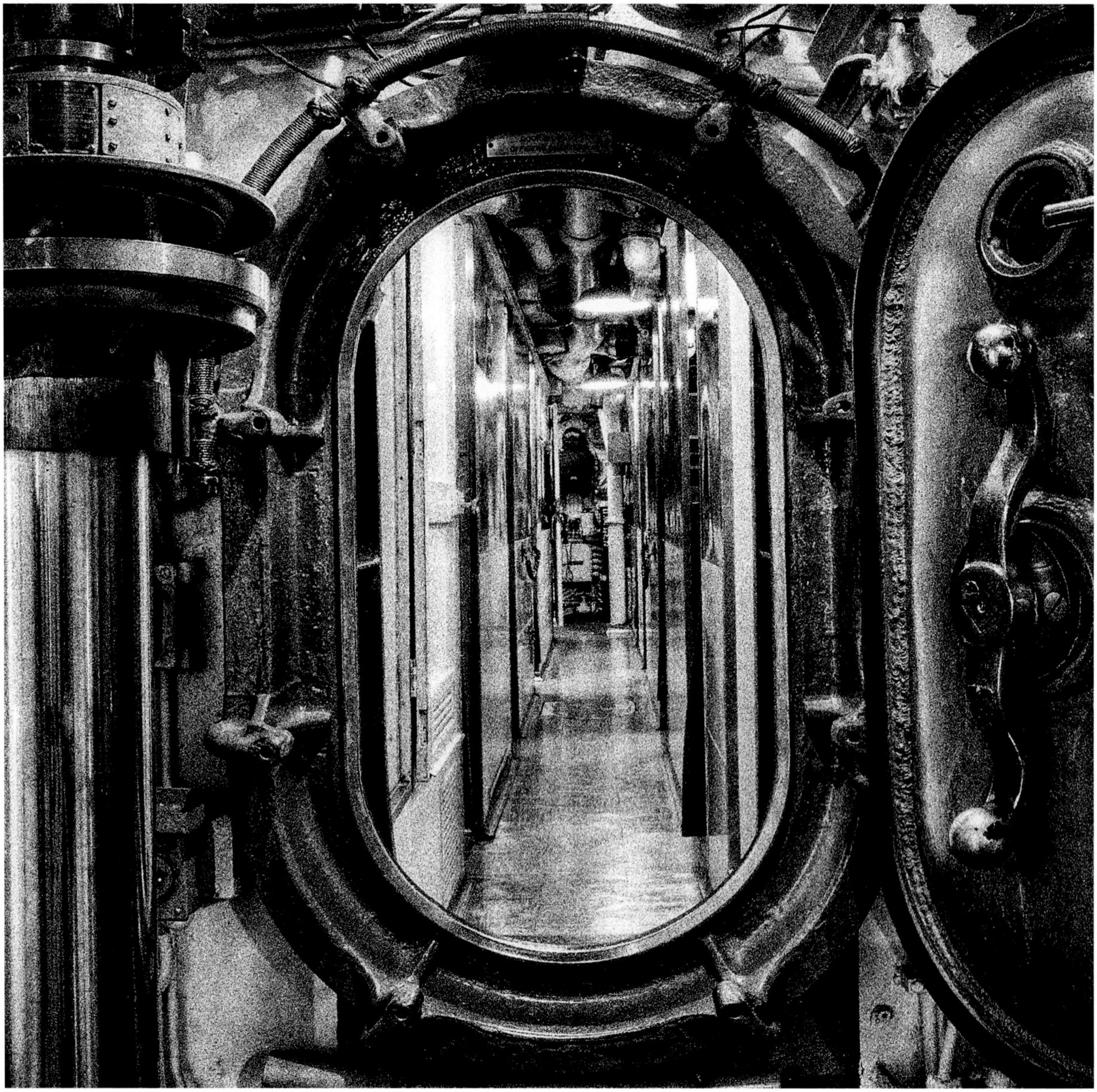

Forward Battery

During the Japanese attack on Pearl Harbor in 1941, much of the U.S. Navy's surface fleet was reduced to flaming wreckage. Within four days of the attack, however, a small U.S submarine fleet began offensive patrols against Imperial Japan.

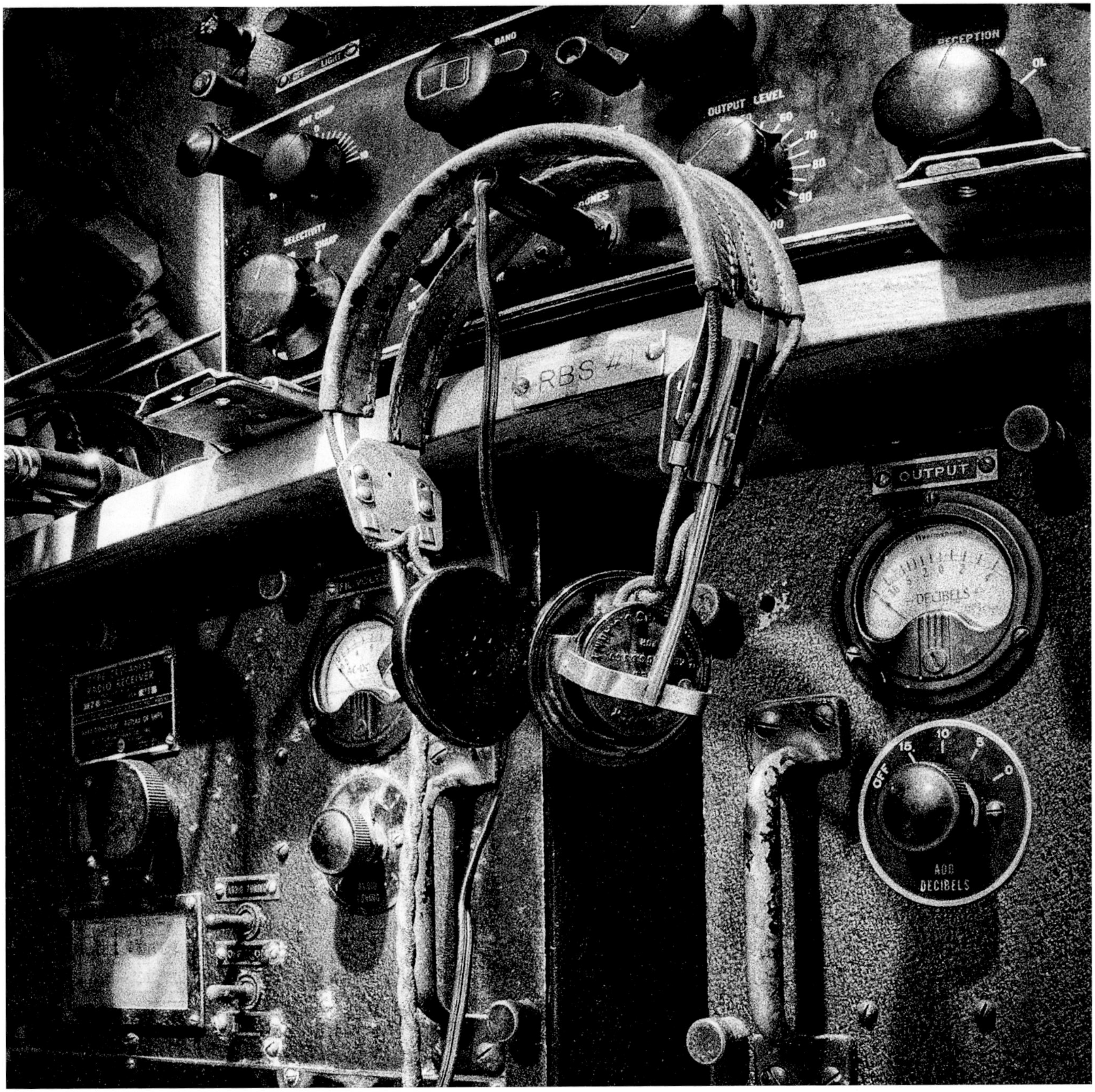

Radio Room

Still in the early months of the war, this small fleet represented the only American warships able to strike back at the enemy. This force represented only 1.6% of the Navy's manpower, yet accounted for more than 55% of Japan's shipping losses.

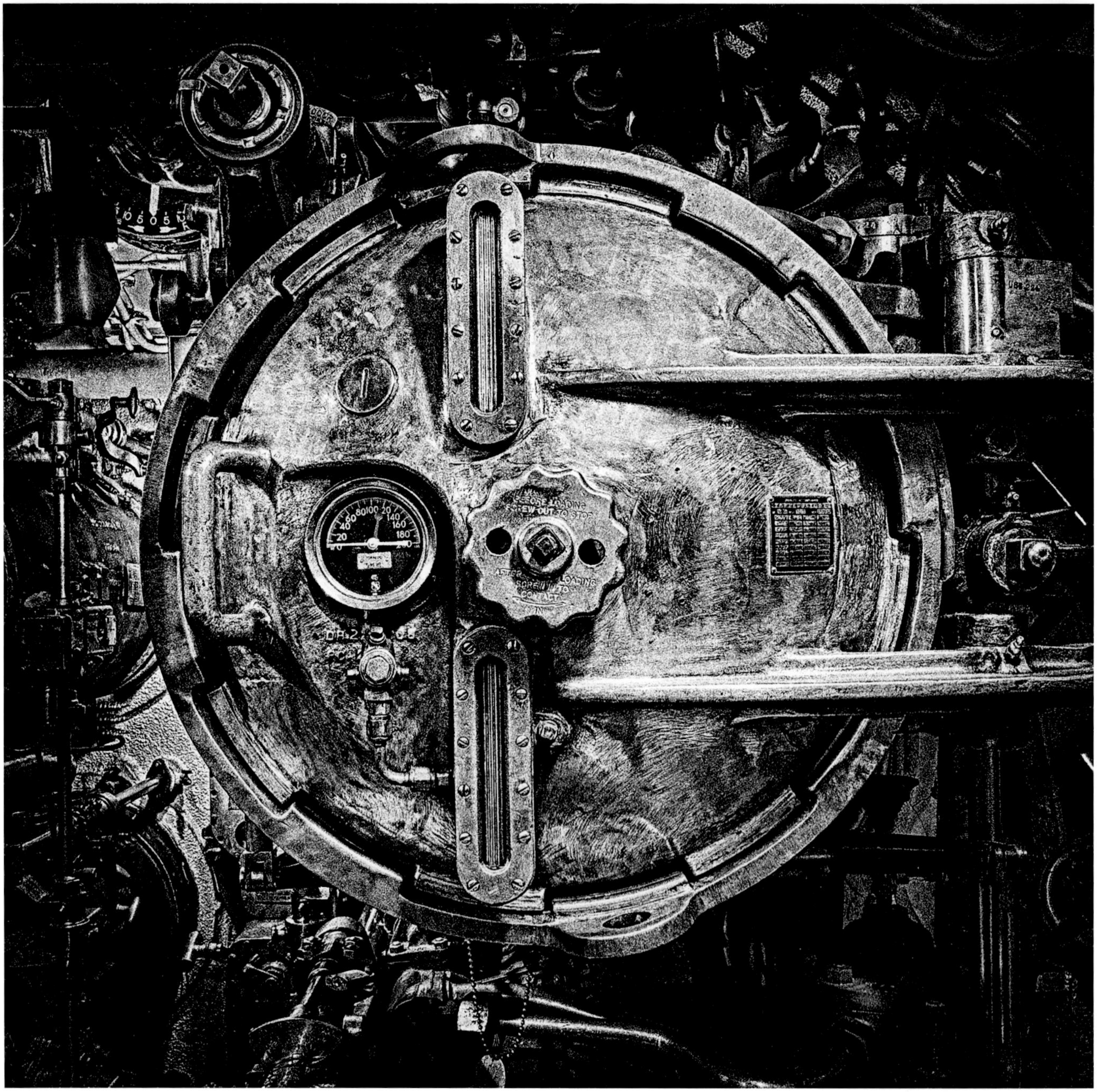

Torpedo Tube

More than 3,600 men died aboard the 52 submarines lost during the war as well as in individual acts of heroism at sea and ashore. Every U.S. submariner had friends aboard subs that were declared "overdue and presumed lost."

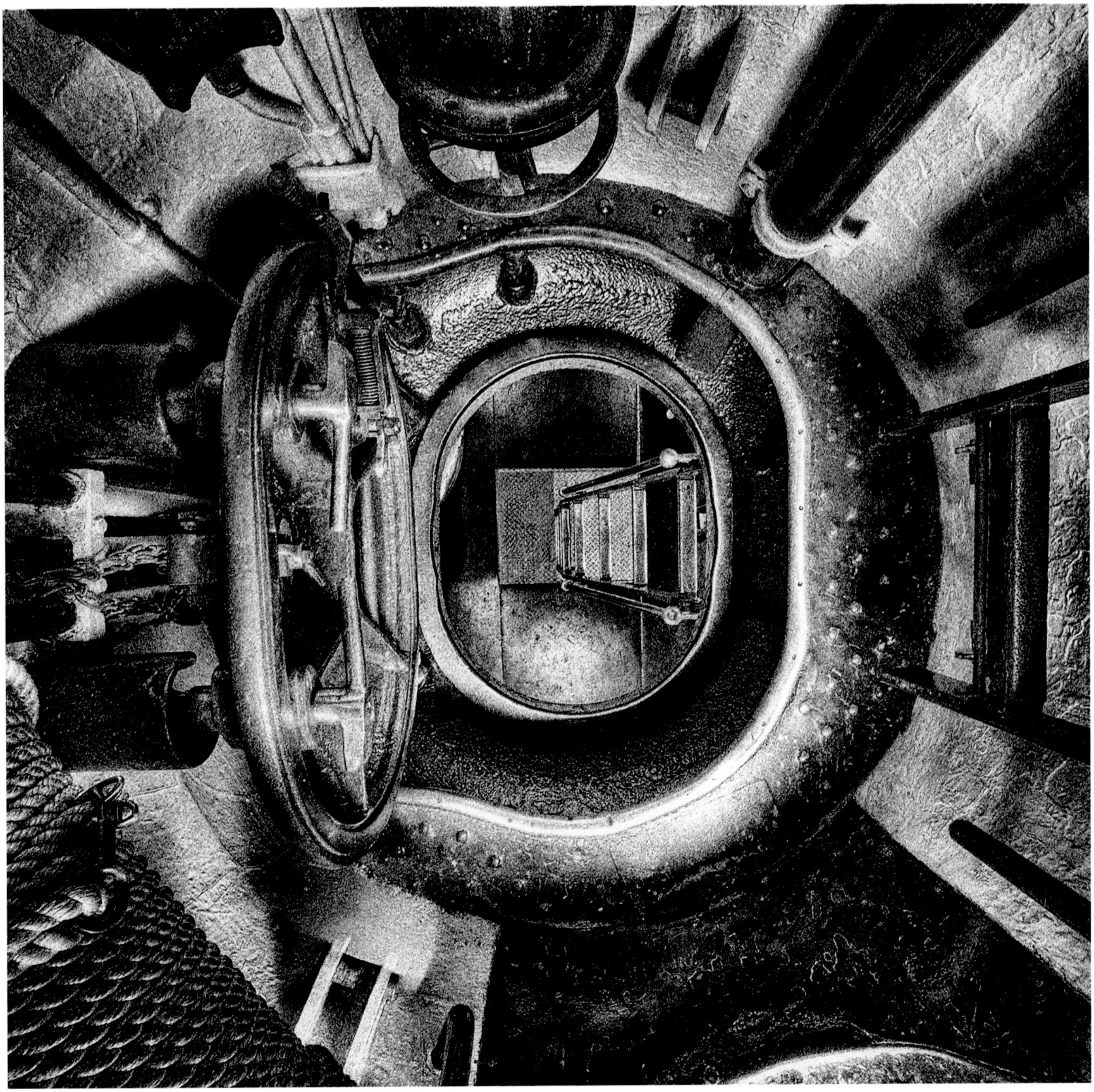

Escape Hatch

The men who served on U.S. submarines were volunteers. For all of them, life on a submarine was difficult. Quarters were cramped, stuffy, and crowded.

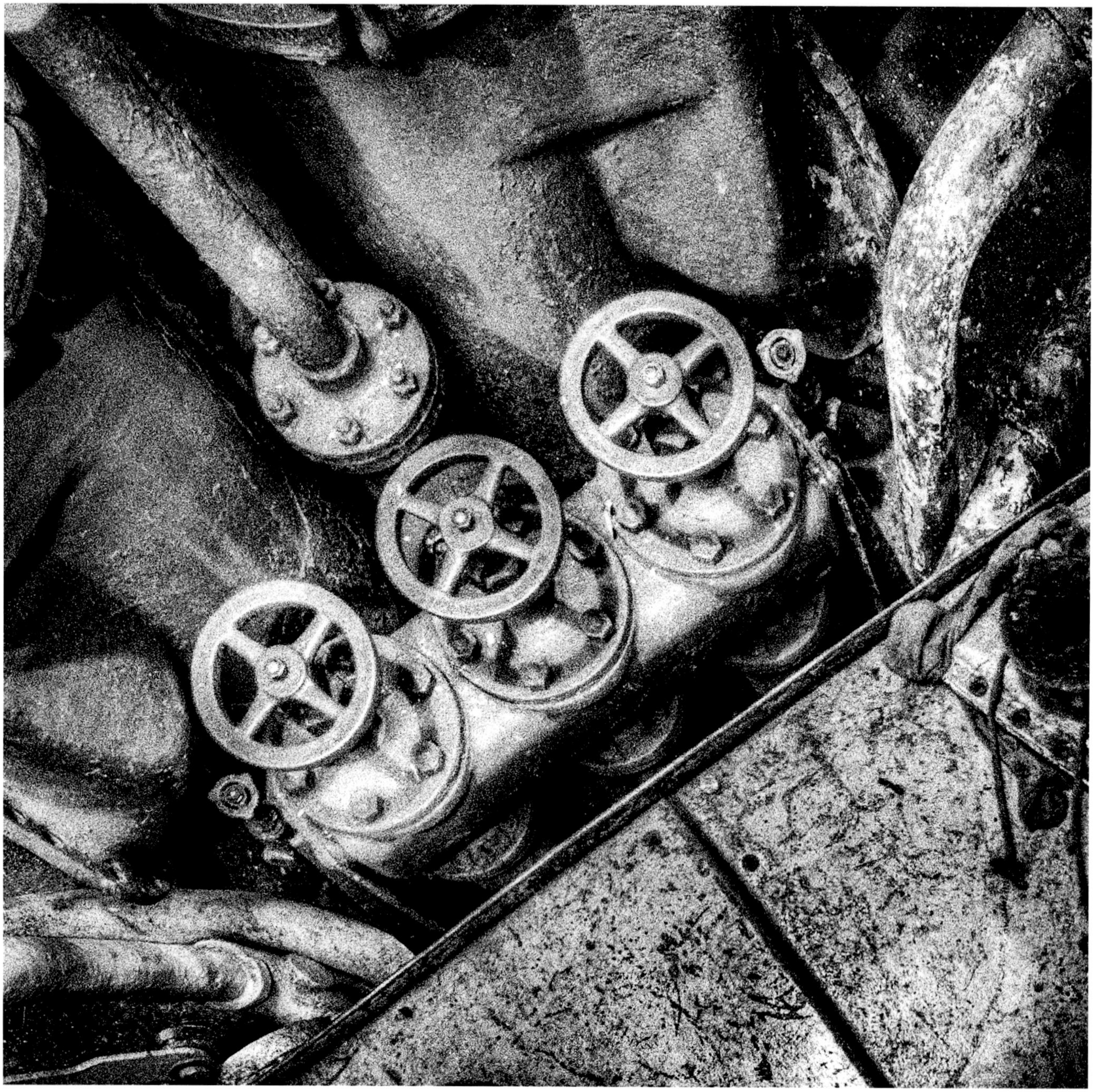

Motor Room

All their risk and hardship was not without rewards, however. Aside from receiving 50% additional pay, submariners also enjoyed the best food in the military and received the most shore leave. They were also held in high regard by the men of the surface Navy.

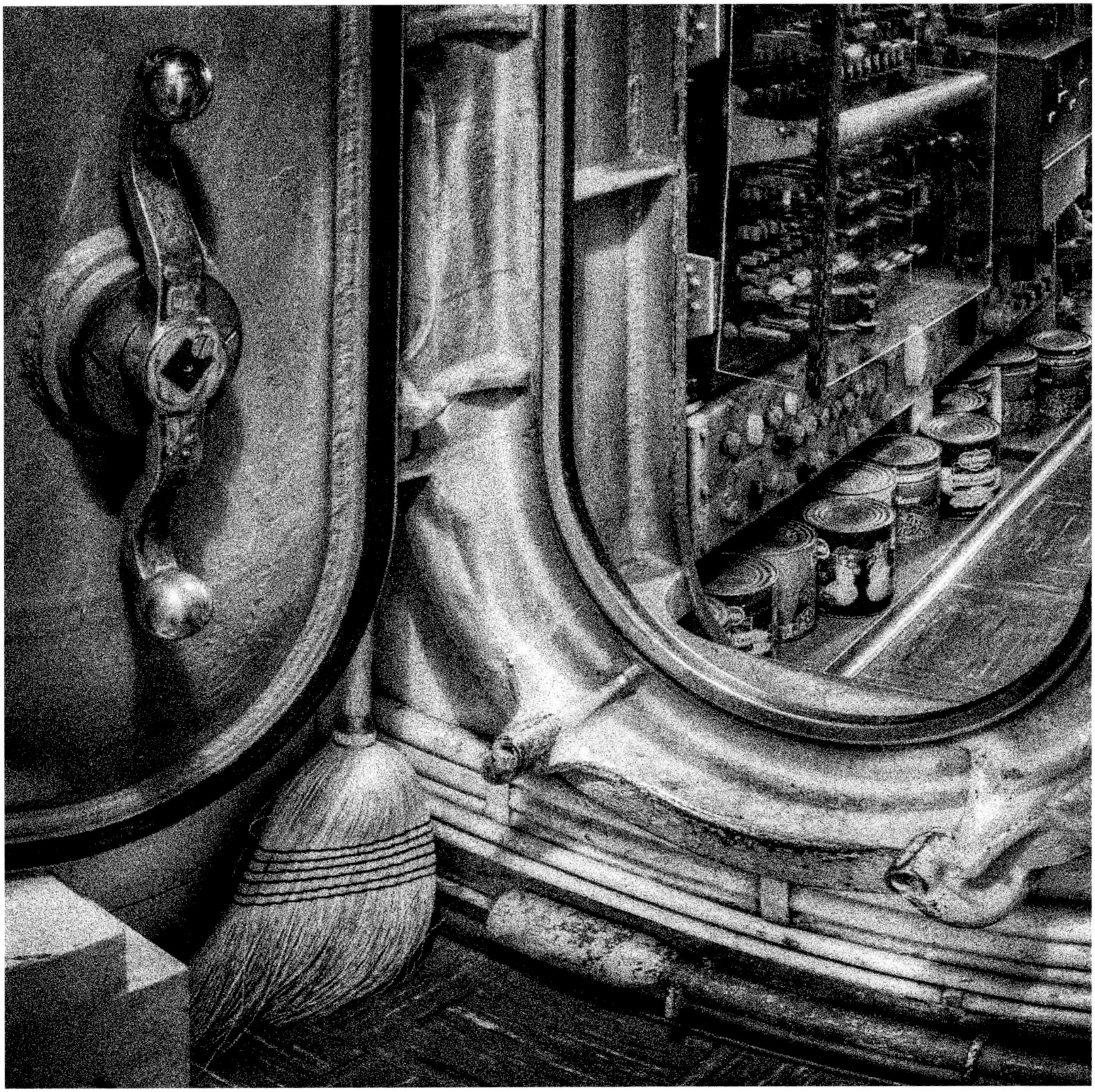

Control Room

These "squares" represent small glimpses into their daily lives. The things they saw, and an environment they had to be conscious of every minute of the day for weeks at a time.

Glacial Silt

by Hal Gage

halgage.com • halgage@alaska.net

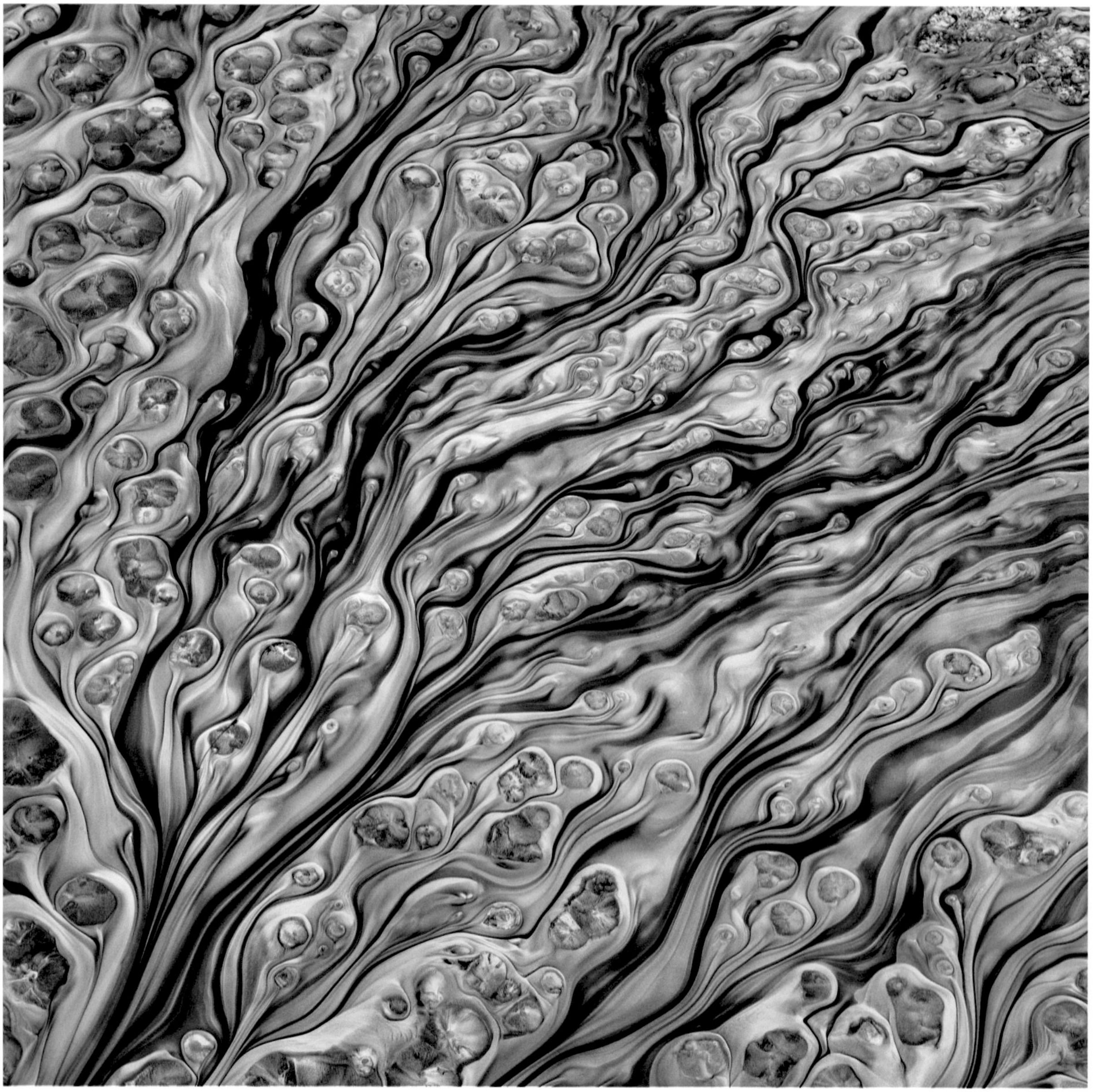

Living in Alaska, I photograph ice. Climate change is always a thought in the back of my mind. In recent years I have seen the results. As the glaciers melt, I notice more and larger pools and streams of melt ice, and along with it the silt and mud that they carry. These runoffs display fascinating shapes and patterns, but it took years for me to really look at them.

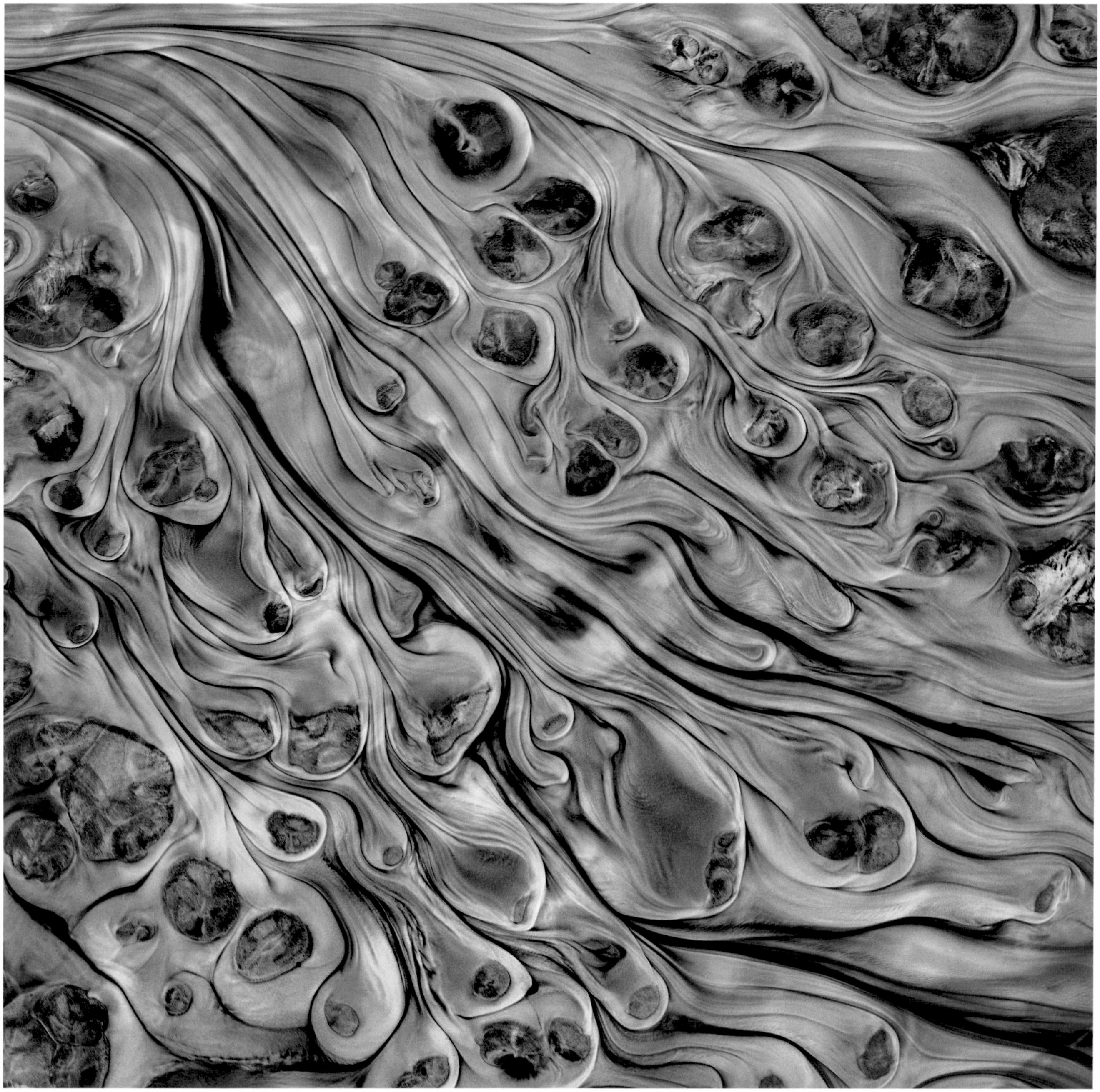

This year I found a grouping of silt patterns on the Matanuska Glacier (100 miles north of Anchorage). The tonality of the silt and water are beyond subtle. Diaphanous and ephemeral, once processed the faint patterns revealed an astonishing maze of sinewy shapes and serpentine lines. The mini volcanos and swimming eyeballs — whatever it is you see in them — are here one moment, gone the next. A fitting metaphor for my disappearing glacial companions.

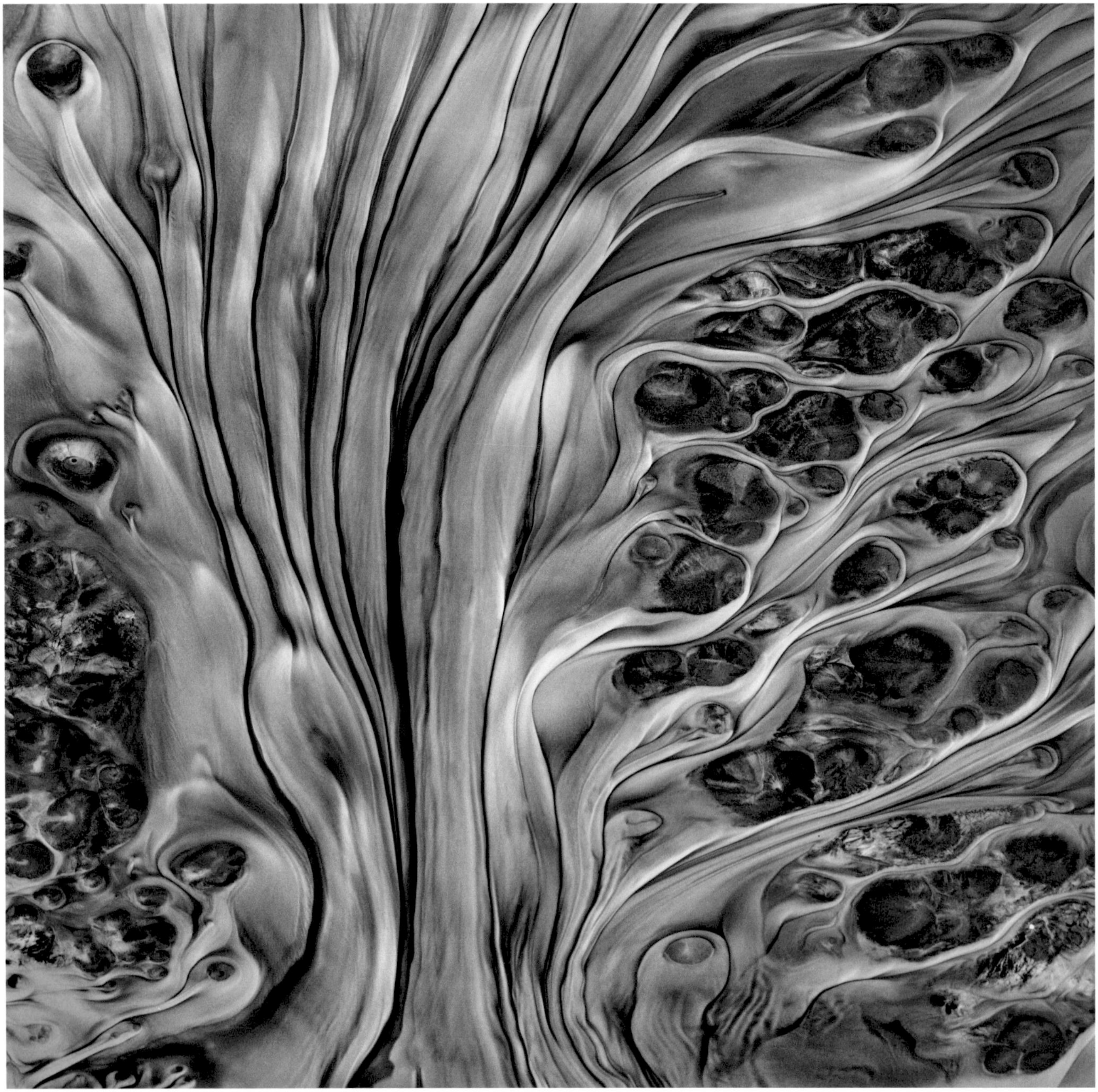

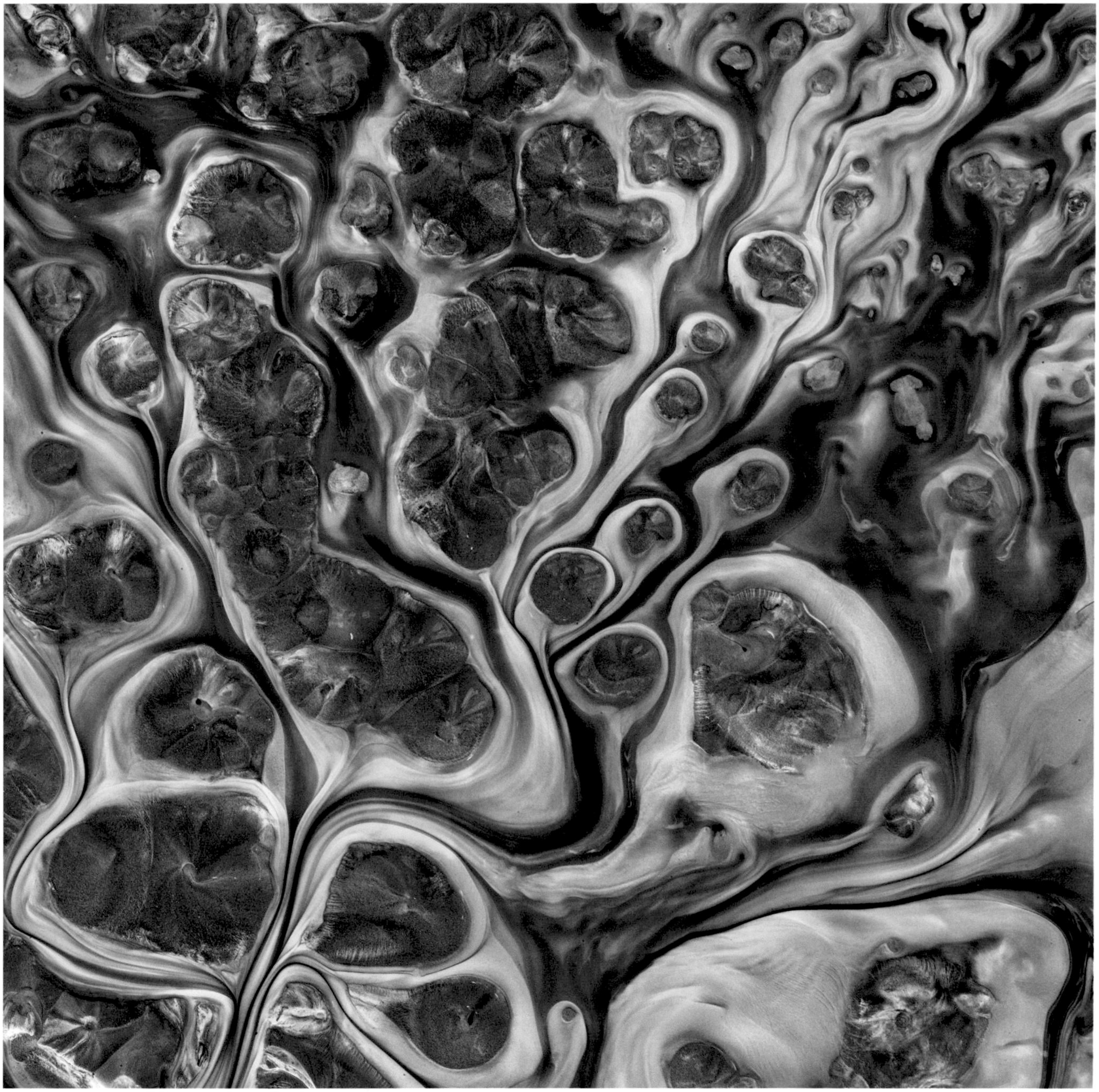

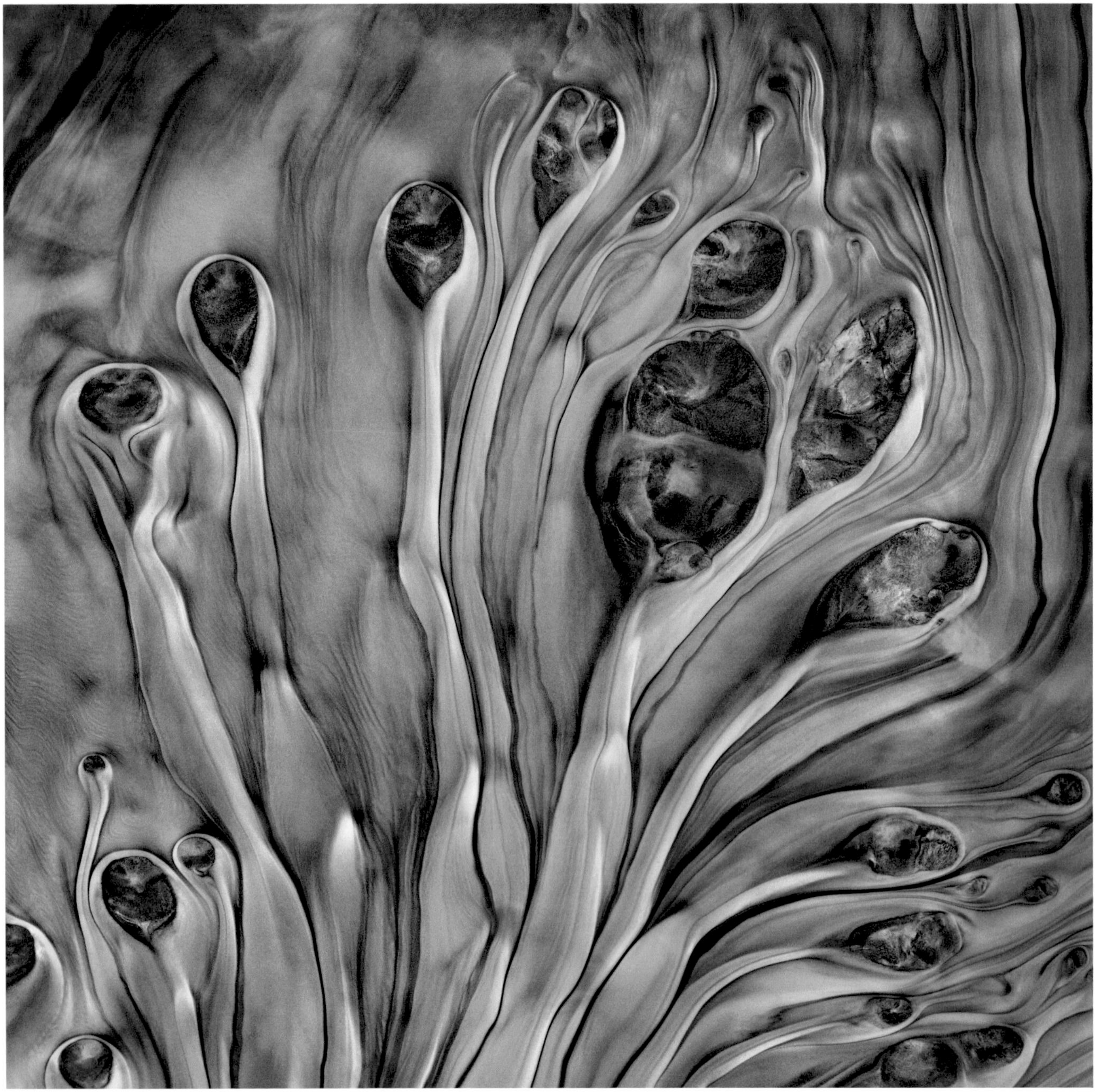

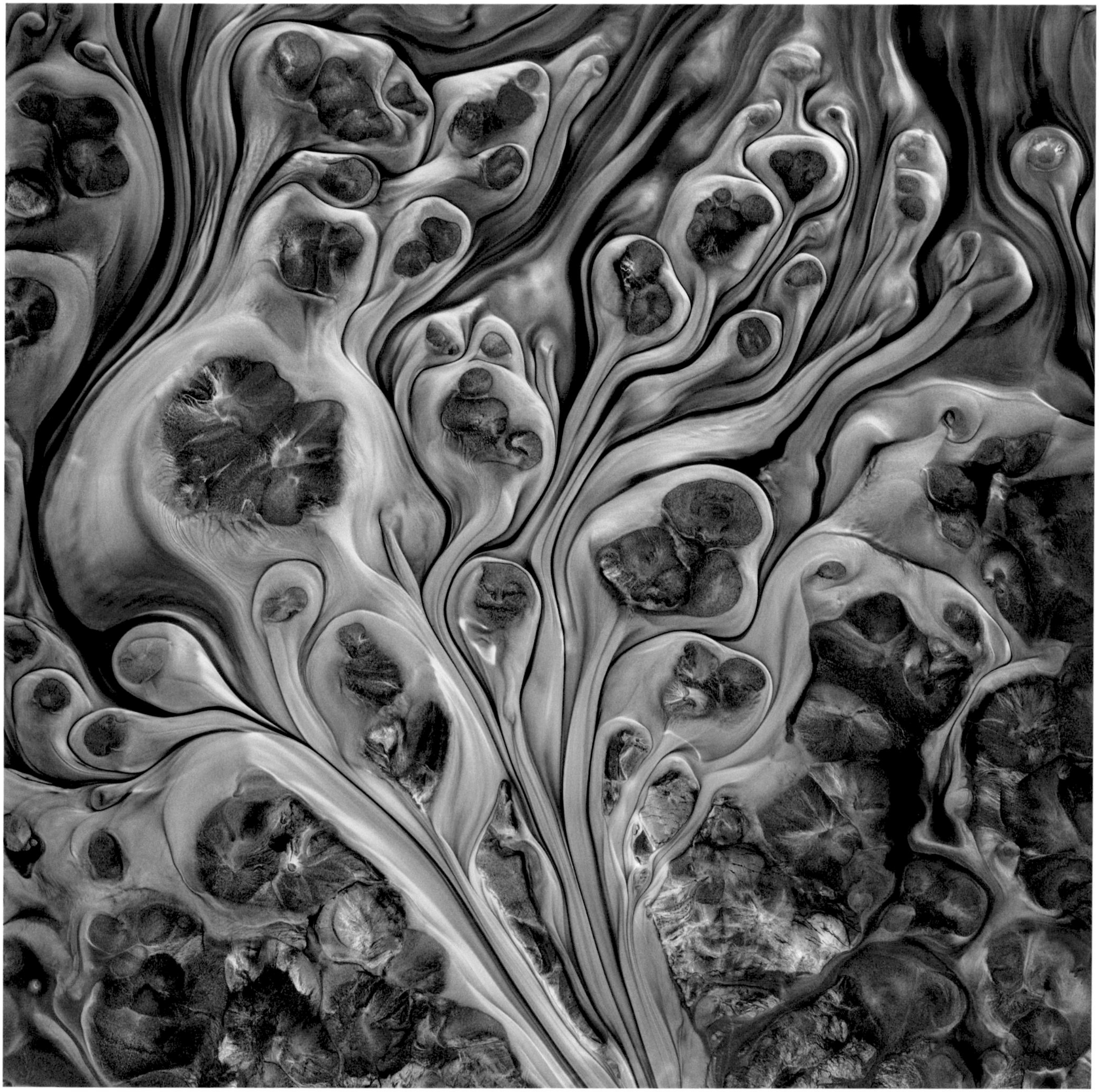

Georgetown Steam Plant Abstracts

by Michael Waller

www.flickr.com/photos/marmot06 ♦ mawaller@gmail.com

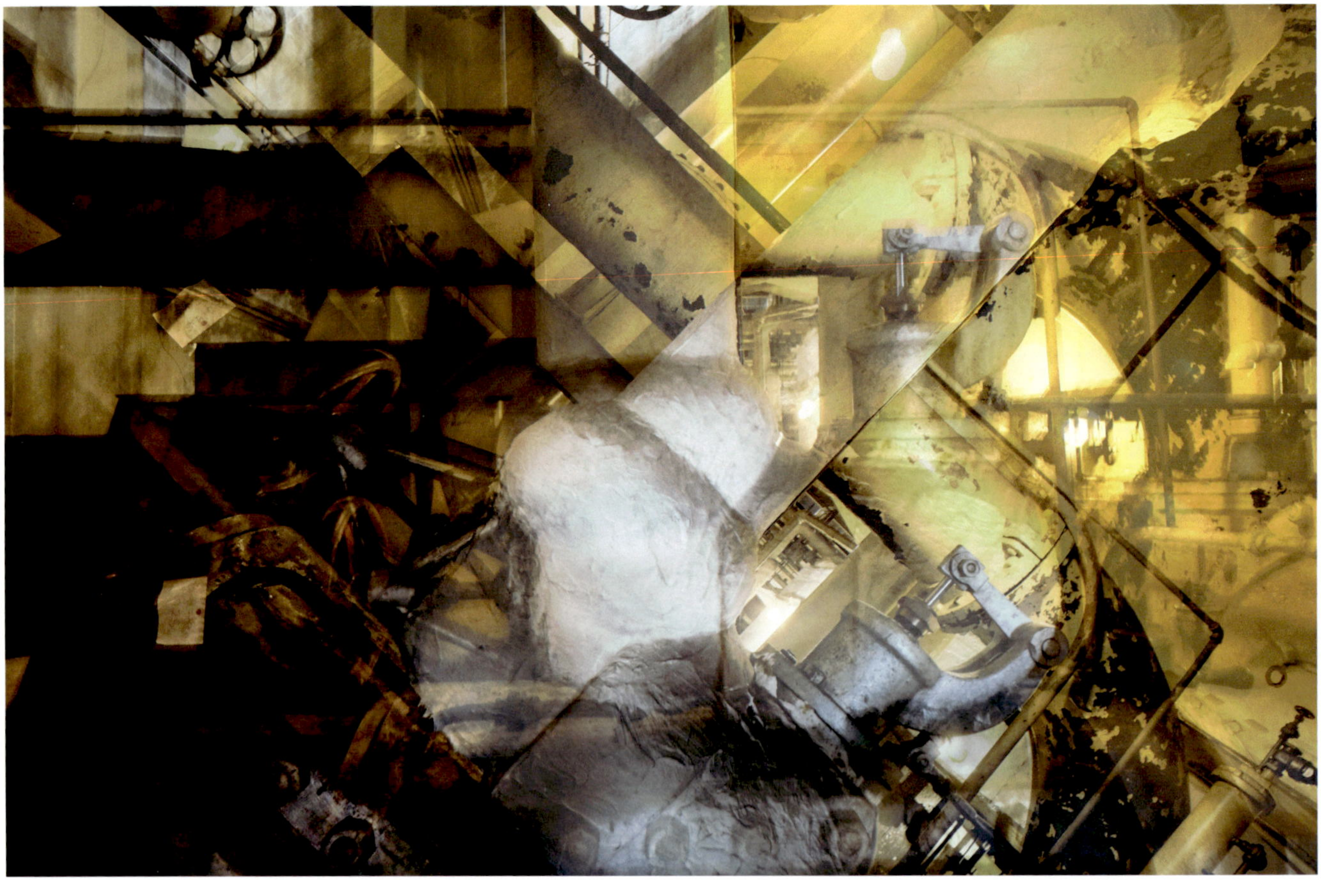

I have been photographing the interior of Seattle City Light's decommissioned Georgetown almost monthly for the past couple of years. The early 20th century plant — recently declared a national industrial historic park — is undergoing a renovation and restoration and is open every second Saturday of the month. It is filled with period electrical generating technology, turbines boilers, and control gear.

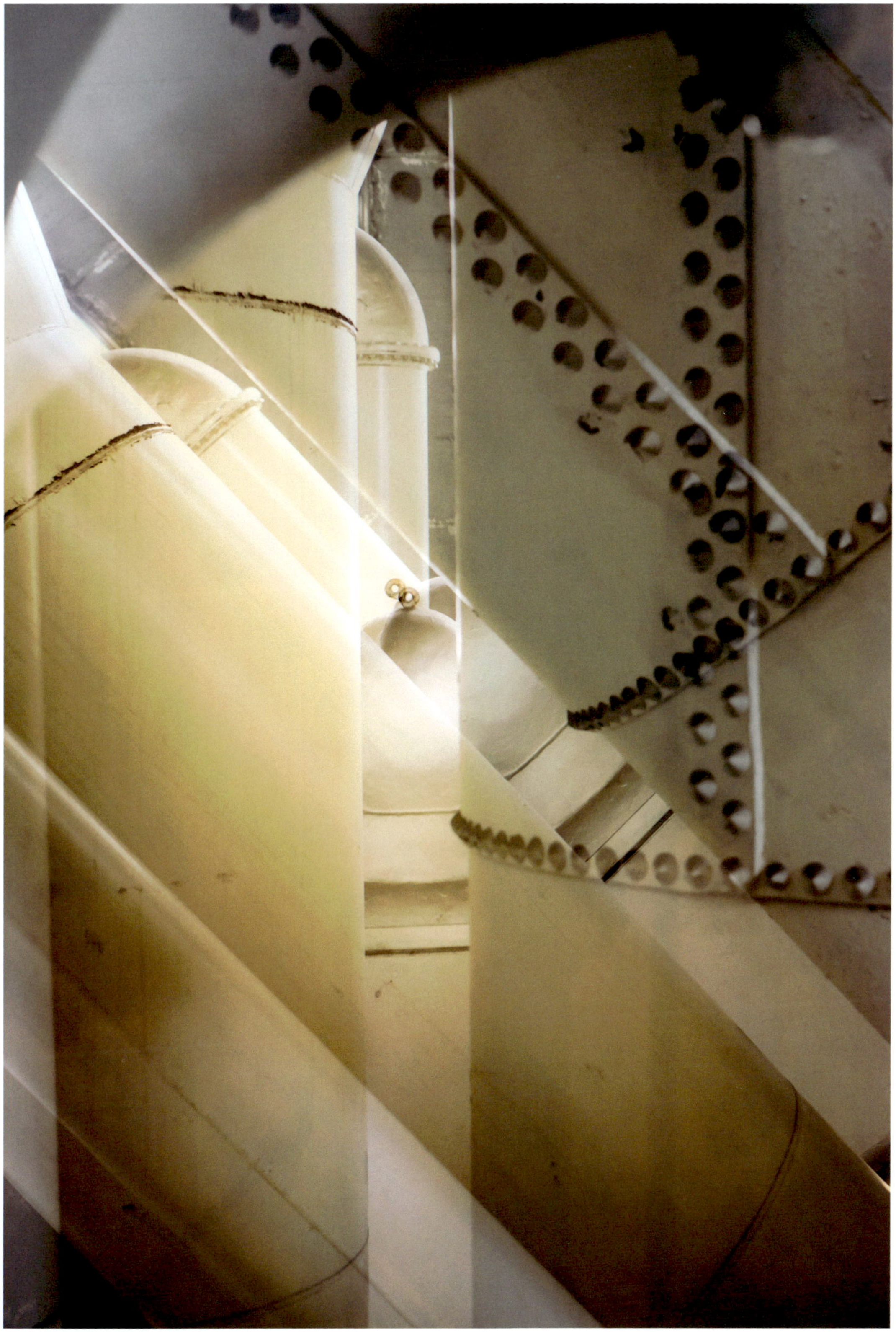

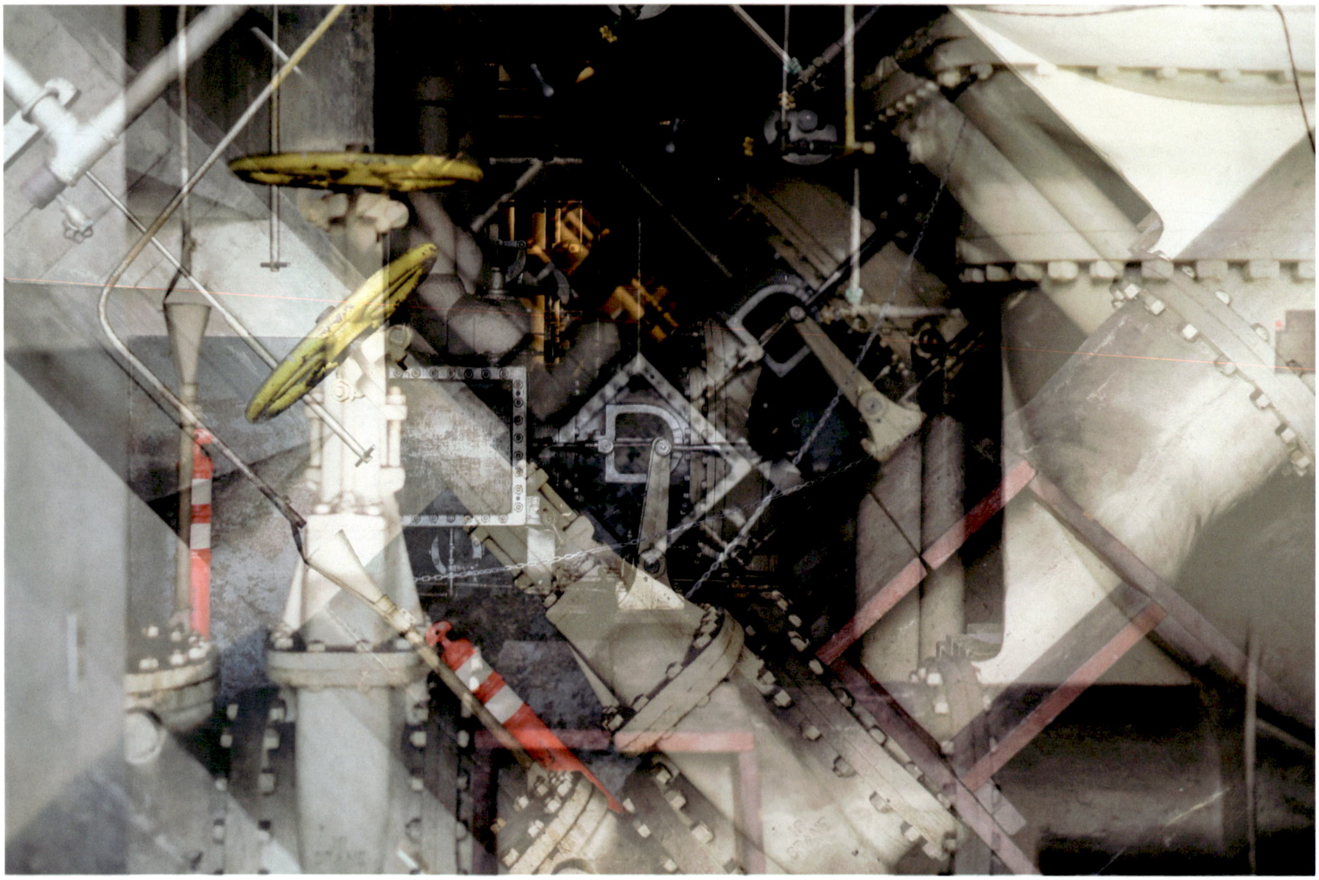

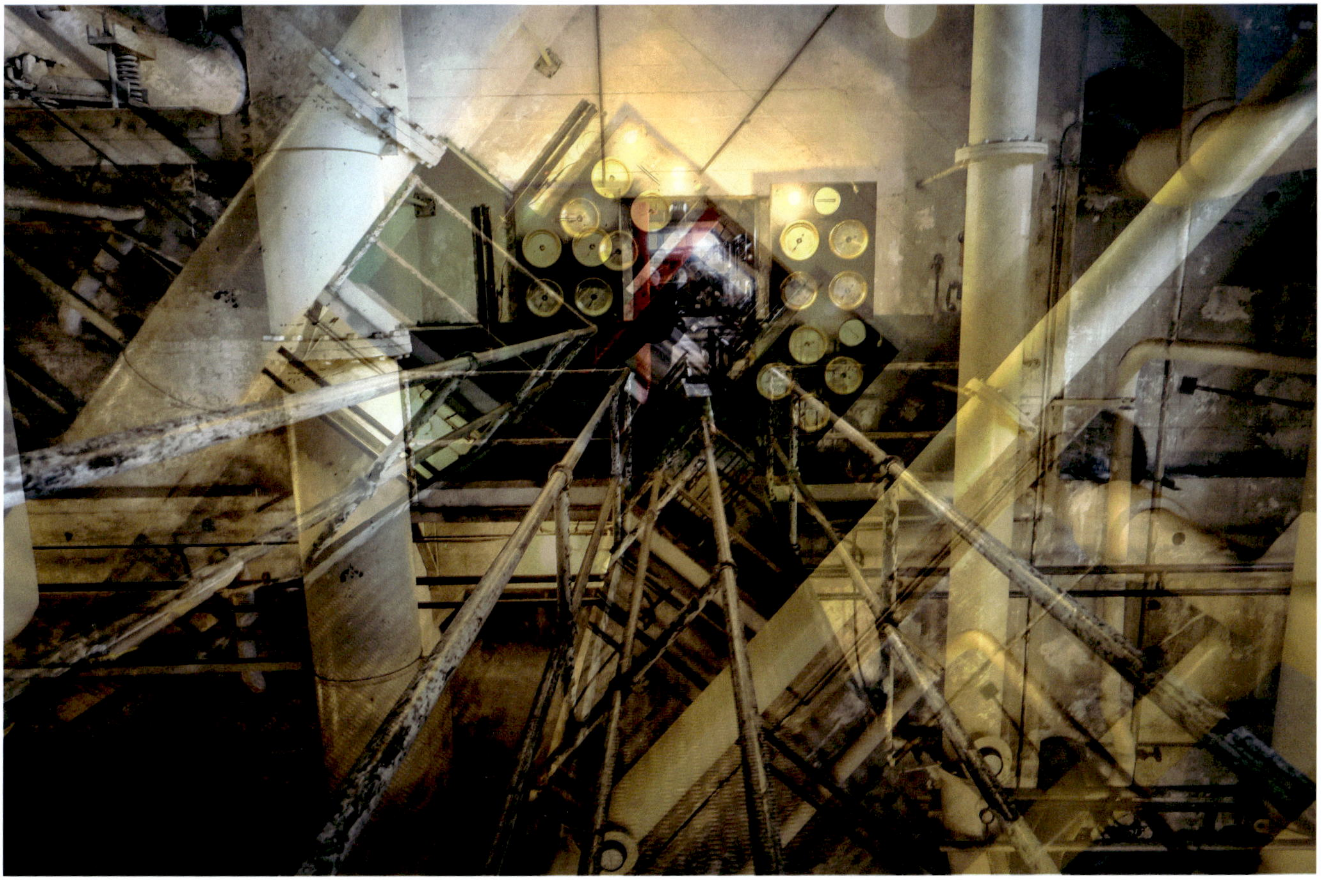

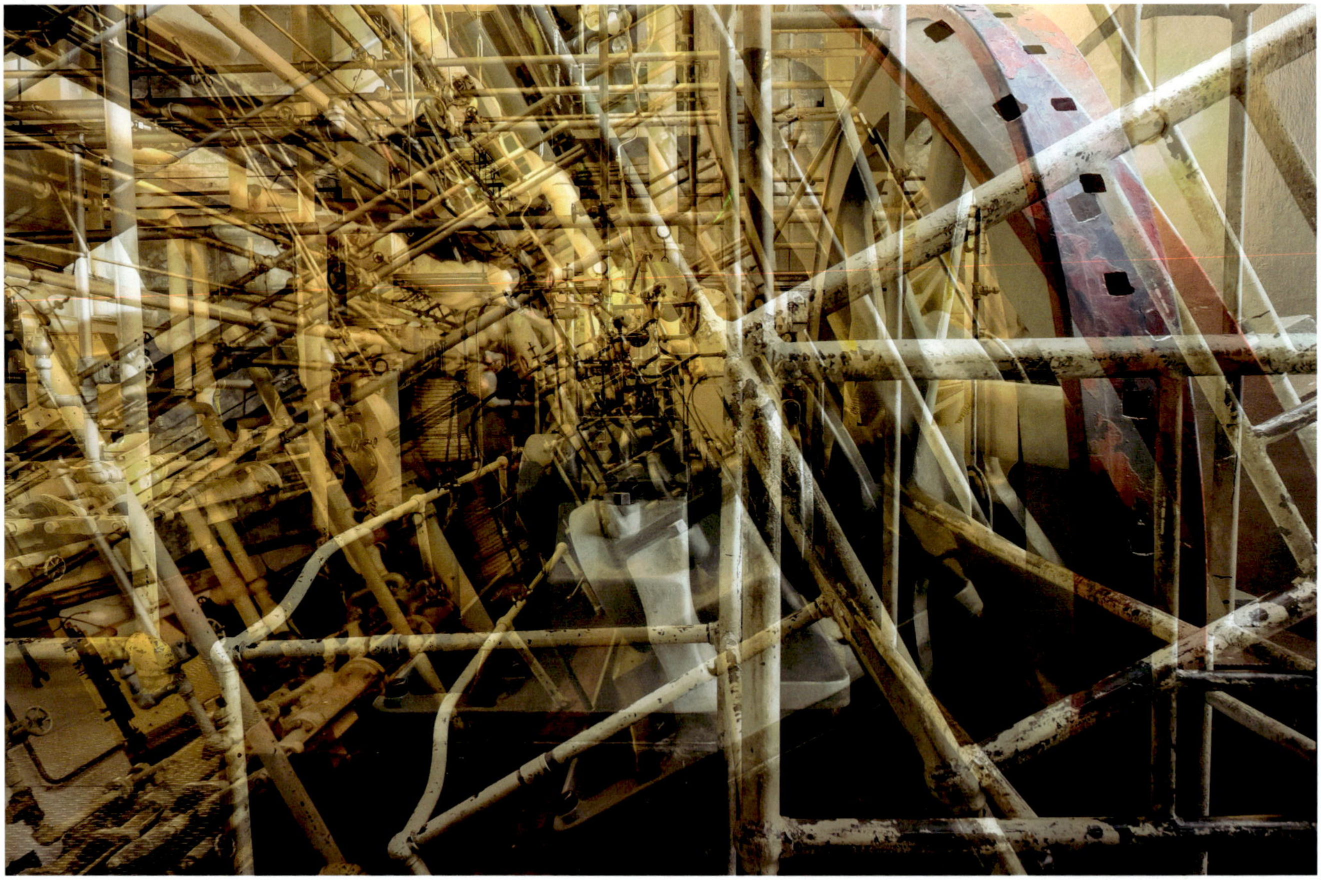

After creating many straight documentary and fine art images, it occurred to me that the site lent itself to a more abstract treatment. So, I began a project I informally termed "Steamplant 45's" and began making multiple exposures that began with a selective straight image overlain with another image of the same subject at a roughly 45 degree angle, done in camera. The soft tones are the result of the natural light from the high windows during Fall and Winter combined with interior incandescent lights. The result is *Georgetown Steam Plant Abstracts*.

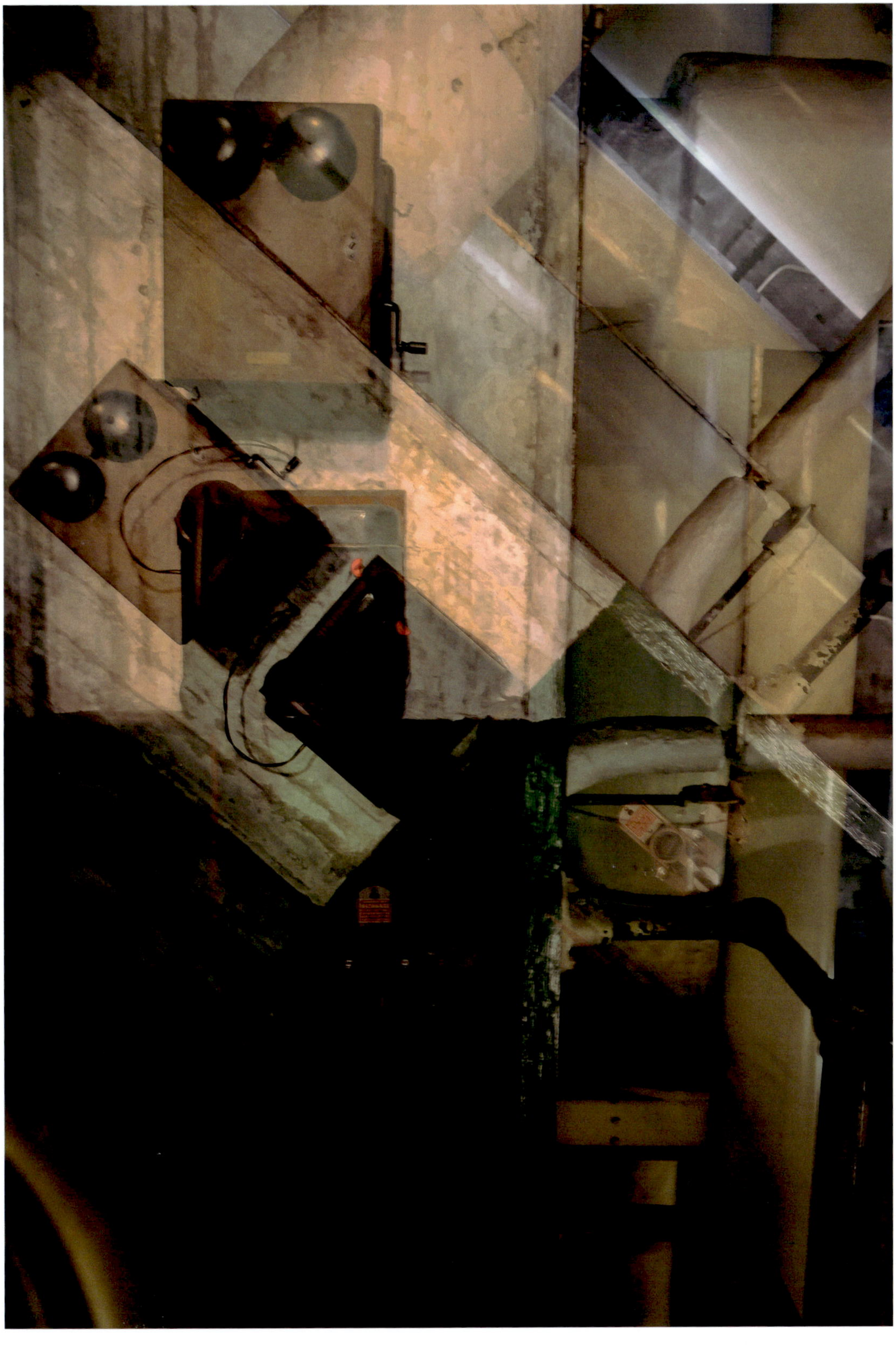

The Fog of Desert

by Jim Hontz

hontzphotography.com ♦ hontzy@comcast.net

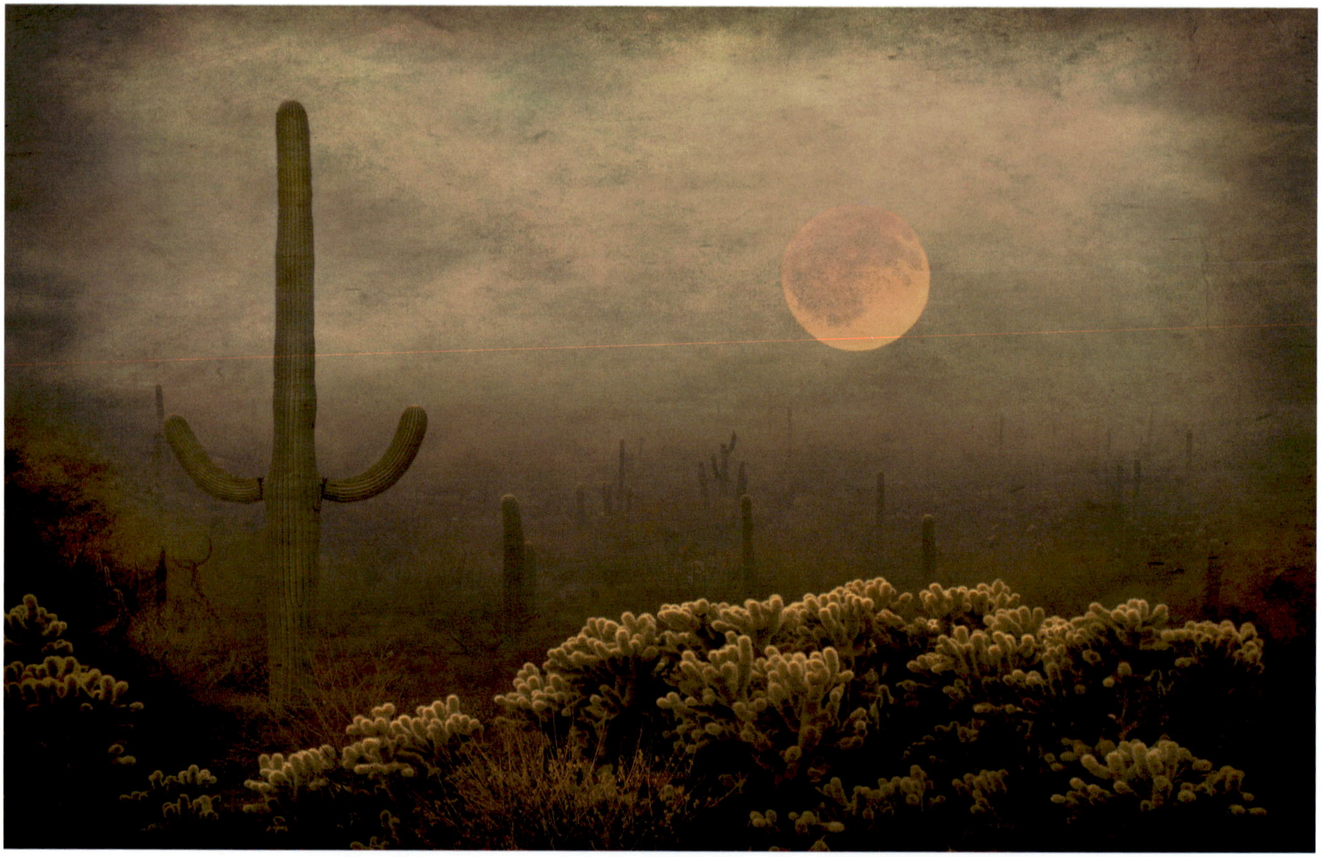

Fog in the desert seems a paradox. It usually follows a heavy winter rain and a cold night. Desert fog is contradictory to one's paradigm of a blistering, arid land inhabited by exotic, specialized life forms designed to conserve every drop of moisture for their very survival.

To wander in this rare Sonoran murk in southern Arizona is to submit to sensory deprivation. The mist subdues footsteps; voices seem muffled in cotton. Distance is foreshortened by a gray curtain through which ghostly saguaros advance and retreat as if from a fantastic, silent dream. The mist is tenuous as it teases those forces which seek to disperse it or enter it.

These blended images are a collective impression of the beautiful mystery of this otherworldly landscape.

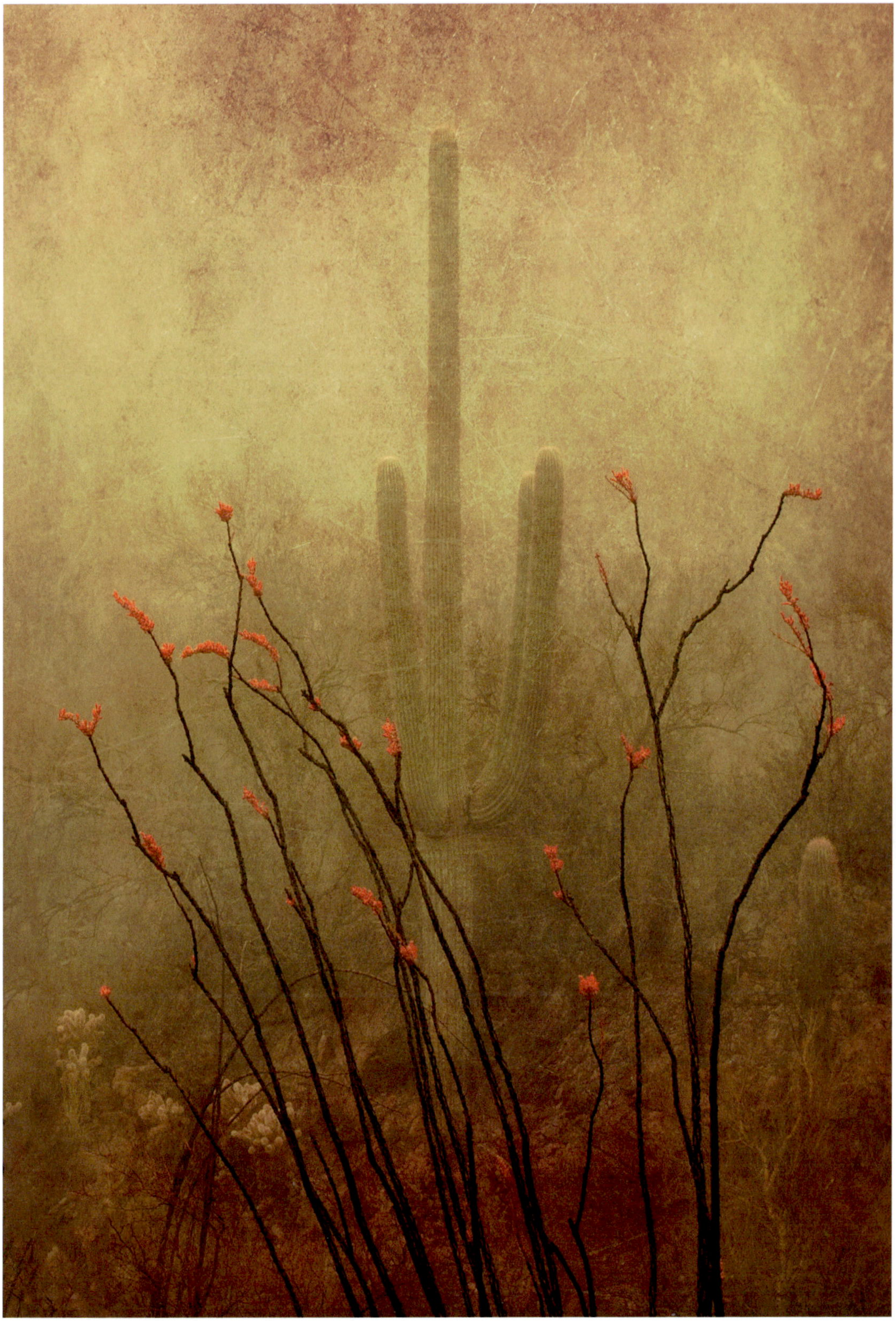

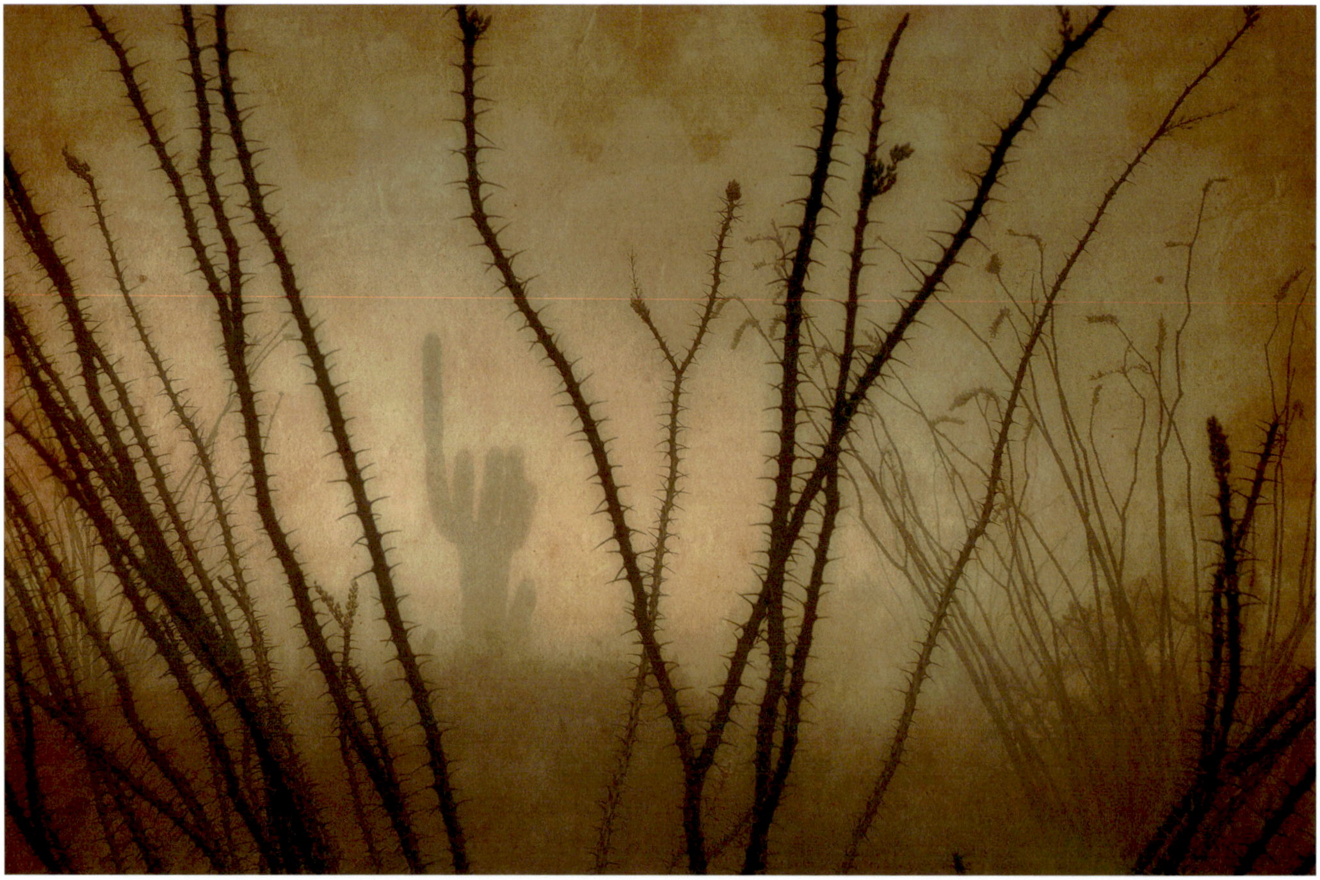

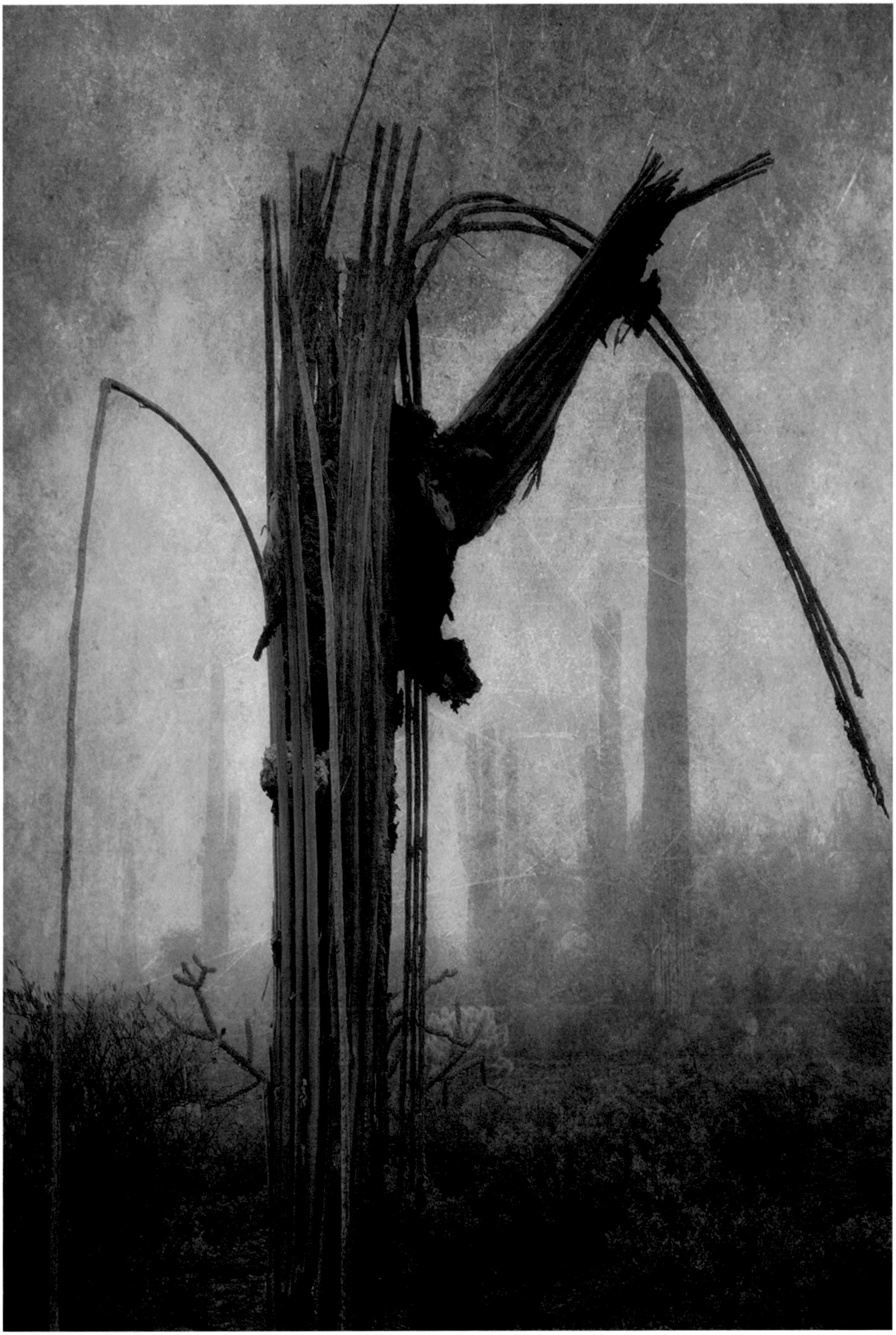

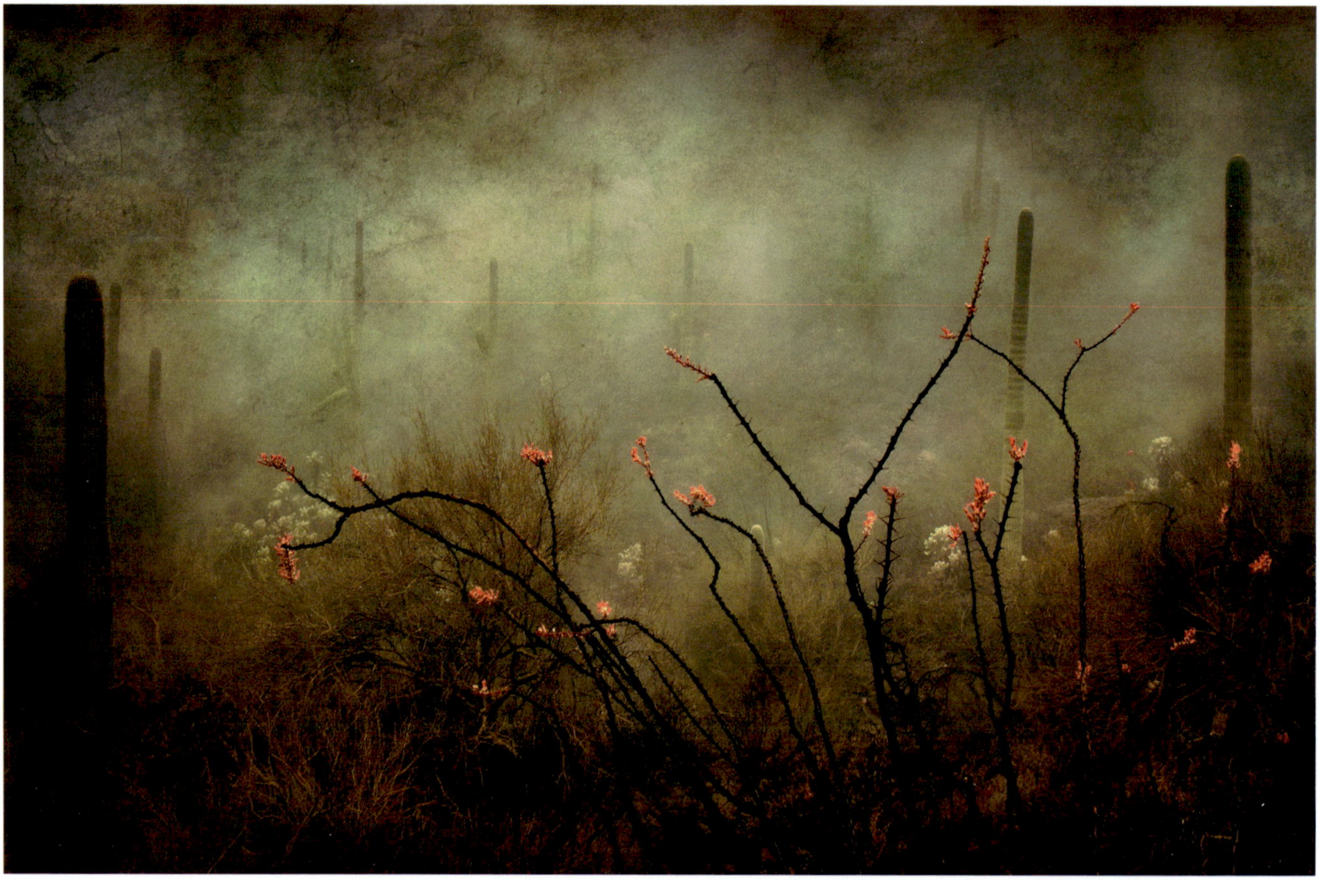

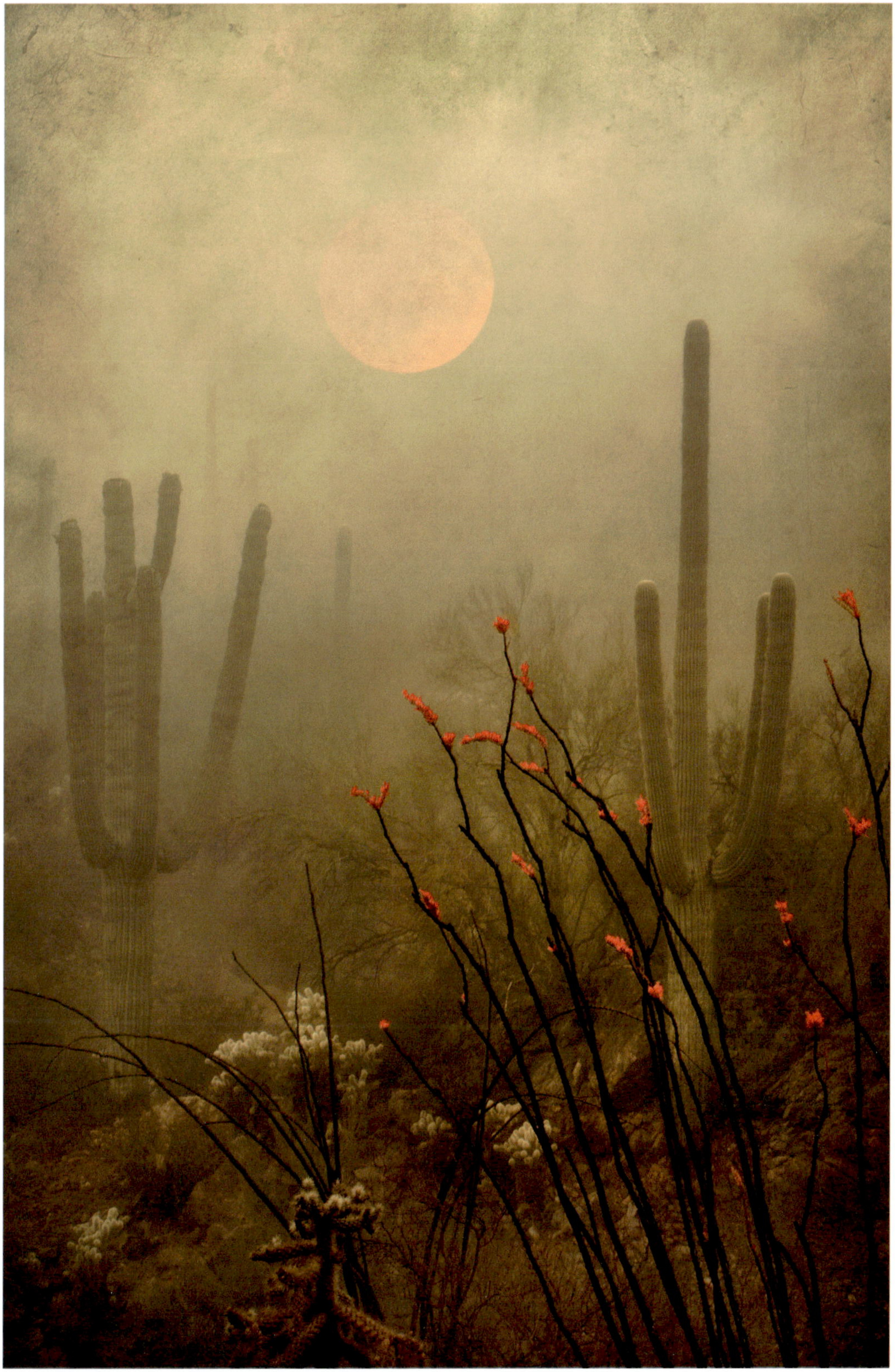

The Wonder of Paper

by Douglas Hall

www.douglashallphotography.com • dhall1000@hotmail.com

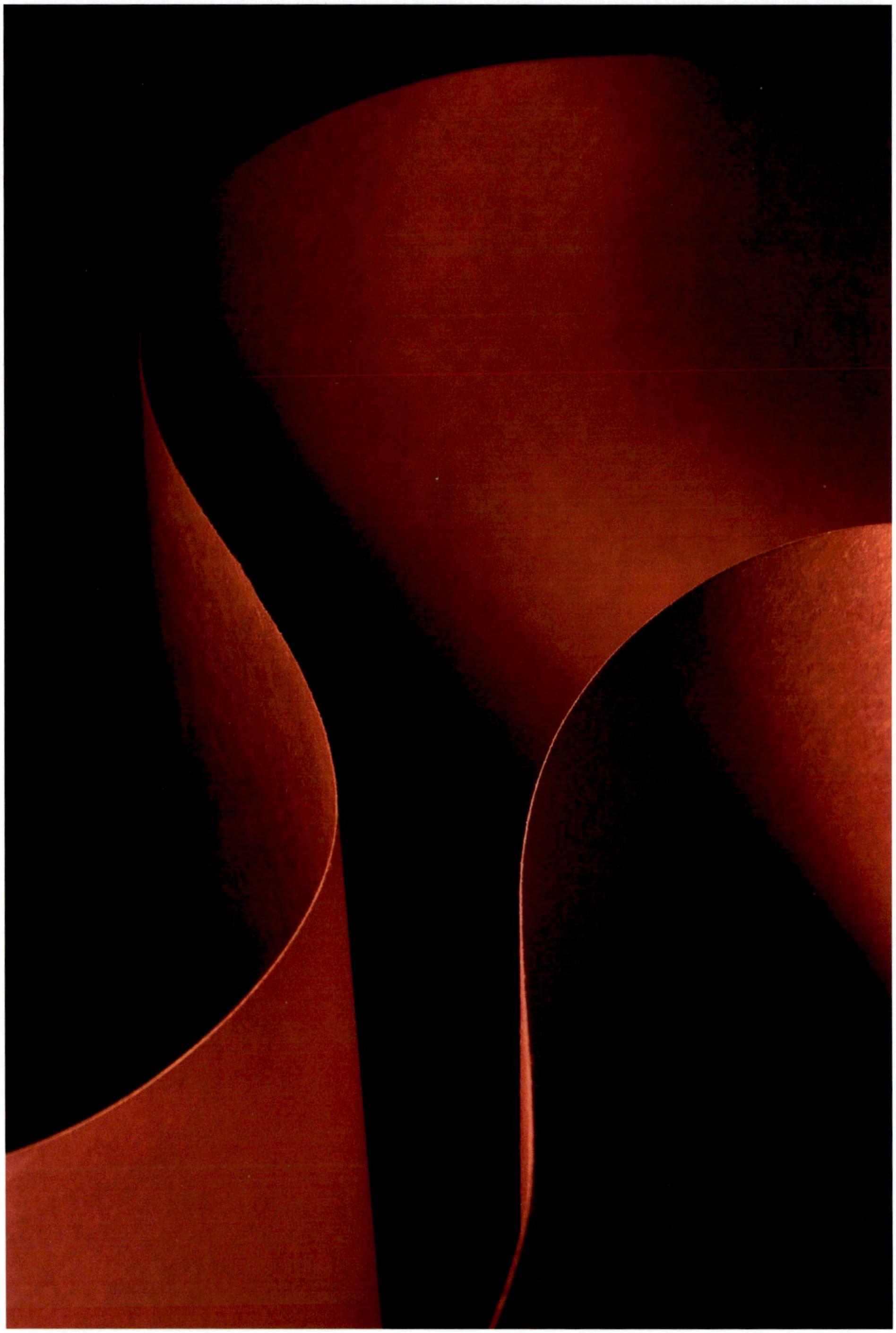

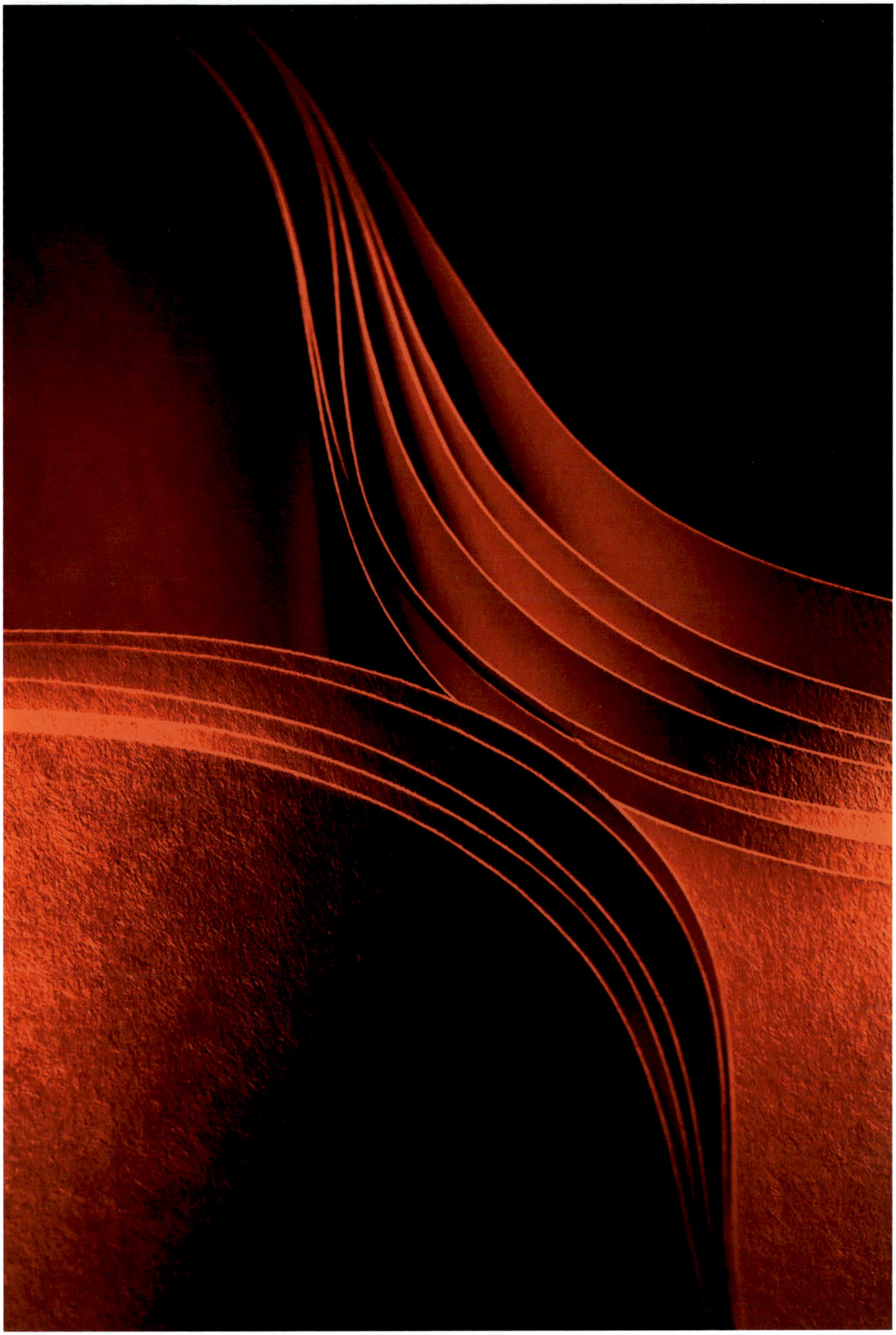

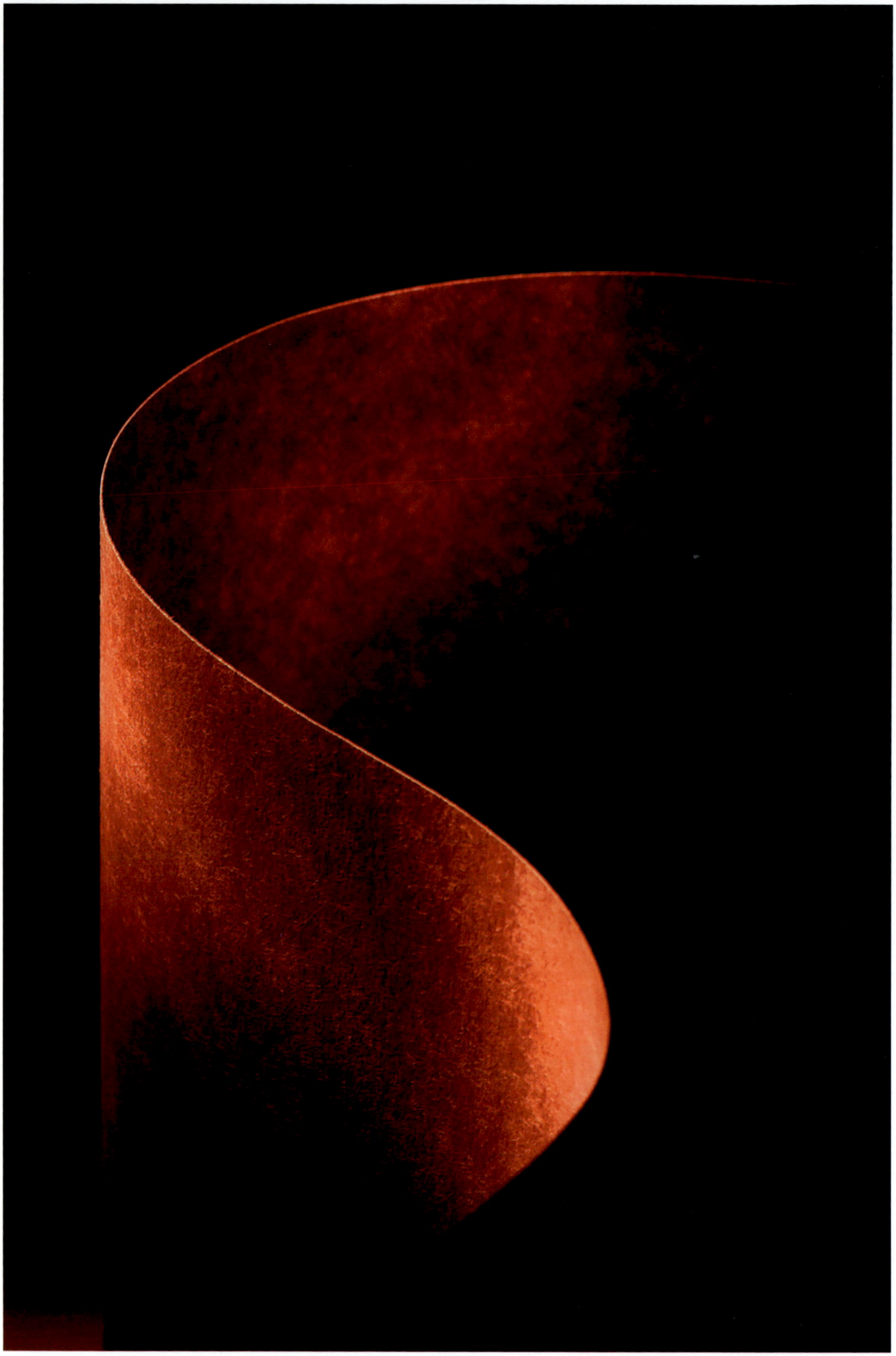

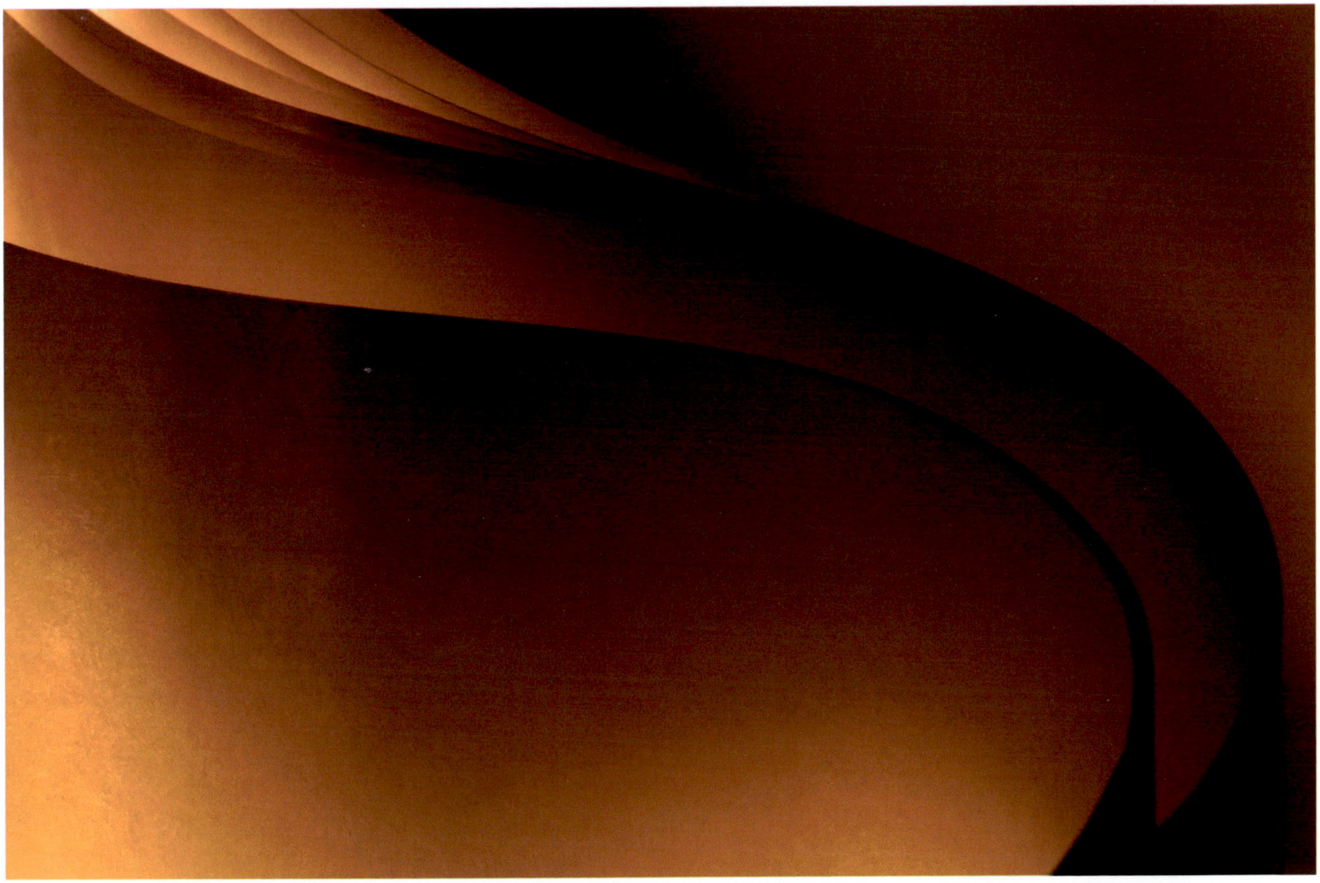

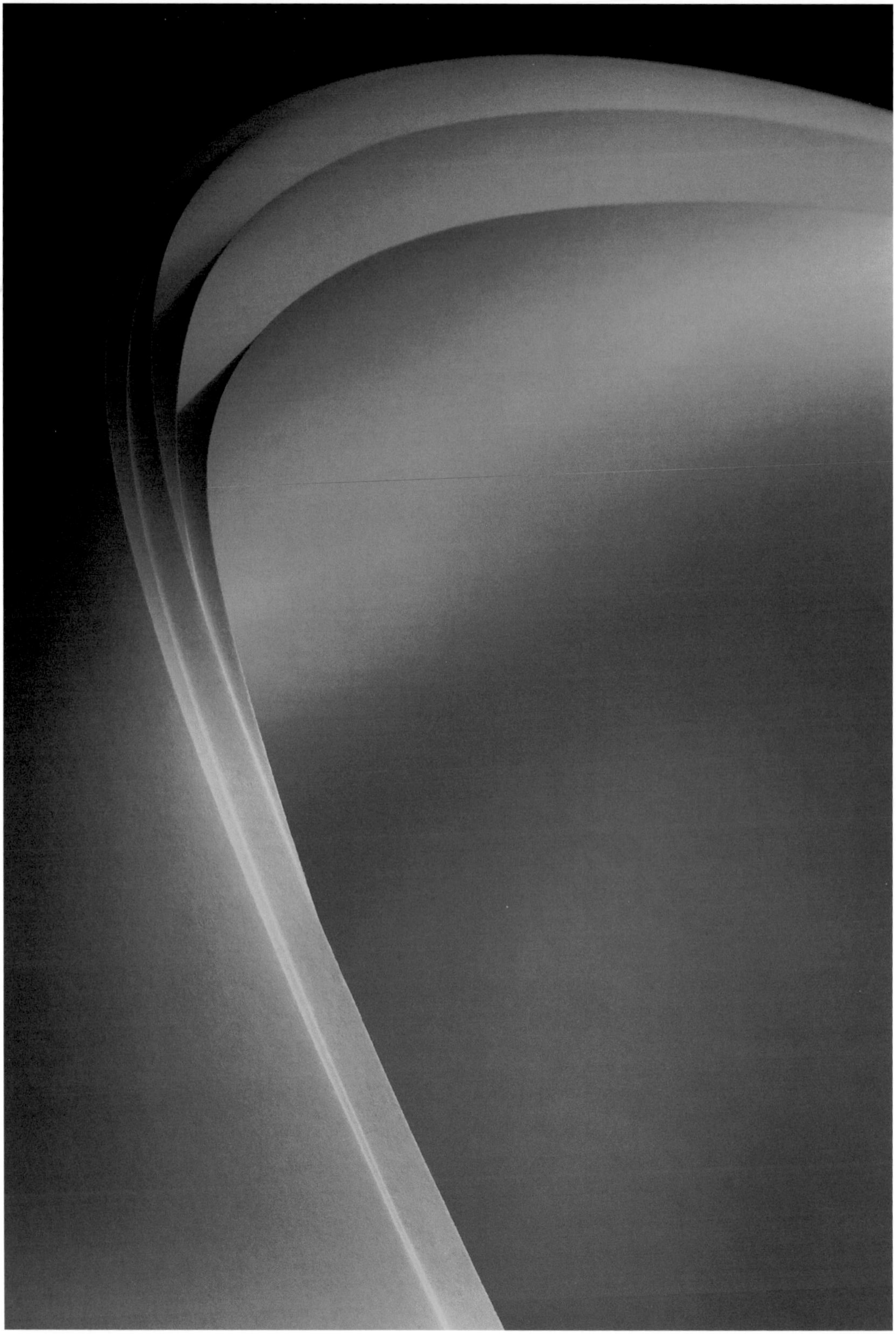

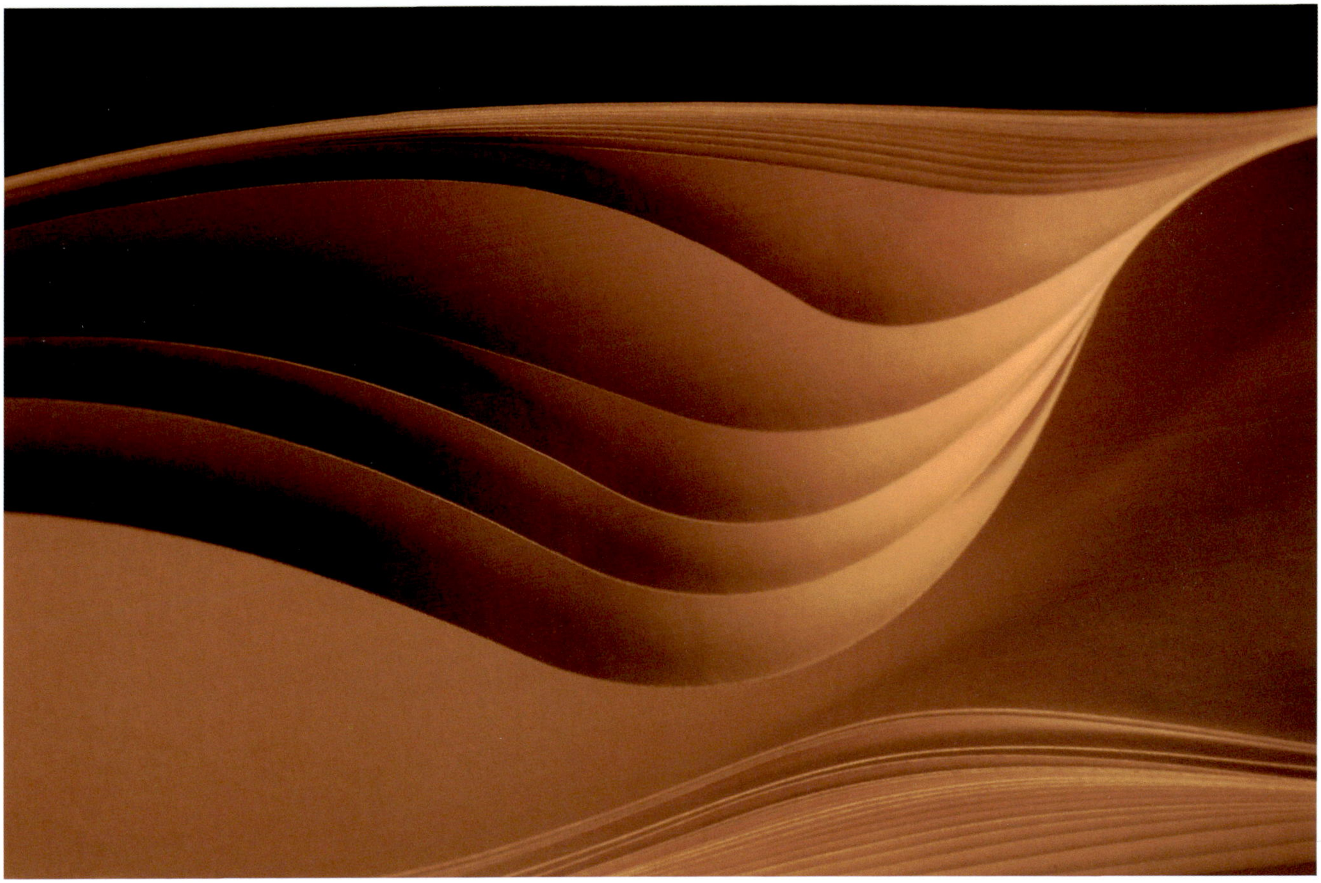

Sleep

by Savannah Bullinger

sbullinger@arcadia.edu

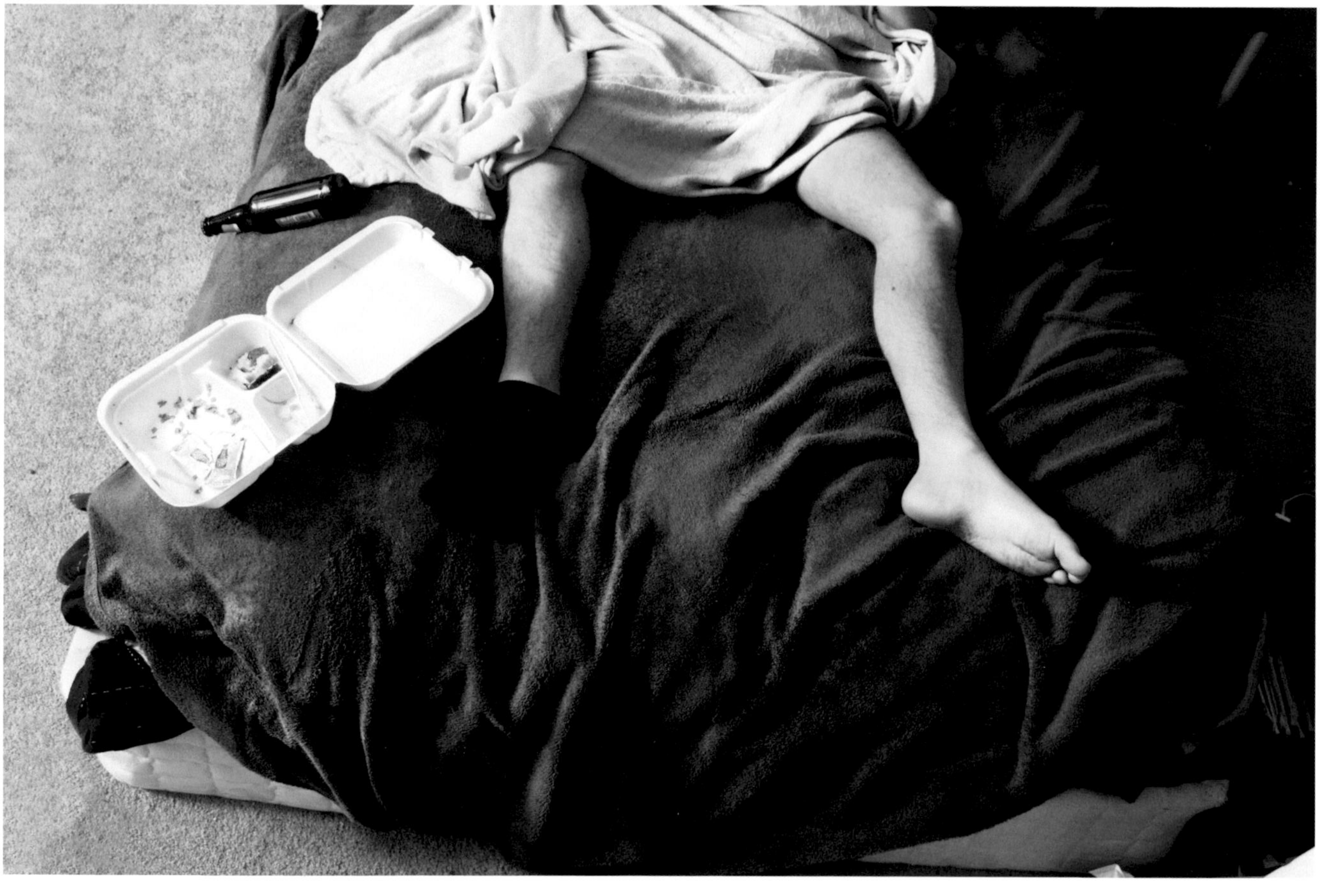

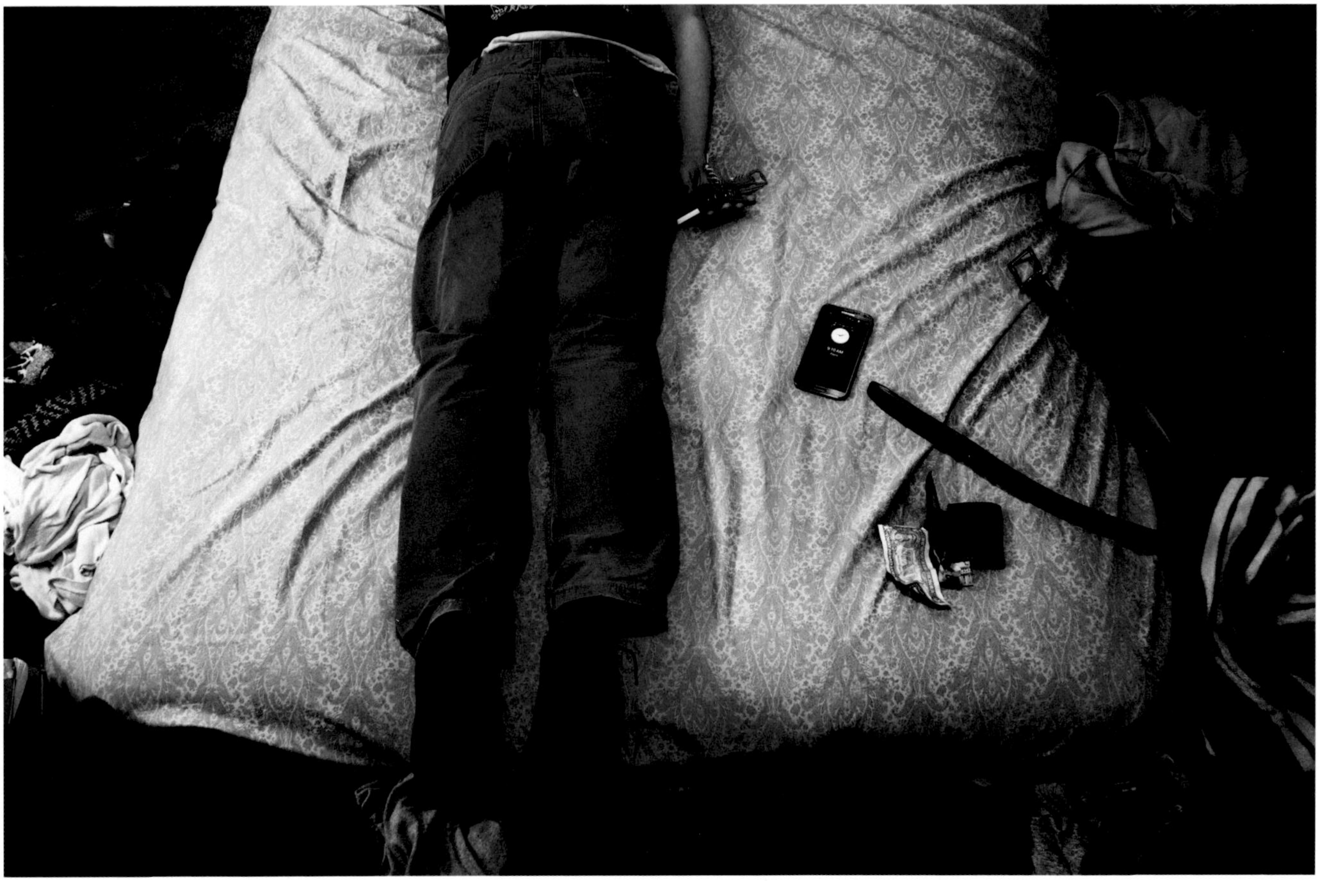

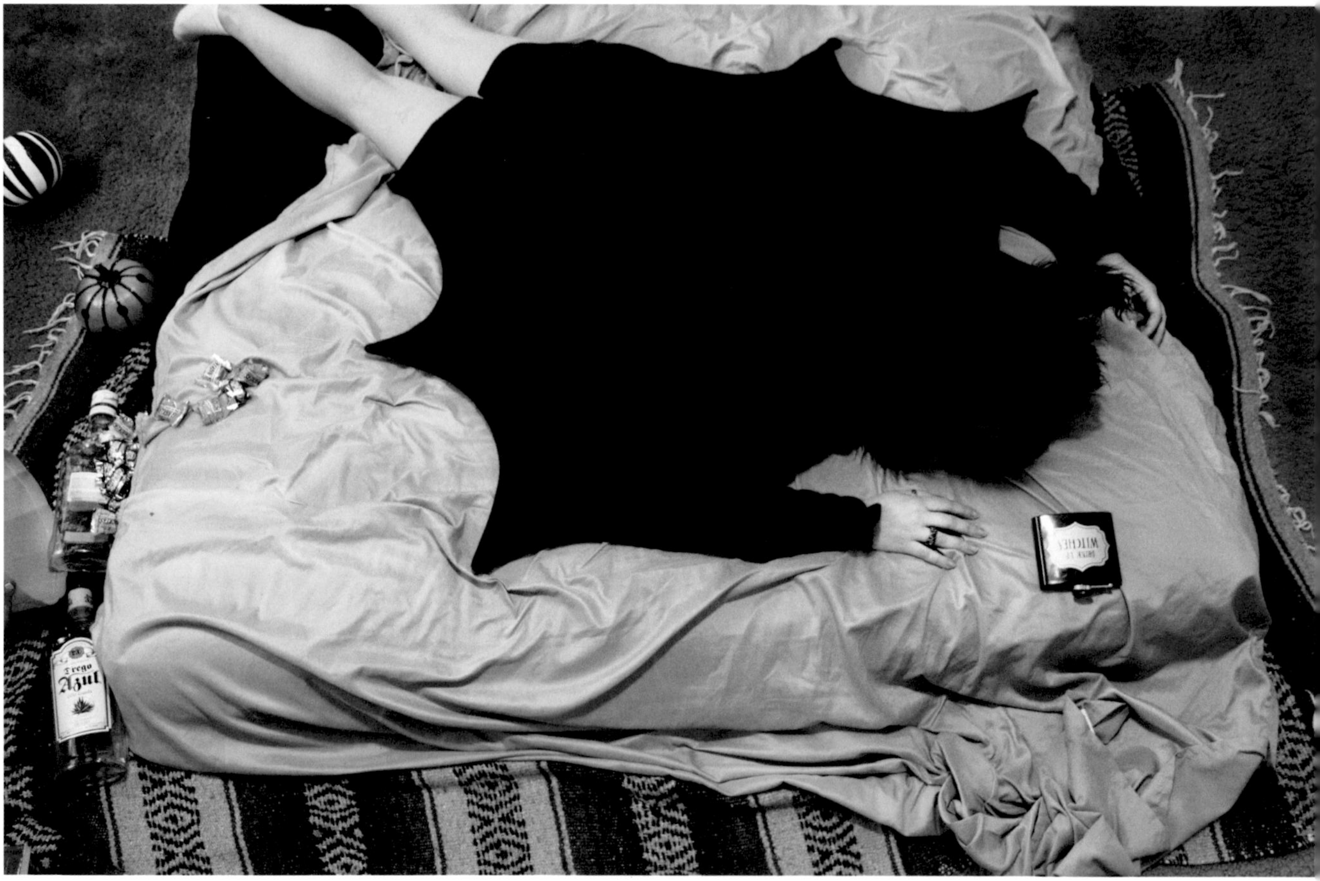
Azul

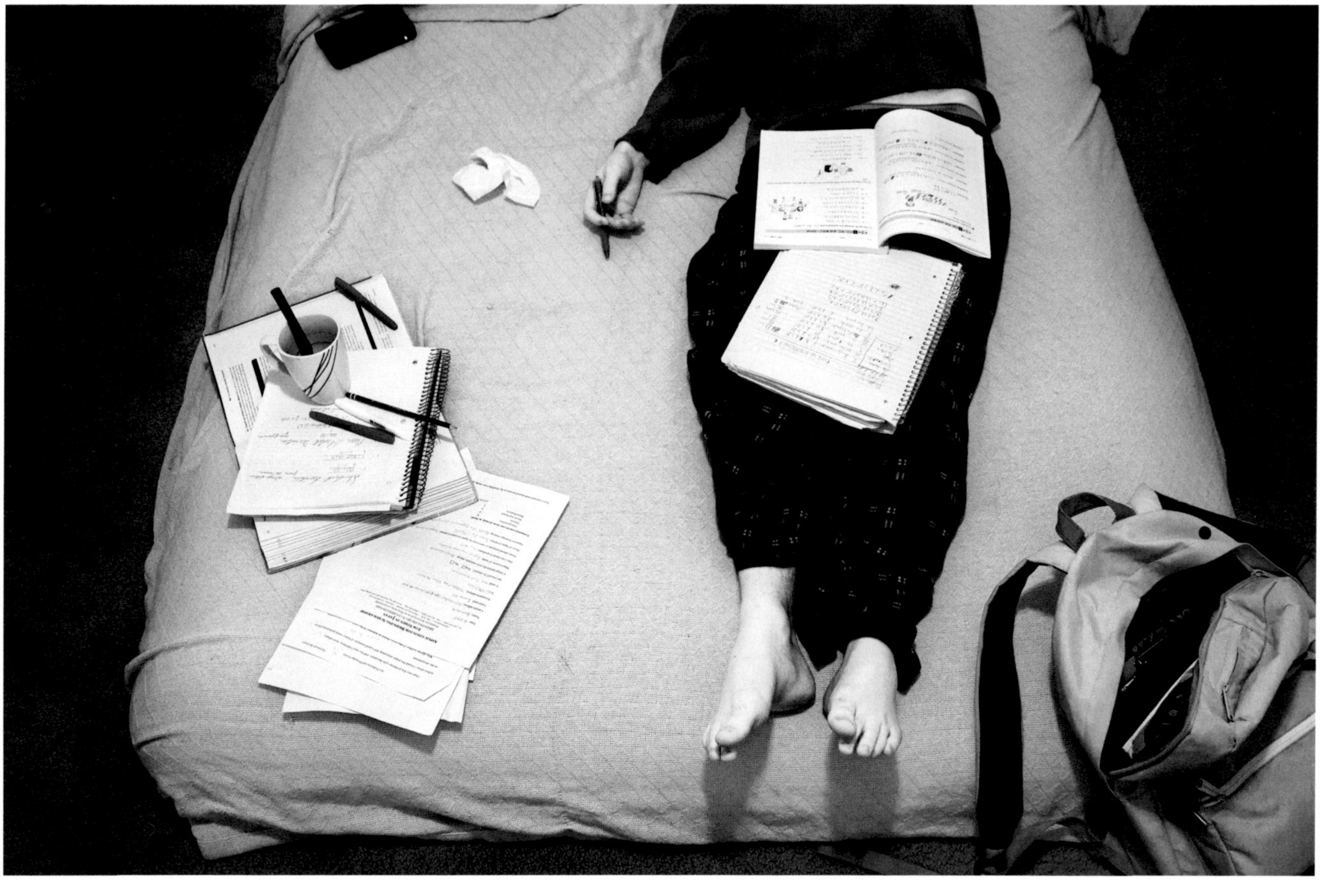

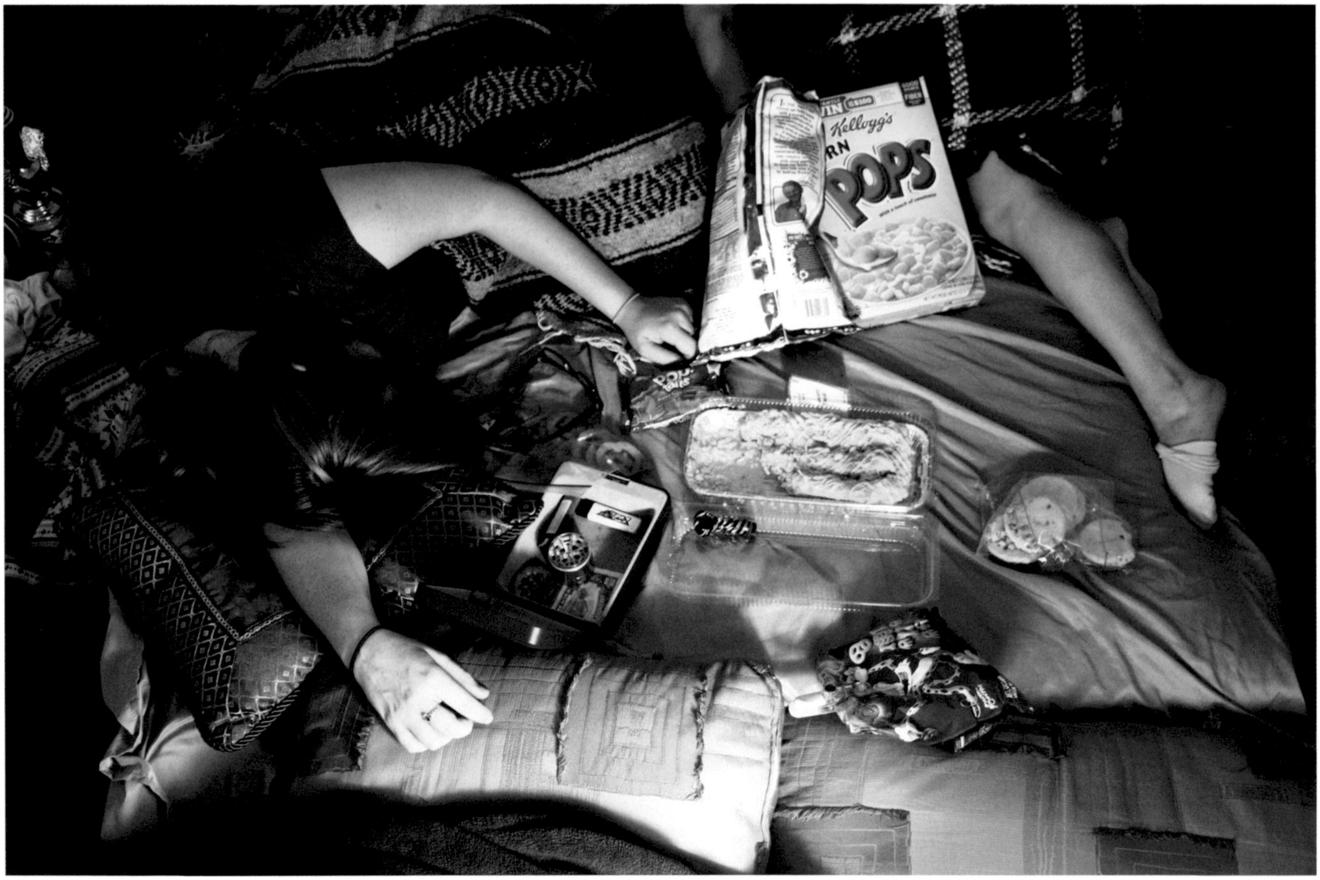
Kellogg's
POPS

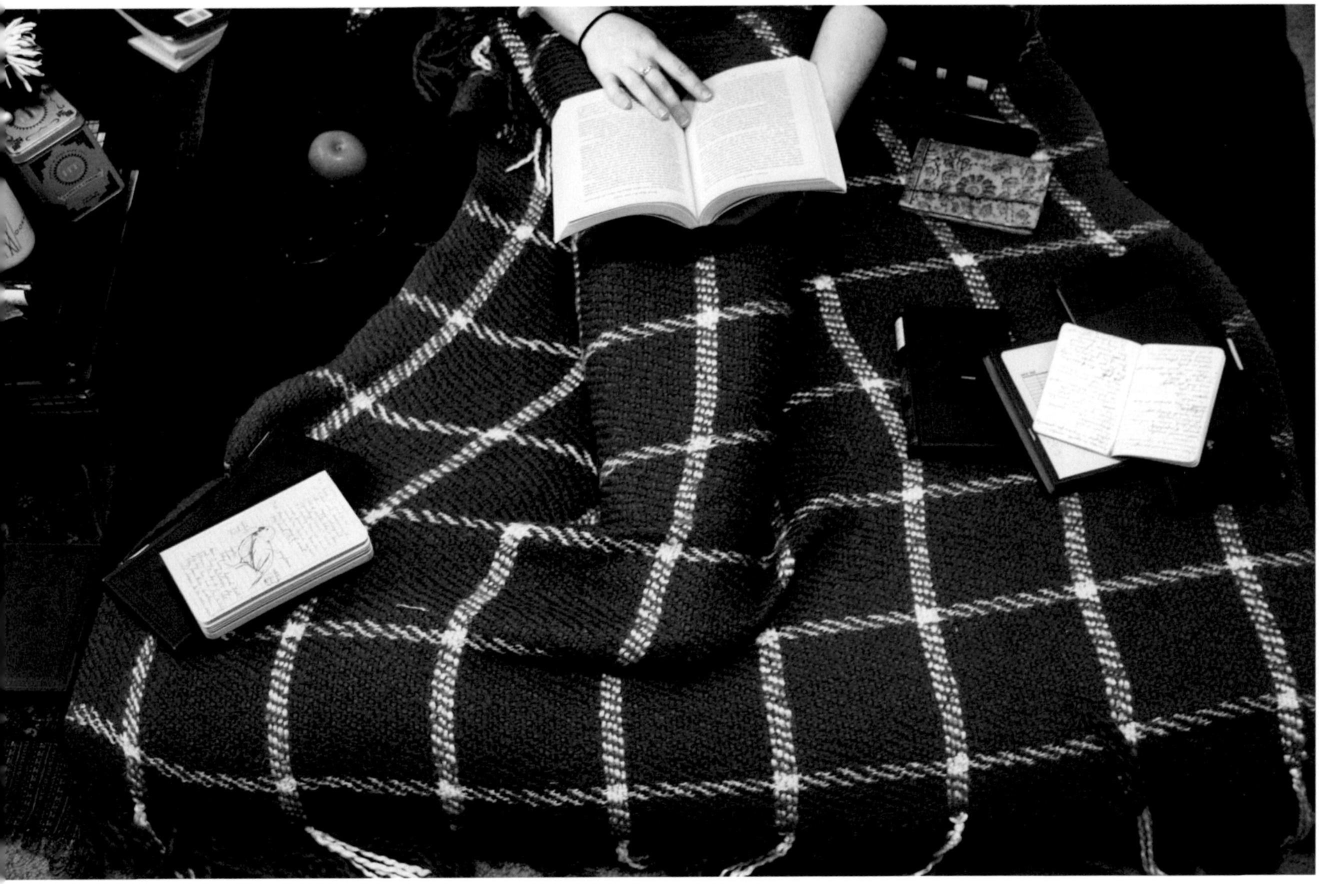

Quiet Hour in the Mannequin Asylum

by Tim Messick

www.timmessick.com • tmessick1@gmail.com

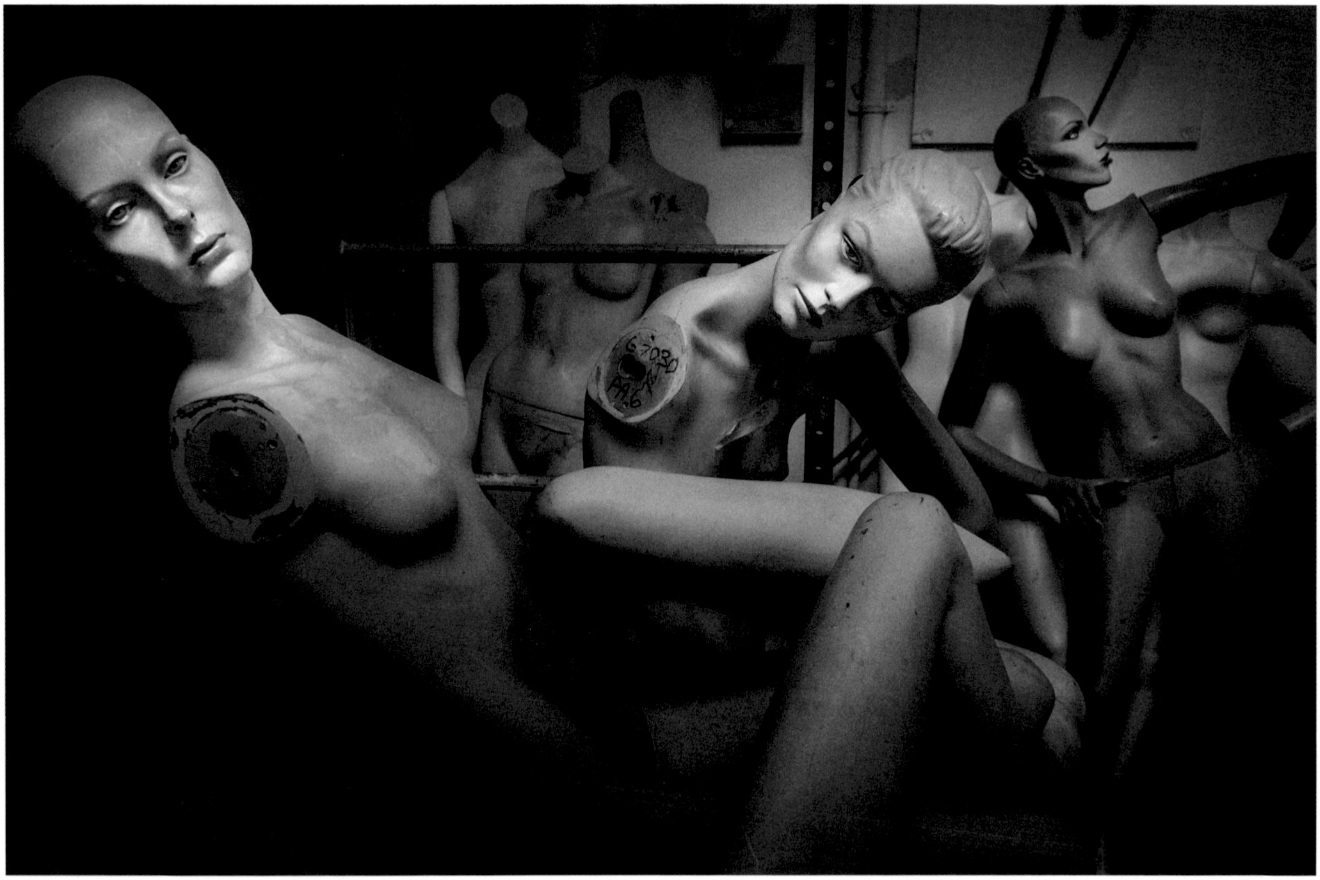

Mannequins Doing their Morning Exercises

There's a store in Sacramento that sells used furnishings and paraphernalia from department stores and clothing shops that have either closed or replaced their damaged fixtures. They have mannequins — many, many mannequins, retired now after years of service or between jobs. They're waiting silently for repairs and the possibility of new homes. But the store where they now reside will itself be closing within a year, so the fate of these mannequins is at best uncertain. I've been there several times now with local photo friends. It's a "target-rich environment" for photography, a playground for image-making.

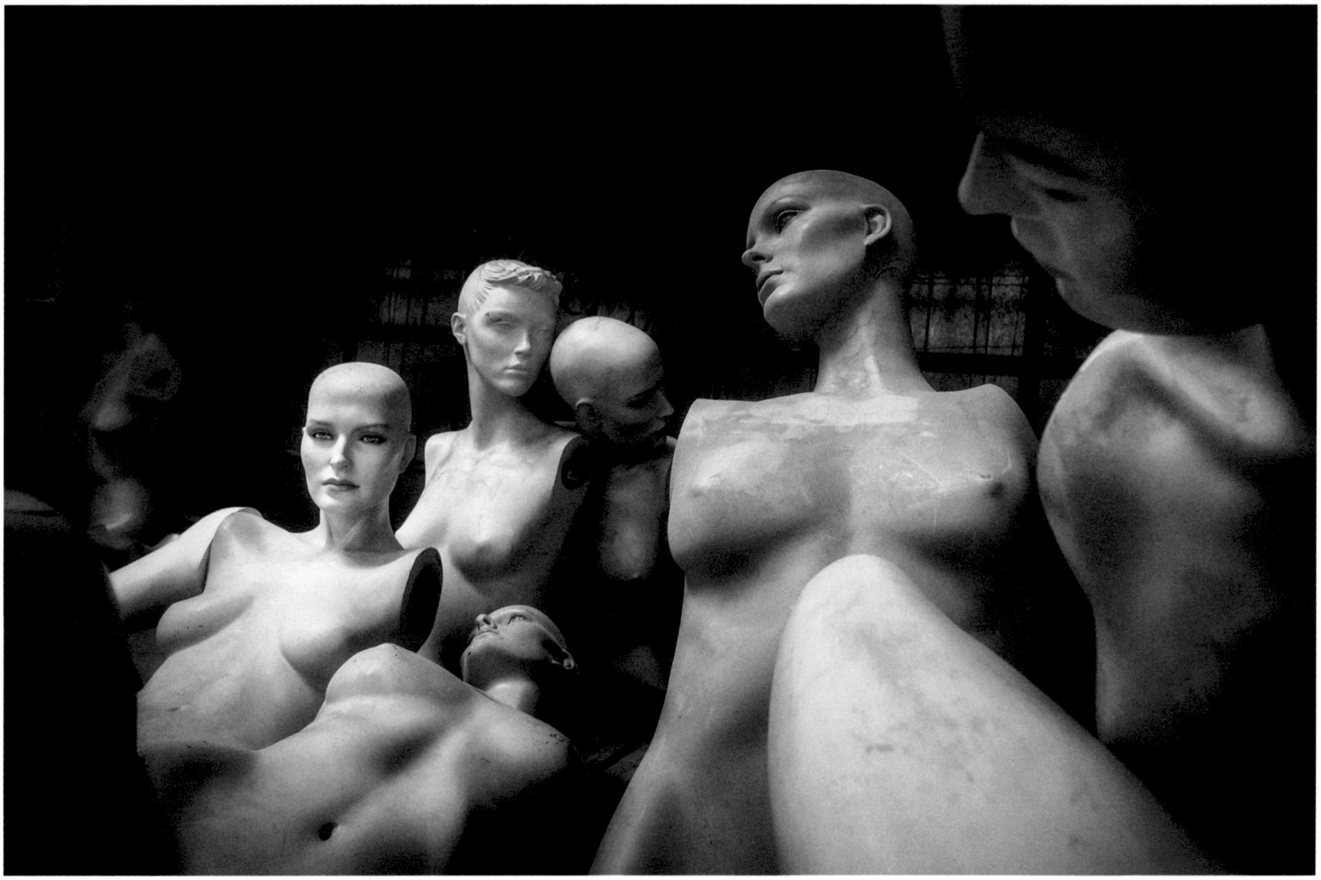

Quiet Hour in the Mannequin Asylum

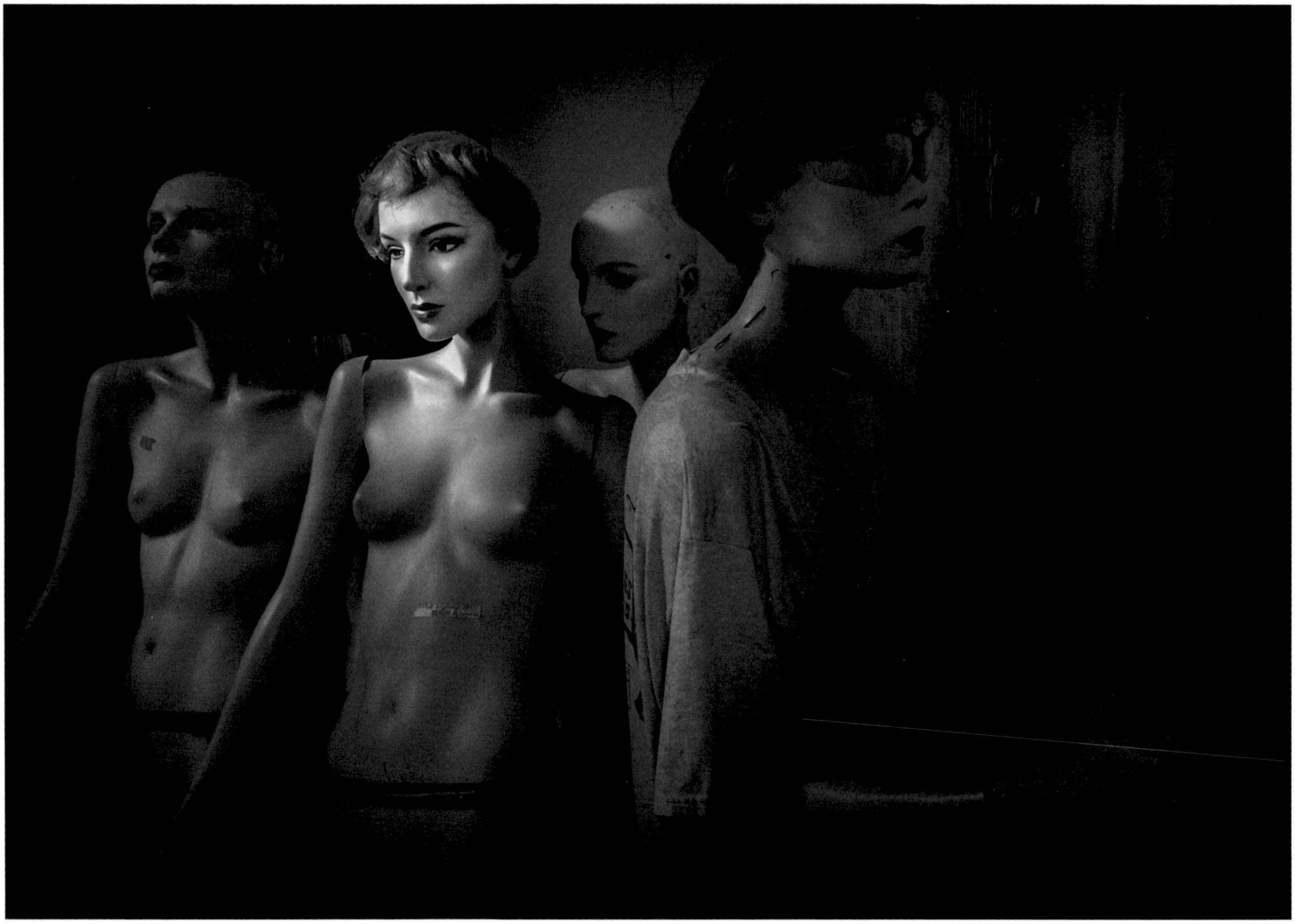

Mannequins Loitering in the Shadows

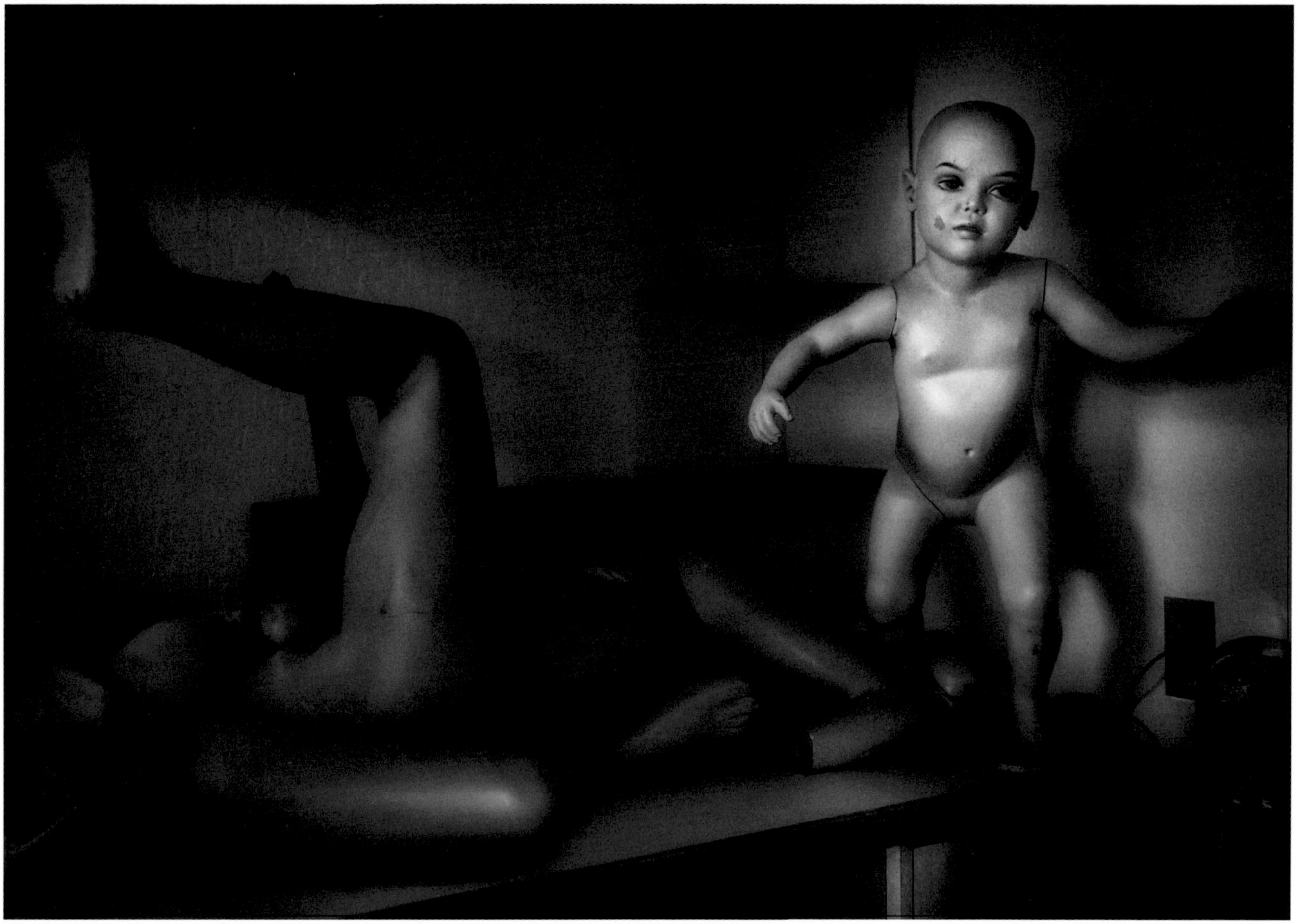

Mannekid Looking for Mom

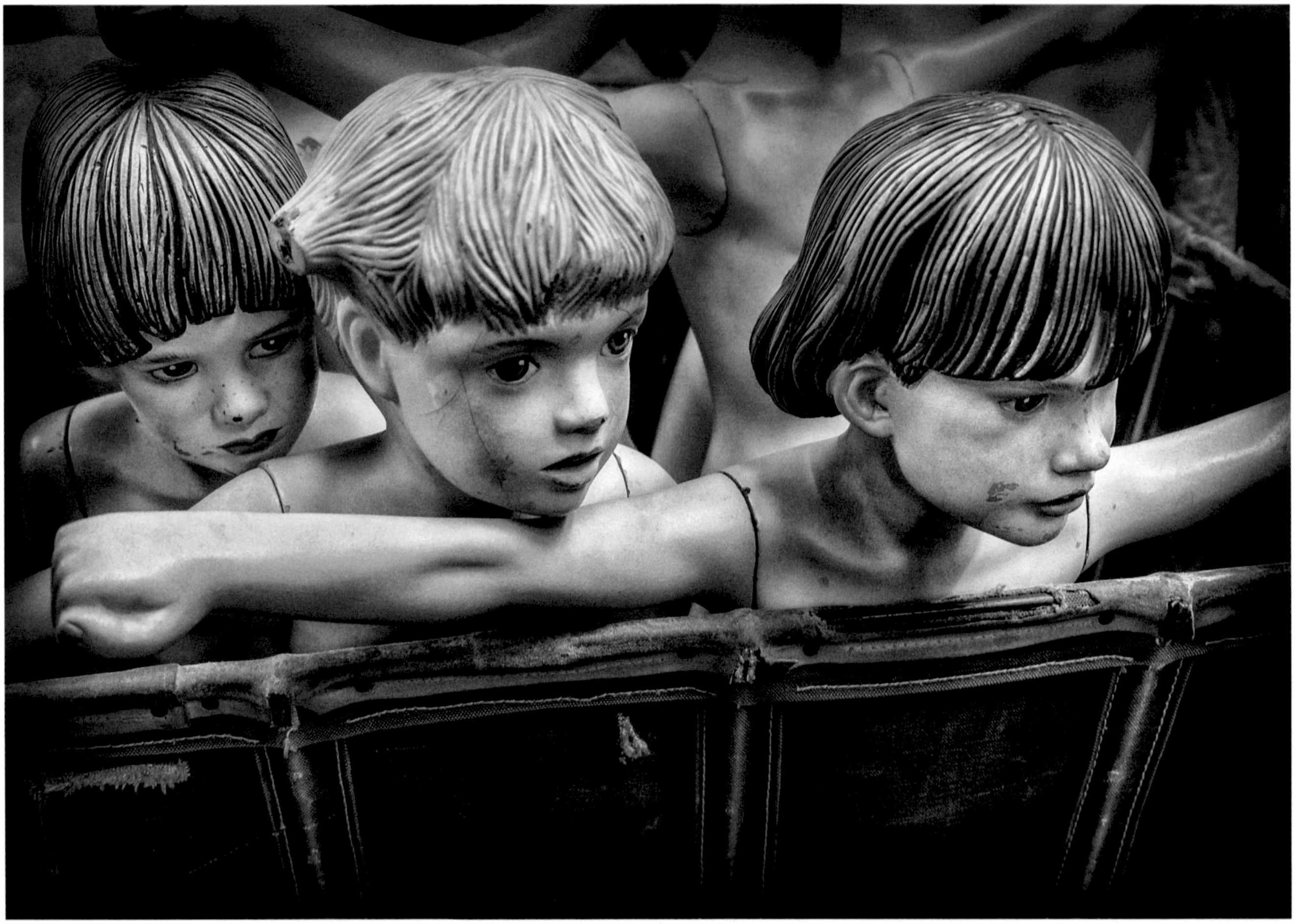

Mannekids Looking Concerned

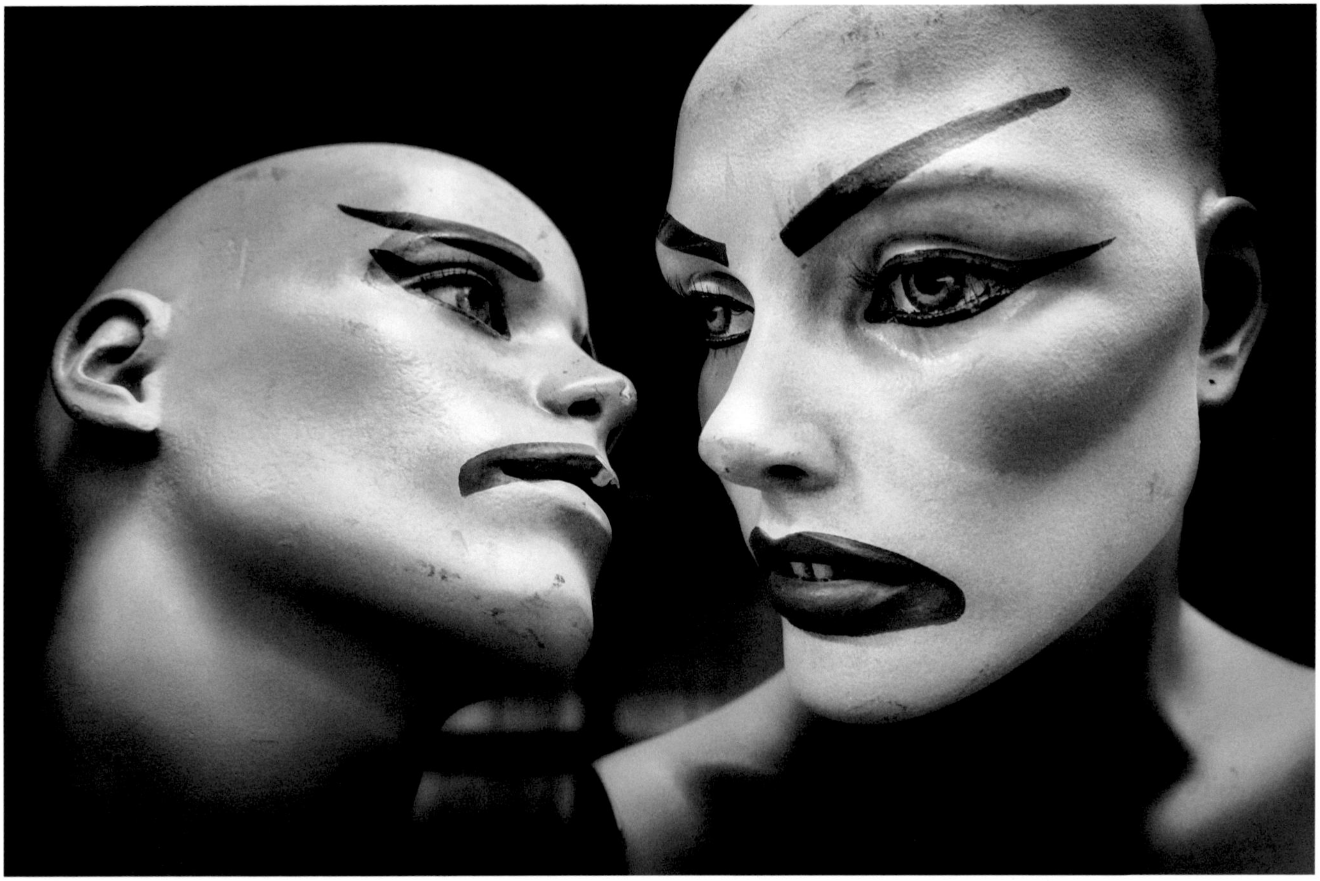

Mannequins Plotting their Escape

Northern Sea Nettles

by Mary Virginia Hall

www.maryvirginiastroud.com ♦ missmerv@yahoo.com

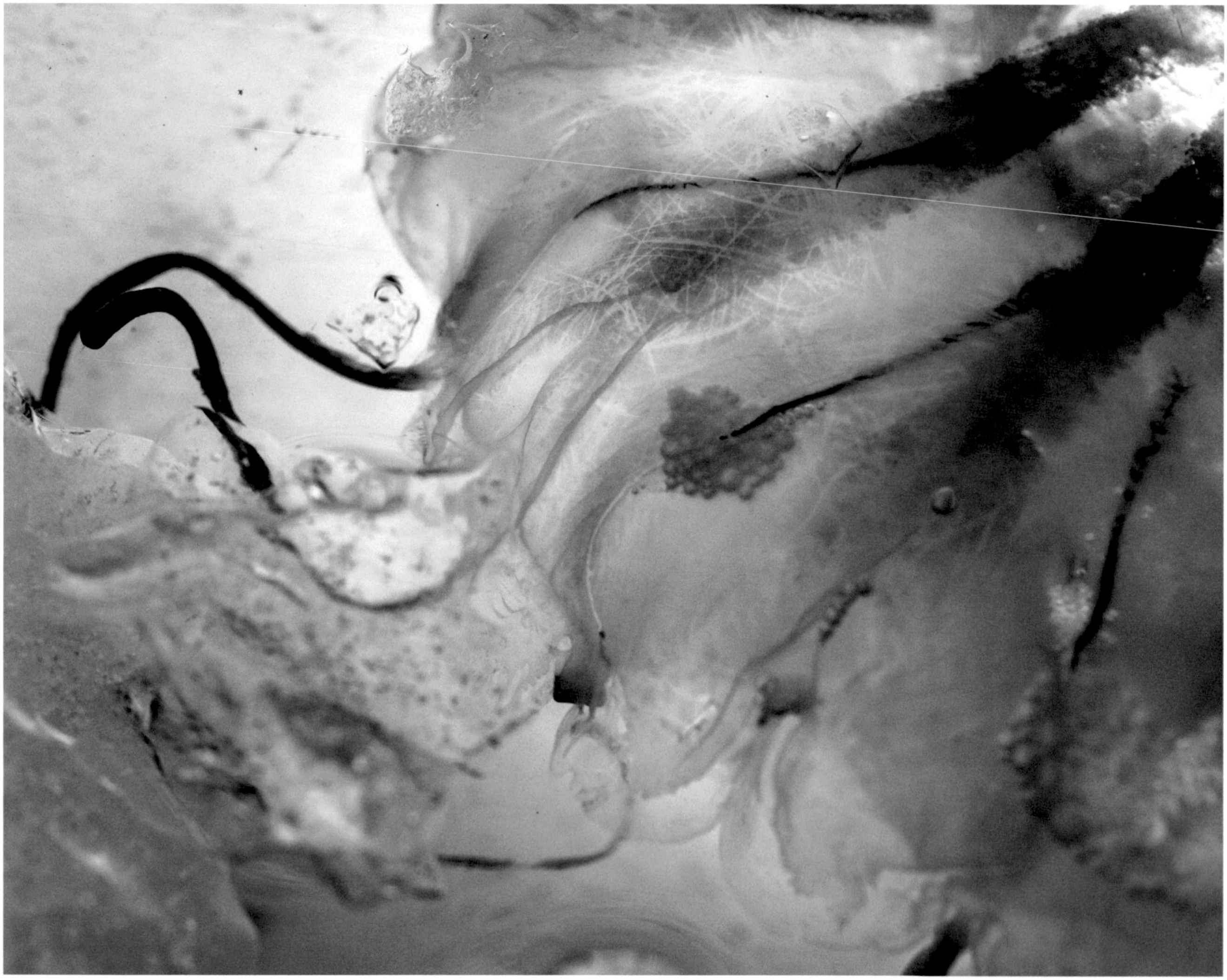

For the past five years I have been documenting the arrival of Chrysaora melanaster, the Northern sea nettle, on the beaches of Barrow, Alaska, through a series of monochrome, macro photographs. Their inner luminescence and grace of movement as they wash ashore is exquisite. Through careful framing and removal of the distracting element of color, I emphasize their diaphanous quality and texture that give them such a unique beauty even in death. Their presence in the arctic, however, is significant. Scientific studies in the Bering Sea fishery indicate that this species' population has increased tenfold in the last decade. Warming ocean temperatures associated with changes in atmospheric pressure patterns is the most likely candidate for the population explosion, but studies are ongoing. What this increase portends for their ocean environment remains to be seen, but it is obvious they deserve closer scrutiny as they may have a role to play in the future of our environment.

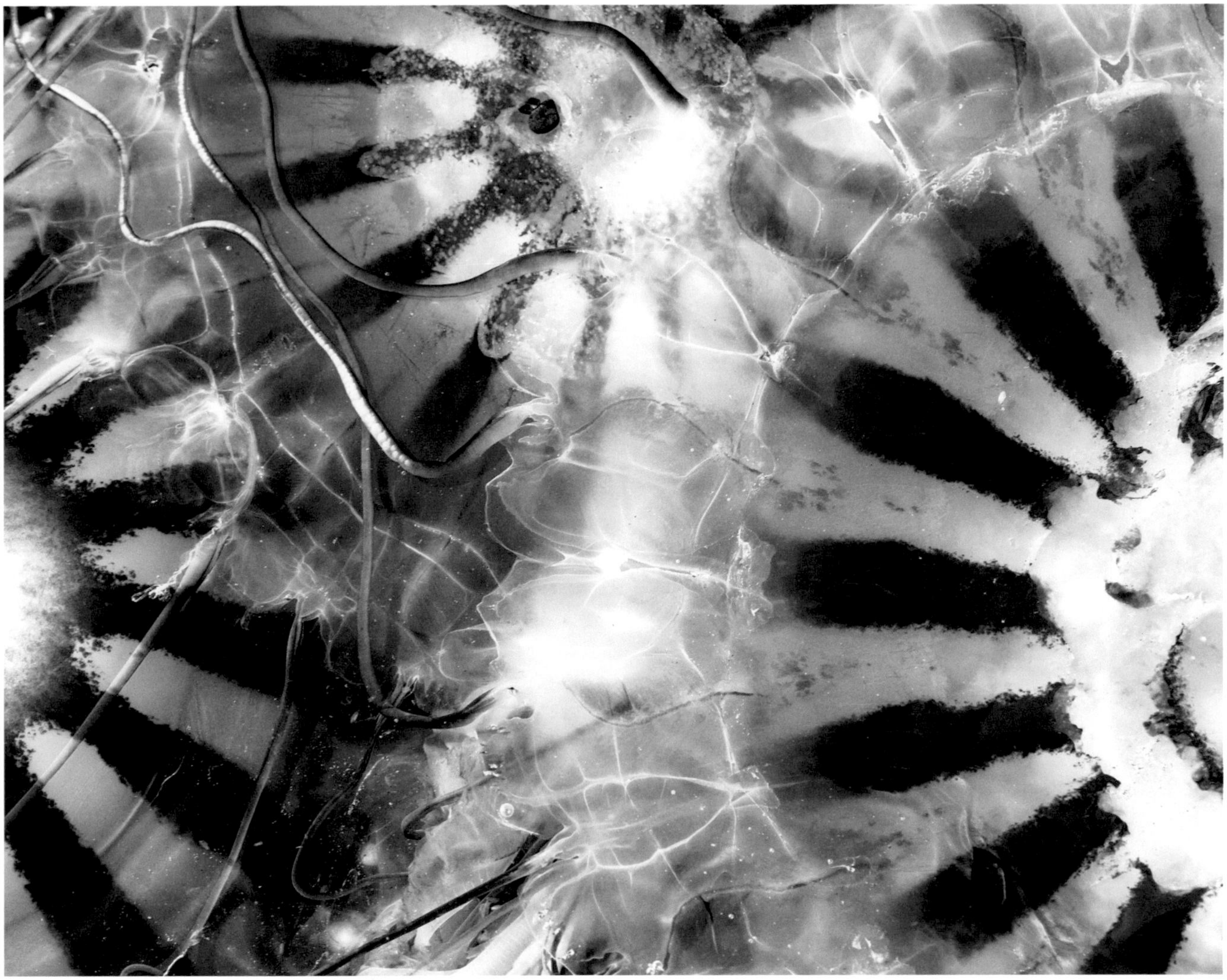

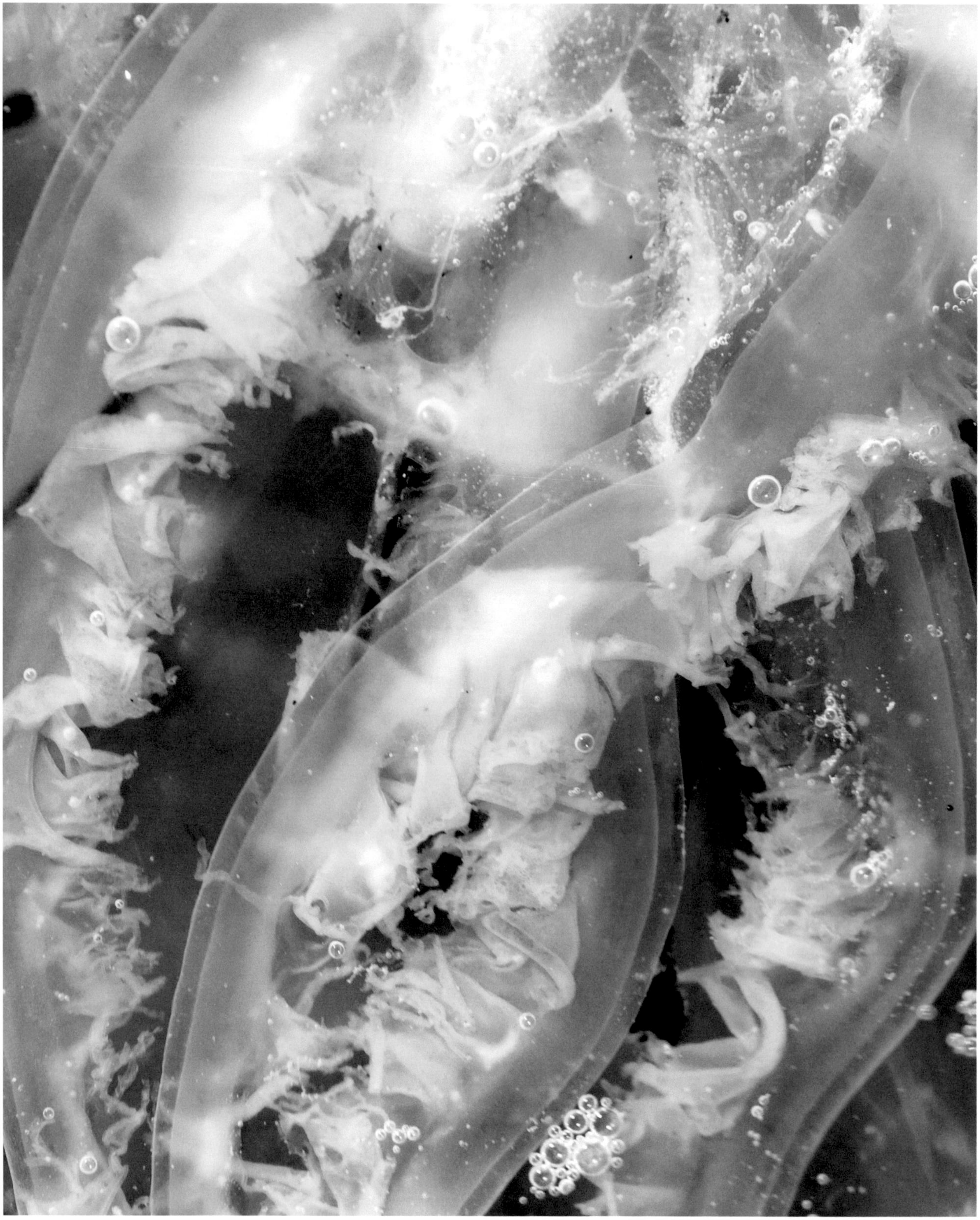

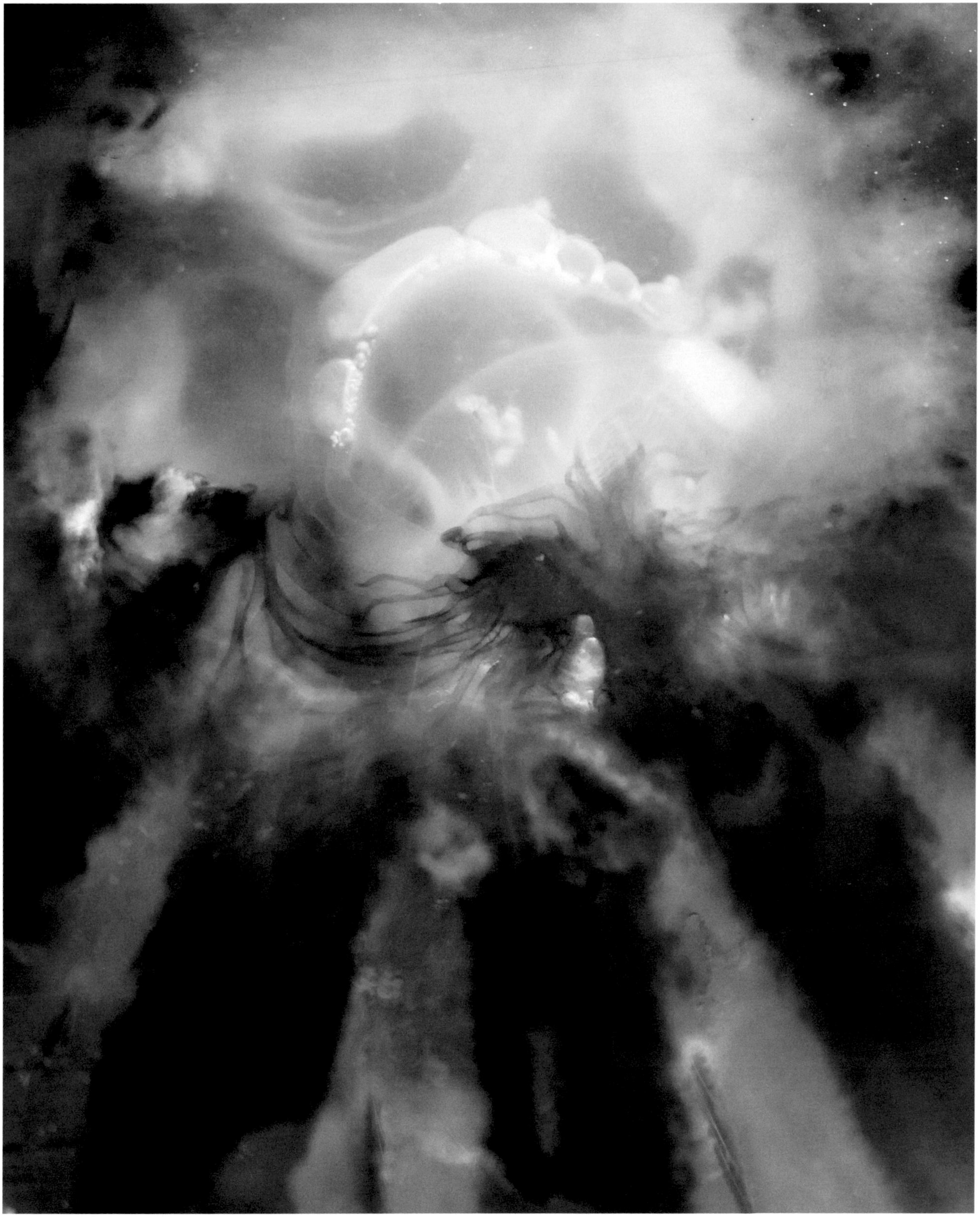

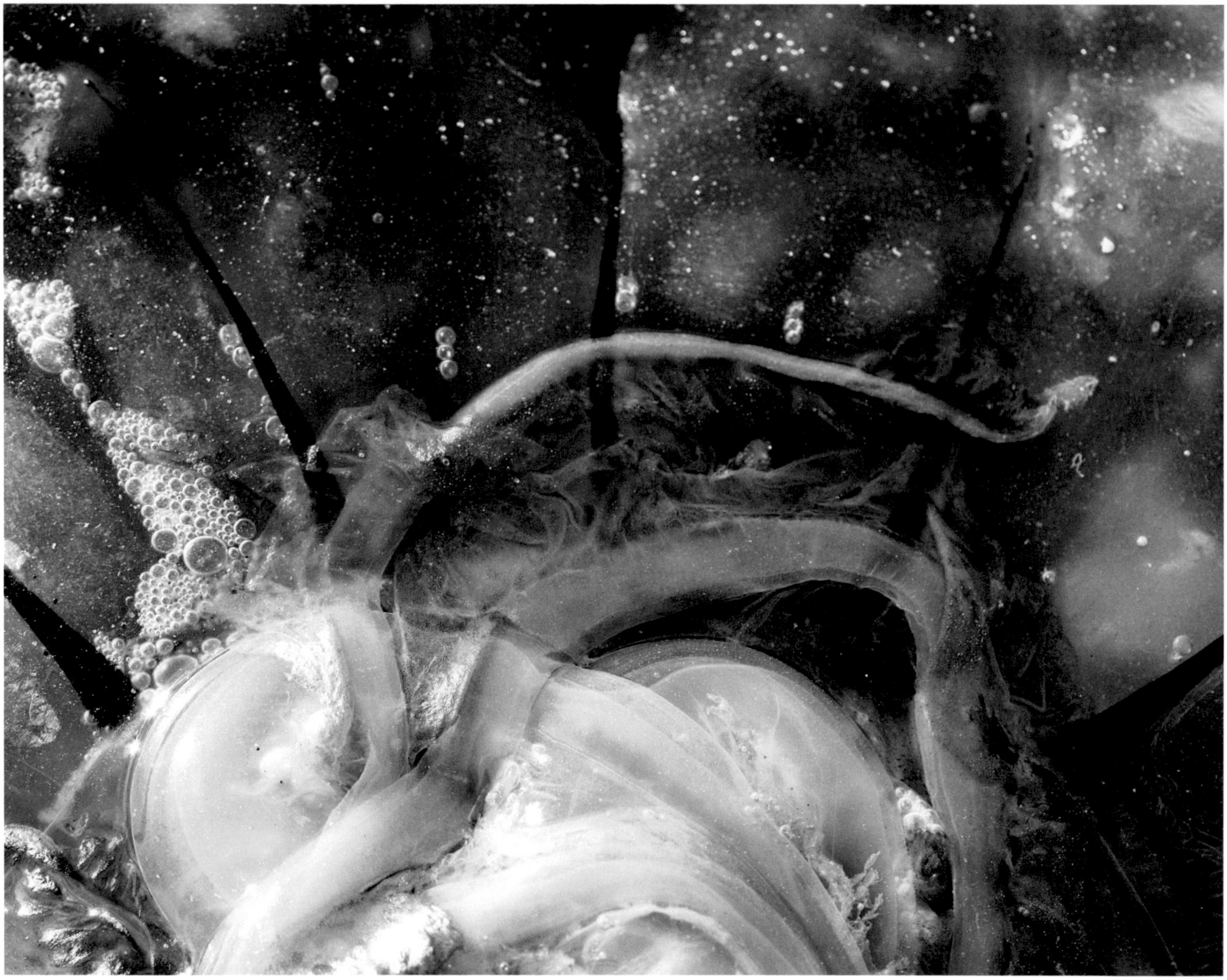

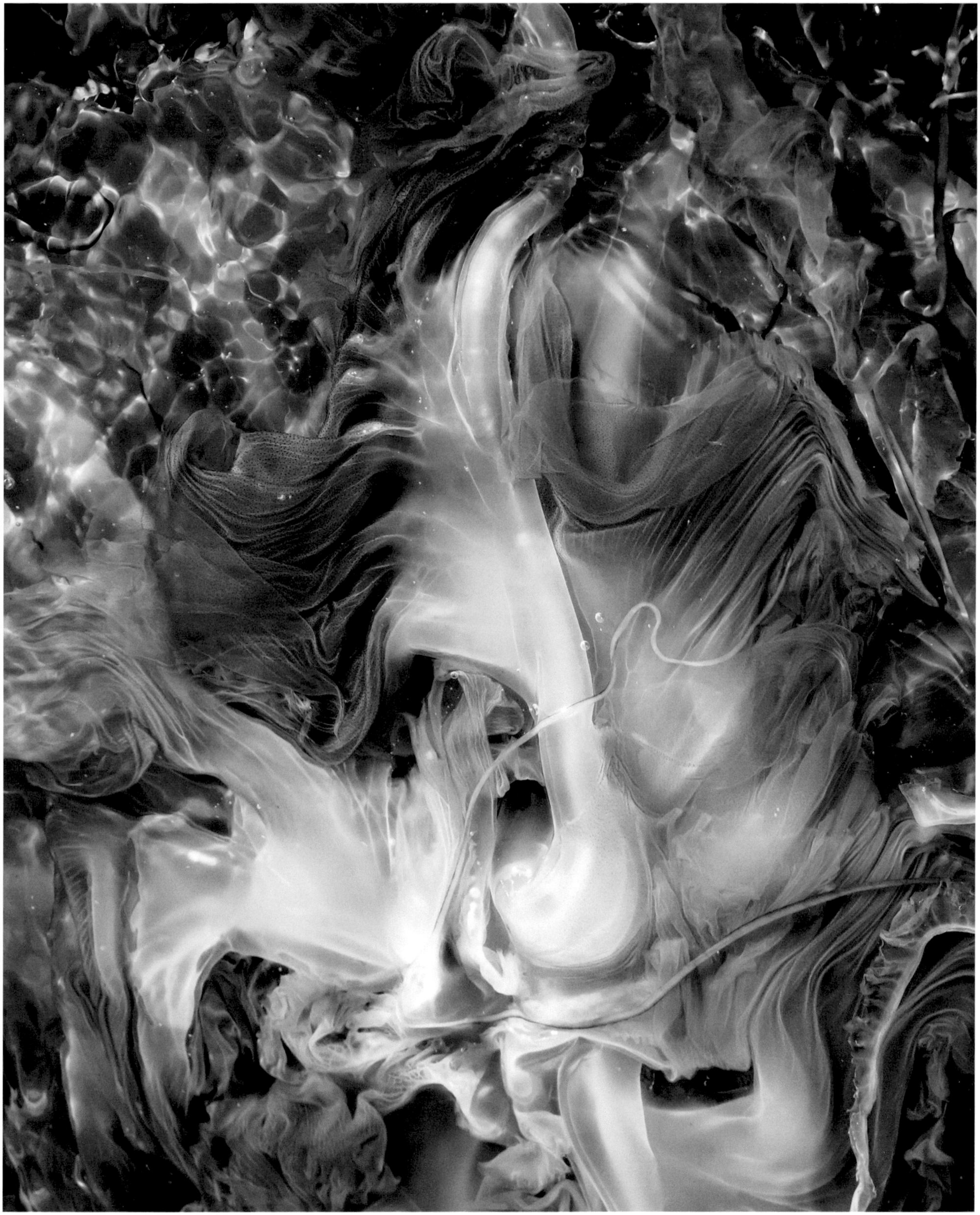

Climb

by Gordon Middleton
GordonMiddletonPhotography.com • gmidd32@gmail.com

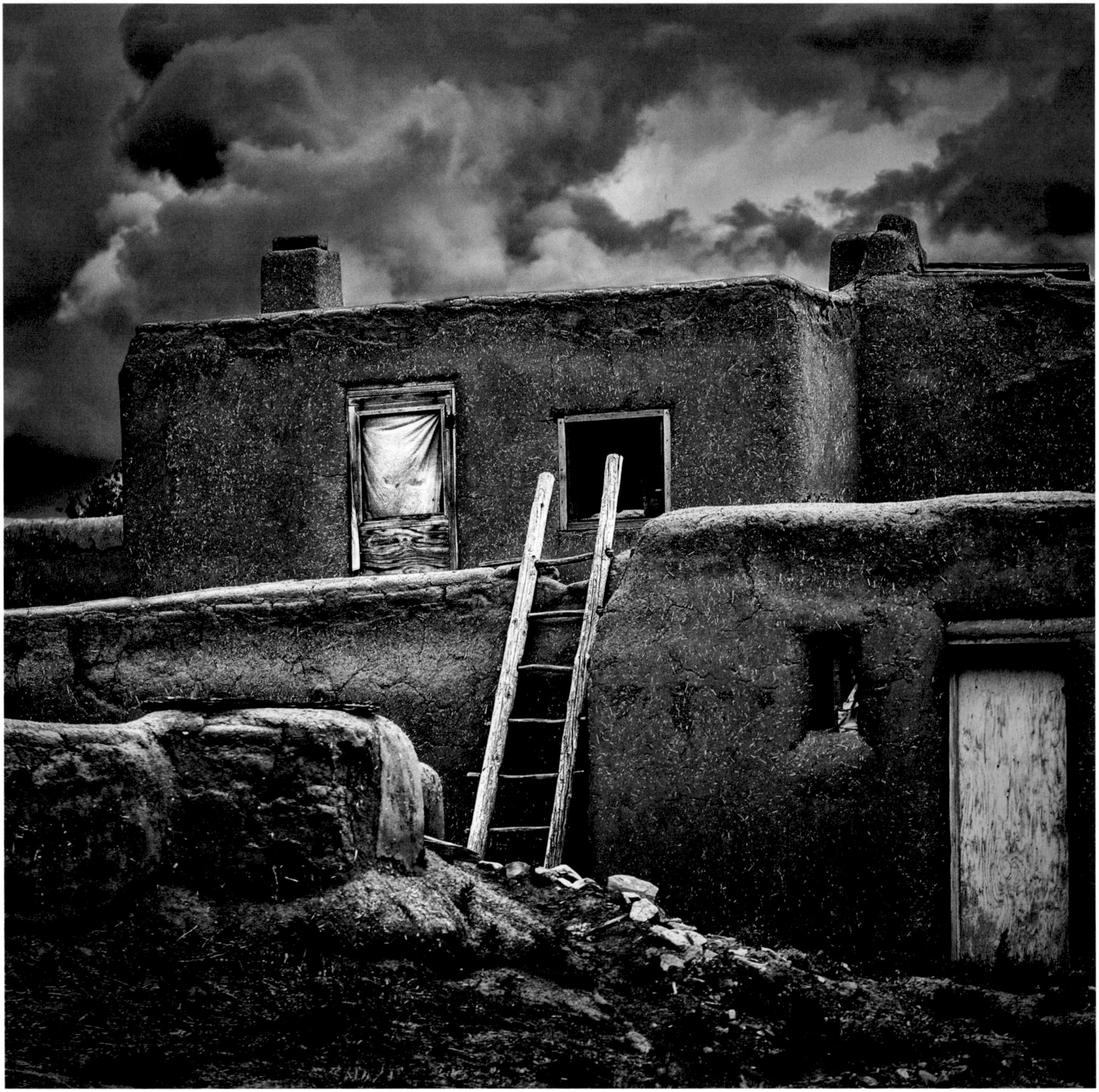

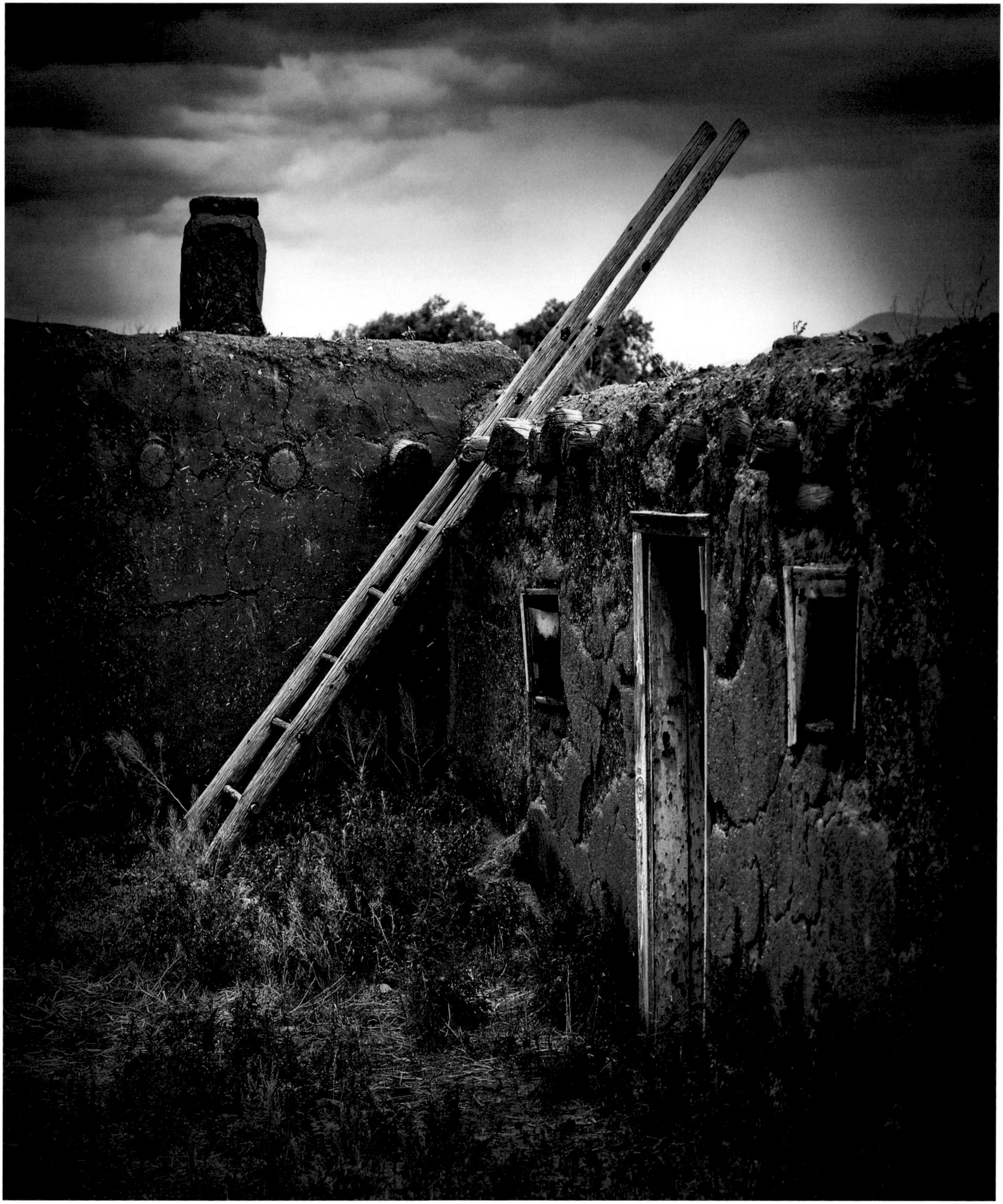

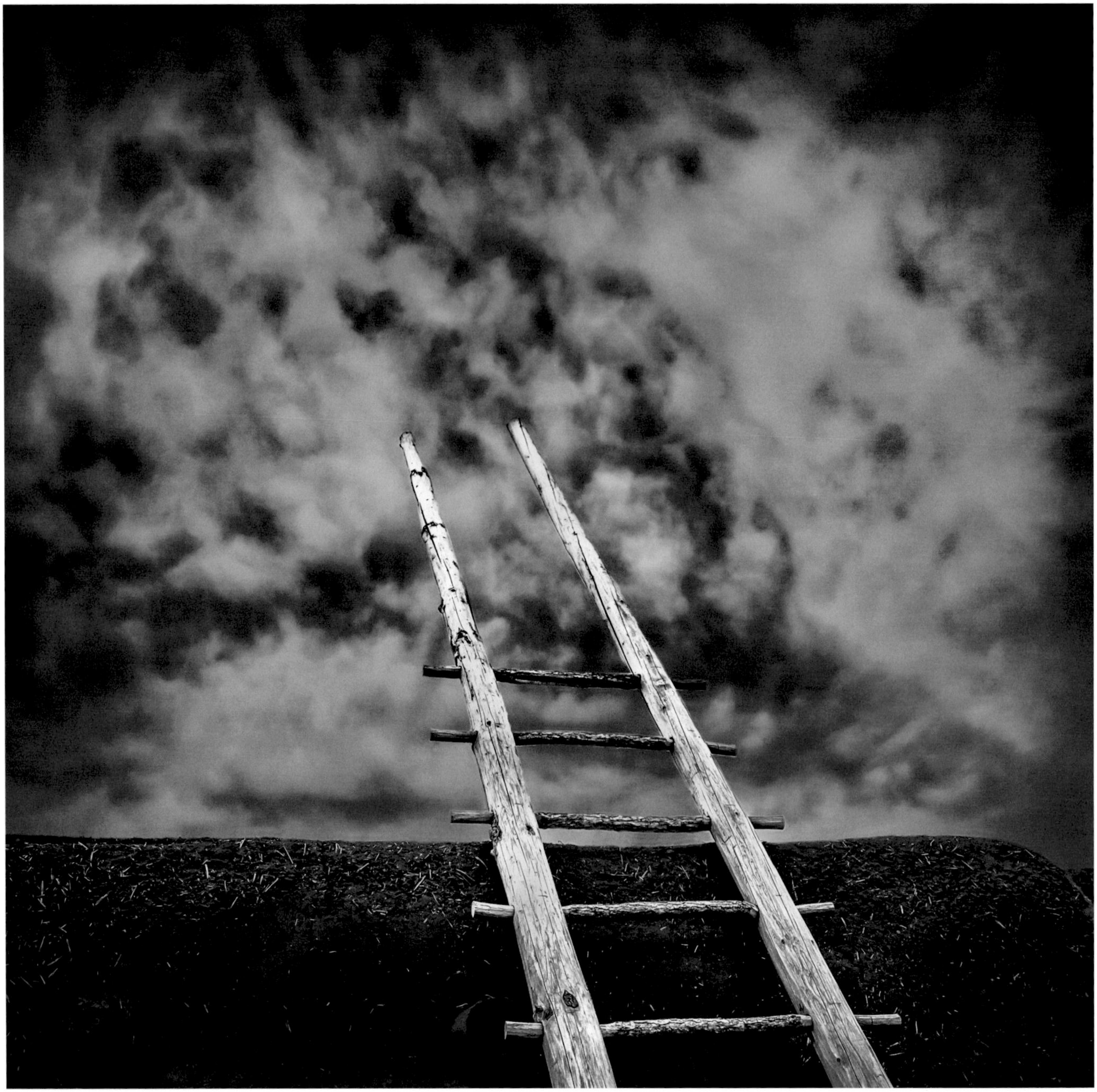

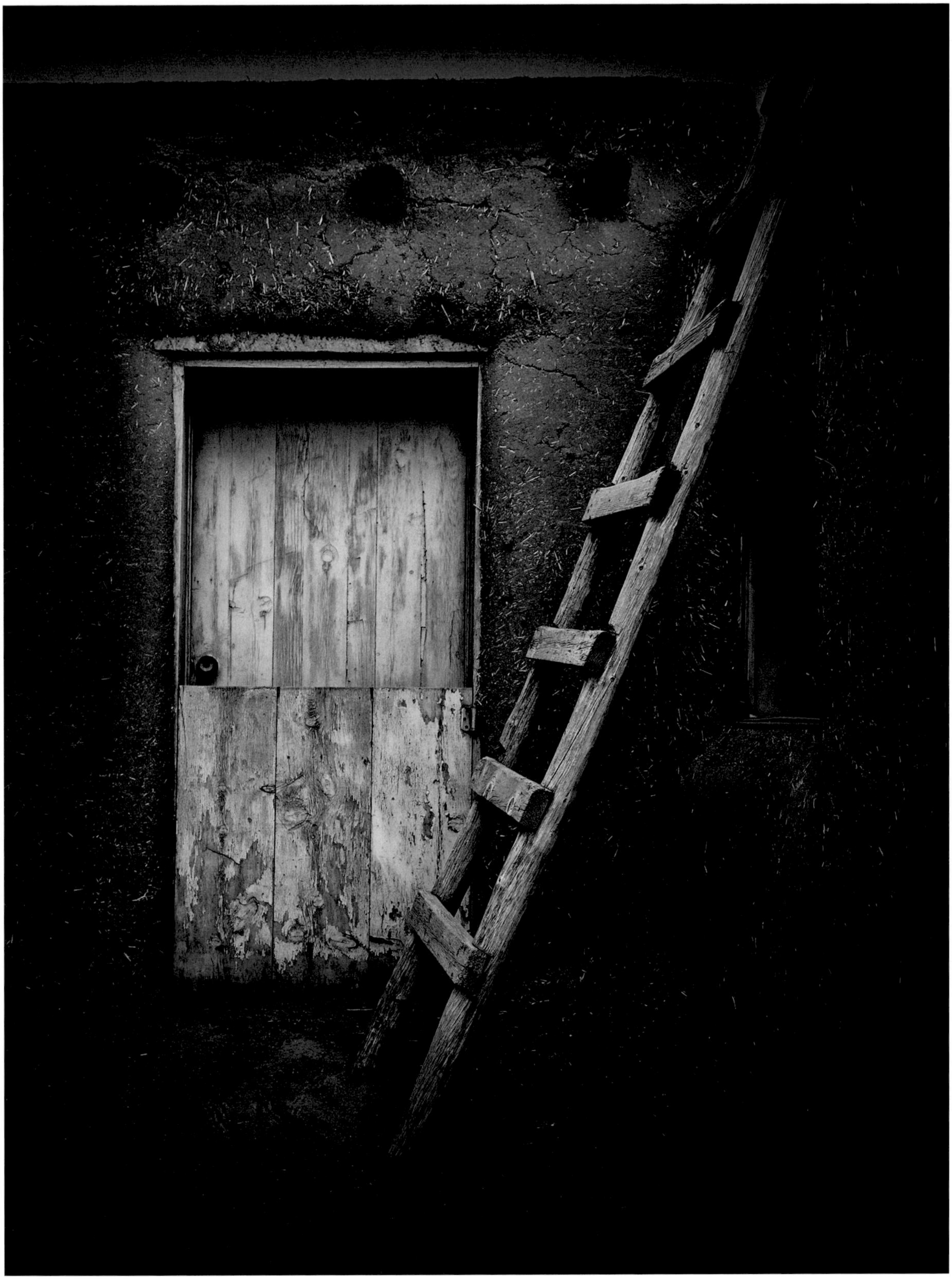

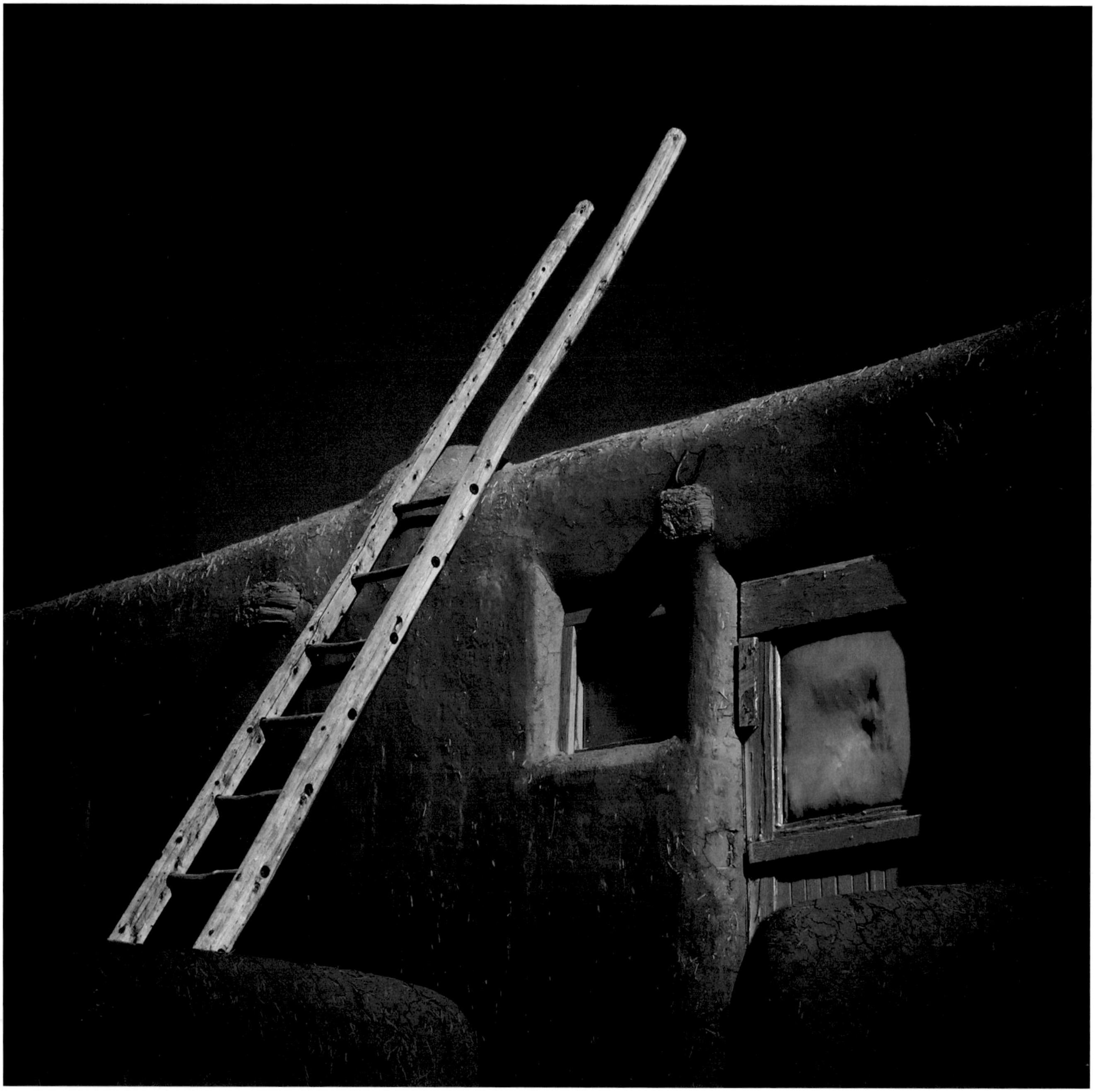

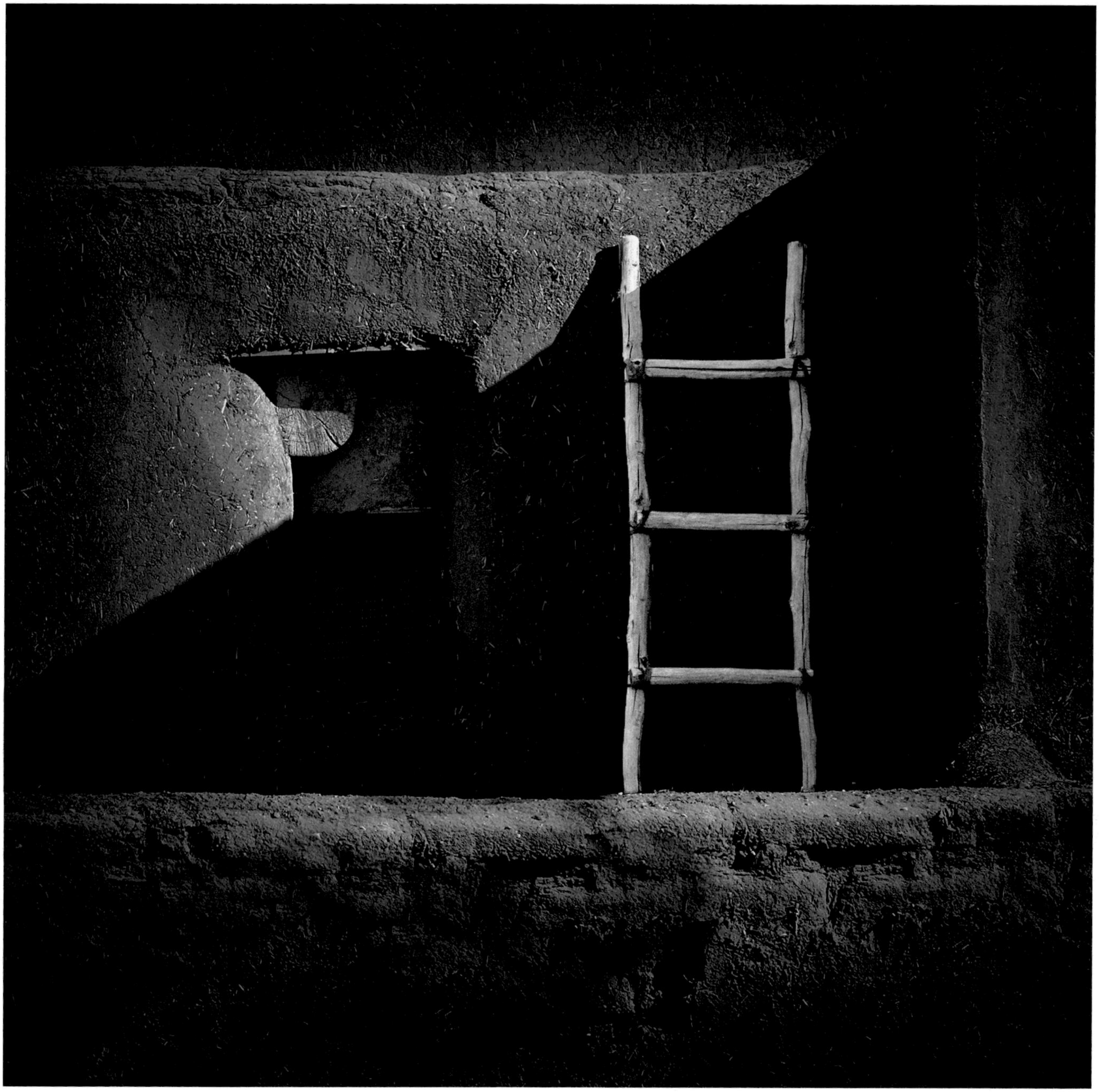

Musical Instruments

by Jim Sinsheimer

sinsheimerphotos.com • sinsheimerphotos@gmail.com

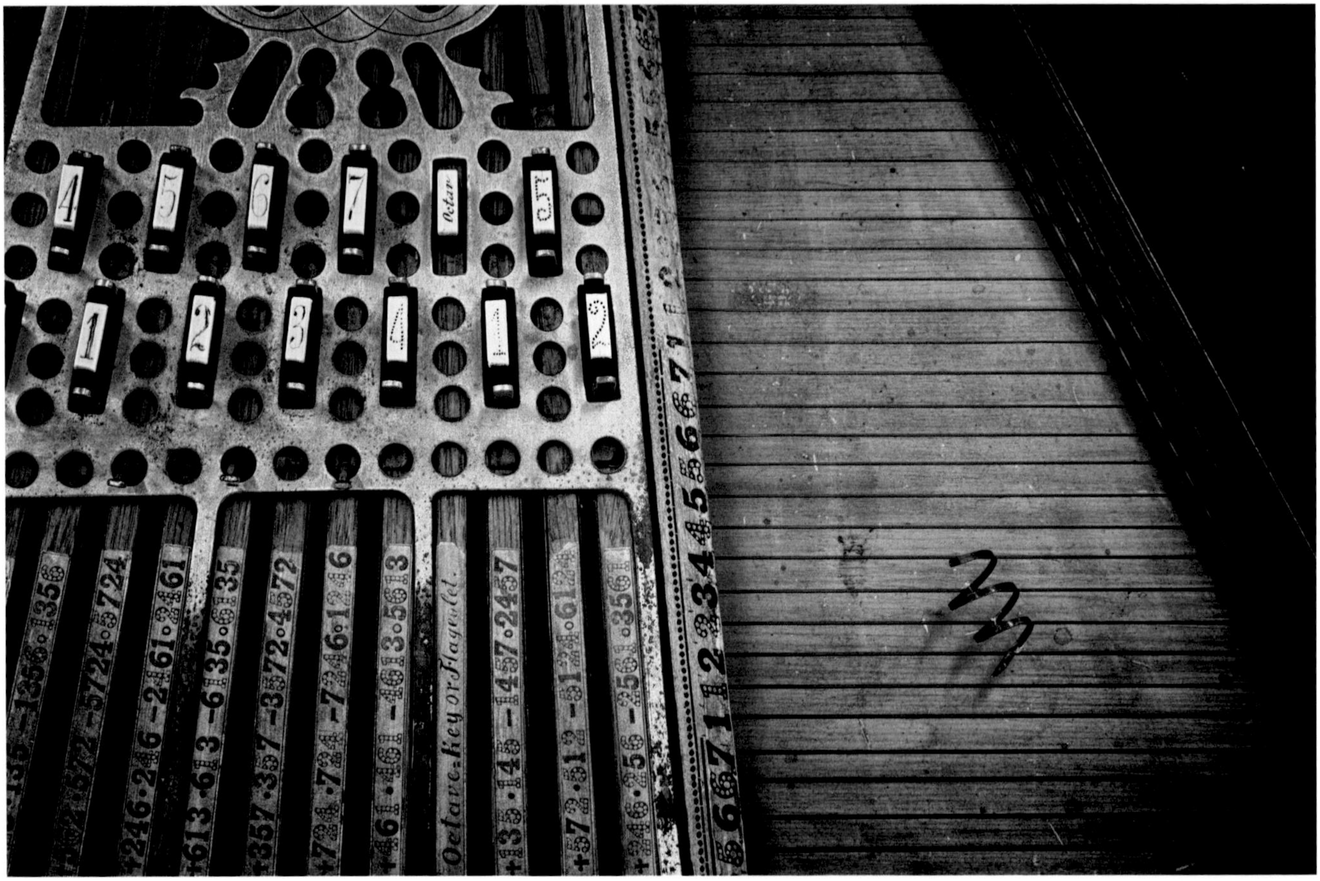

Autoharp

While in Scottsdale, Arizona, a friend arranged an after-hours visit to the Musical Instrument Museum (MIM), a giant two story facility exhibiting instruments of every kind from around the world. With permission to photograph and no one around, it was a great opportunity to explore their visual designs and detailed craftsmanship. The variety of string, wind, and percussion instruments is astounding and offered almost endless compositional opportunities and color/texture contrasts. My concentration was mostly on capturing portions of each instrument to reveal it in a more abstract manner. Though we only had three hours, there certainly was enough subject matter to prepare this portfolio.

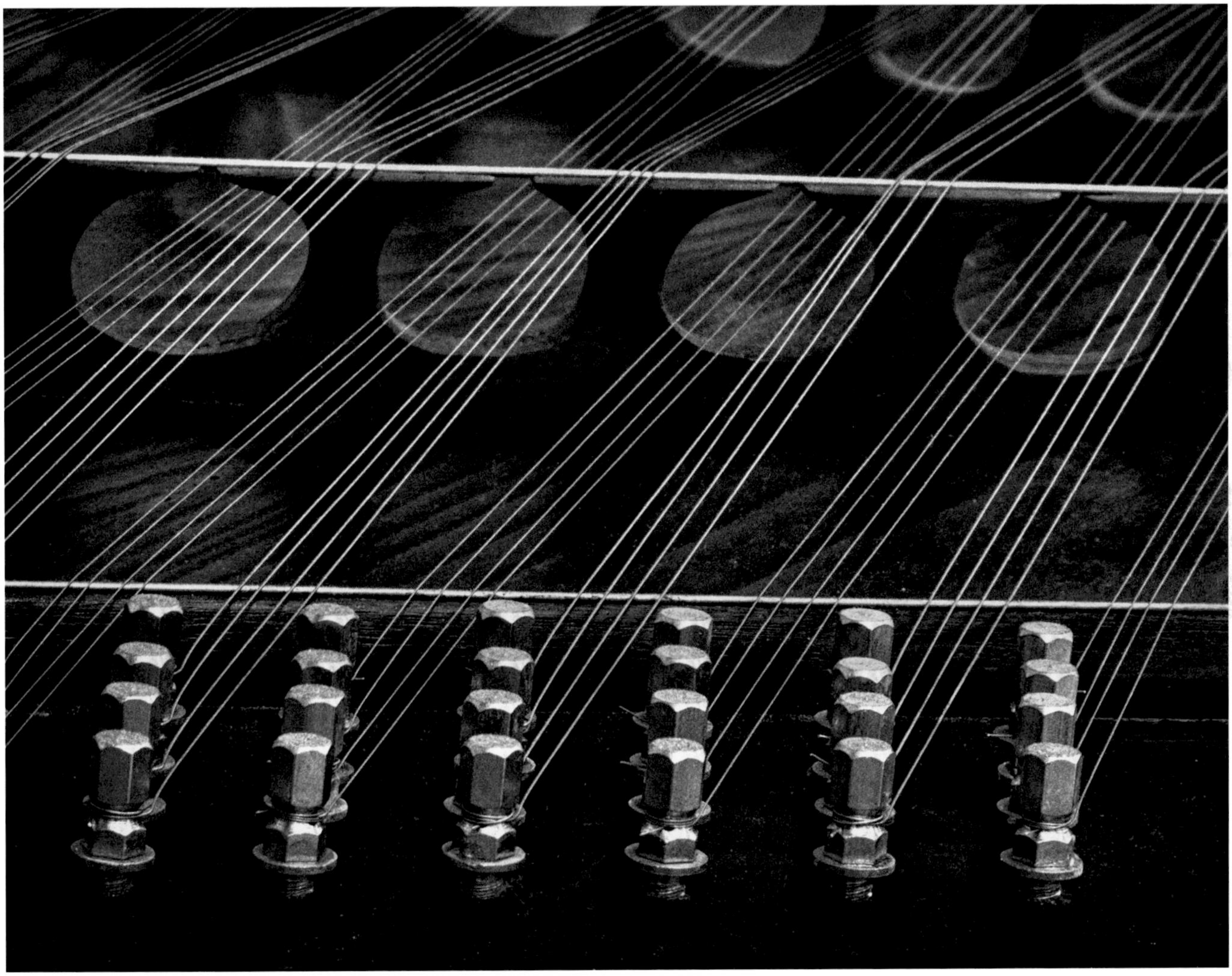

Cimbalom (Struck Zither)

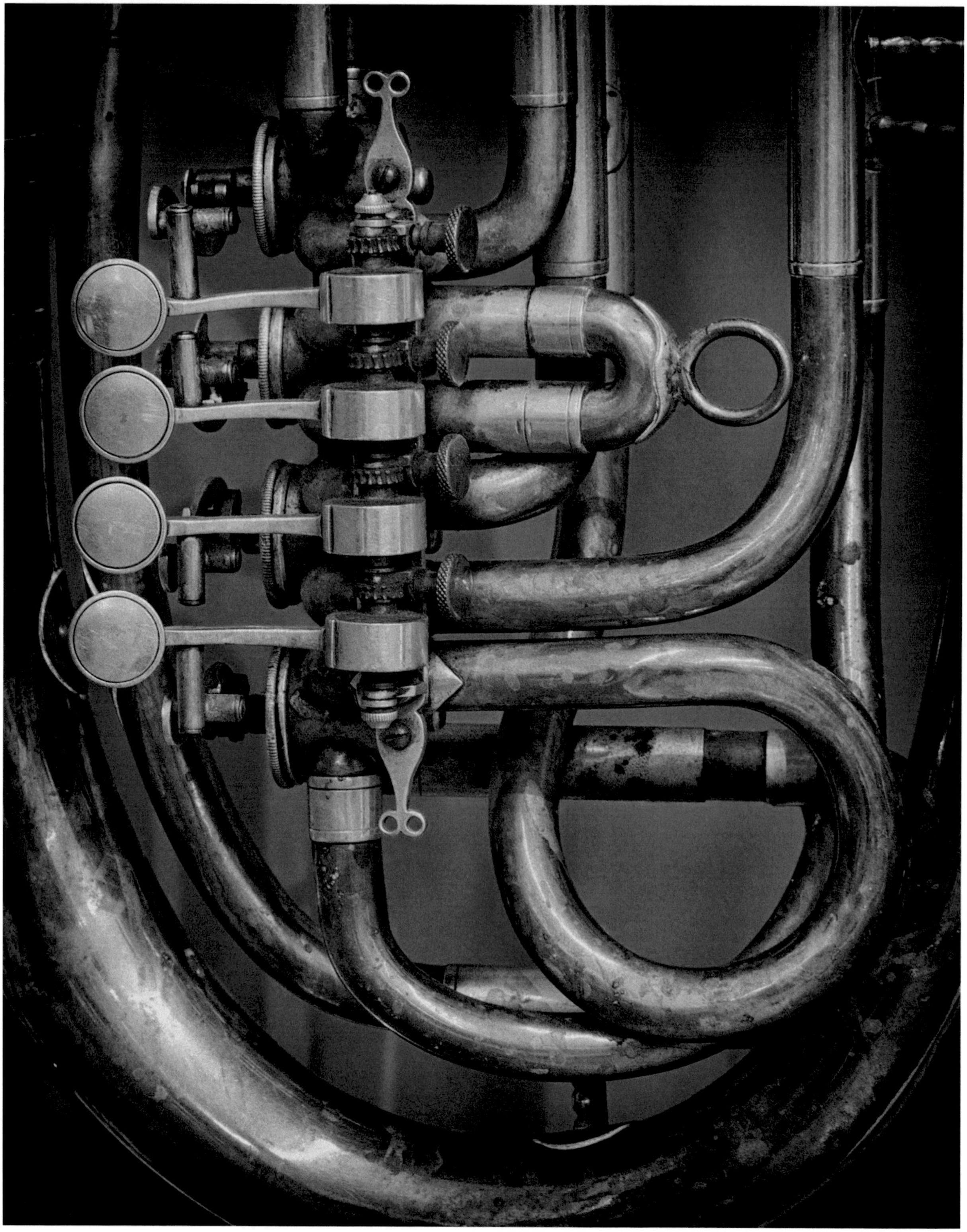

Heligon (Valved Horn)

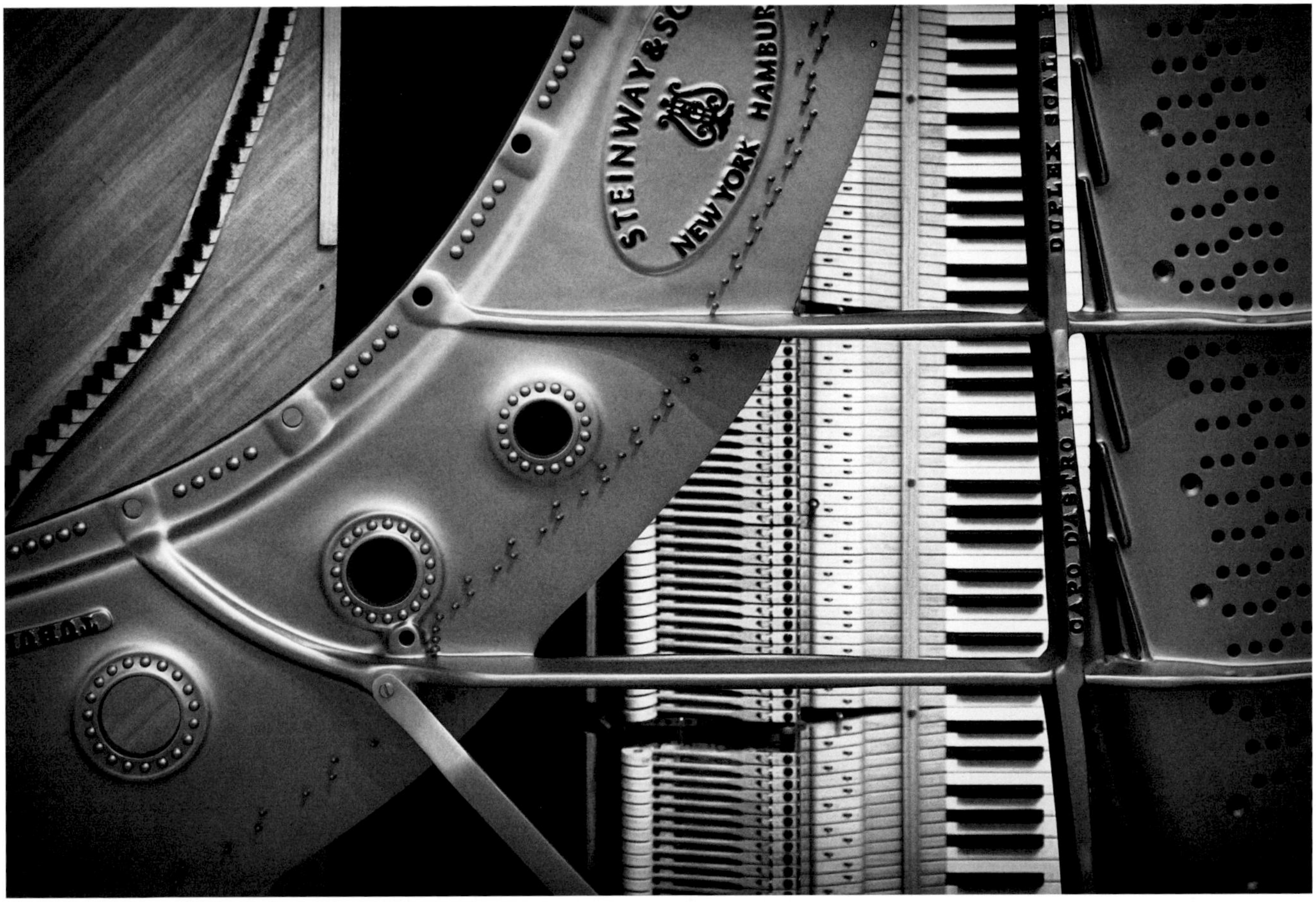

De-constructed Steinway

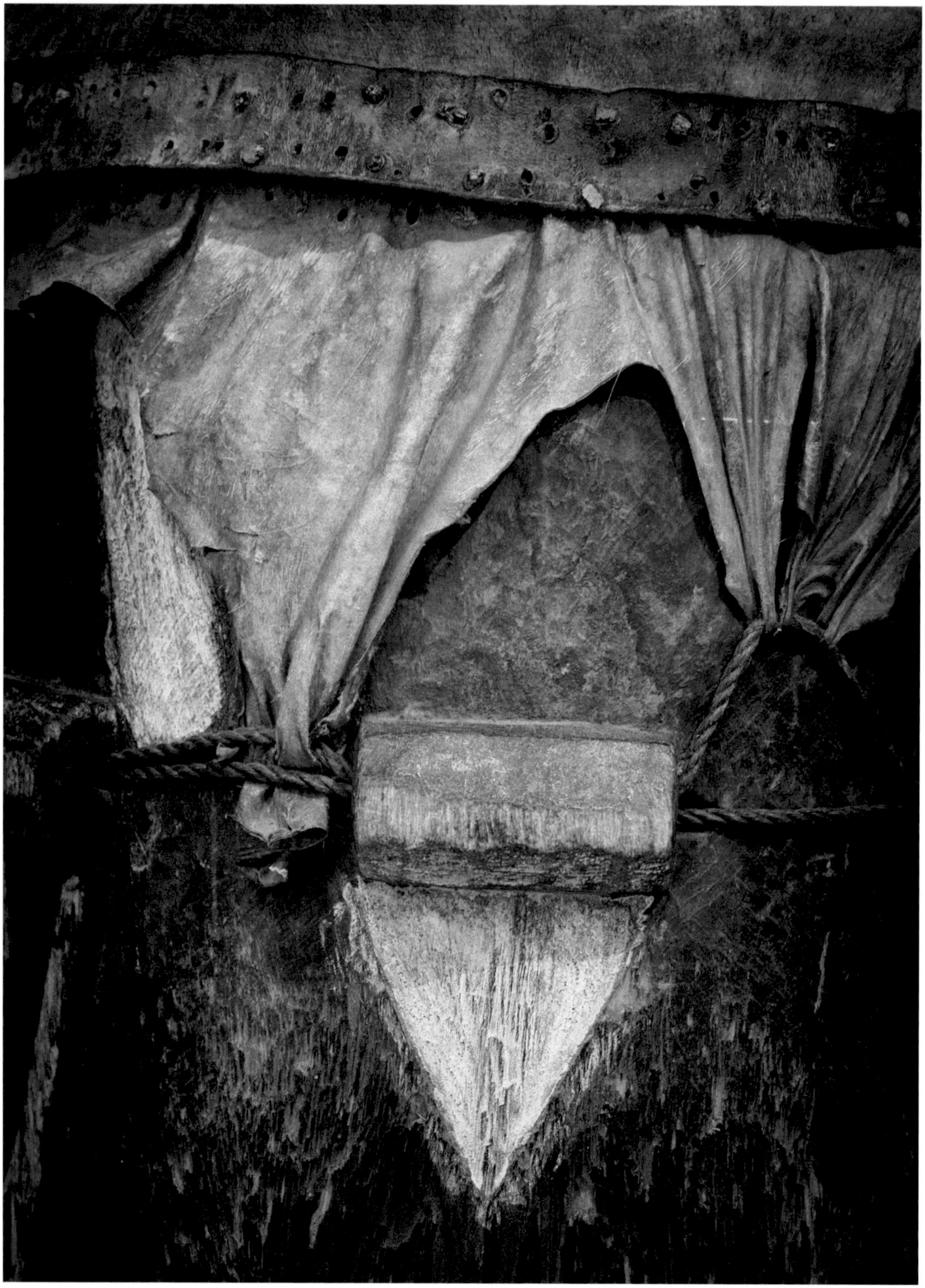

Lomonda (Cylindrical Drum)

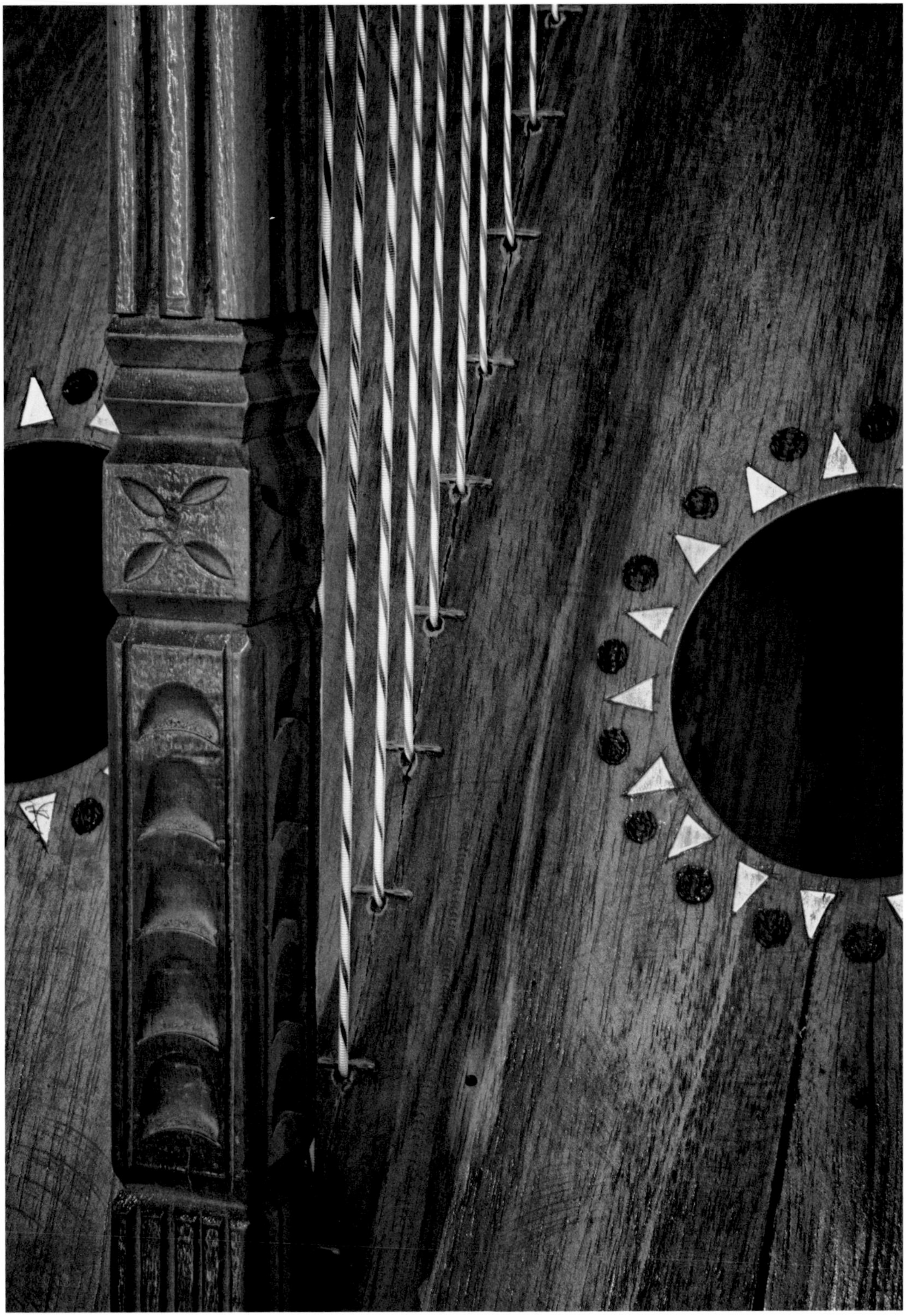

Leona (Plucked Flute)

Bosch Redux

by Lori Pond

loripond.com ♦ lori@loripond.com

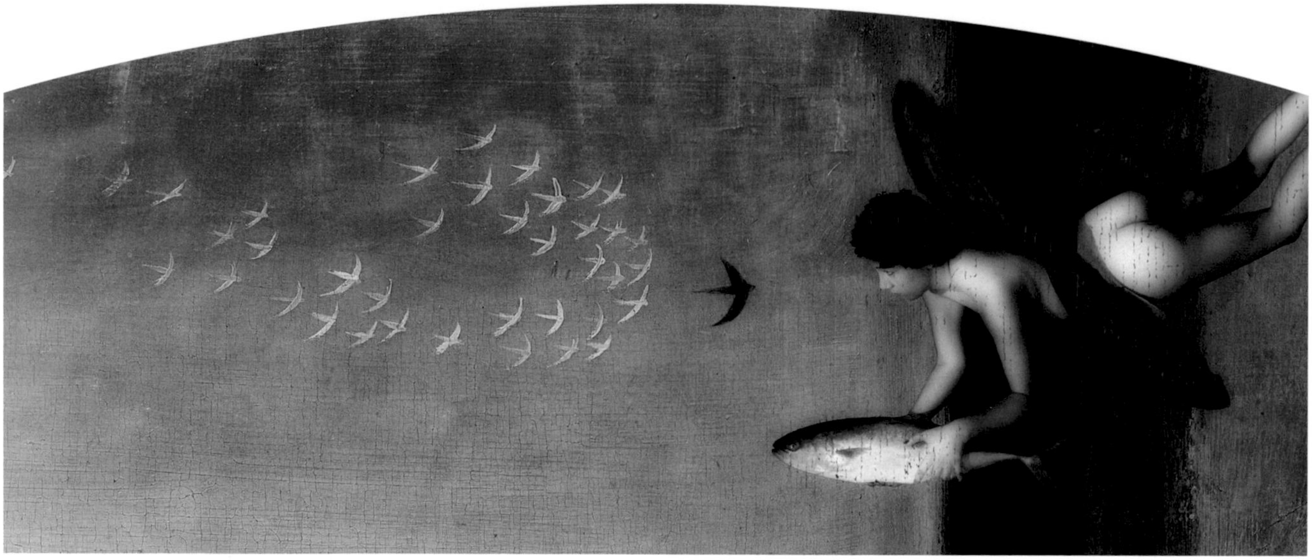

Bosch Redux takes flight from the unprecedented imagination of the painter Hieronymus Bosch (16th century), using photography to emphasize the sacred power of details, sing hallelujah to the bizarre, and marvel at how art connects people across centuries and continents.

I became fascinated with Bosch's *Garden of Earthly Delights* as a teenager. His limitless imagination and intricately detailed images captured my mind. In *Bosch Redux*, I hone in on details that occupy the background of his work. I put them center stage, lingering on what could otherwise be passed by. By bringing to the forefront the marginal, I confront my sense of smallness and unimportance in a vast world.

Bosch's bizarre images also speak to my own fascination with oddities and outcasts. As a kid, I was absorbed by horror movies and shows like "The Twilight Zone." On my bedroom door I taped a photo of the fattest twins in the world riding minibikes side-by-side. My mom would periodically throw out this picture, but I always found it and re-taped it to my door. I cherished weirdness in all forms, since I grew up in Anaheim, where everything and everybody looked the same. (In the '70s, that is...)

Bosch further intrigued me because there was so little known about him — what he believed in, what he thought, who he was. I felt compelled to use my medium of photography to try to understand him, to inhabit his world and his mind. By painstakingly recreating in photographs the details that sprang from the mind of a painter five hundred years before I drew breath, I seek to understand: What draws people together? What creates affinity?

The photographs that comprise *Bosch Redux* bring out of the margins and from the past, new images that challenge, push, disturb, prod, and delight the senses and minds of those seeing them.

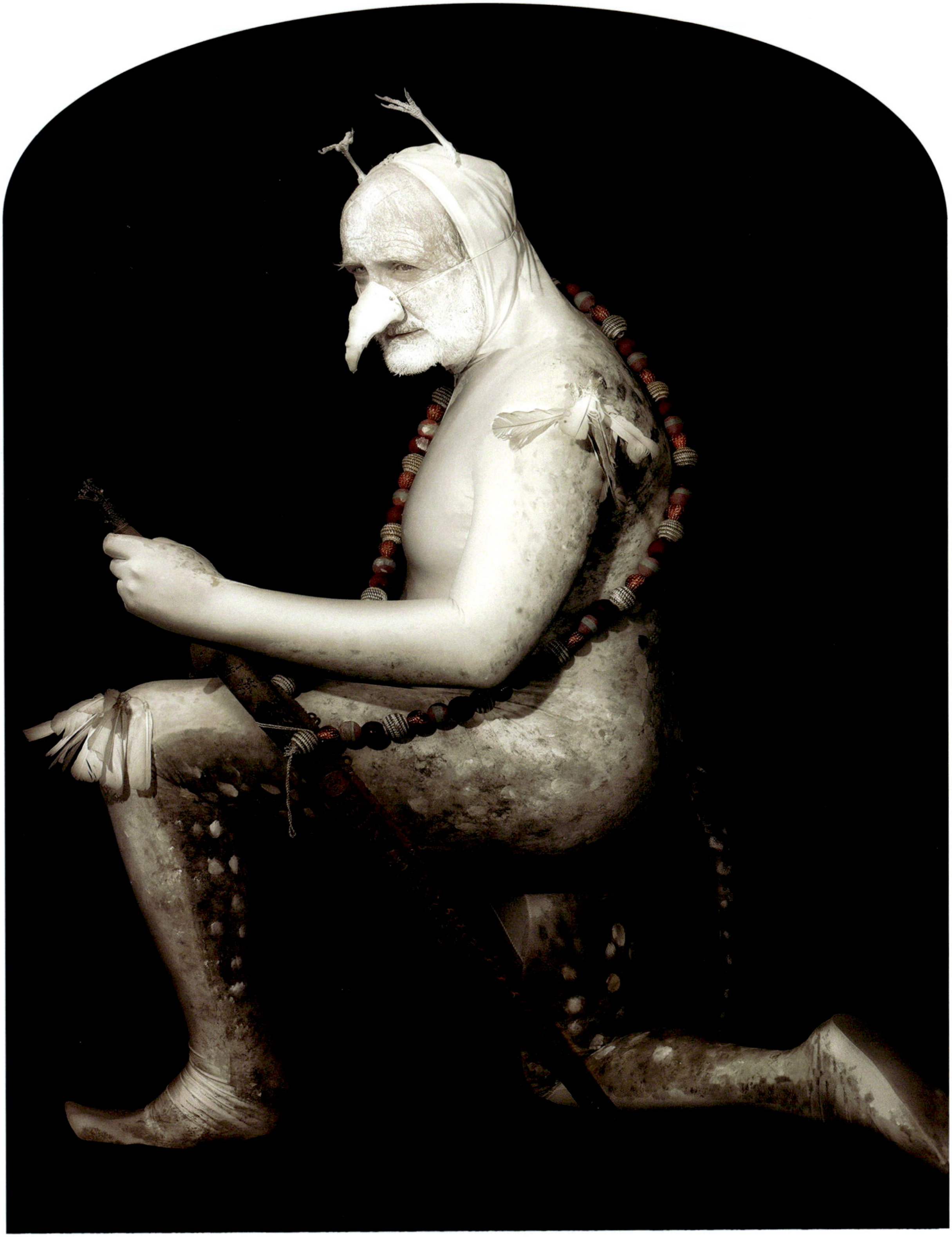

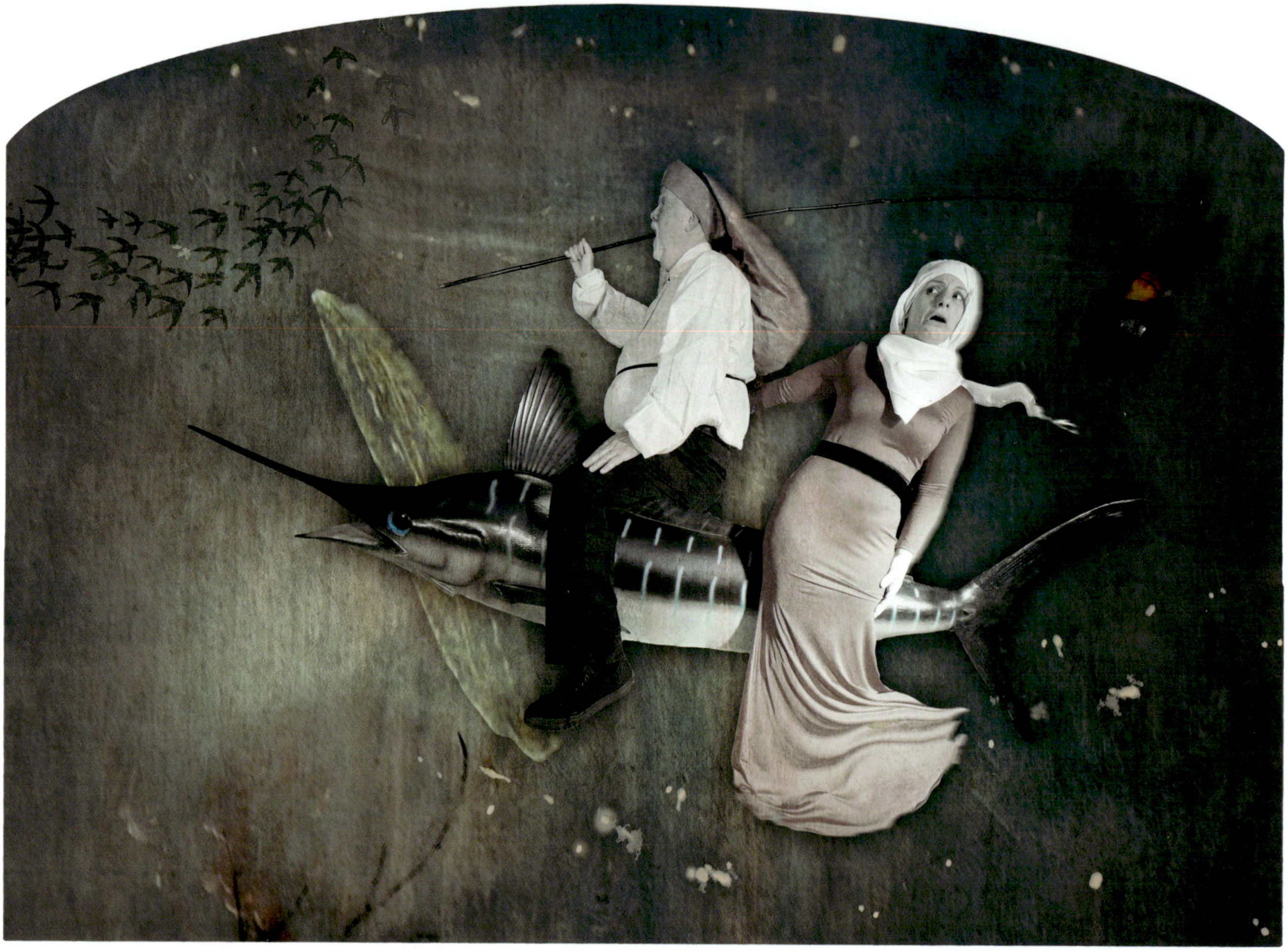

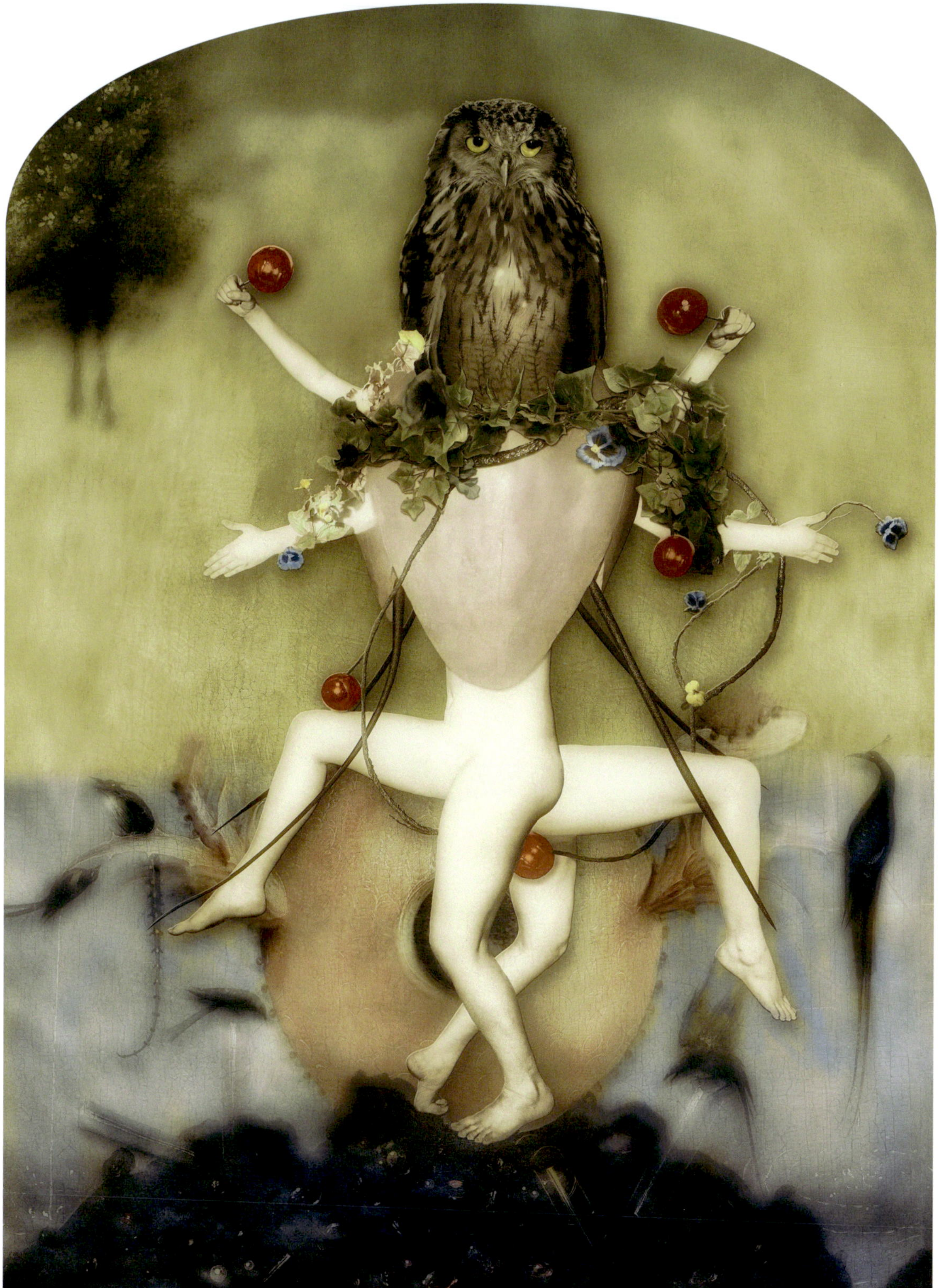

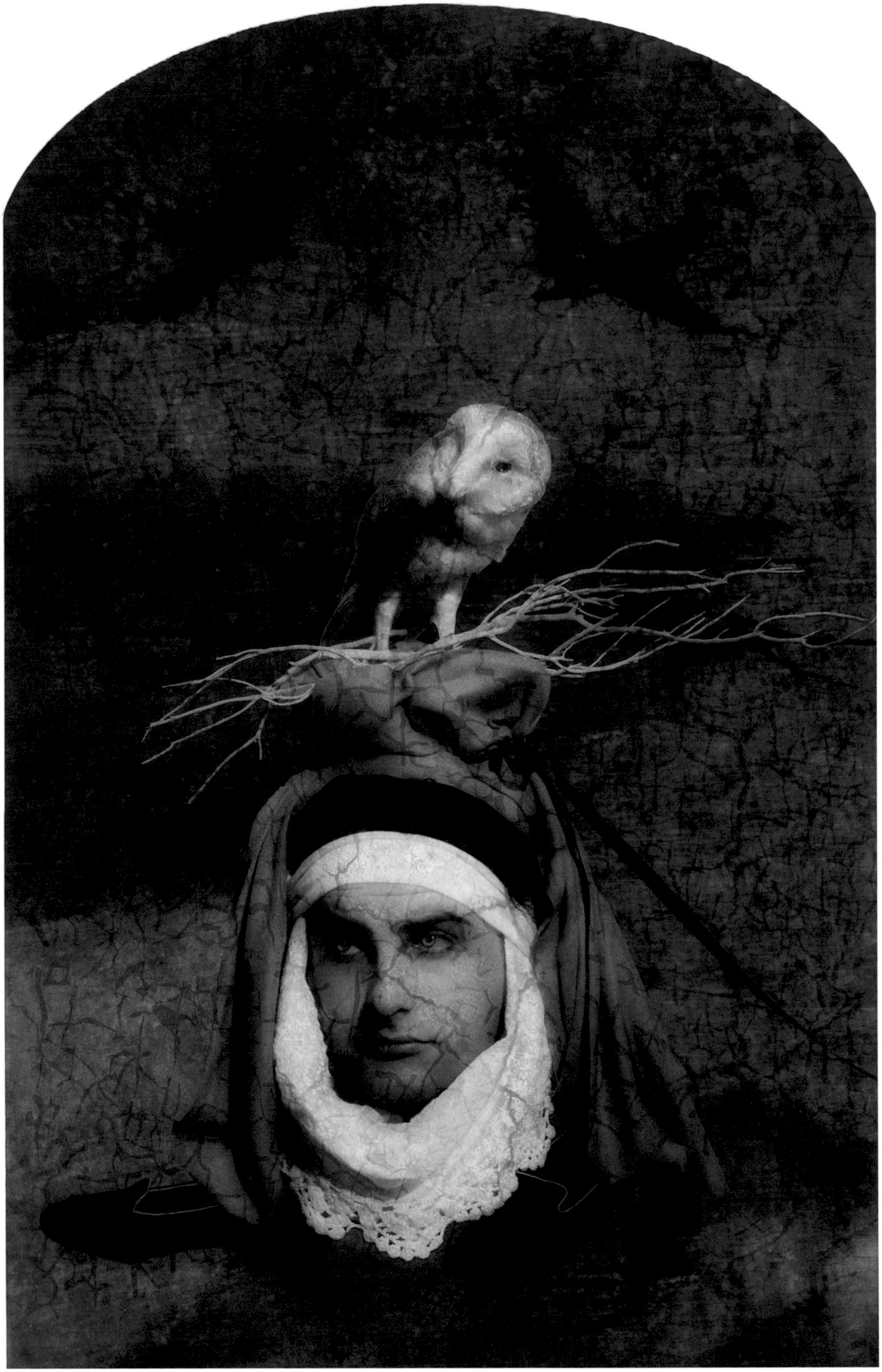

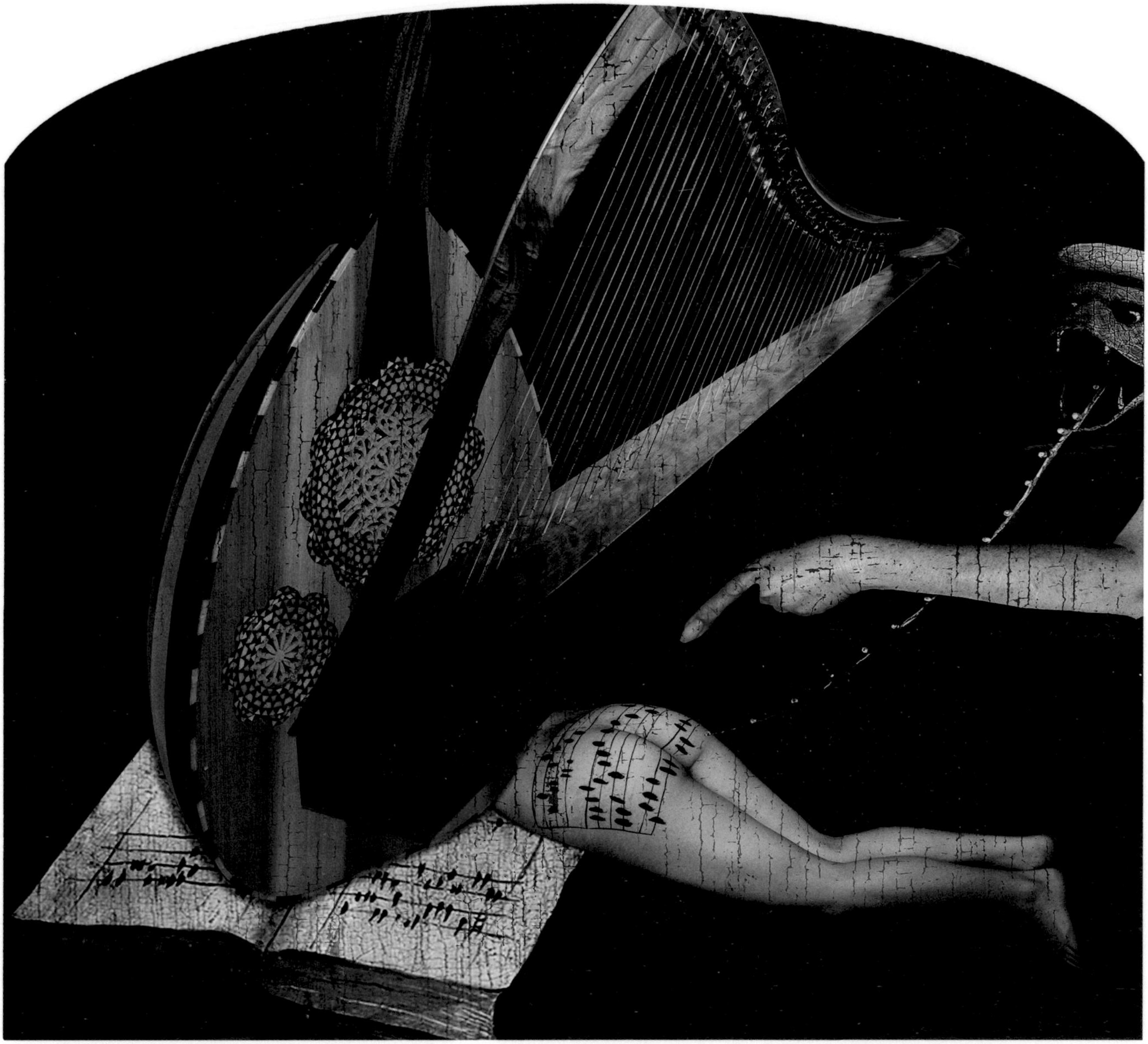

The Dressmaker's Daughters

by Emery Roth, II
rothphotos.blogspot.com • erothii@gmail.com

The Ansonia Opera House is a real opera house, built in 1870 in Ansonia, Connecticut. The architect, Robert Wakeman Hill, designed other opera houses and armories and firehouses all over Connecticut. Once the Opera House made a huge contribution to daily life and culture in this once busy mill town. In addition to hosting shows and plays, the Opera House was the place to gather. Graduations, social events, and meetings brought people here to the center of town, and on Saturday mornings the chairs were set so children could roller-skate around the perimeter of the floor.

The Opera House faded from importance after the strikes of 1919 when the armory was built with an "all-purpose" meeting space, but the Opera House continued to serve as a secondary meeting place through WWII. Today it is decaying while quietly hoping to be rediscovered, and many young people and newcomers don't know it's there.

I met the dressmaker's daughters on my first visit. Modest as they are, it took several visits before a few would let me photograph them in their boudoirs. My muses are local, and my photography is often about "Place" even while striving for universality.

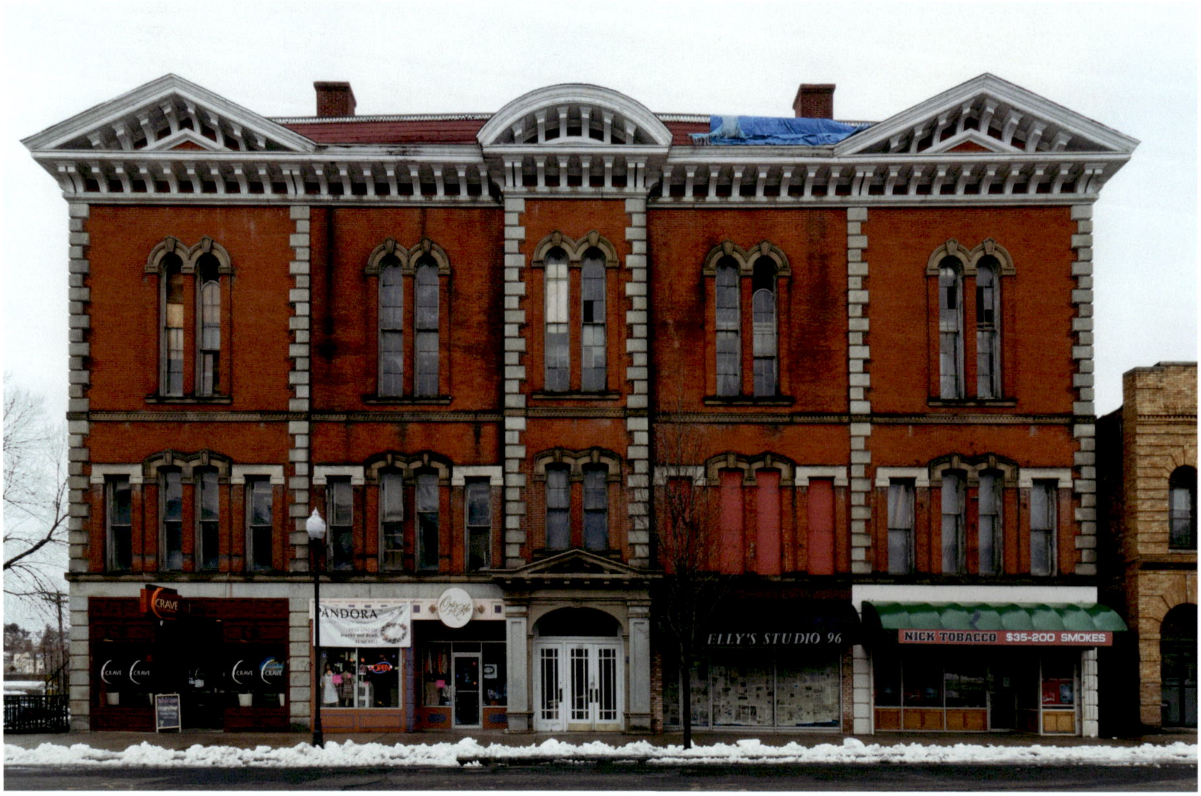

Above the bustling shops and beneath the majestic opera house

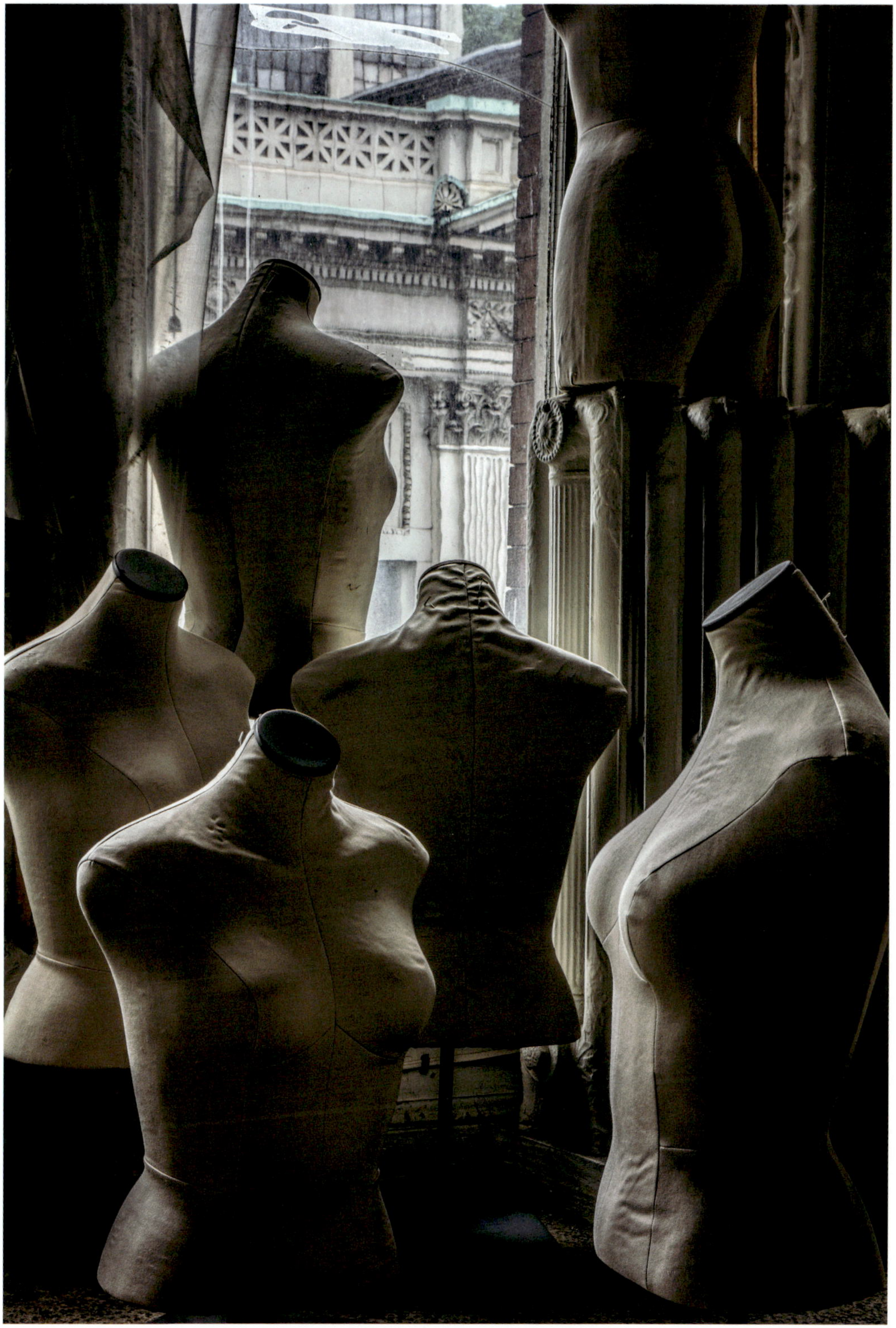

they lived in a narrow flight
where they dreamed in arias.

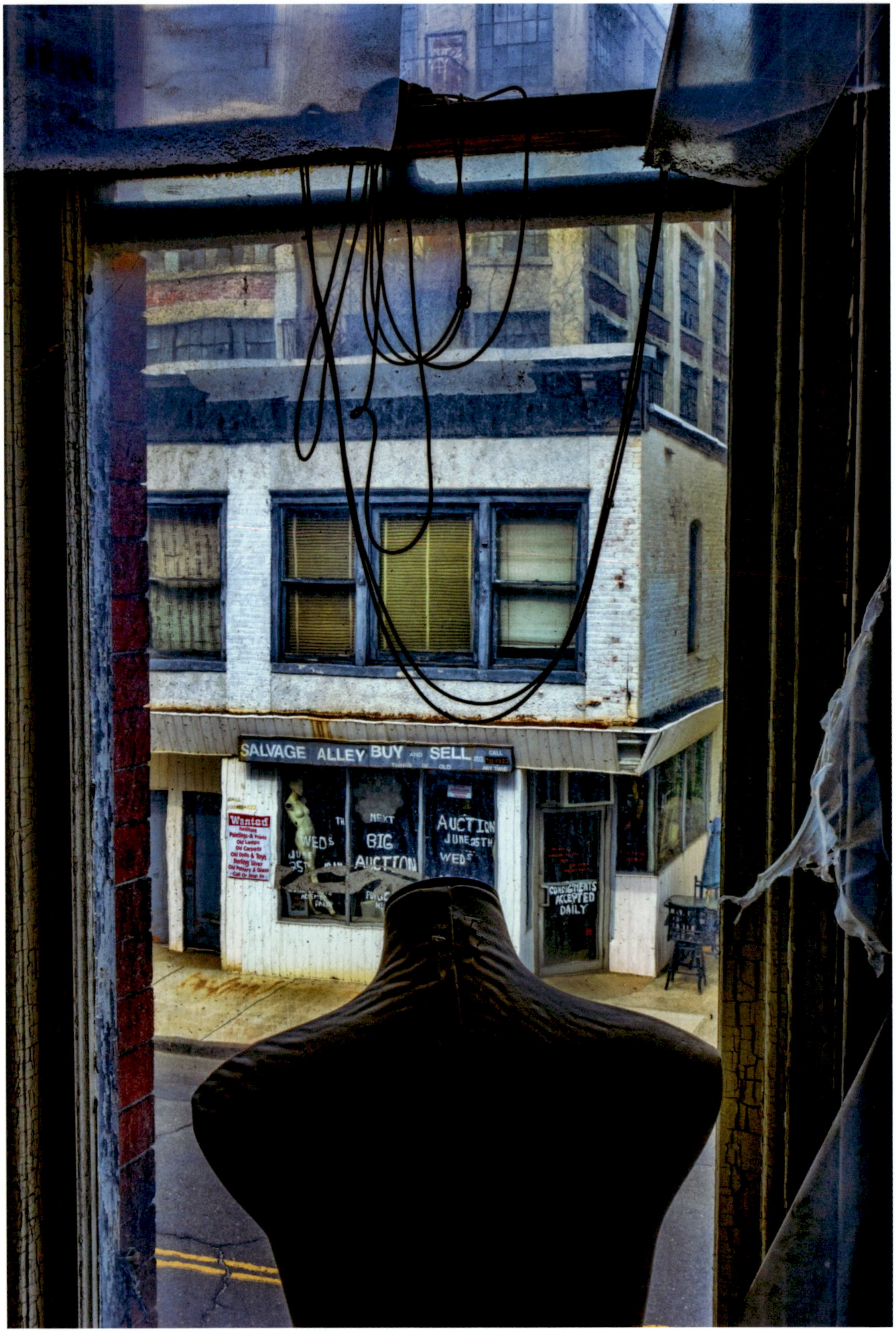

Leonore longed for a vagabond lover…

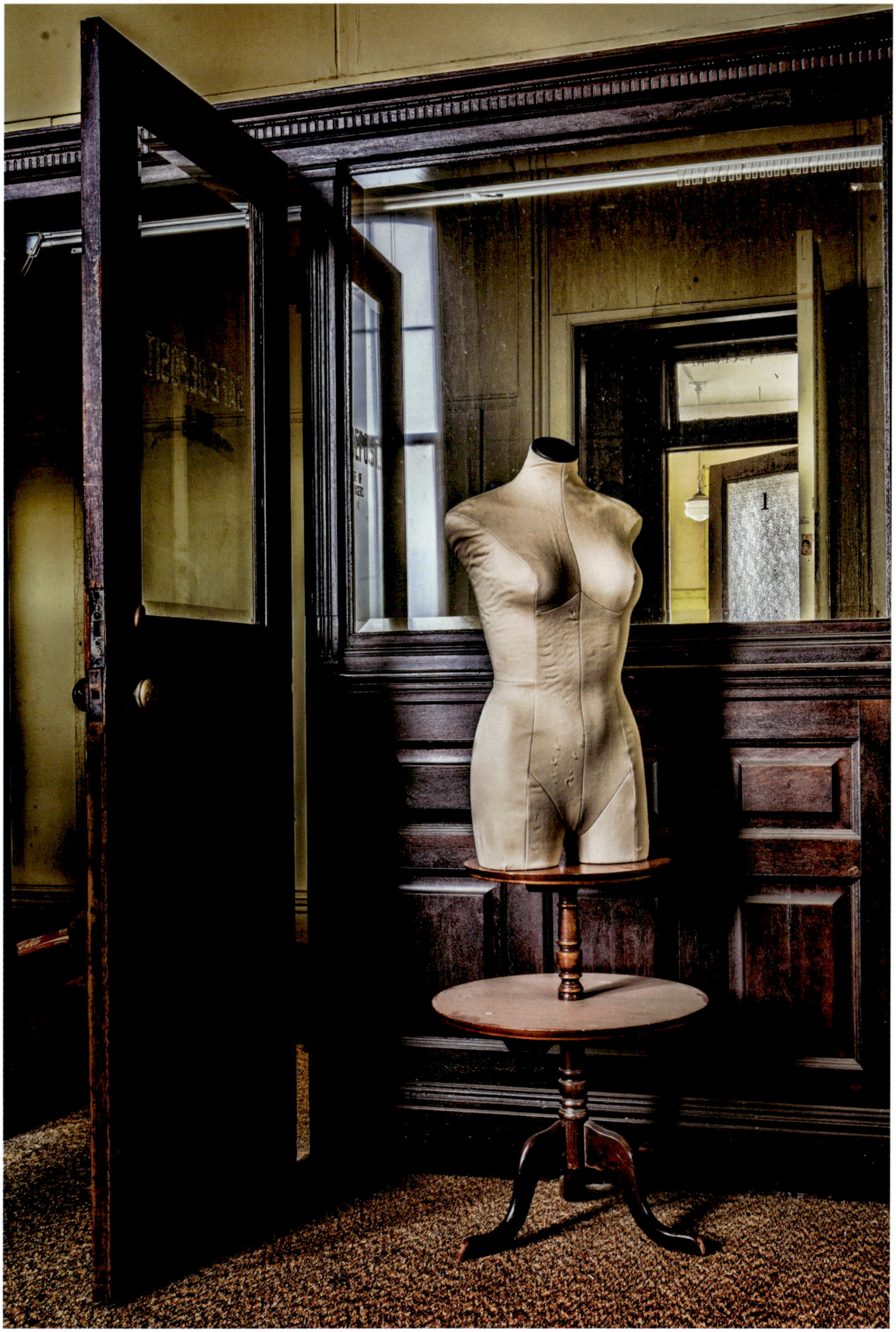

as Cleo waited for Mr. Number One.

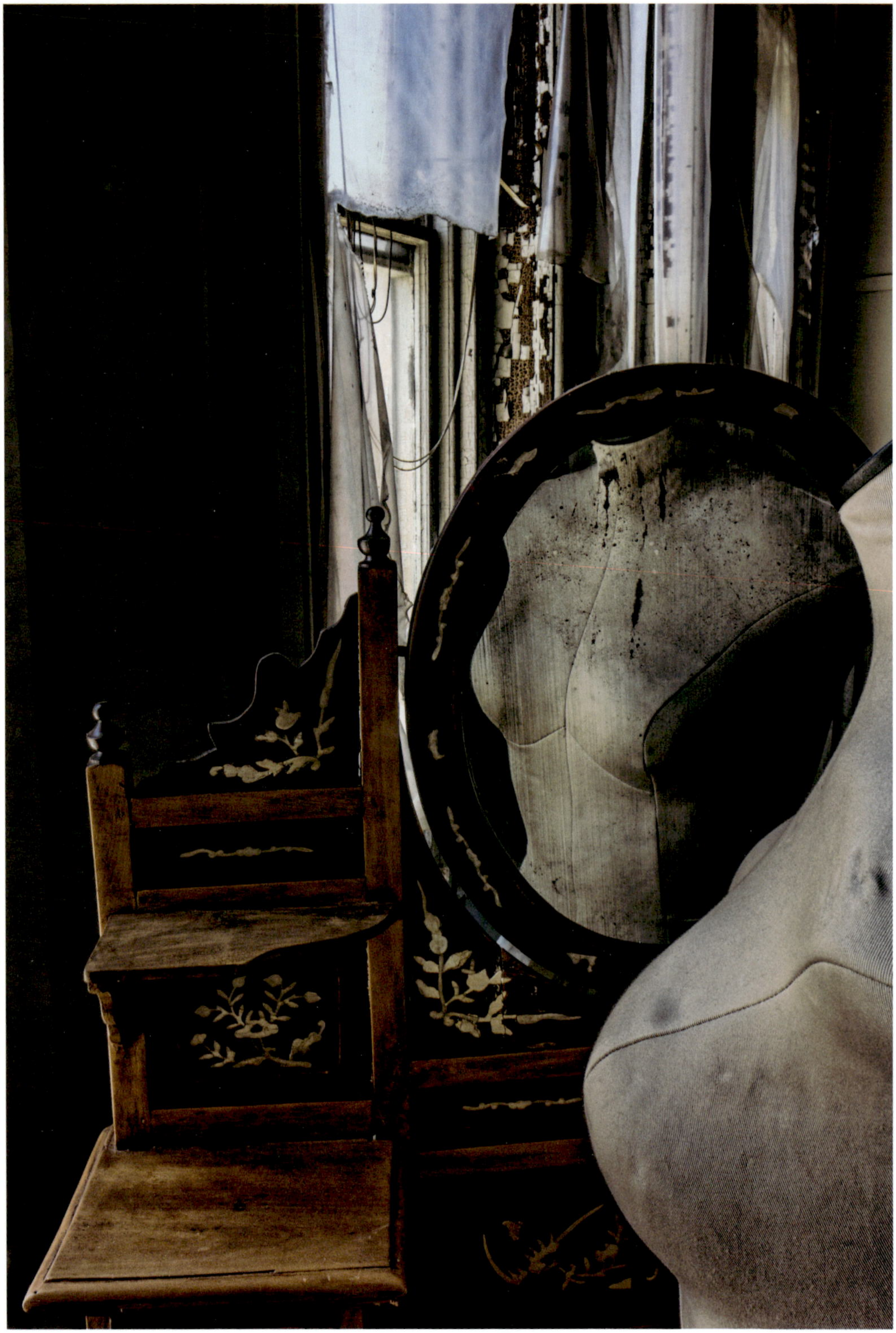

Carmen dreamed of distant places,
foreign tongues, and uncommon rituals...

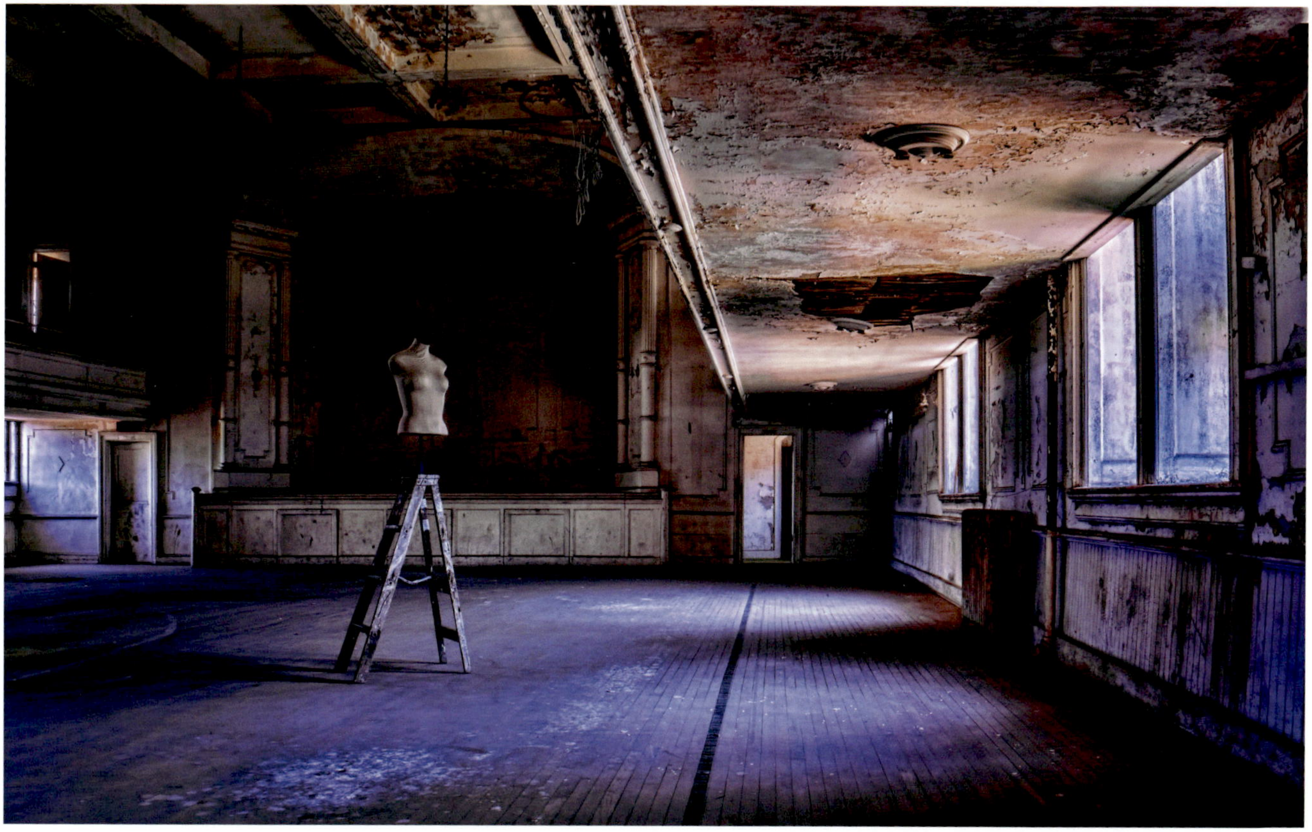

while Brünnhilde, the youngest, was star-struck.

Winter Vitrine

by Kathleen Pickard

RaraAvisPhotos.com • kathleenmpickard@gmail.com

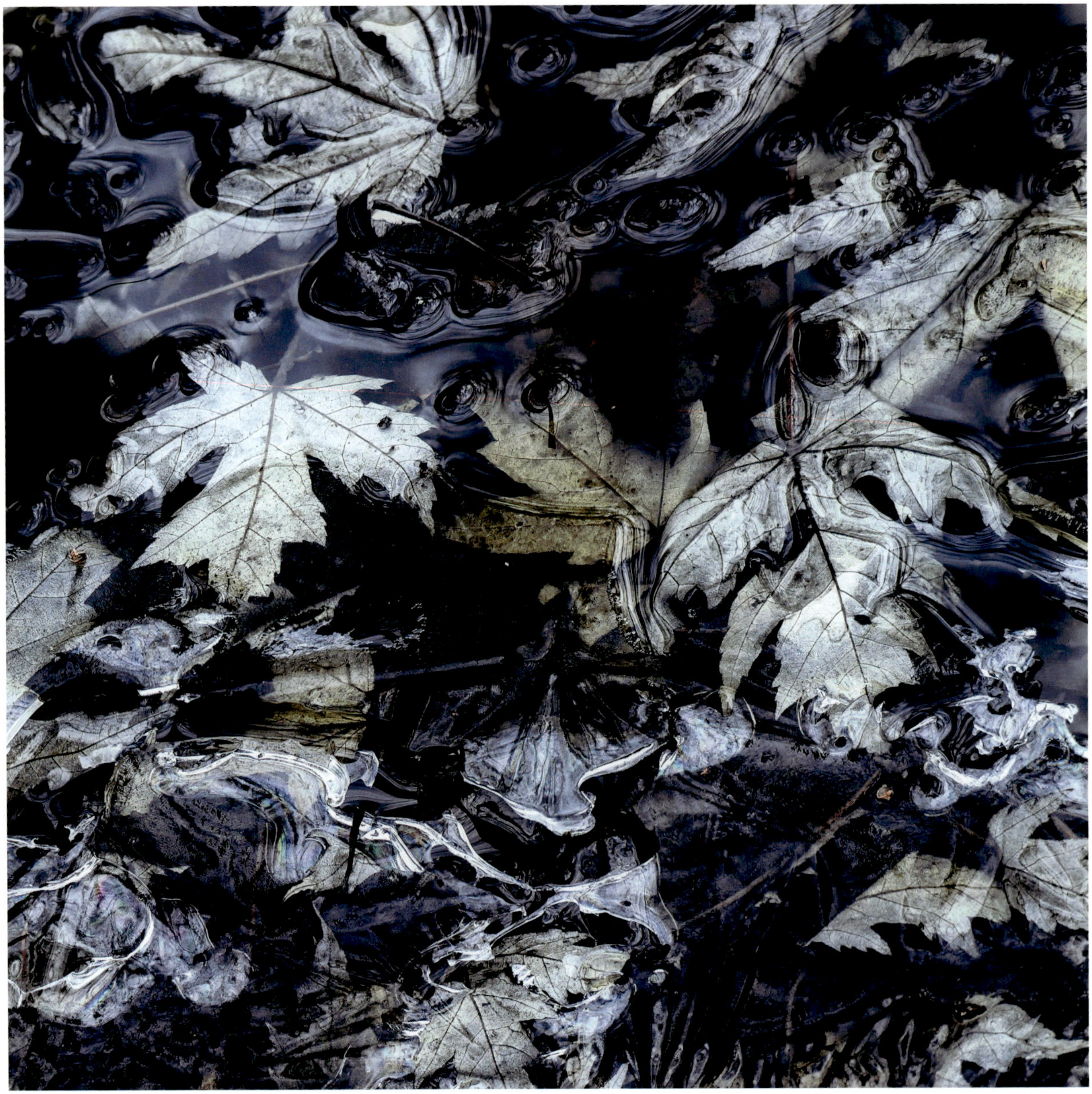

There was a rare convergence of weather conditions in Southern Ontario during the winter of 2014/15. Unusually heavy autumn rains refilled the vernal ponds in the low lying areas of a local woodland. Then, a long spell of extremely low temperatures arrived, unaccompanied by snow. The surface of the ponds froze into a sheet of glass that was transparent, pebbled, full of bubbles, cracks, and swirls. Leaves, fallen not long before, became encased in the ice as if arranged for display.

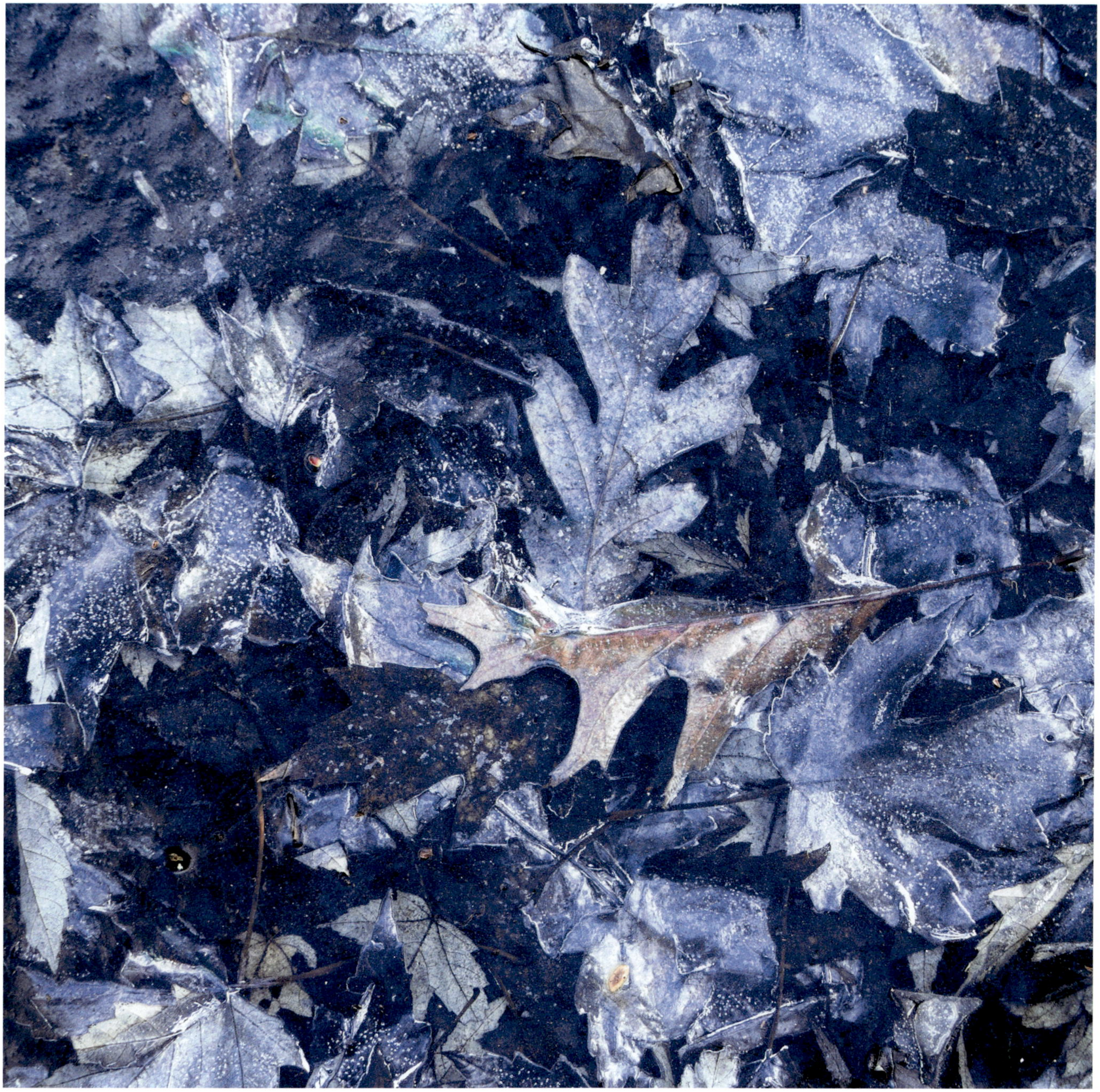

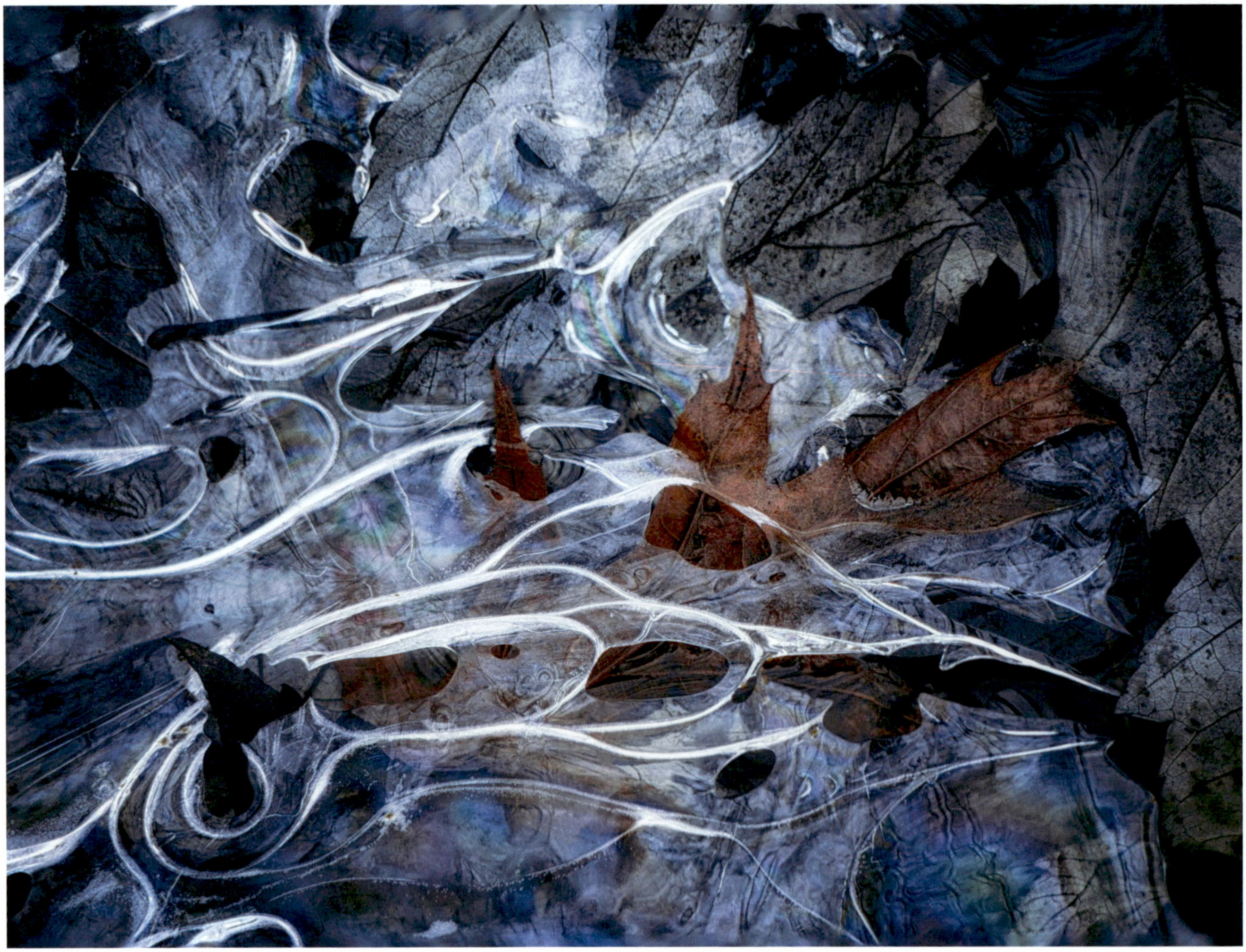

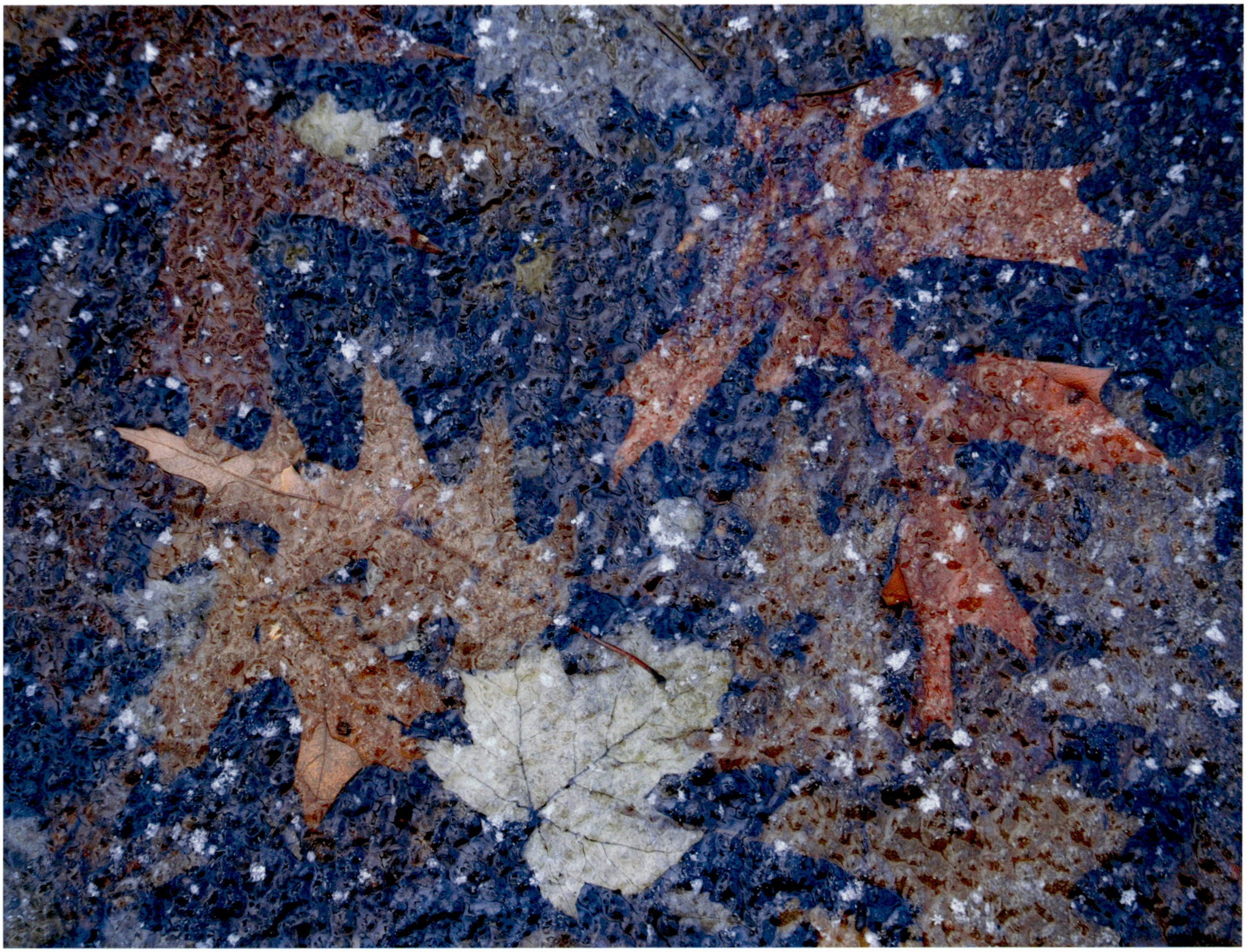

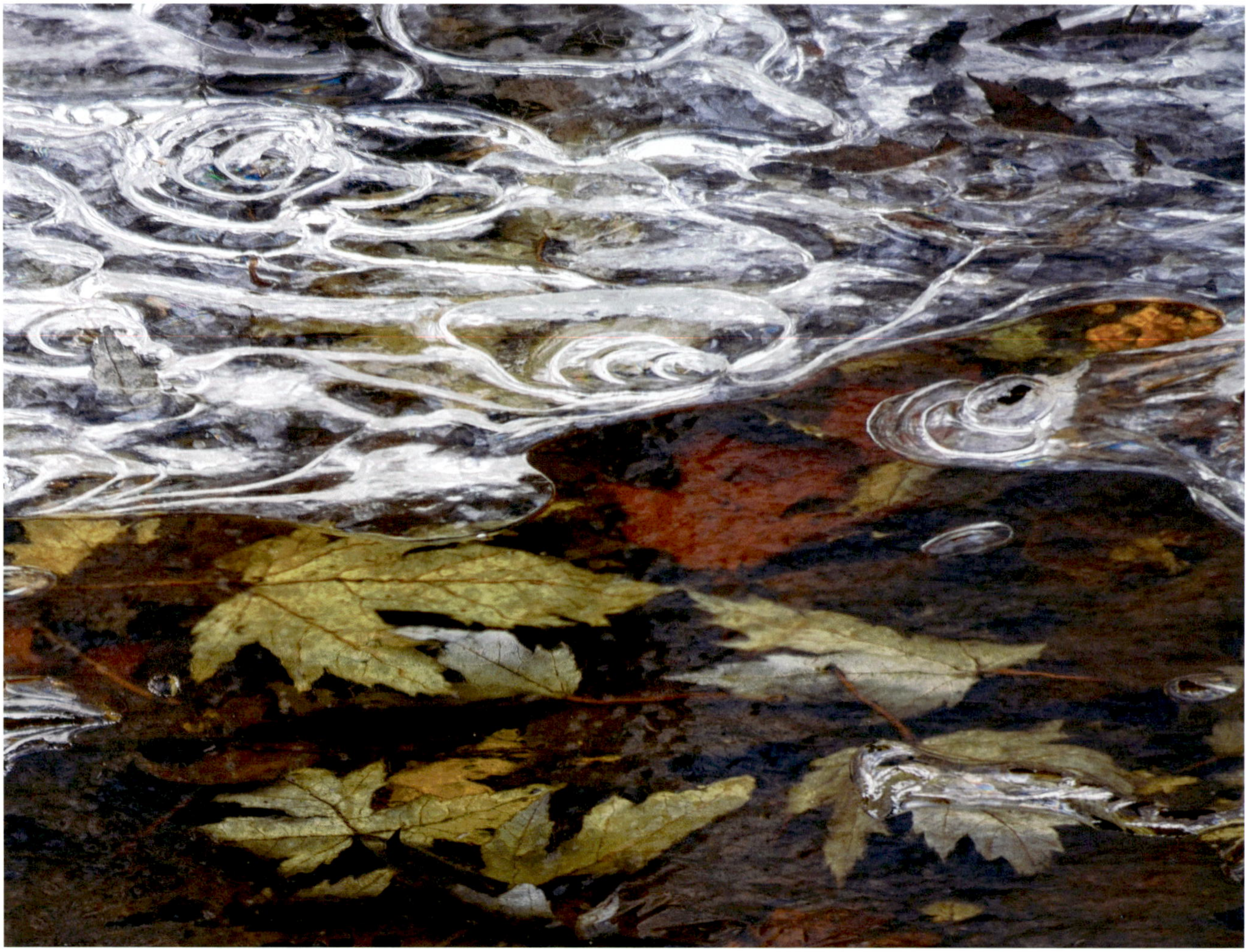

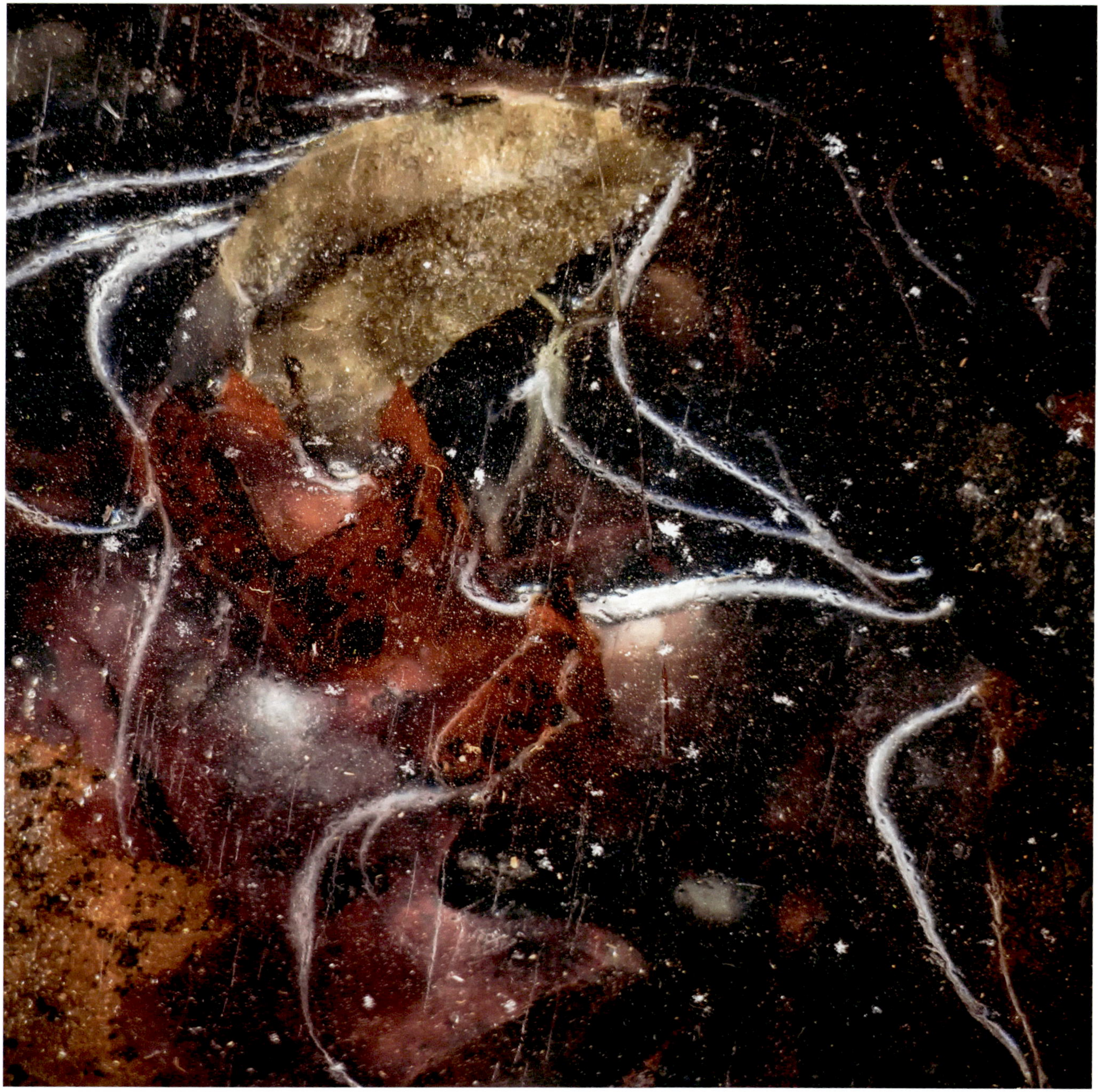

Pontiac

by Bill Young

www.byoungphoto.com • b.young100@gmail.com

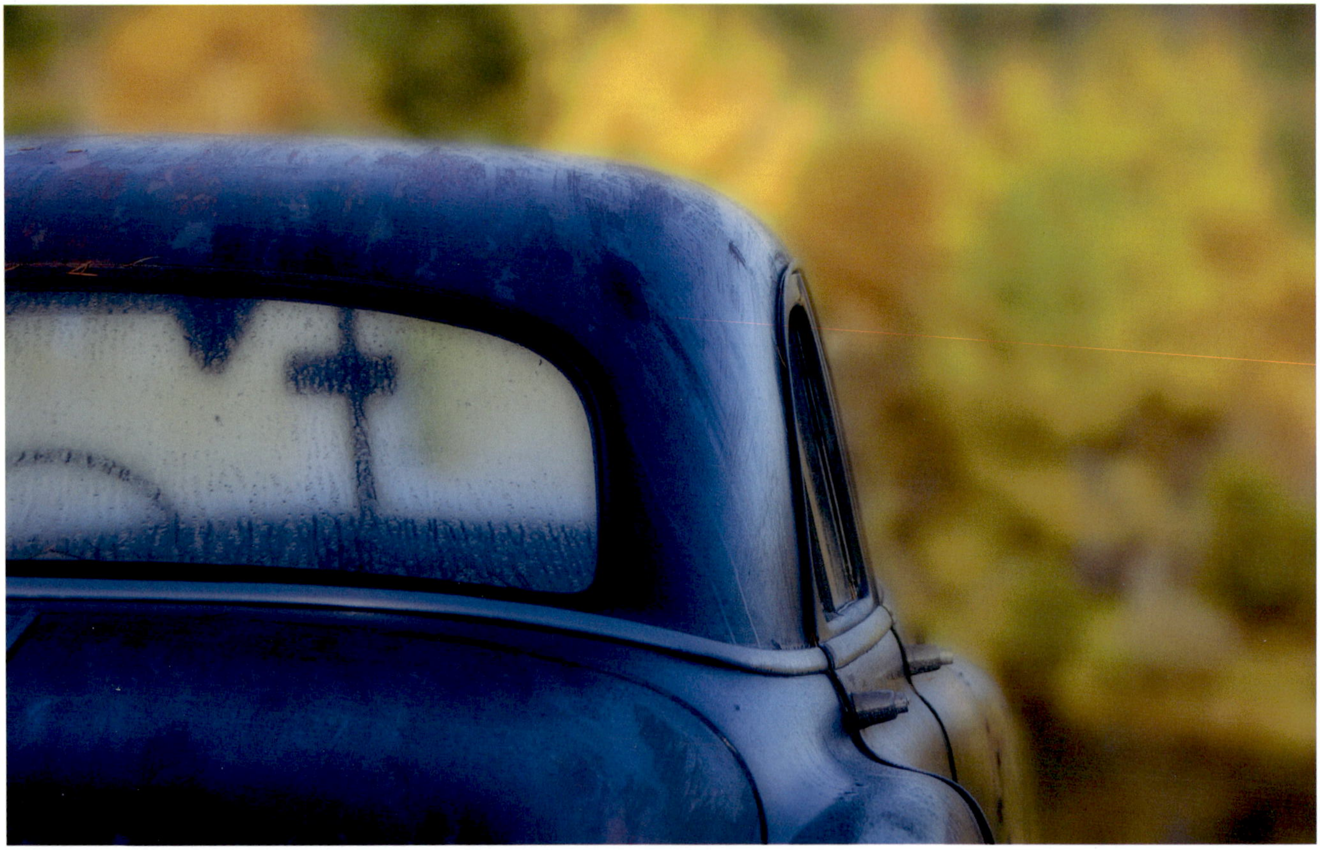

For the last hundred years people have had a love affair with the automobile. It's not only the car itself, of course, but rather the experiences, the special times we associate with them that matter most. From family vacations, learning to drive and getting your license, drive-in movies, your first car, and yes, even some conceptions and births in the back seats — automobiles have played a huge role in most of our lives. Little wonder that older vehicles evoke a sense of nostalgia, the longing for simpler, happier times of filtered remembrances.

In these images one old Pontiac coated with morning dew is proxy for all the cars we have collectively owned, sparking fond recollections of times past.

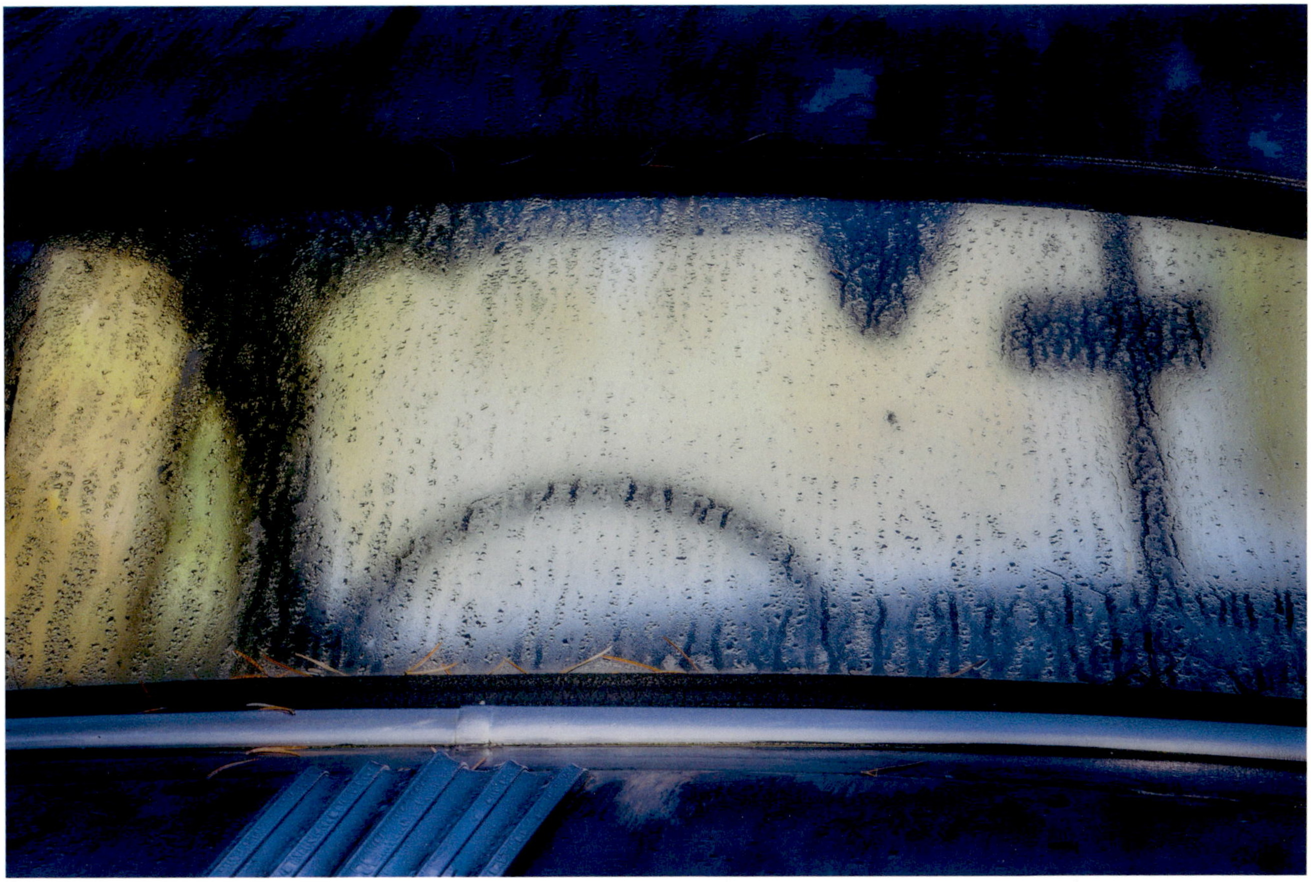

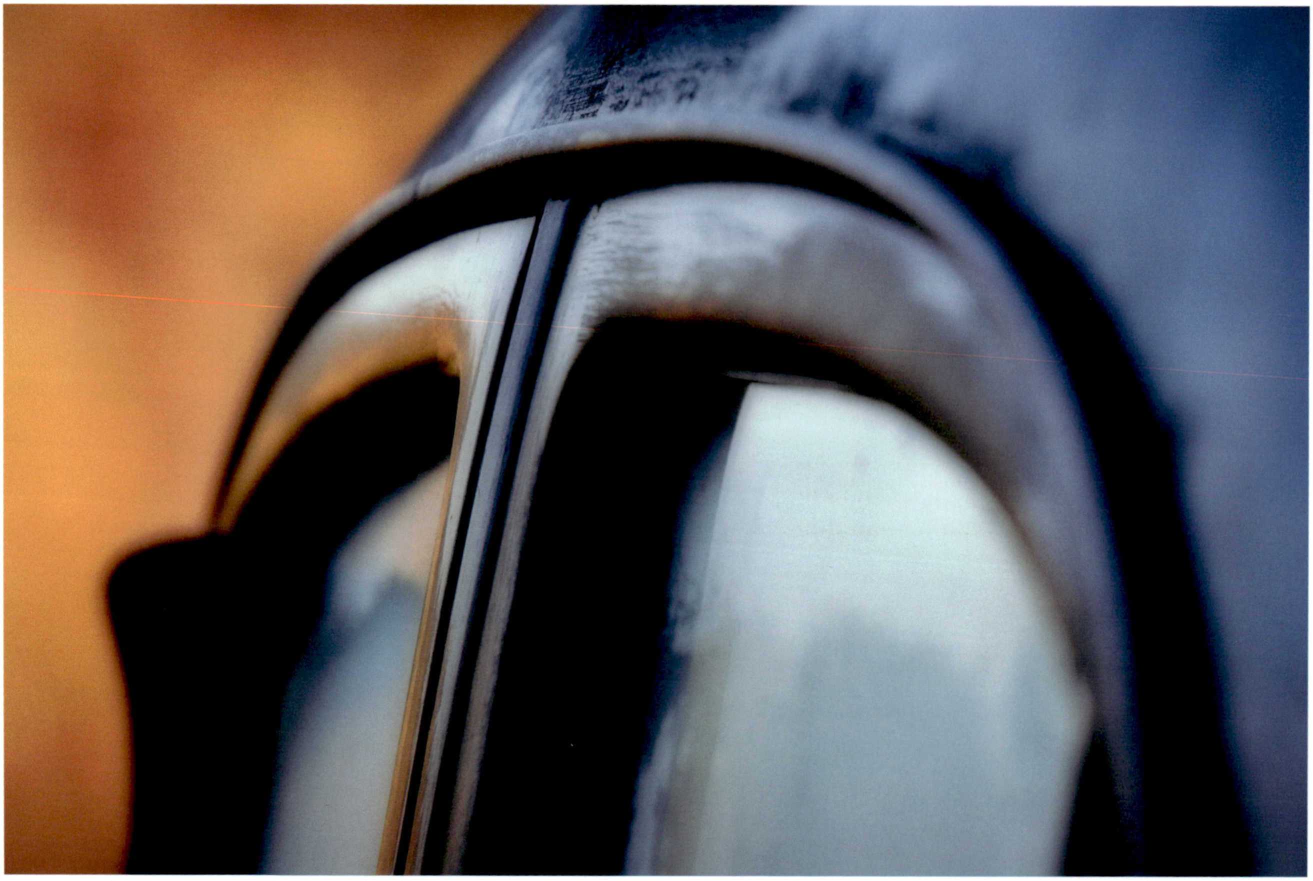

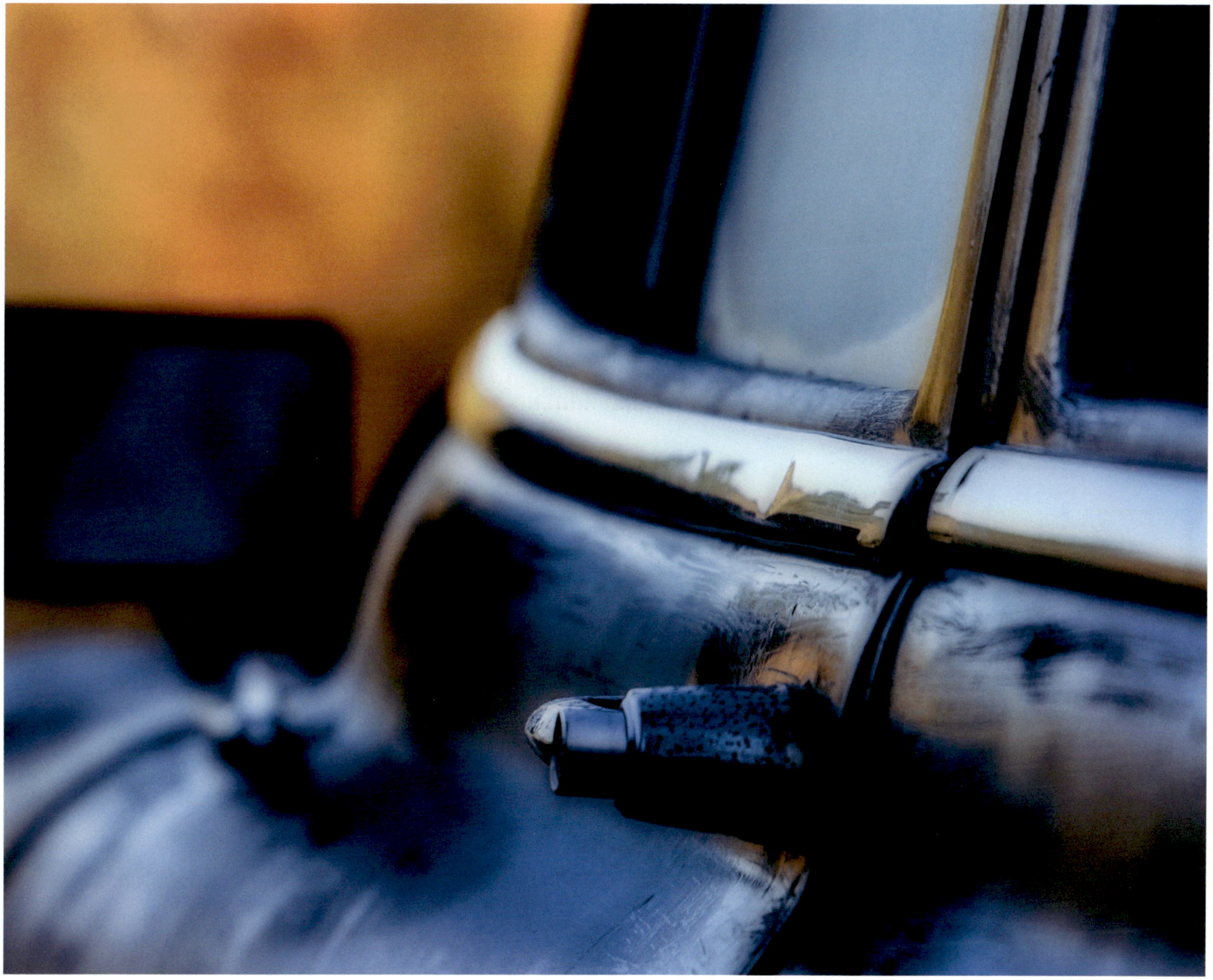

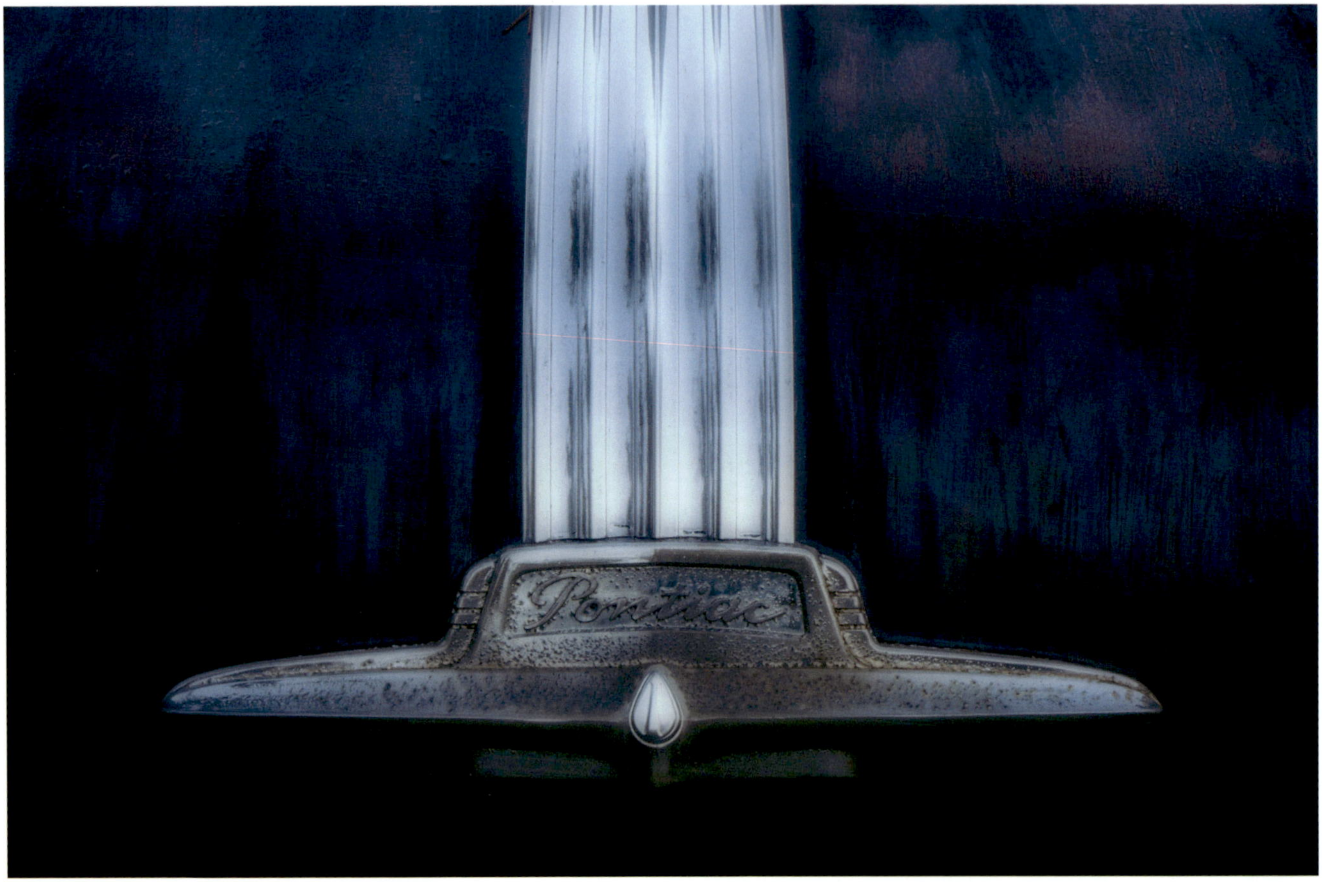
Pontiac

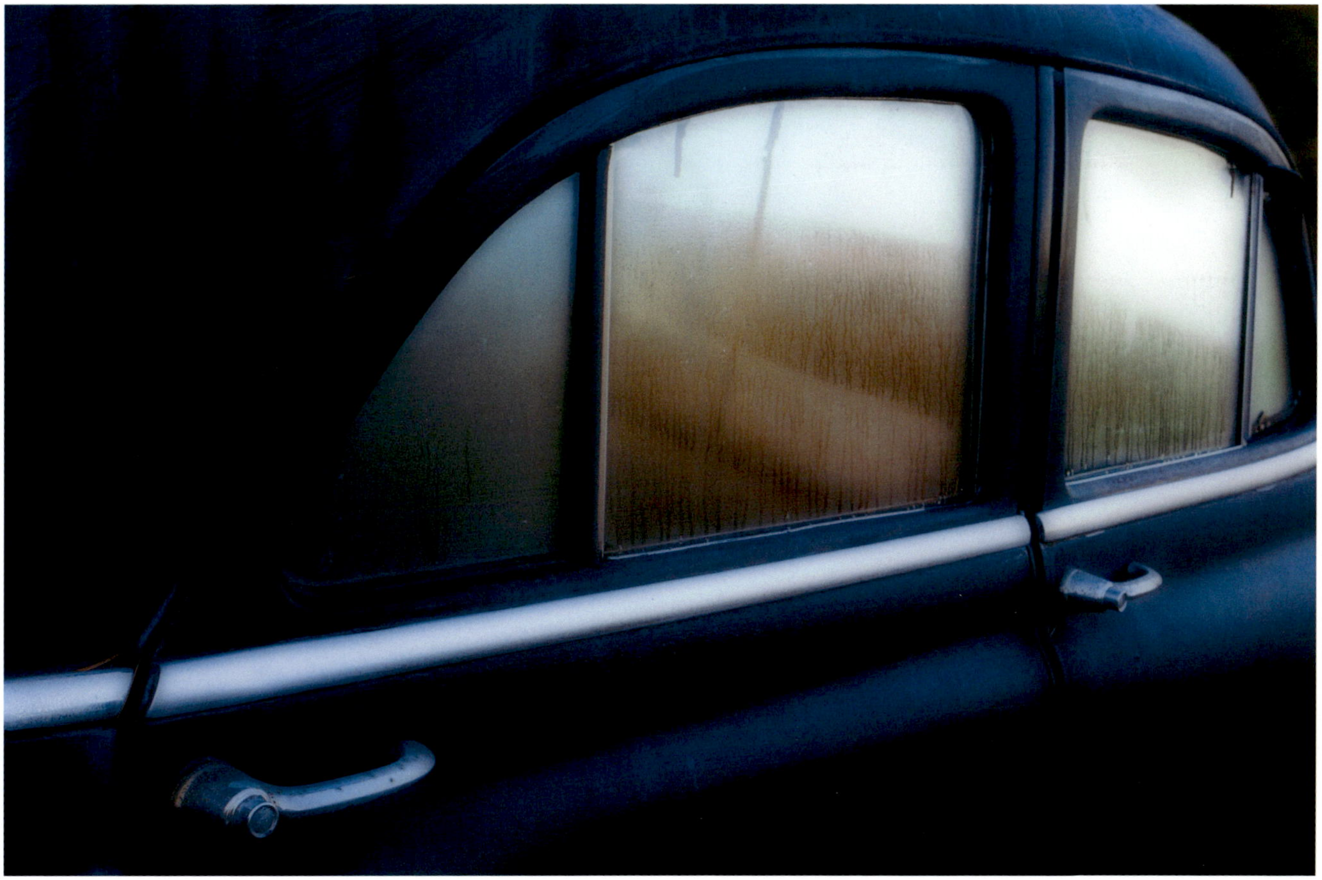

The Train to New York

by Daniel Goldberg

www.dcgphd.smugmug.com ♦ dcgphd@yahoo.com

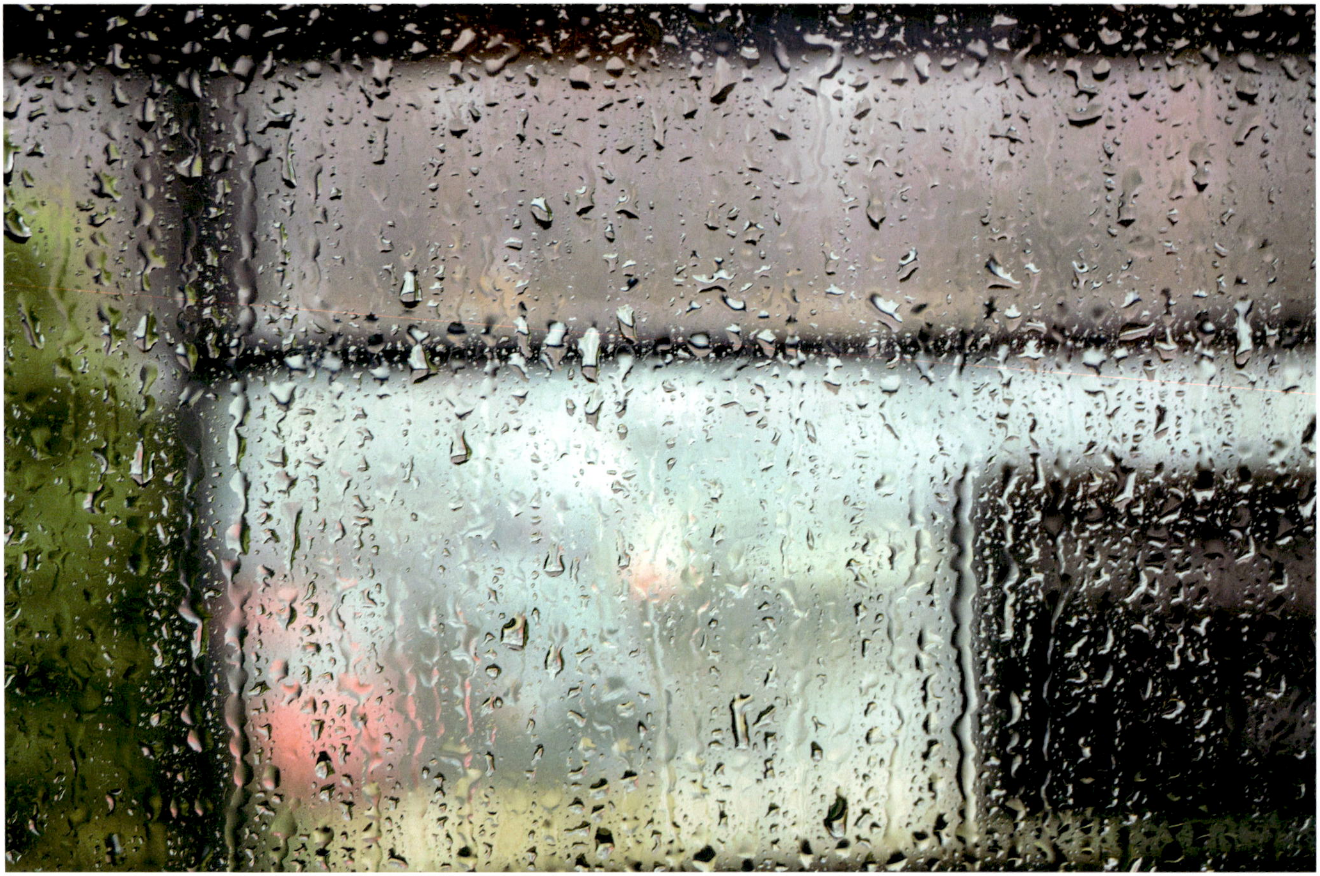

It's the 9:36 AM local to New York City. The train rocks to and fro. Its rhythm calls for sleep and my eyes begin to close. Rain pours from above covering the windows with these interesting streaks. It's an interesting state, this halfway point between sleep and being awake. A comfortable place. As I look at the windows, this visual play begins. What's in the foreground? What becomes the background? Everything becomes dreamlike in the distance as I focus on the foreground of the rain pouring down the windows. I want to drift back to sleep, but something keeps calling me to notice what's right in front of me.

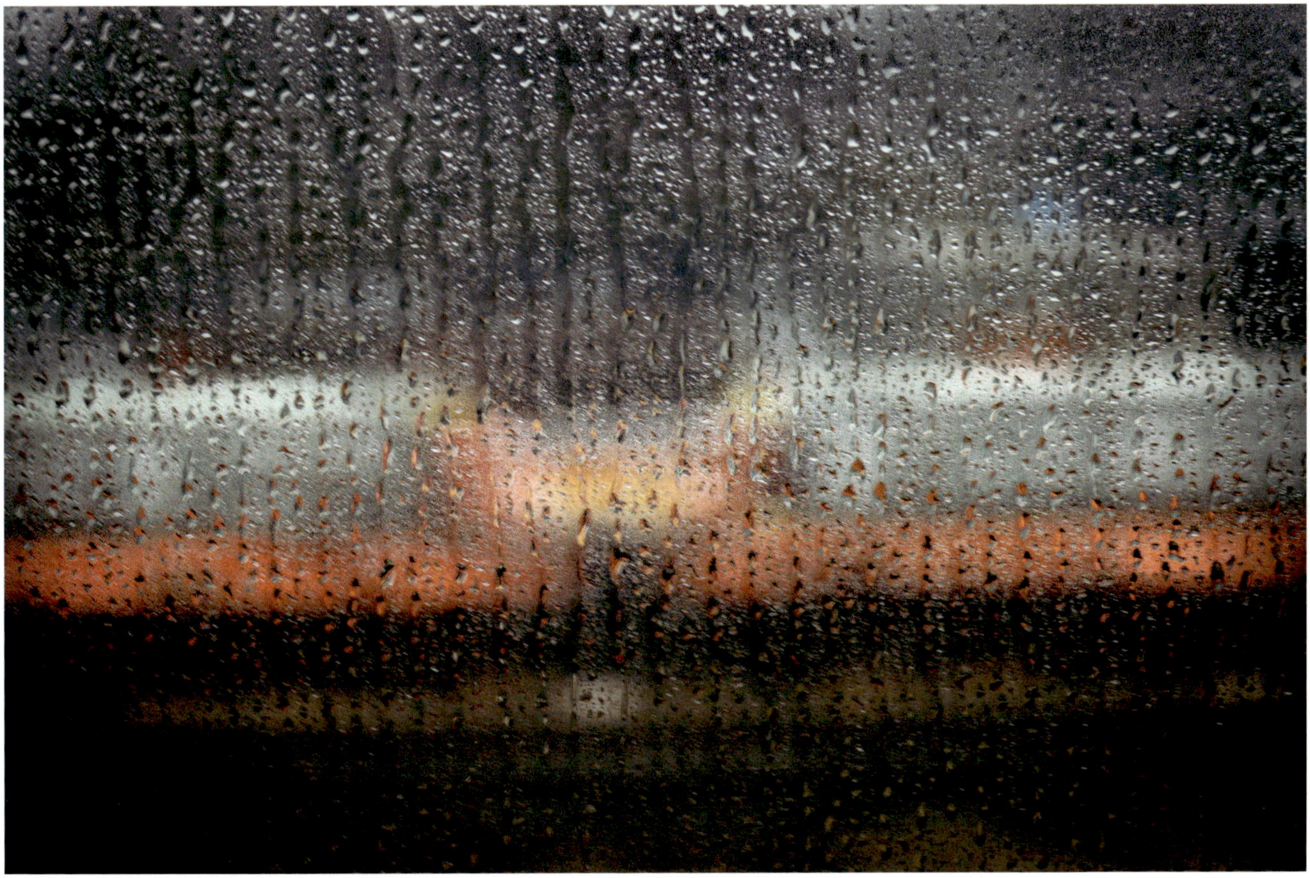

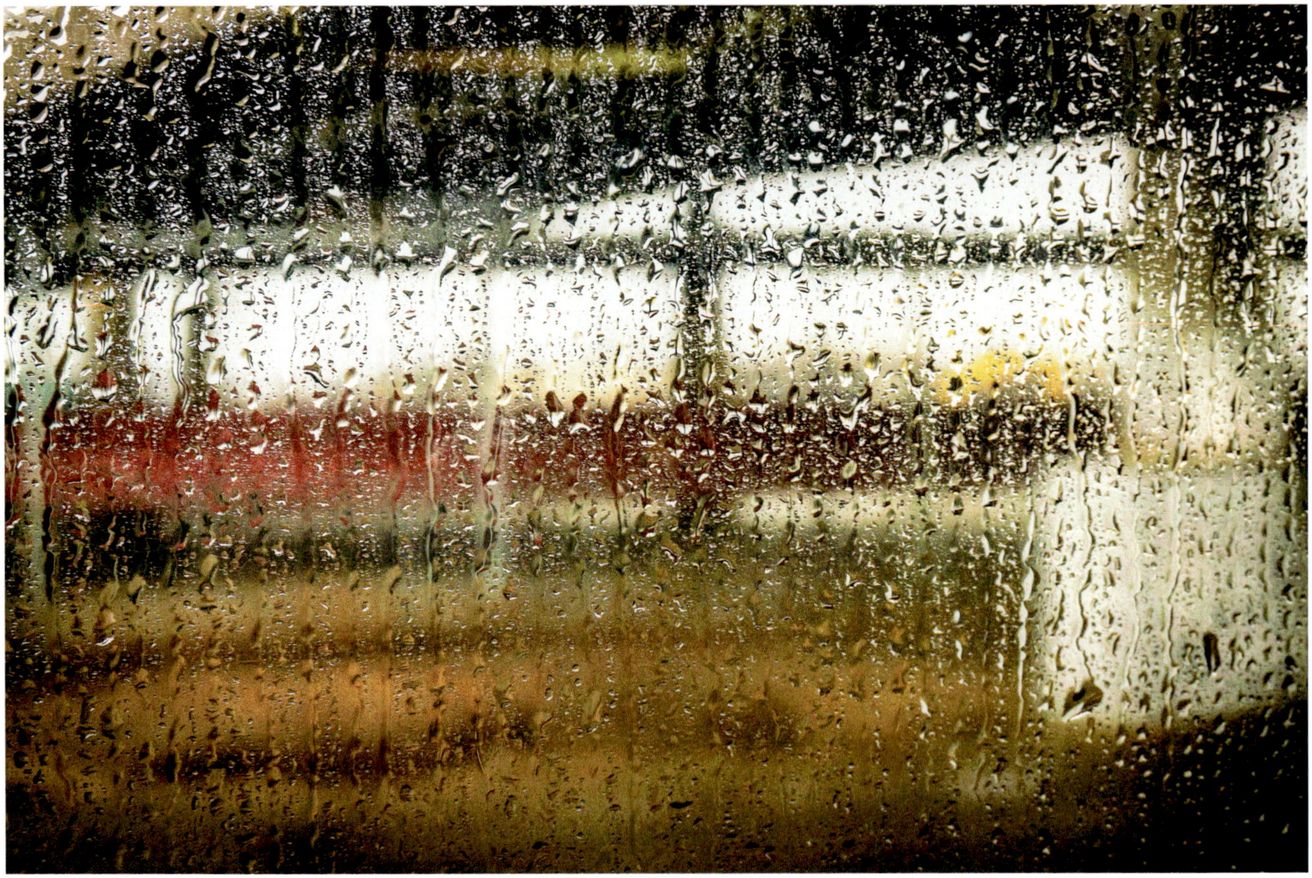

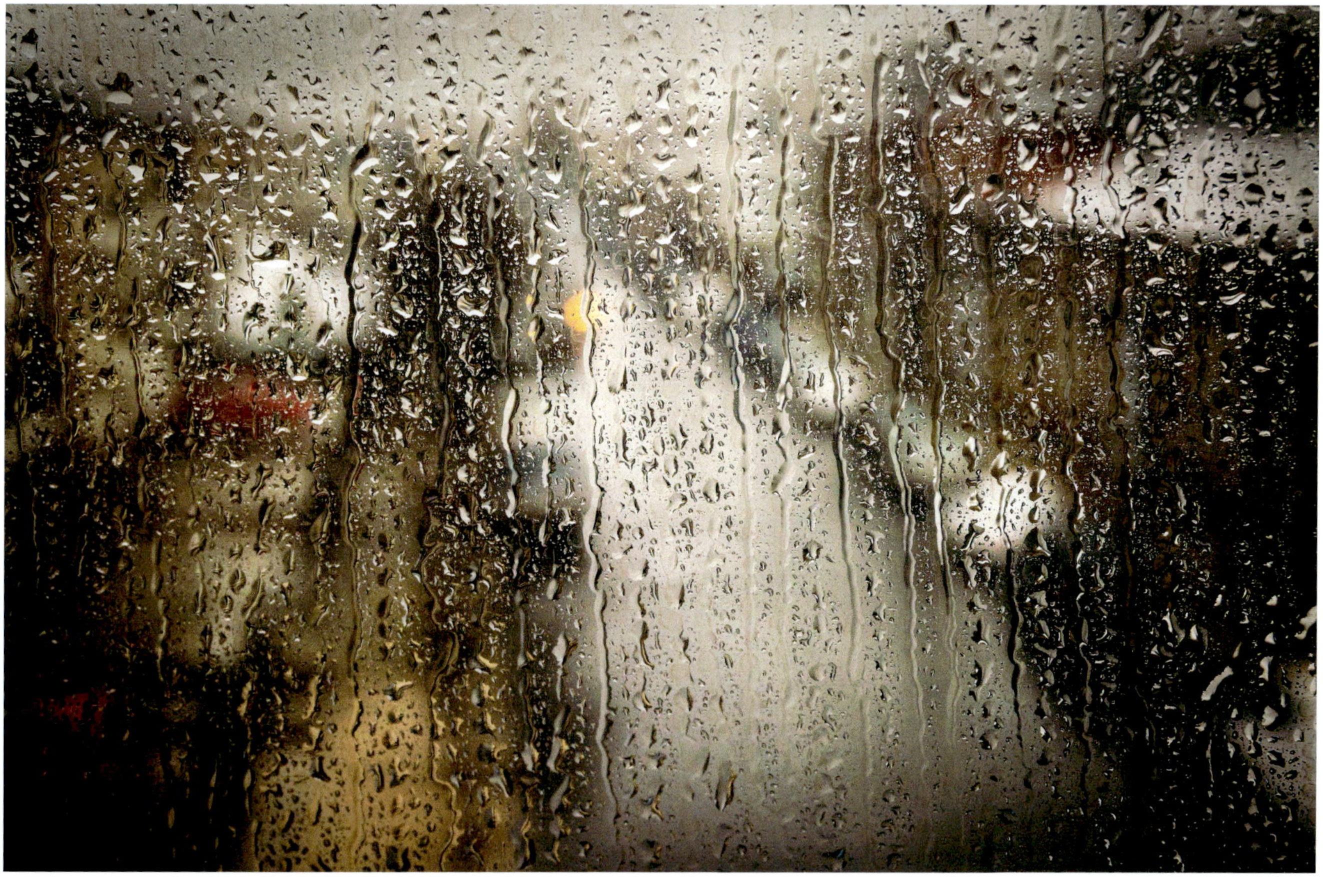

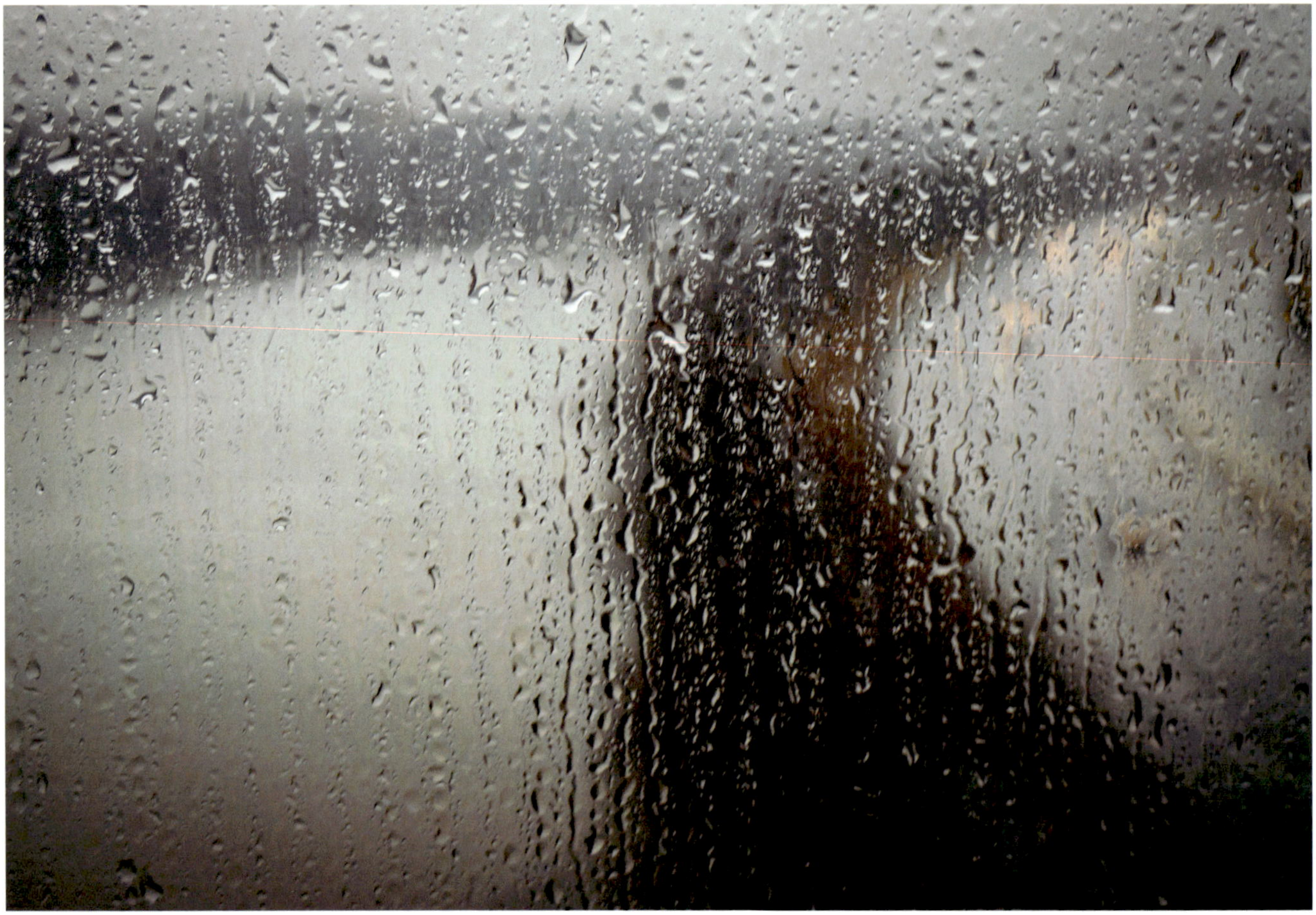

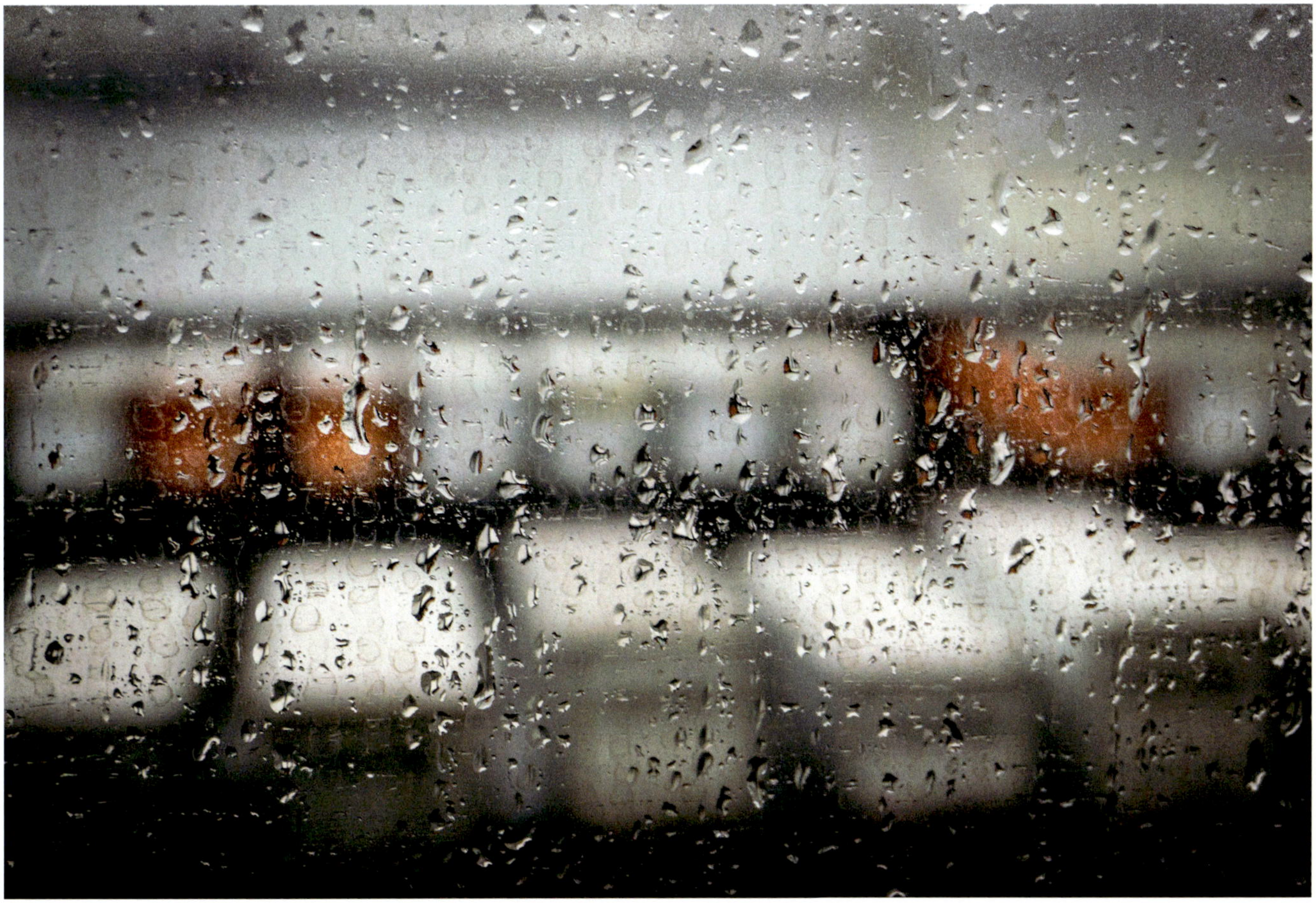

Alien Architecture

by Jack Curran

www.jackcurranphotography.com • jack@jackcurranphotography.com

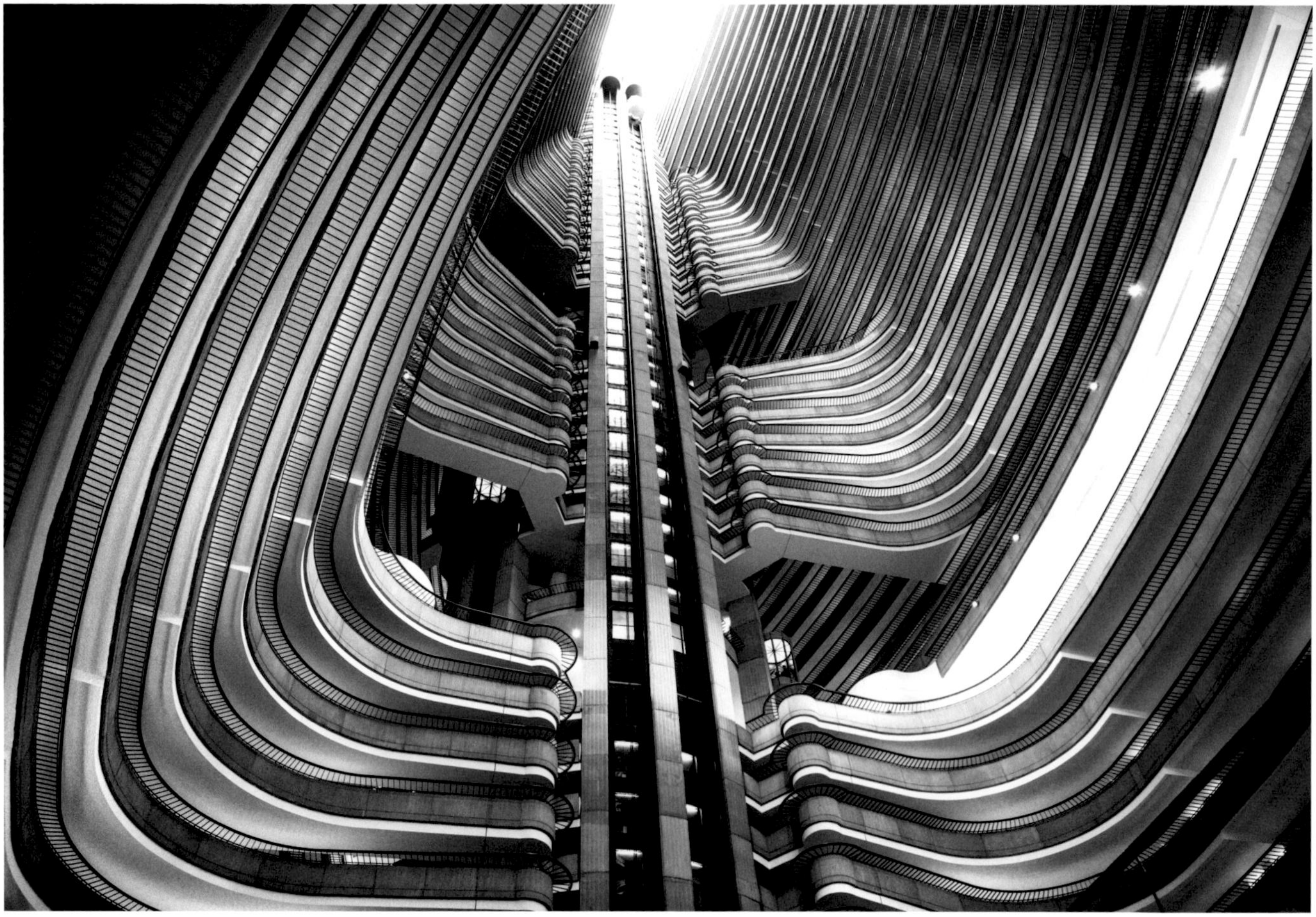

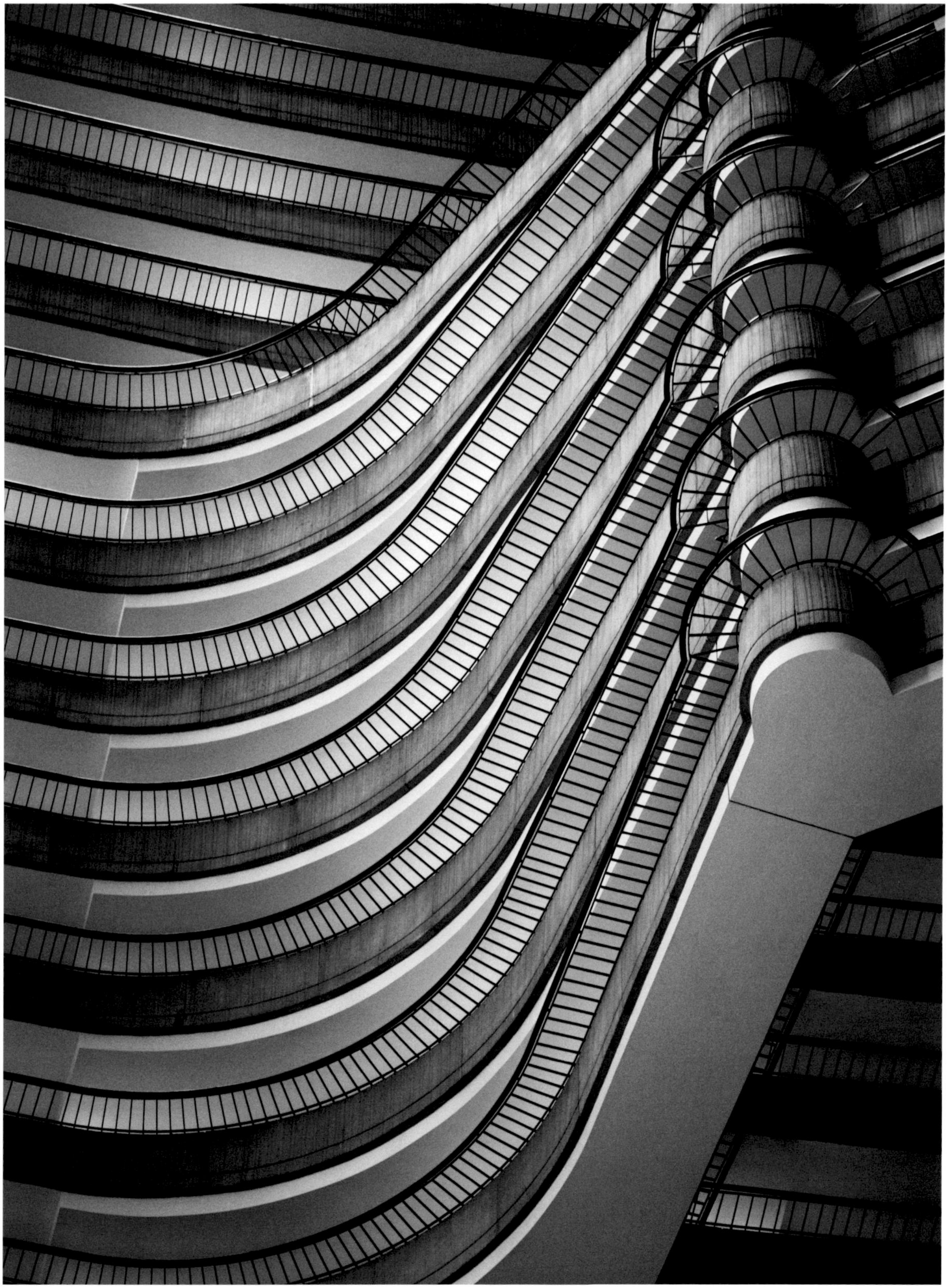

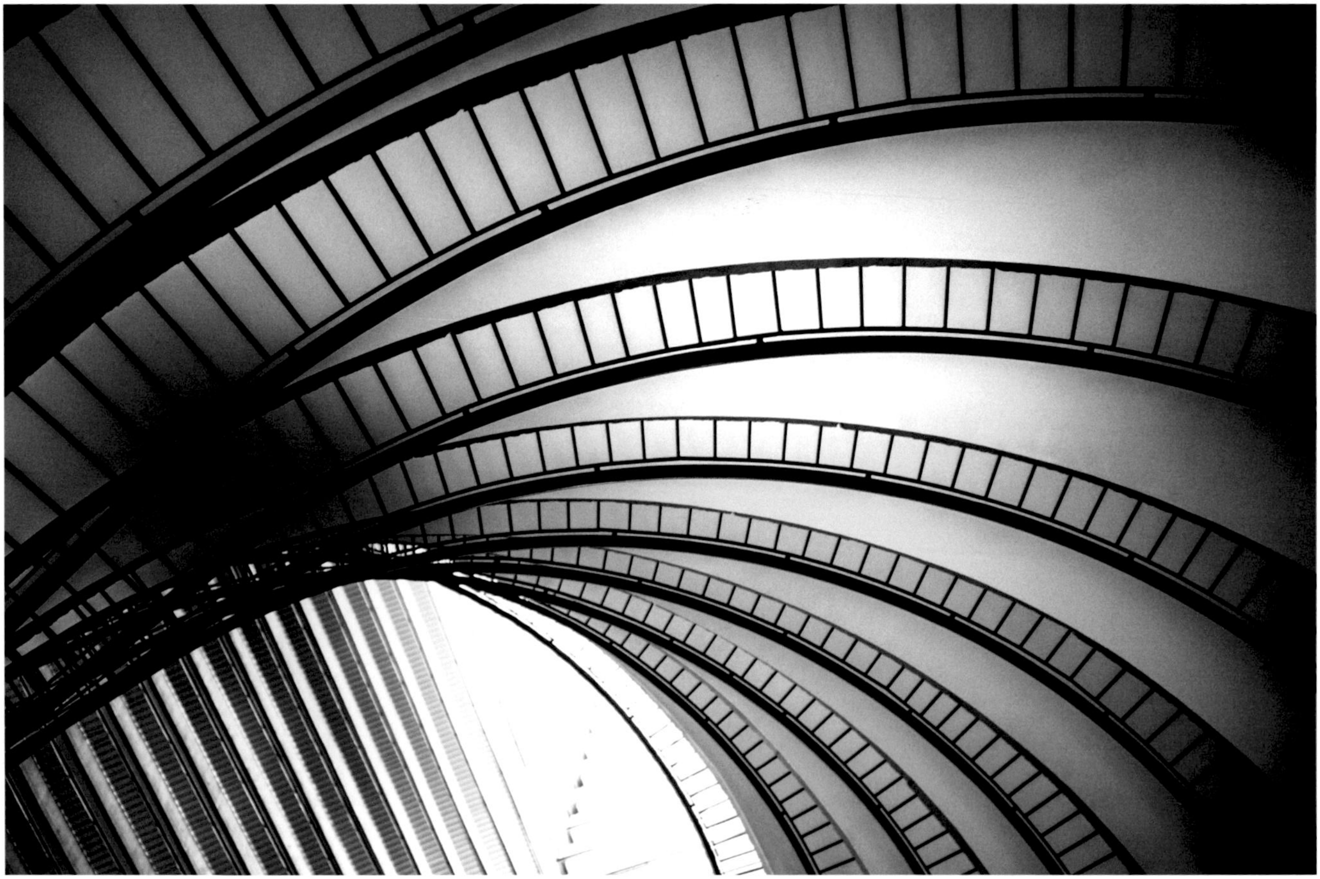

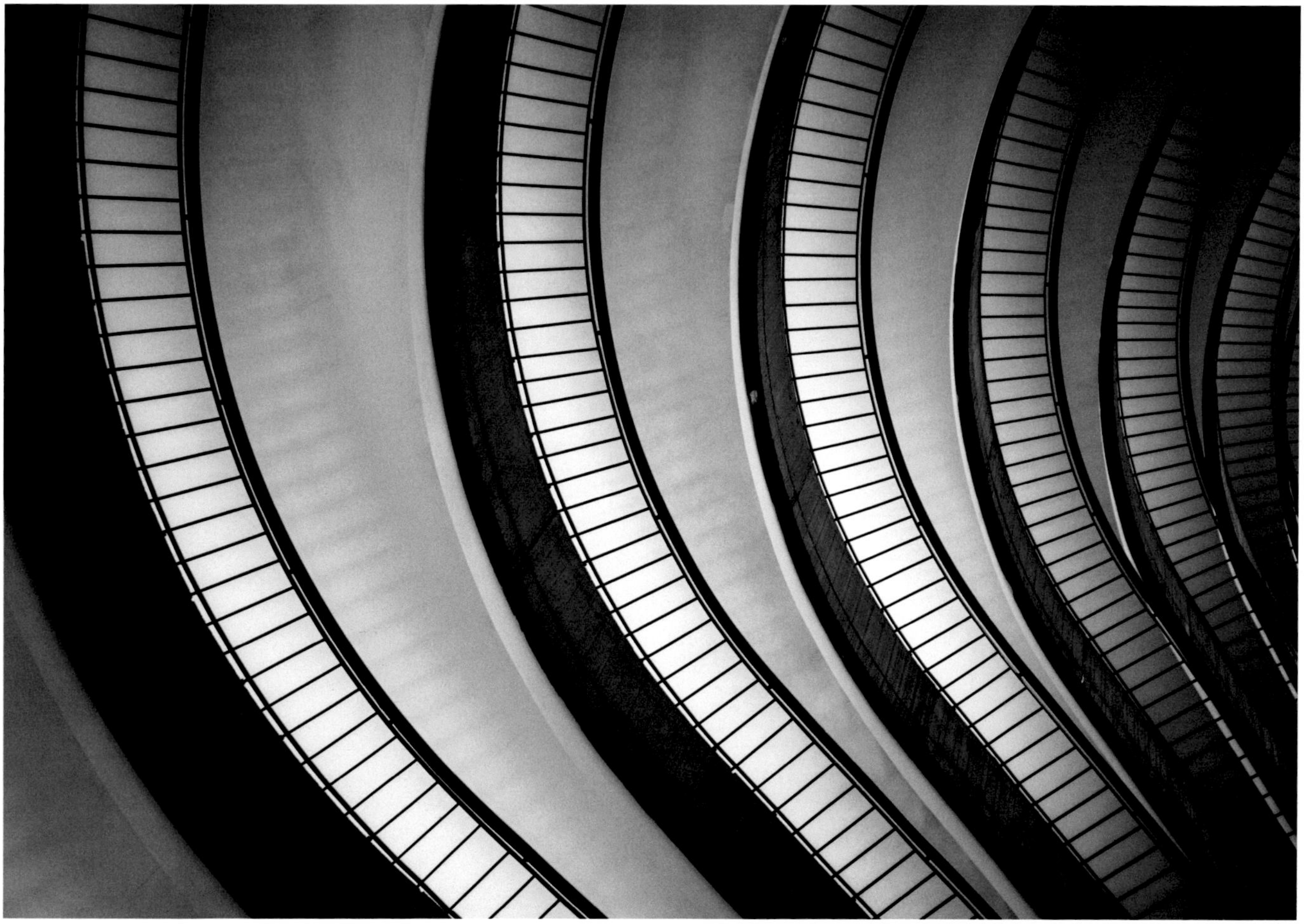

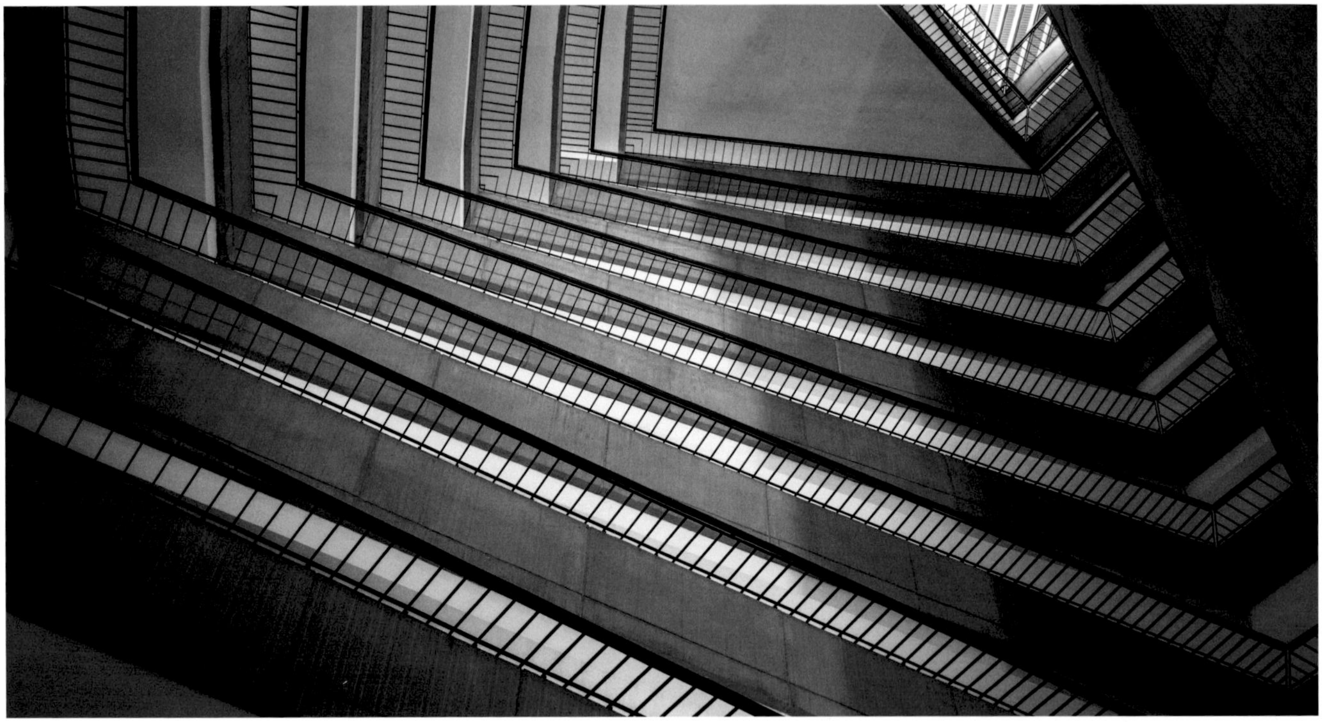

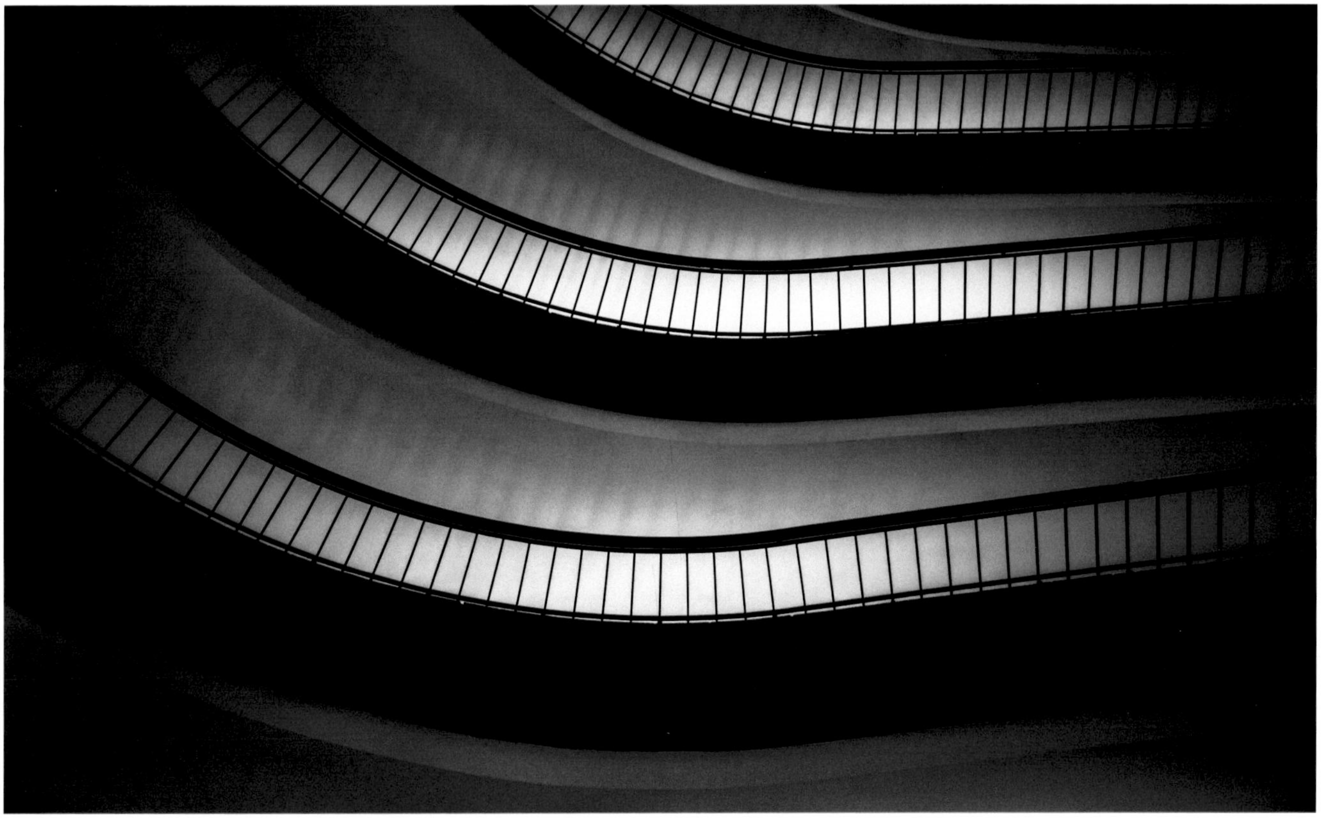

City Flow

by Moises Levy

moiseslevy.com ♦ moises.levy@gmail.com

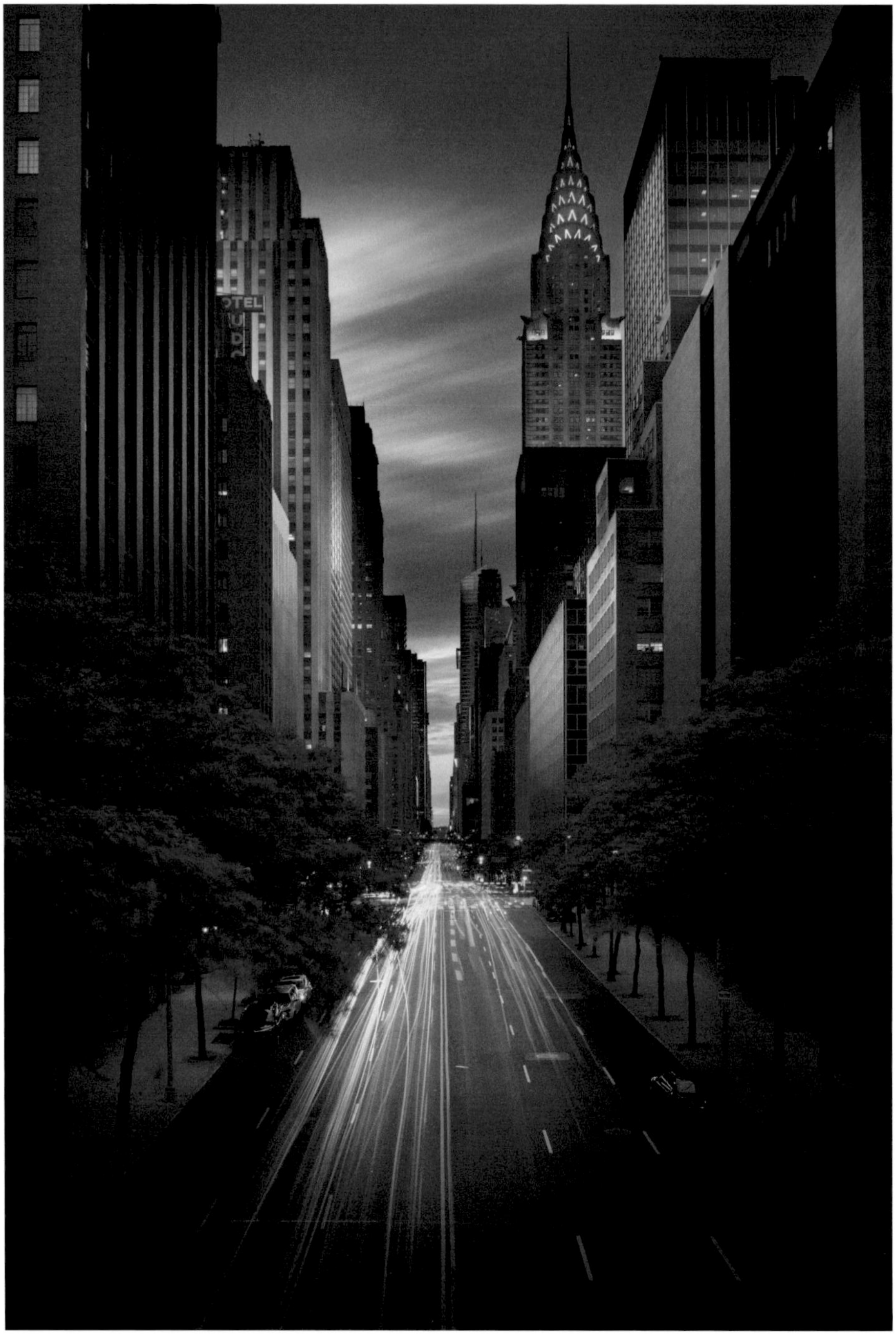

42 St Sunset

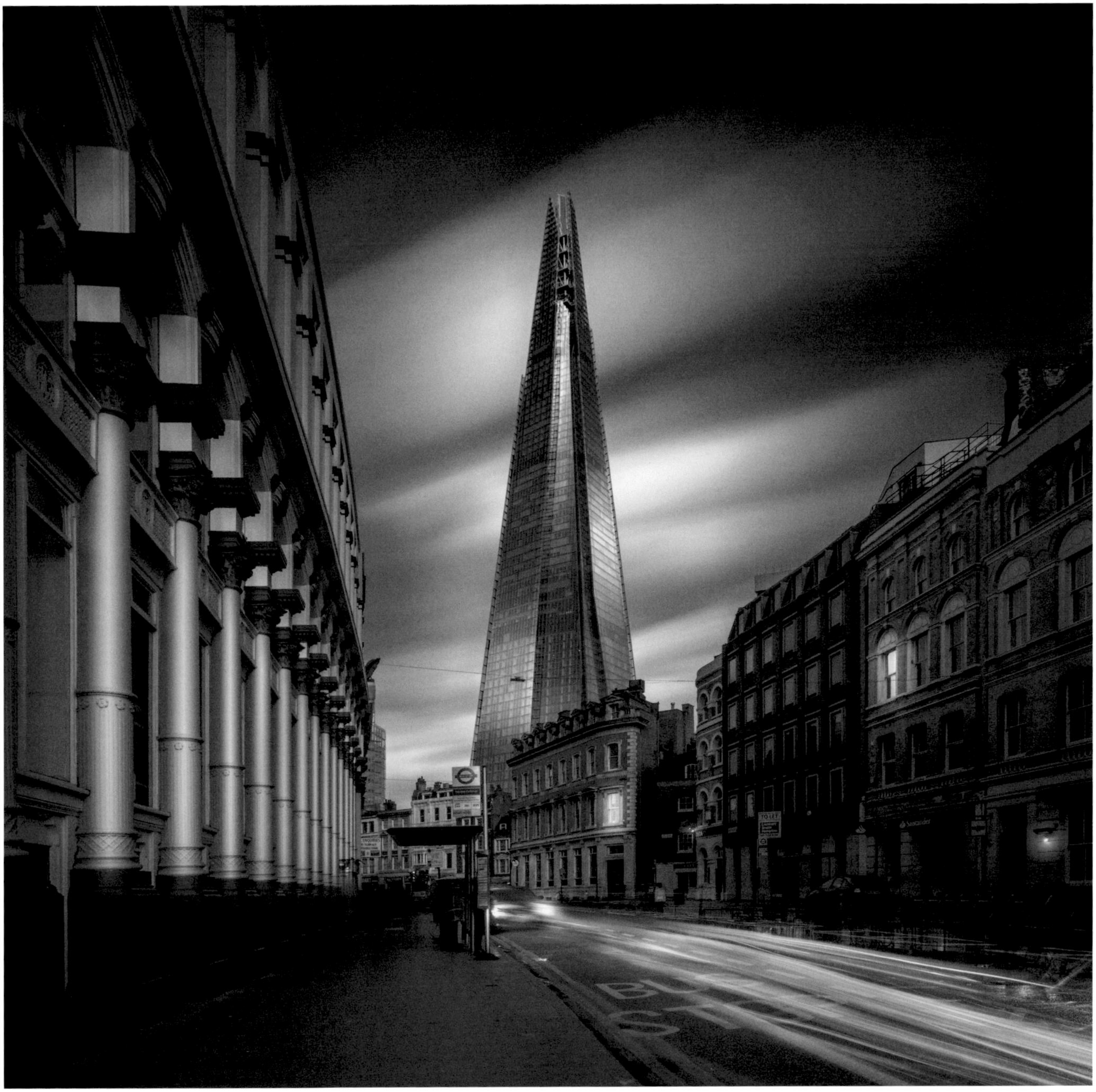

Connections

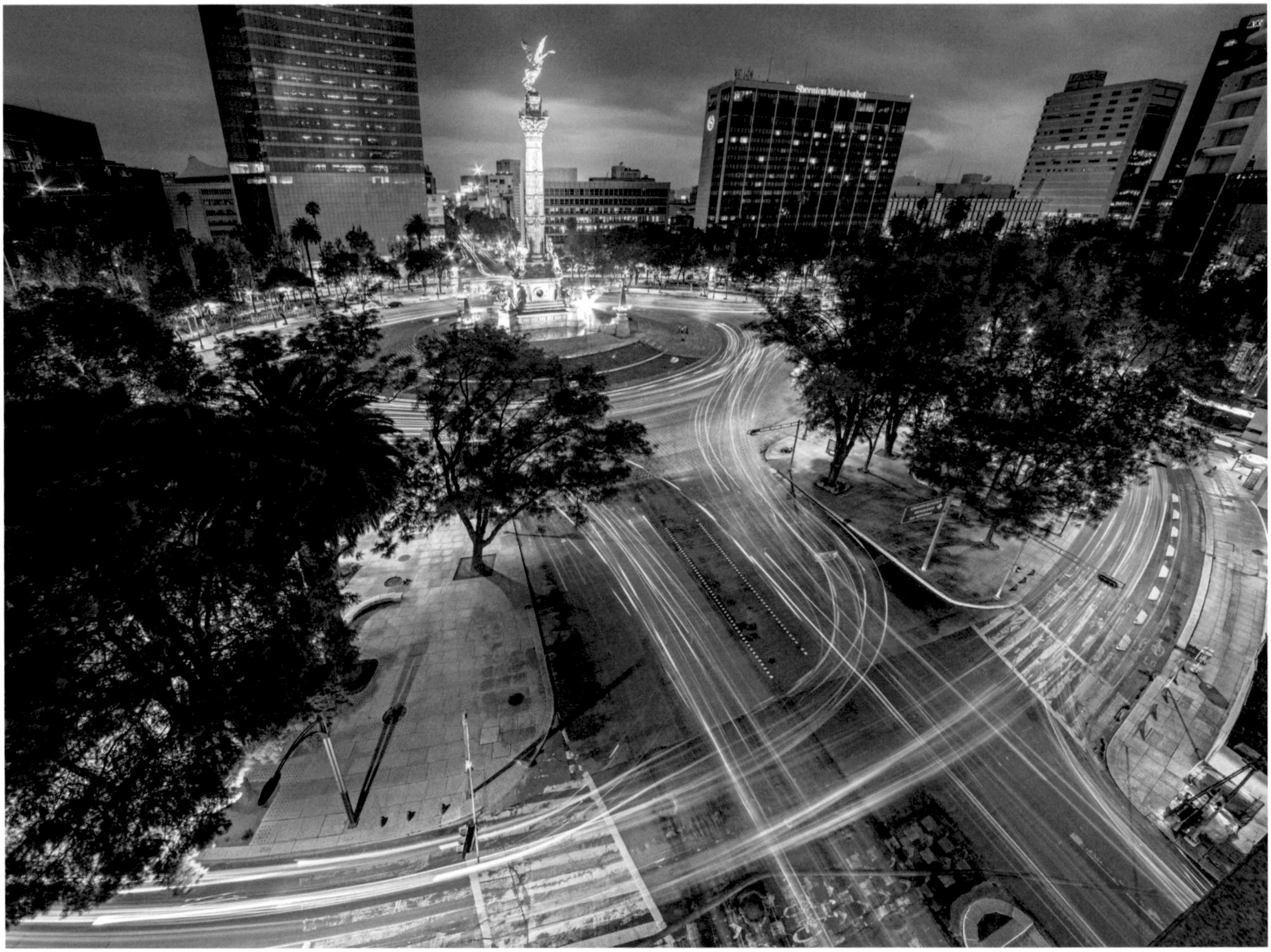

El Angel

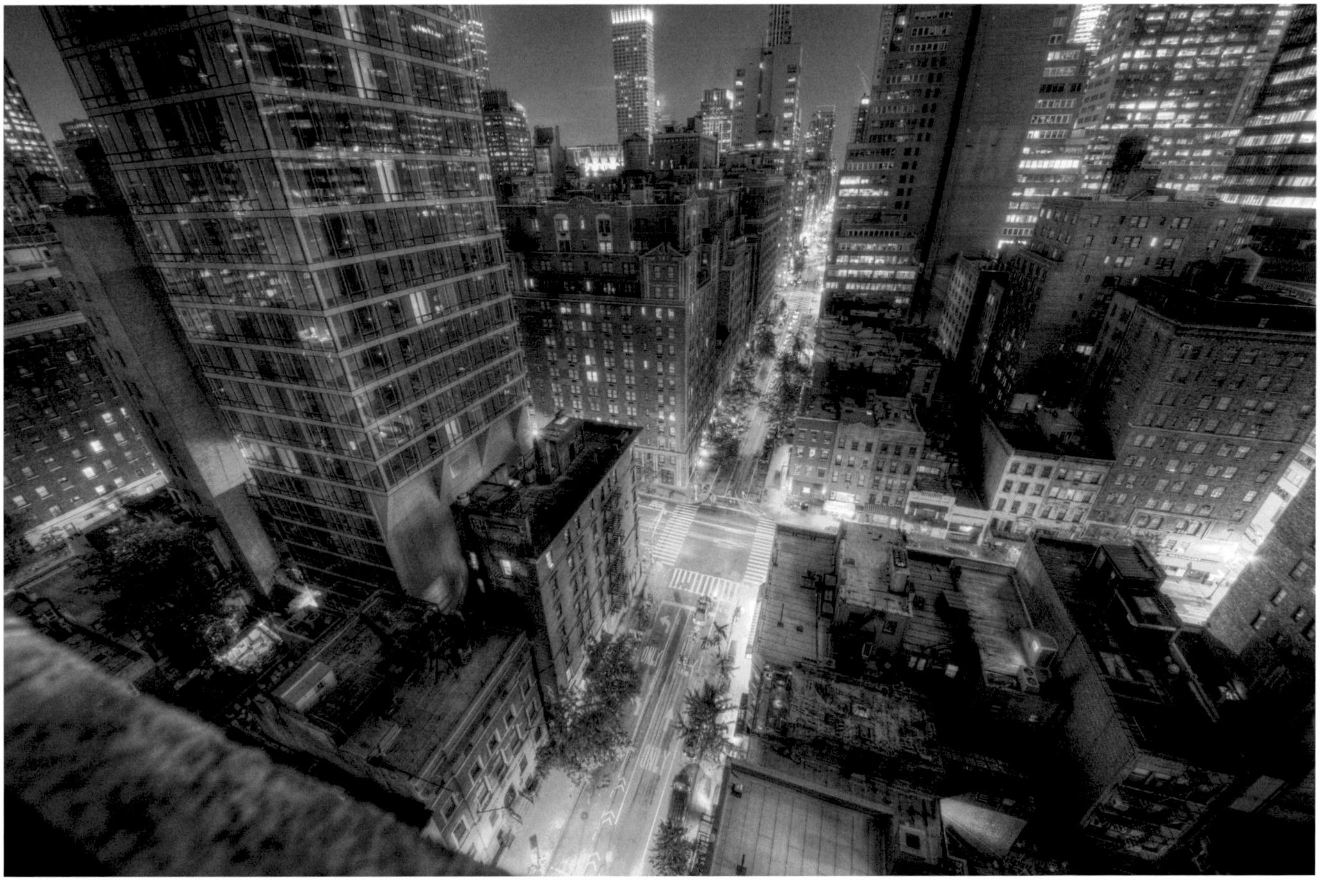

Energy

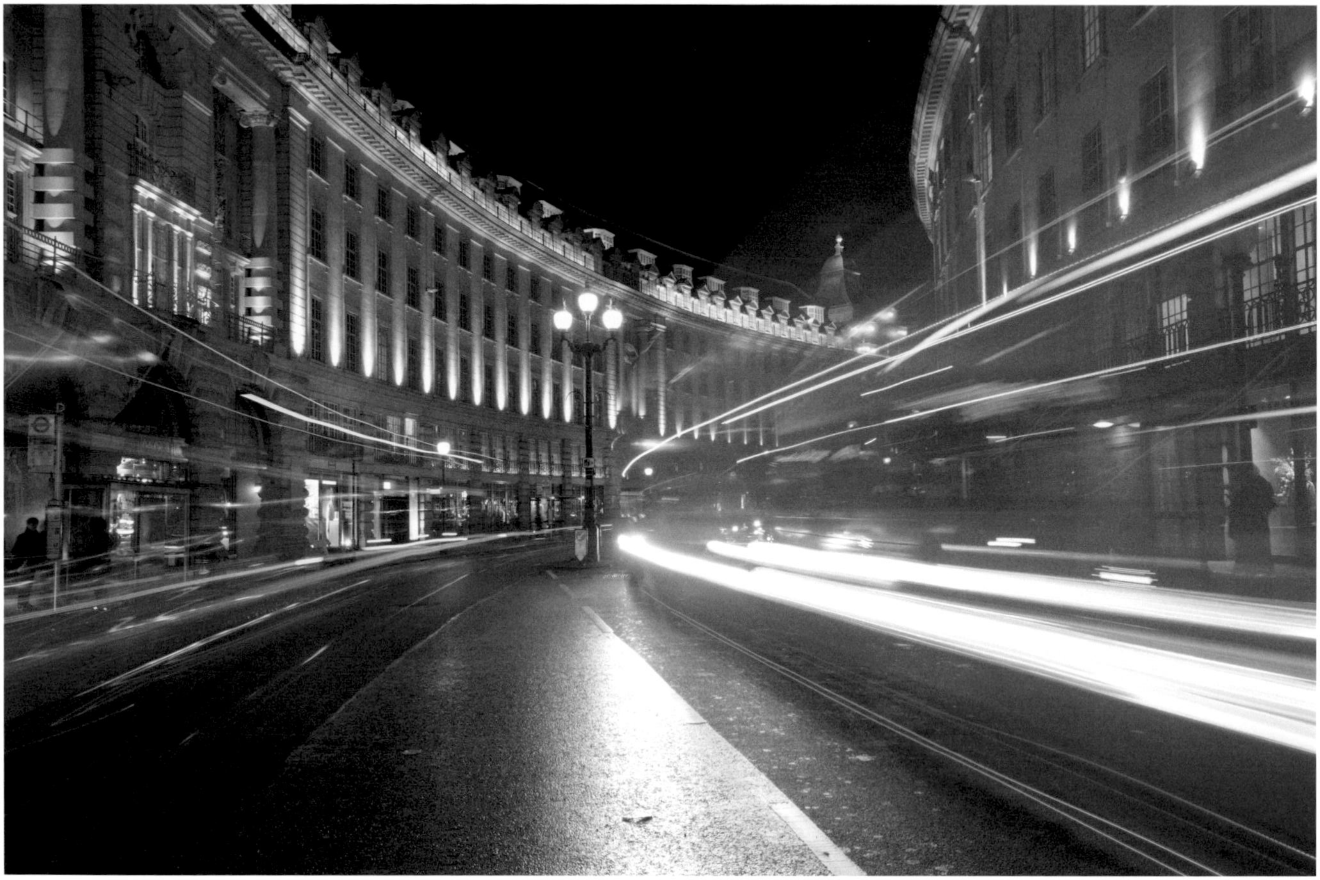

Flow

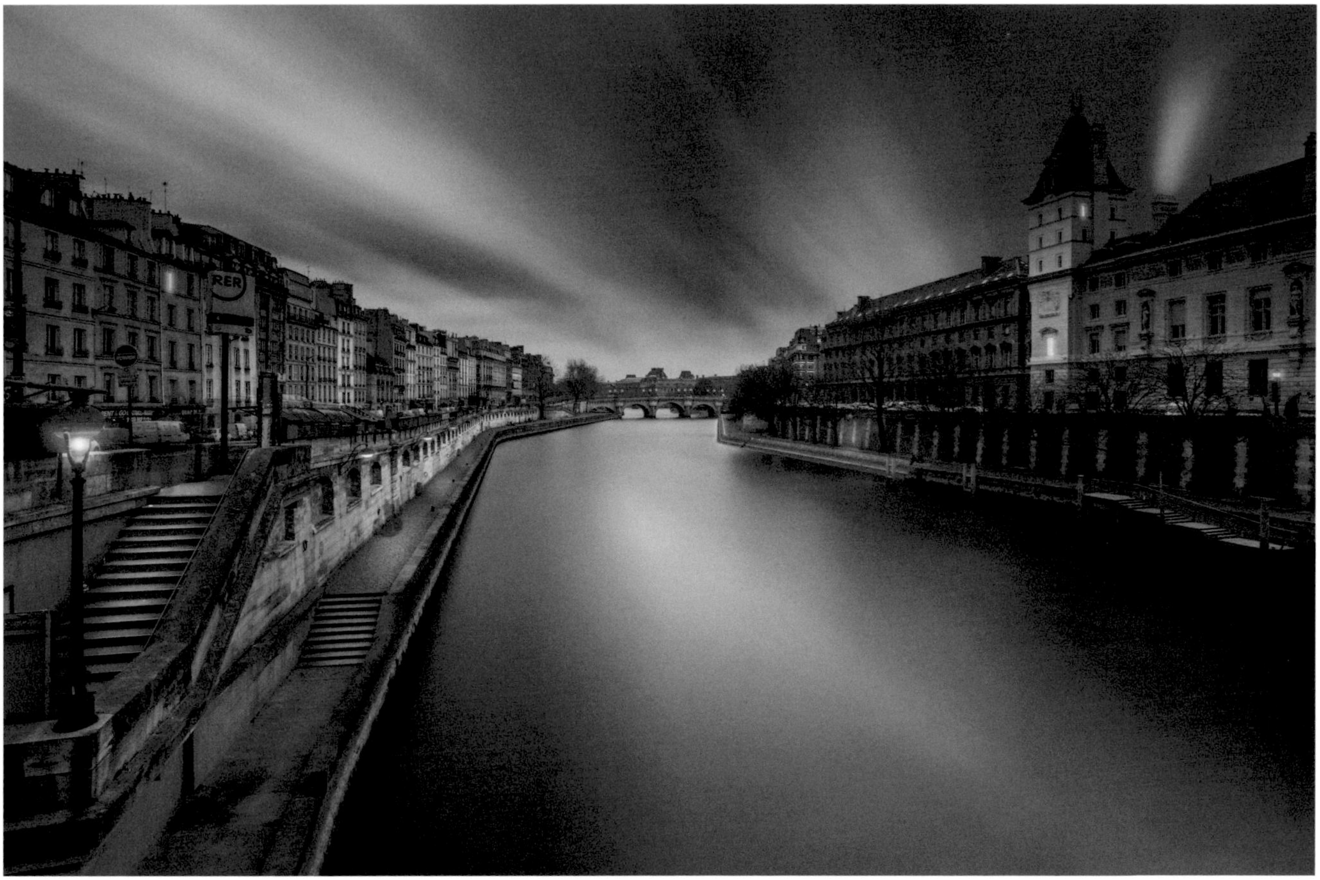

Rio Senna Flow

Ouroboros, The Circle of Life

by Barbara Warren

www.barbarawarren.com ♦ barbwarrenphoto@gmail.com

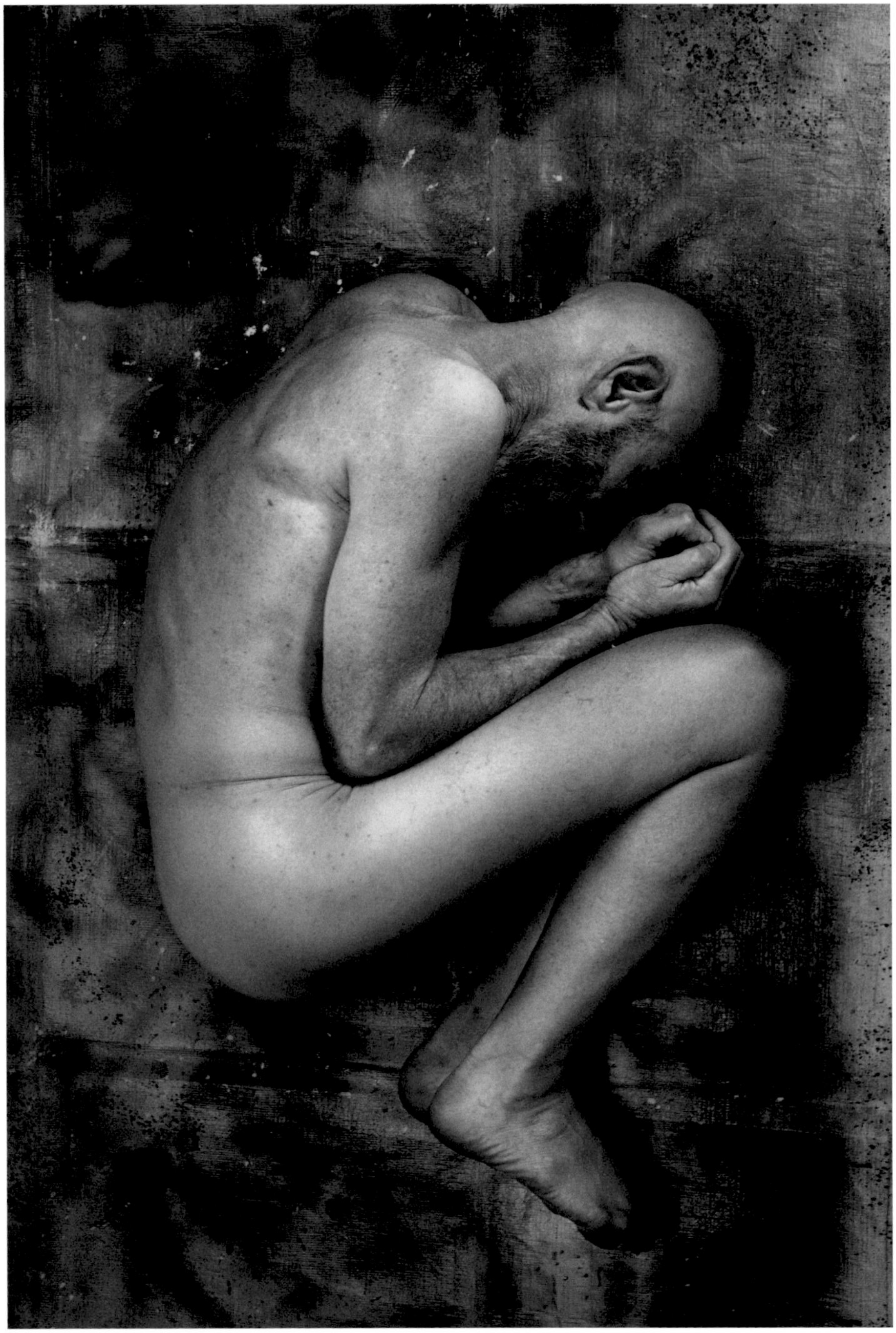

Birth

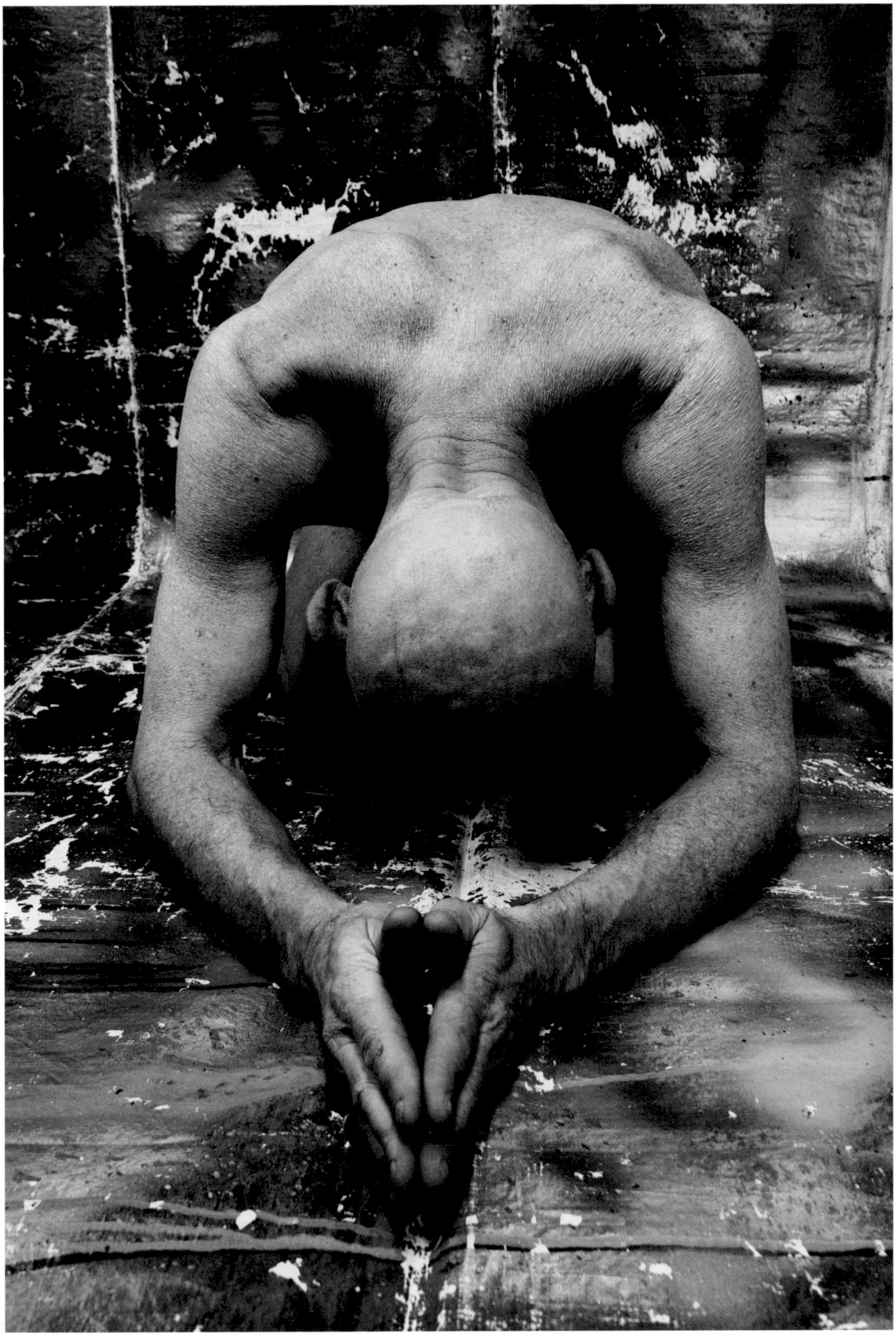

Deference

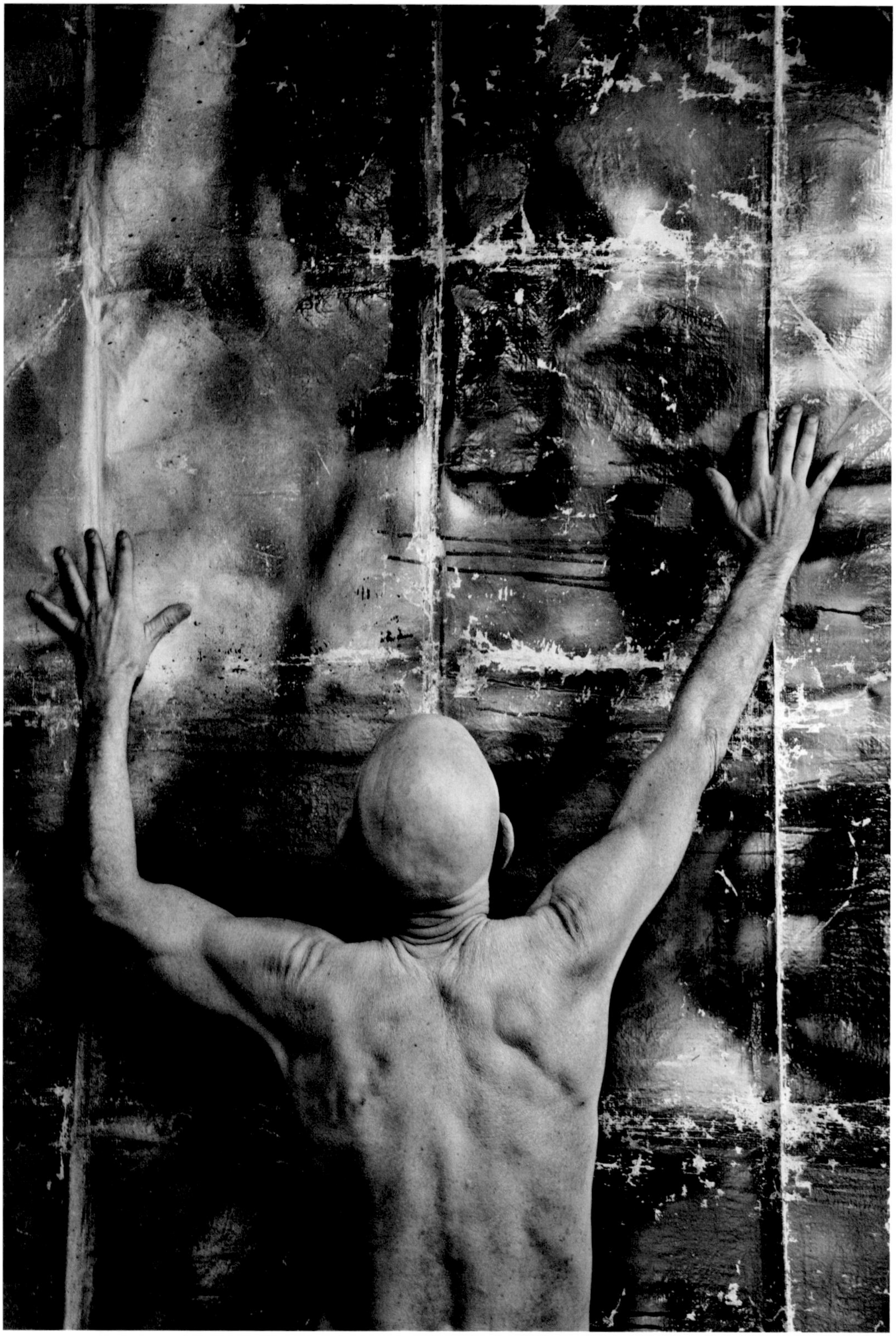

Ambition

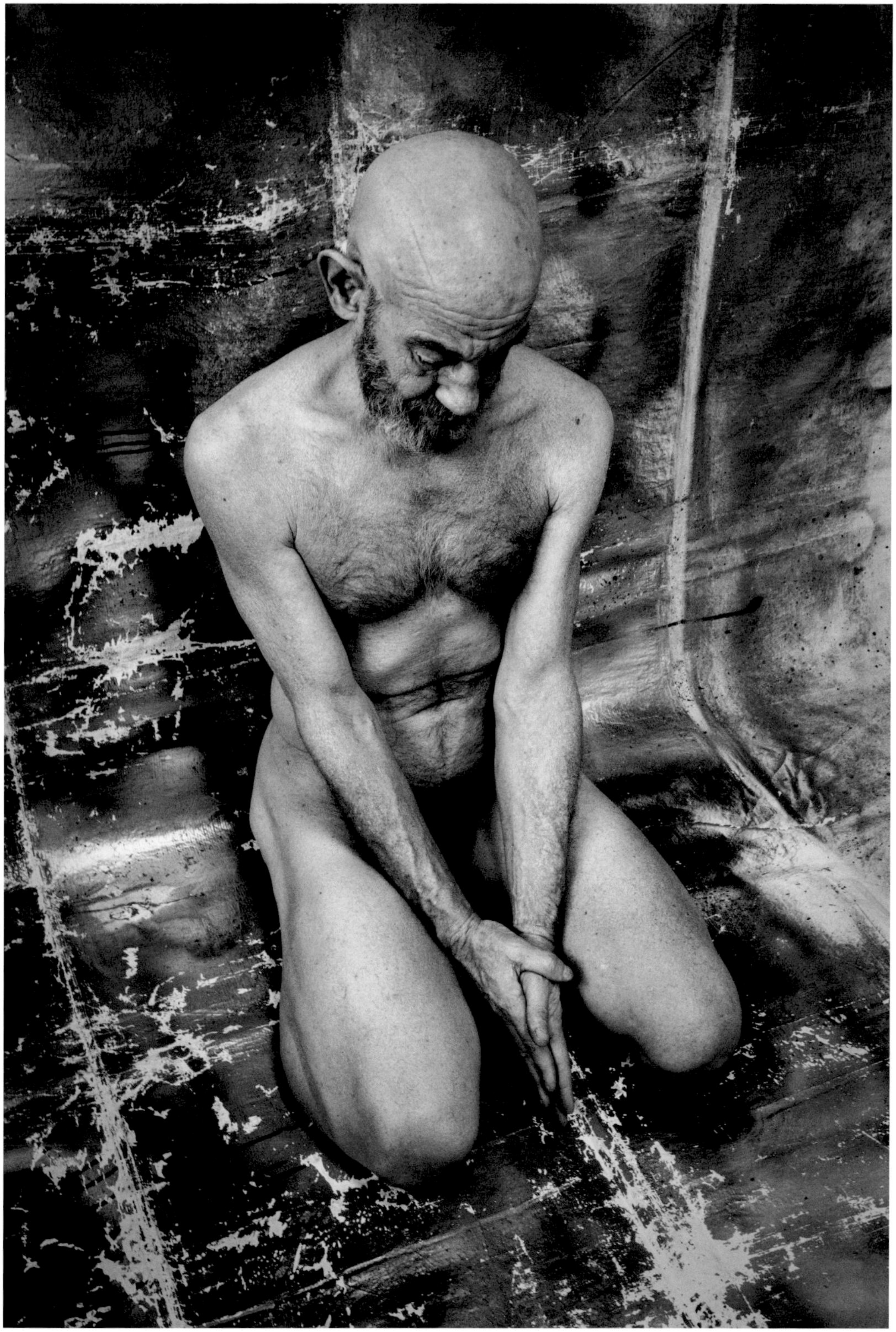

Sorrow

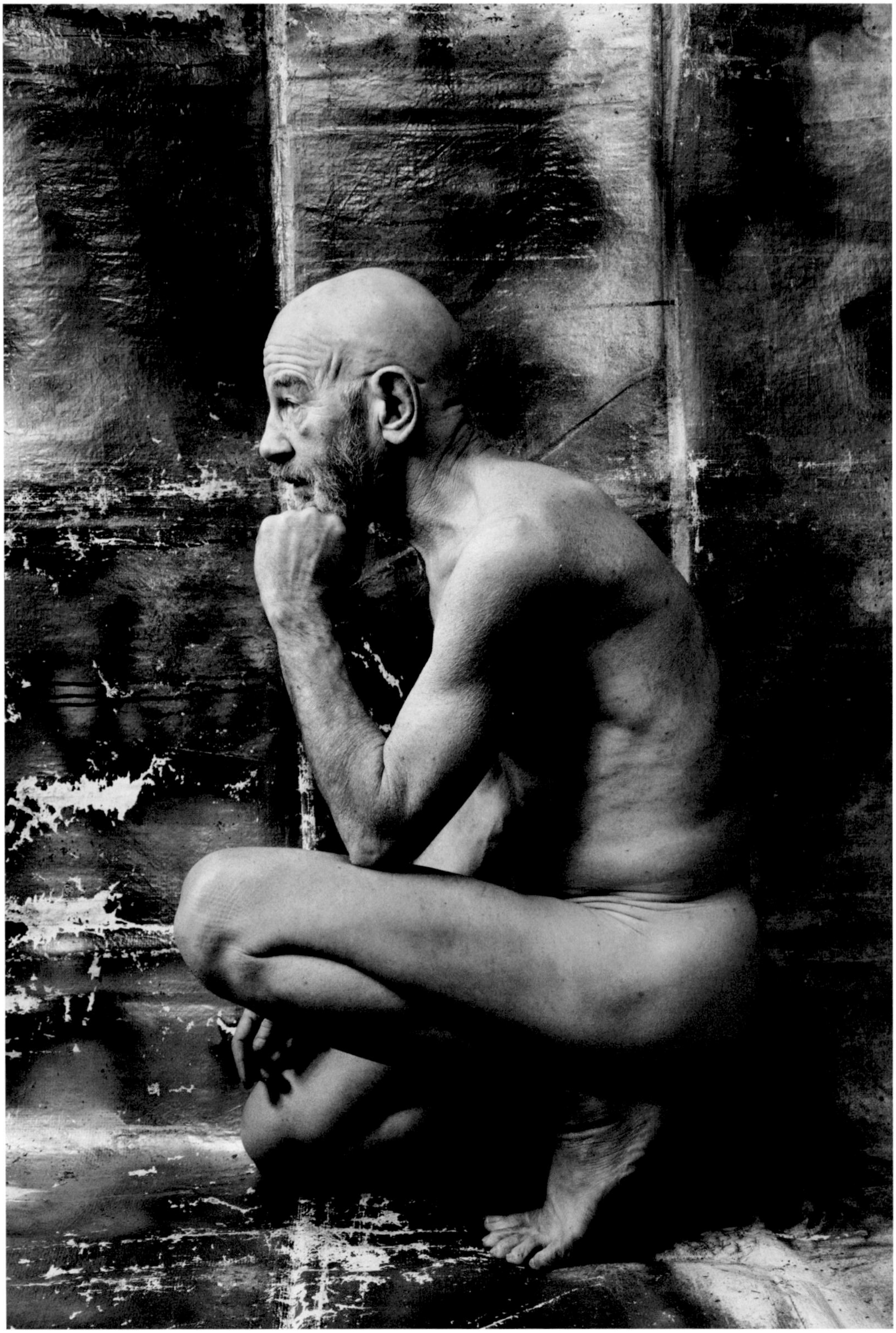

Contemplation

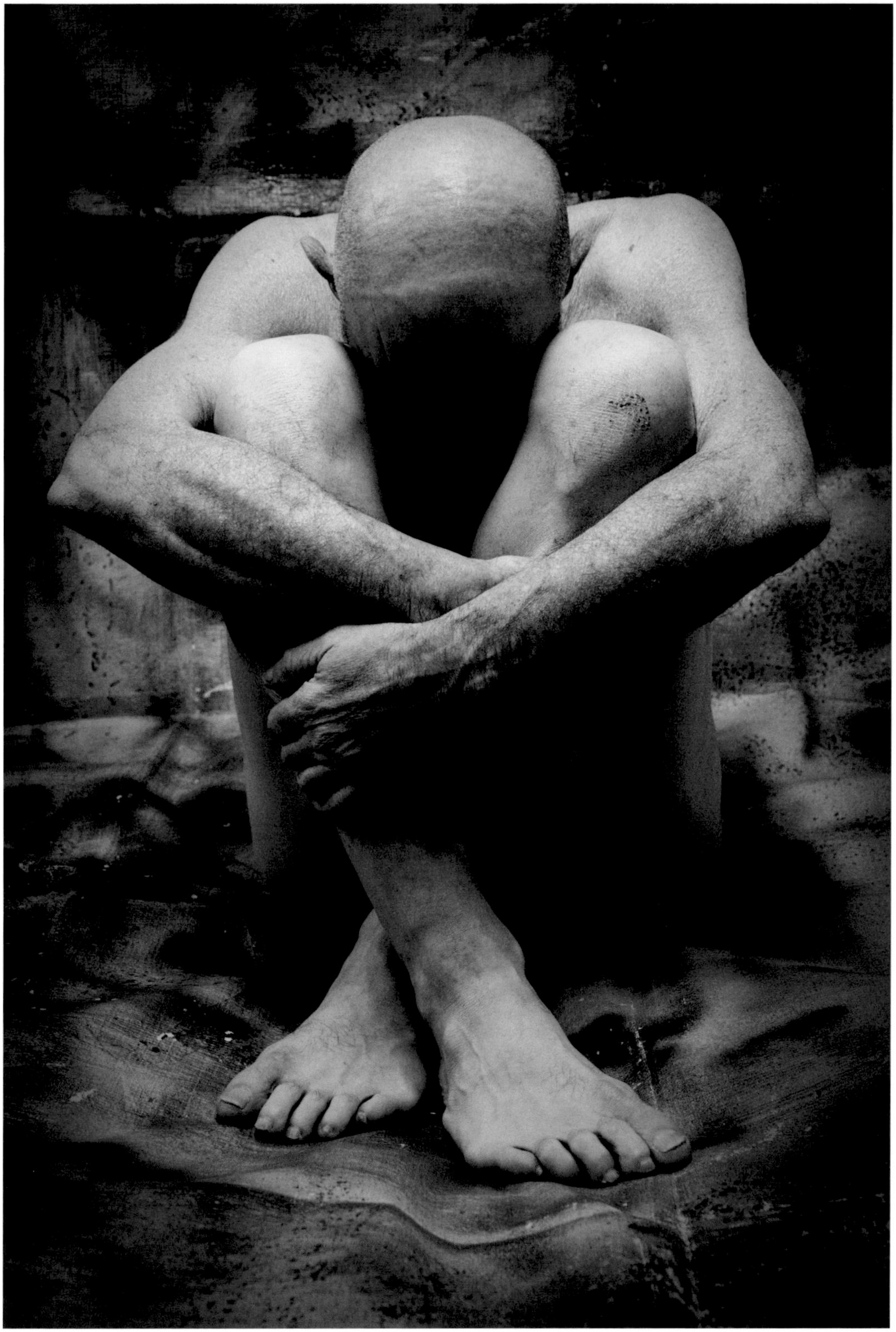

Death

New Shoes

by Mary Aiu

www.maryaiu.com ♦ marymea@aol.com

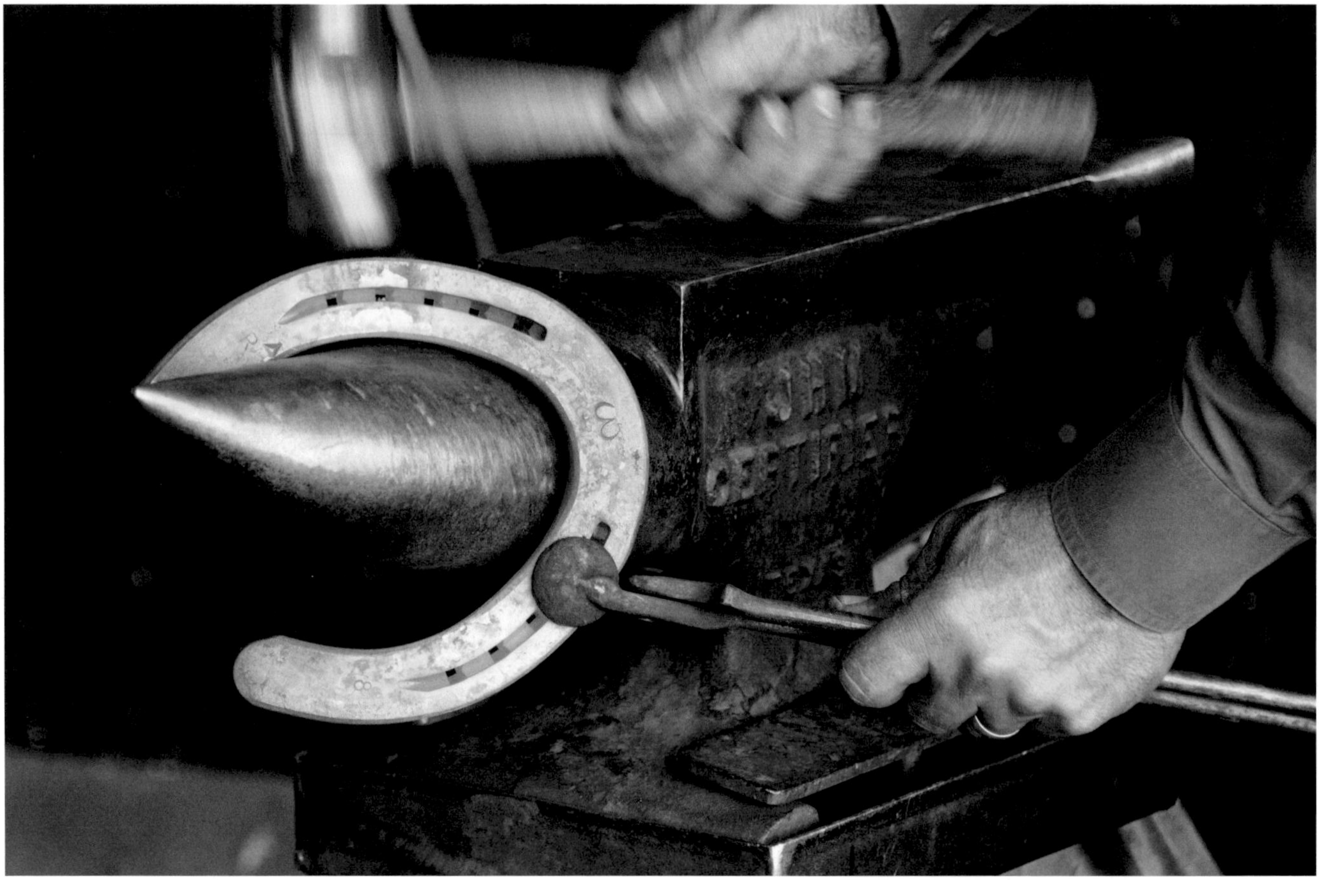

With the skilled hand of the farrier, heated forged iron is seared briefly to the wall of a horse's hoof, which is part of the process in preparation for new shoes.

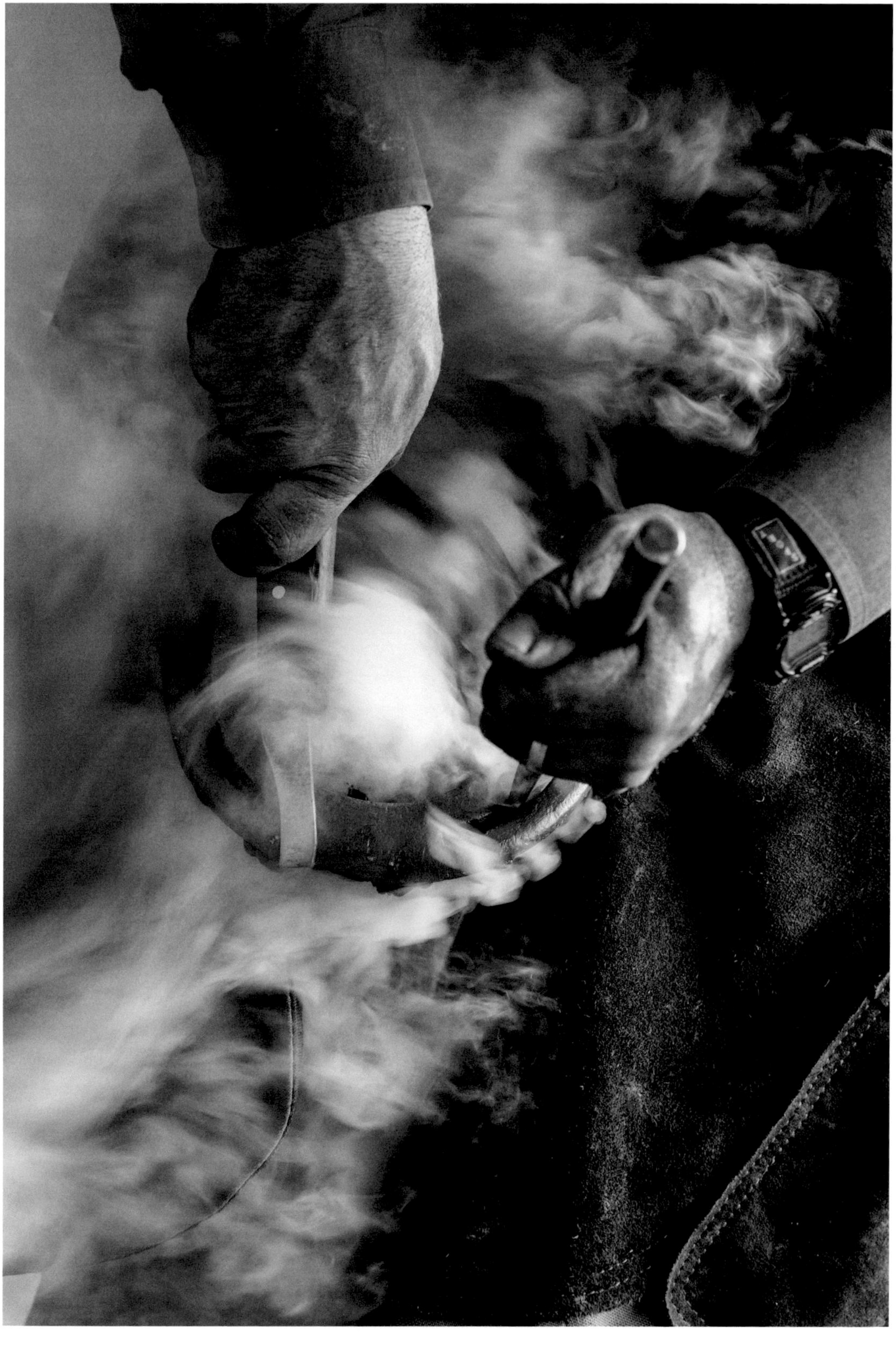

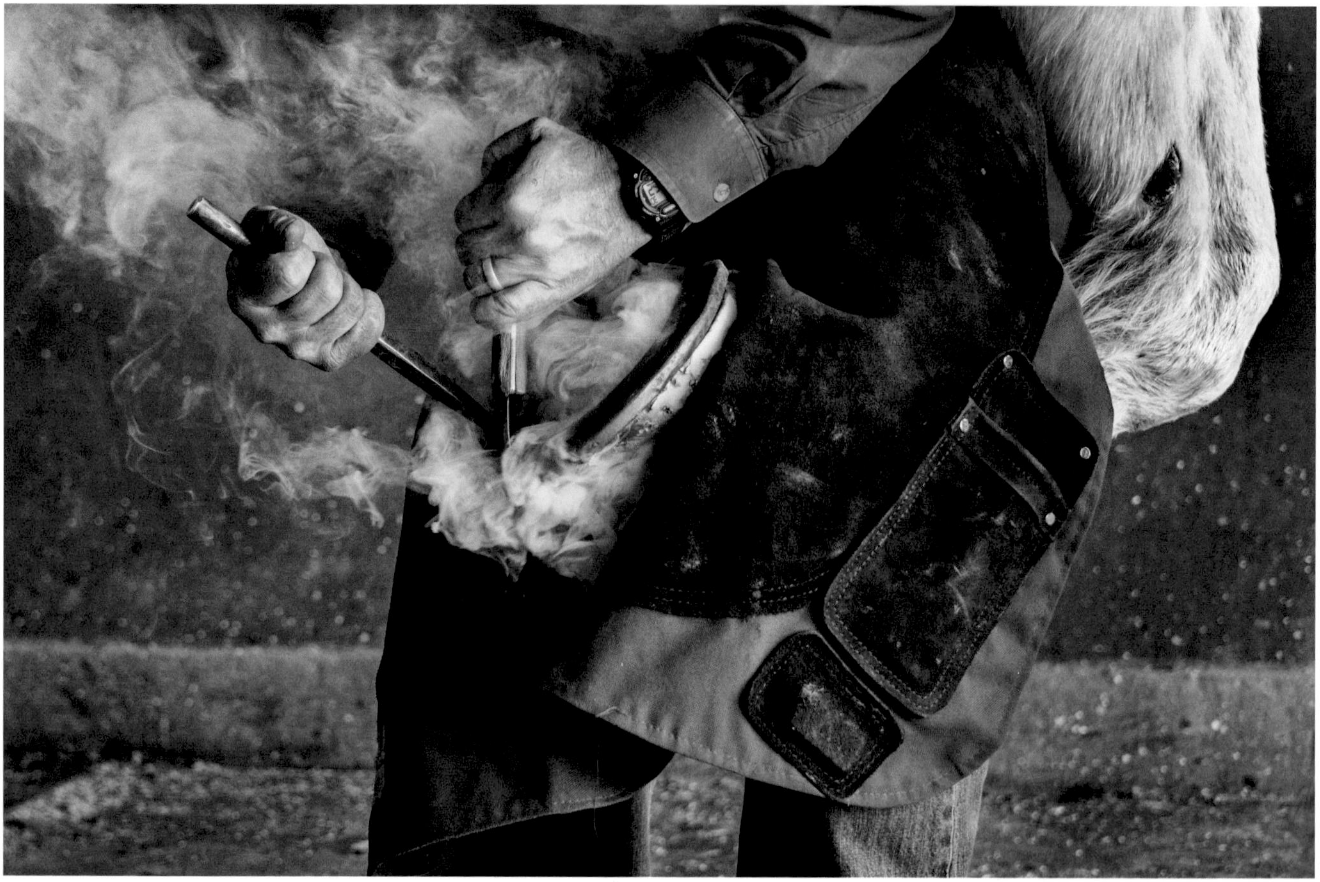

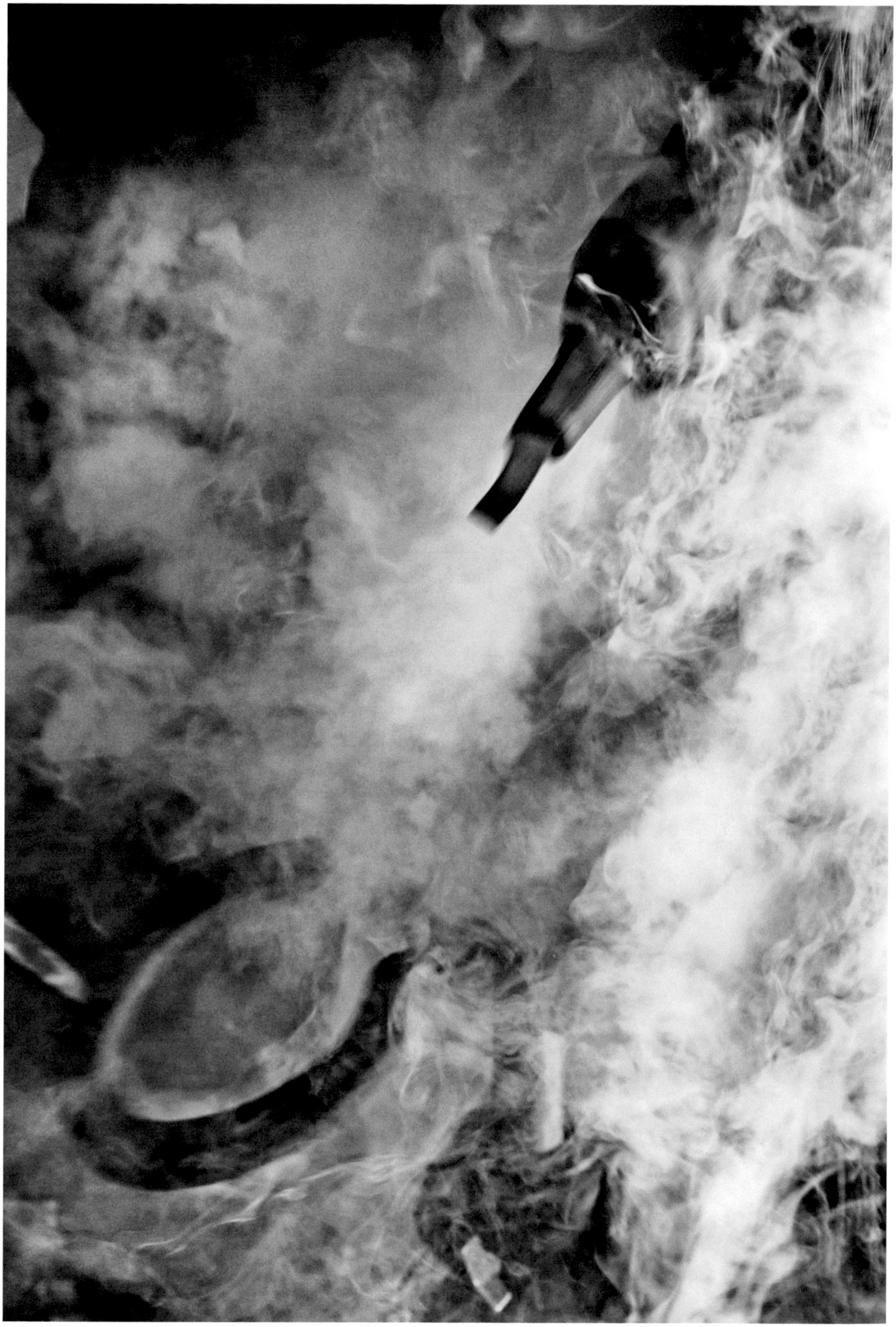

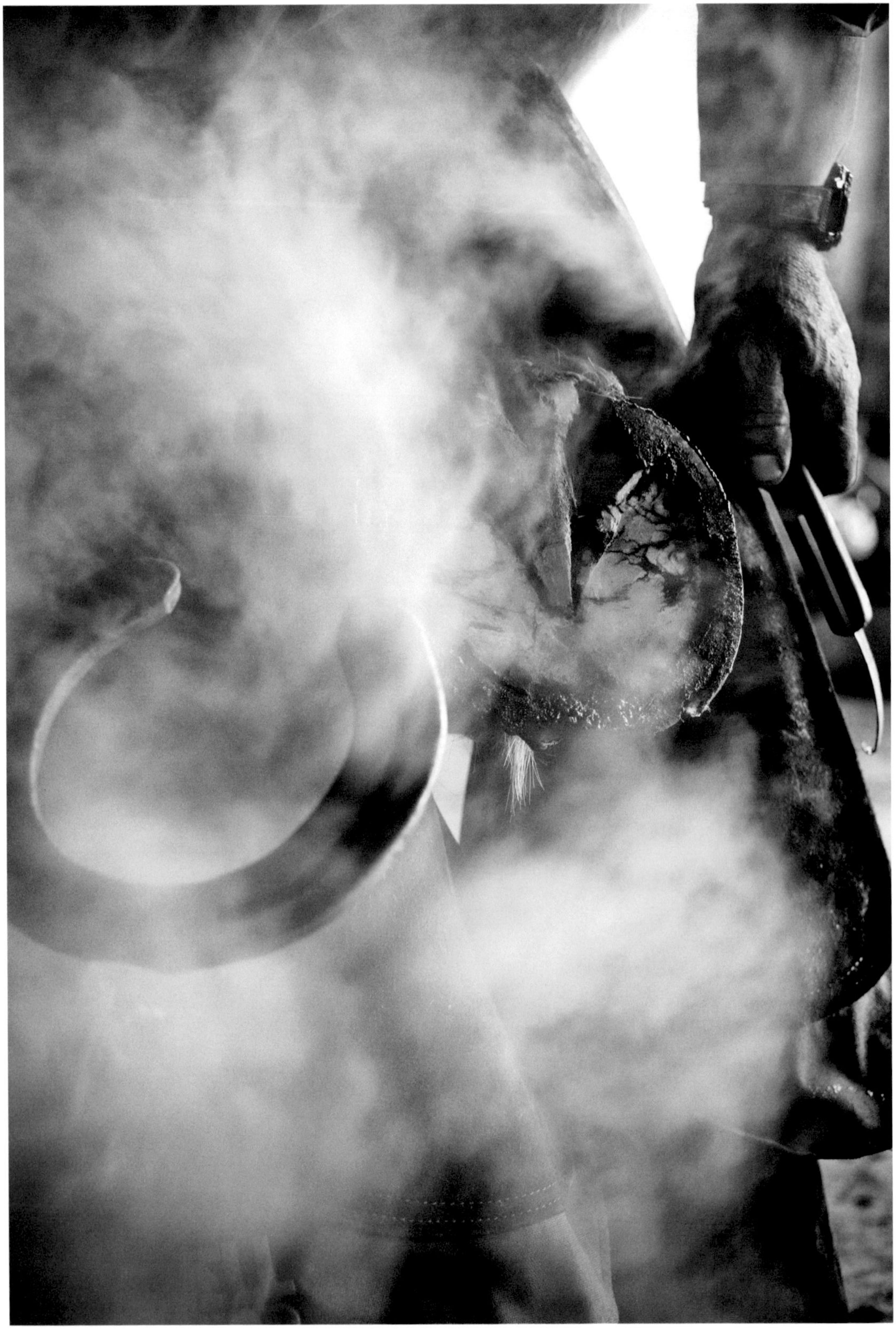

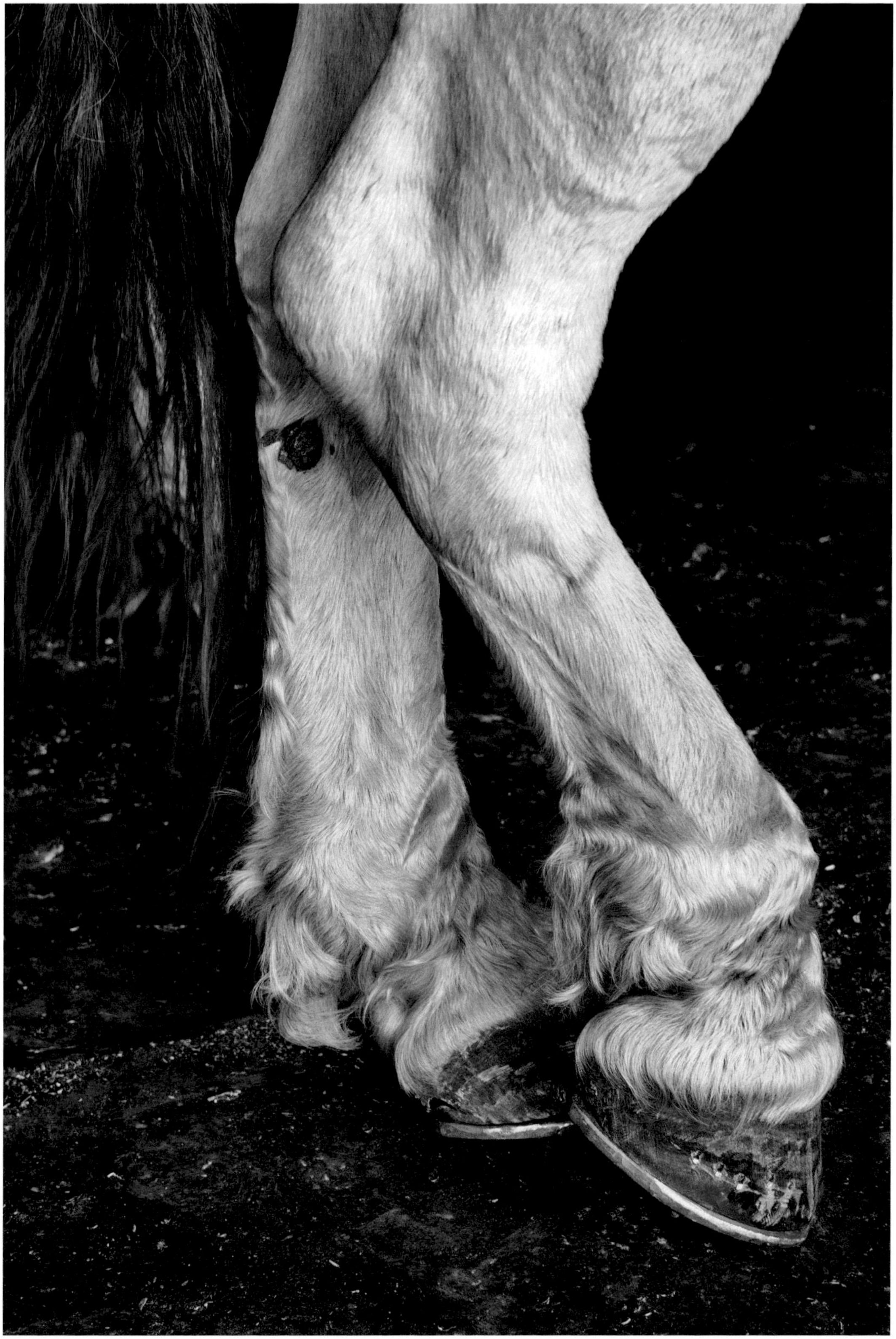

Old Hands: A Life

by Mark Gardner

www.photographybymarkgardner.com • photobymg@rockisland.com

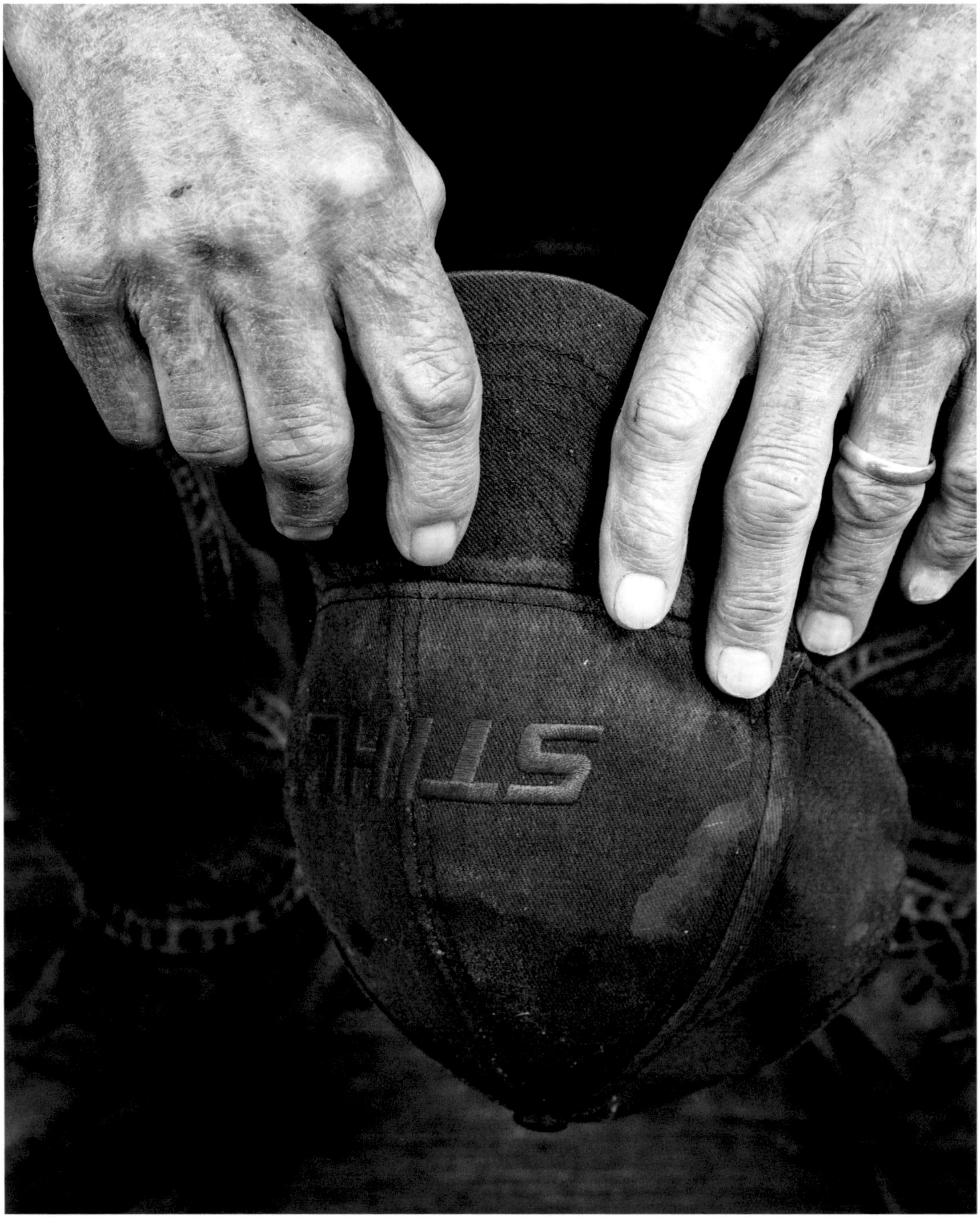

Work I

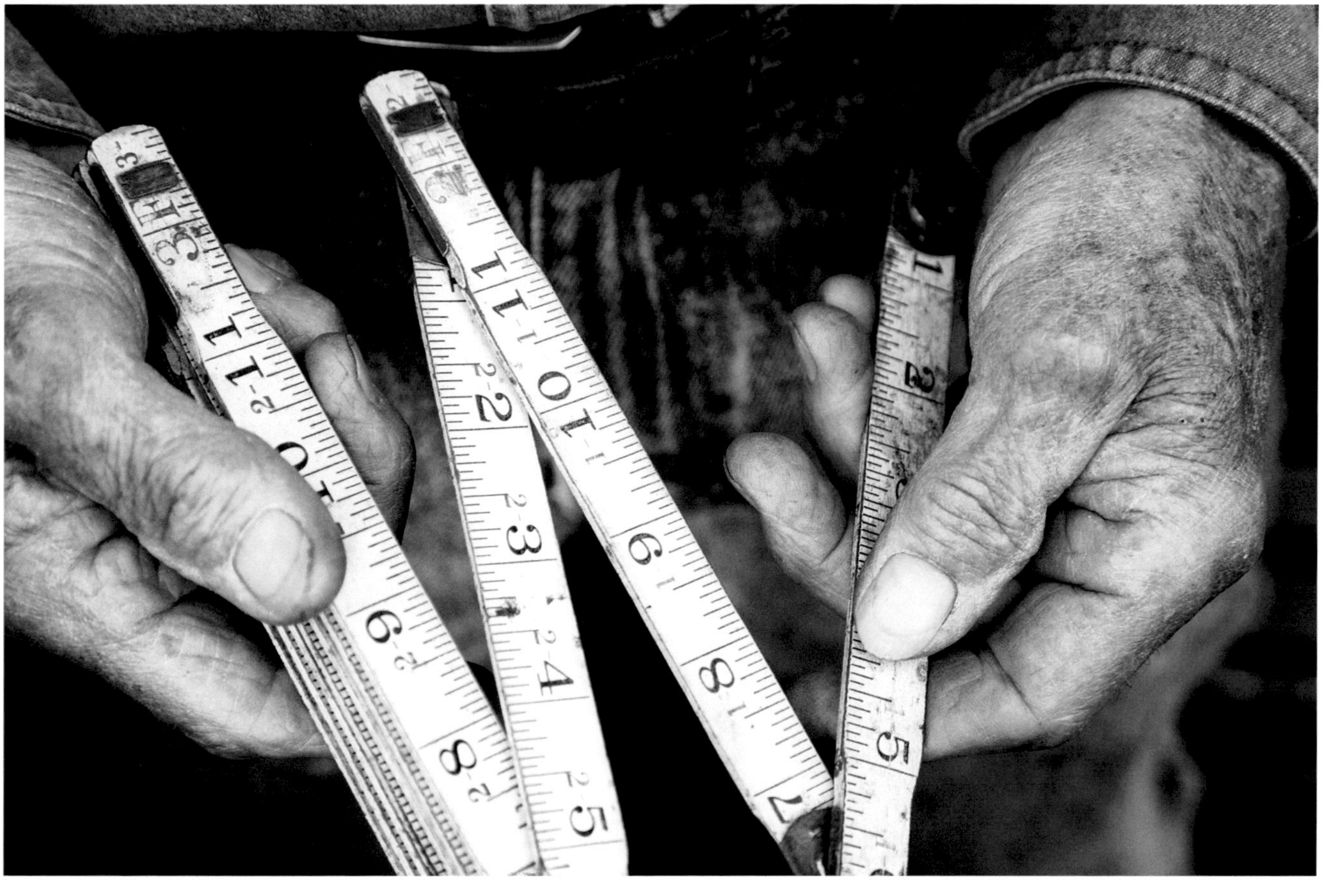

Work II

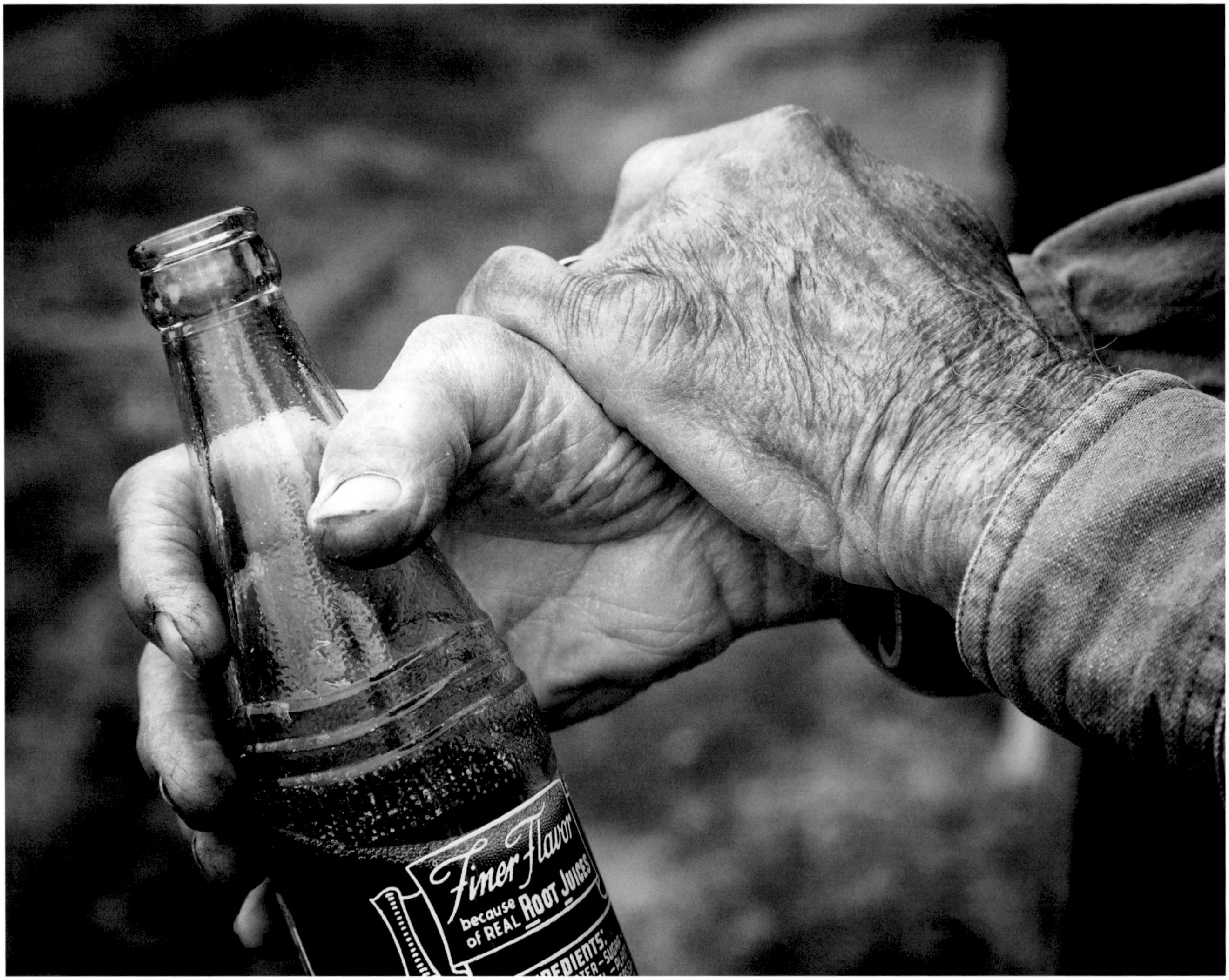

Rest

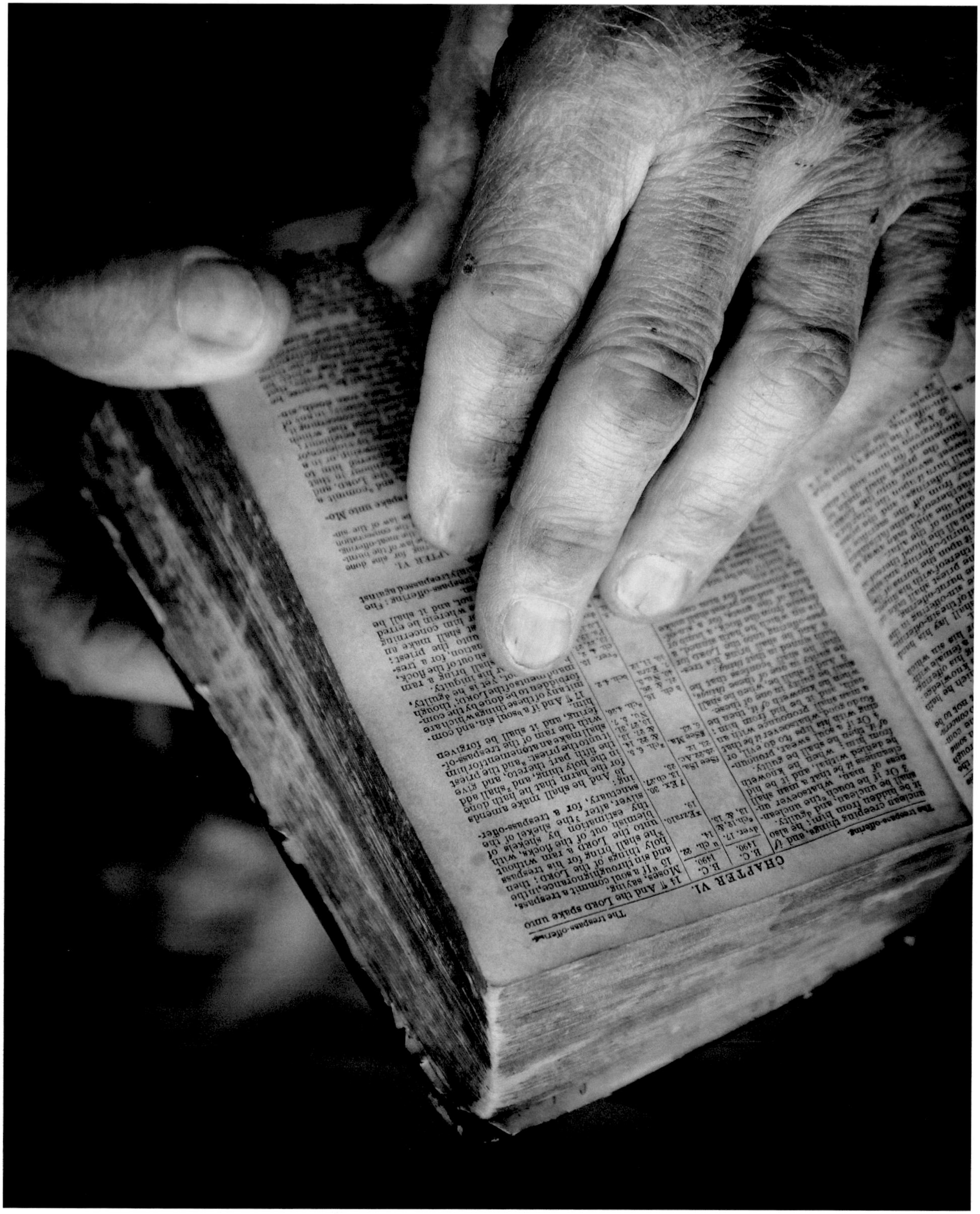

Faith

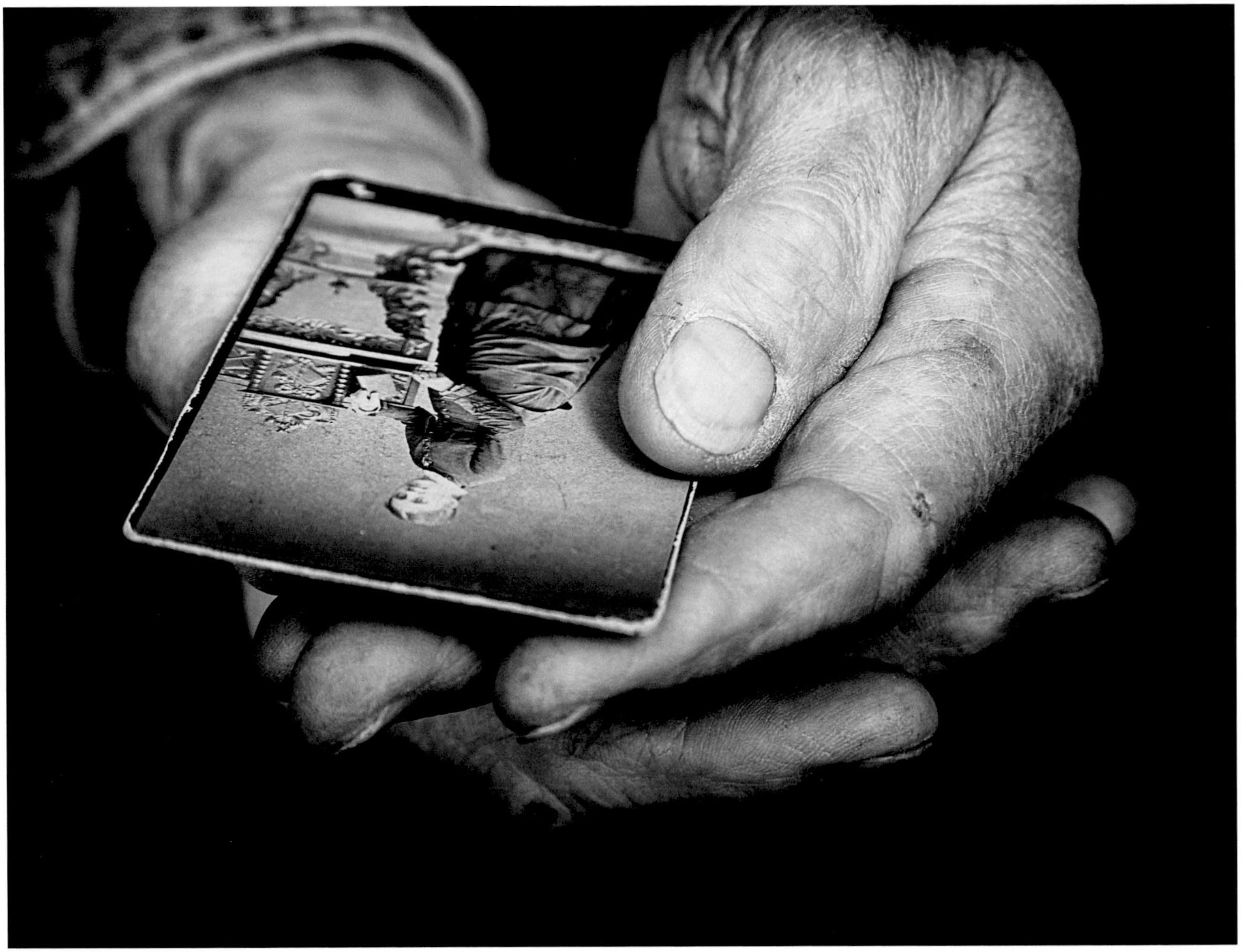

Family

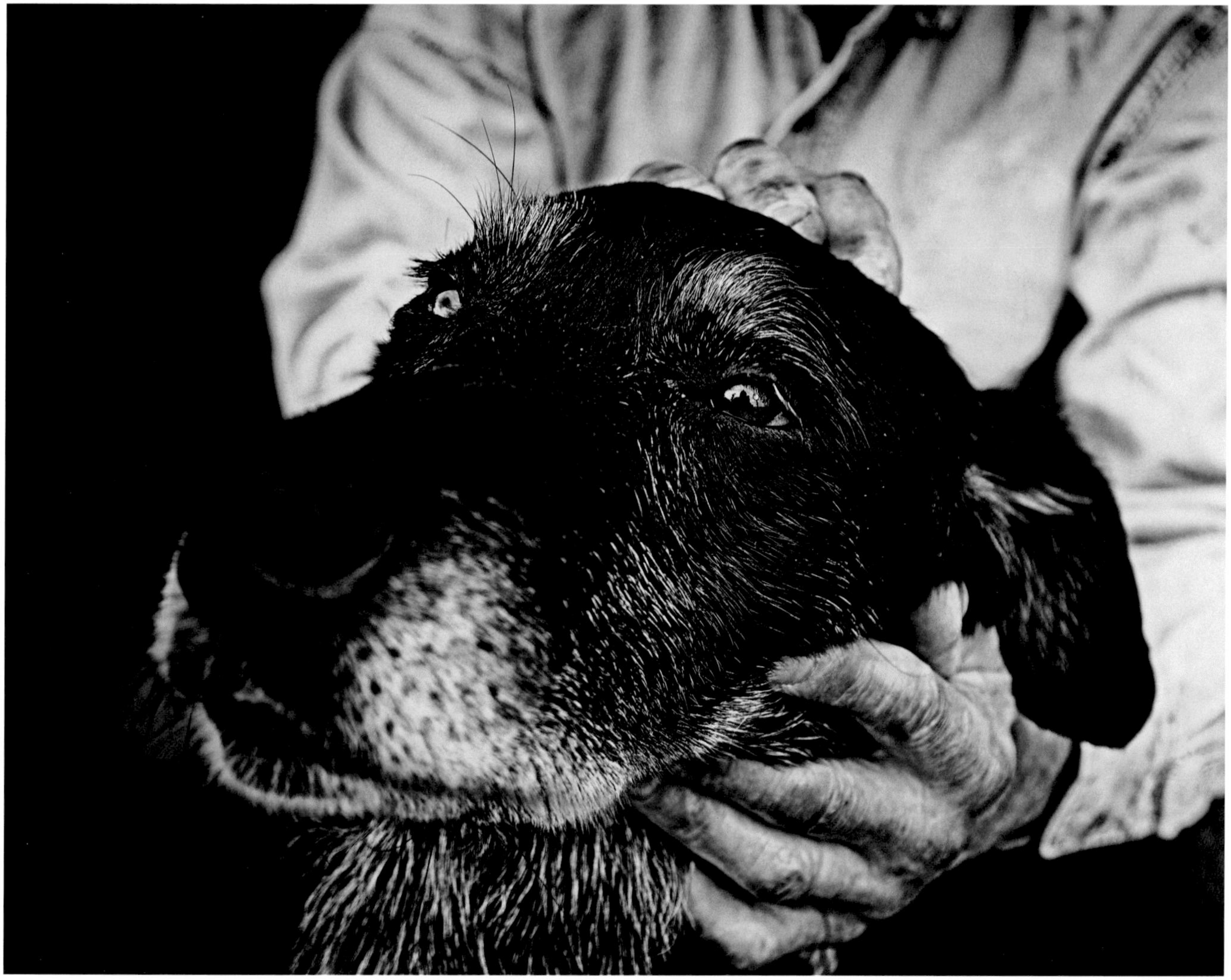

Best Friend

The Wool Shop

by Hugh Templin

hughtemplin@hotmail.com

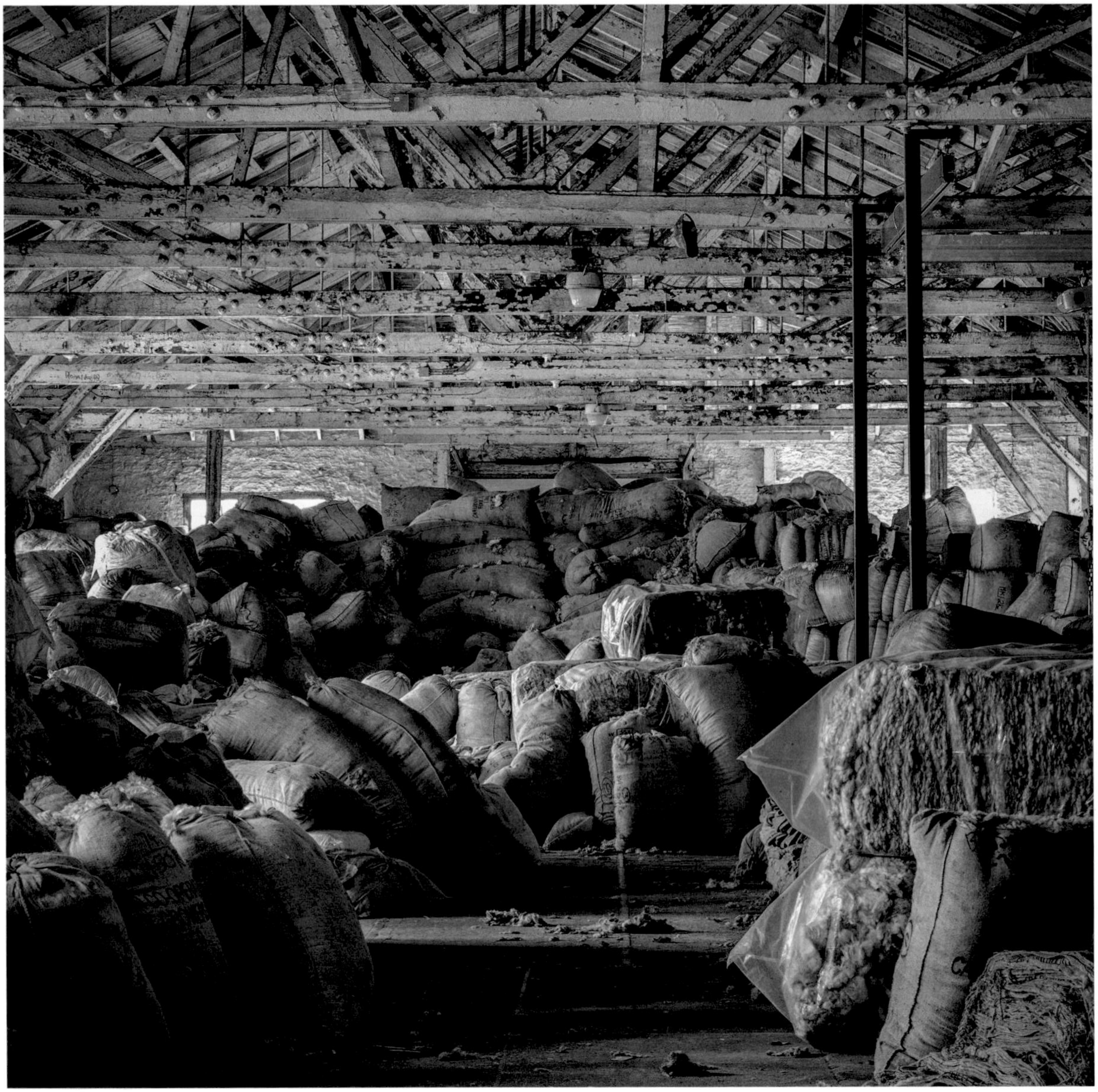

I went with my wife to a wool shop that she had heard about in a small town outside of Ottawa where we live. While we were browsing through the woolen goods sold there, one of the shop ladies saw the camera around my neck and asked — since I appeared to be interested in photography — if I would like to see what was "out back."

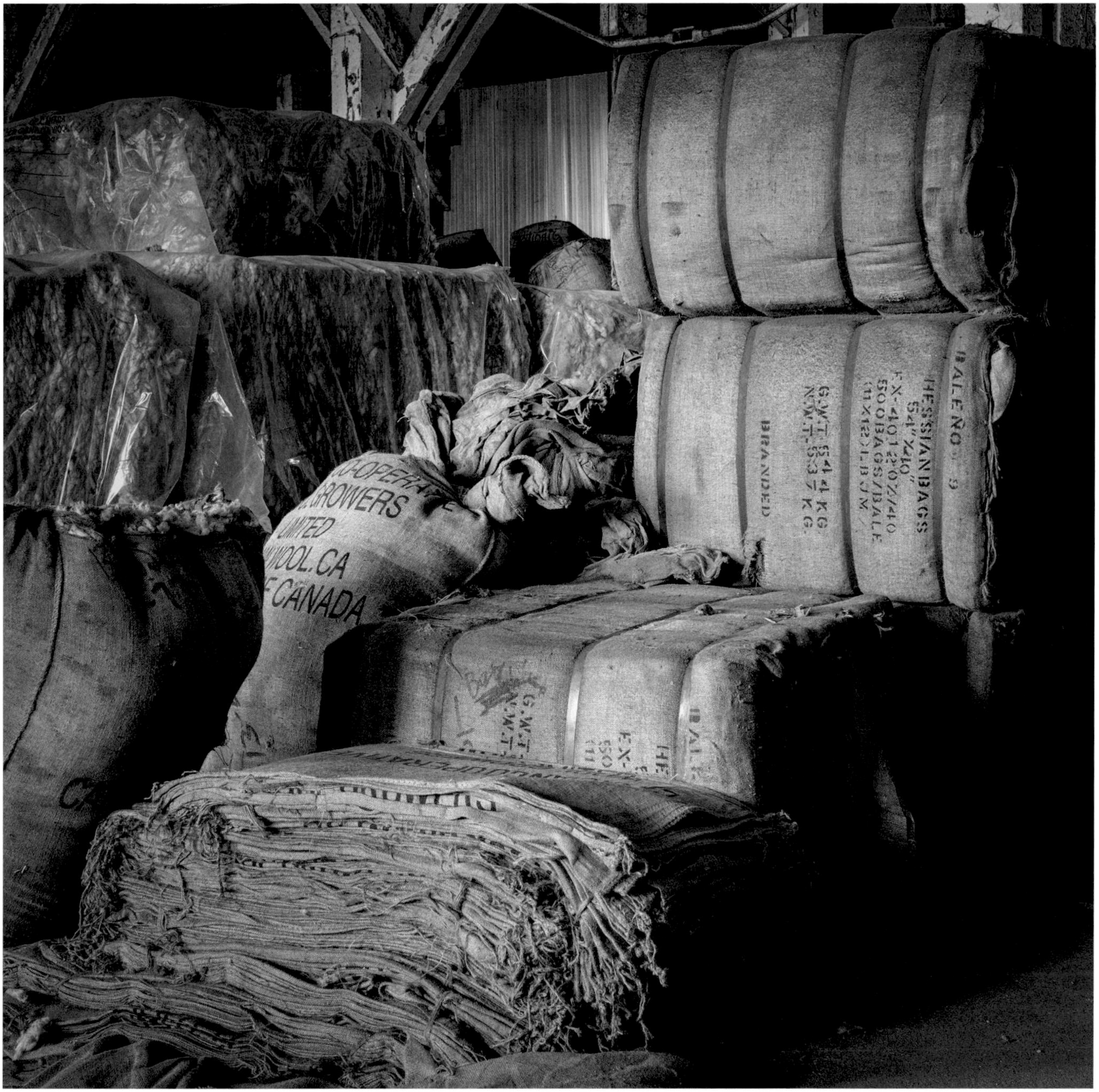

I said, "Sure," without hesitation. She led me through a back door which turned out to be a portal into another world. I entered a cavernous warehouse full of bales of raw wool, which was not expected from the modest front of the store.

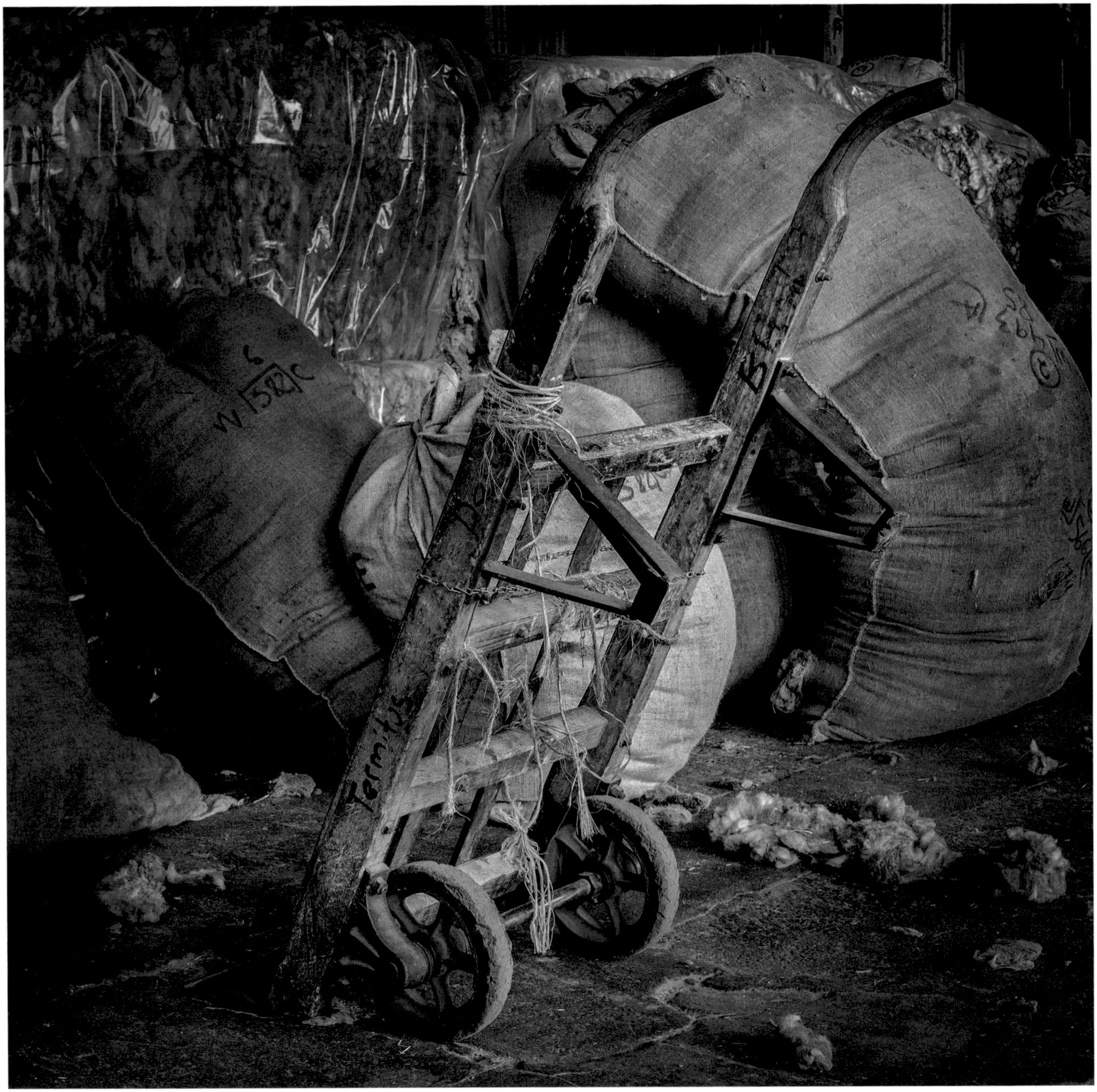

She explained that the building was originally a railway roundhouse built in 1890 and was taken over by the Canadian Co-Operative Wool Growers in 1940. Approximately 95% of the wool produced in Canada comes through this facility for grading, sorting, and shipment to all parts of the world.

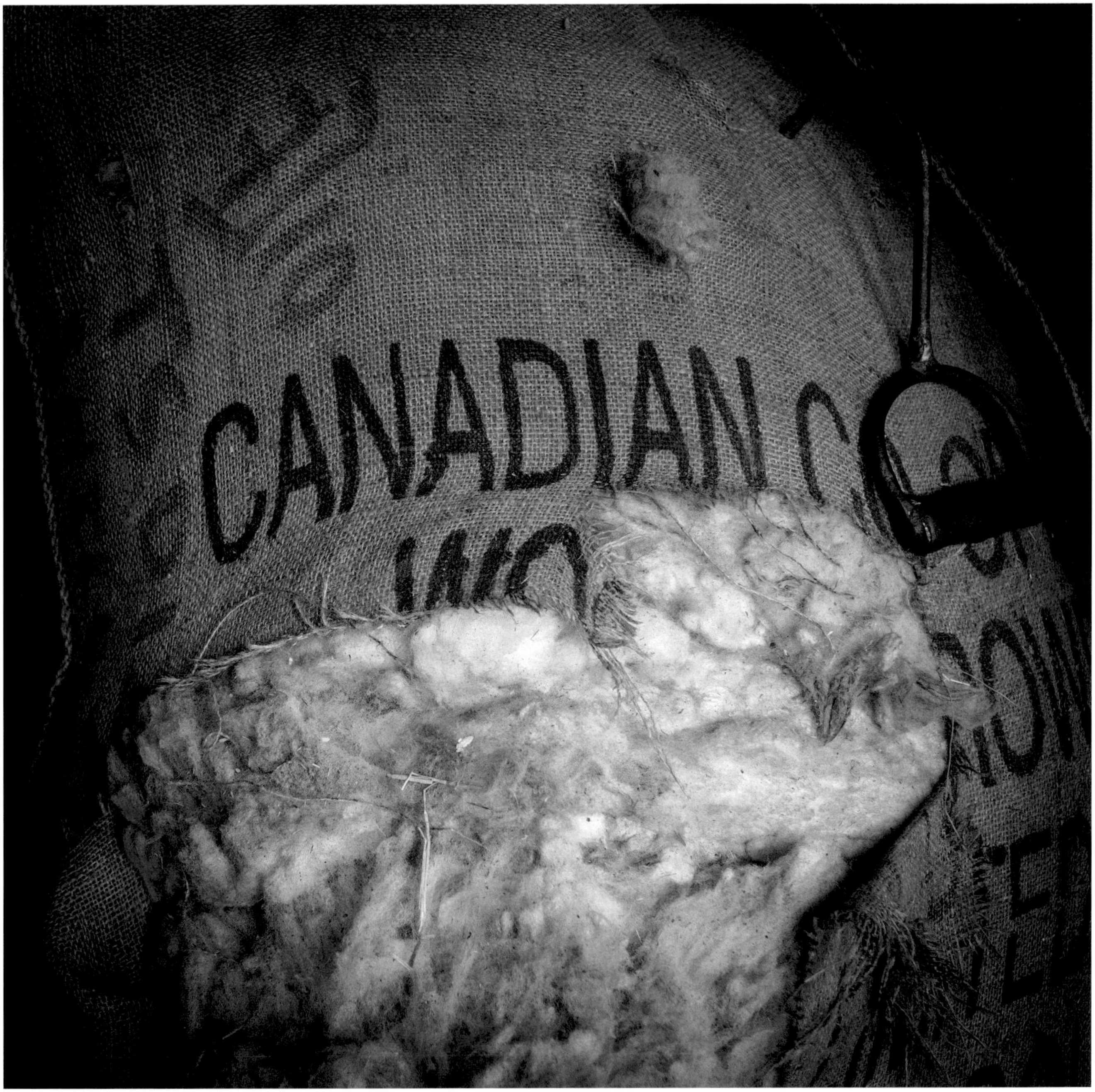

The place was abandoned since it was a weekend and the workers must have left everything as it was at the end of their shift on Friday, which could also have been 75 years ago, ready to resume on Monday morning.

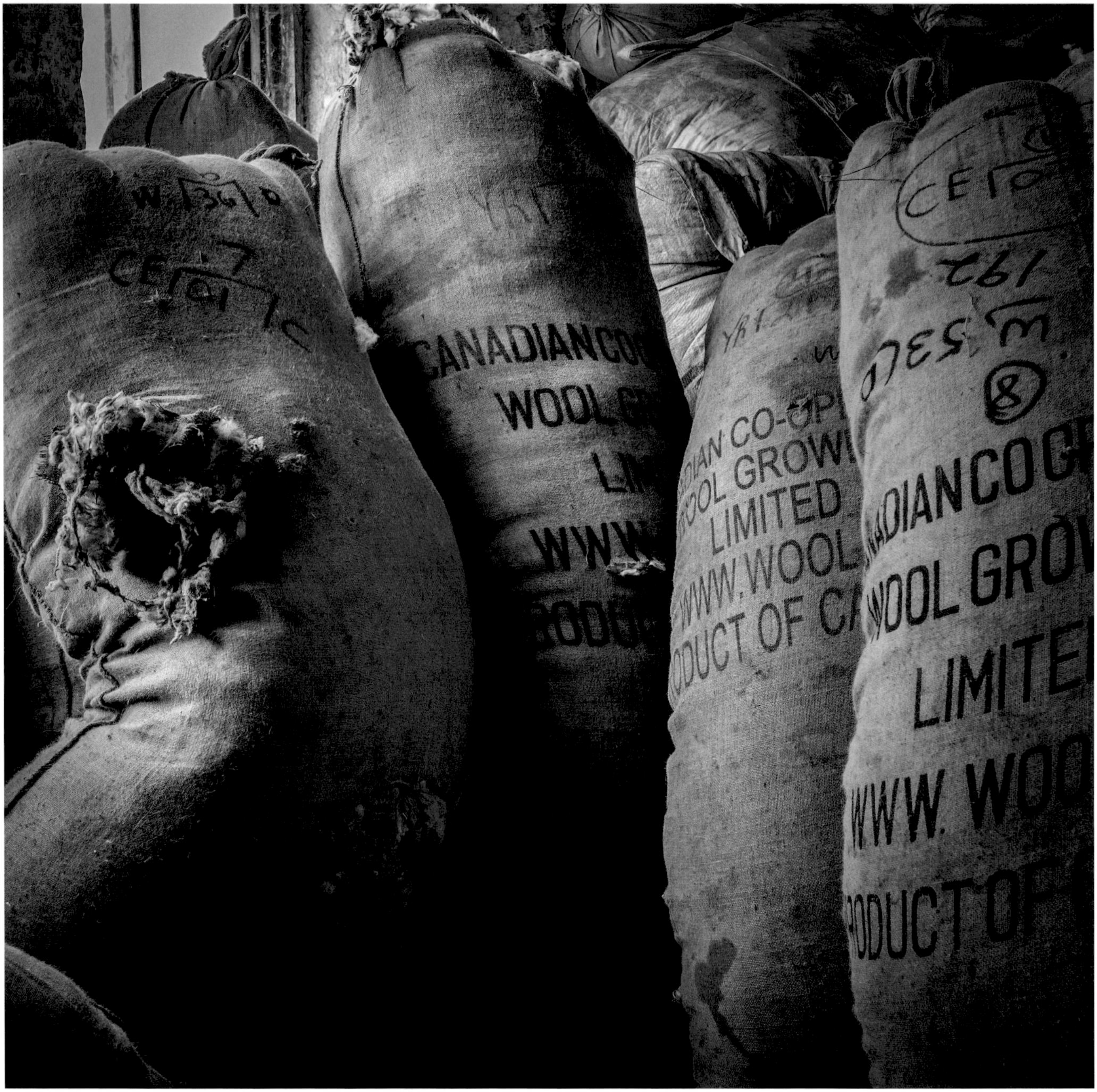

There in front of me was a veritable medley of shapes, objects, and textures with the only lighting provided from the large windows on two sides. The space had a mixed aura of more past than present and it gave me the impression that the tradition of wool production had been preserved in this living time capsule.

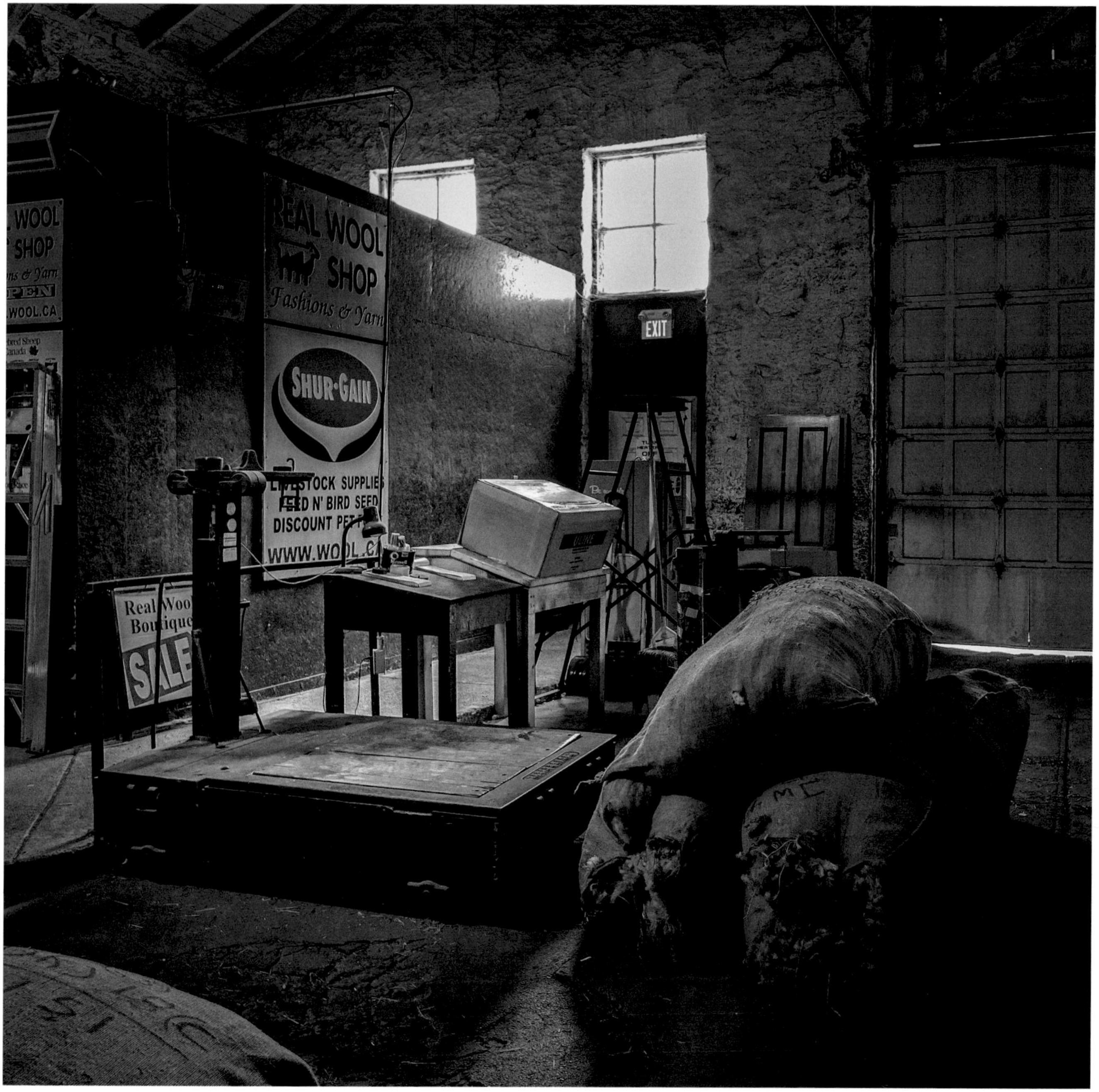

These photographs are my interpretation of the feelings I experienced on that fortuitous visit to the wool shop.

Redwood Portraits

by Darcie Sternenberg

darciesternenberg.com ♦ dsternen@charter.net

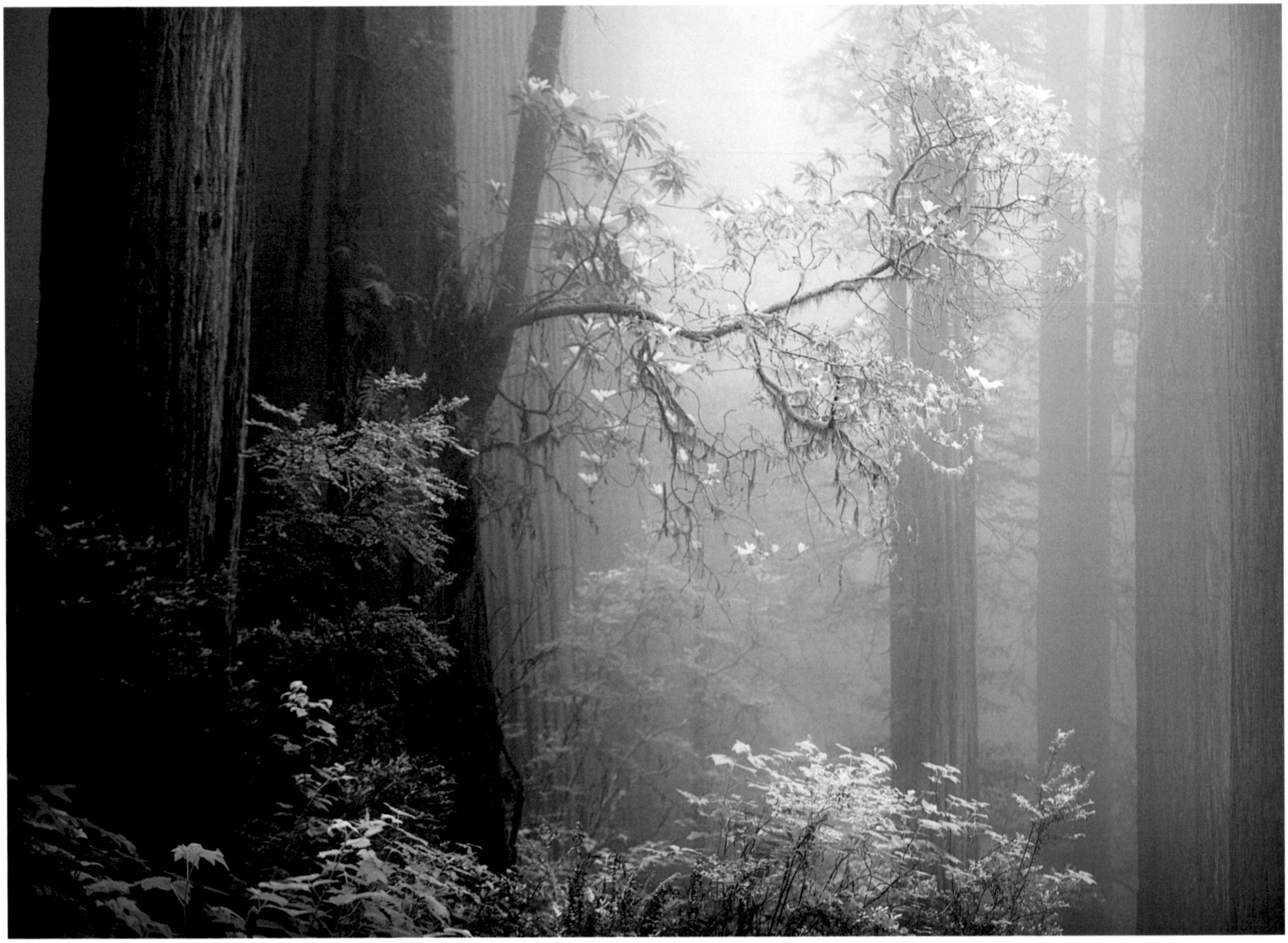

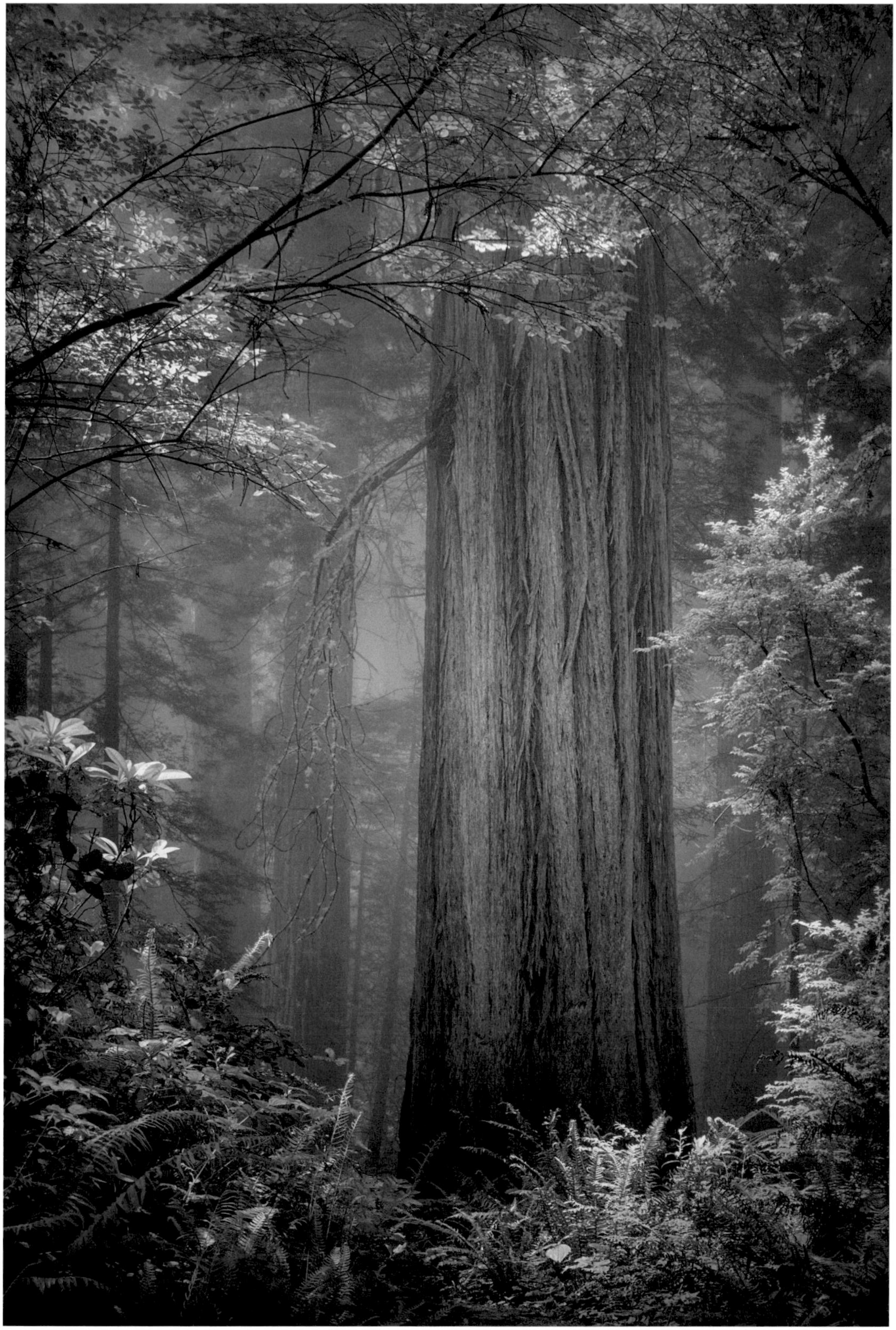

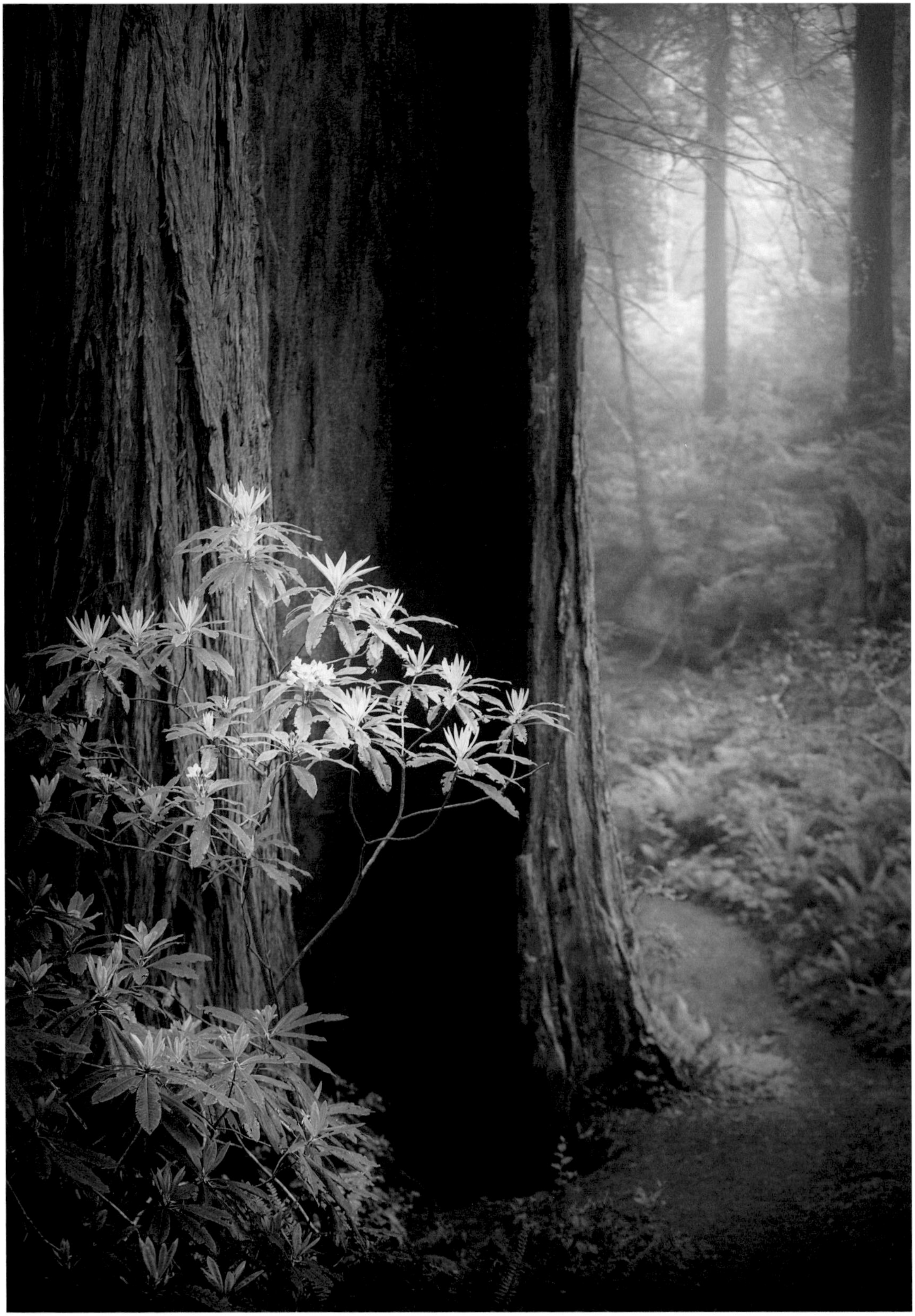

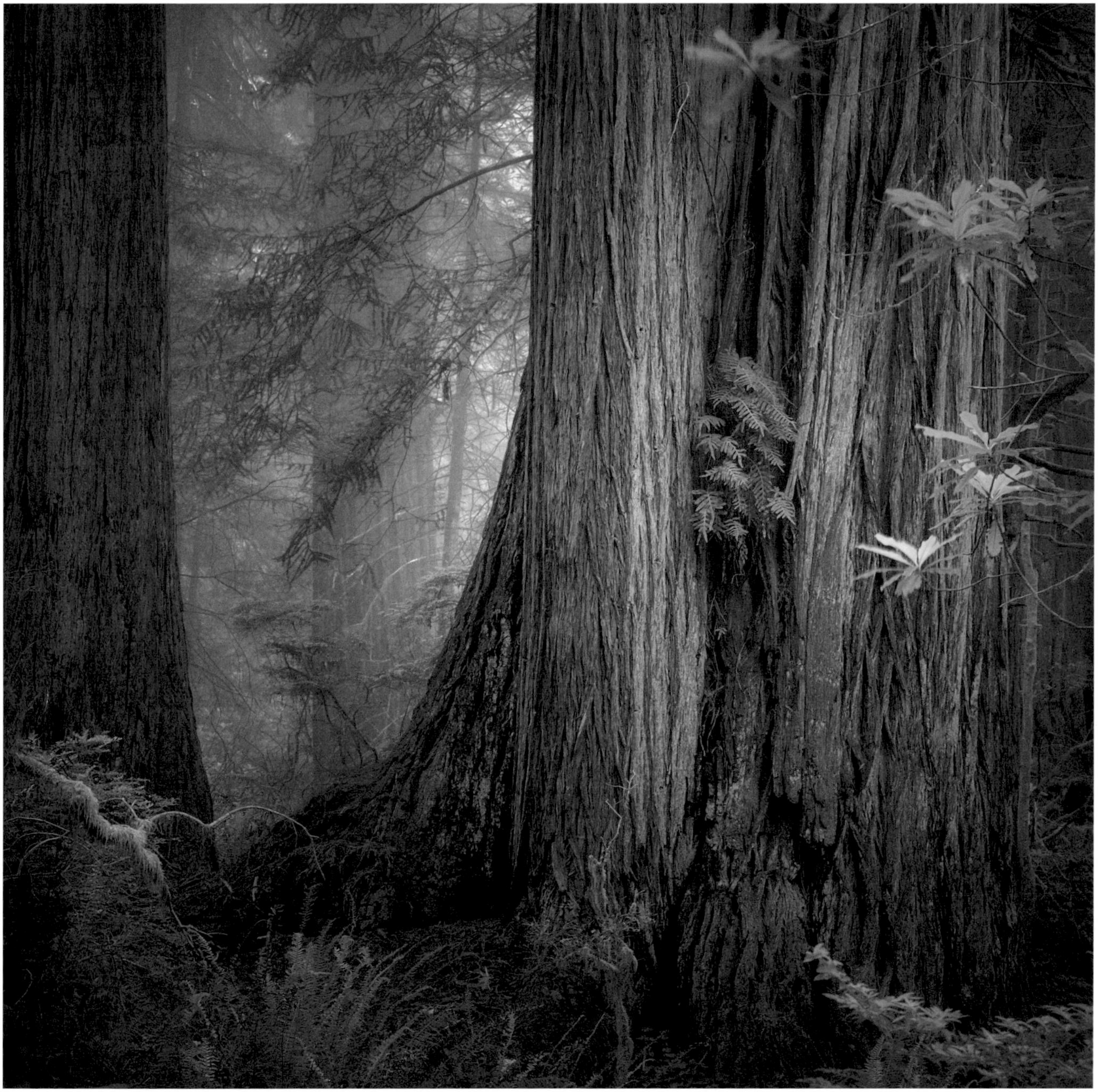

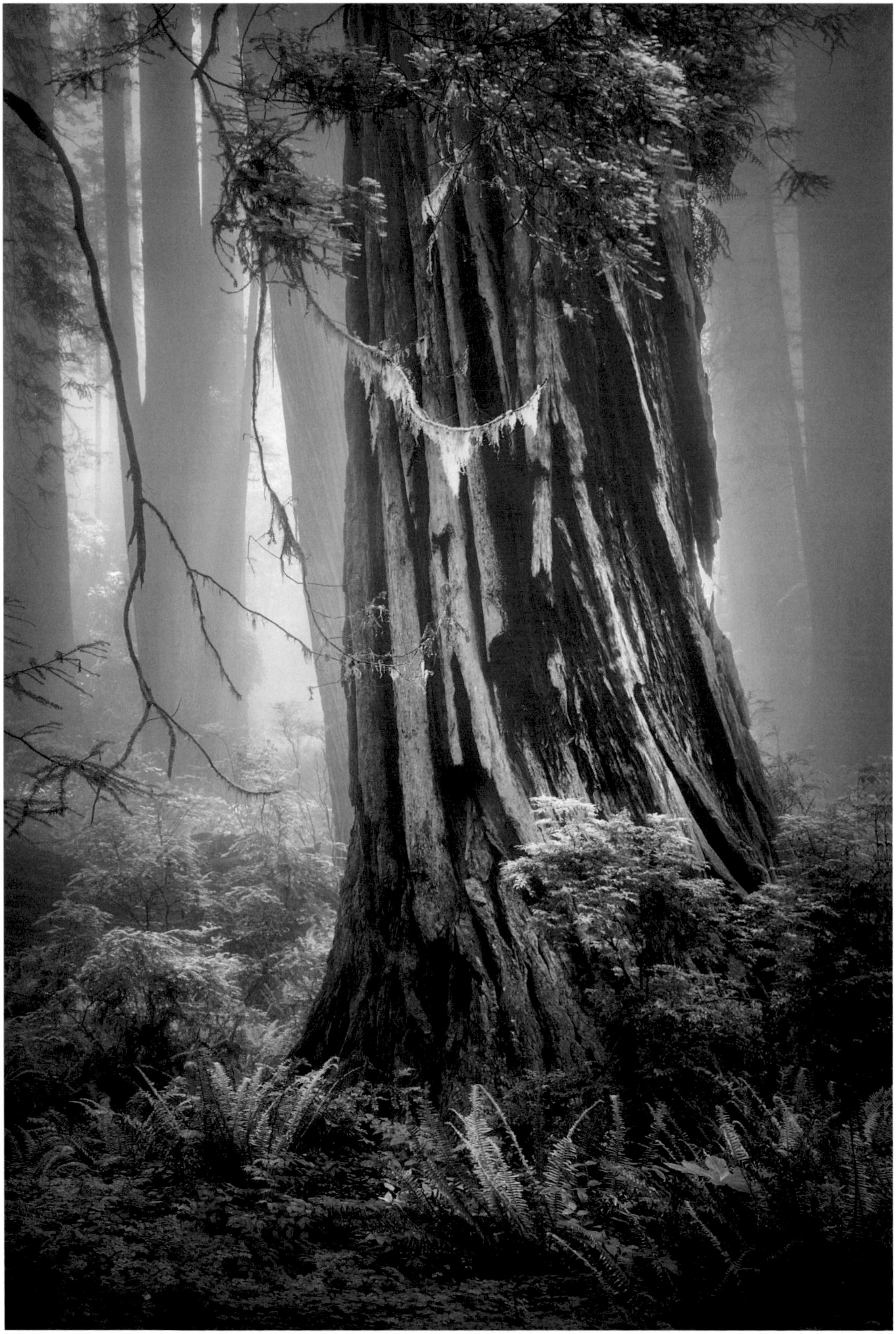

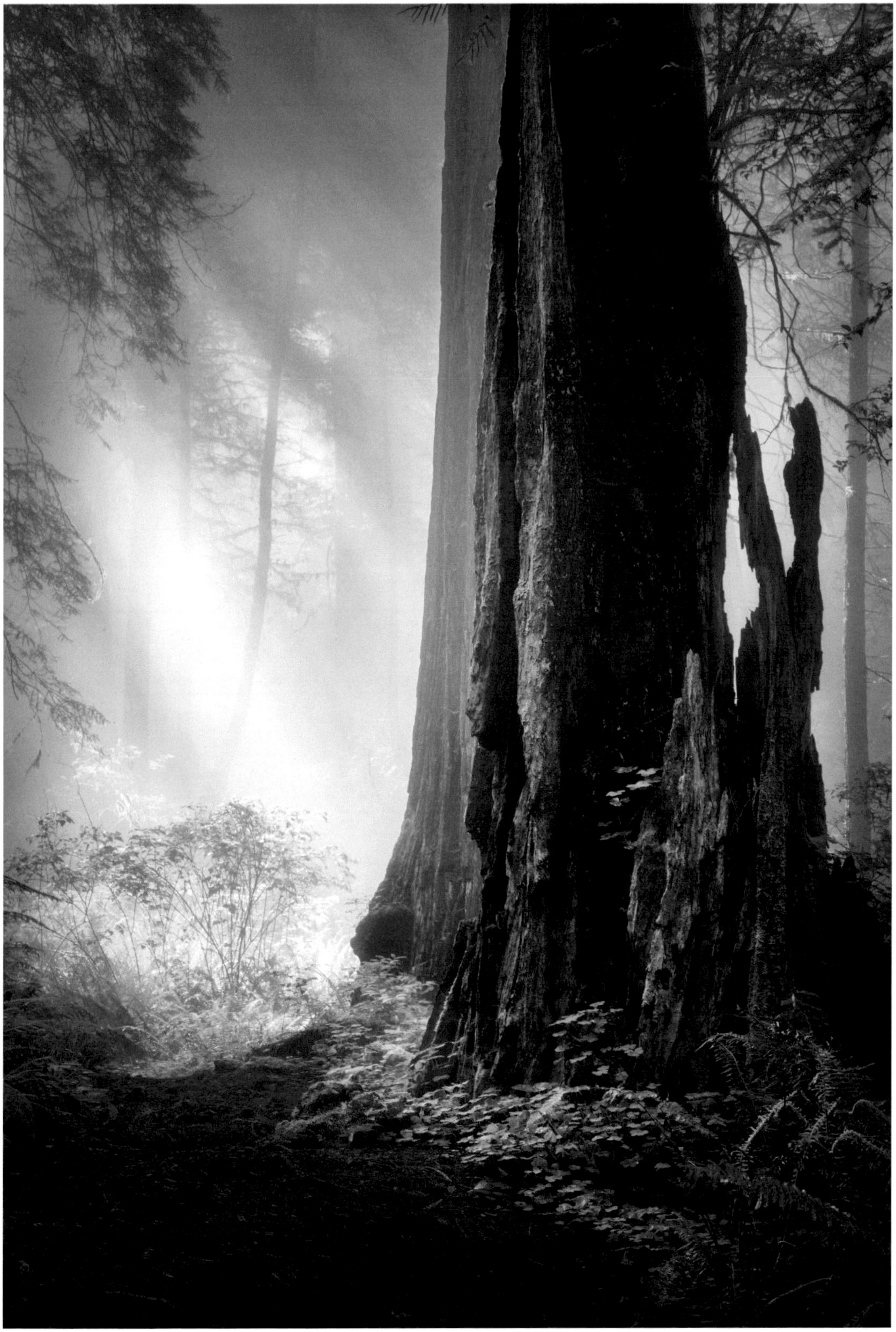

Debris

by Mark Rindflesh
markrindfleshphotography.com • mrindflesh@comcast.net

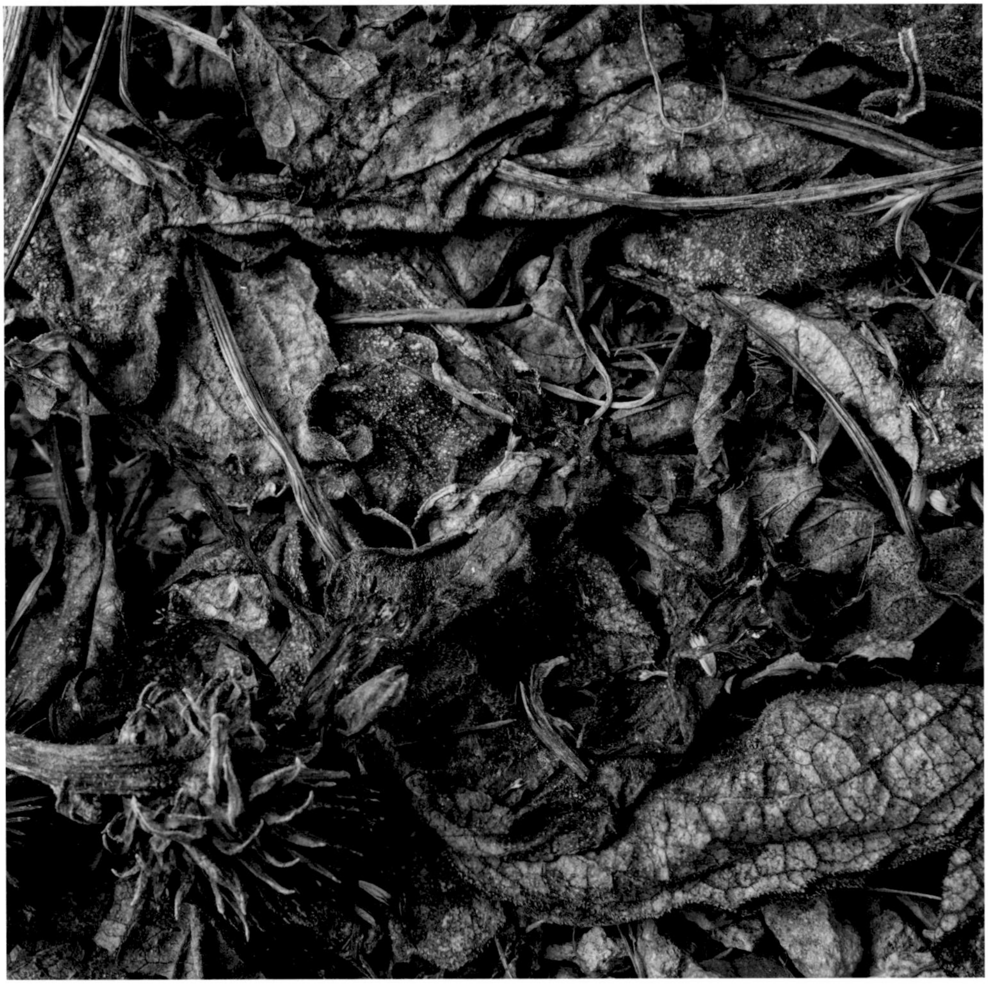

The treachery of March
reveals winter's ravage.
In its debris,
death and dissolution,
the turning of the wheel.
Hurrying by, carelessly, I see nothing.
Crouching deeply, on my knees, I discover the dark beauty of past stars.
Observing fearlessly, I realize the full truth of the turning wheel.

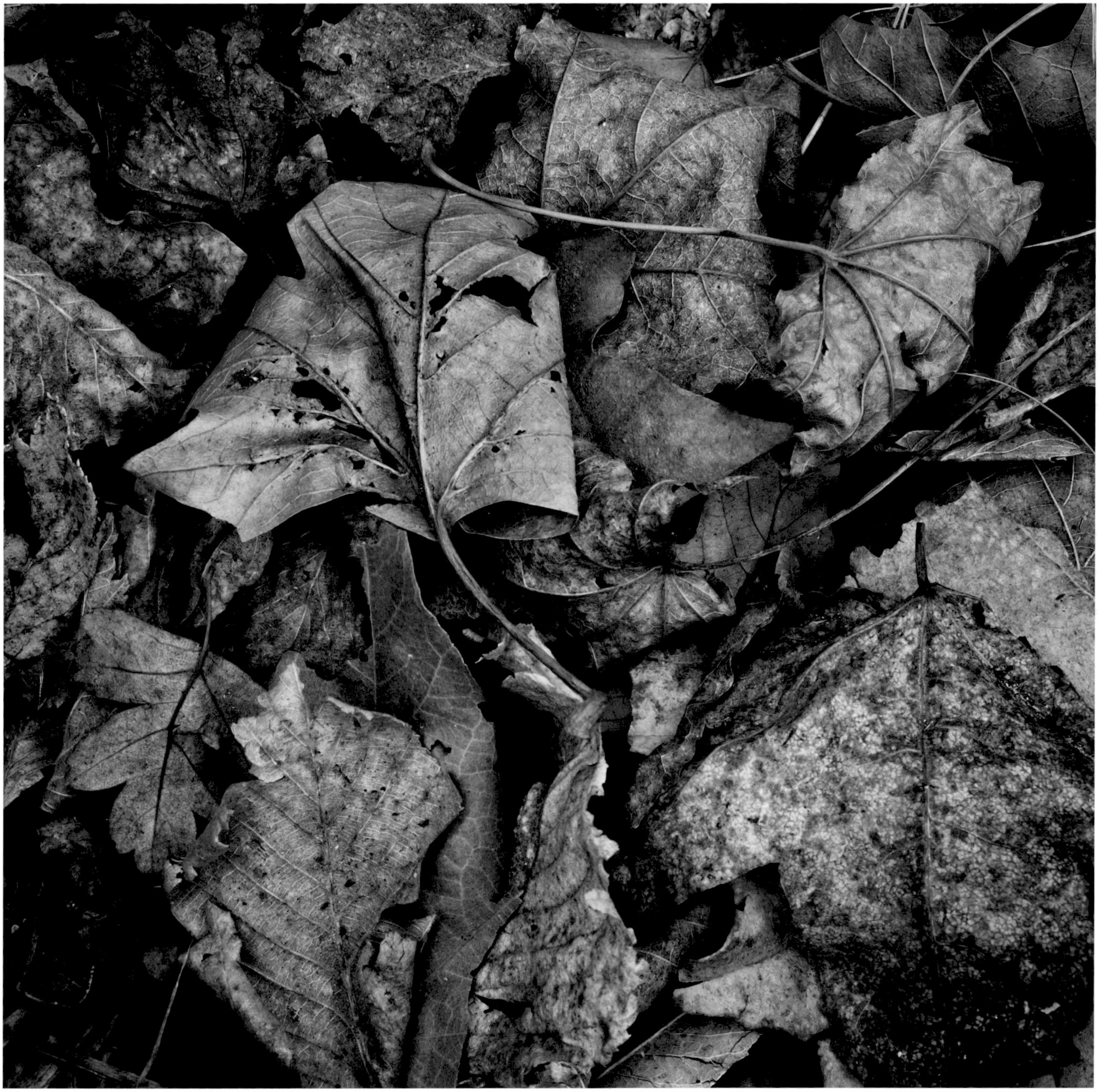

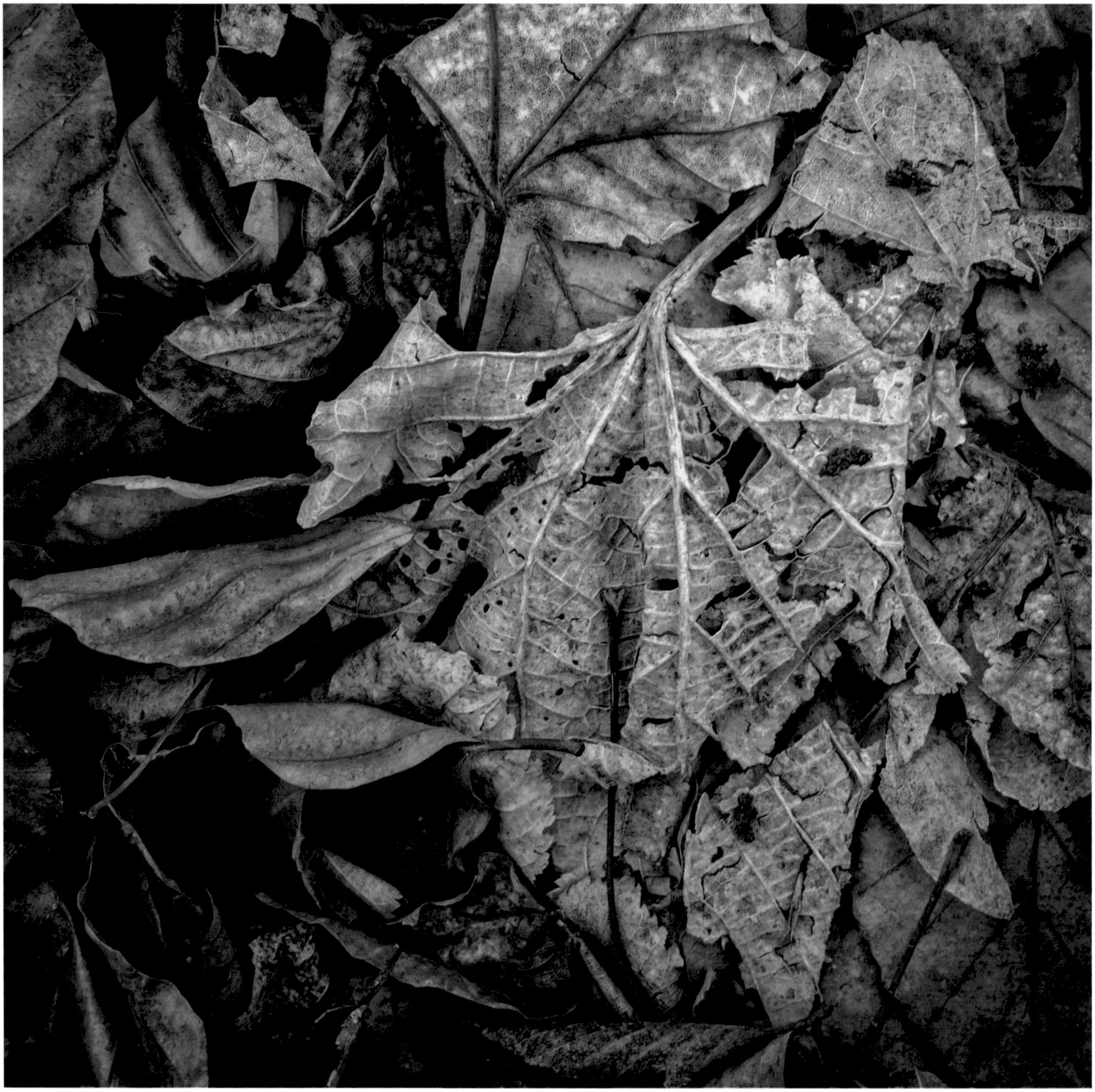

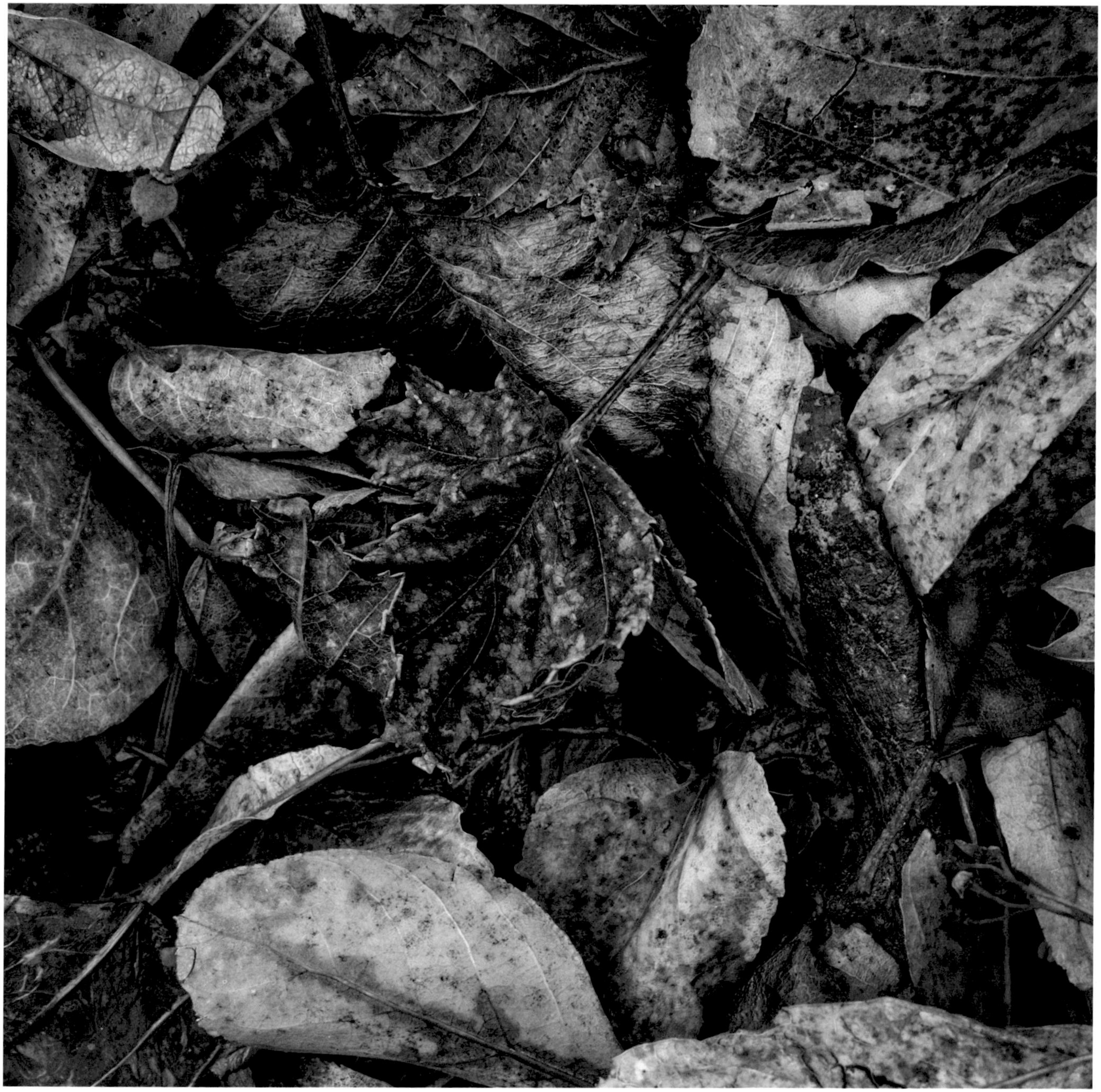

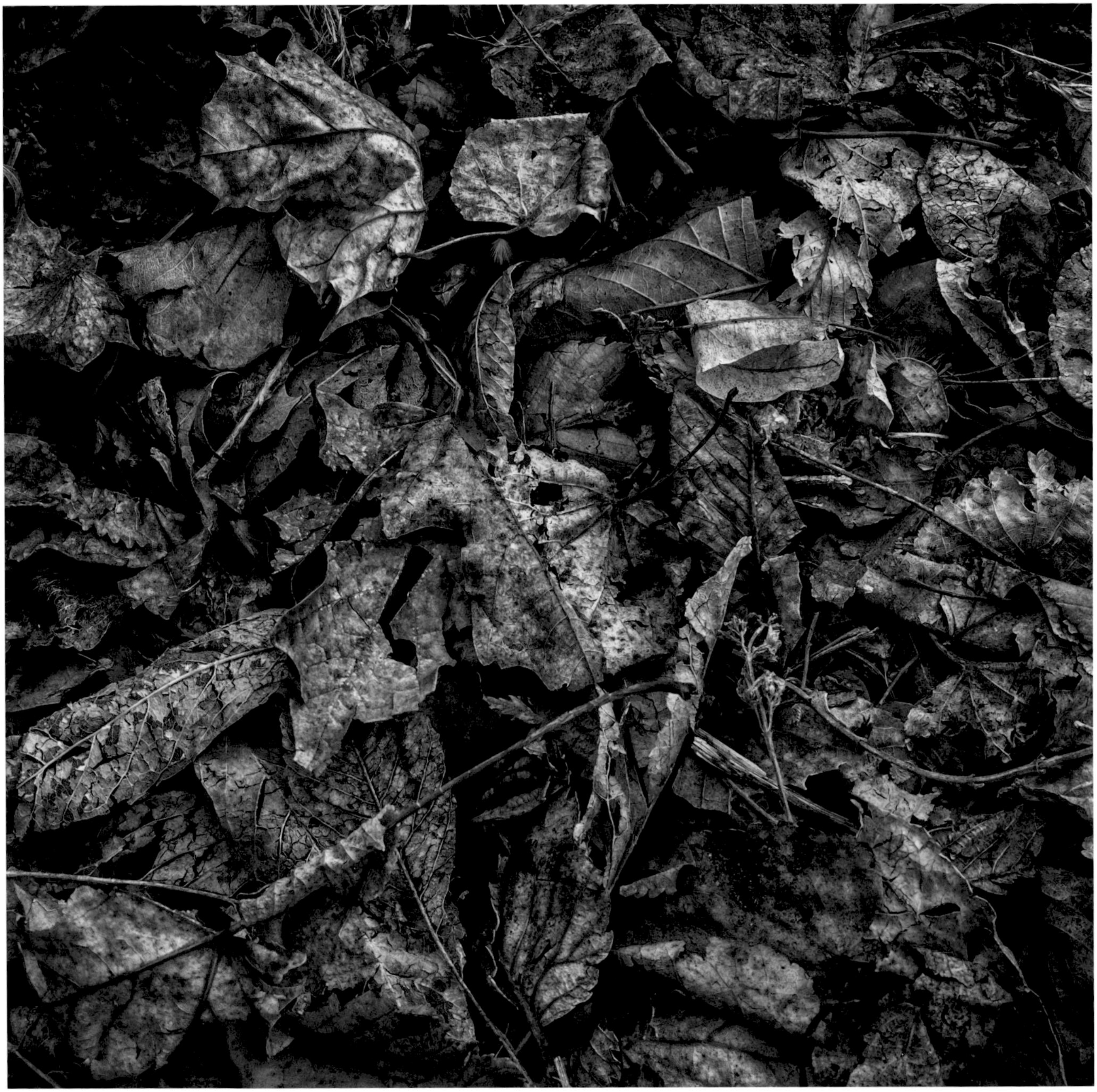

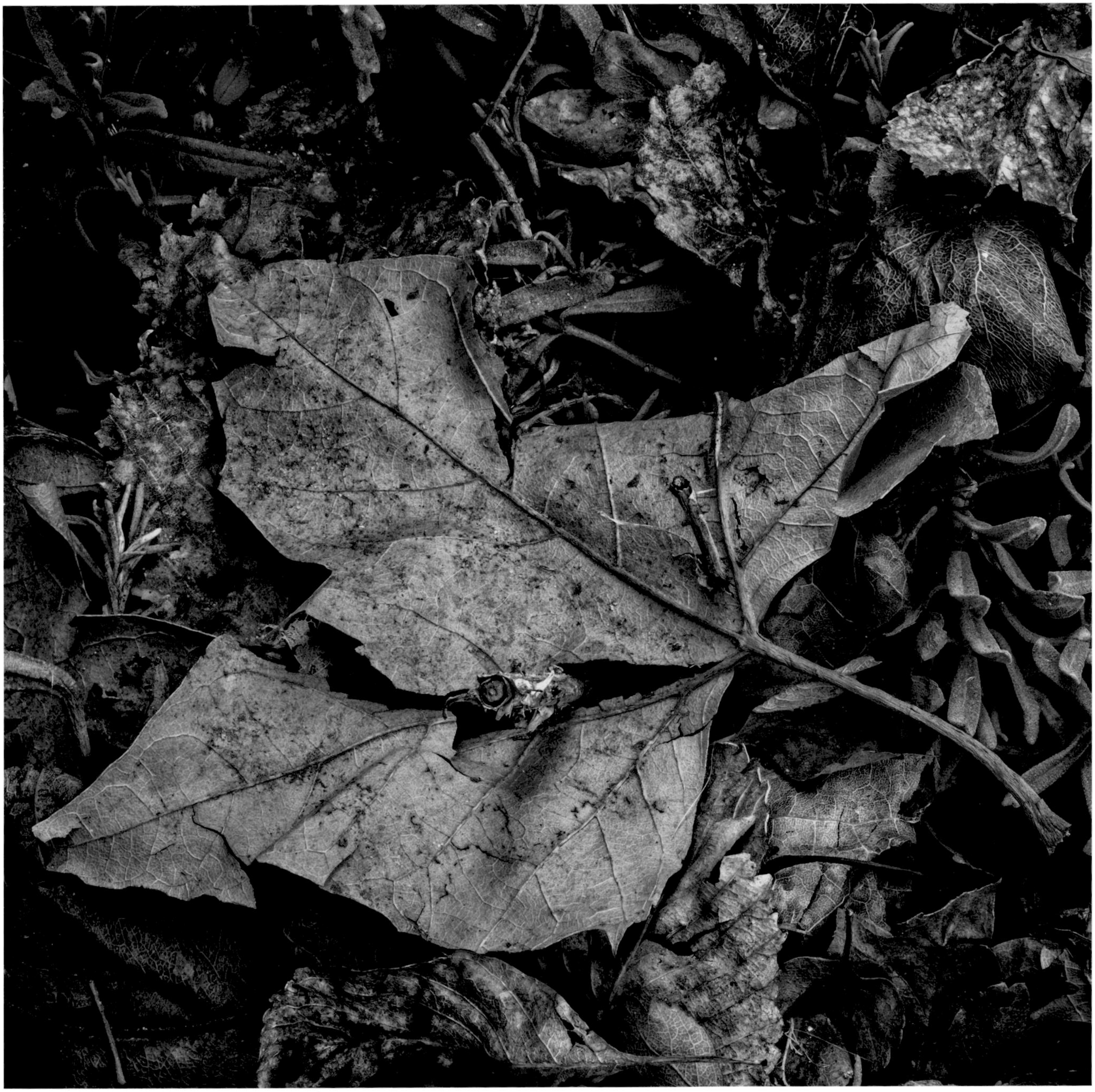

Medieval Steel

by Christopher Mark Perez www.flickr.com/photos/christophersoddsandsods/ • smilingmonk@gmail.com

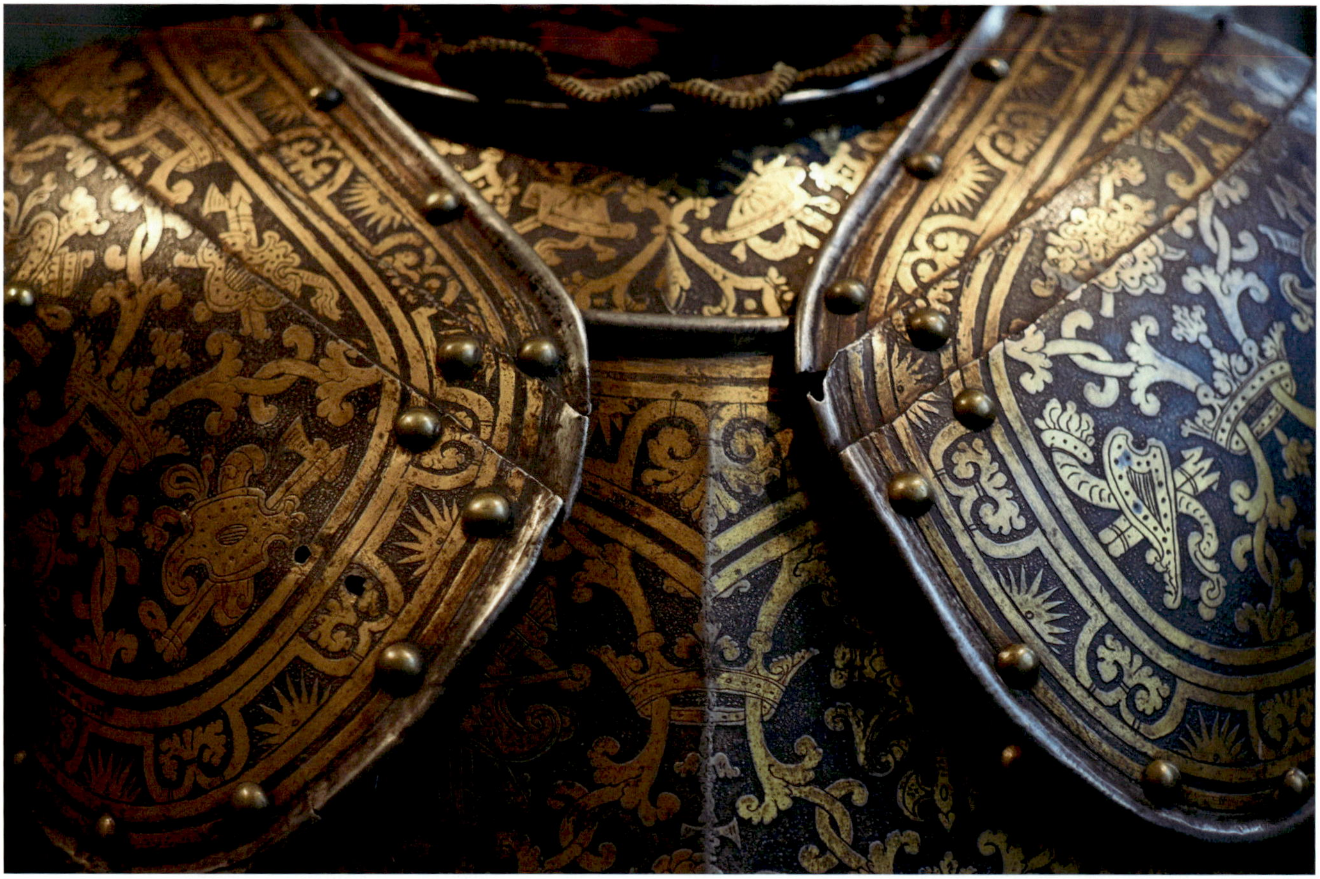

...Thus, seamed with many scars,
Bursting these prison bars,
Up to its native stars
My soul ascended!
There from the flowing bowl
Deep drinks the warrior's soul...

from *The Skeleton in Armor*
Henry Wadsworth Longfellow

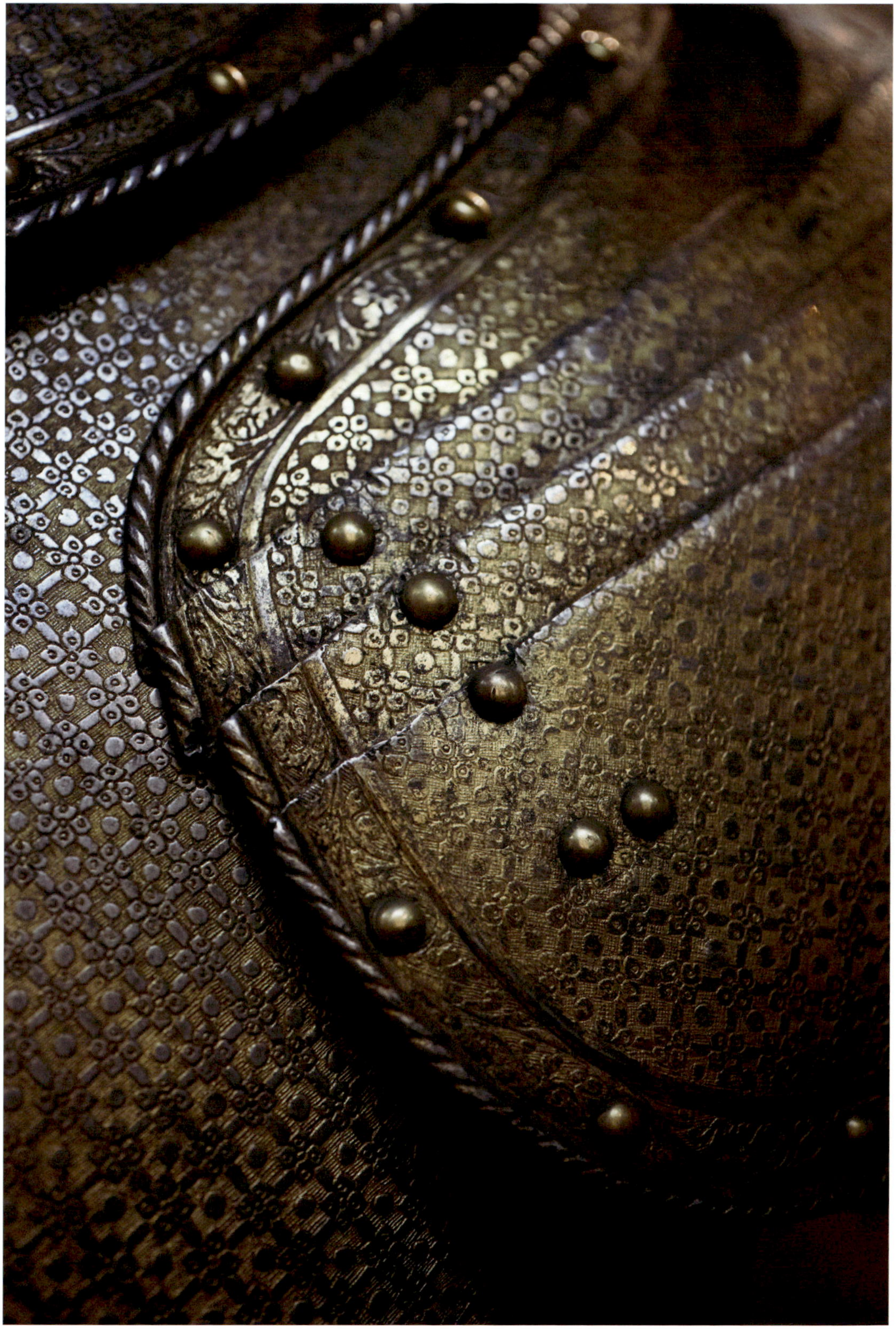

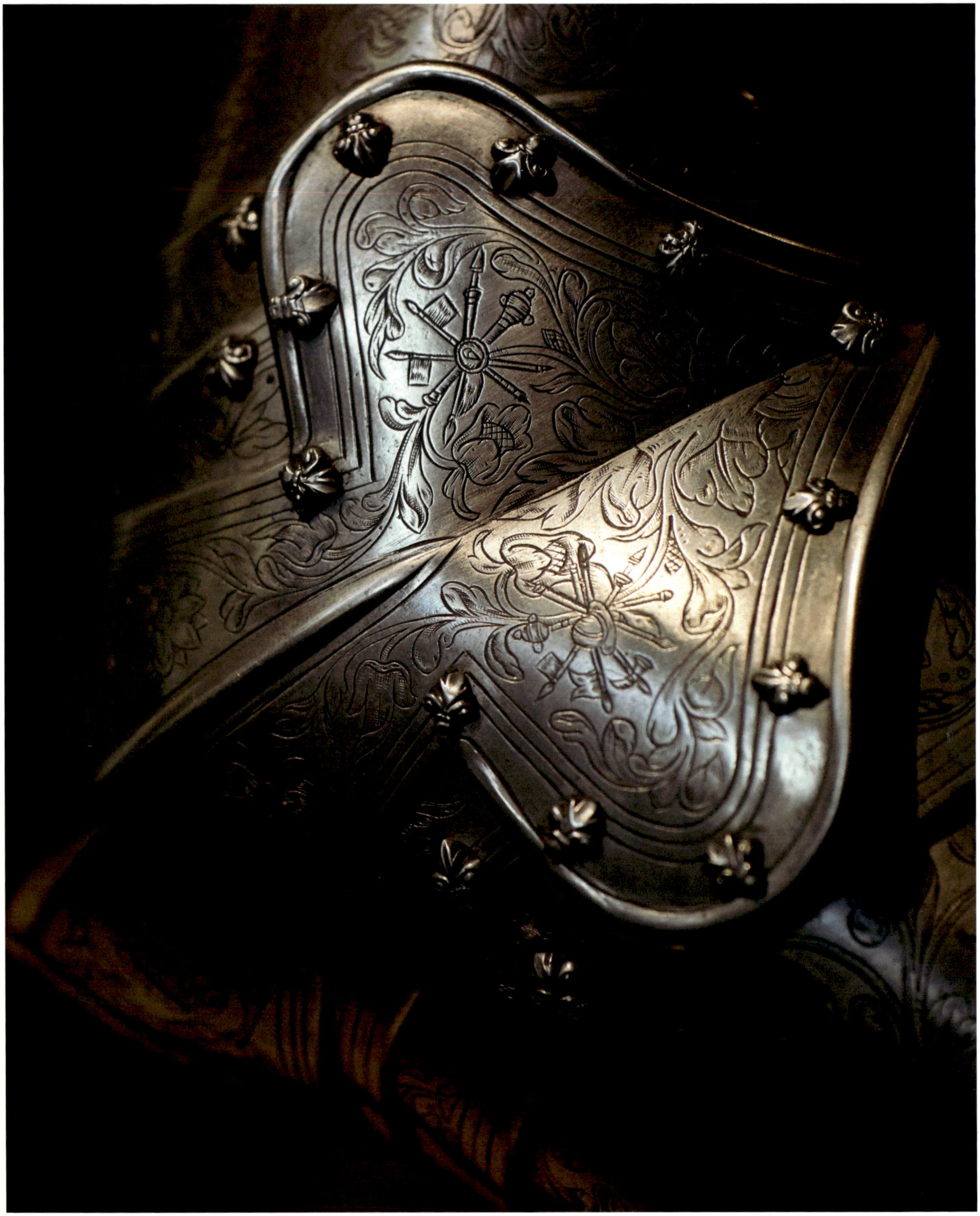

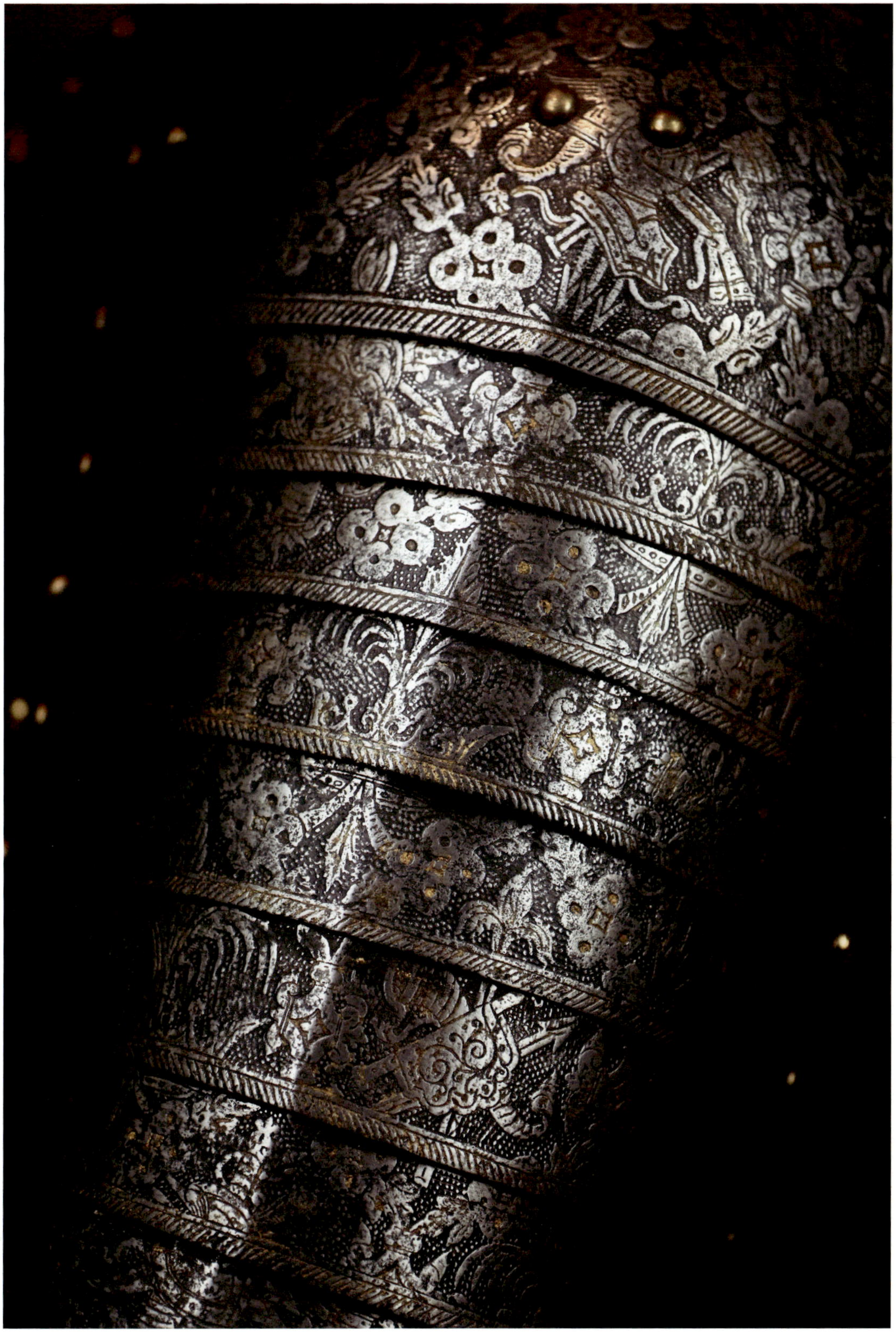

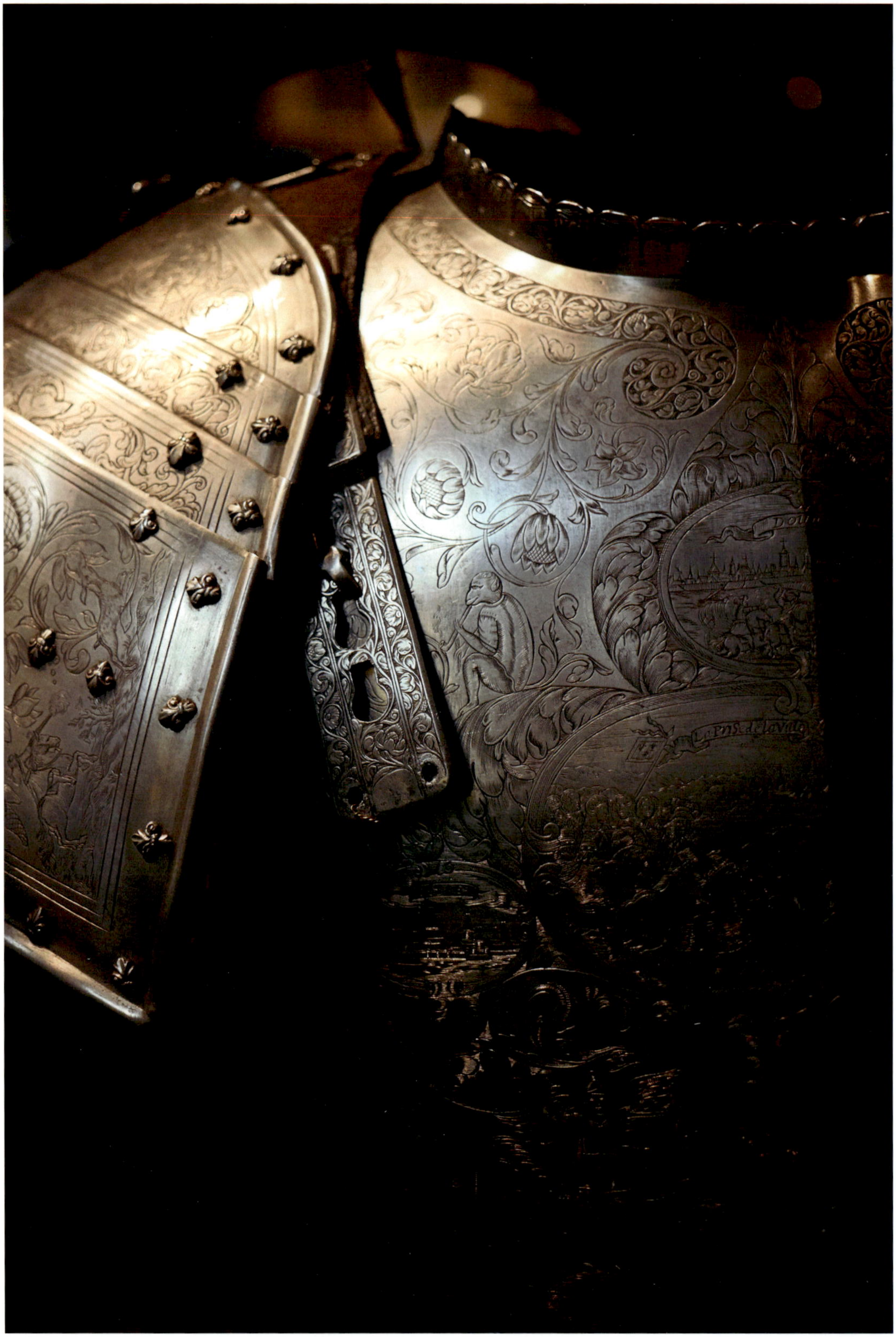

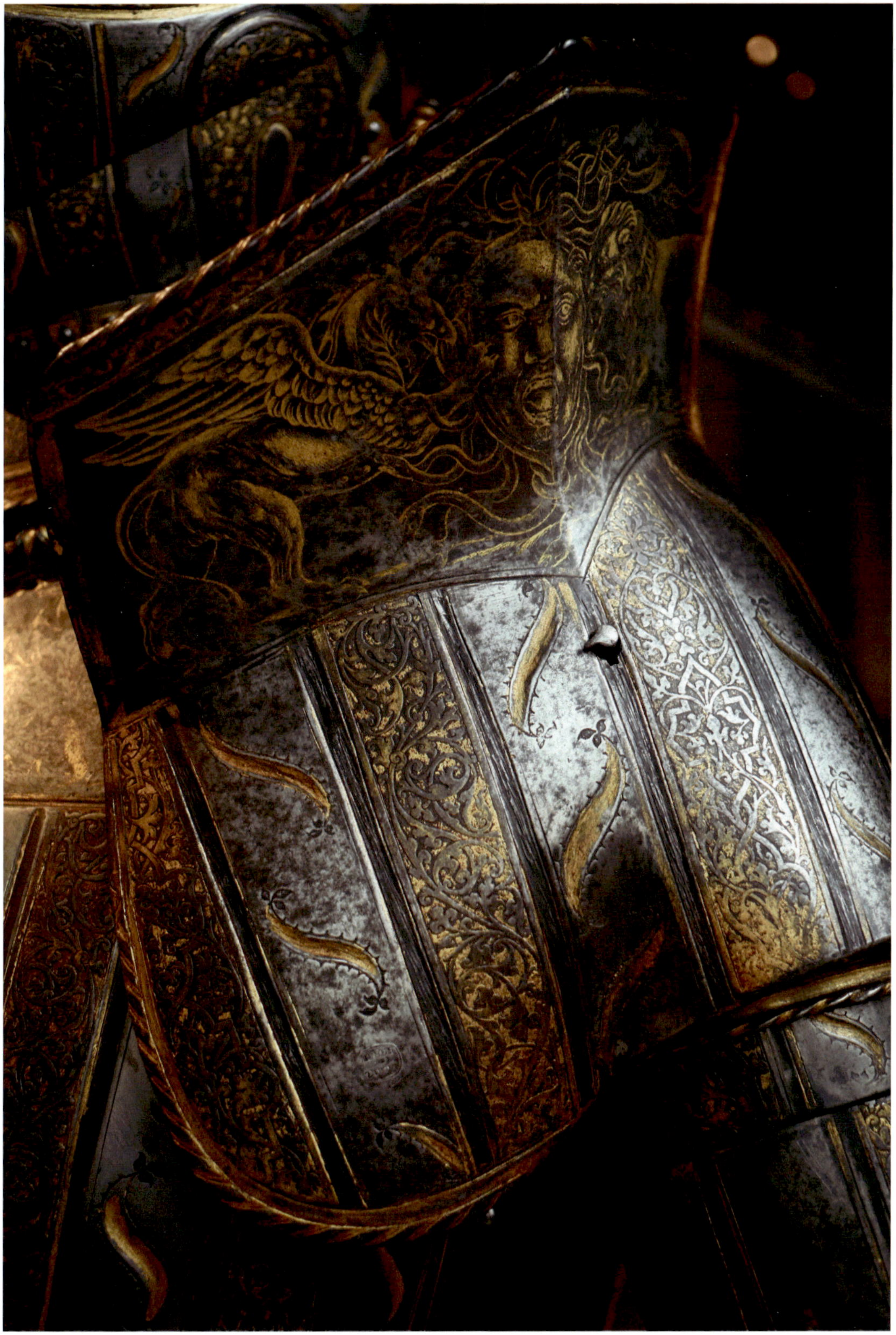

Niagara Mist

by John Conn

johnconnimages.com ♦ iconn55555@aol.com

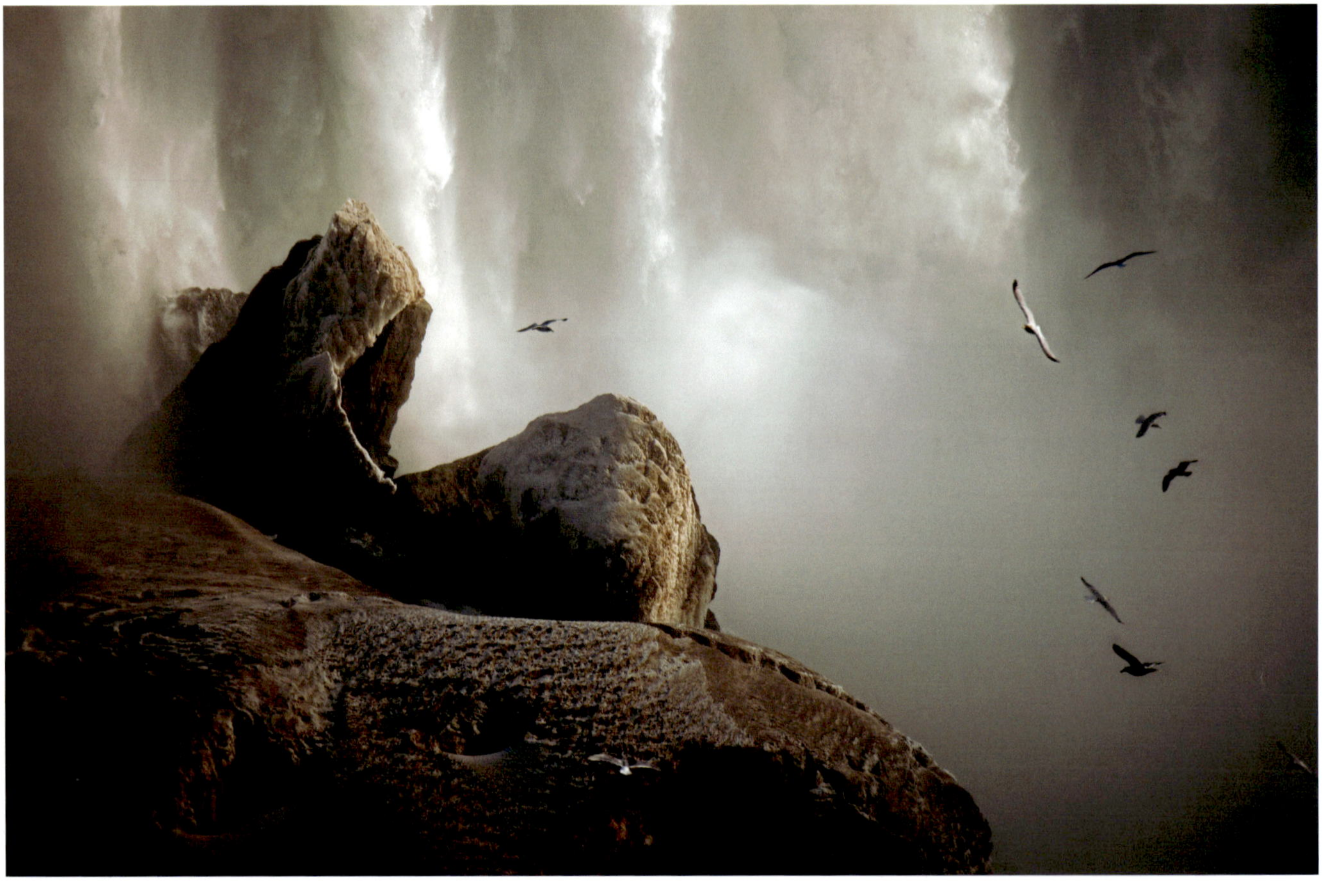

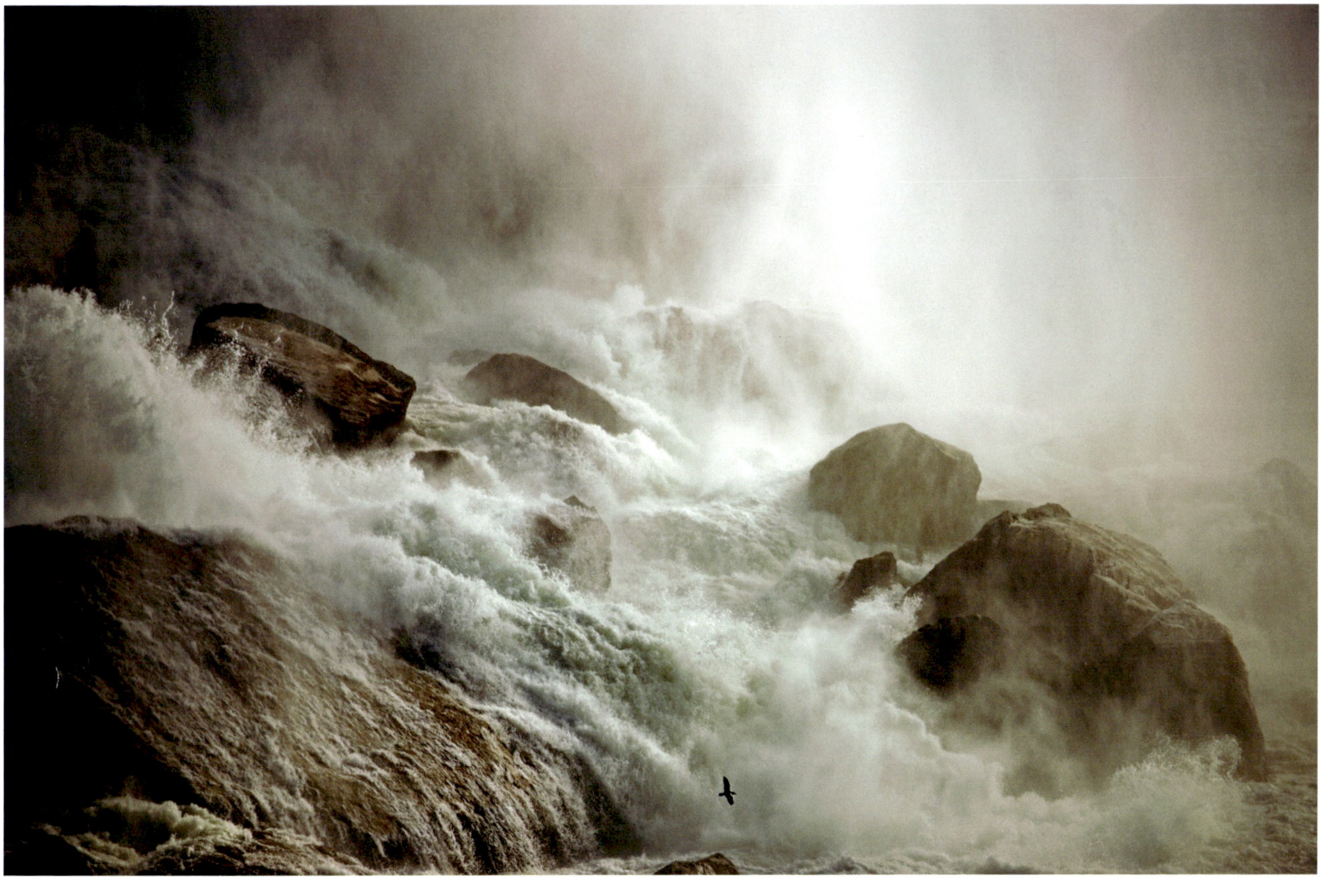

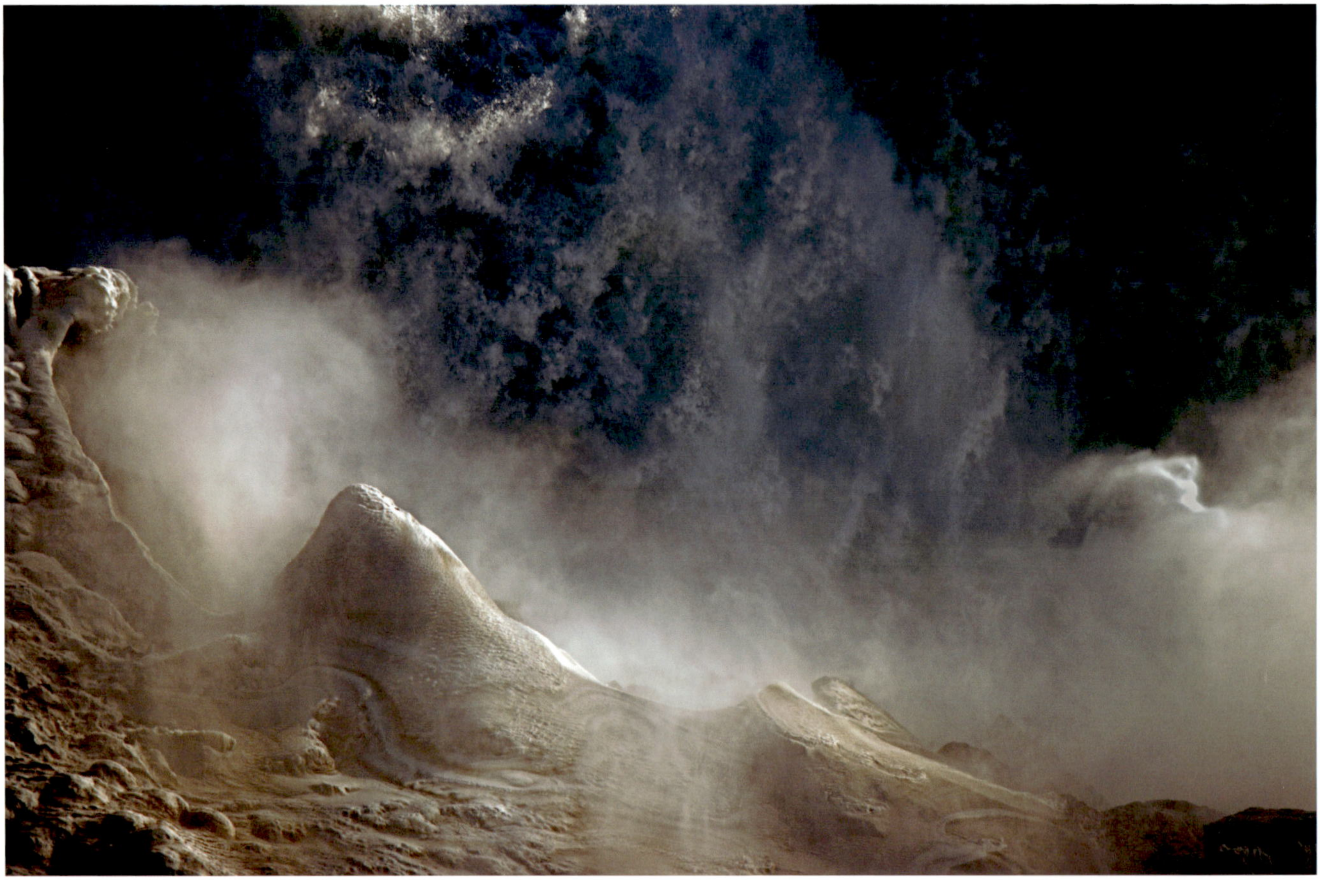

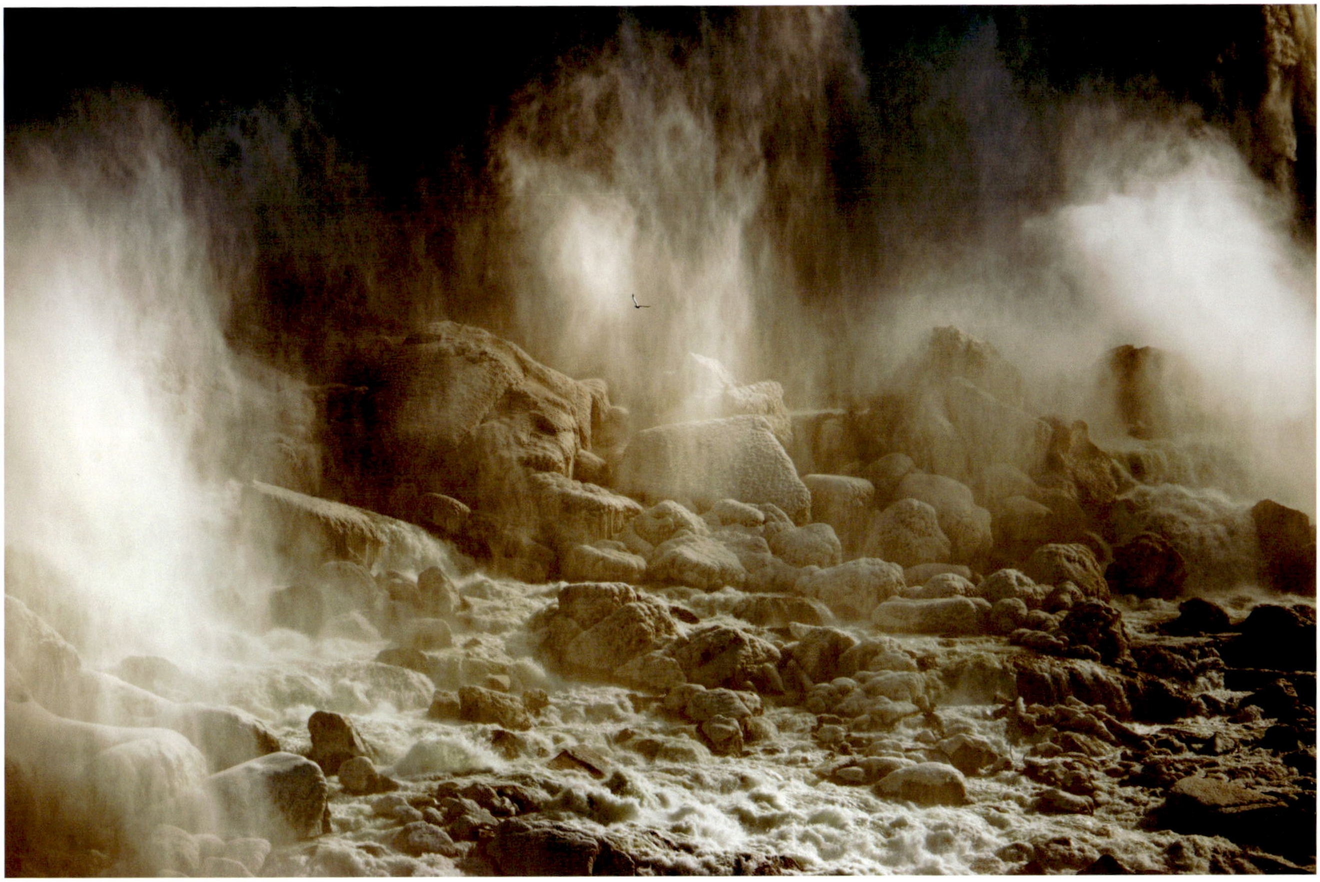

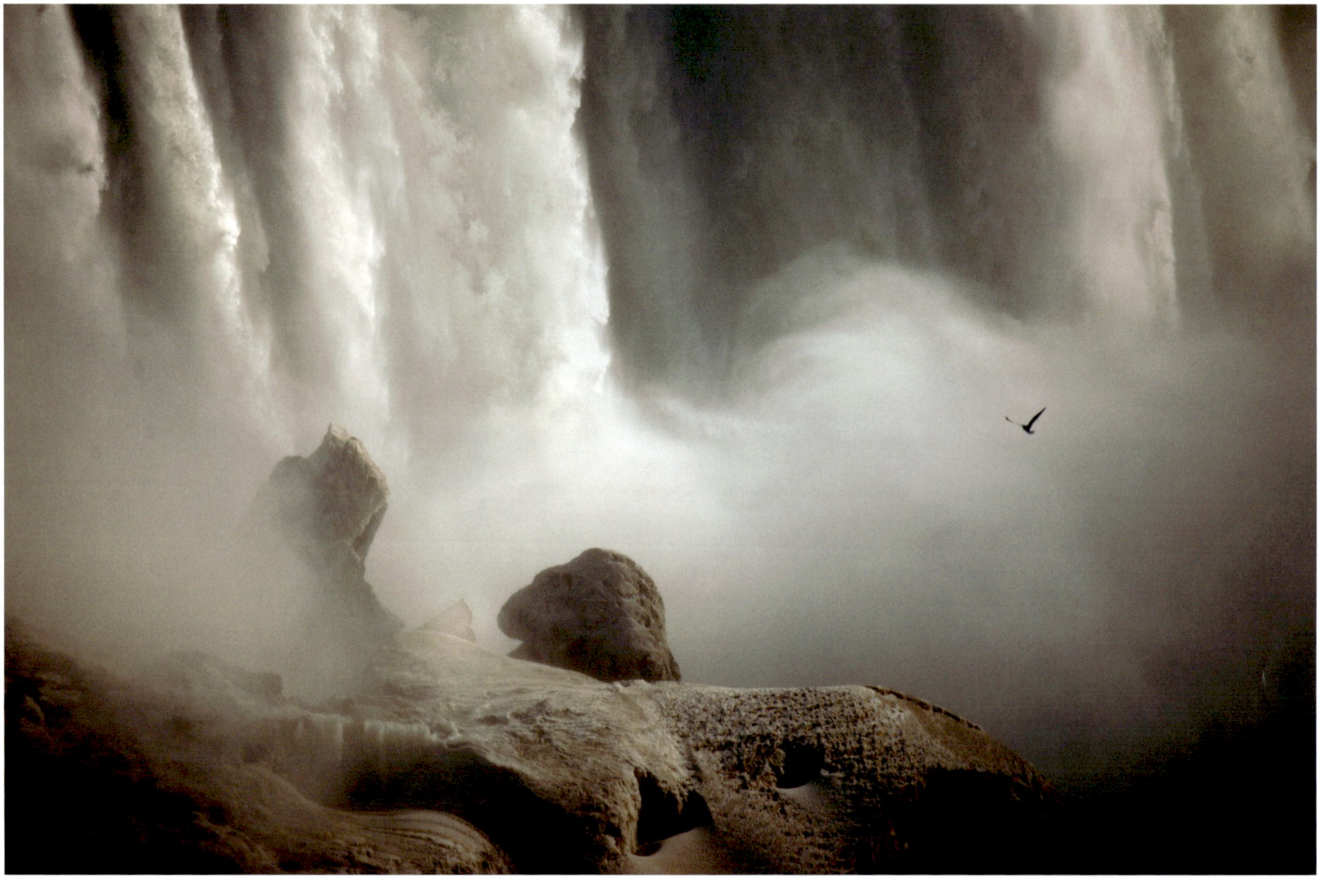

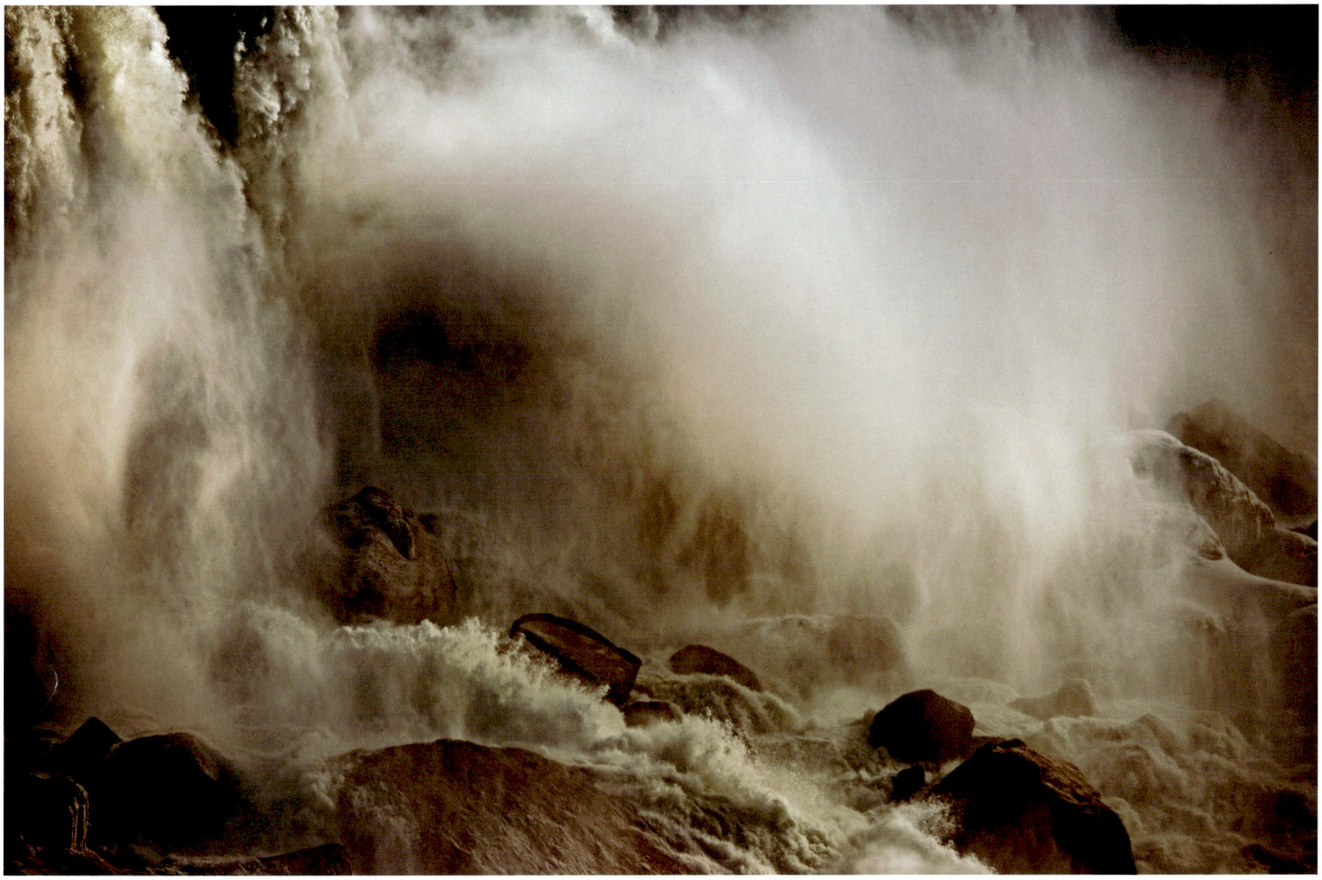

These photographs were taken at the beginning of February (2016) on the Canadian side of the Falls. There was a mixture of sun, rain, heavy mist, cold, and the gulls winging themselves through it all. The action was happening at the base of the Falls where all of these elements came together. Thank God for the birds. (Do you know how hard it is to throw a bird that far? It does confuse them.)

The Magic of Flight

by Anne McGrath

www.gerardandannephotography.com ♦ annemcgr@gmail.com

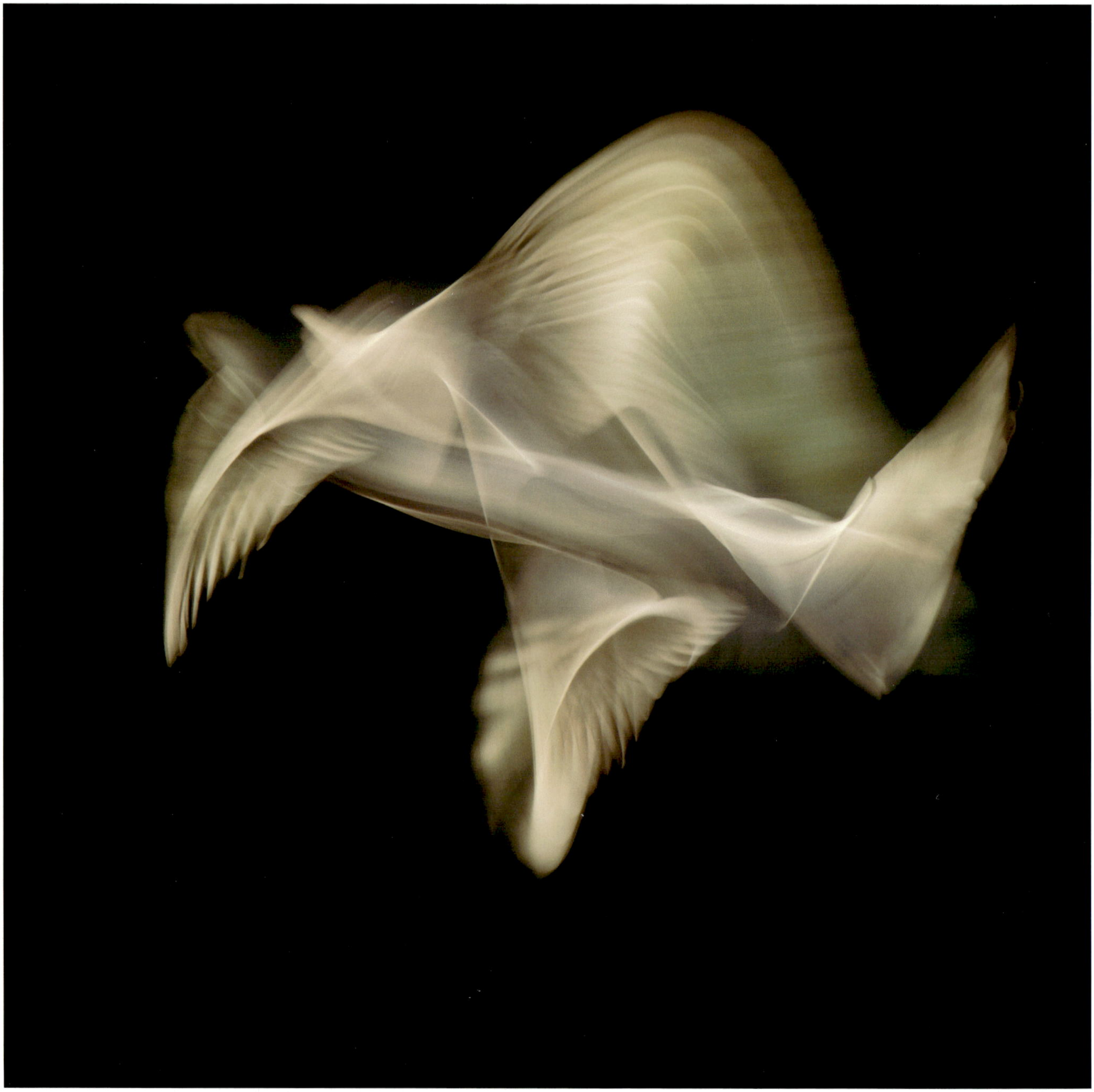

Abstraction

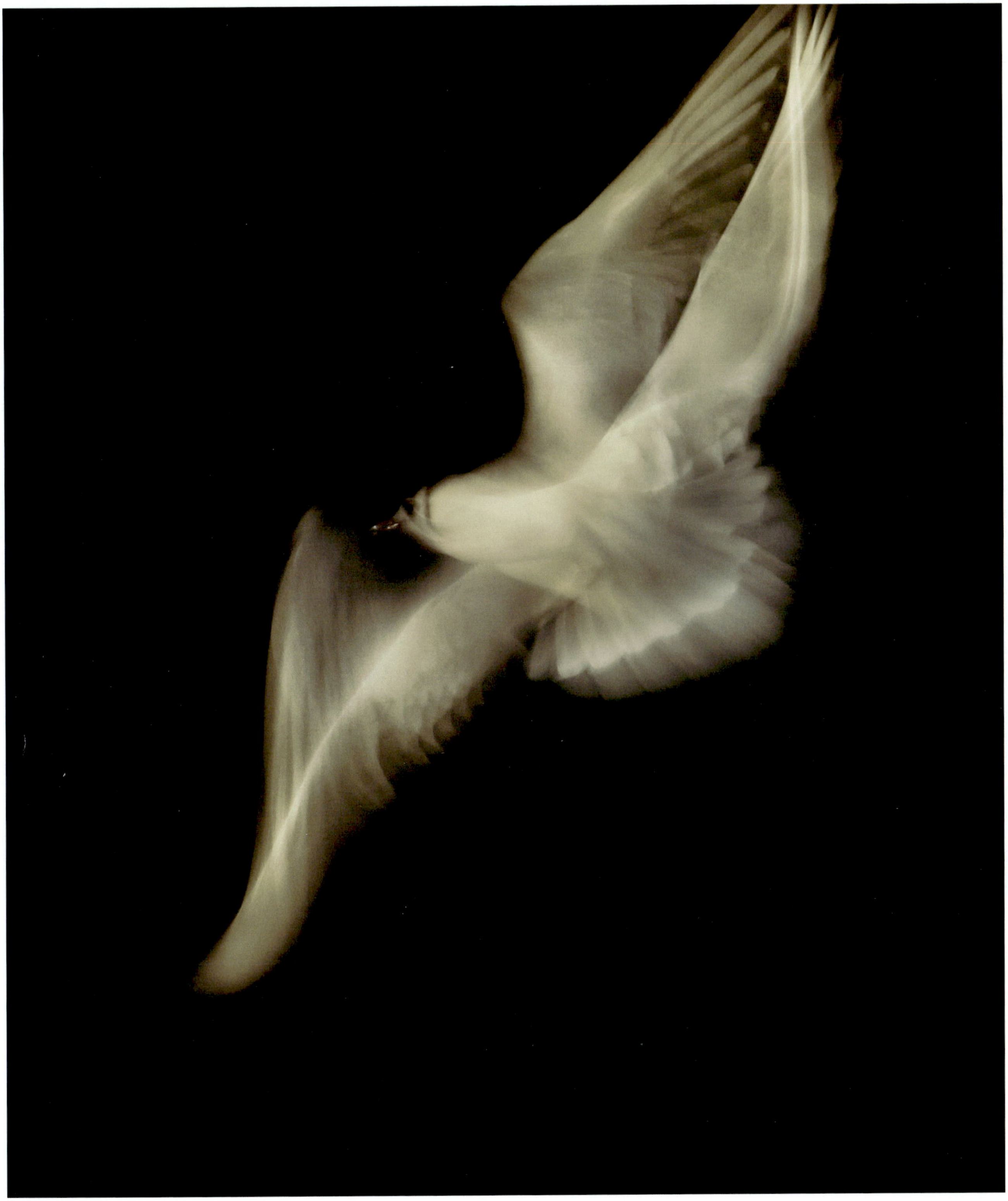

Wing Movement

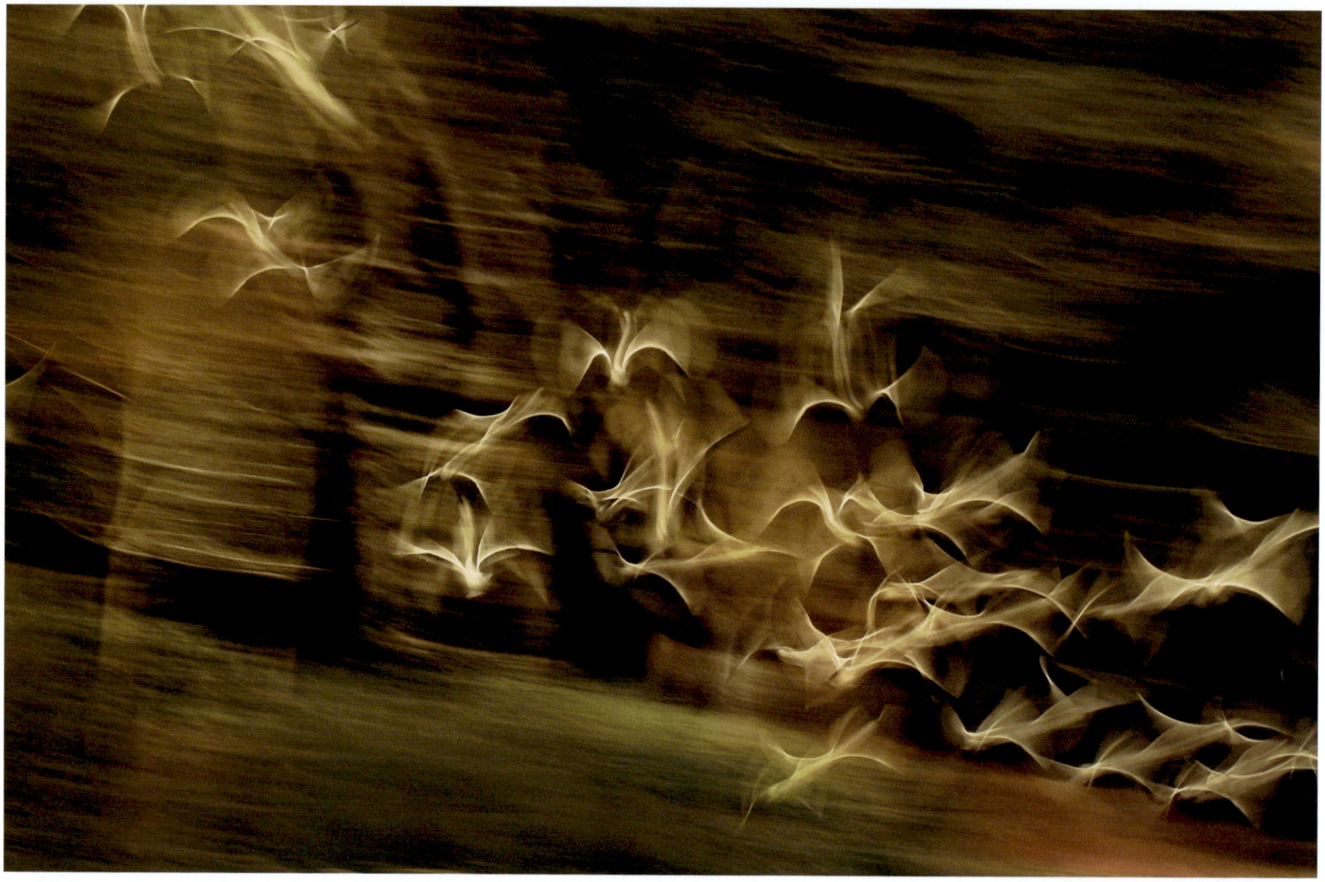

Blurred Flight

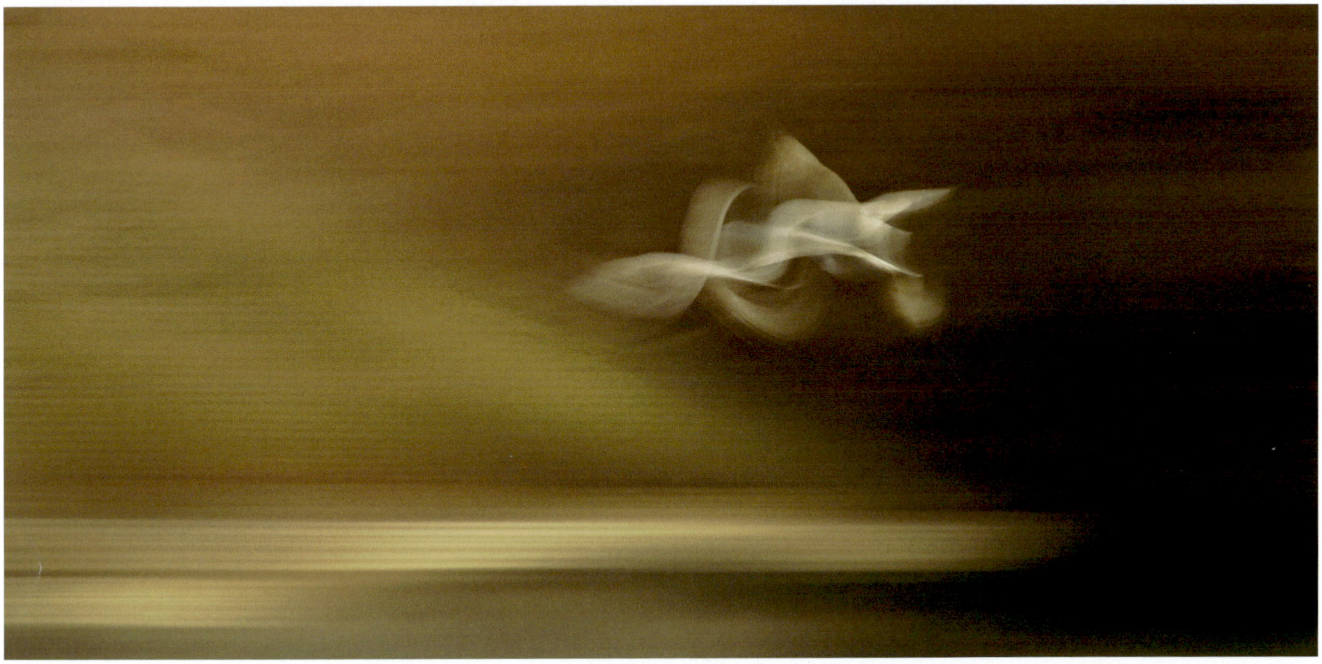

Light and Shadow

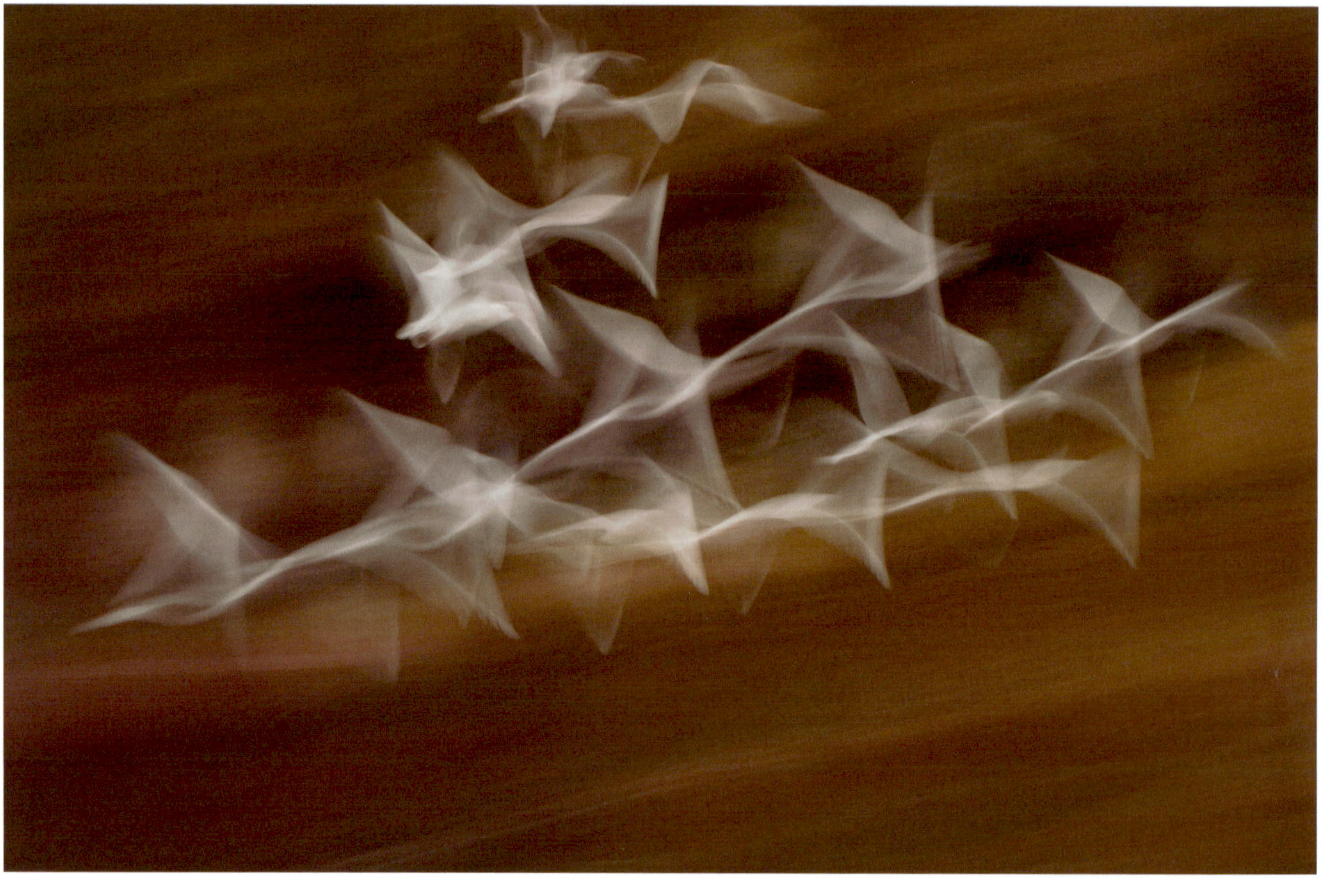

Beating Wings

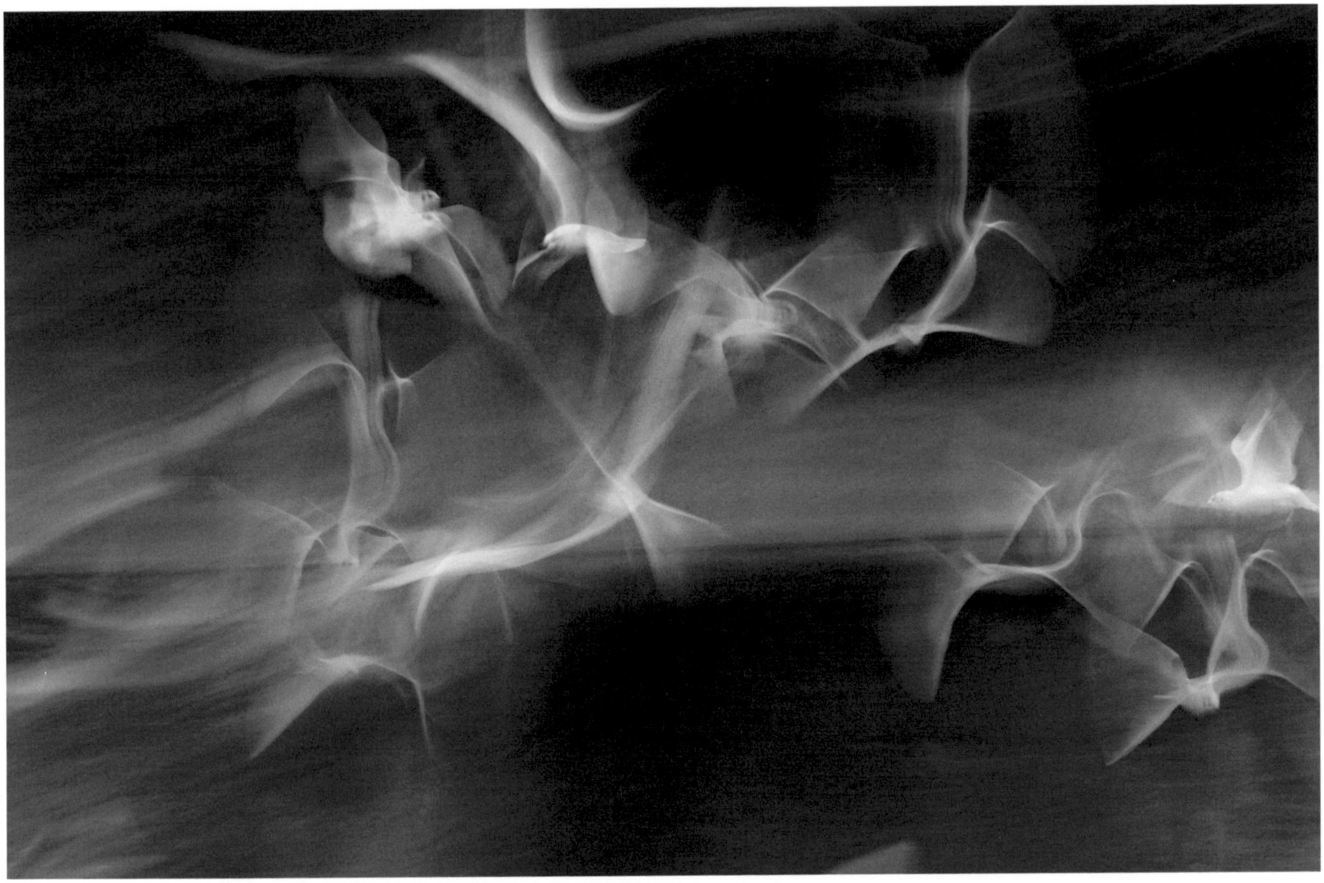

Ethereal Flight

All these images are of seagulls in flight, taken at slow shutter speeds to capture the motion of beating, flapping wings or the beautiful abstract shapes created by the movement of flight. The pale coloring of the seagull contrasts with the dark background of trees, so the eye homes in on the bird, and its shape and form, and the background often becomes irrelevant.

Trees of Rittenhouse Square

by Richard L. Davidson

rdavidson1x@gmail.com

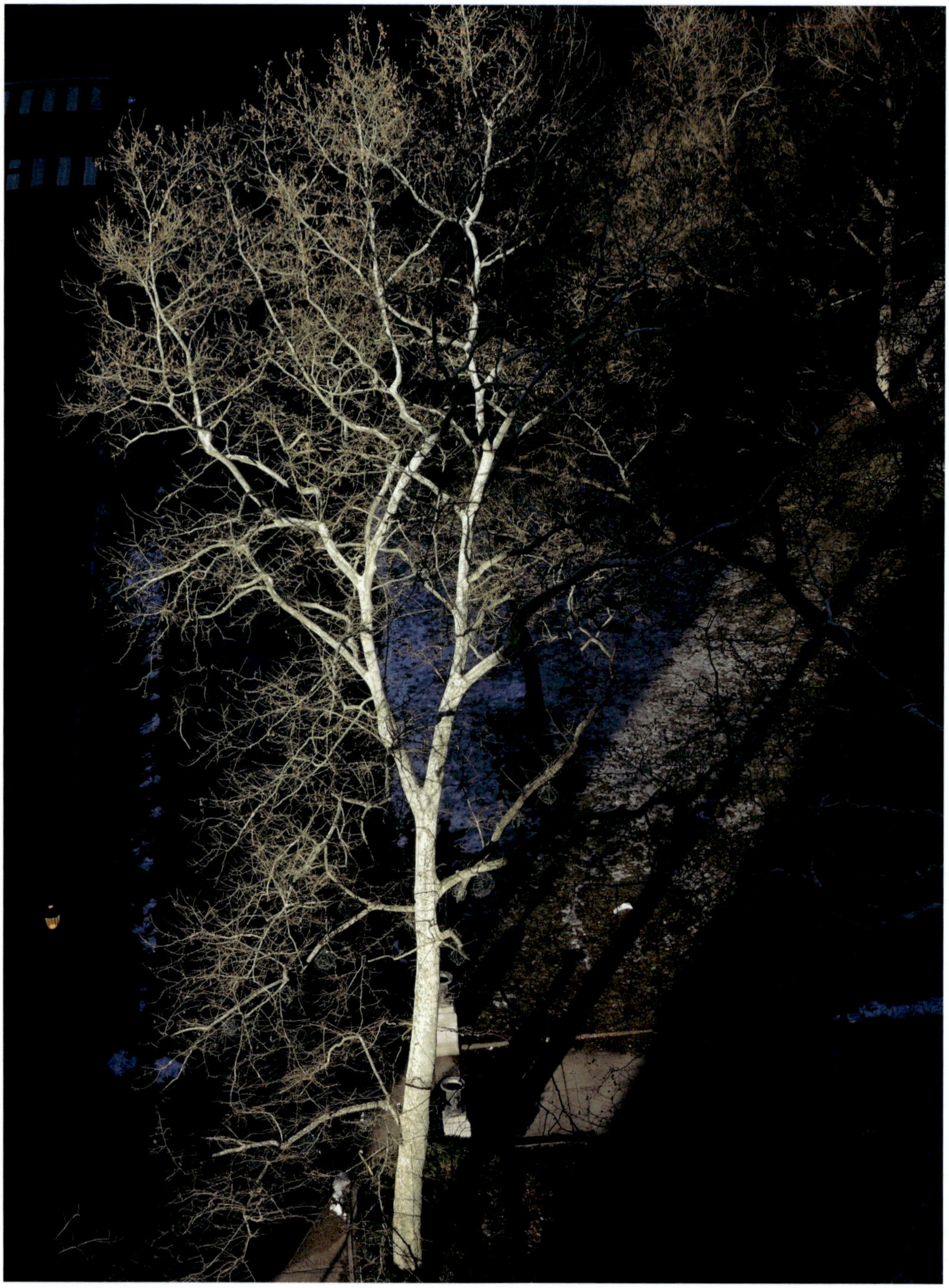

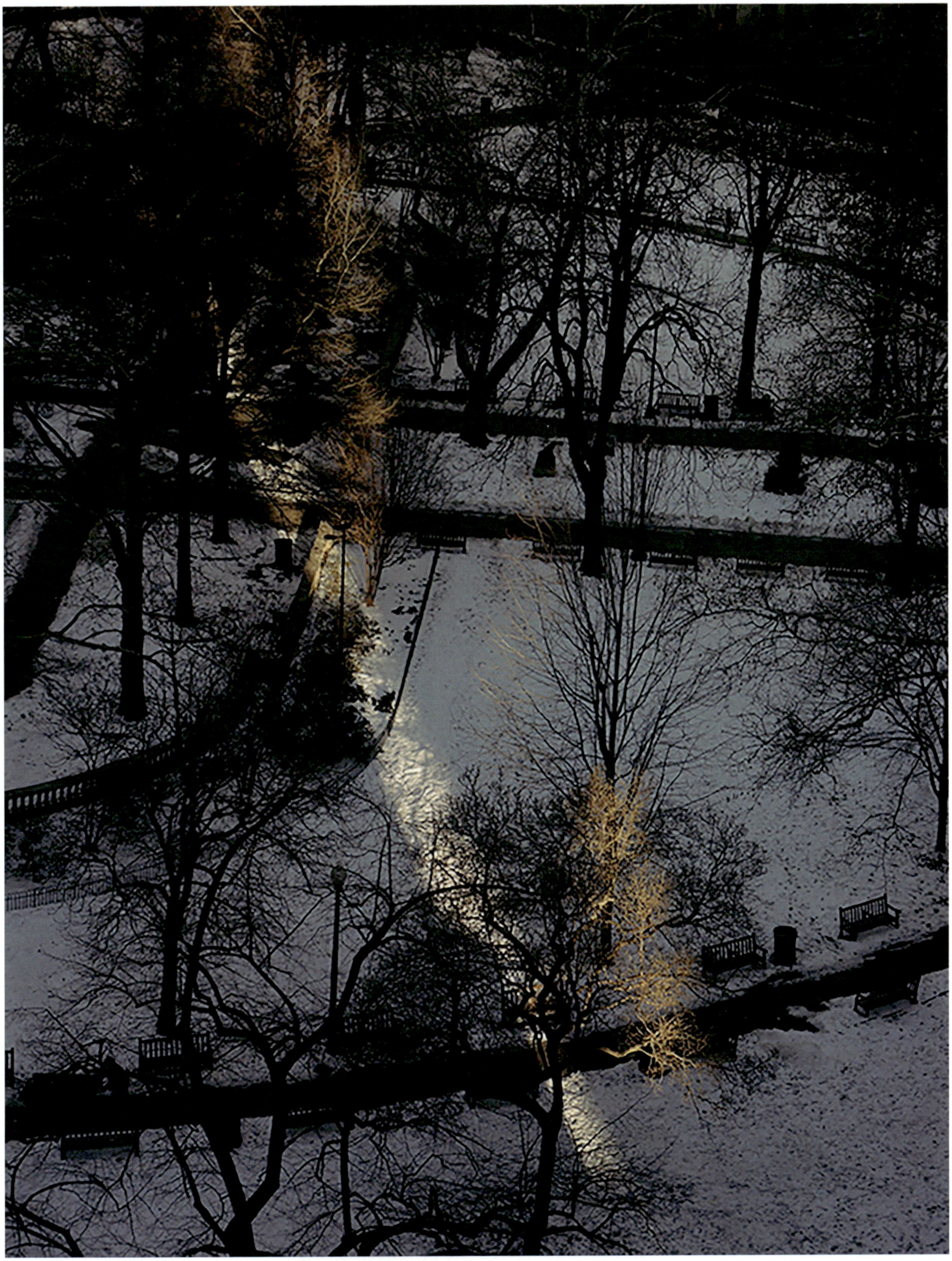

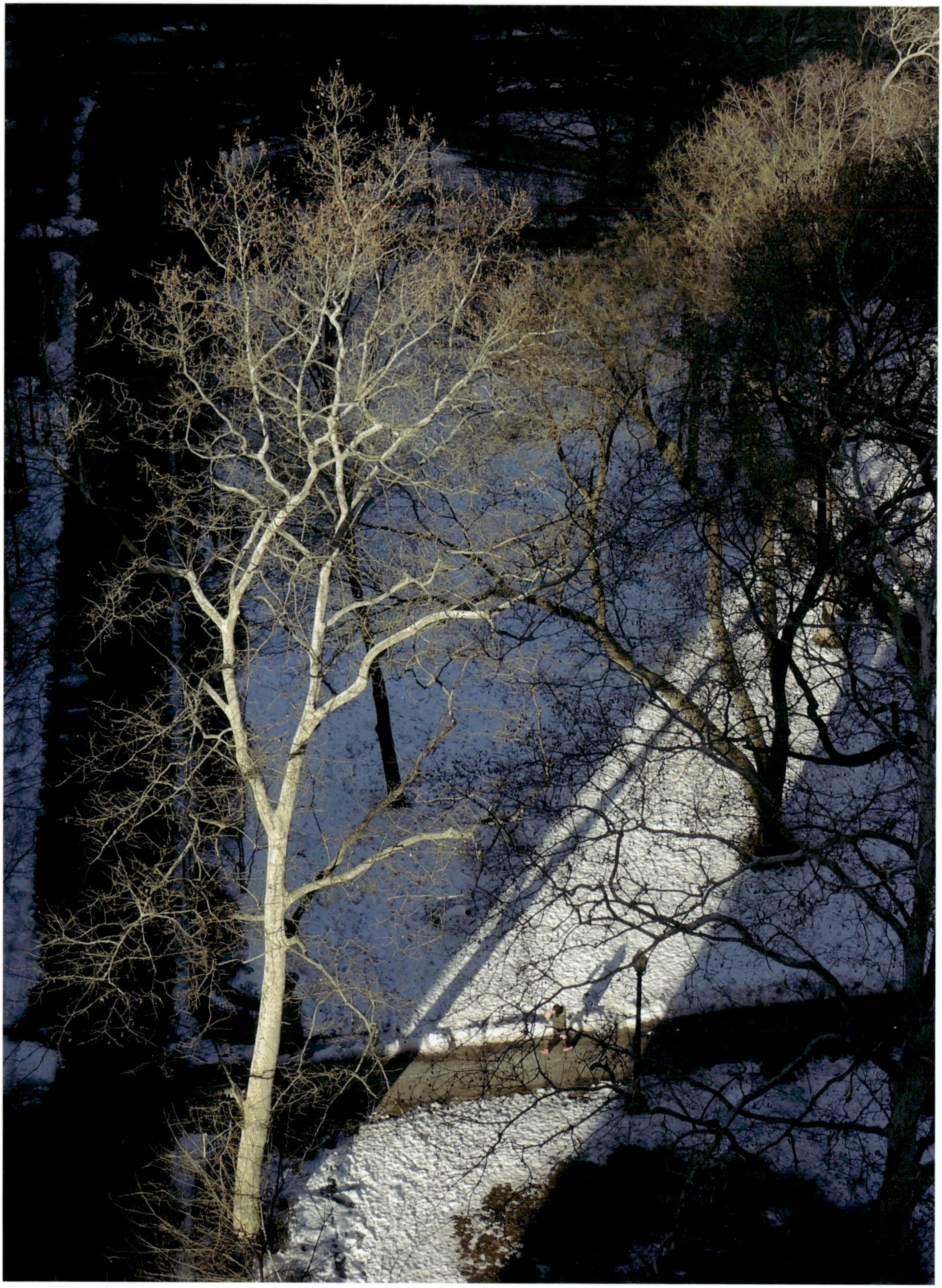

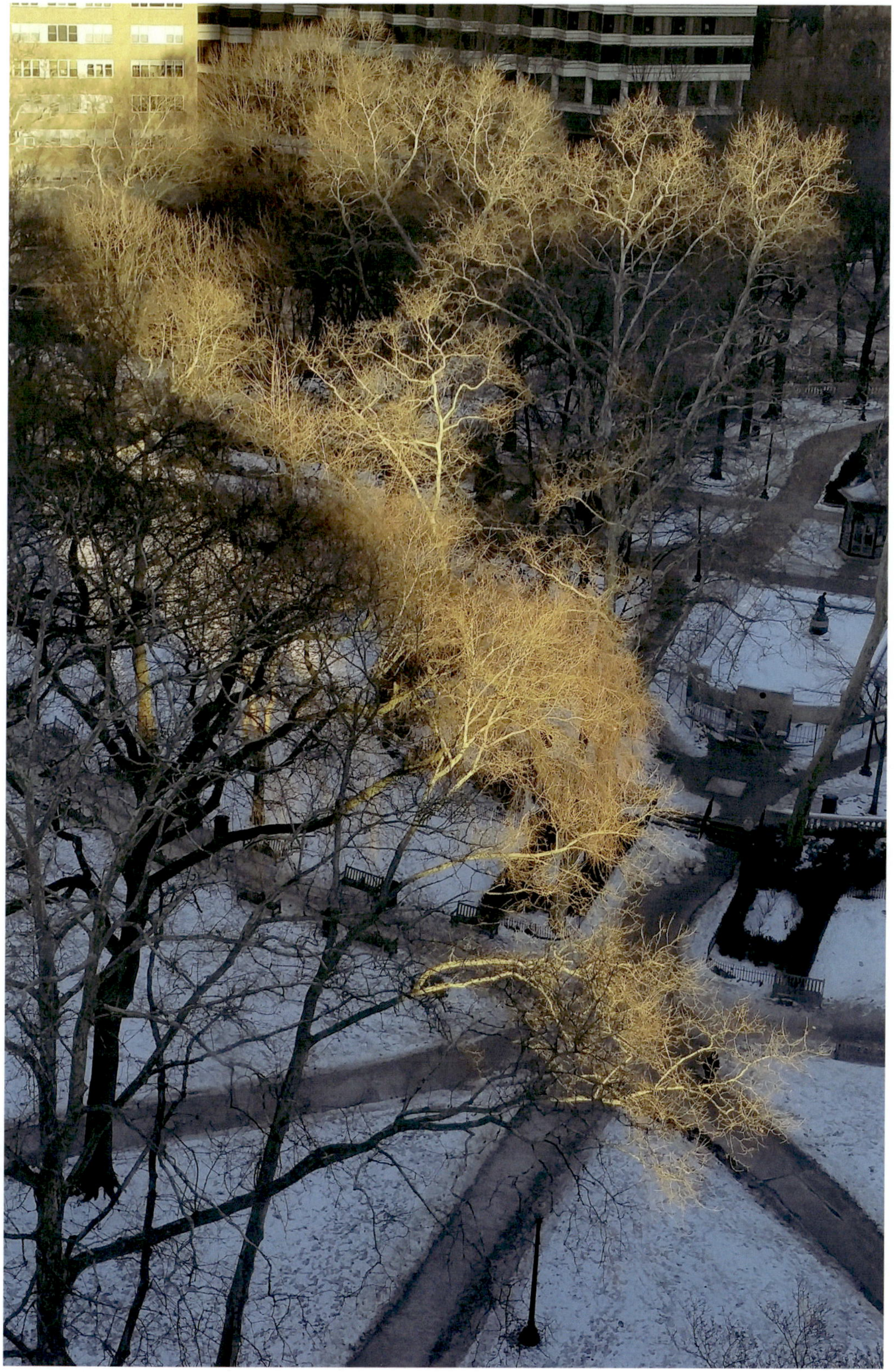

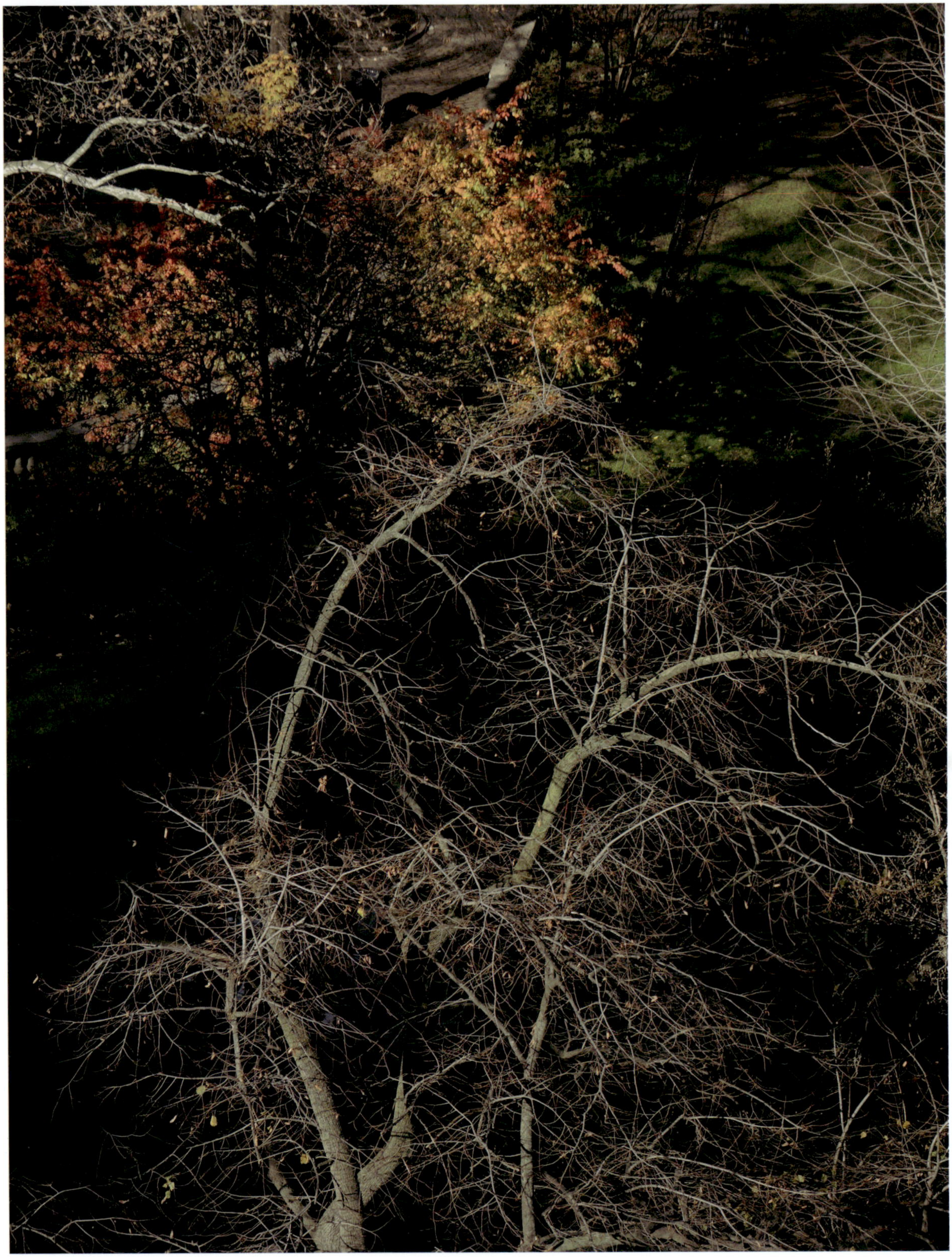

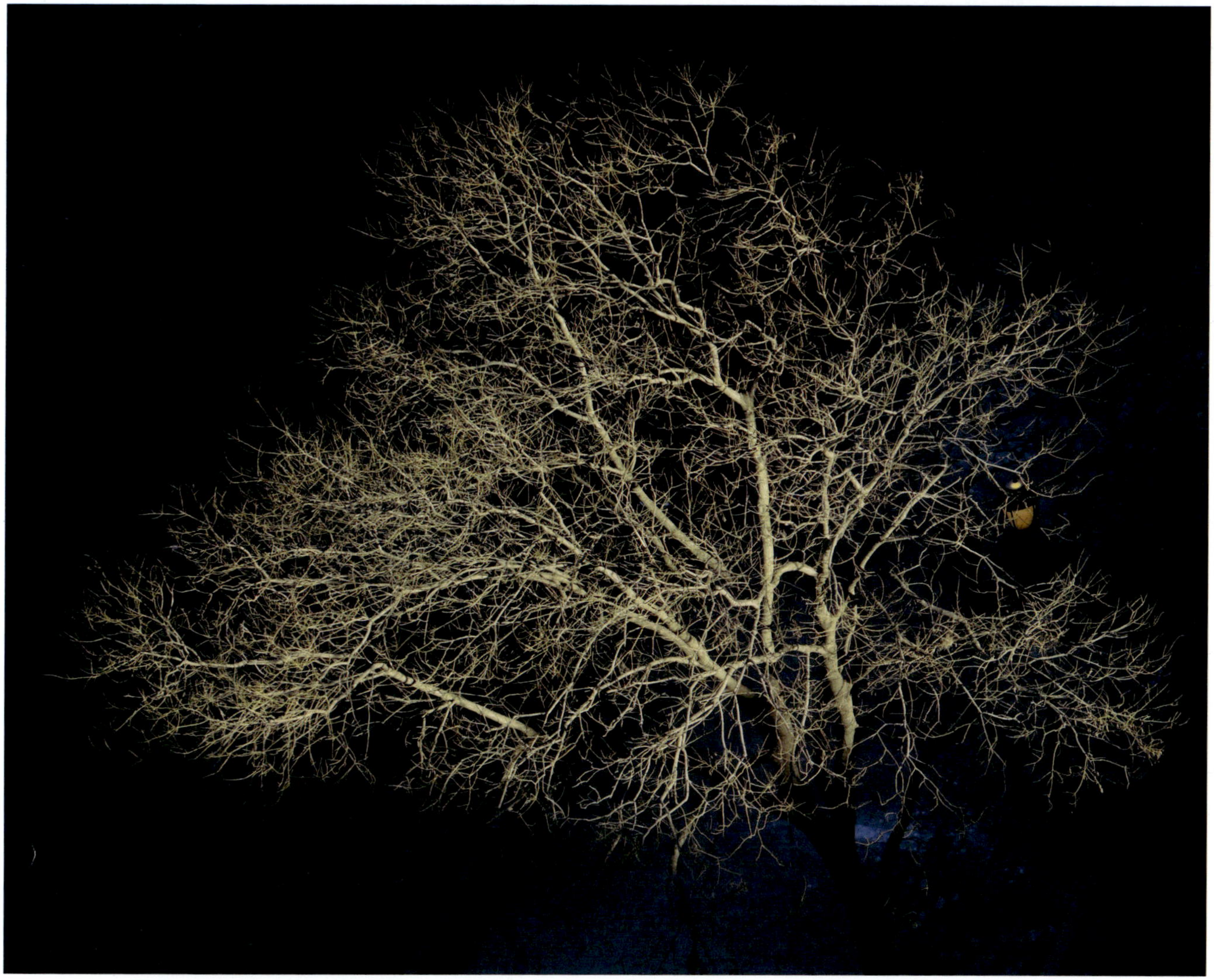

This series of photographs is based on the trees in the park across from my apartment on Rittenhouse Square in Philadelphia, and they were largely taken through only one window in the apartment. The photographs are from different seasons and different times of the day, and the effects of narrow beams of light highlighting just the tips of branches or the tops of trees are highly dependent on the time of day and the angle of the sunlight. A number of these photographs arise from a time of day when there are only long narrow traces of light across the park. These narrow beams of light come from the rays of sunlight streaming through the gaps between the closely-adjoining buildings around Rittenhouse Square. The directions from which the beams come (and also their intensities) vary according to the seasons and the time of day. There is absolutely no digital manipulation in any of these photos to create the beams of light or their effects of creating highlight among the trees in the Square.

Hosta La Vista

by Michael Rich

mcrich.net ♦ mcrich11@comcast.net

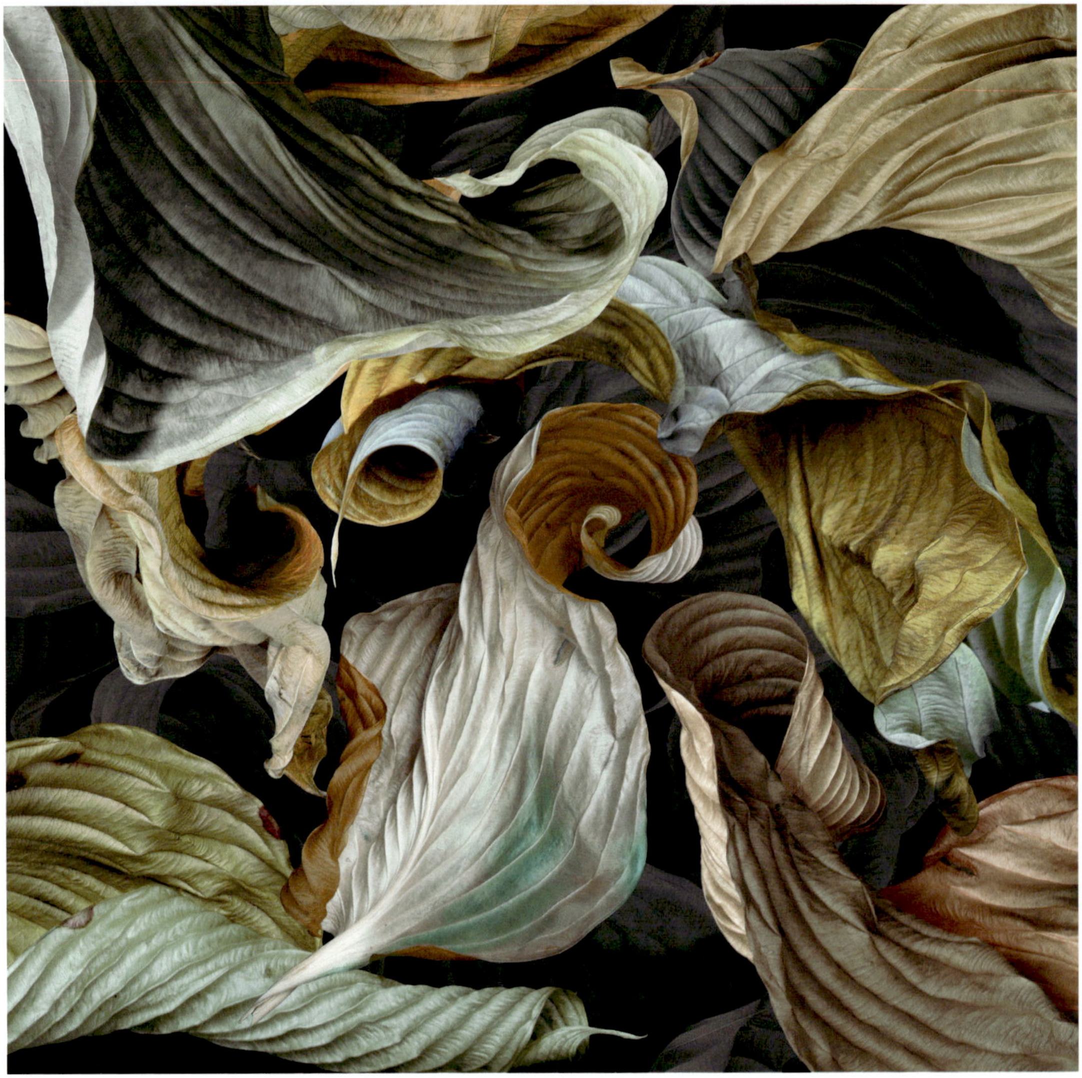

Loving summer eons on
We desiccate and twist
And yet in yellow leaf we band
The flowery binding kiss.

"Florilegium of Decline"
Nick Drake, the Far Leys notebooks

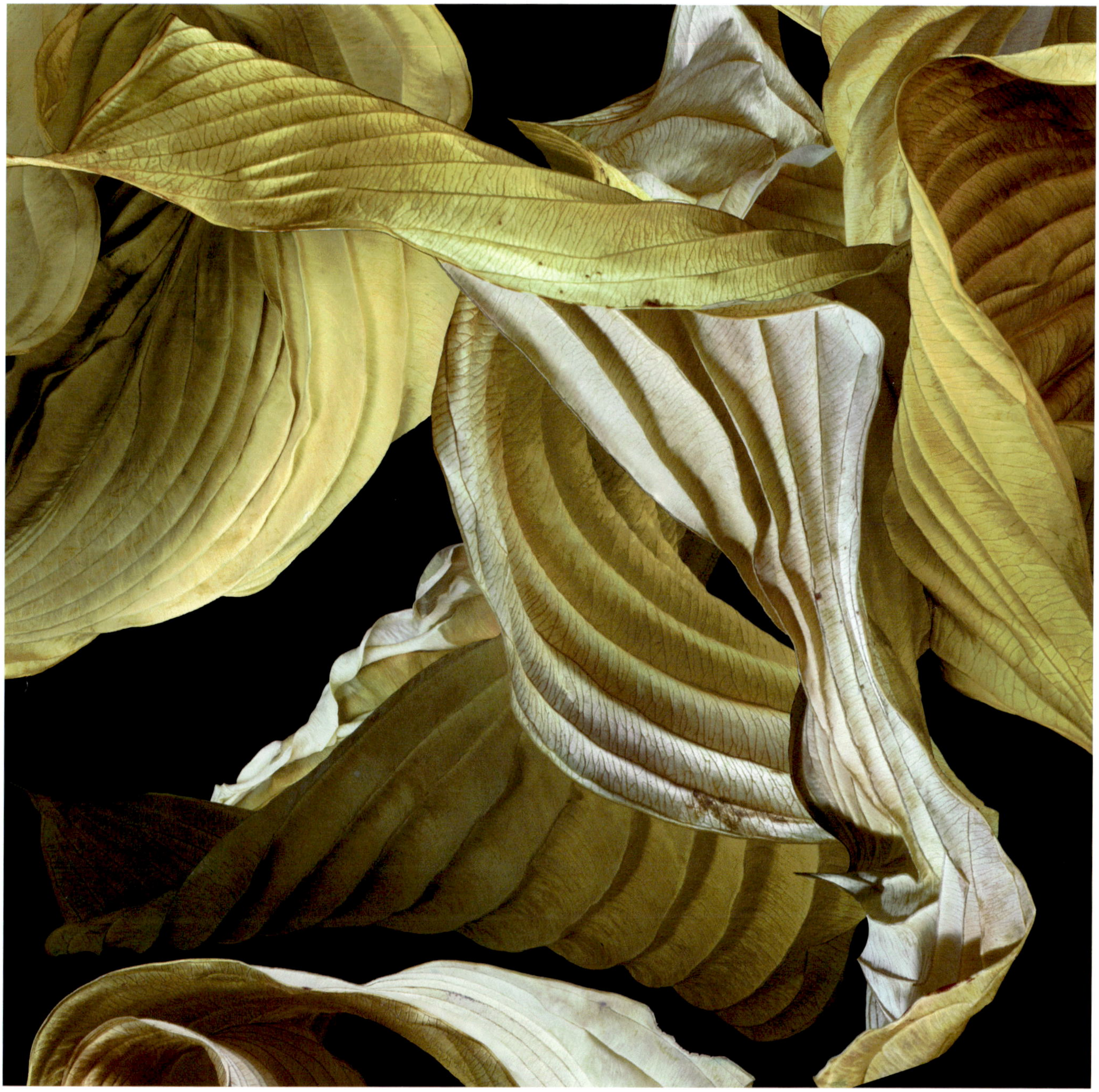

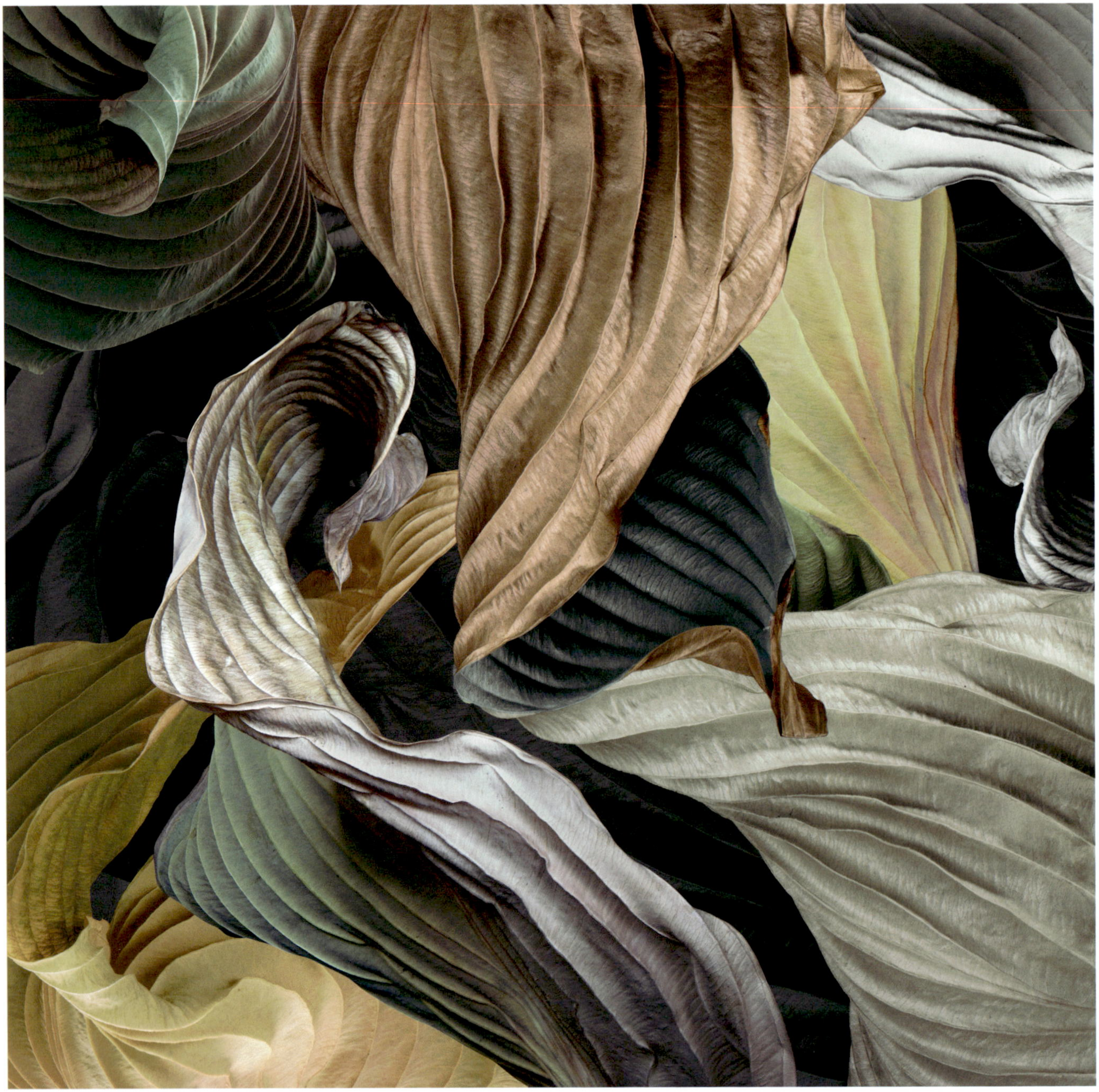

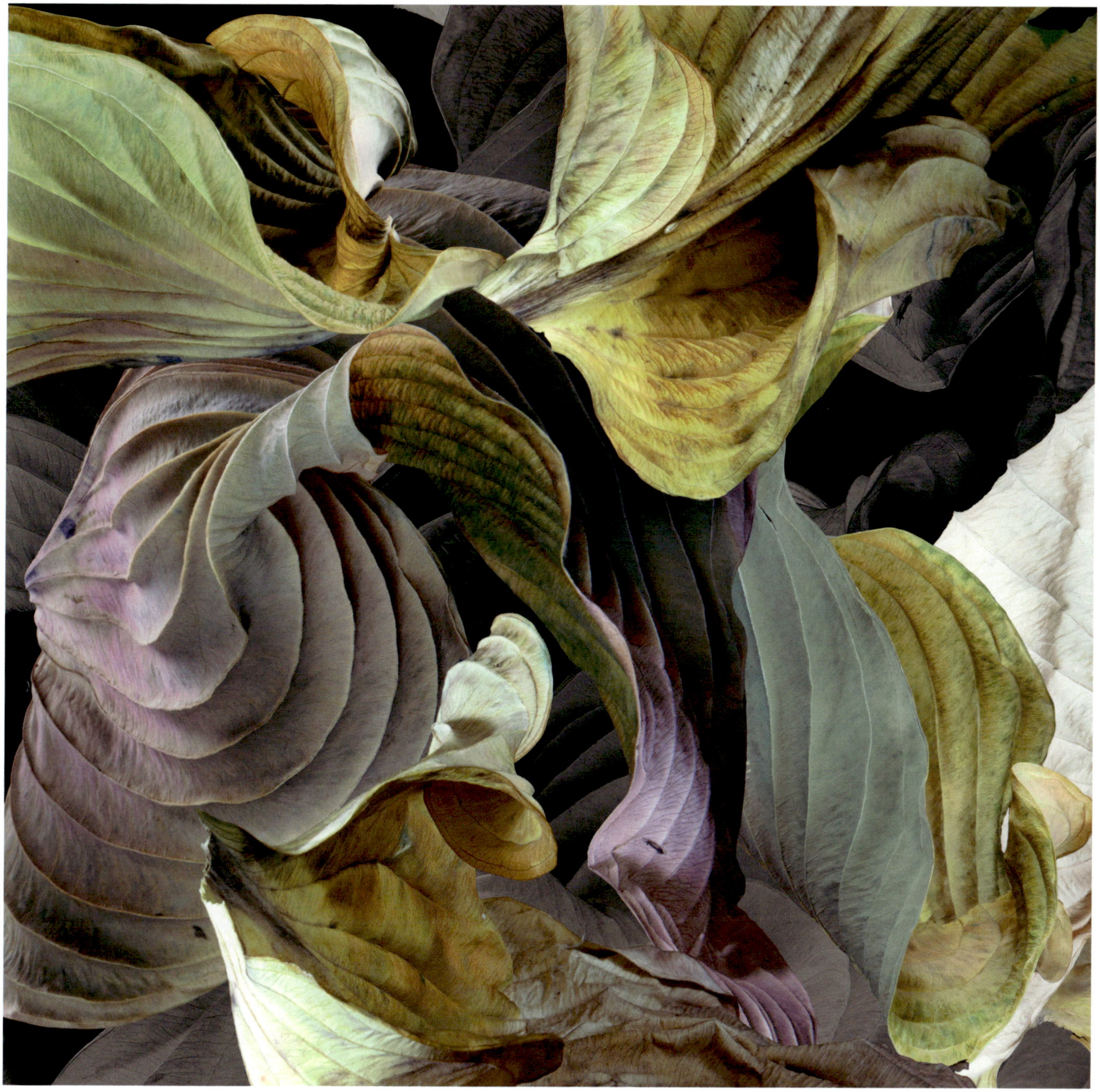

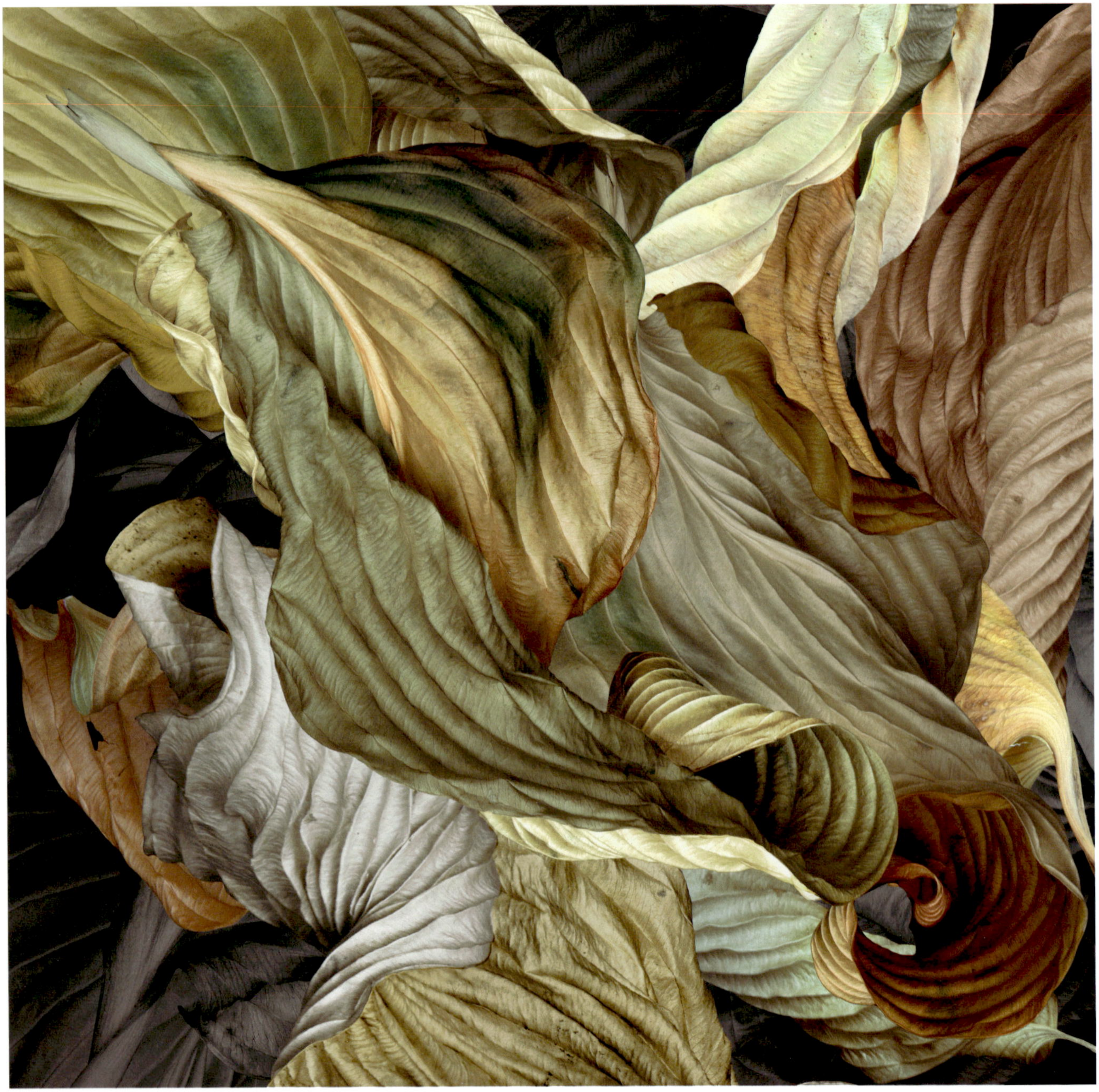

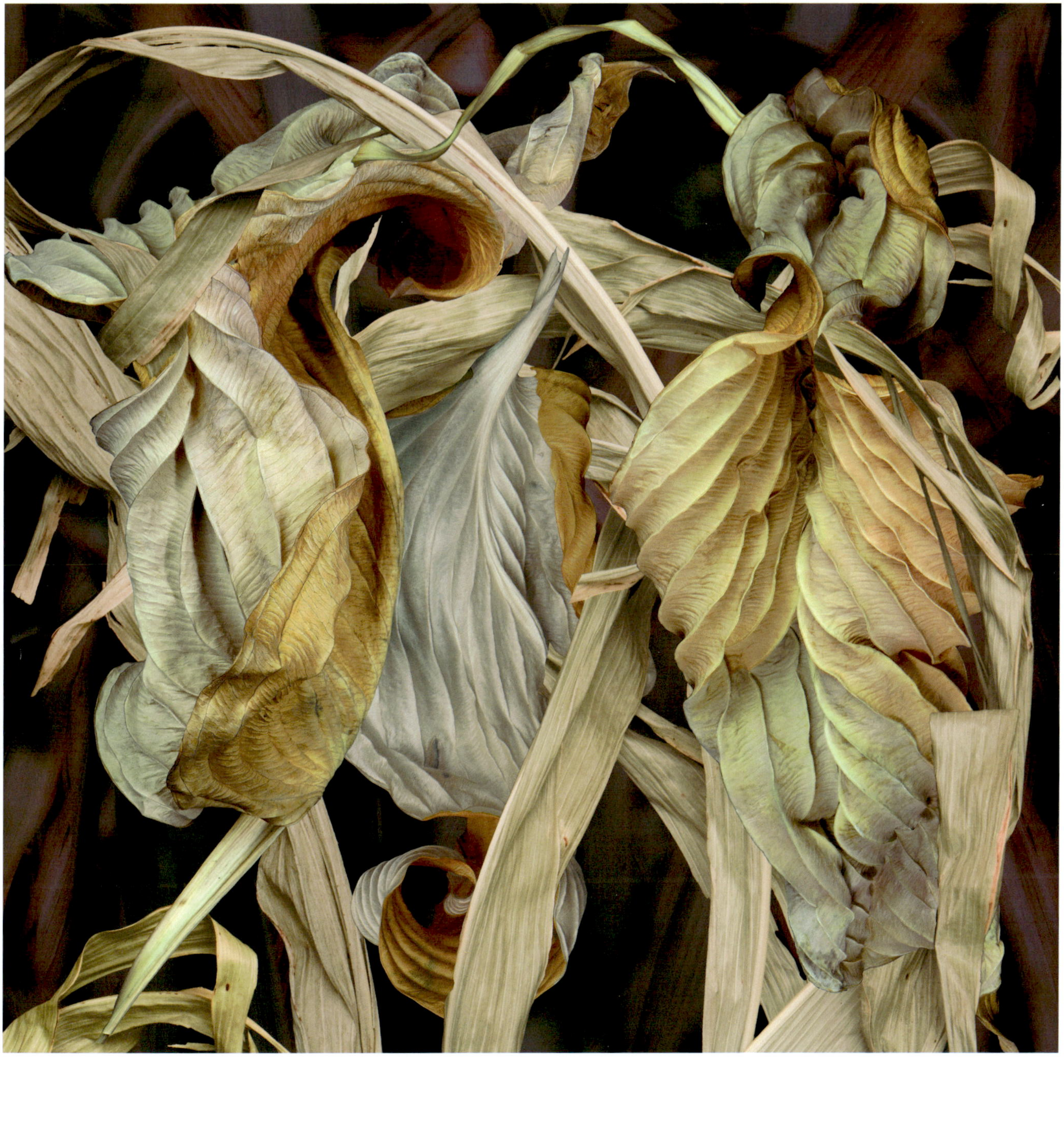

Into the Woods: A Pathless Pleasure

by Joanne Scherf

www.joannescherf.com • joanne@joannescherf.com

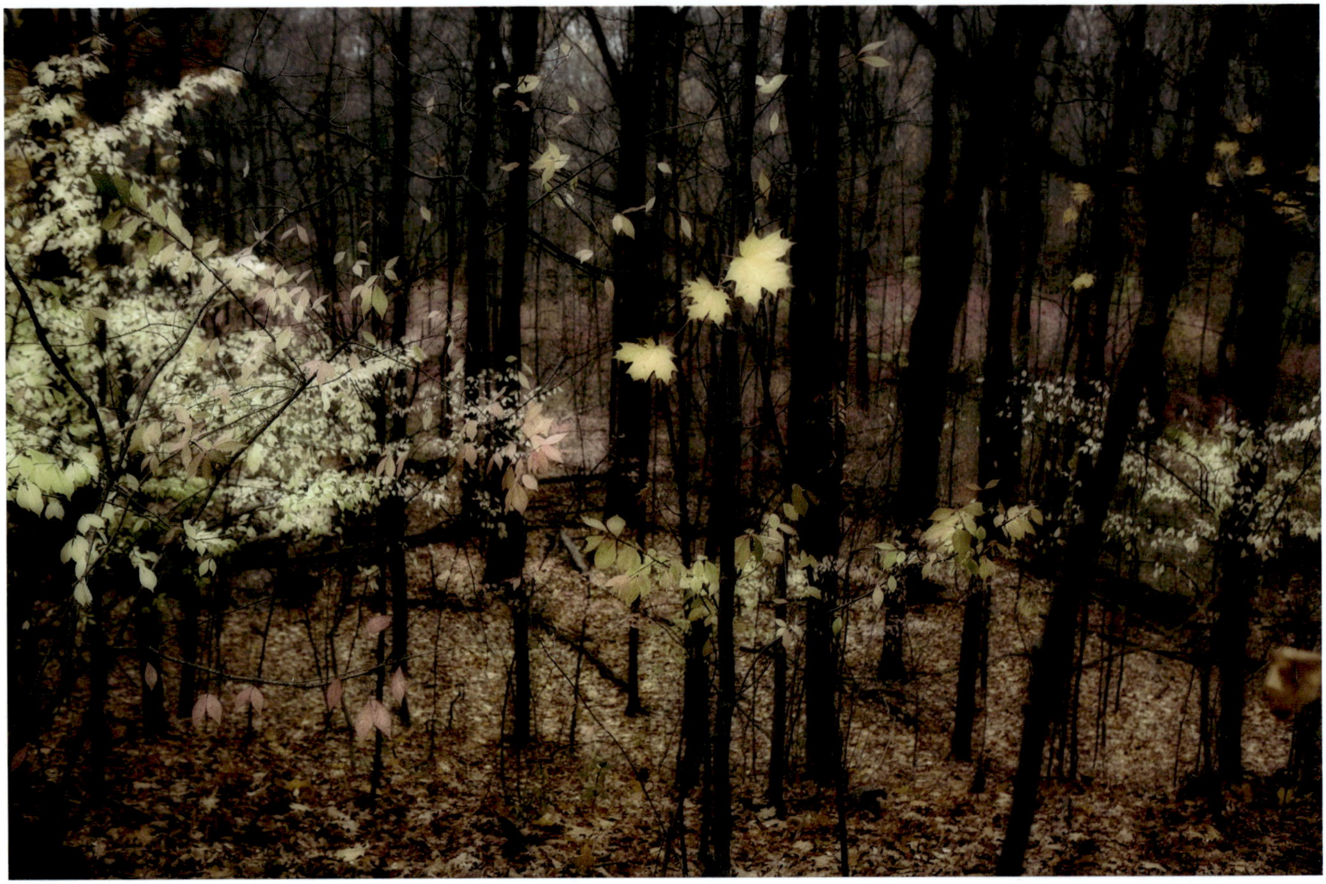

A visit to my mother's gravesite is a familiar place that offers many opportunities for serenity and joy in embracing the quiet solitude. On this day, as I made my way to the exit, I took a different route and found myself in an enchanted forest that bordered the cemetery. Standing atop the ridge, the scene before me was breathtaking—an absolute spectacle of dramatic and austere beauty with a hint of haunting elegance. Drawn to this priceless discovery by the spirit of my mother, I was inspired to create images that convey the essence of her soul.

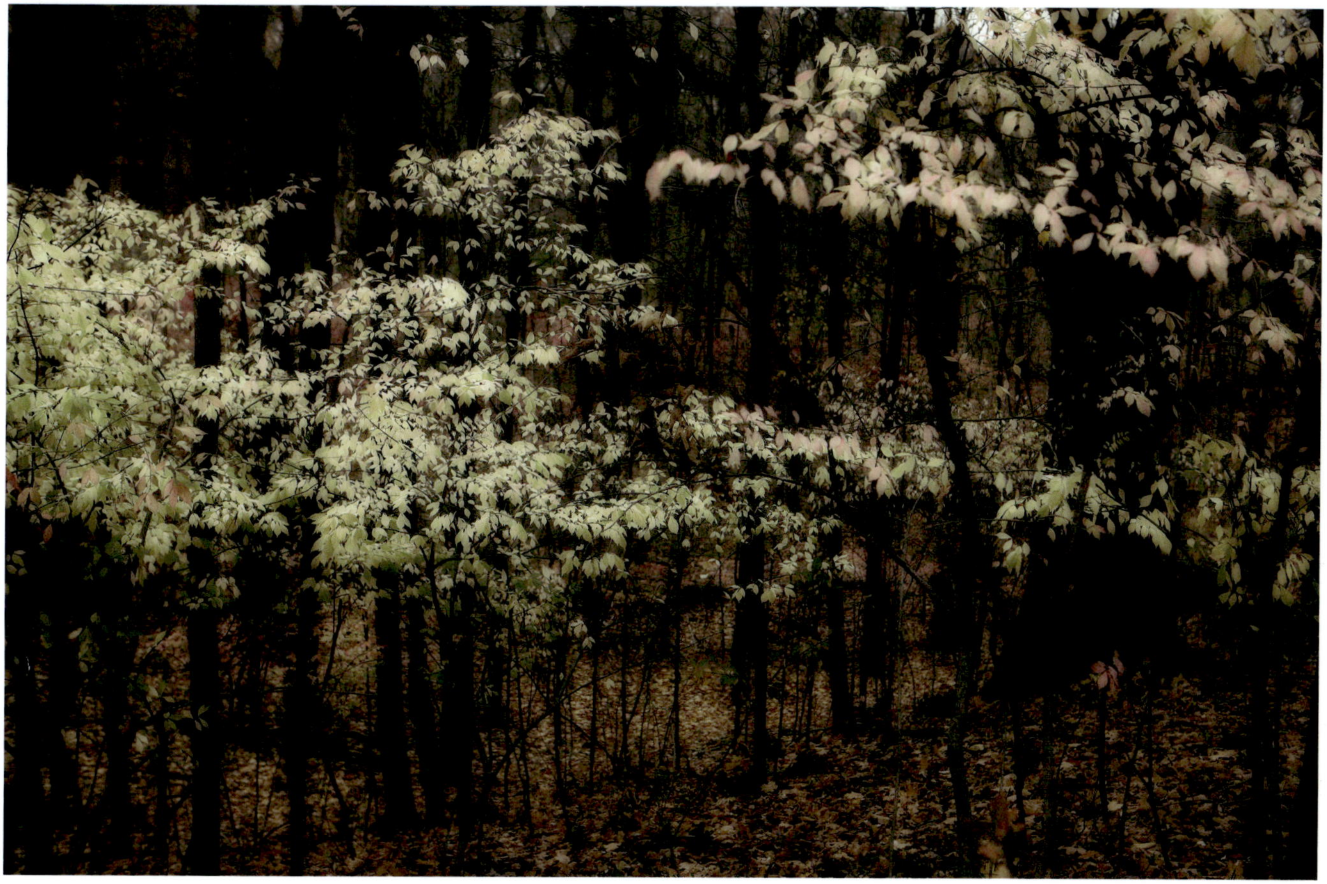

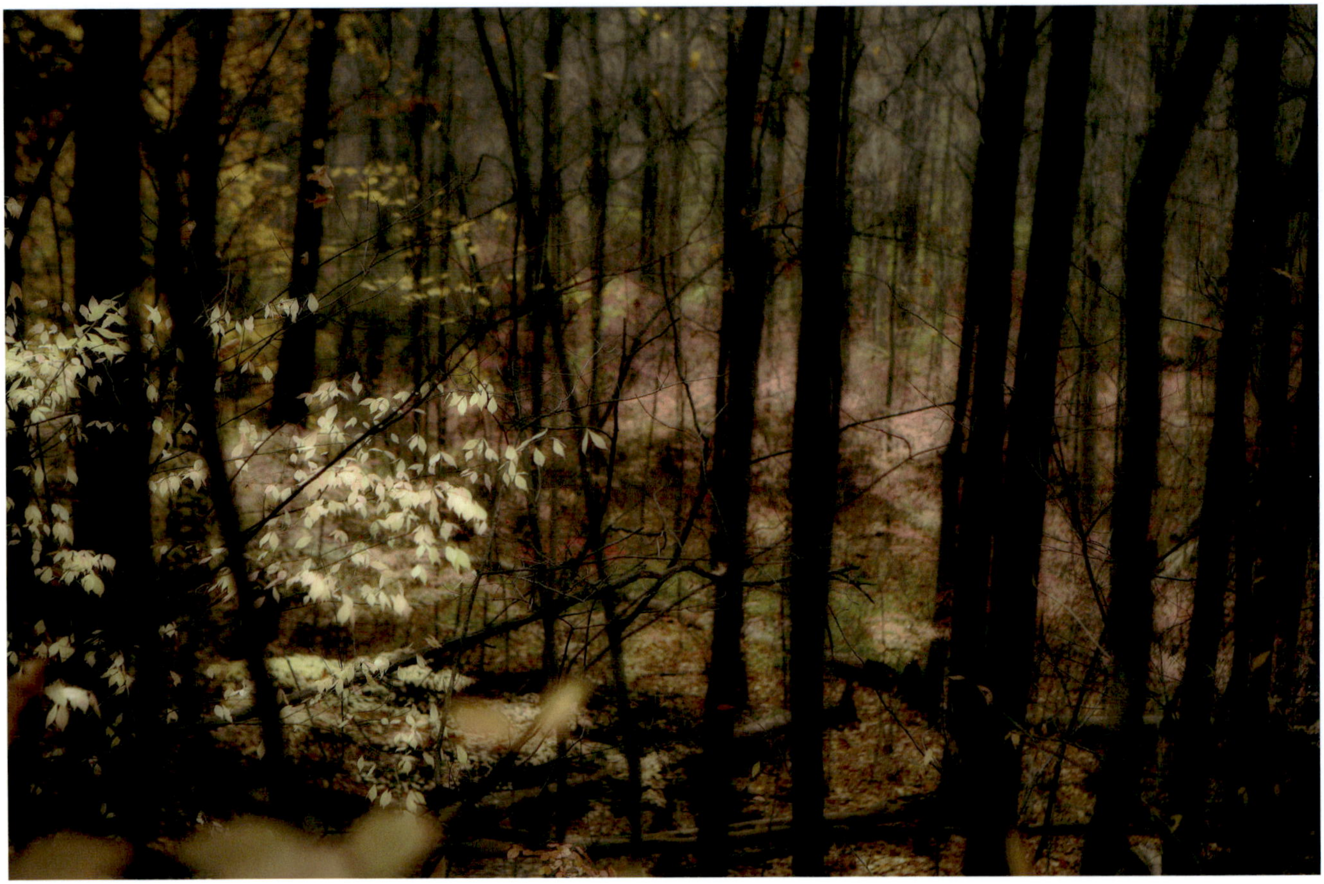

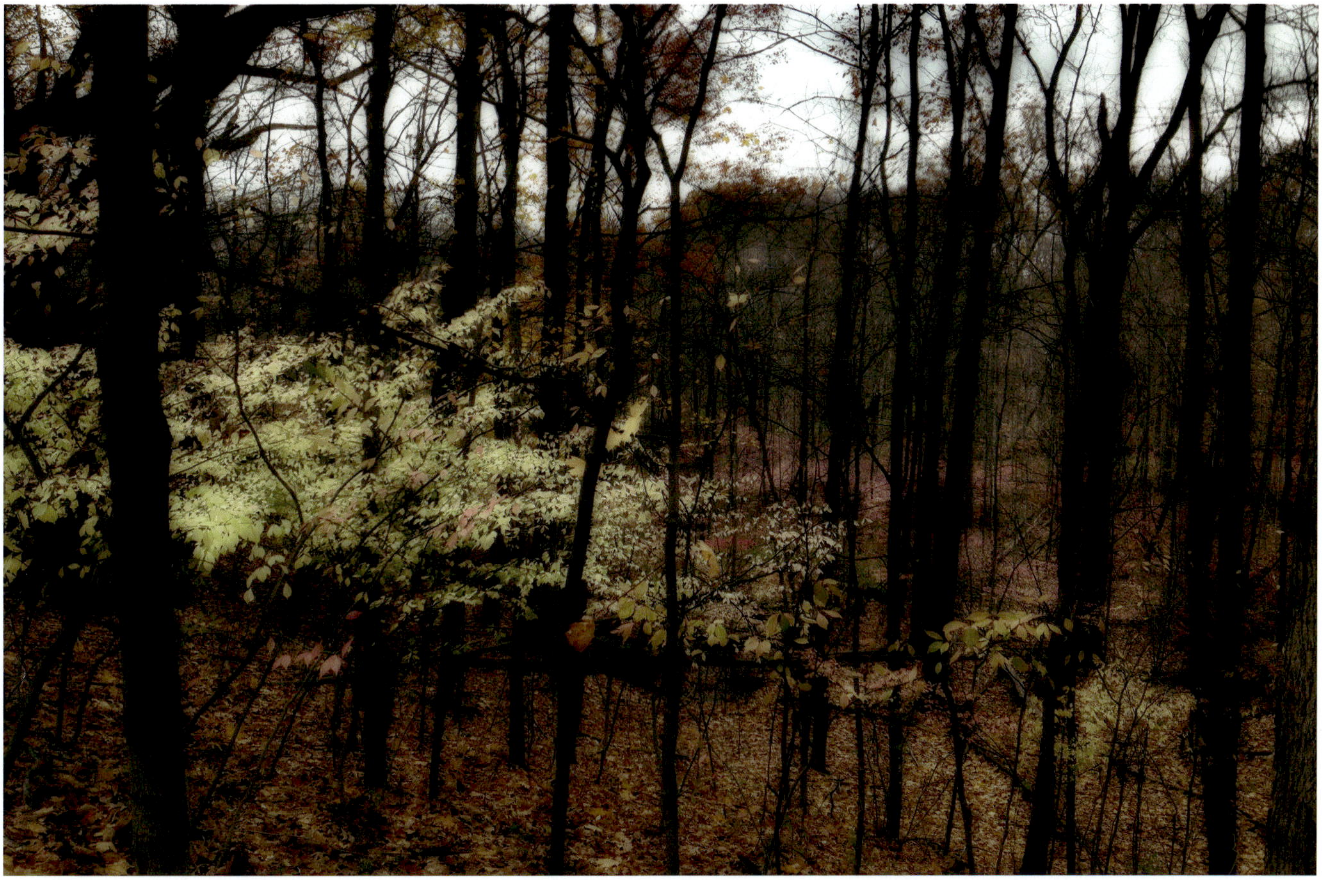

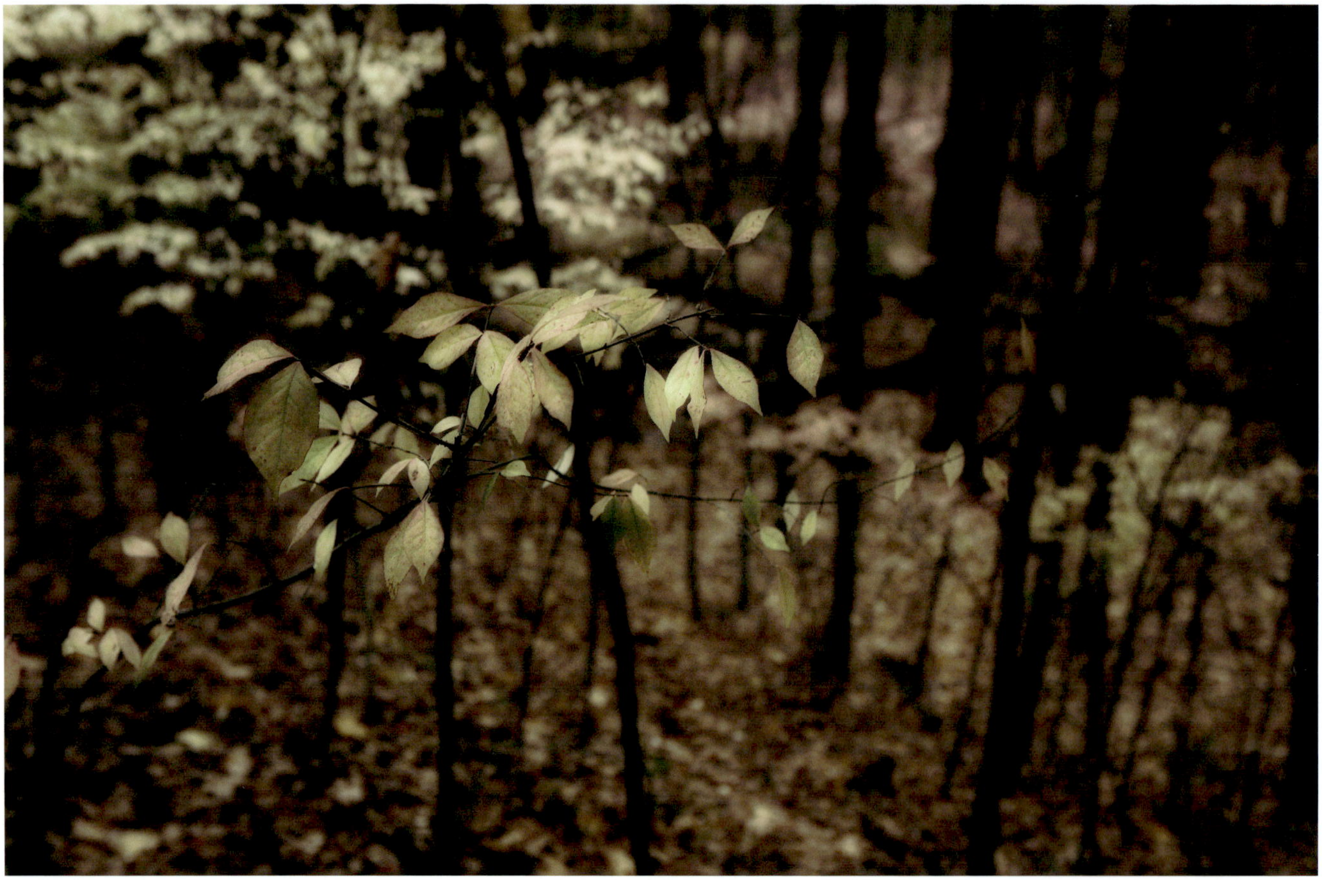

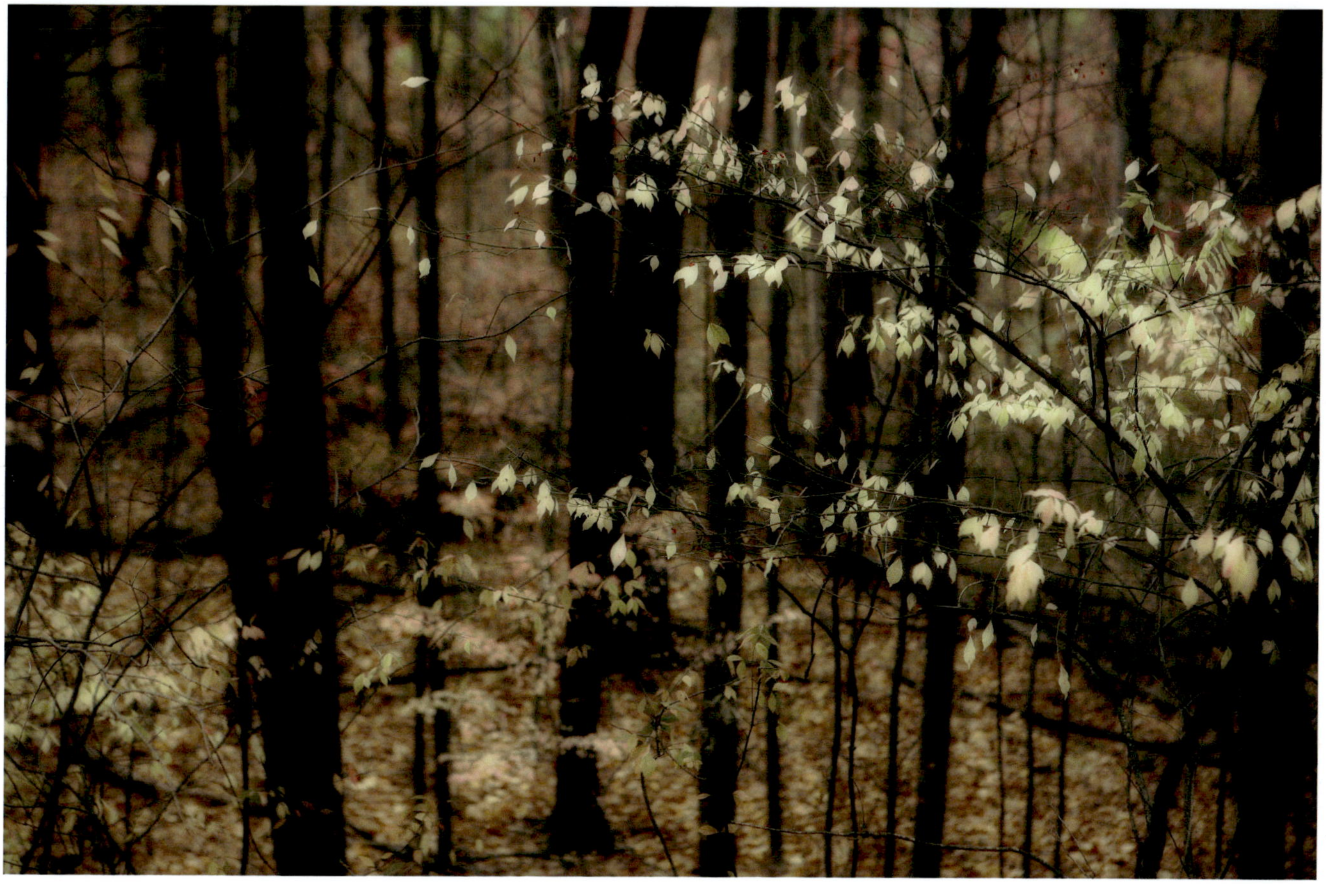

Rogue River Illuminists

by Lewis Anderson

www.lewisanderson.net • madzub@lewisanderson.net

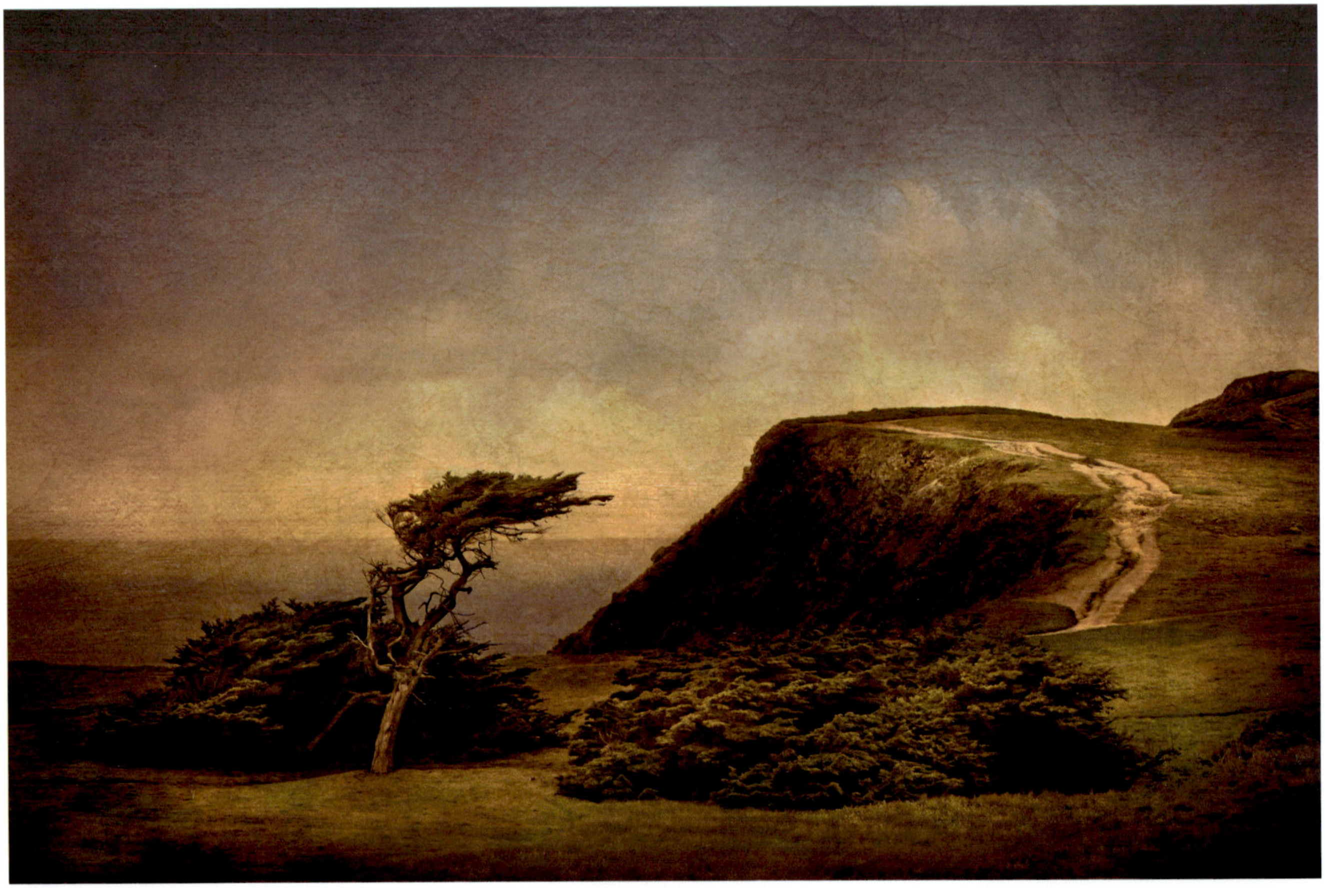

Cypress Road

This series is an homage to the romantic Illuminist painters of the Hudson River Valley School. They were convinced that if one looked deeply enough at the landscape one could see the Divine. Seems like a lofty ideal worthy of consideration and emulation. The Illuminists were also some of the first artists to make work in purposeful pairs and small series. They used the natural landscape to communicate a deeper allegorical meaning found not only in each individual painting but a more complete narrative when all the individual pieces are seen in juxtaposition to each other in the series.

My heart seems to resonate with the magnificence of nature and especially with pastoral landscapes. In my effort to avoid the dreaded "post card effect," and to infuse something more, I have purposely hung my images on that fine line between a painting and a photograph.

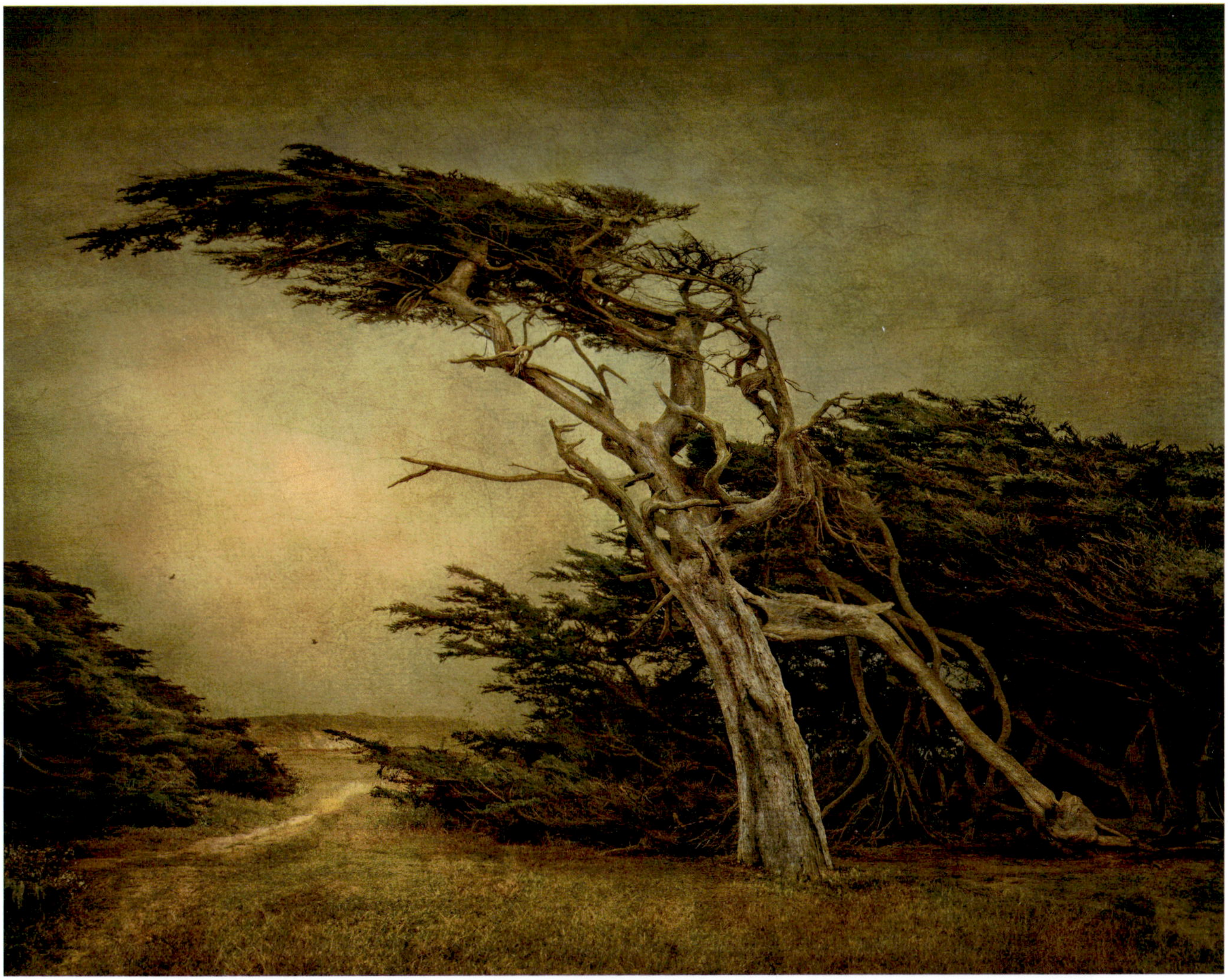

Bodega Way

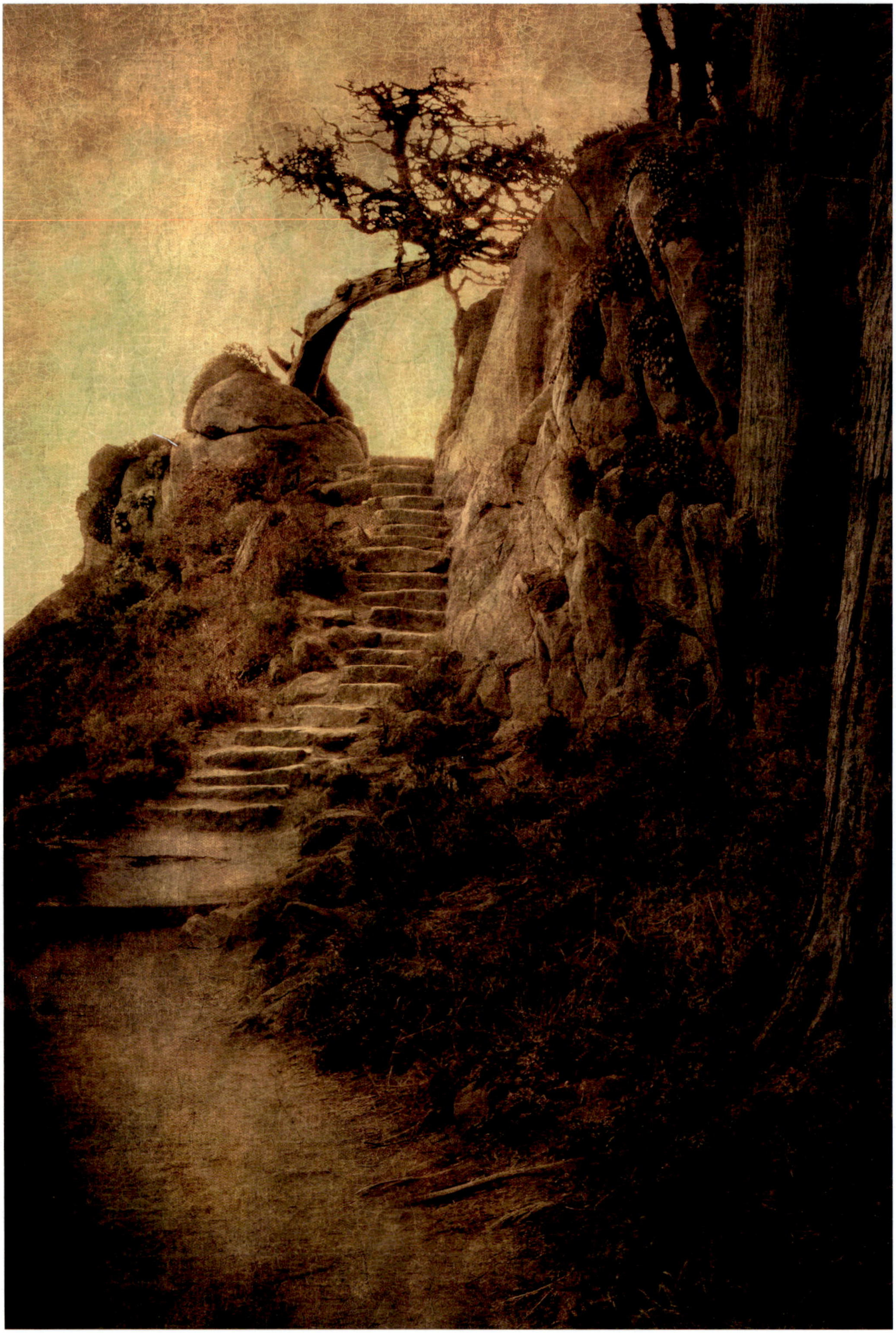

Ingress

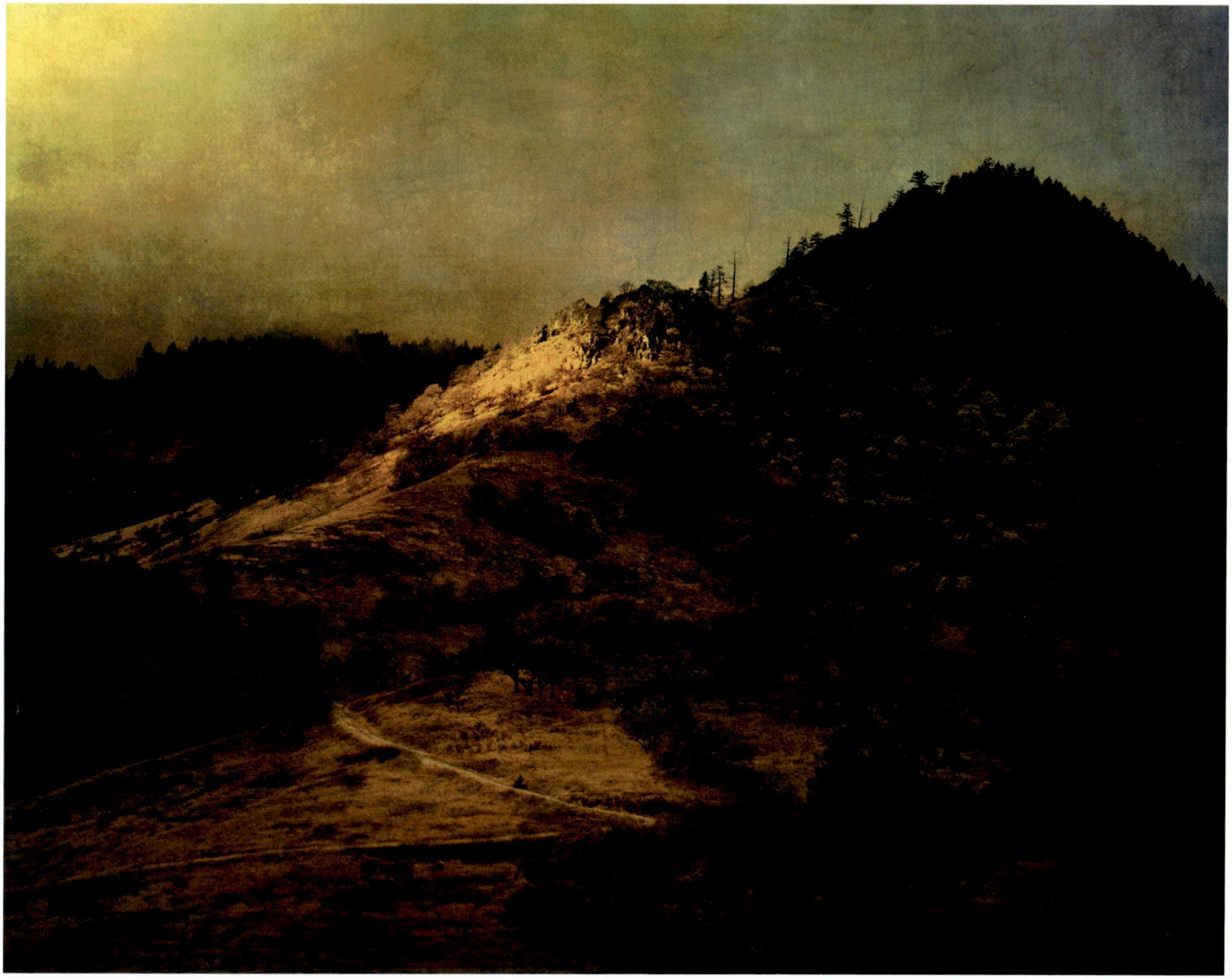

Guided Again

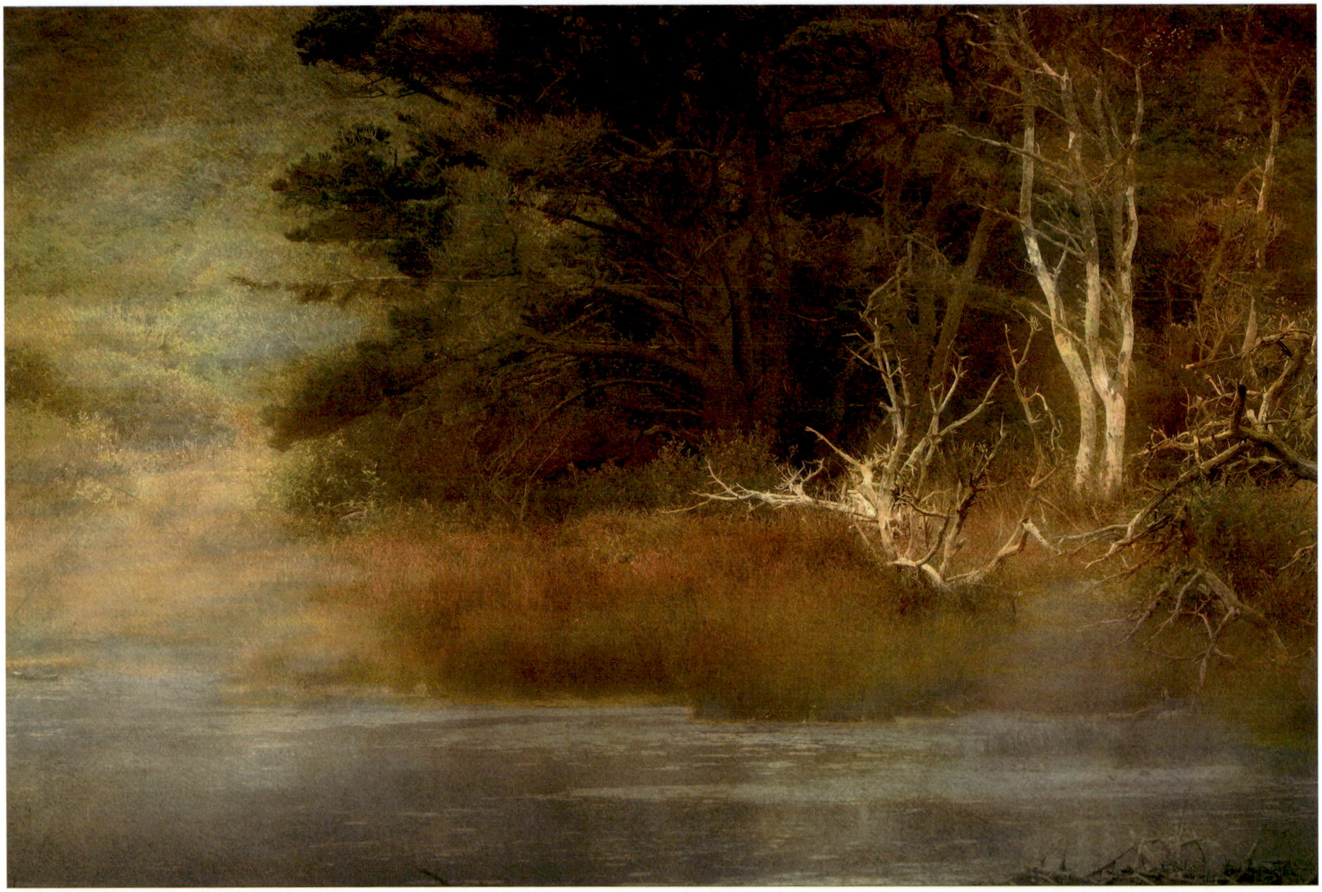

Coastal Swamp

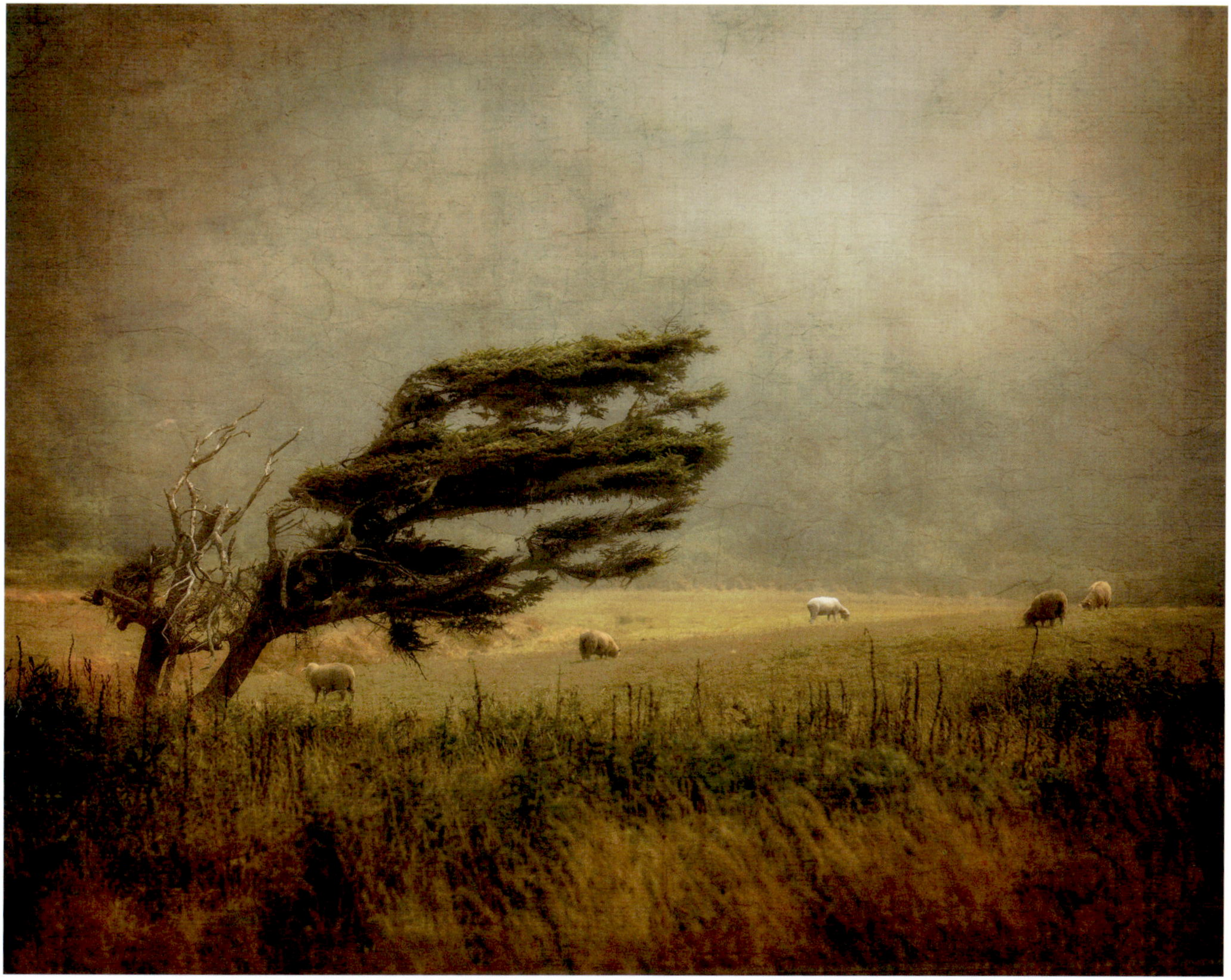

Scotland, Oregon

Reflected Glories

by Julius Kassovic

www.photojulius.com ♦ jkbiz4@yahoo.com

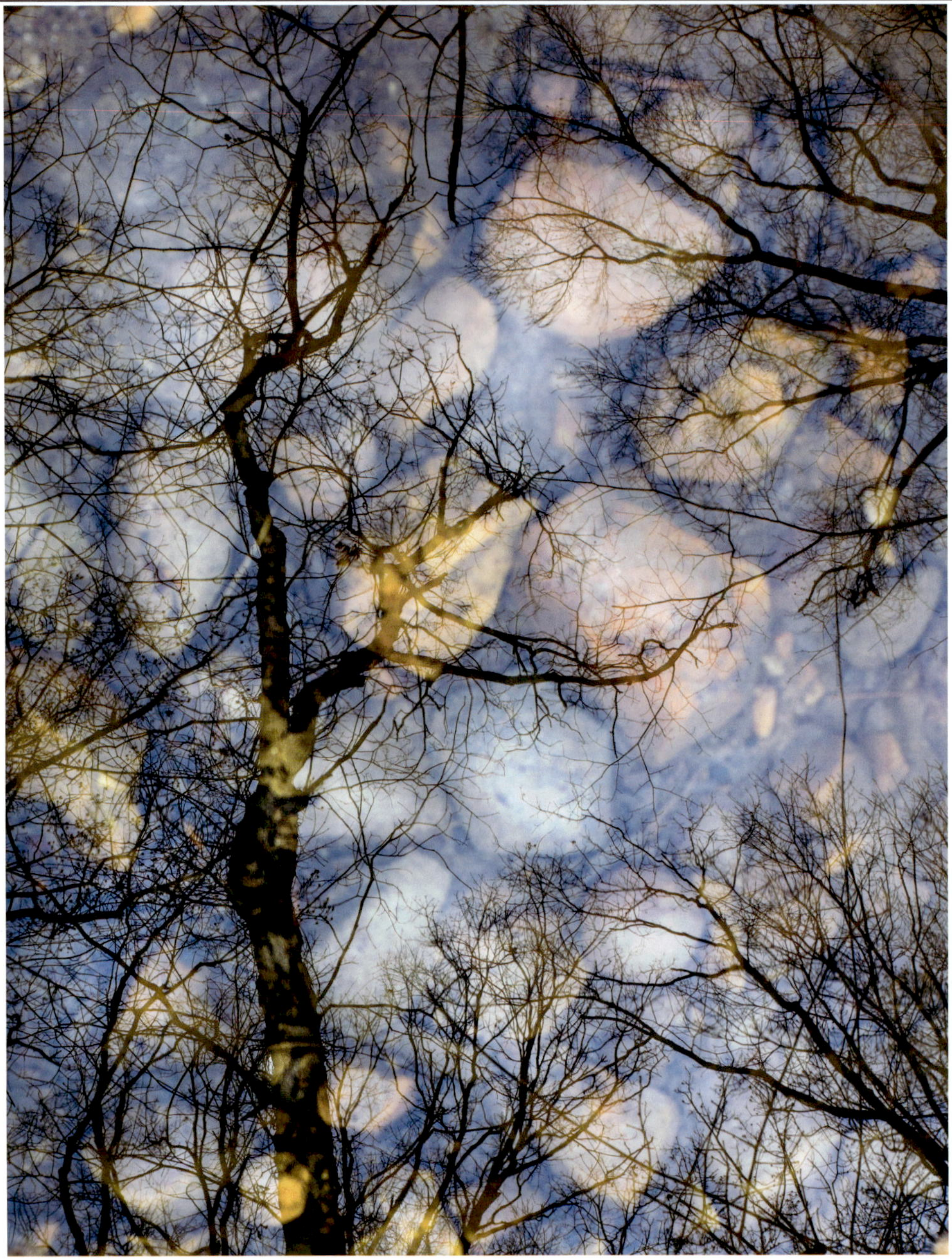

Petrous

Trees overhang a shallow waterway. Sometimes reflected, sometimes casting tree-shaped shadows, their images blend with the water, rocks, leaves, and creek bottom.

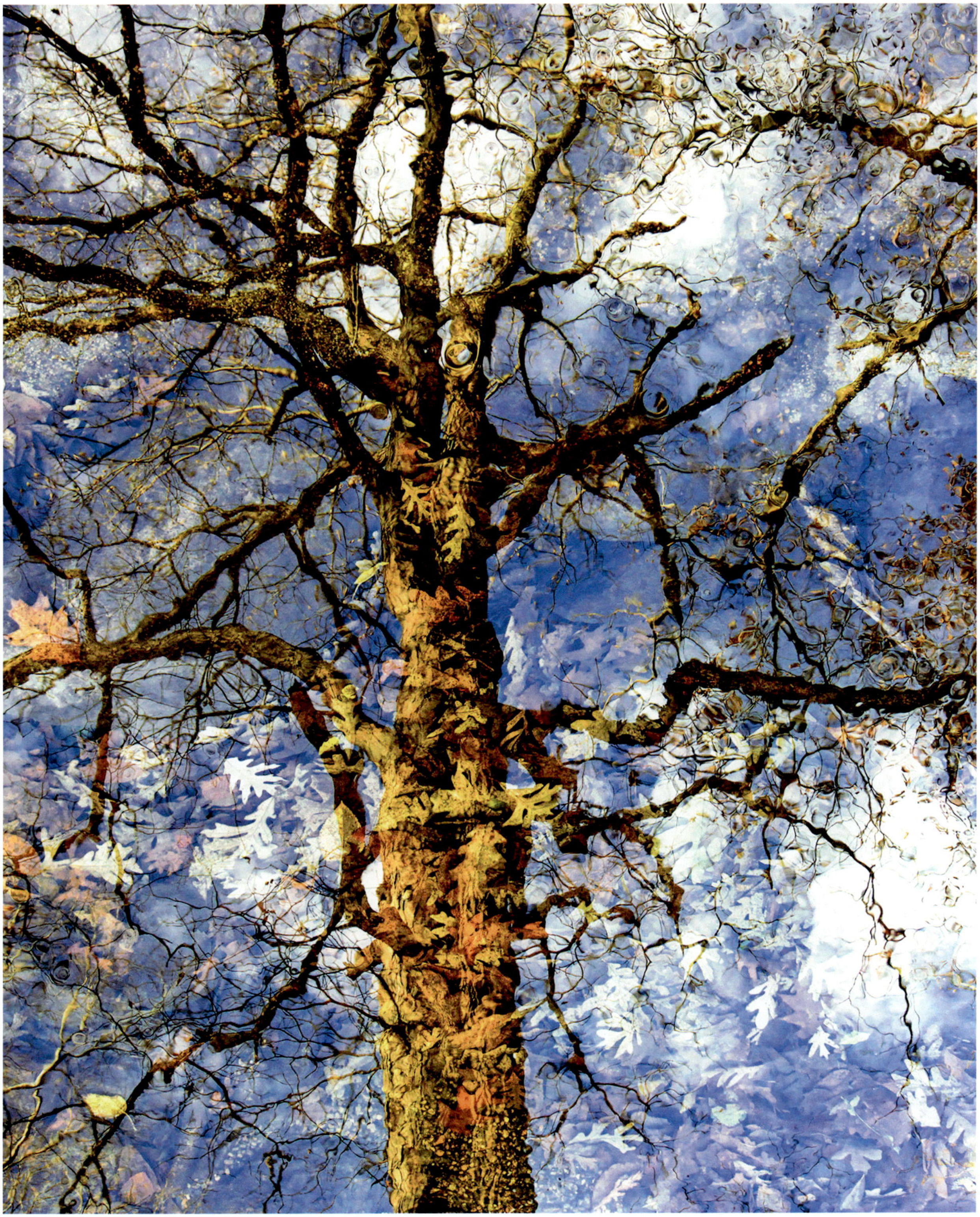

Vestment

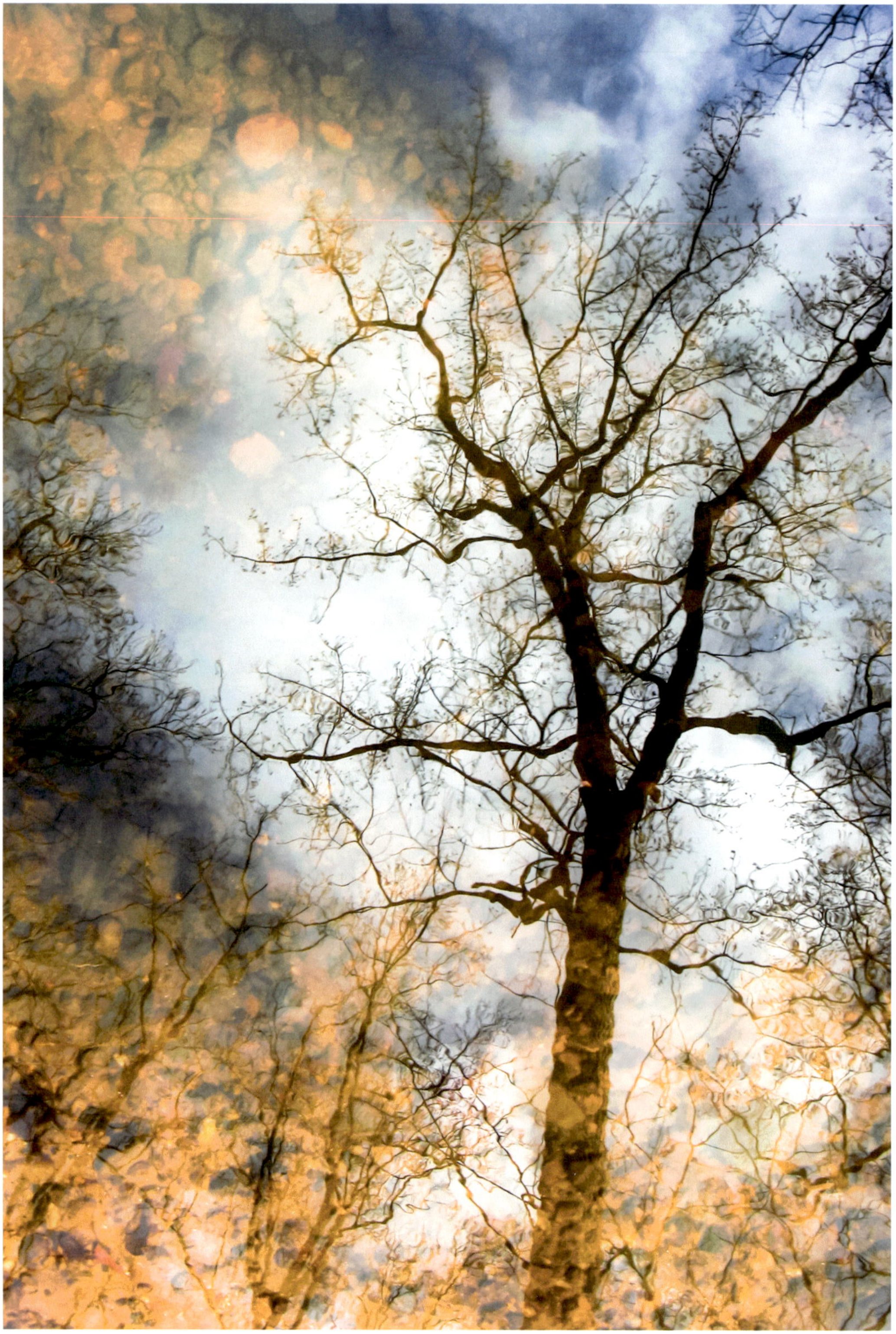

Dorado

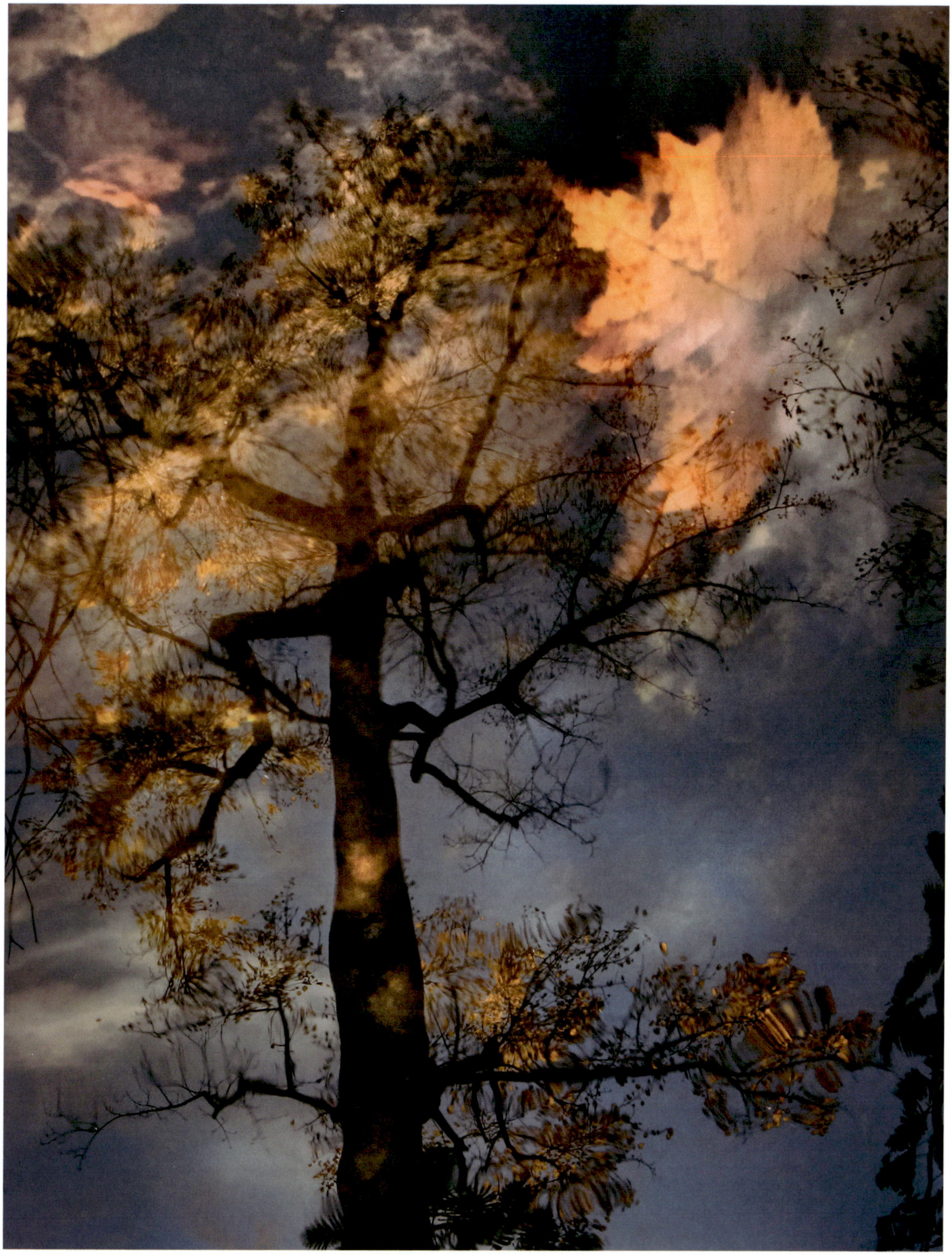
Gloaming

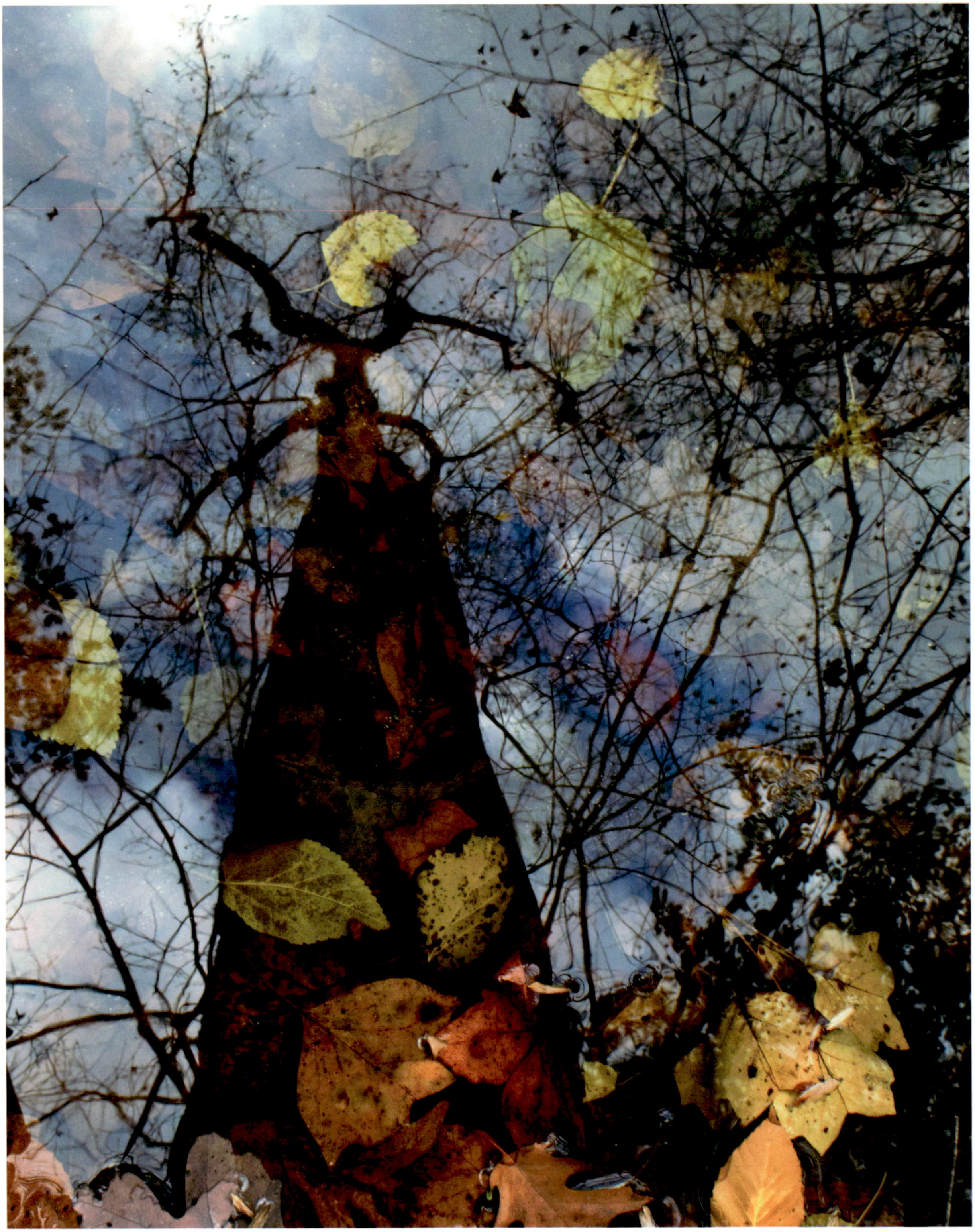

Obelisk

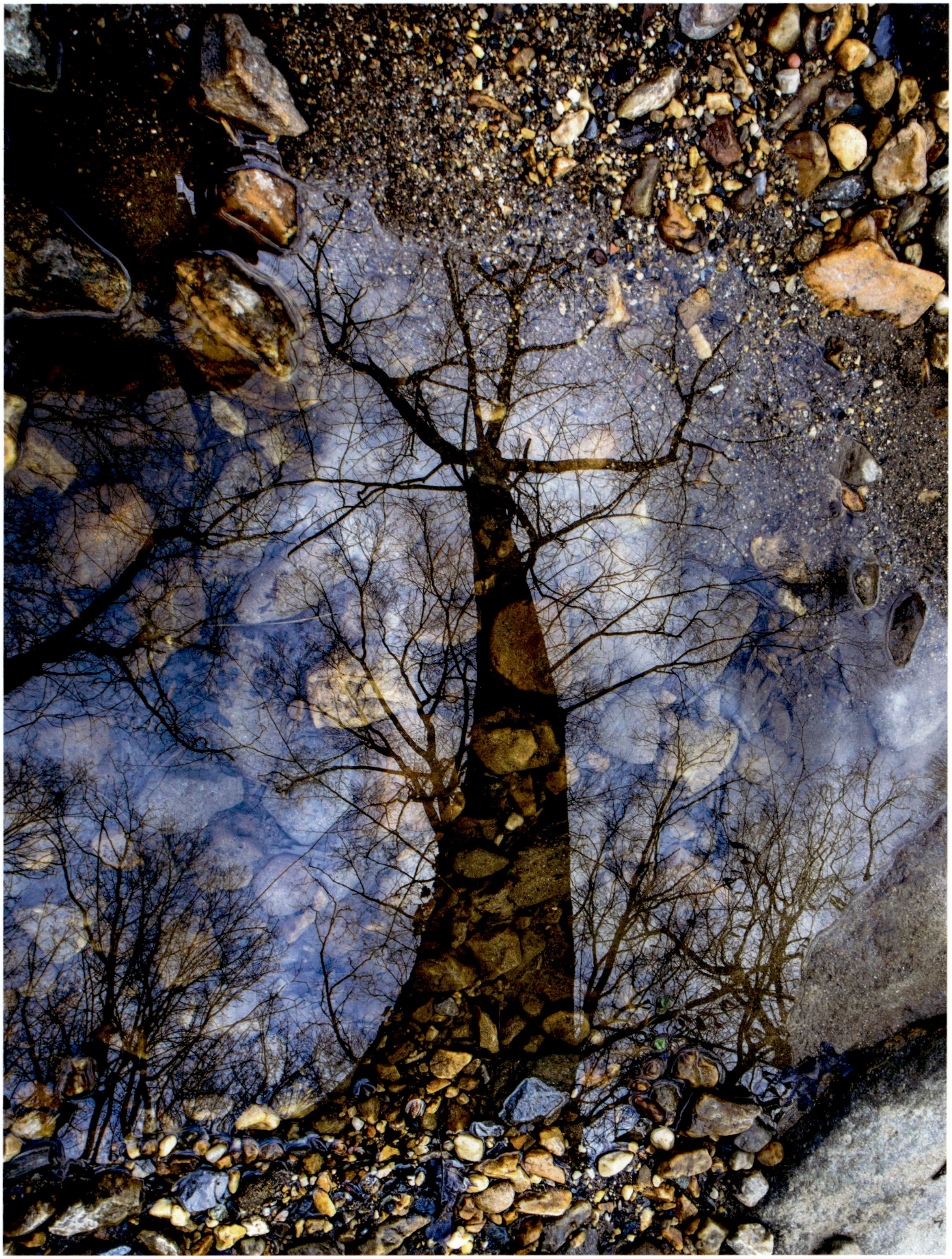

Lithic

Water Tapestry Triptychs

by Lisa Redburn
www.lisaredburn.com • lisa.redburn@gmail.com

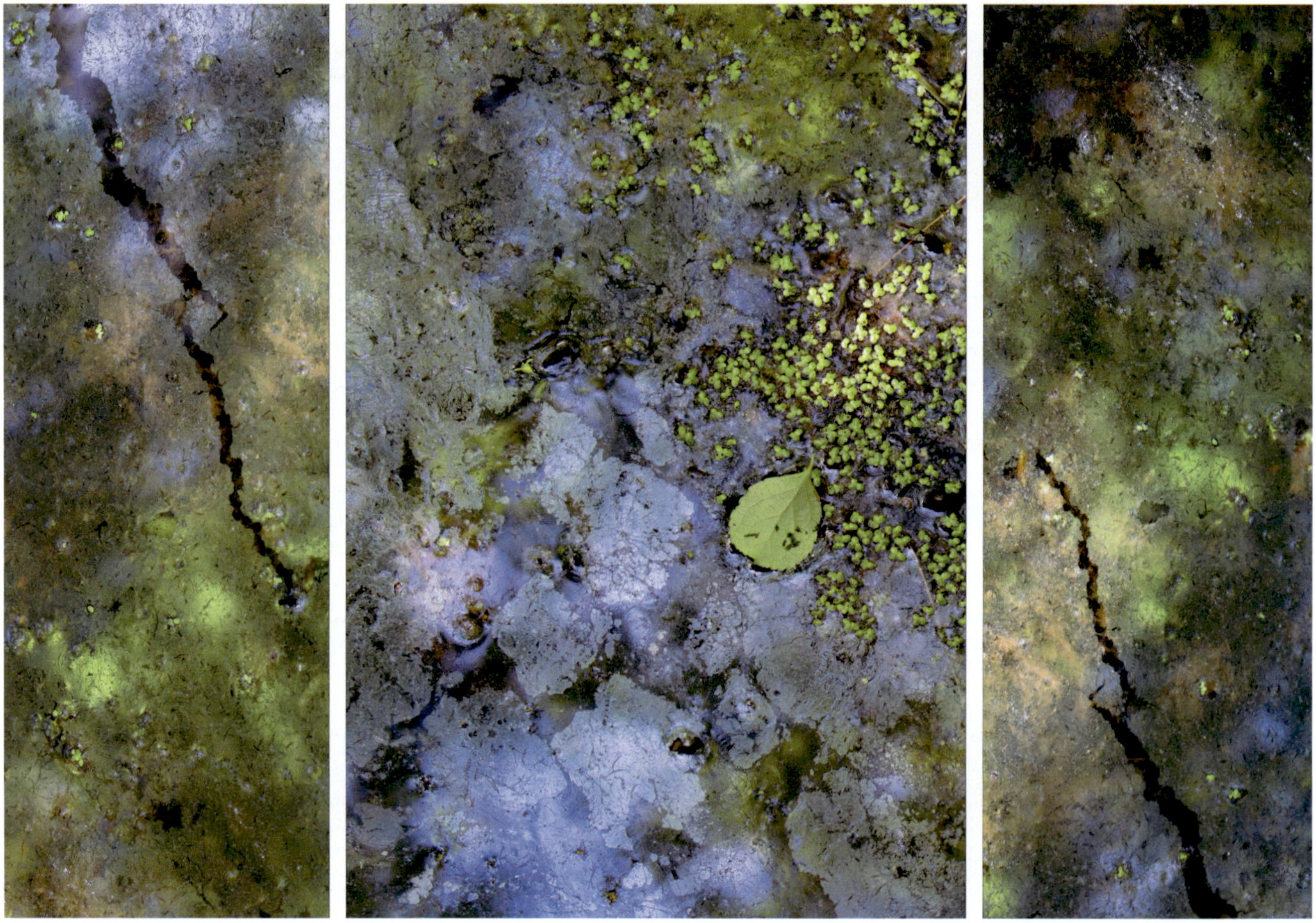

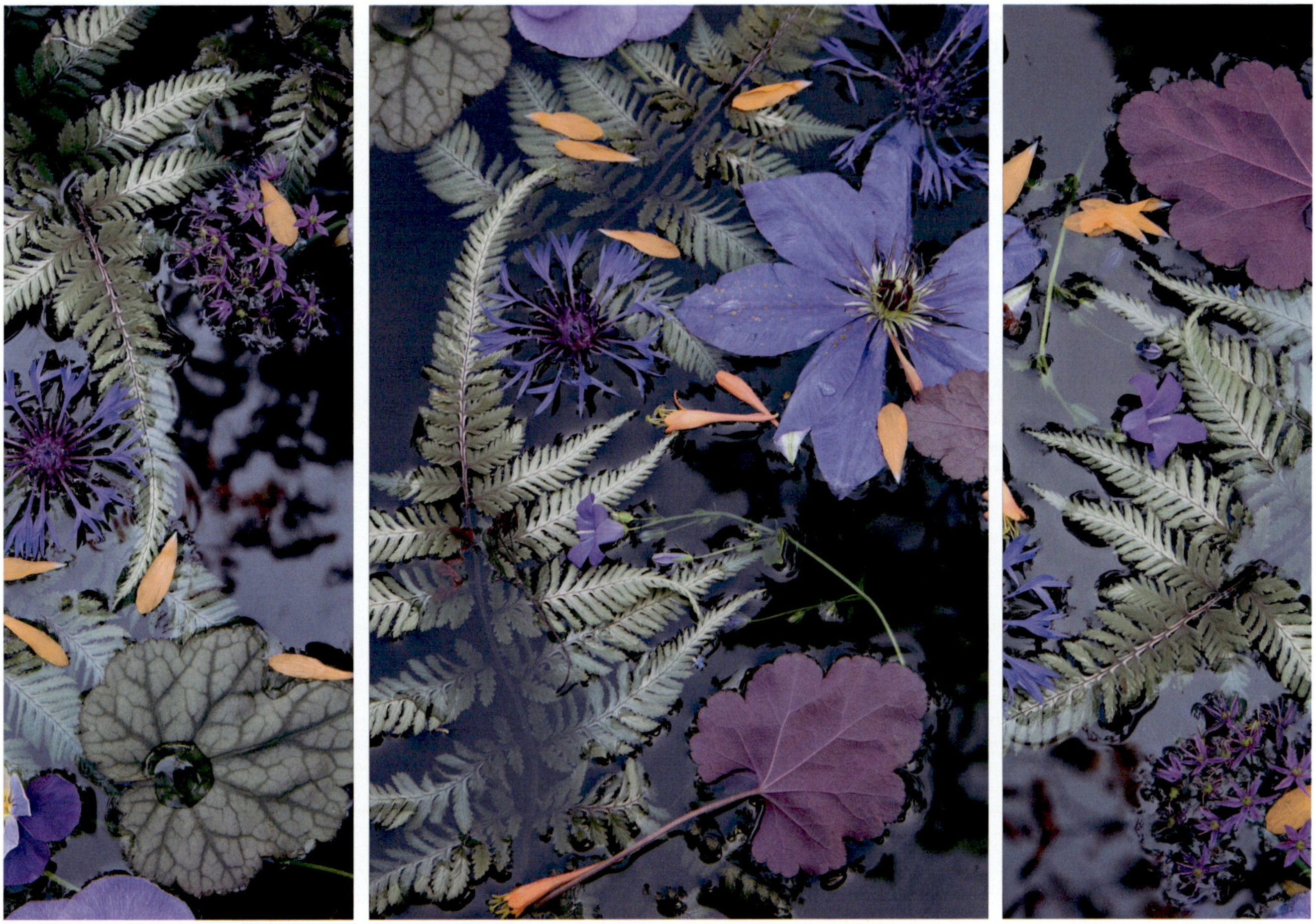

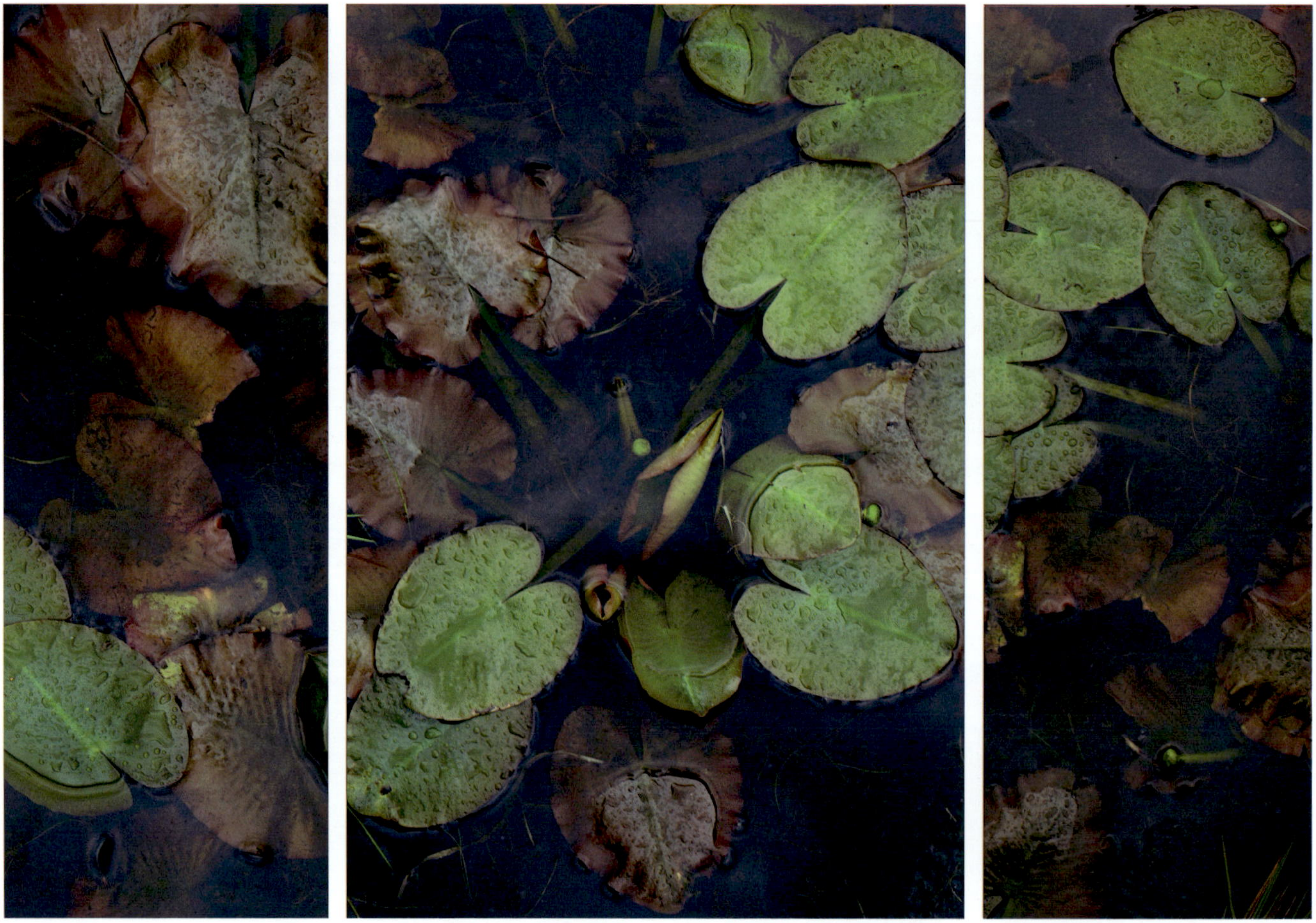

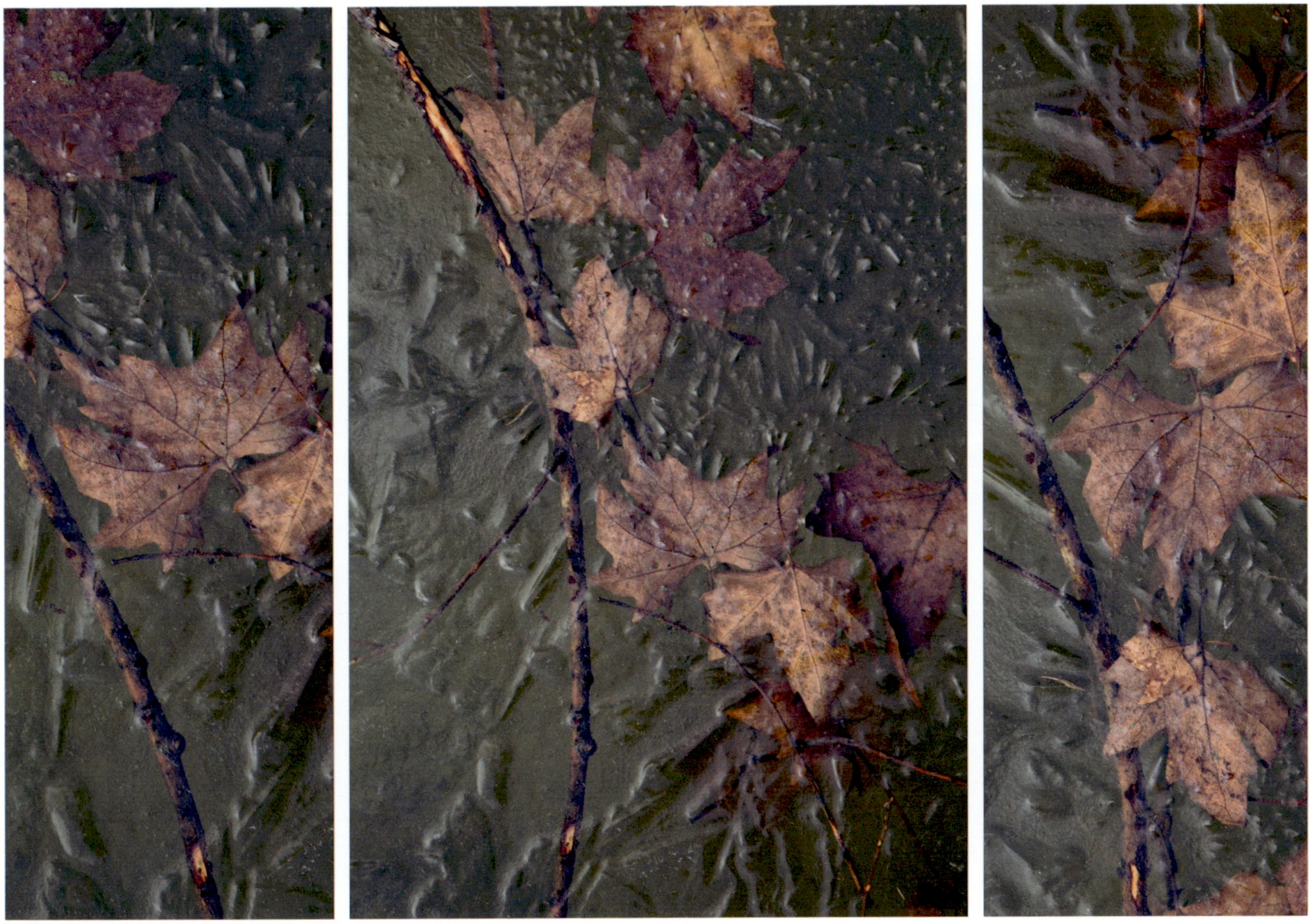

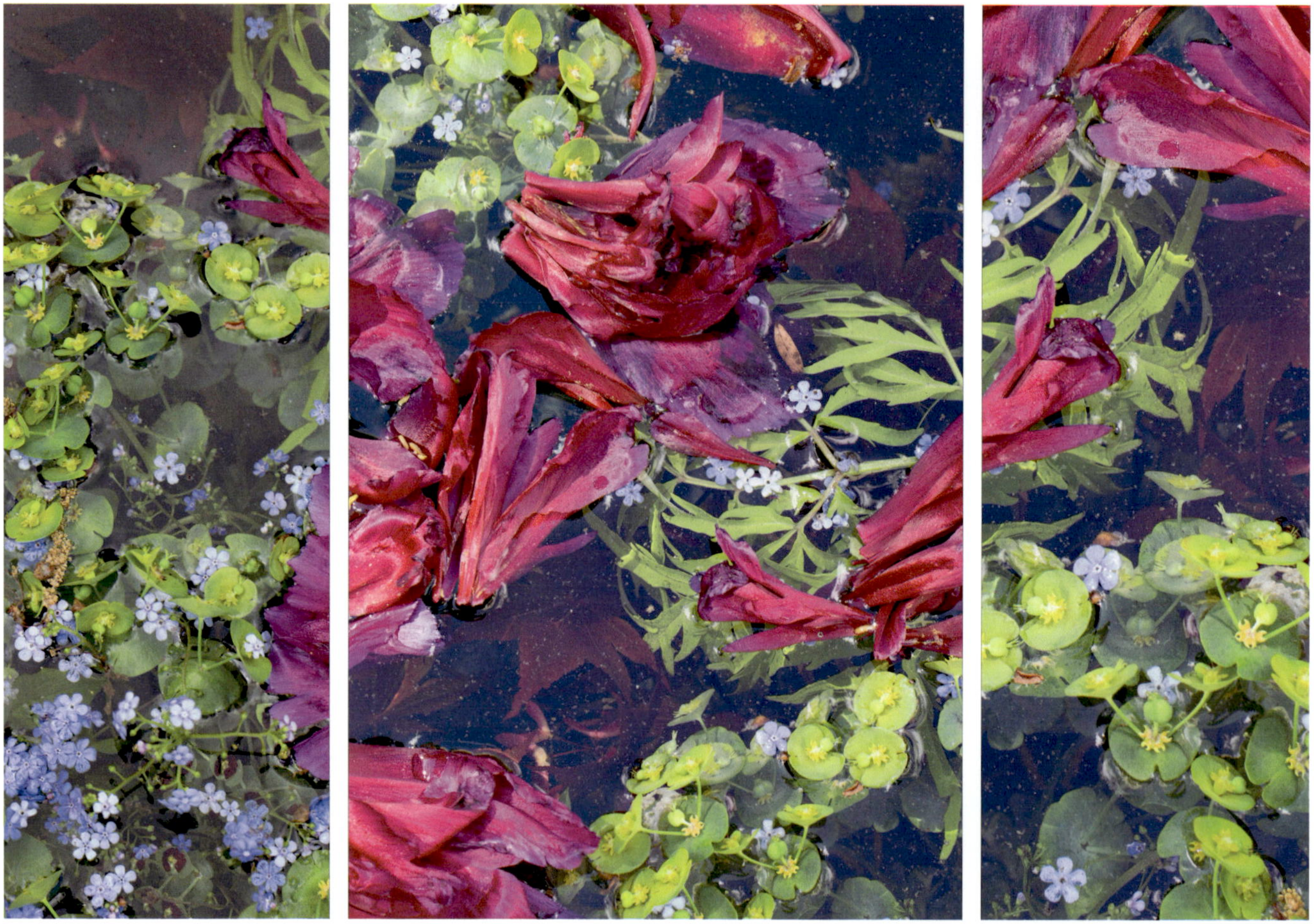

My camera lens is my looking glass into evanescent wonderlands. I'm particularly drawn to water scenes where the boundaries between real and reflected are fluid. And where layered beauty is revealed in the shifting relationships between the richly textured surface, the reflections from above, and the mysteries below. Much of my imagery includes leaves, which so vividly evoke the cycles of life.

I often shoot in overlooked places, where I find intriguing juxtapositions and ambiguous stories. In swampy spots, the interplay of generations of growth and decay. In moving streams and ponds, the ballet of reflected trees and leaves. In winter landscapes, the tension of a world trapped in ice.

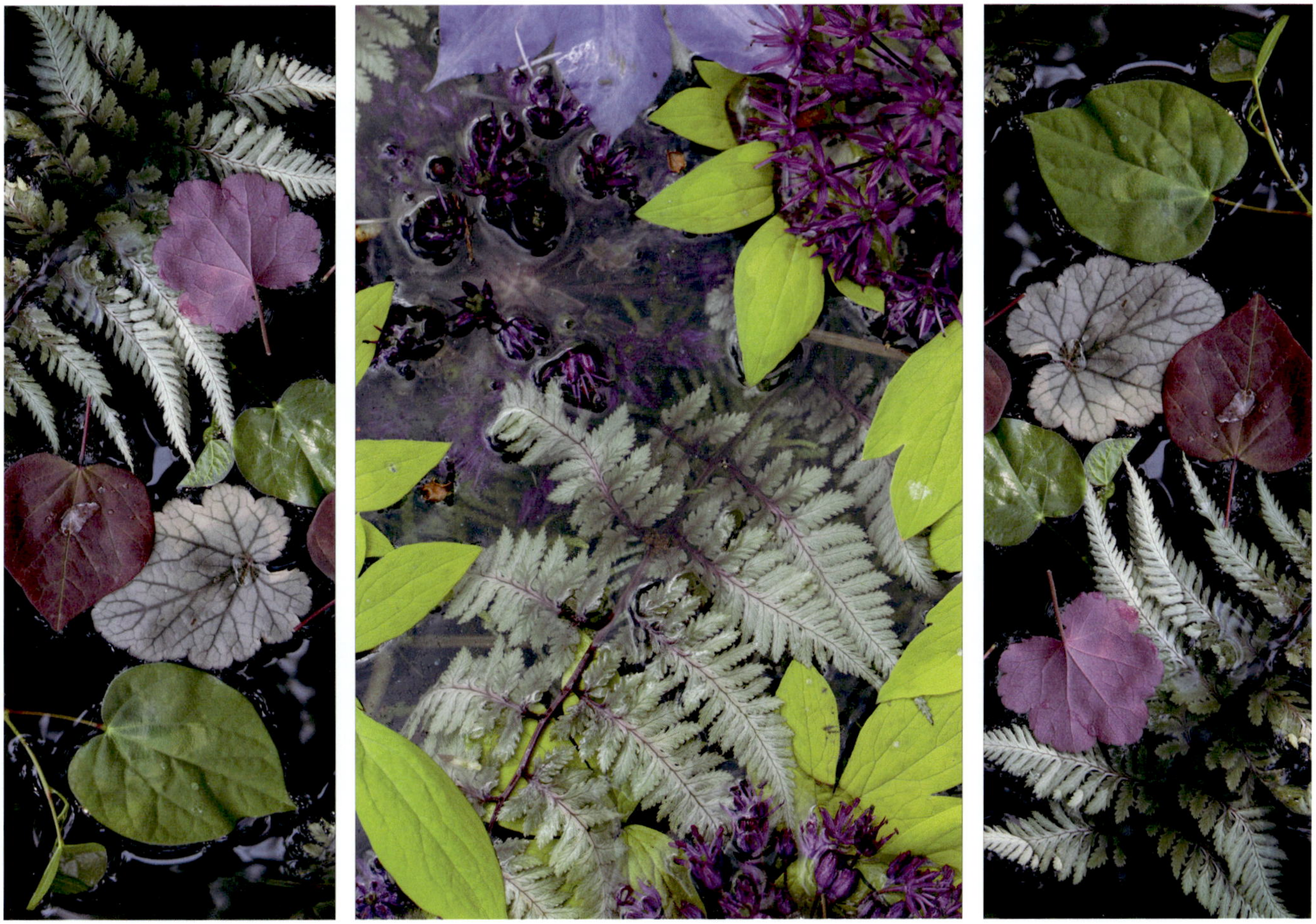

I also shoot in my garden, where I create floating "still lifes" with leaves and flowers in my pond.

As I look at these scenes — in the wild and at home — I use my camera to create "water tapestries" of the shifting elements, spinning their stories and weaving them together. Light reflects color and illuminates patterns on the surface, but light and color also seem to emanate from deep within.

In this series, I've created triptychs with several of my water tapestry images, introducing a fresh dimension to the ways I'm exploring these interrelationships.

Succulent Garden

by Mark Wainer

markwainer.com • mark@markwainer.com

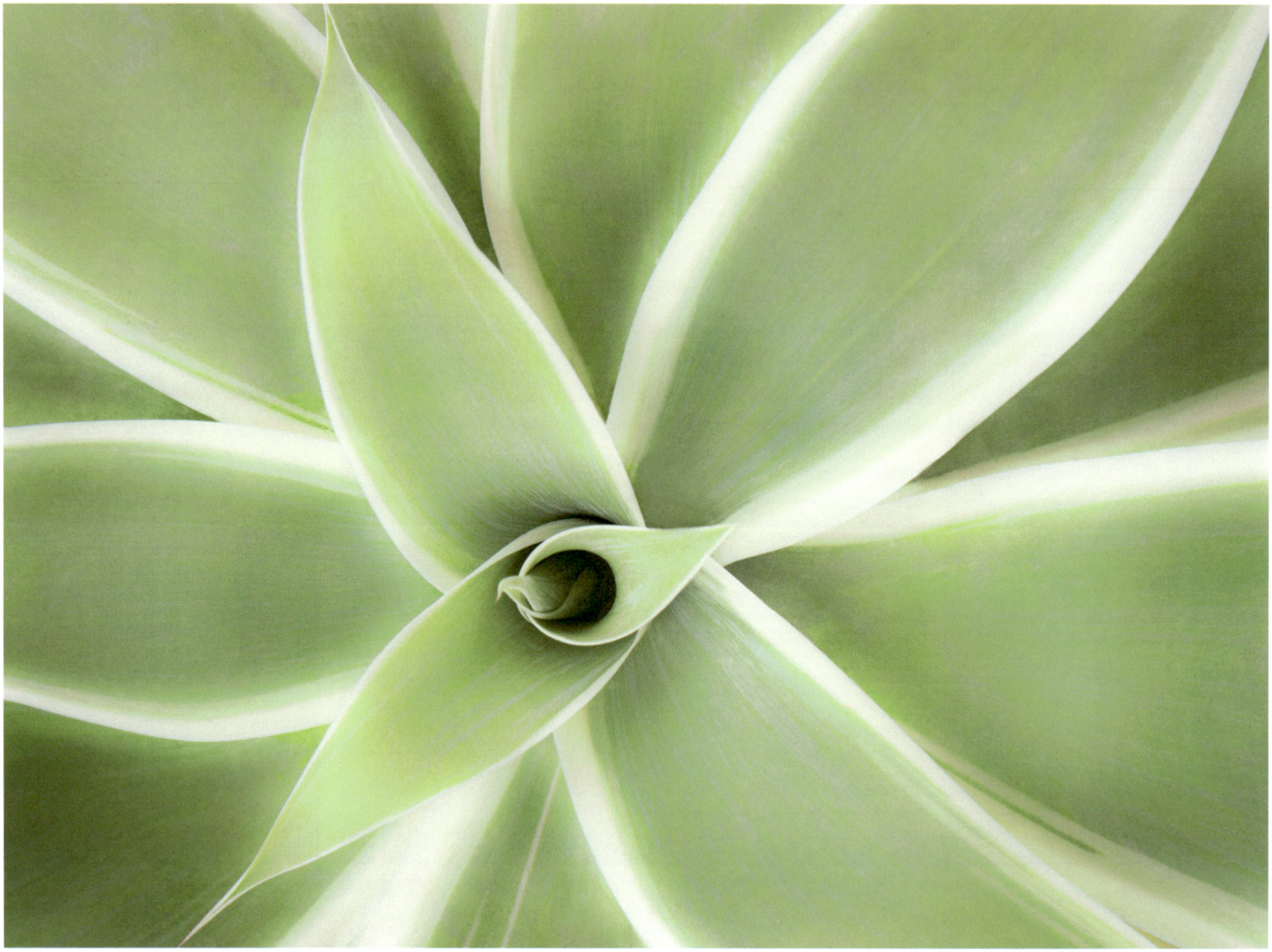

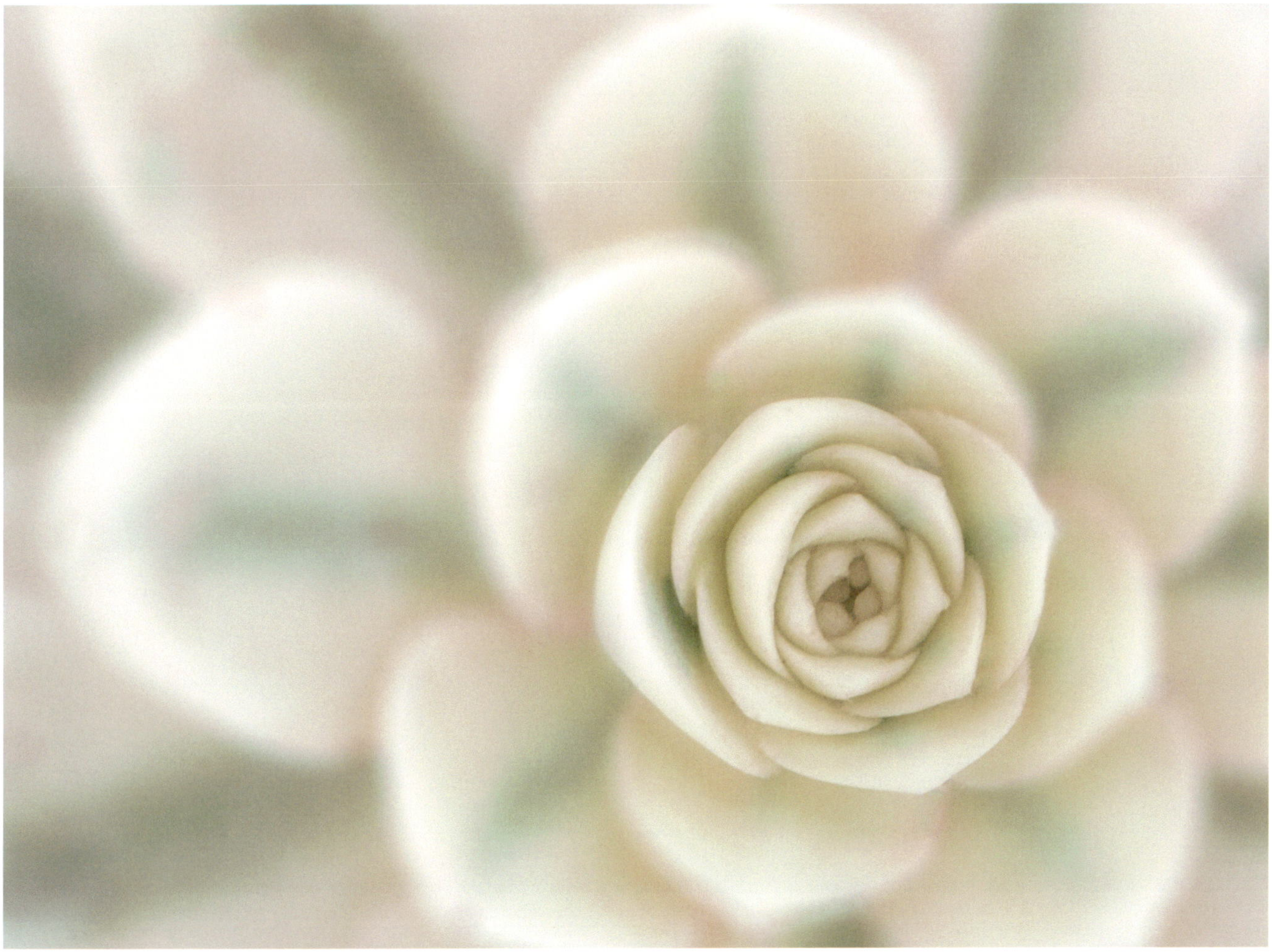

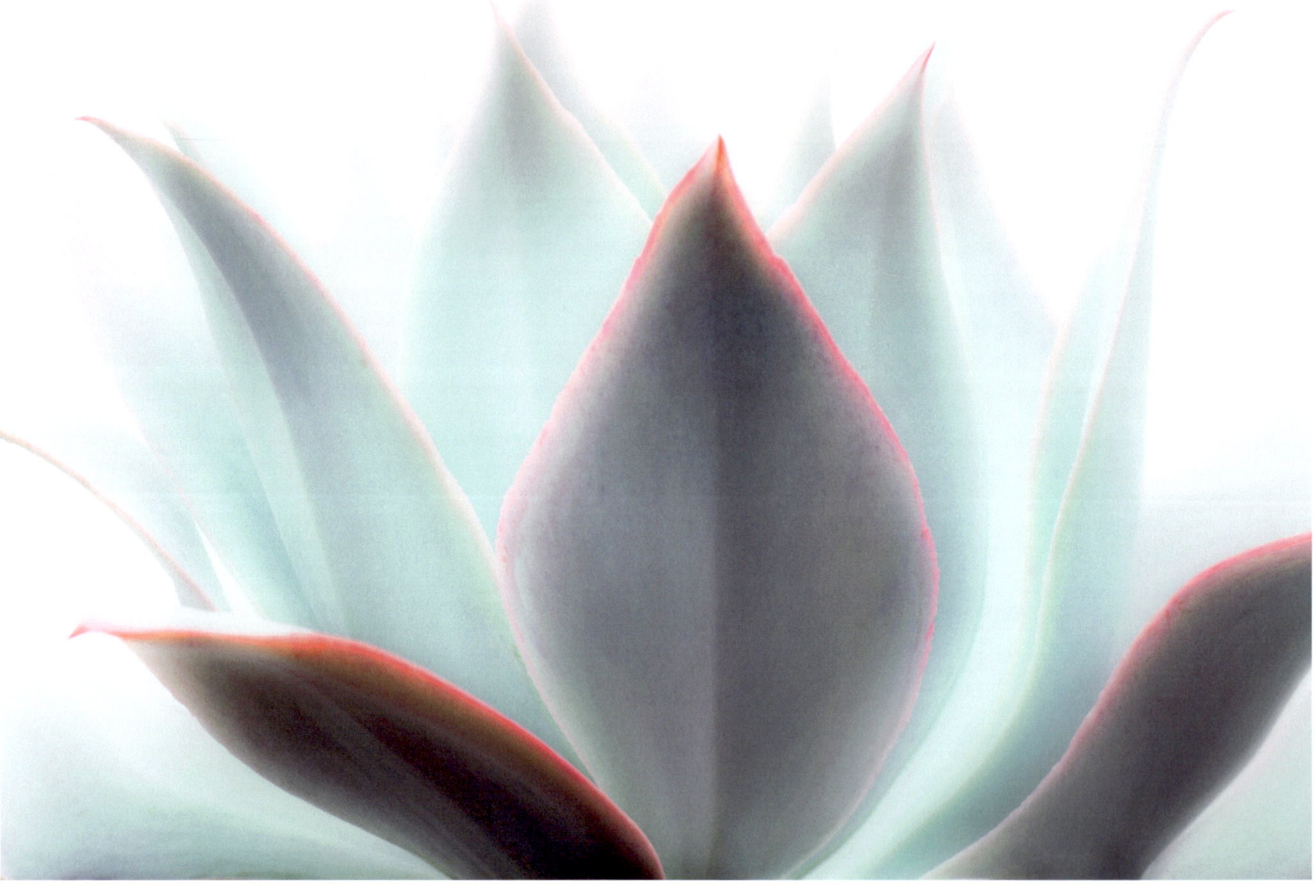

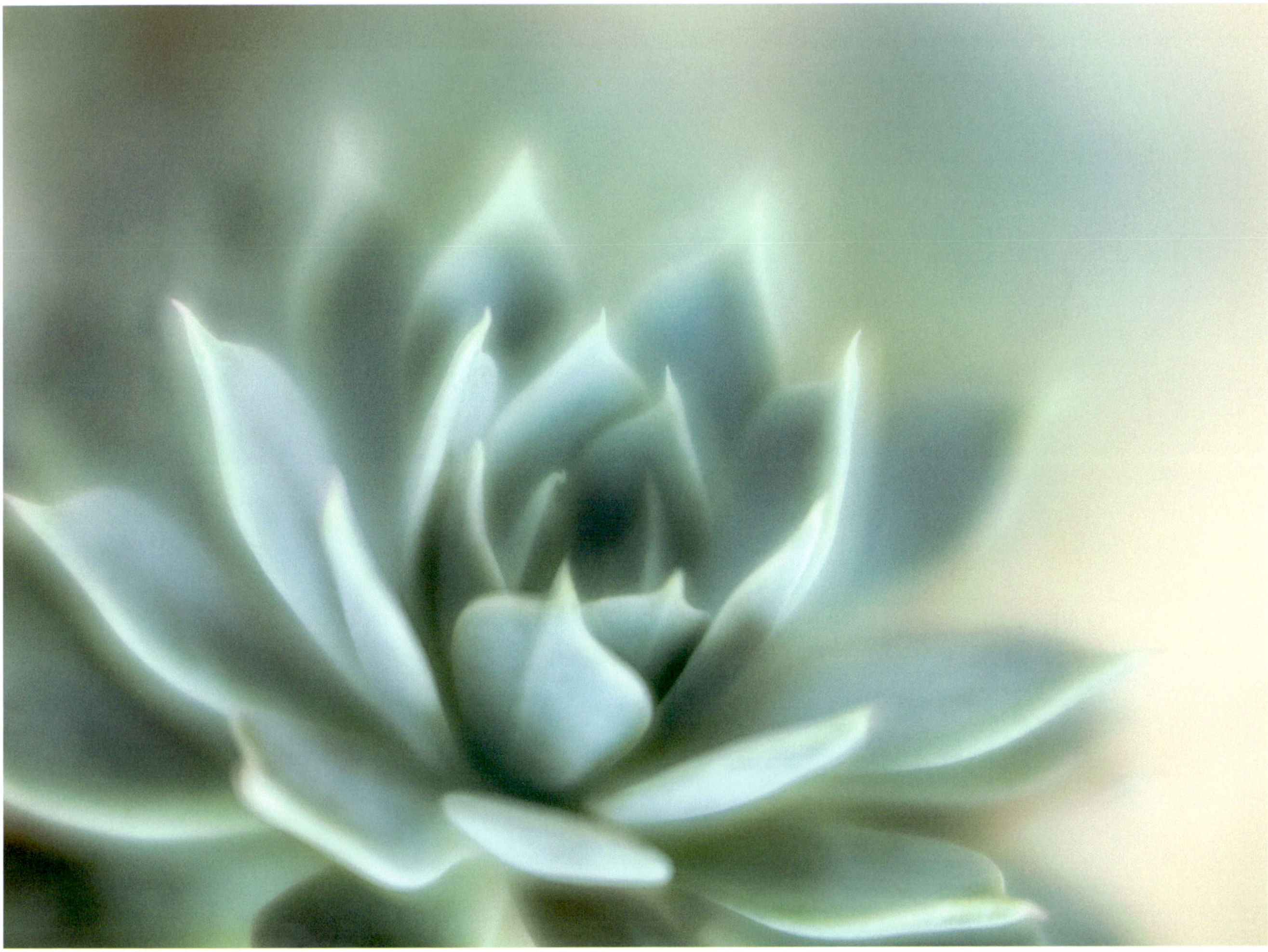

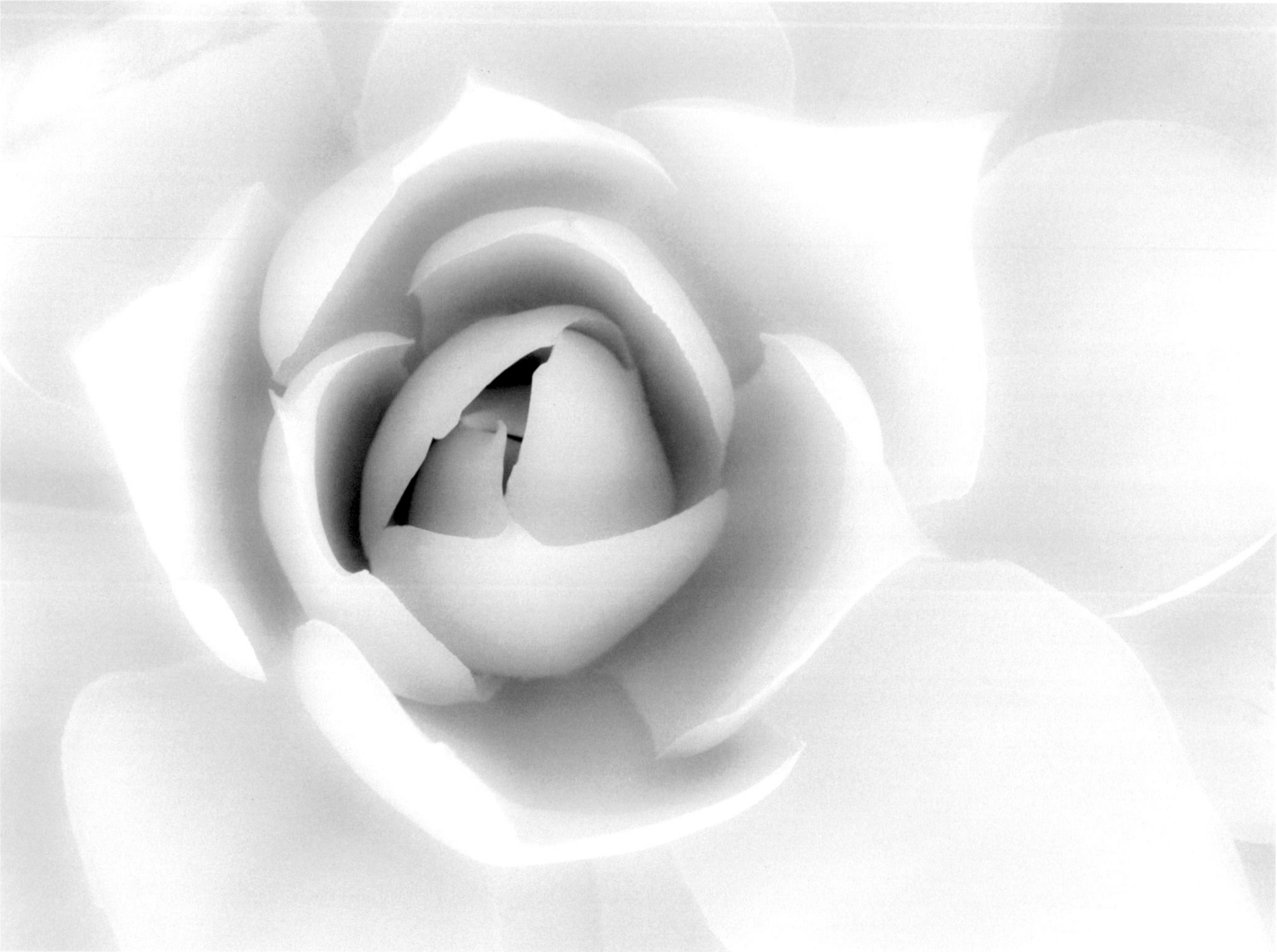

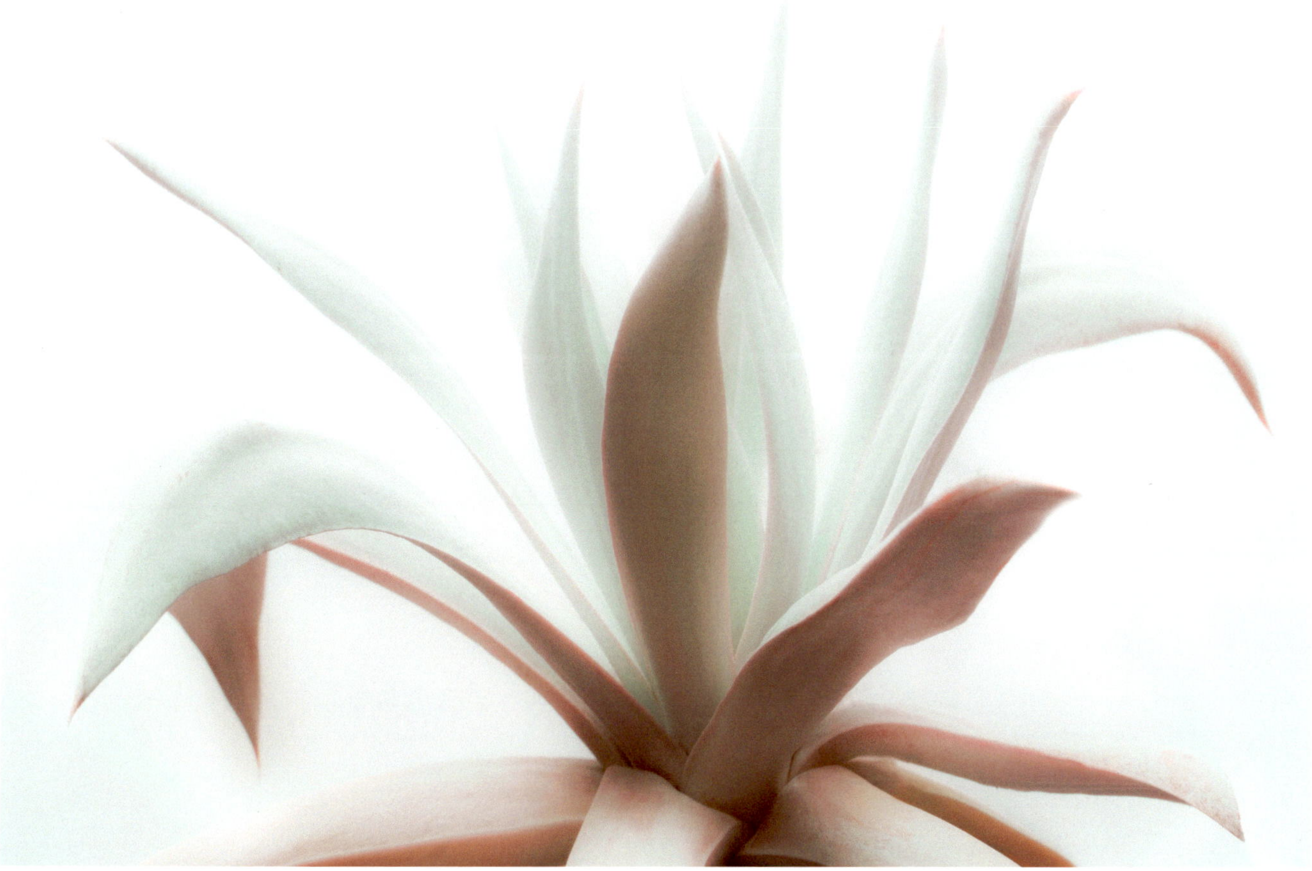

Elemental

by John Miskelly

www.johnmiskelly.co.uk • john@johnmiskelly.co.uk

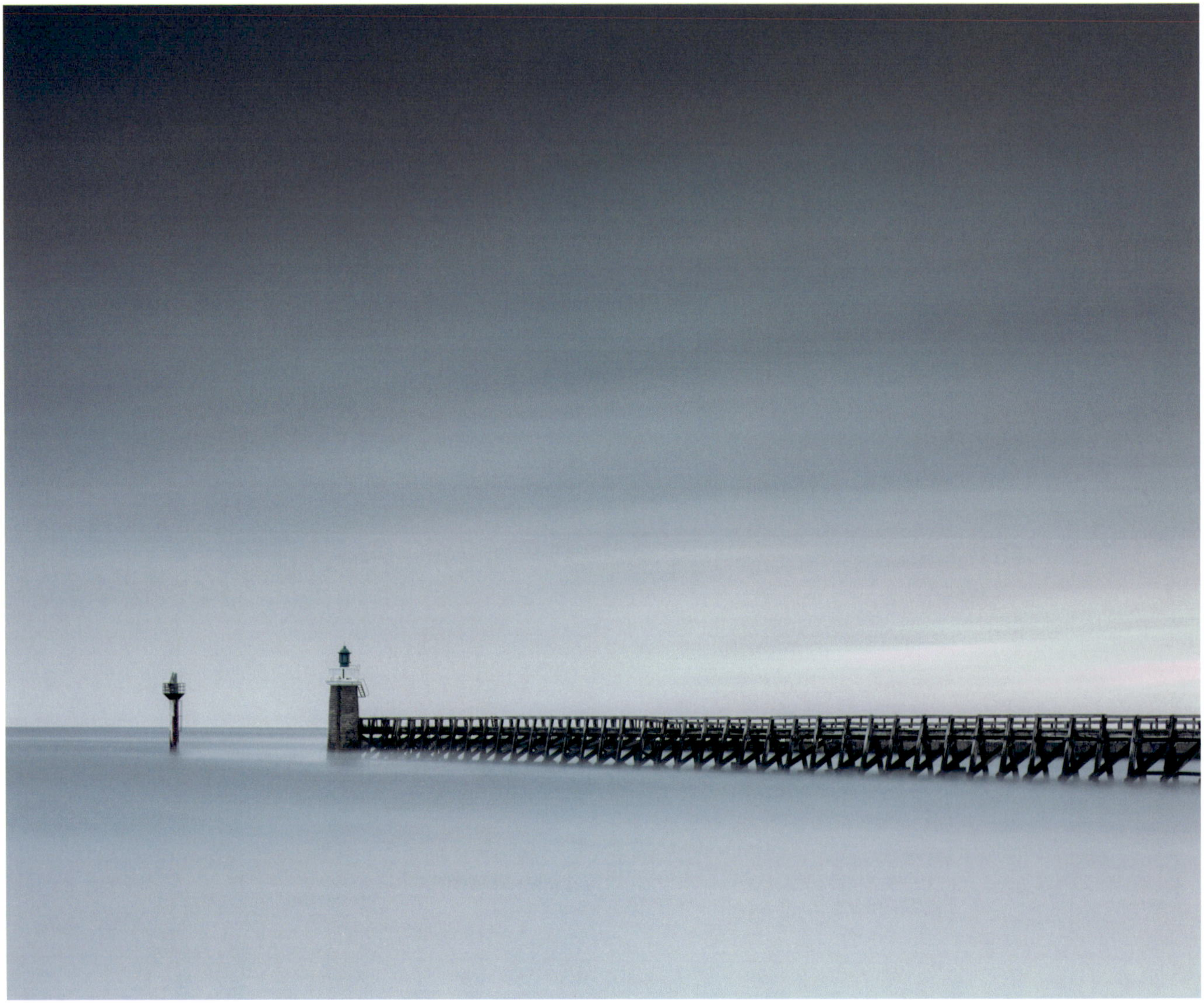

Sentinel
Pier at Capbreton on the West coast of France

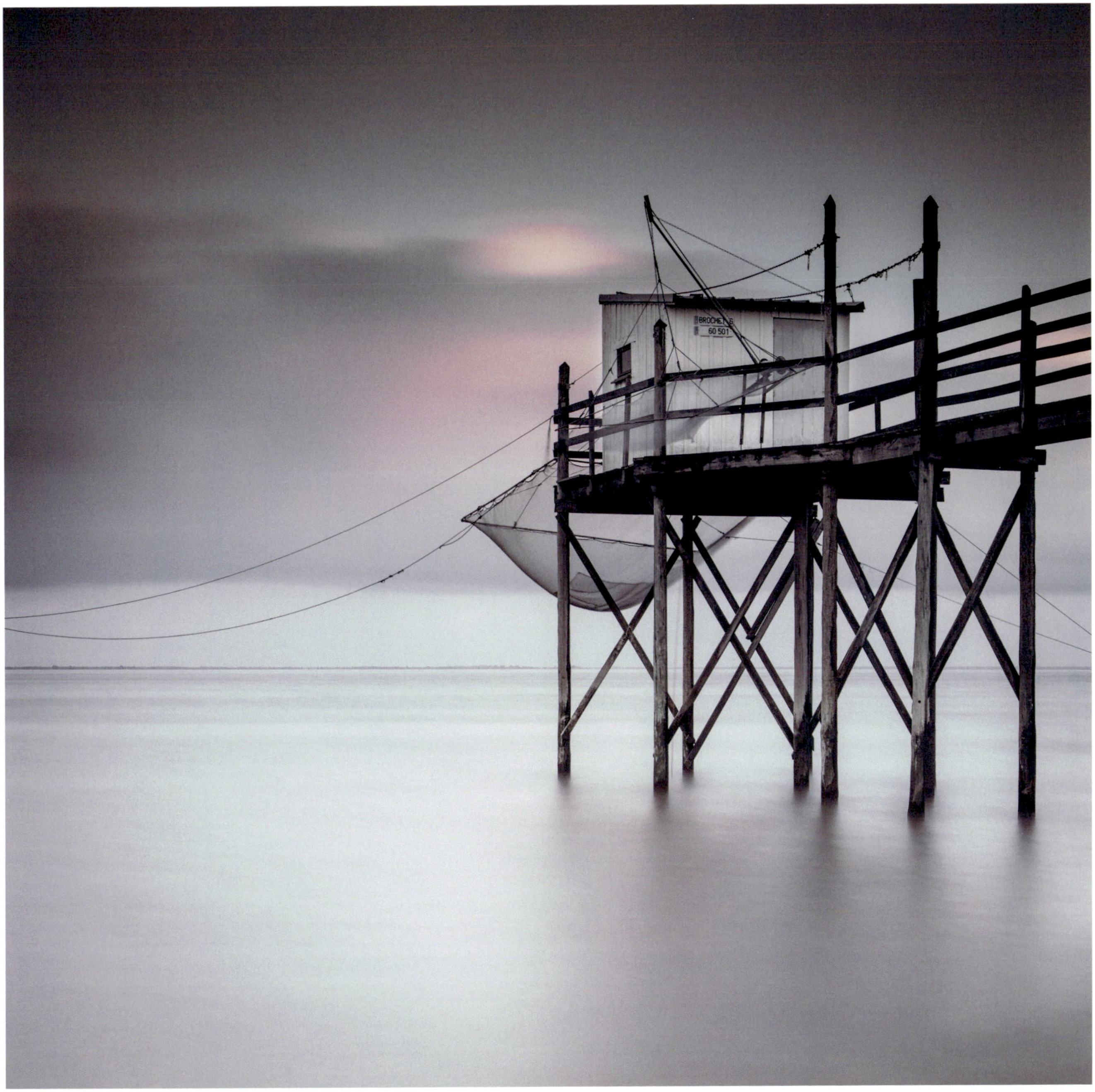

Fishing Hut

One of around 400 fishing huts along the Gironde Estuary in France

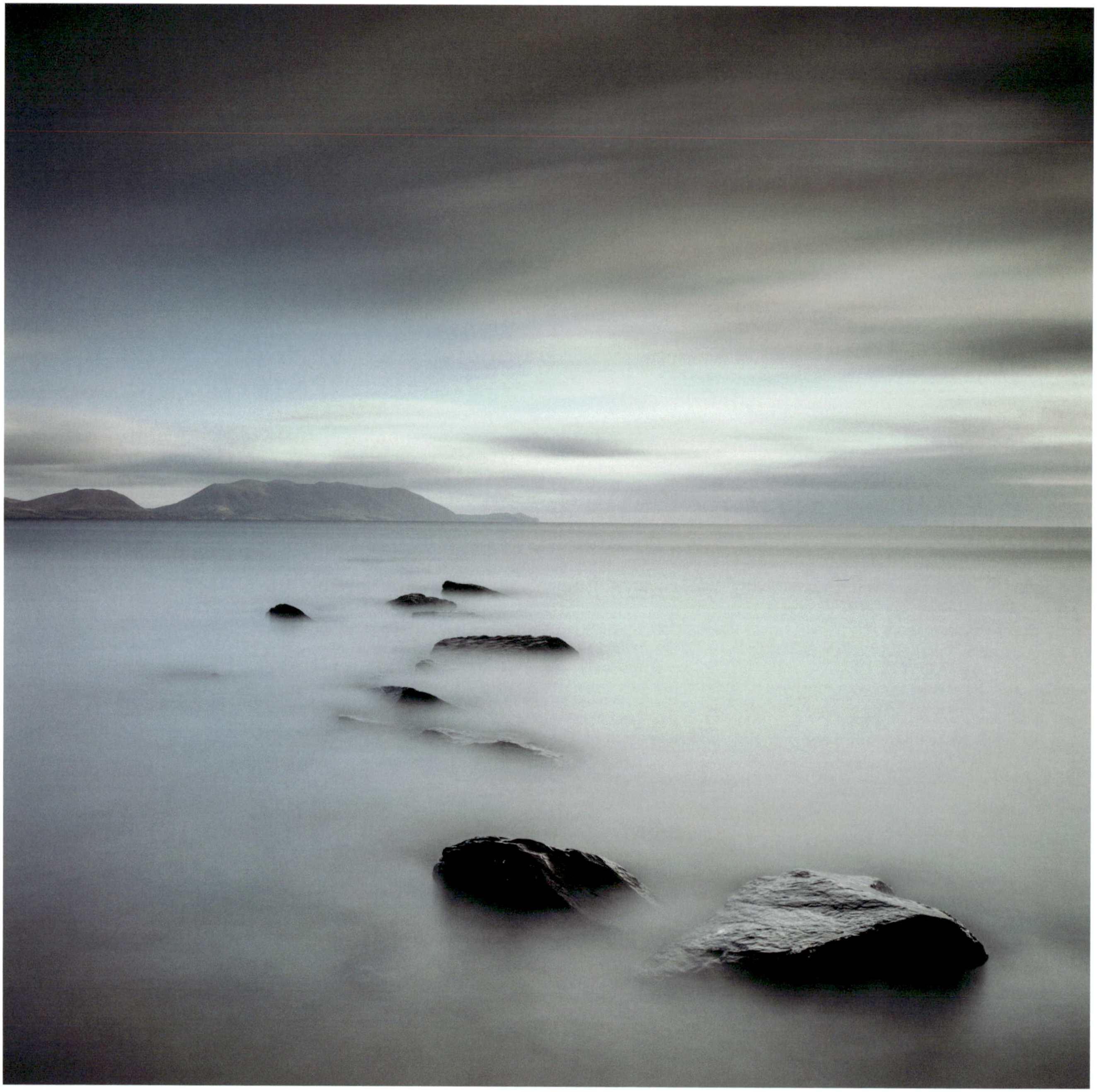

Stepping Stones
Rocks on Inch Beach, on the Dingle Peninsula, in the west of Ireland

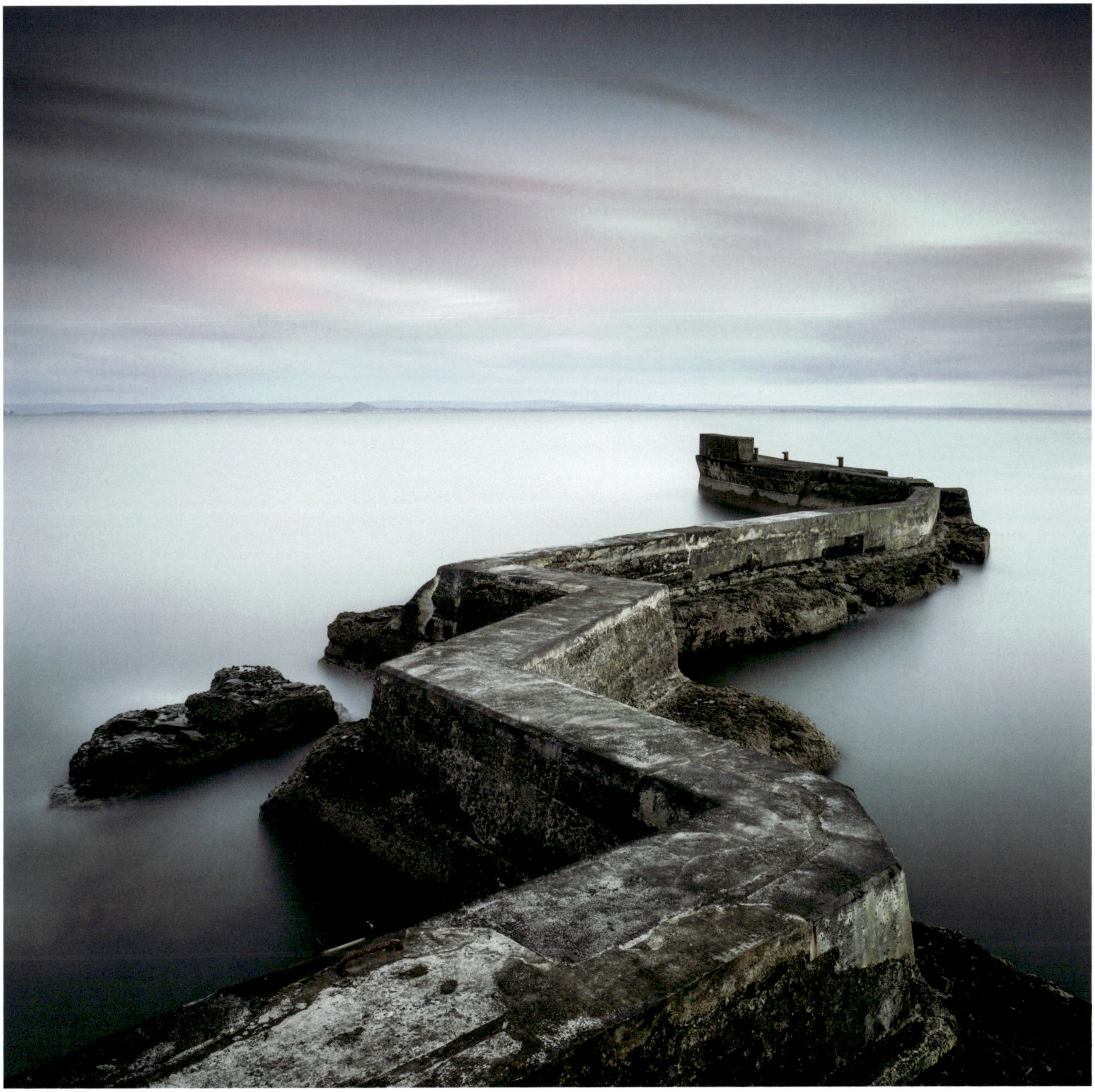

Breakwater
St Monan's breakwater on the east coast of Scotland.

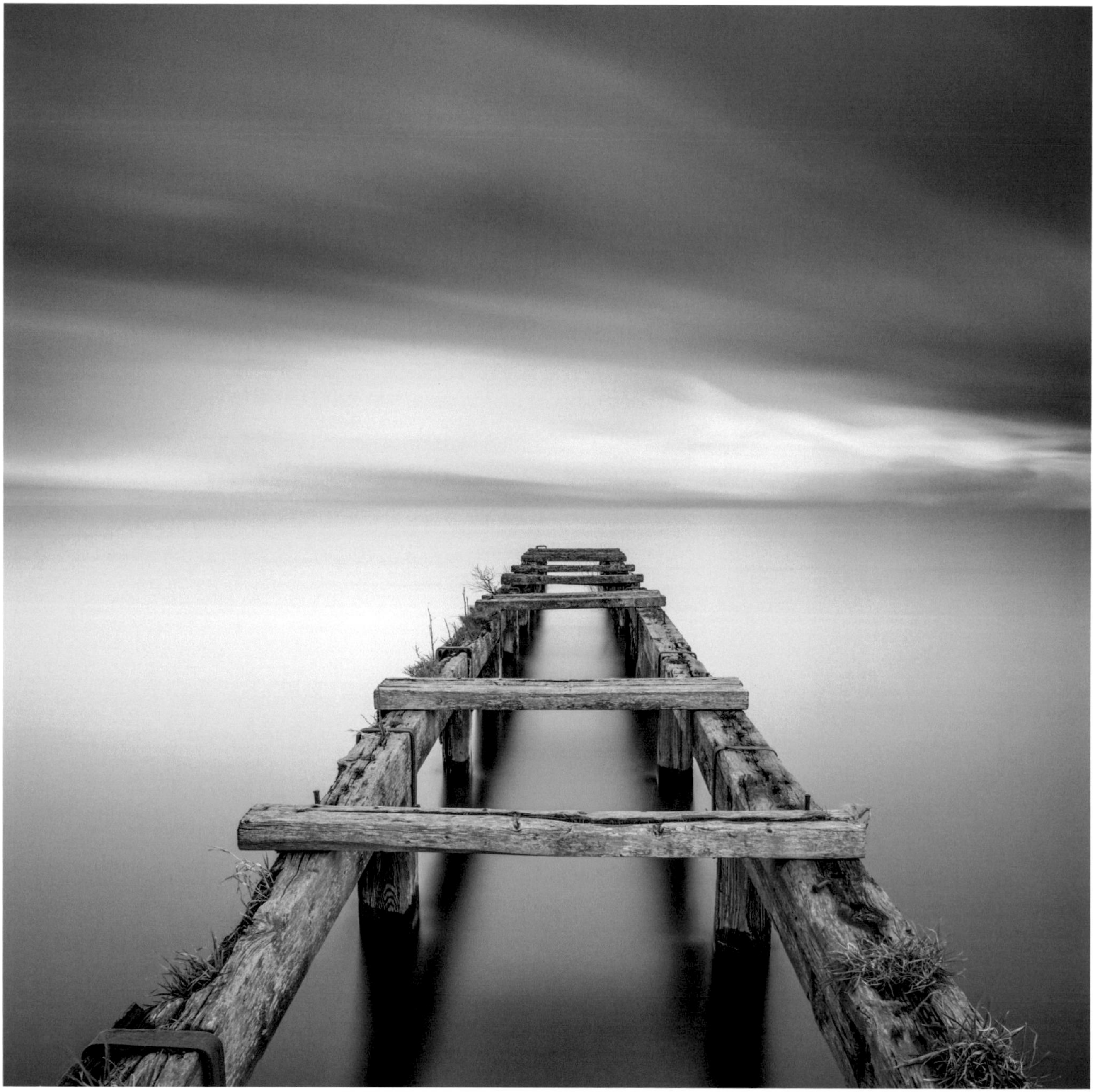

Abandoned
The old Derrytrasna Jetty on Lough Neagh, in Northern Ireland.

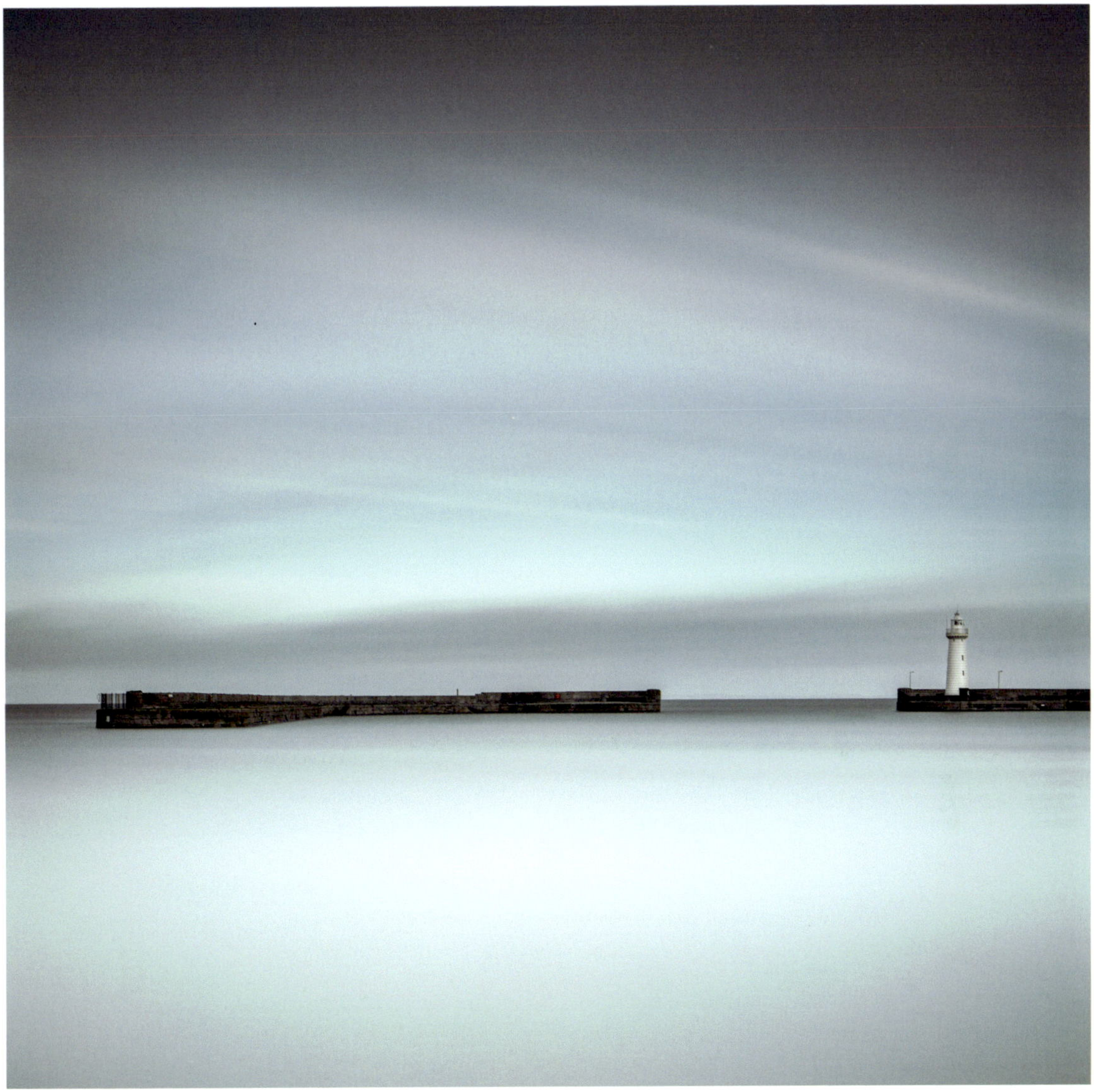

Lighthouse
Donaghadee lighthouse in Northern Ireland

My landscape photography is an exploration of time, not the split second photographic exposures that we so often see, but rather an attempt to capture some element of the passage of time. I use very long exposures, ranging from 2 minutes duration to 8 minutes or even longer, aimed at giving a sense of time passing, whether that be in the movement of clouds across the sky or the smoothing of the water. My work is often about the connections and relationships between the natural elements around our coastline and the structures that have been created by man. I have chosen to work in colour, where my intention is to show the muted palette, most commonly found at the beginning and end of the day.

Beyond The Veil

by Al DaVal le

davallephotography.com ♦ adavalle@jkbcapital.com

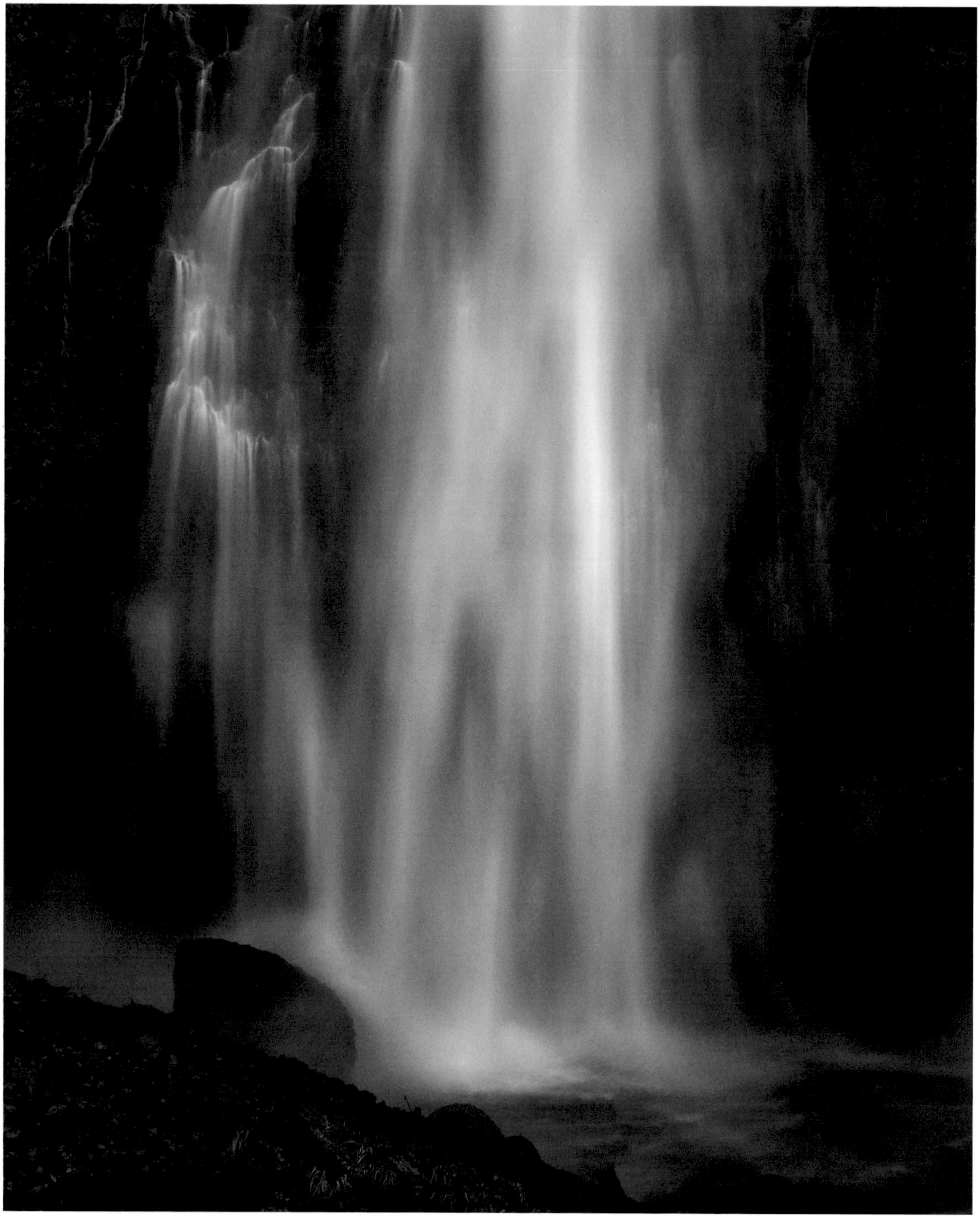

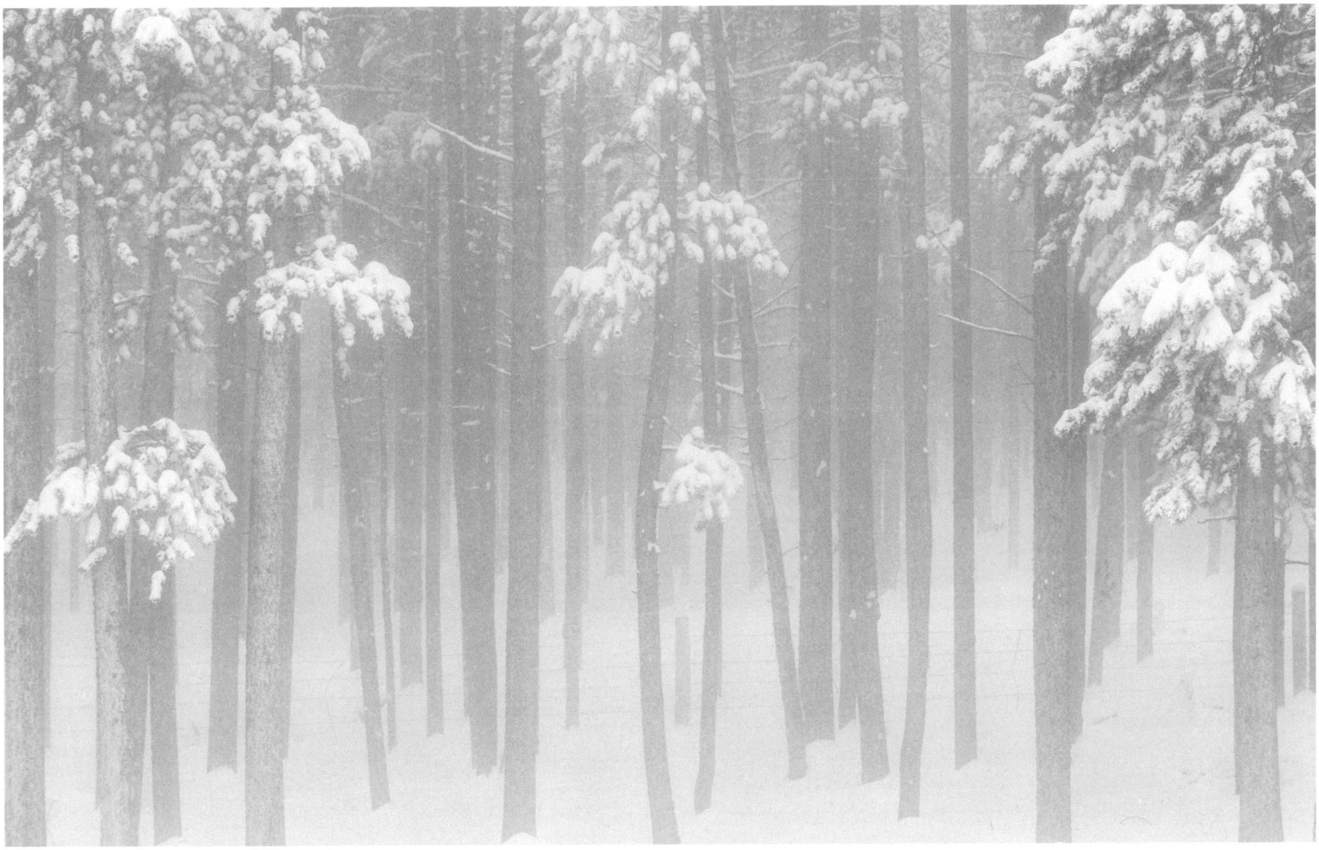

These images are inspired by the mysterious beauty and "unresolved stories" brought to the surface by mist, fog, and flowing water moving across the landscape. For me, these elements bring just the right amount of mystery, intrigue, and questioning to an otherwise common scene. It allows the maker to put enough of himself into the image in order to create art.

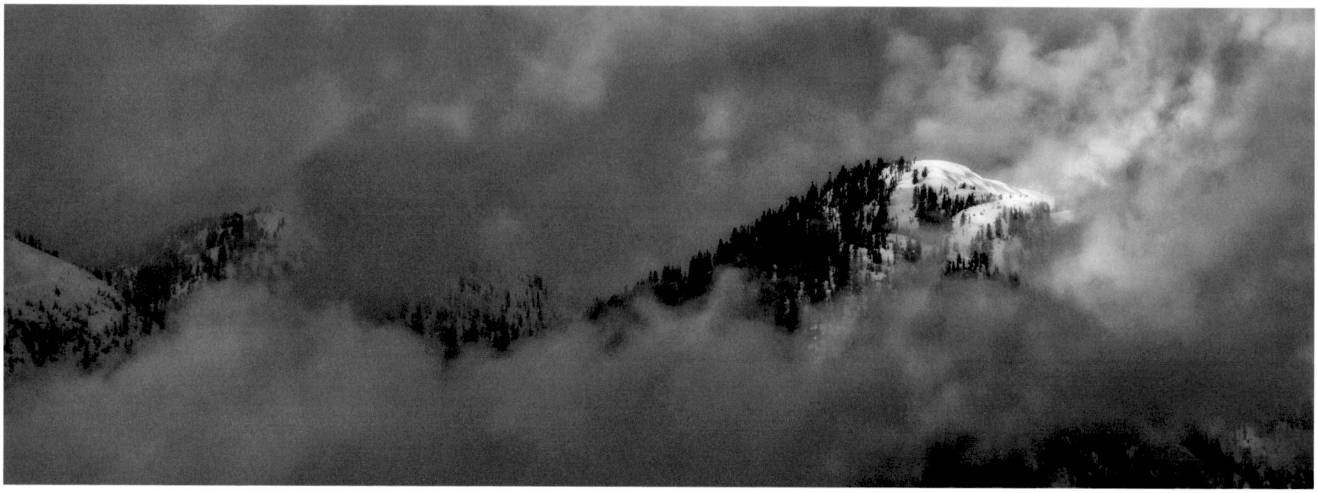

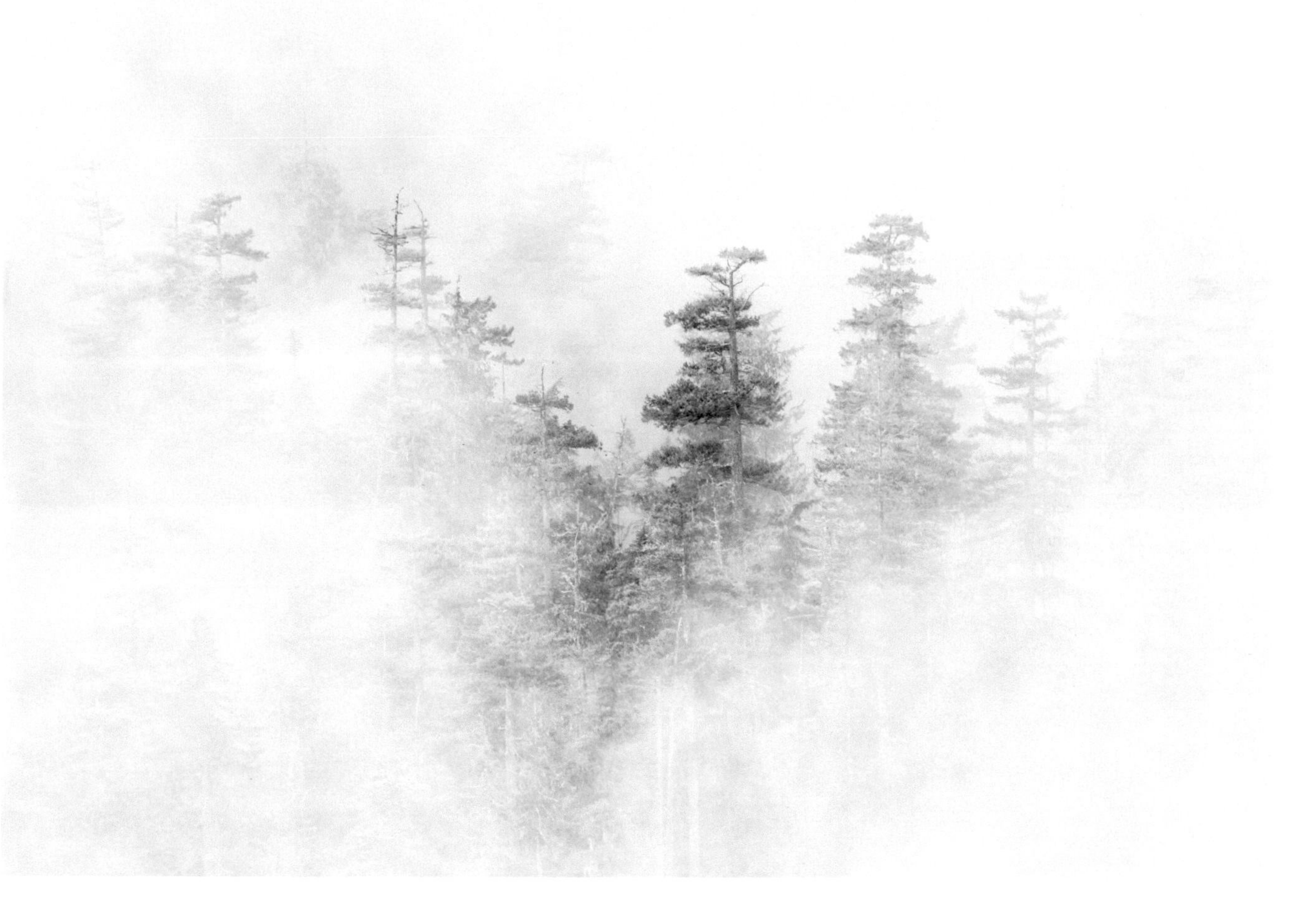

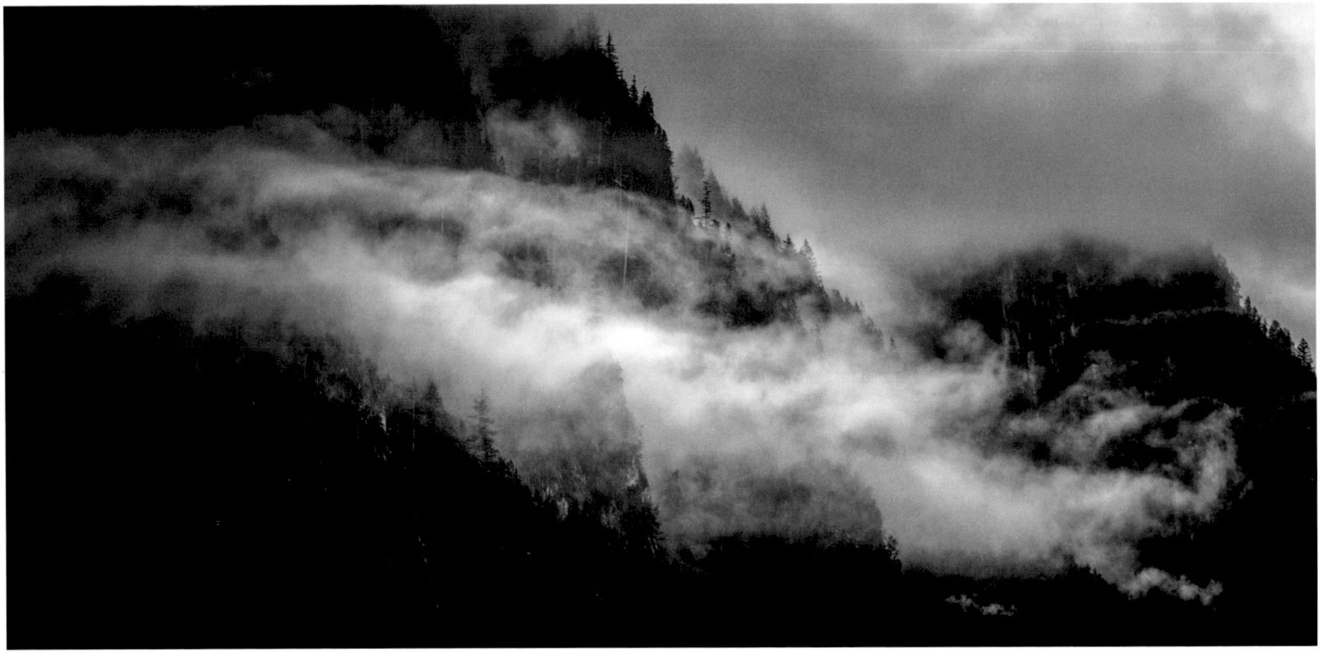

Were I called on to define, very briefly, the term Art, I should call it "the reproduction of what the Senses perceive in Nature through the veil of the soul." The mere imitation, however accurate, of what is in Nature, entitles no man to the sacred name of "Artist."

~ Edgar Allan Poe

I ran across this quote from Edgar Allen Poe while researching for this small project. Poe's words haunt me! I present these six images as art, yet there is something in his words that strike deeply and painfully. It's an open question.

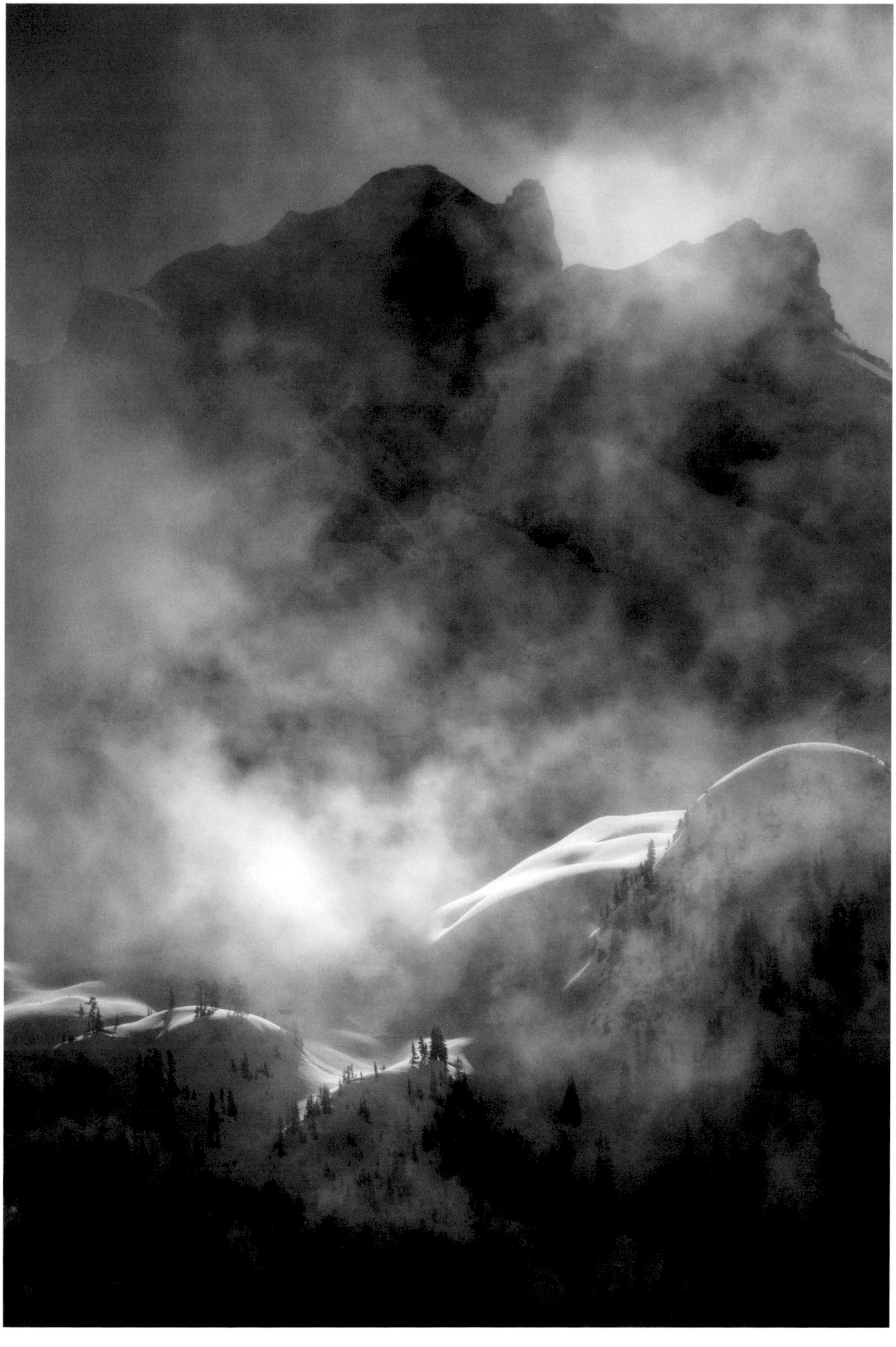

Relinquish

by Adrienne Defendi

www.adriennedefendi.com • adrienne.defendi@yahoo.com

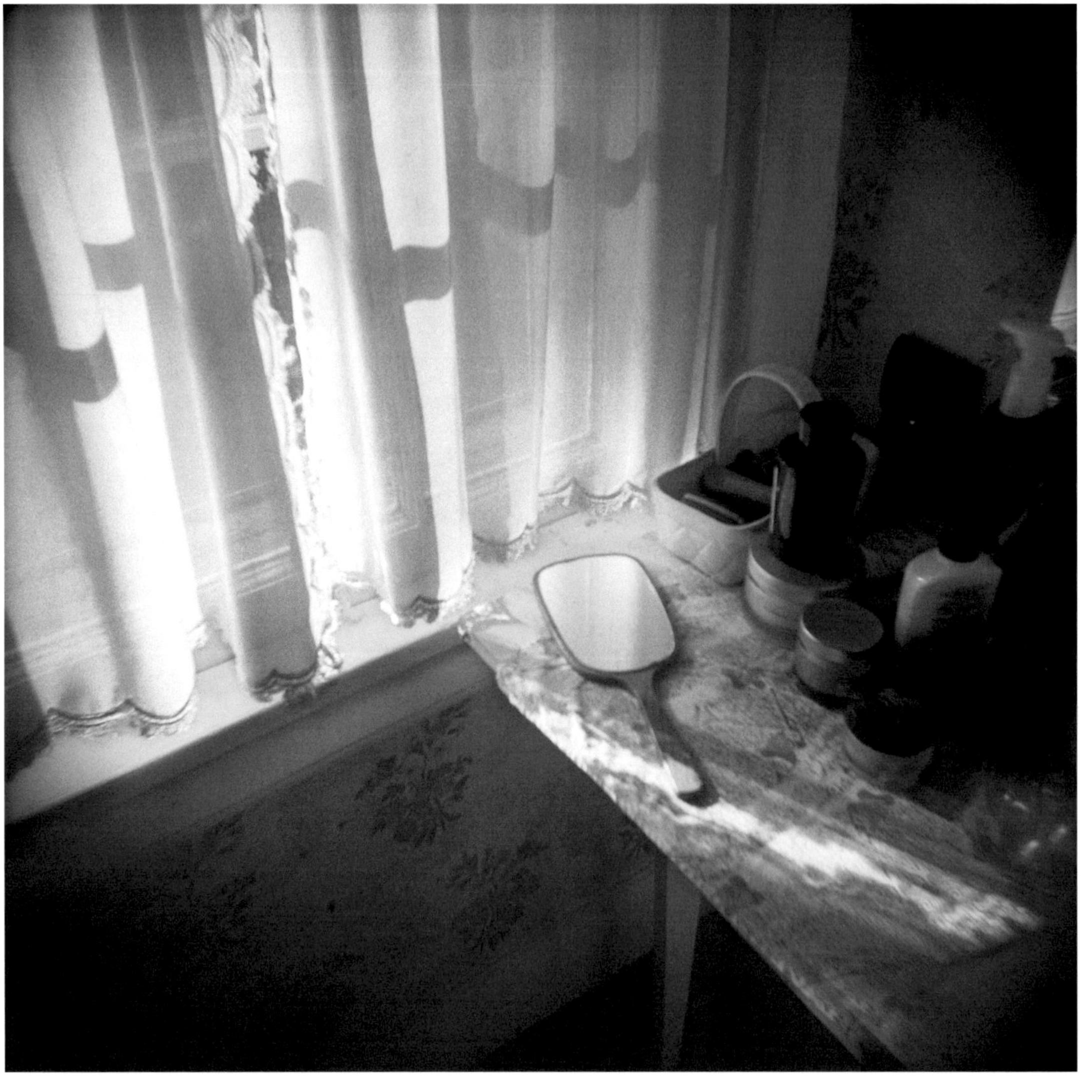

Afternoon Toilette

These photographs document the home where my aged parents have resided for over forty years and explore their hermetic lives within. Through this project I have come to understand how my parents and I, gracefully and lovingly, are letting go of each other — relinquishing each other to the natural cycle of life. Accepting this allows me to revere and record their now quiet and meditative lives.

To relinquish them is to remember them anew.

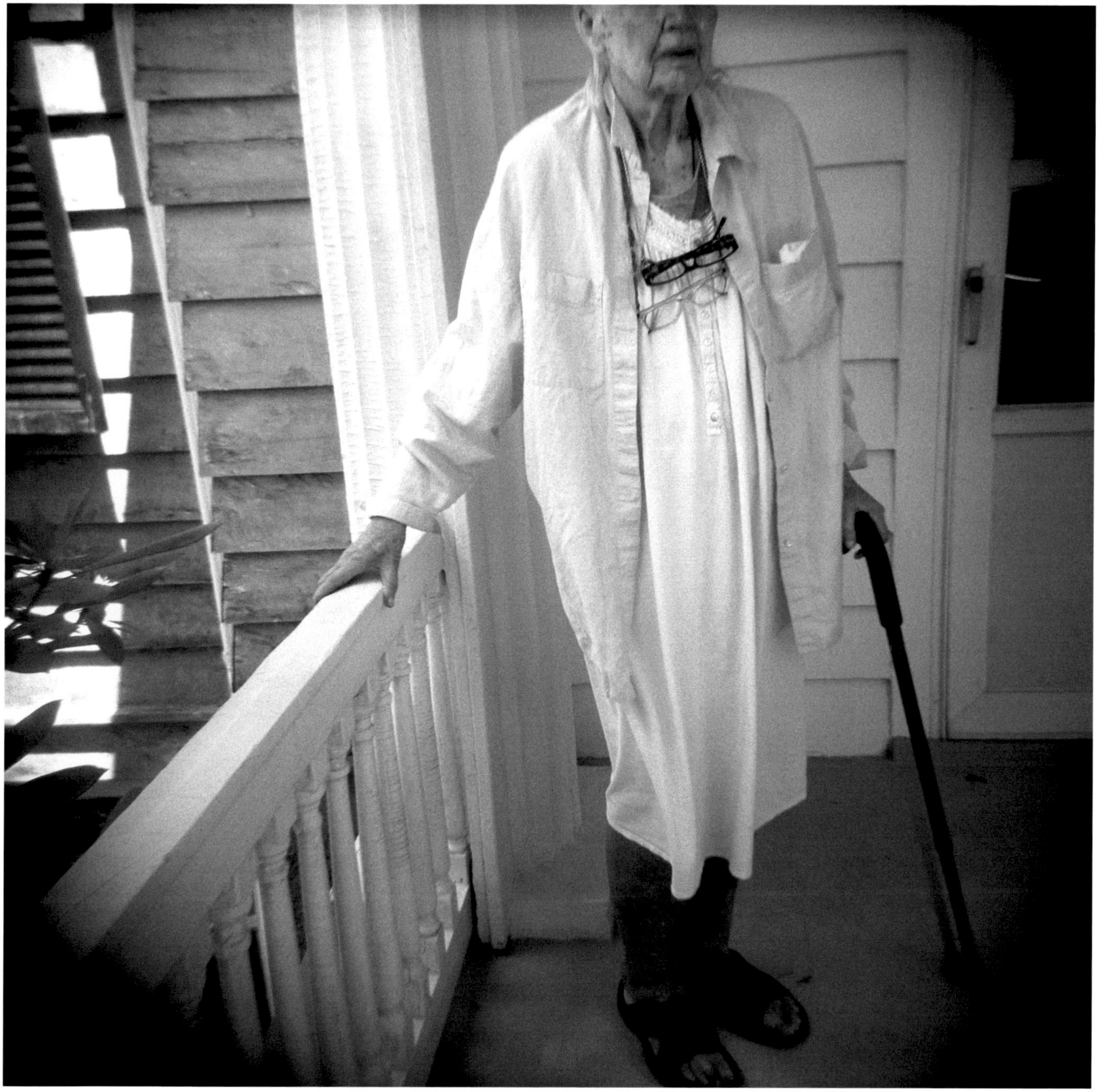

June Chrystal

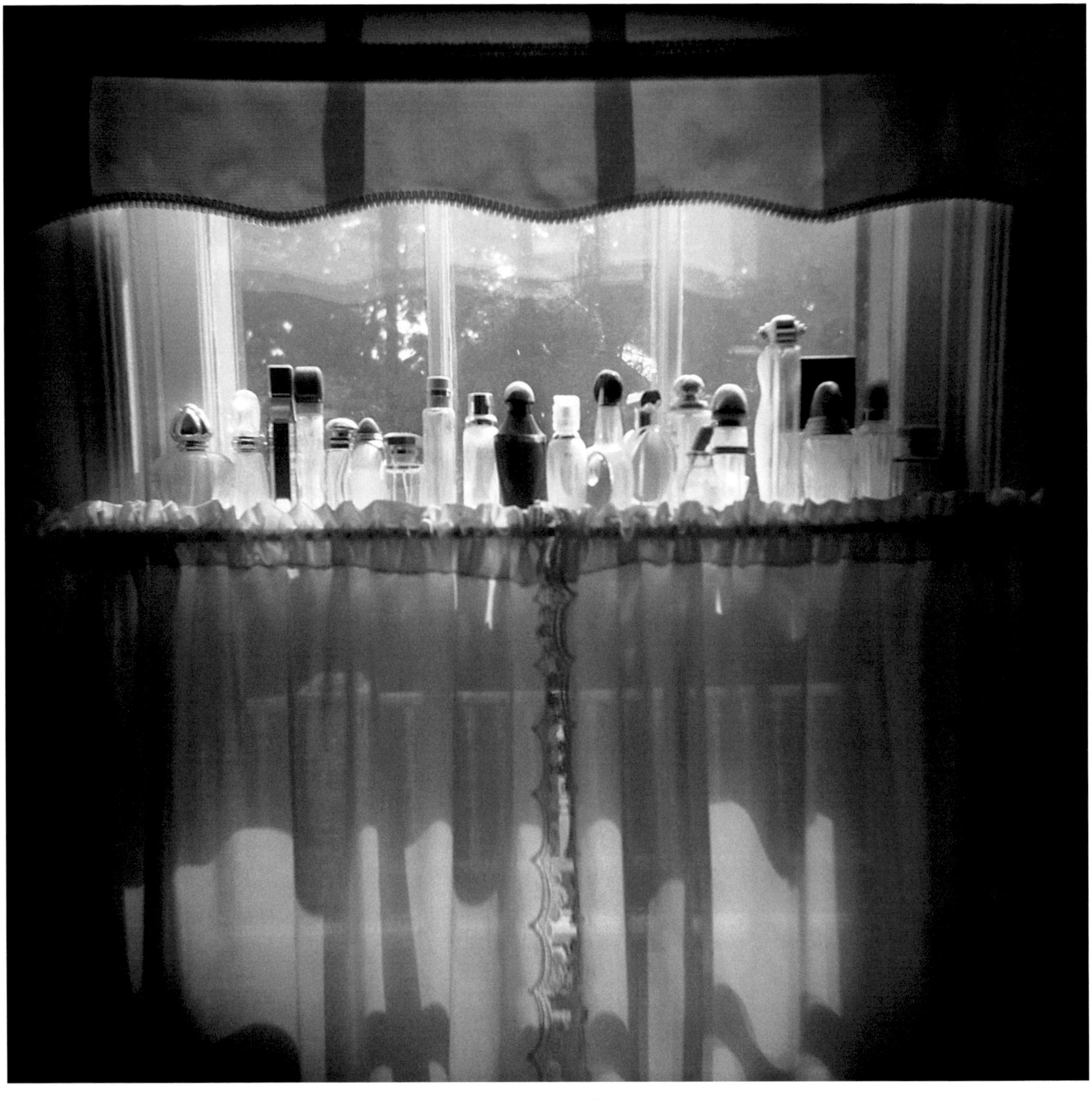

My Mother's Perfumes

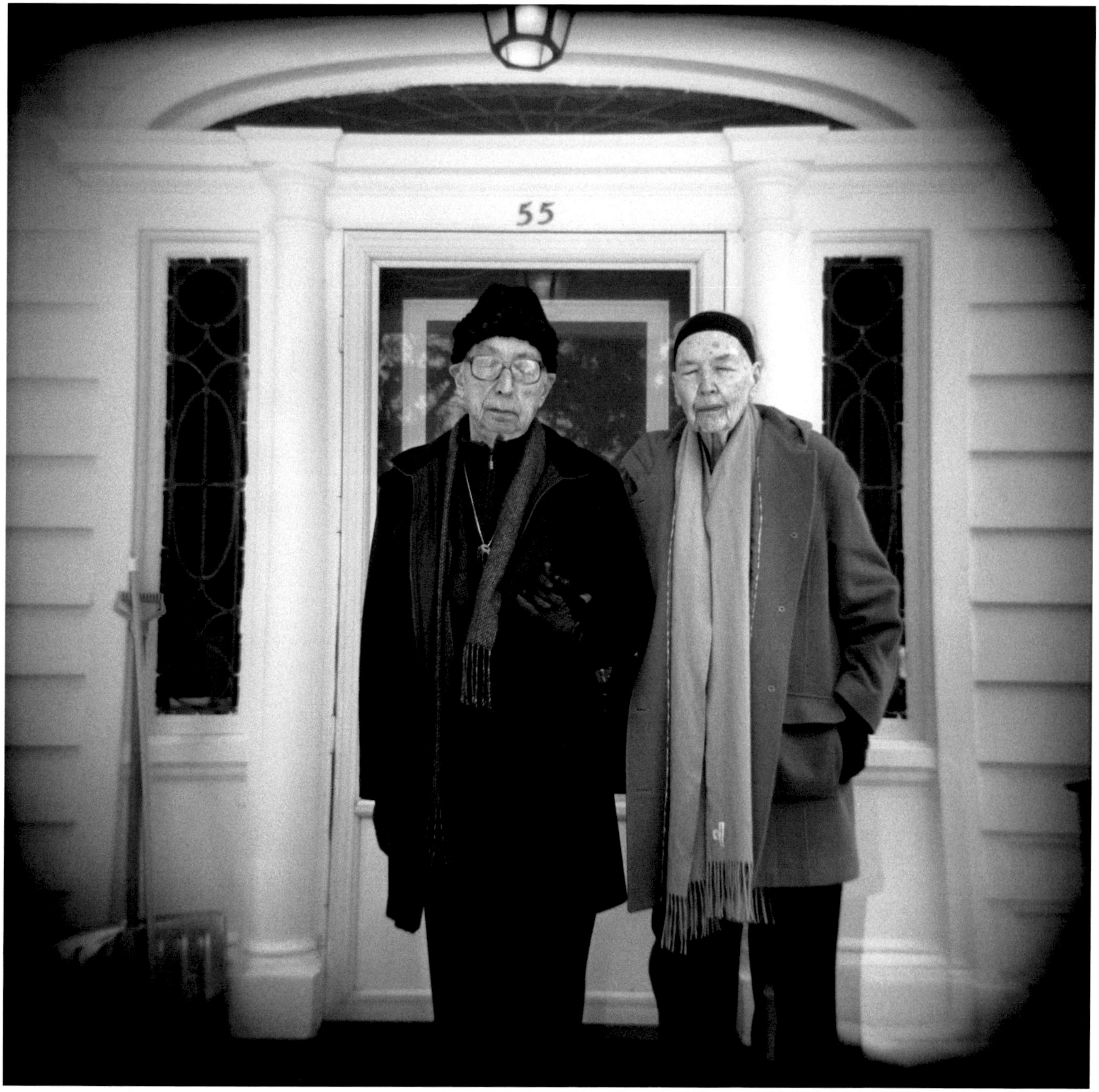

Beautiful Death 55

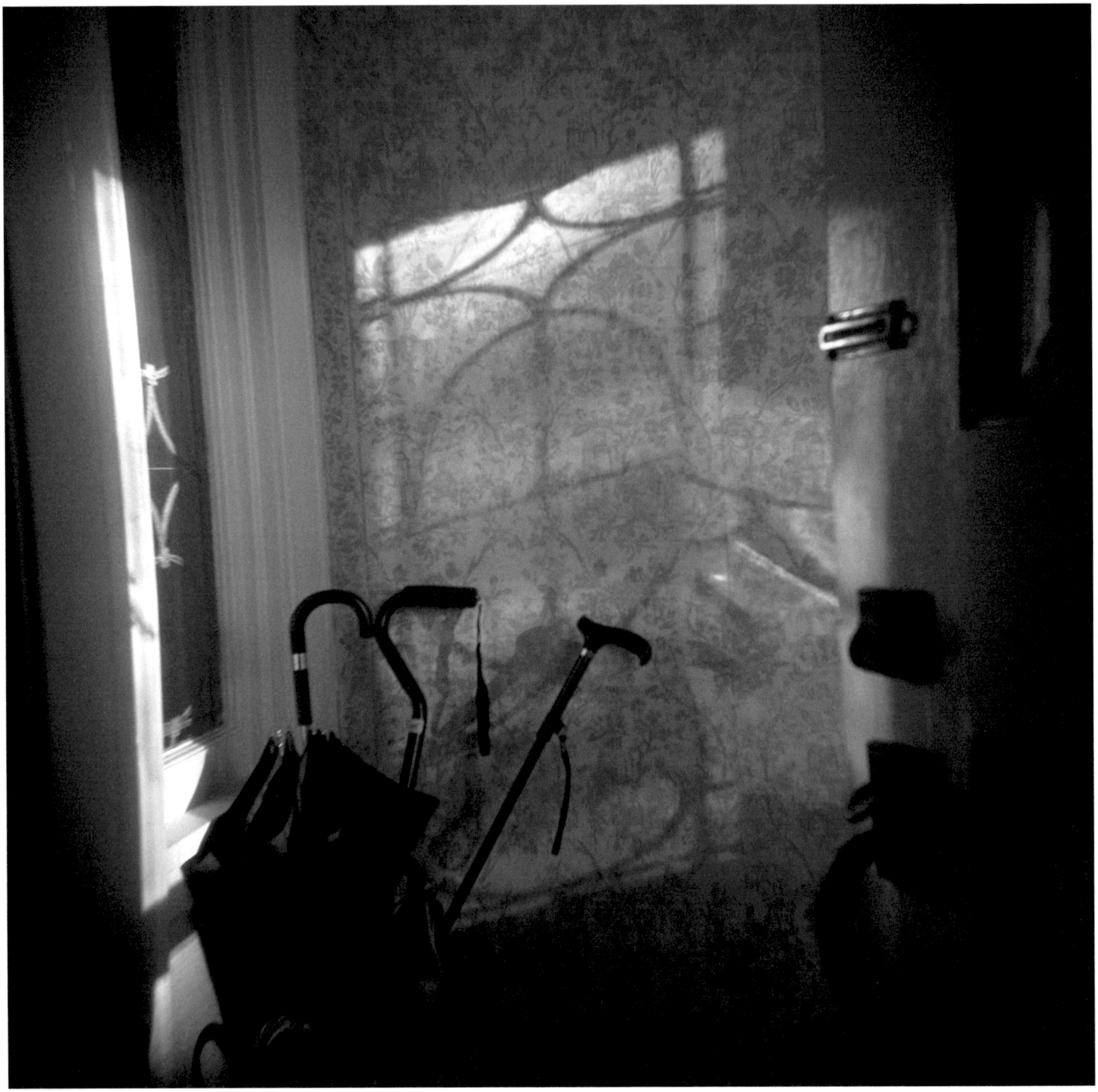

Passing Through

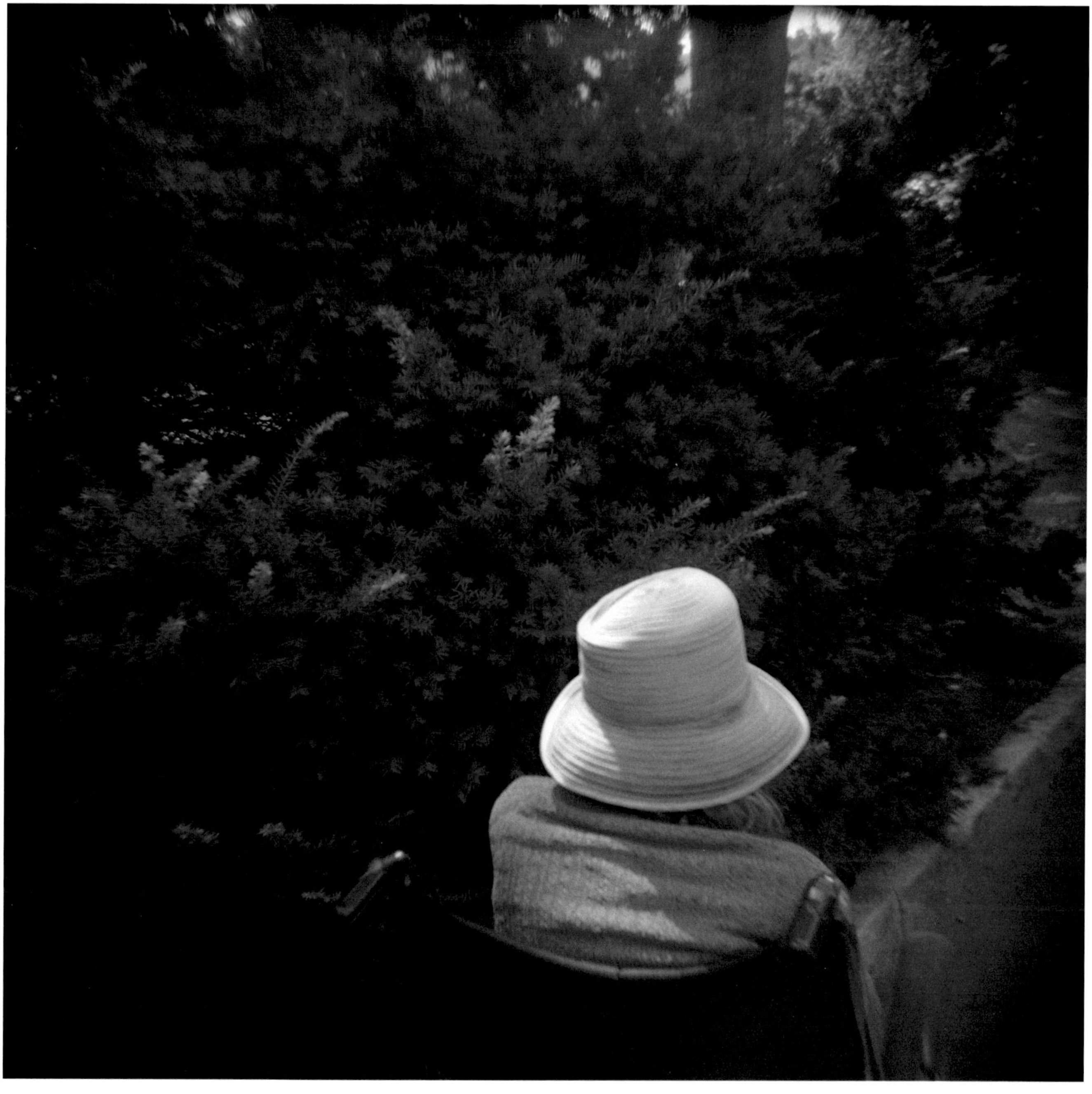

Last Summer Hat

The Fall Morning Light

by Montie Talbert

www.AmbientSilver.com ♦ montie@earthlink.net

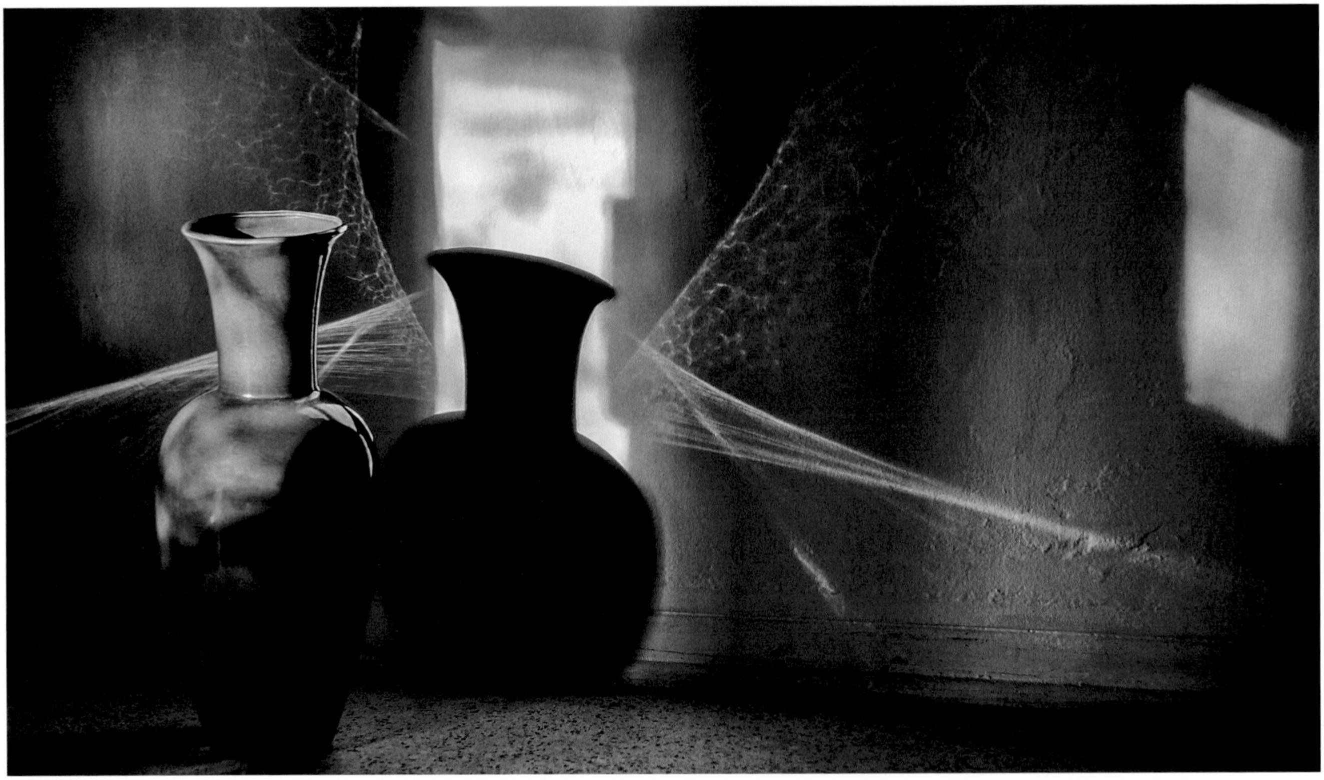

. . .Awakens my space.
Not Spring or Summer bright
Shines the transient grace.

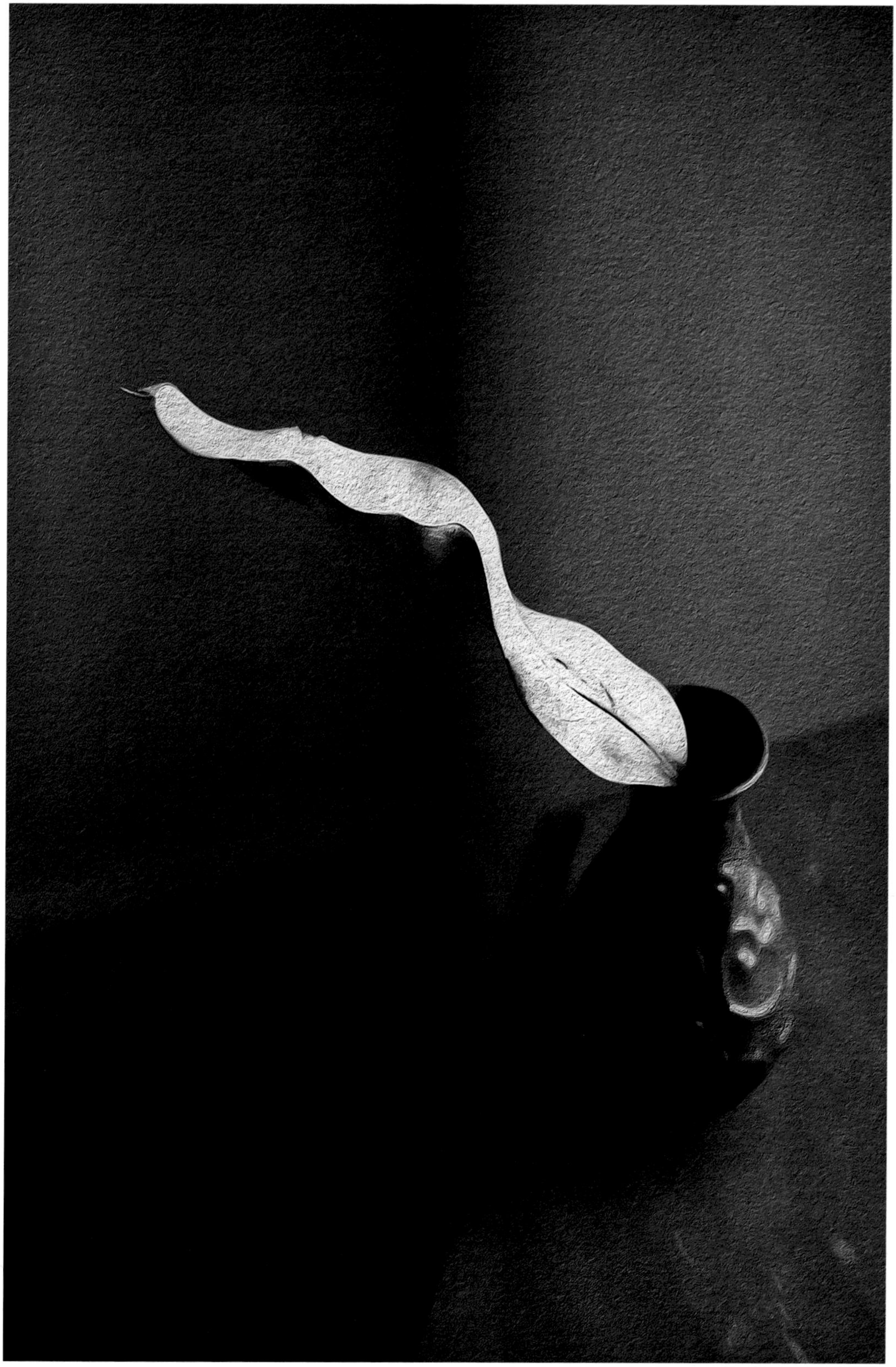

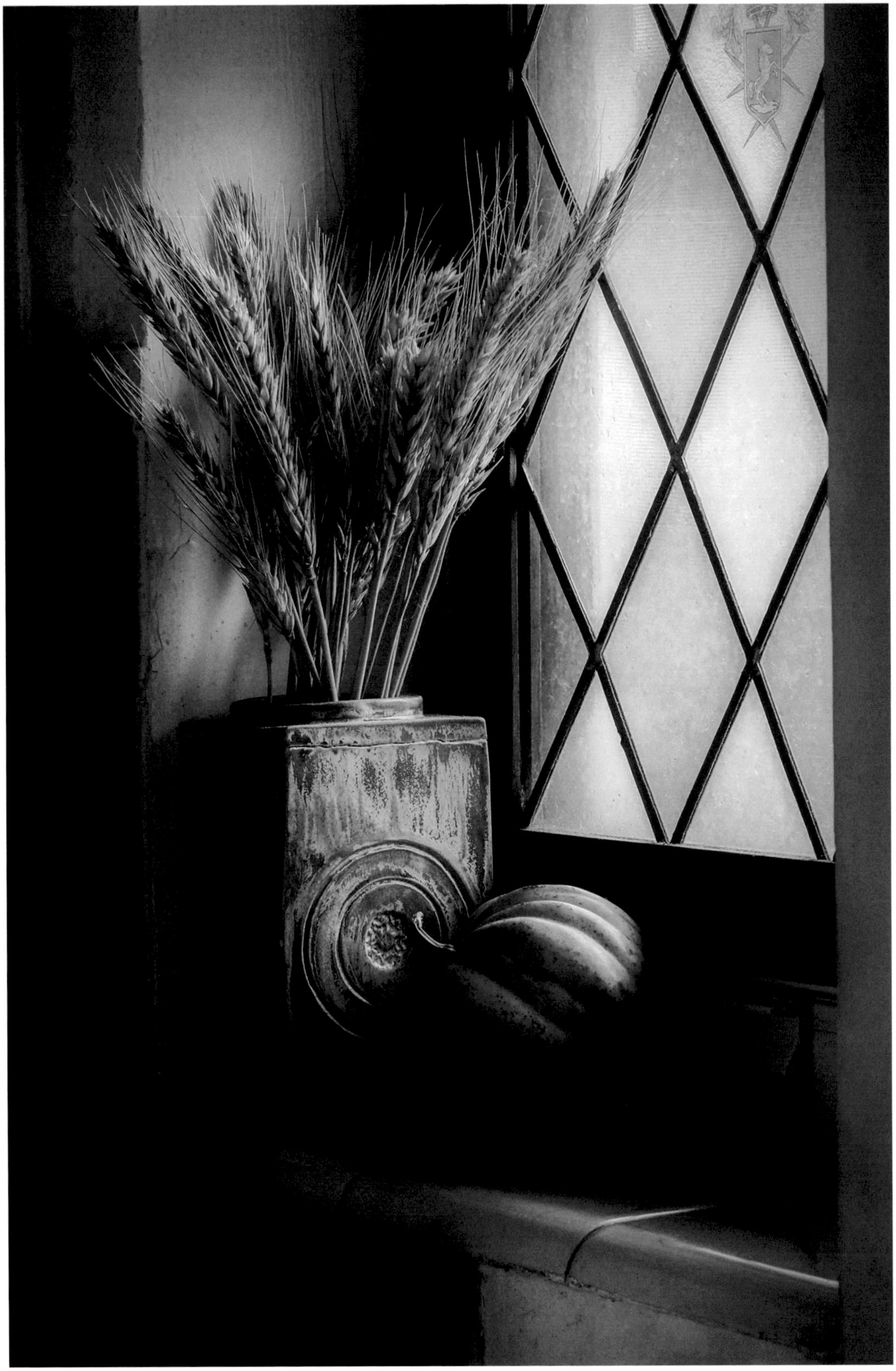

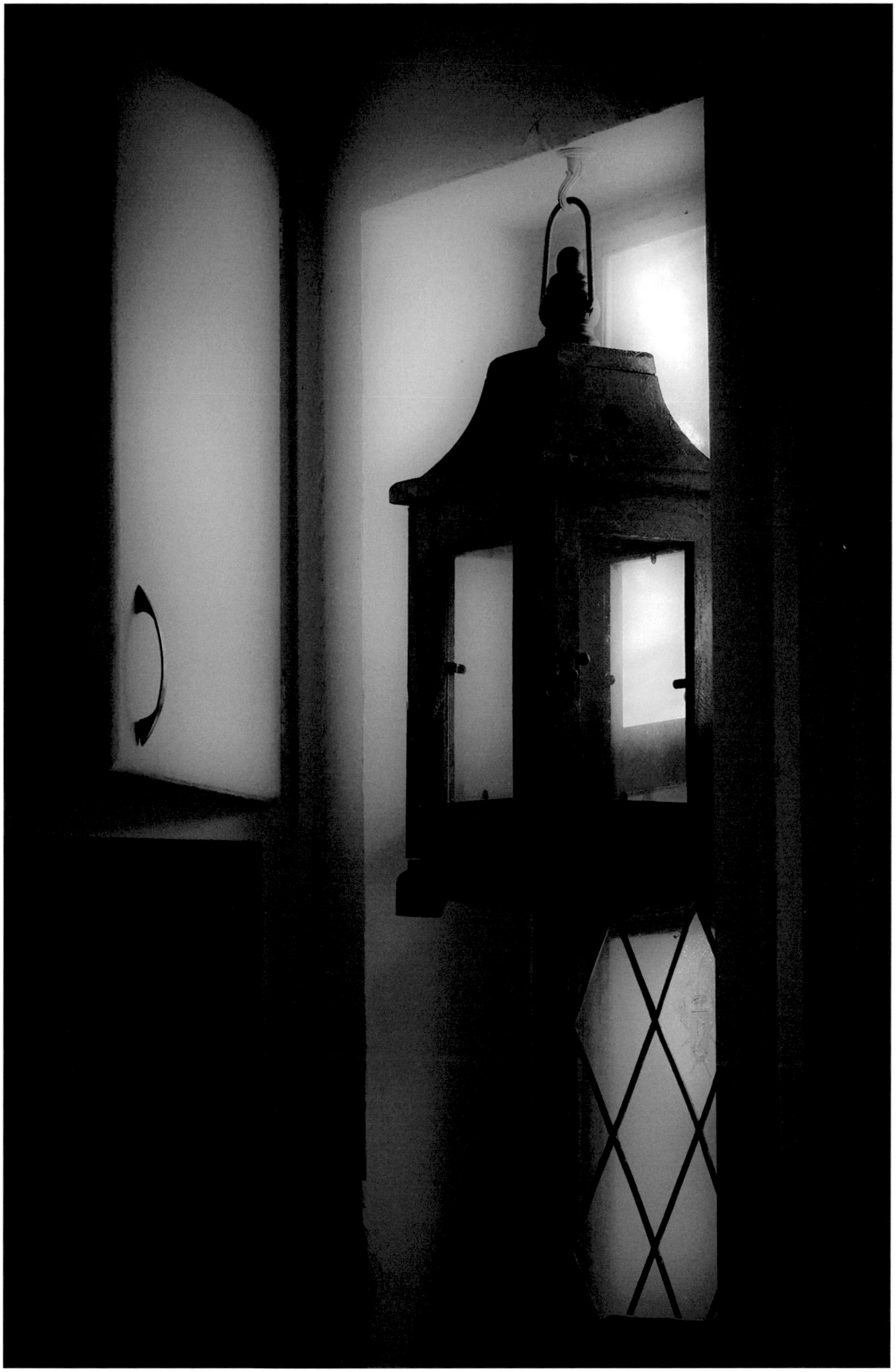

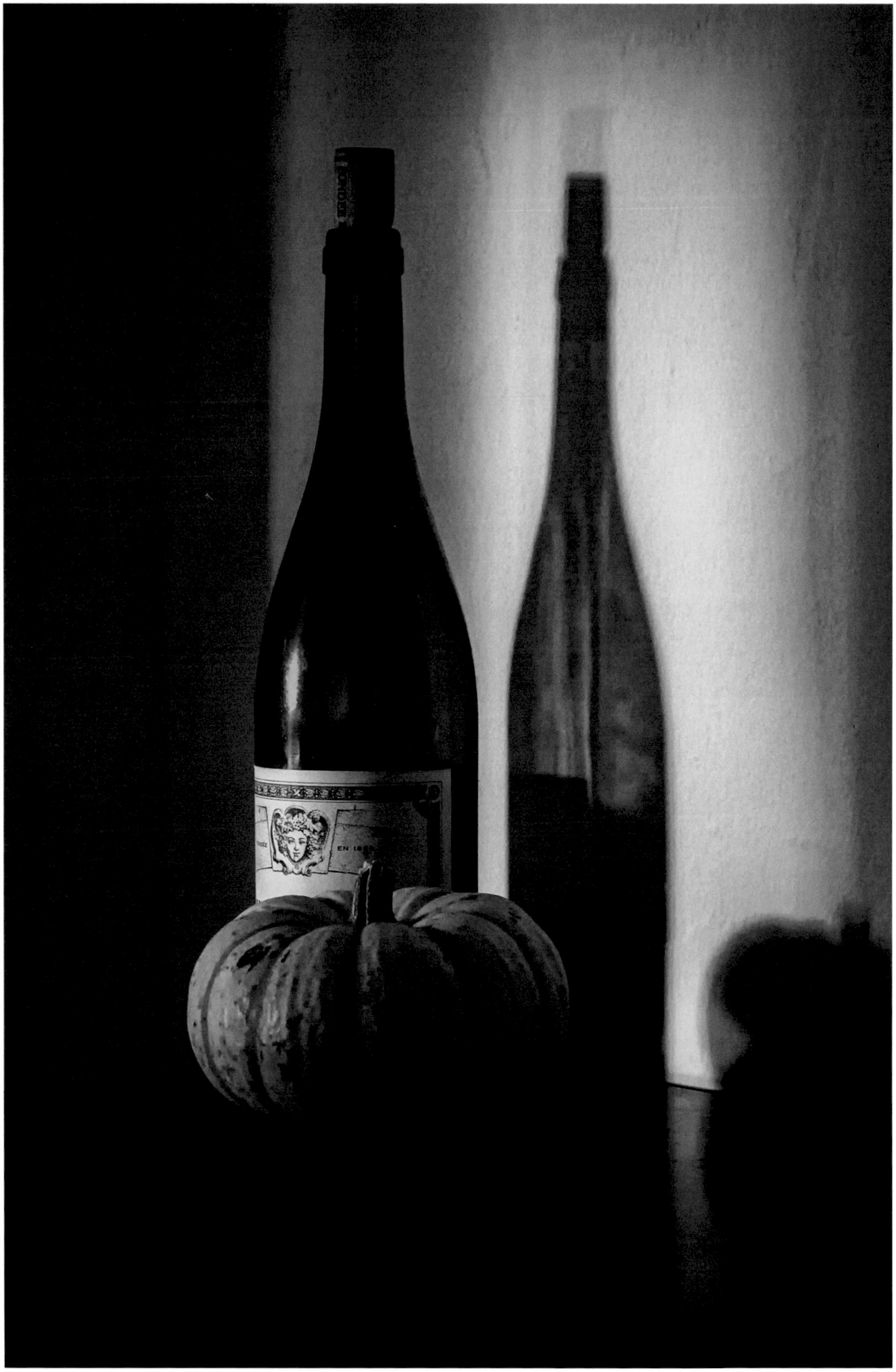

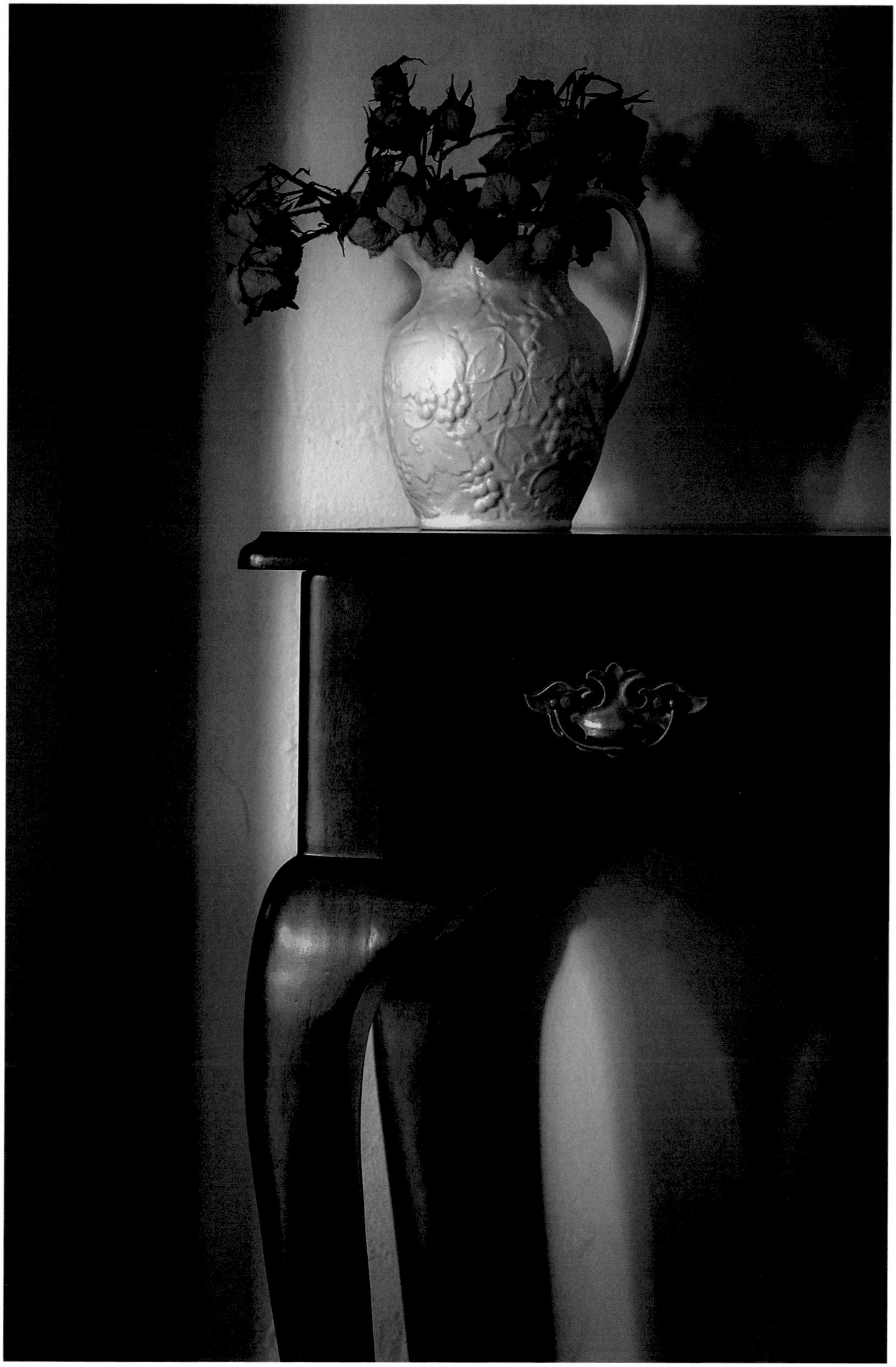

A Study of Architectural Details

by Stefan Bäurle

www.stefanbaeurle.com • sbaeurle@gmail.com

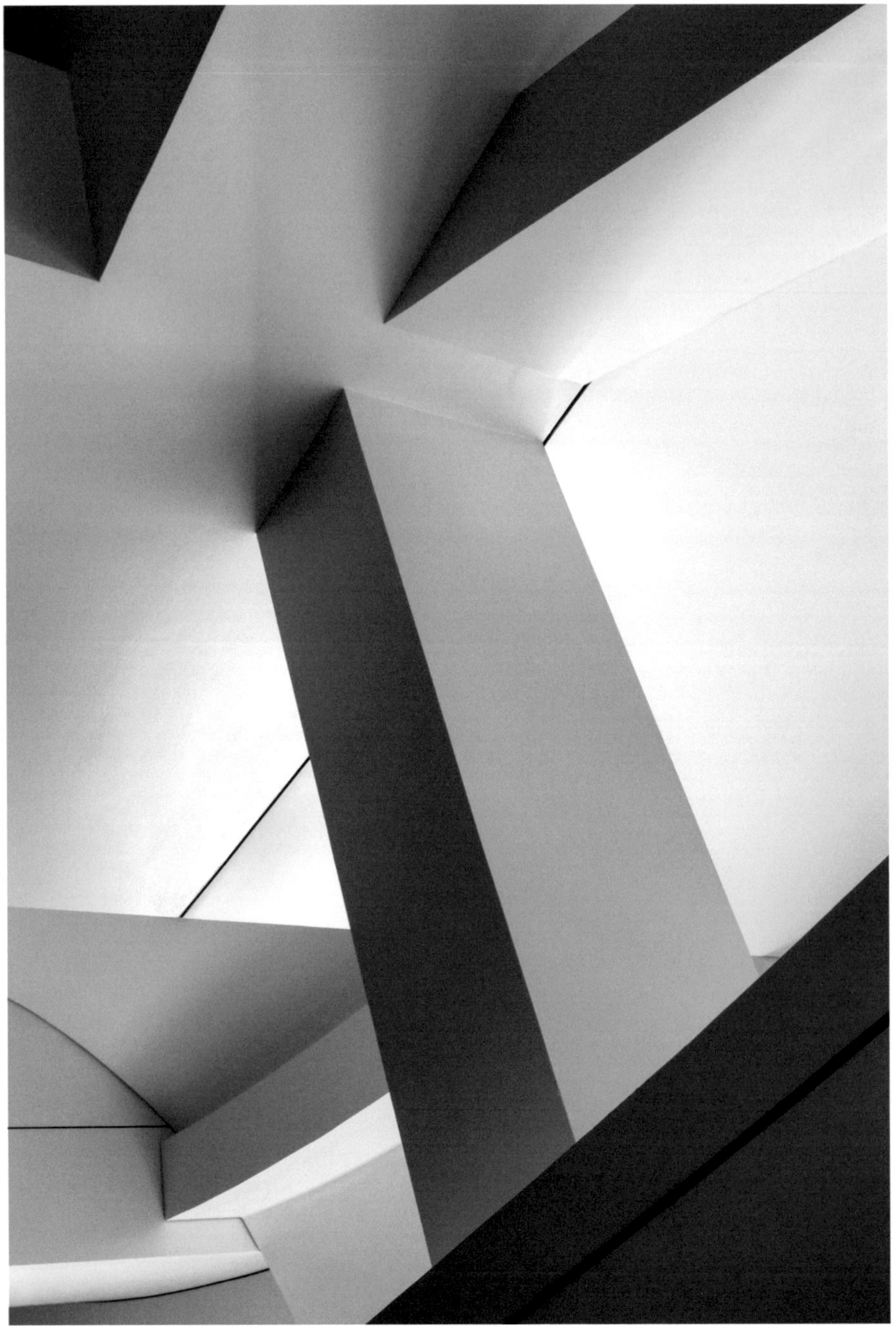

Shapes Study 35
Packard Electrical Engineering Building, Stanford University, California

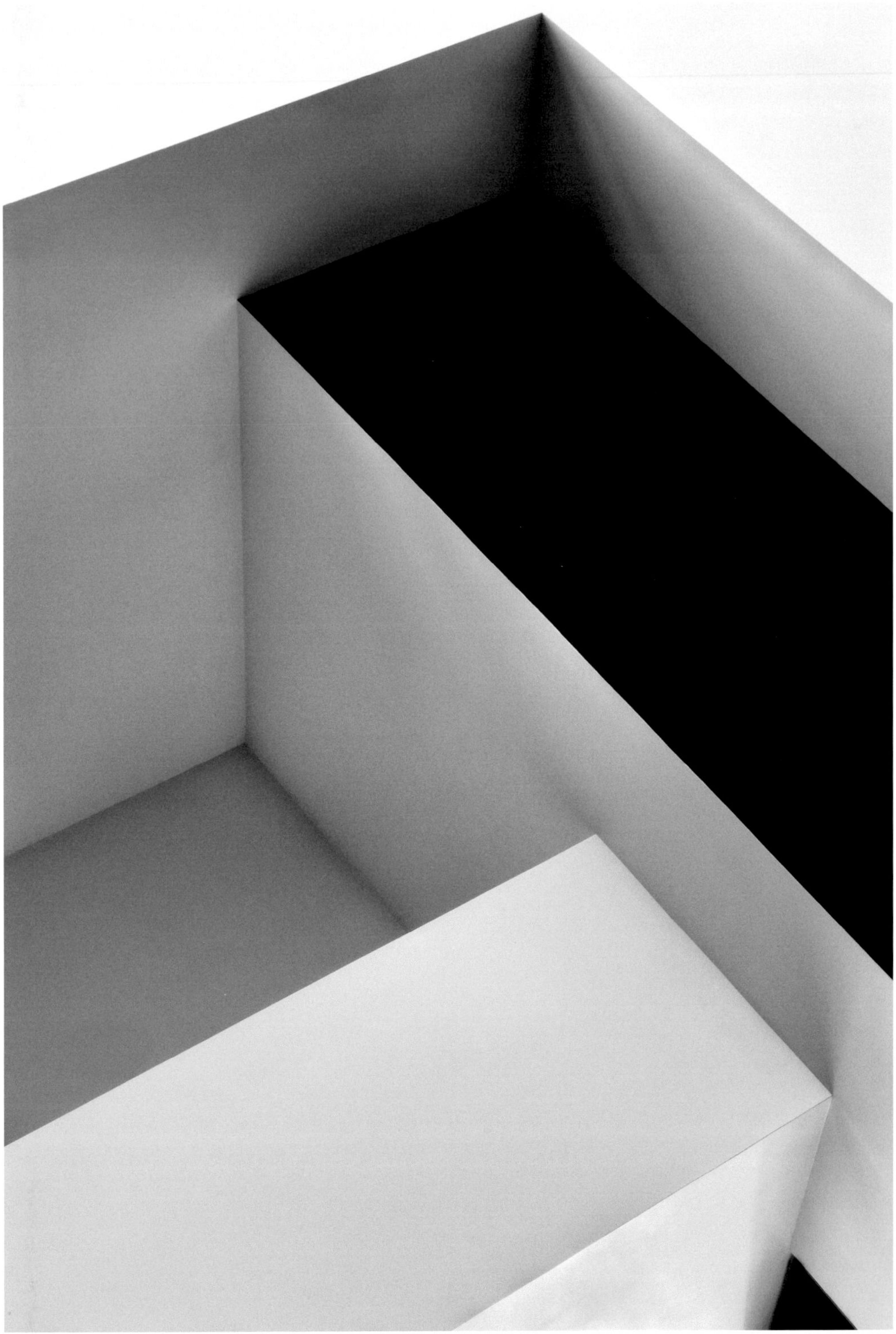

Shapes Study 29
Convention Center, San Jose, California

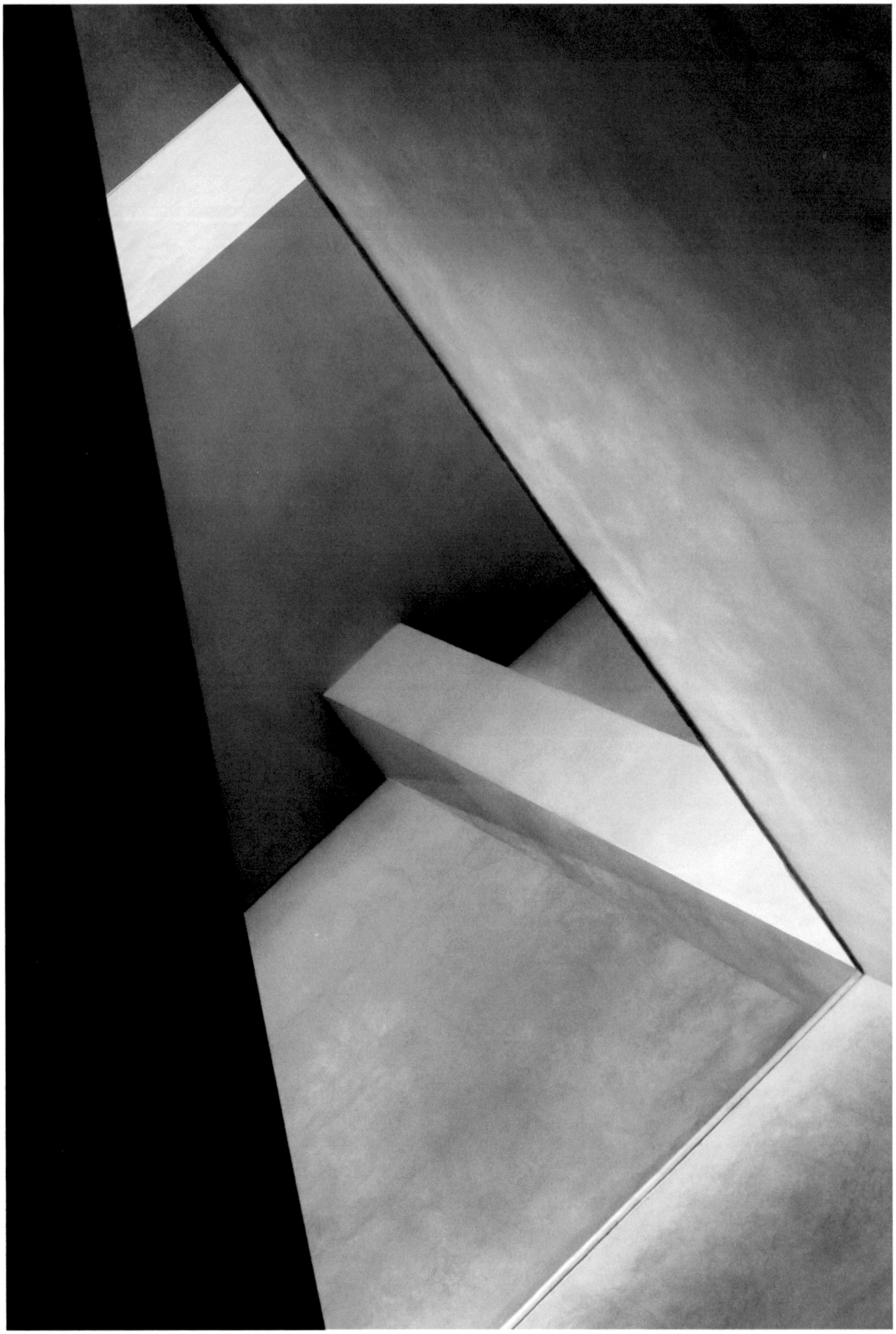

Shapes Study 12
The Tech Museum of Innovation, San Jose, California

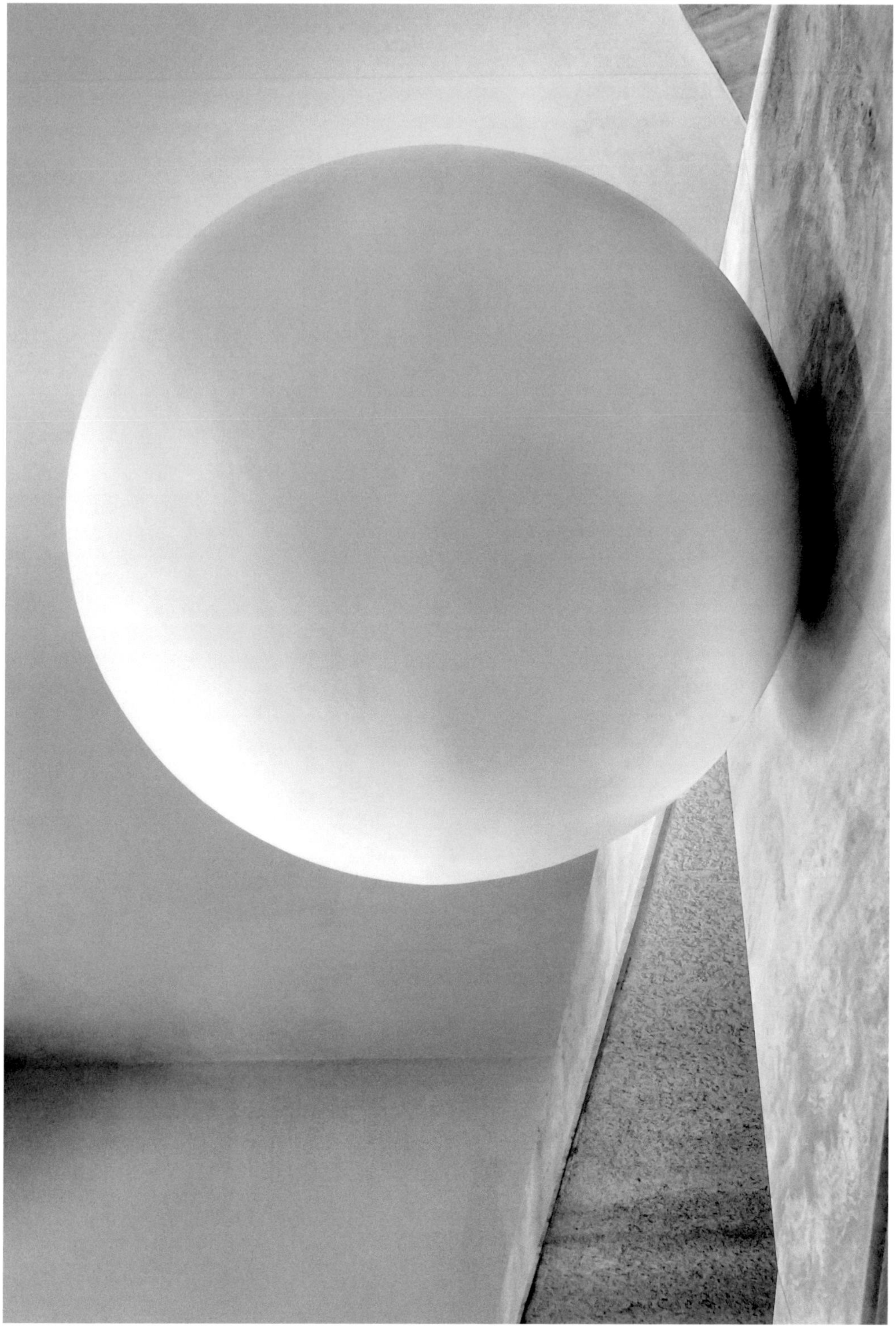

Shapes Study 13
The Tech Museum of Innovation, San Jose, California

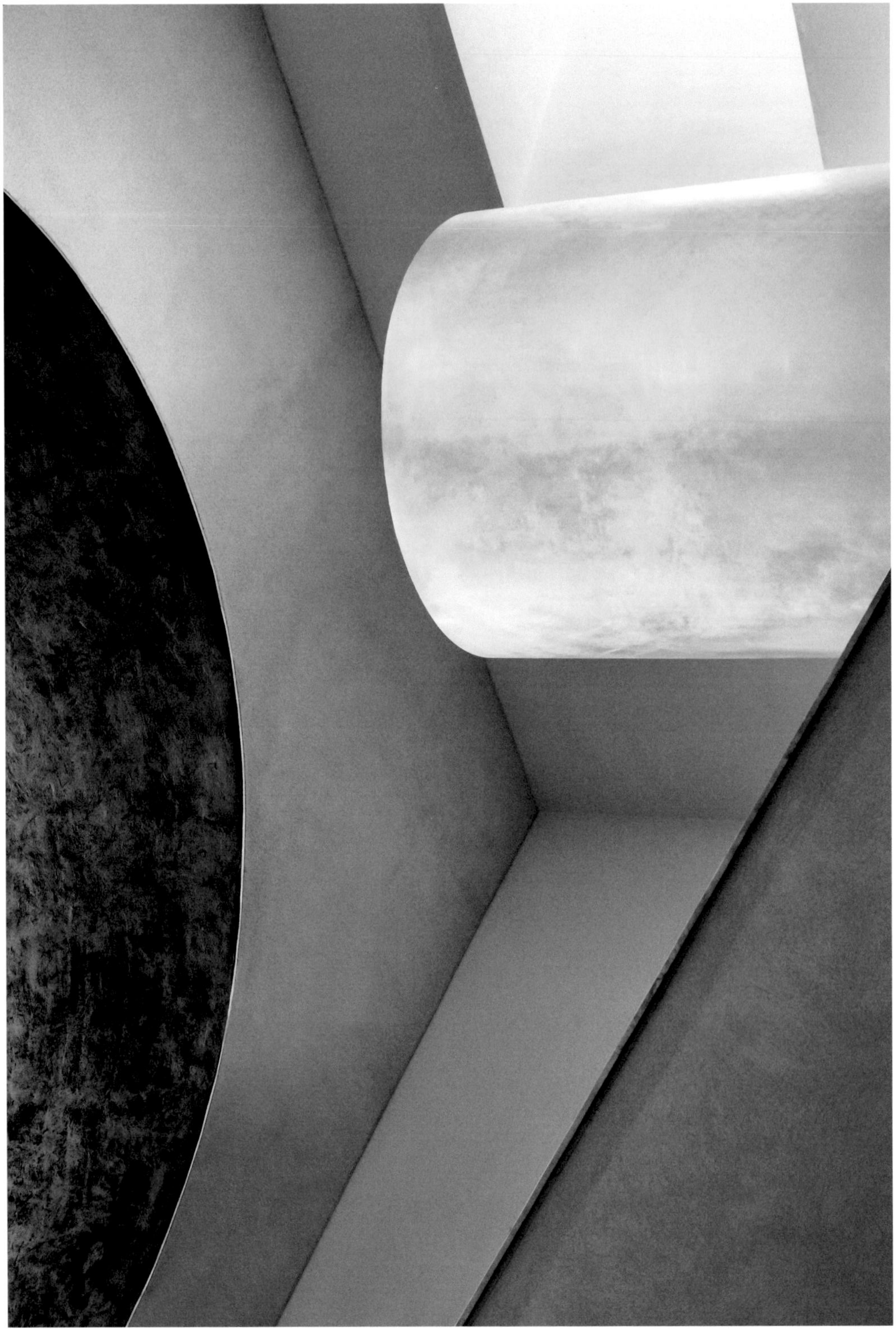

Shapes Study 16
The Tech Museum of Innovation, San Jose, California

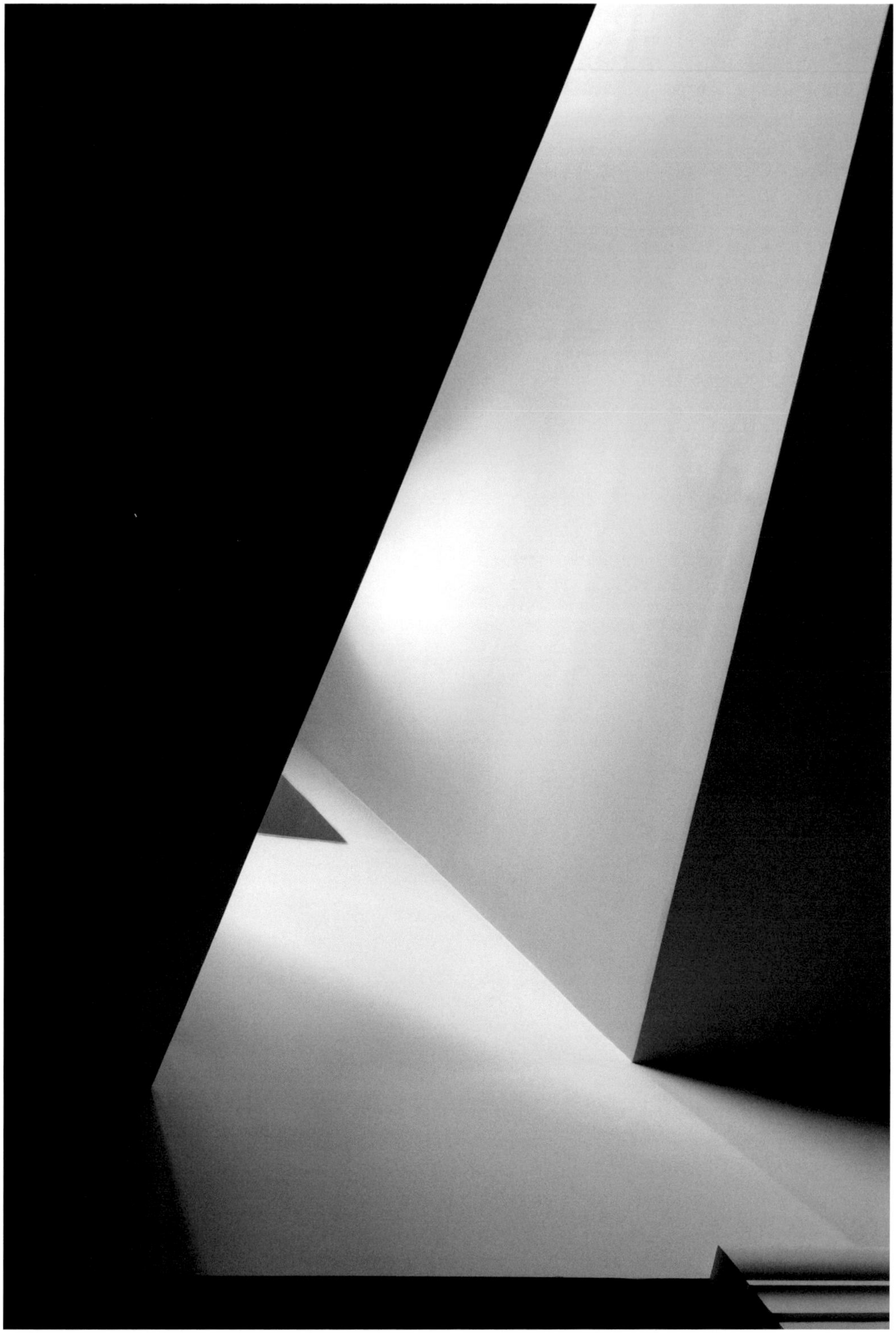

Shapes Study 8
The Fairmont Hotel, San Jose, California

Reflecting on Bodie

by Tim Messick

www.timmessick.com ♦ tmessick1@gmail.com

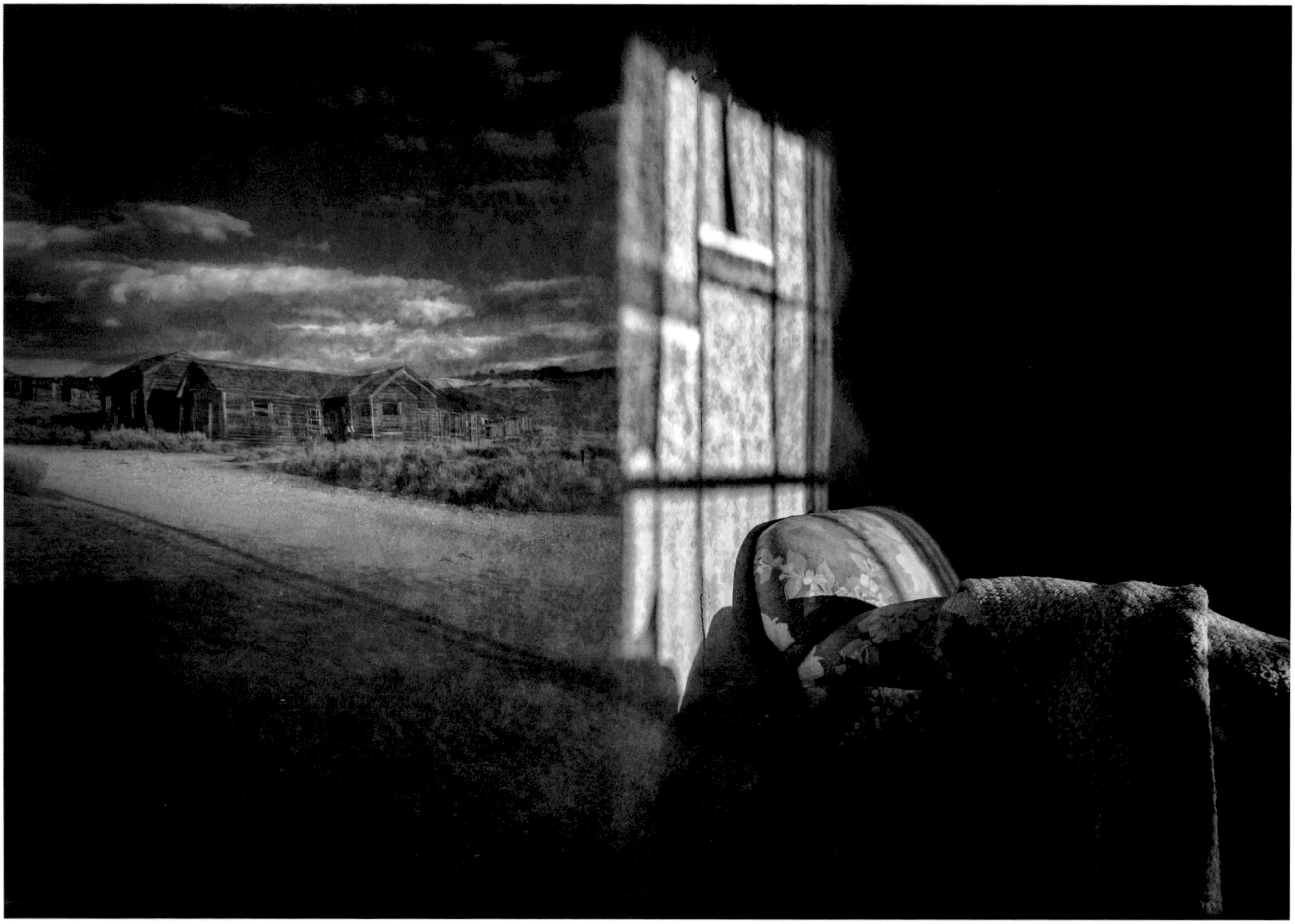

For years I've made pictures in and around the buildings at Bodie State Historic Park in Mono County, California — a favorite destination for many photographers. I looked through the windows at the artifacts inside, trying to shield the reflections of the bright sky behind me. Then one day, after reading an e-book about photographing reflections, I realized the reflections I had been fighting might add new depth and complexity to these images. My initial results changed how I see Bodie and what I look for there. Now I'm hooked on seeking out reflections, composing these ephemeral found collages of interior and exterior light.

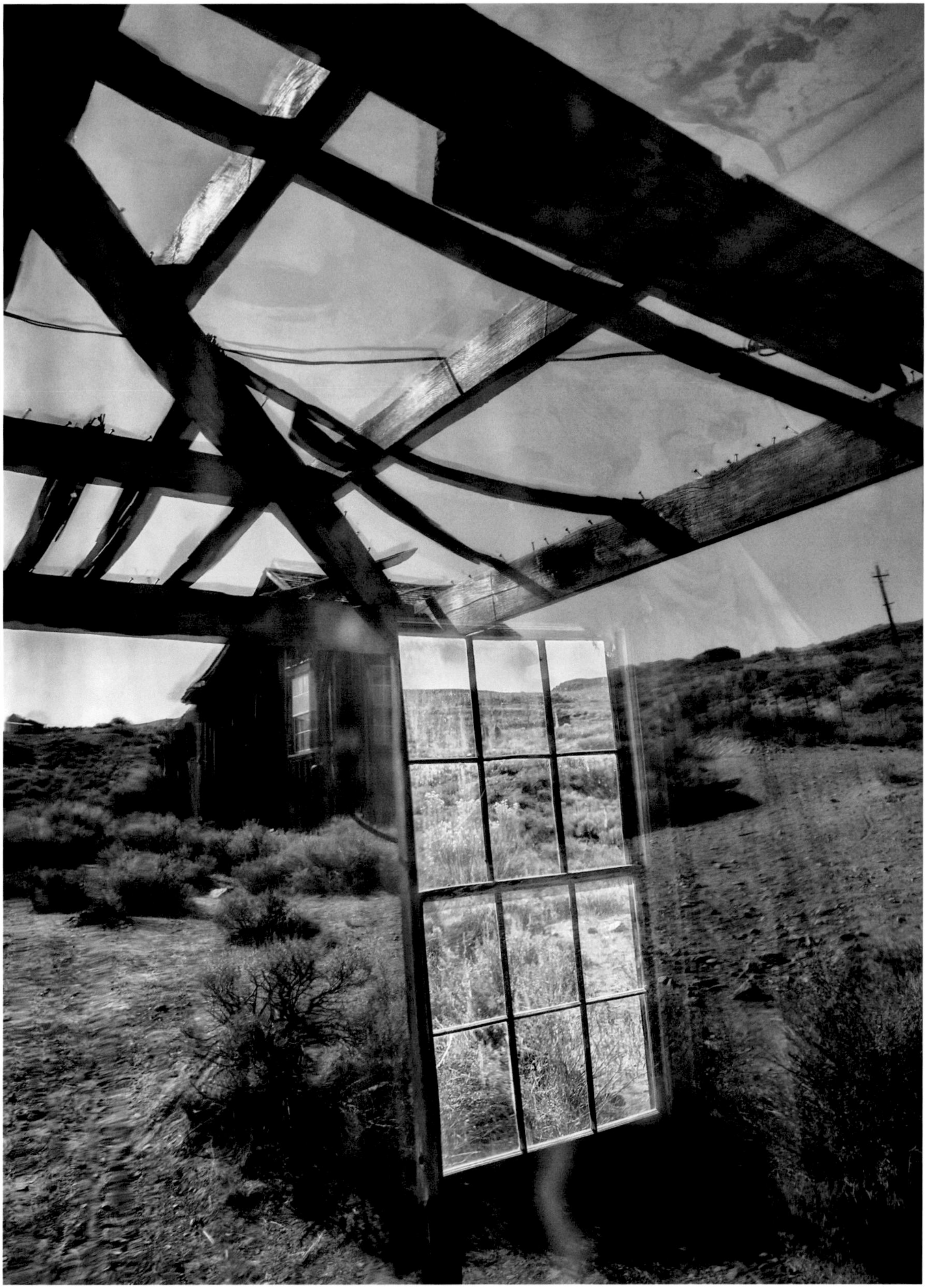

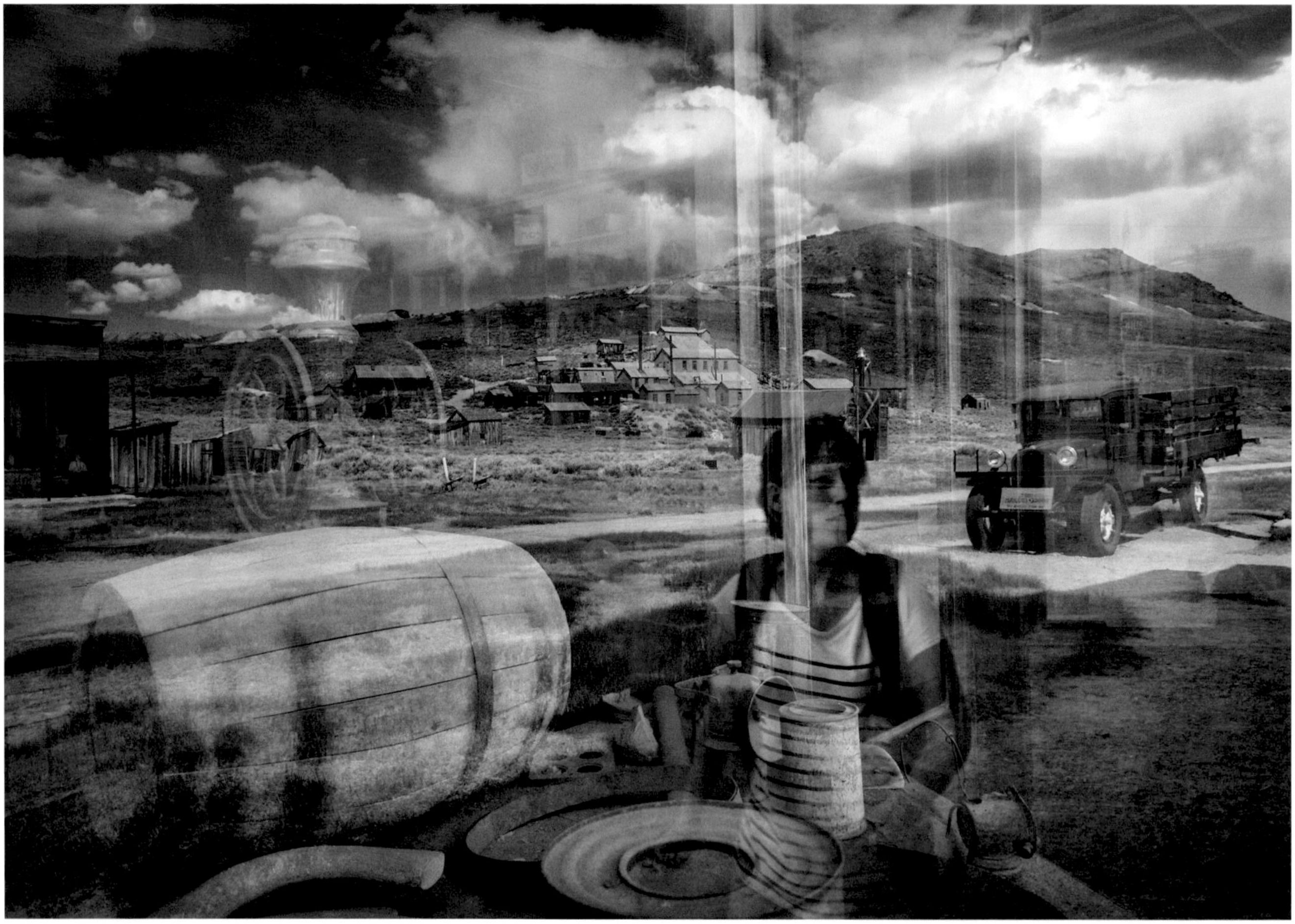

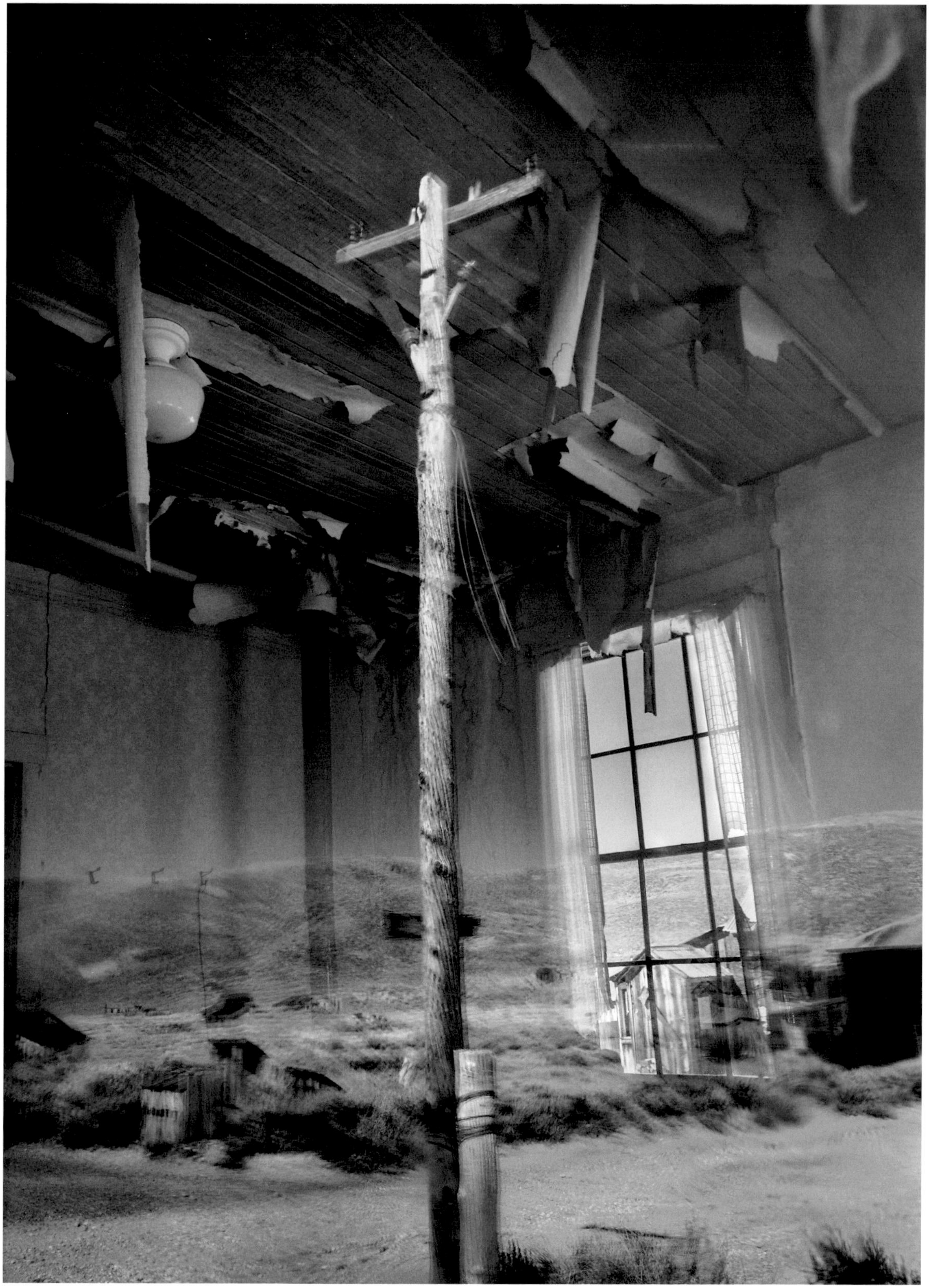

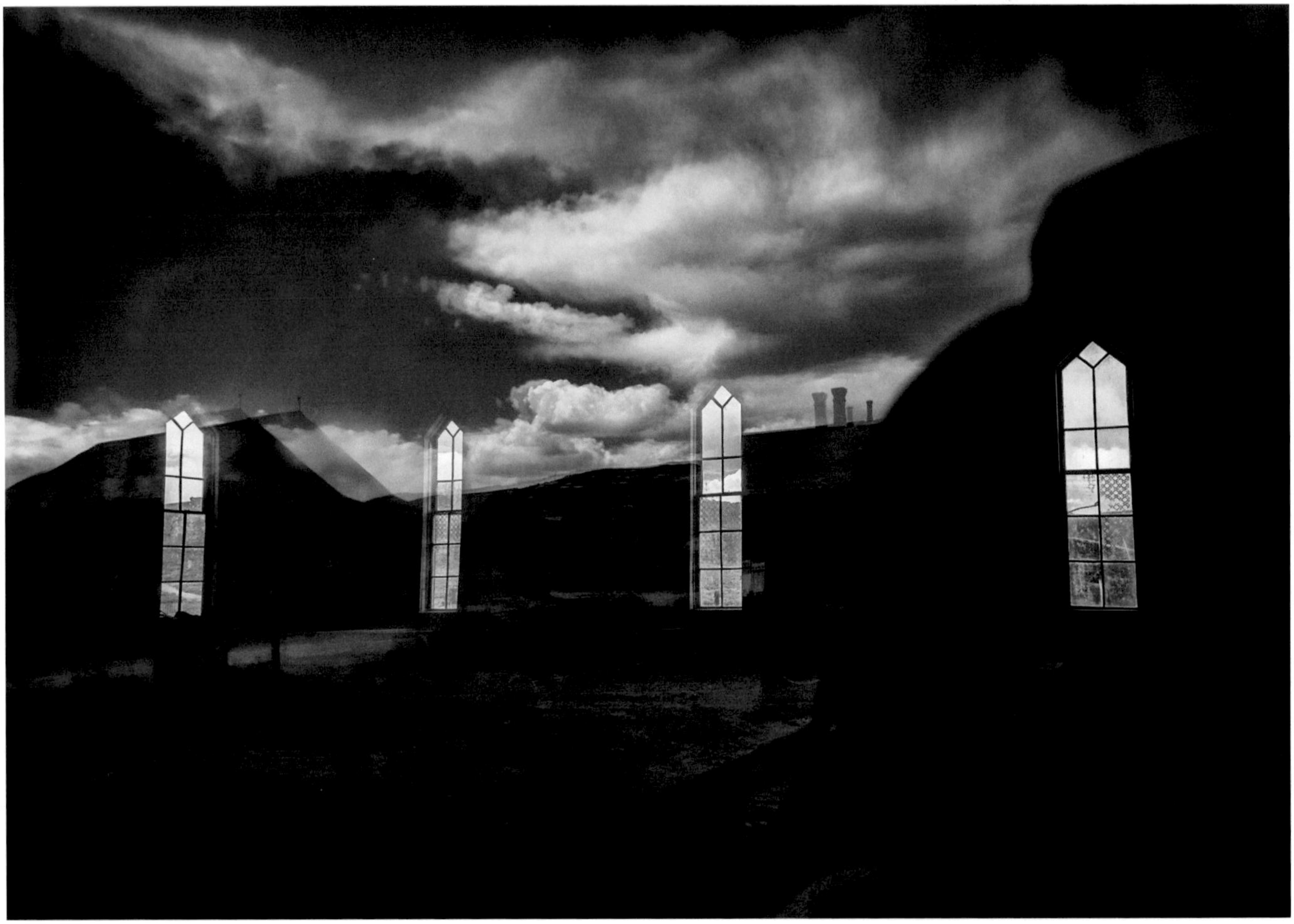

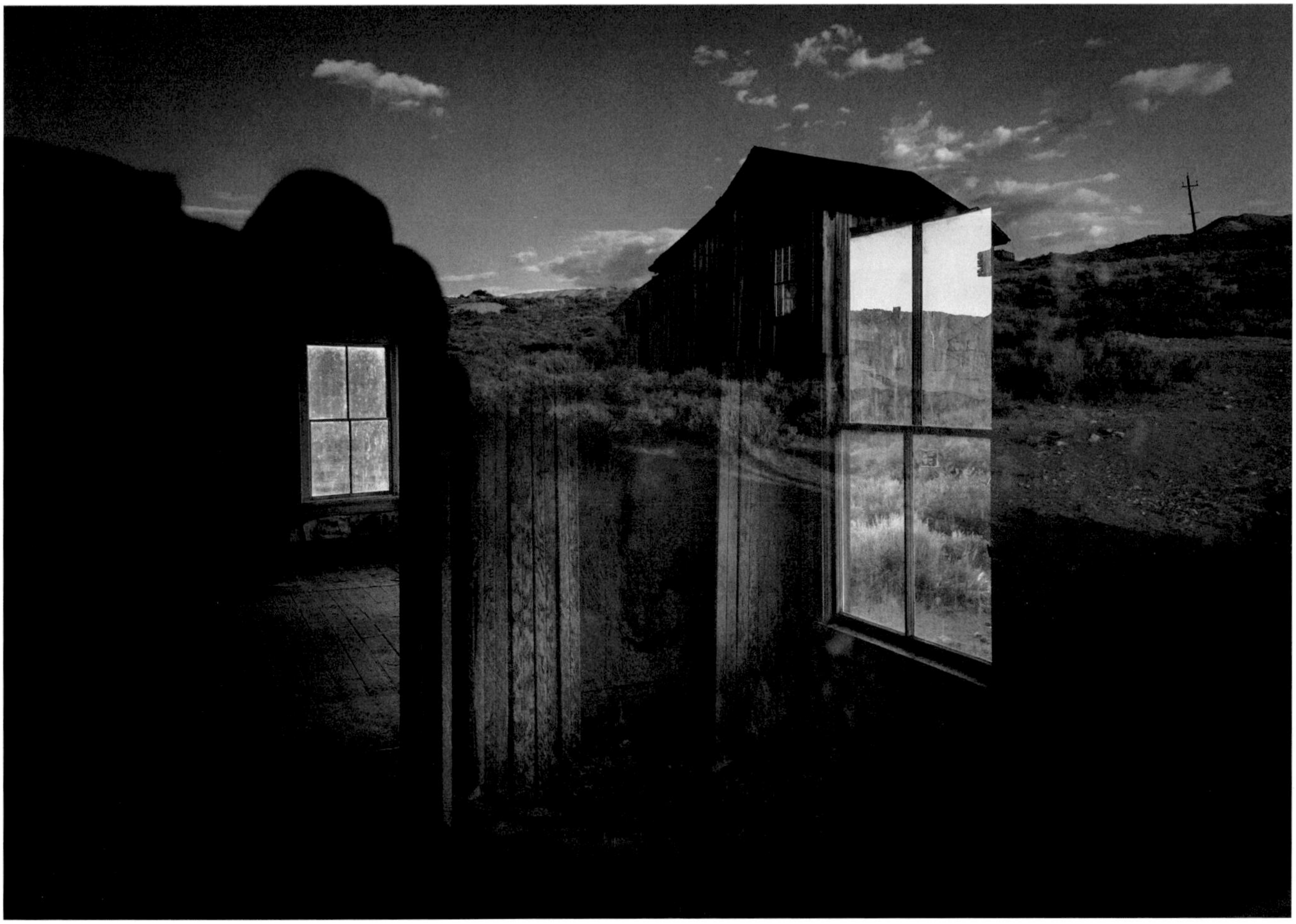

The Village Distilleries of Maramureş Romania

by Ian Macilwain

www.broombank.co.uk ♦ ian@broombank.demon.co.uk

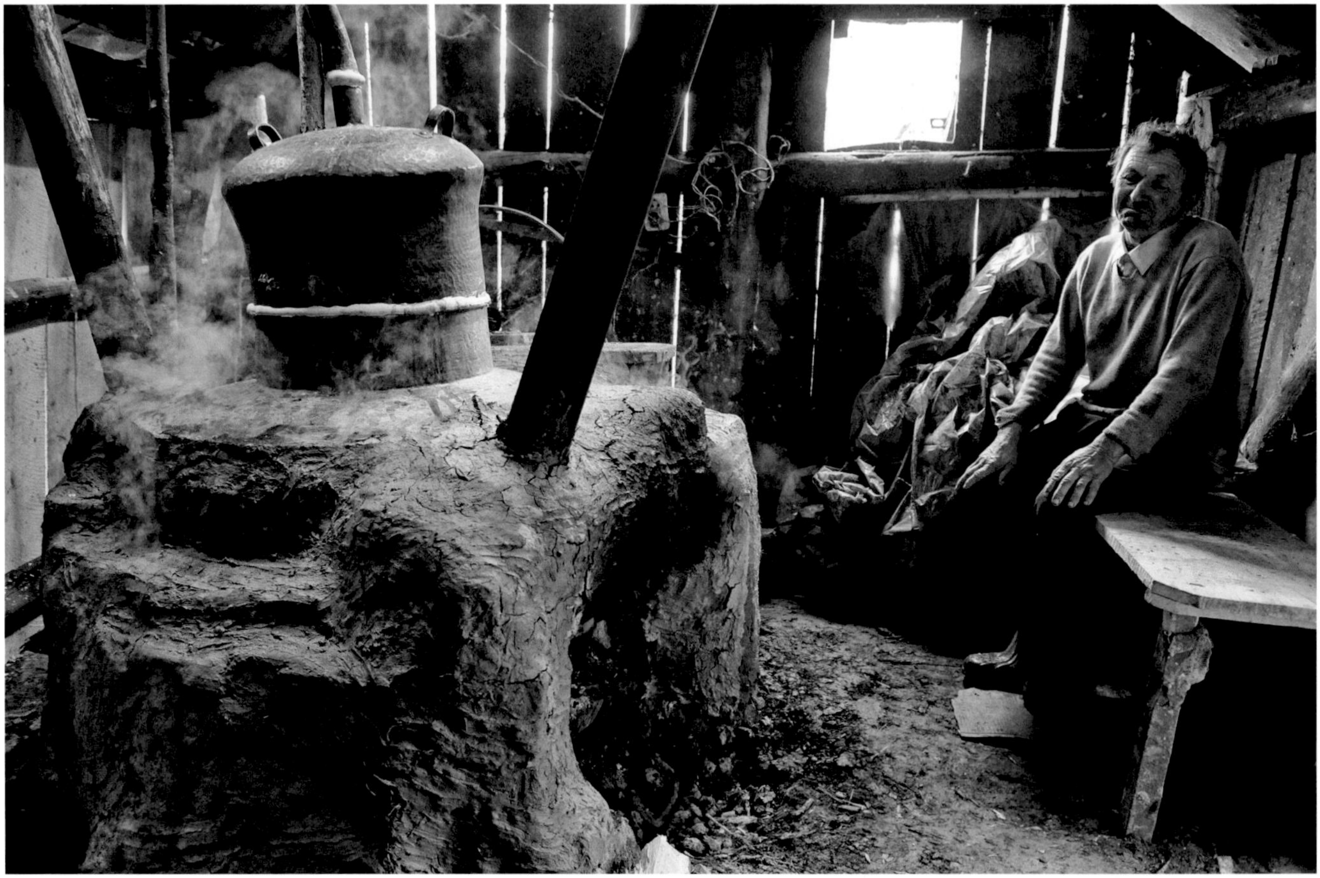

I first went to Romania on a Honda 50 scooter in 1968. I was captivated then, as I am now, by its untouched rural culture, unchanged for hundreds of years. Family loyalties are intense. Nowhere is that more apparent than in the distillation of "Horinca," the fruit brandy which is at the very centre of Maramureş village life.

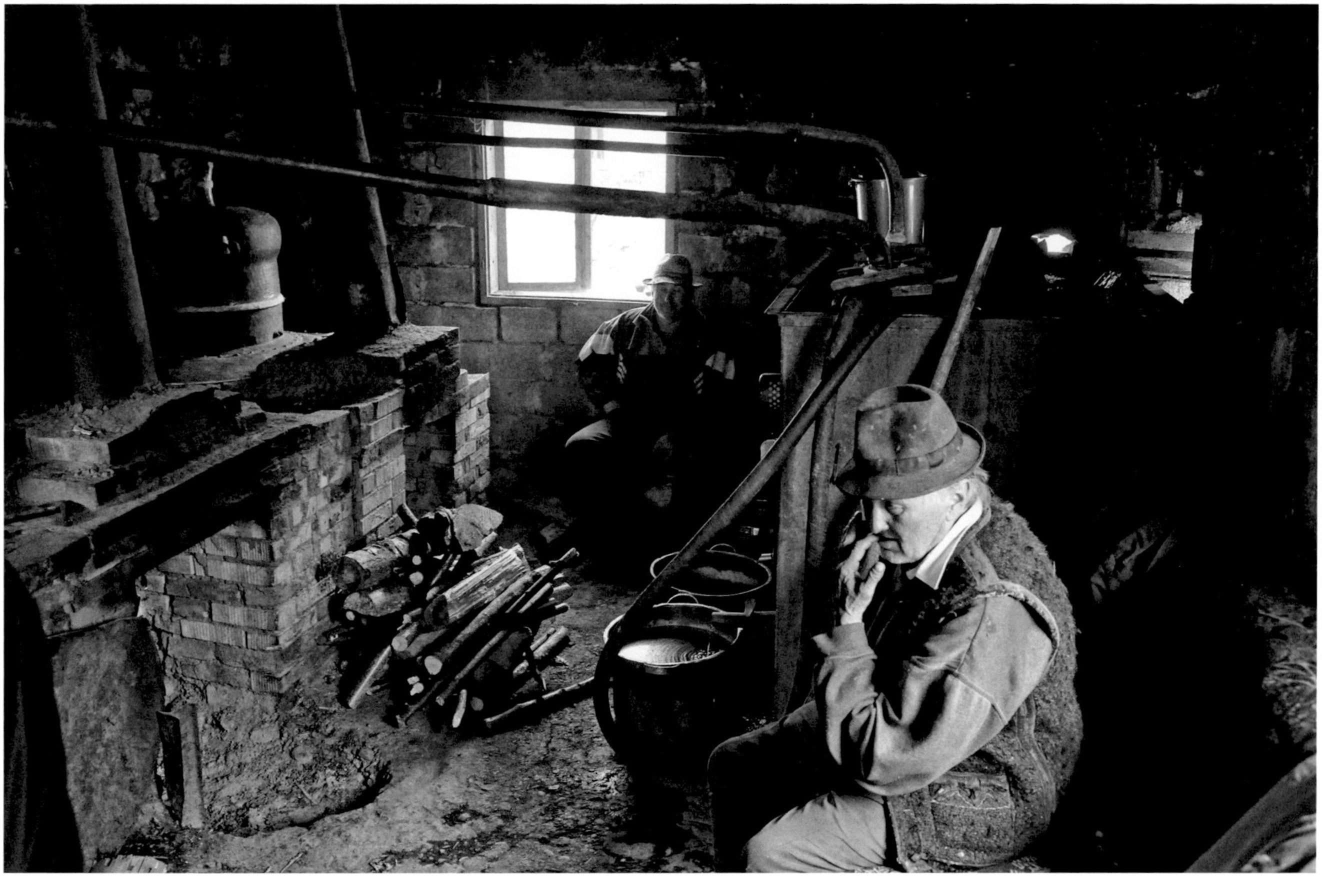

The *cazane* or stills are owned by one family, but used by many, who bring their own fruit pulp after months of fermentation to be distilled in the copper still.

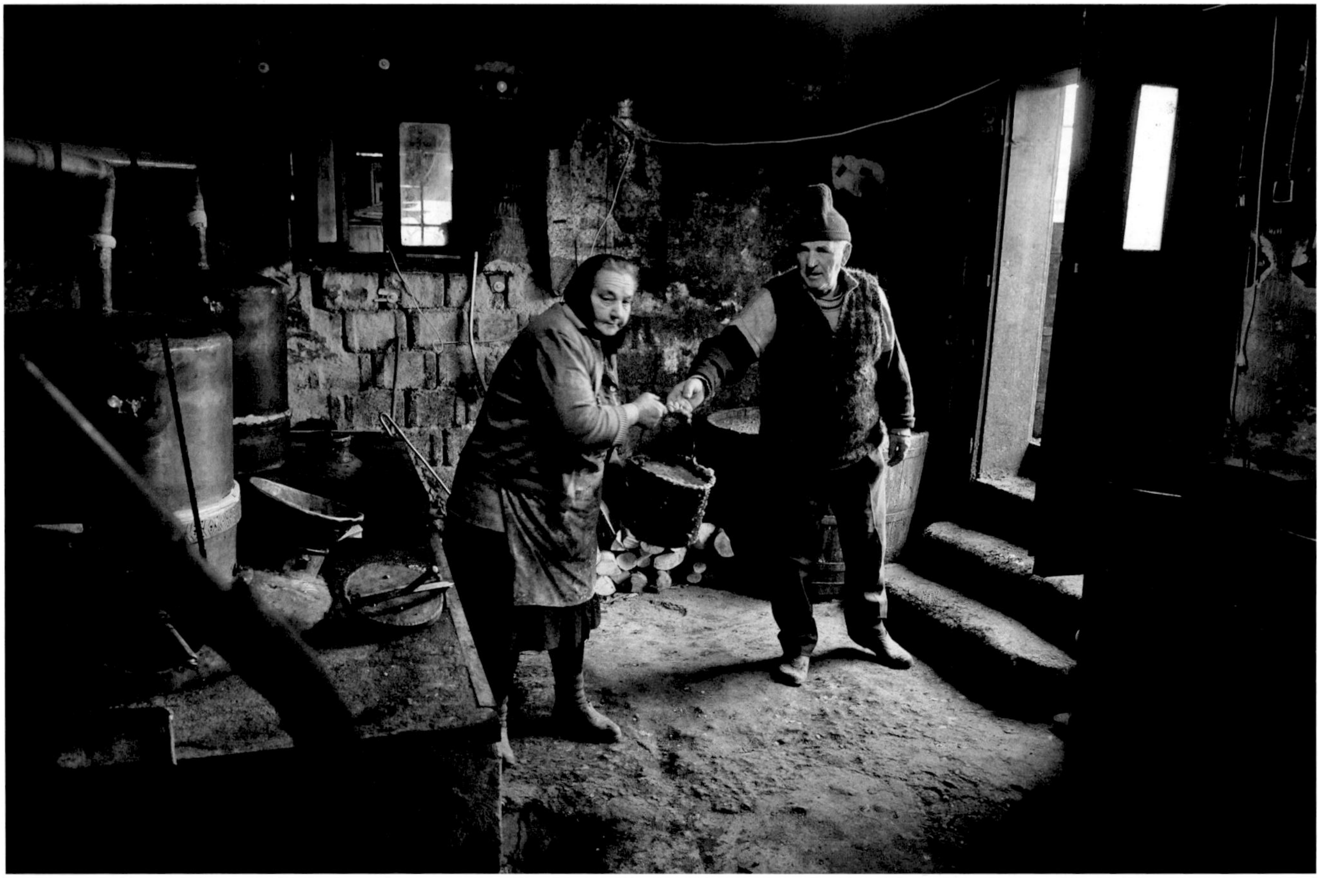

Everybody helps, from older children to grannies in their 80s.

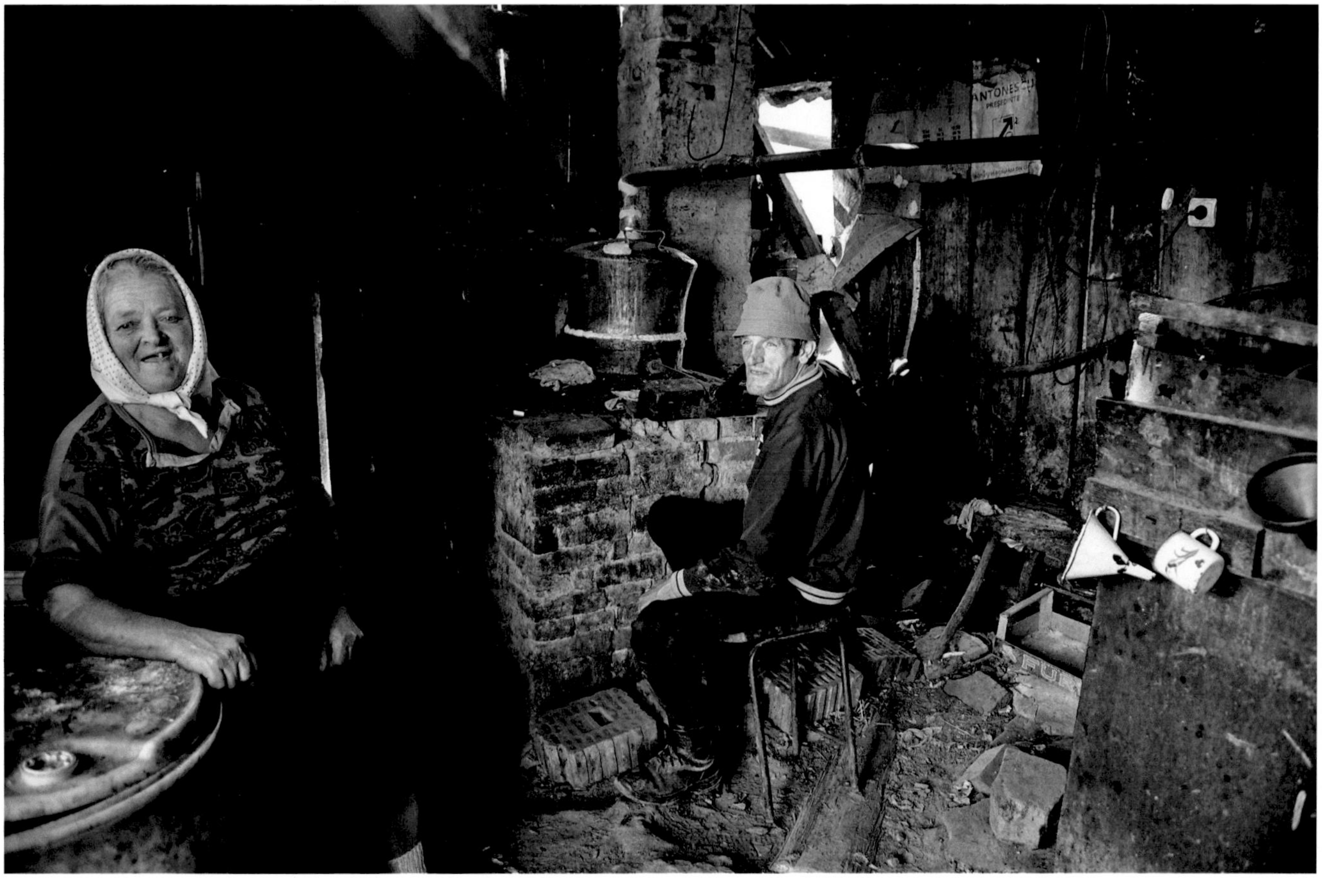

There is an atmosphere of camaraderie and good cheer
with lots of joking and humor.

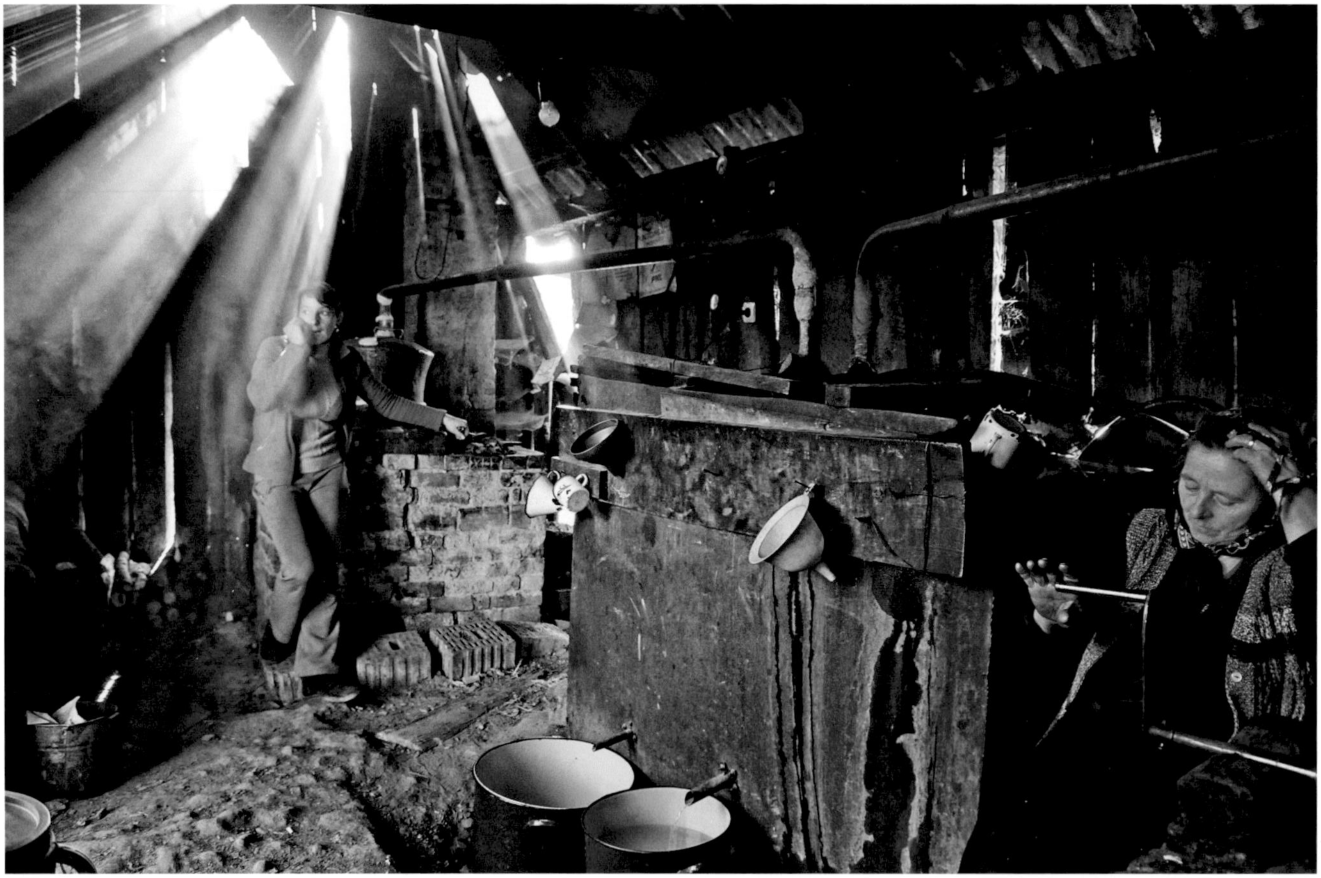

It is hard work. The still must be turned with a crank handle for two hours in between each filling to stop the pulp from sticking to the sides.

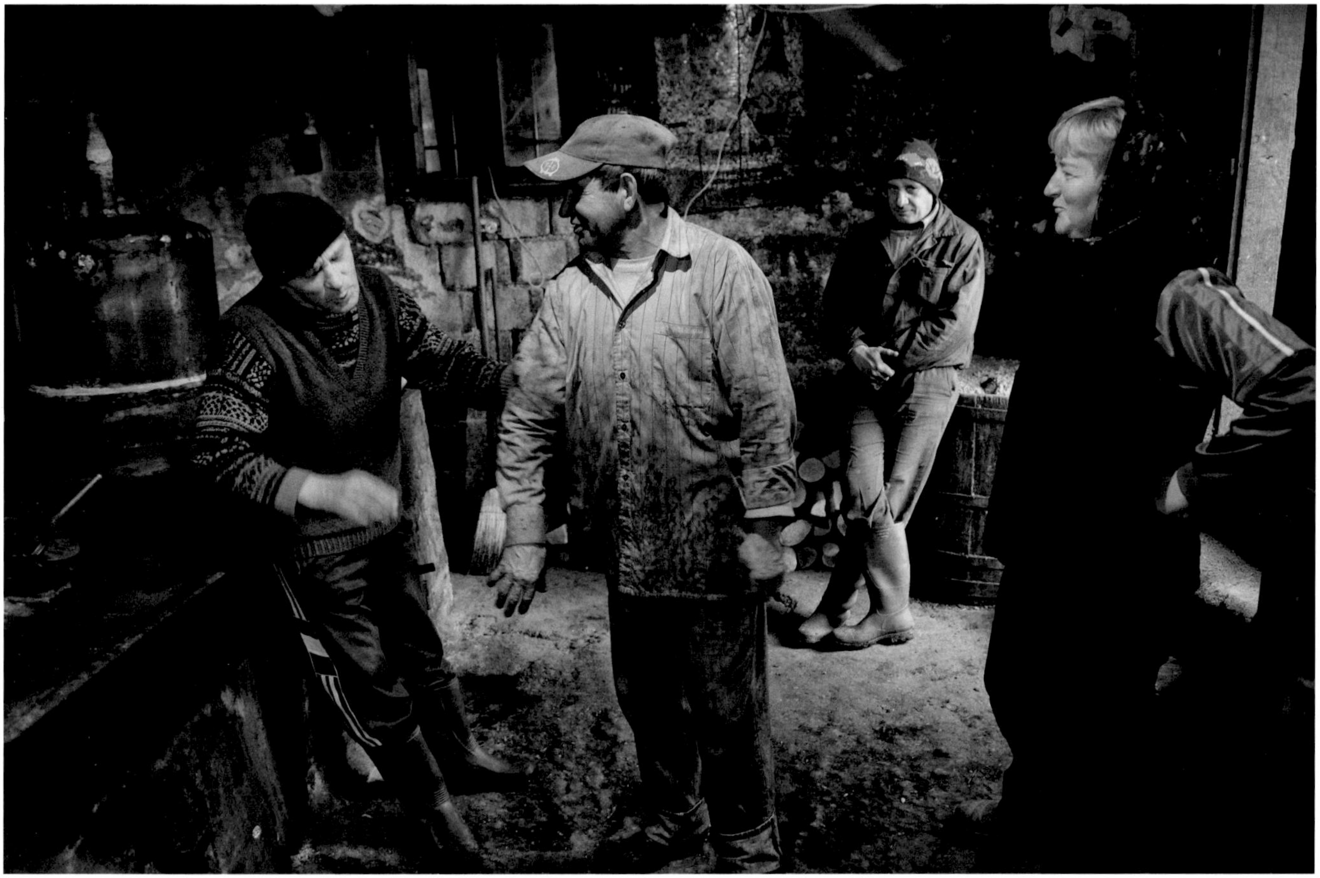

I have "distilled" my large collection of pictures (which contributed to the book, *In search of the village distilleries of Maramureş,* published in 2015) down to just six images for this project. As black-and-white conversions (the book is in color) they seem to represent the very essence of this atmospheric place.

A Portrait of Shadows and Light

by Amy Kanka Valadarsky

www.amykankaphotography.com ♦ amykva@gmail.com

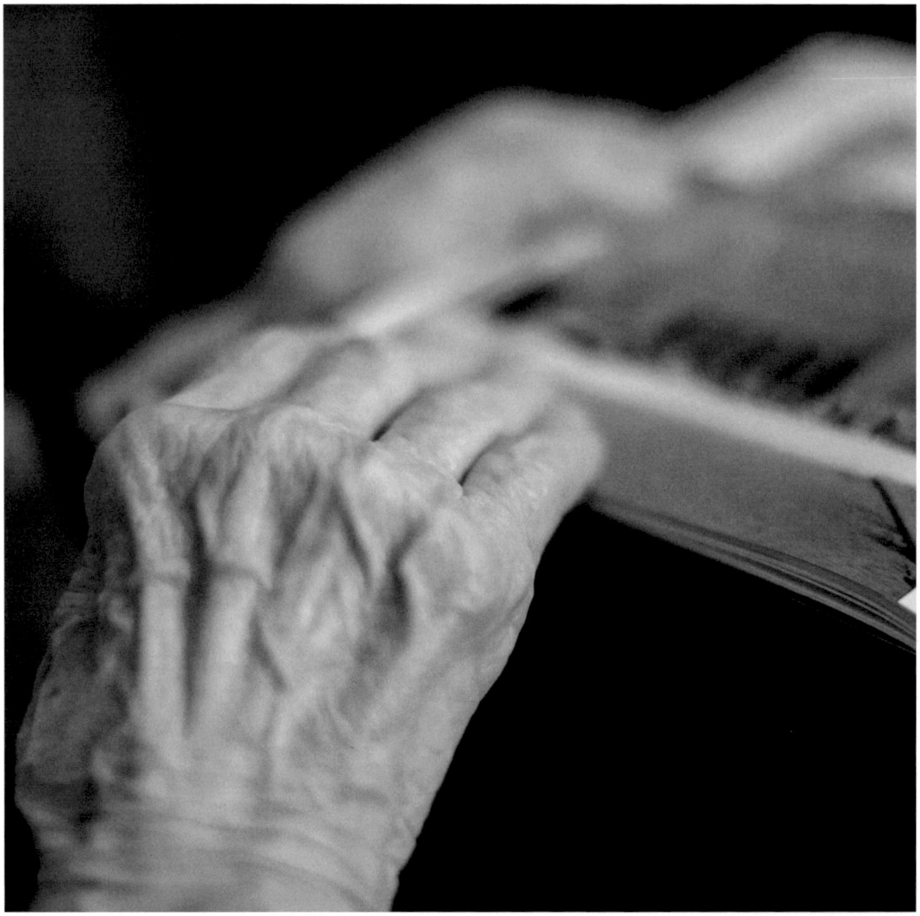

Neither houses nor people remained

Leafing through an old book with images from Bratislava, the place where she was born. "Those were the best years of my life," she says.

I created *A Portrait of Shadows and Light* as gift of love to my mother-in-law, Irene Kanka, who never understood why I insisted on photographing her. Irene is one of the few lucky survivors who came out of the Auschwitz concentration camp walking on their two feet. Four of her sisters did not. Despite going through the darkest of time, she still, at the age of 94, radiates an aura of goodness and light.

Her daily life is a blend of the ordinary and the remembered. Framed images in her bedroom, a few surviving photographs from "before." Whenever I visit, "those times" are as present as the sun shining through the lace curtain, creating patterns of shadow and light.

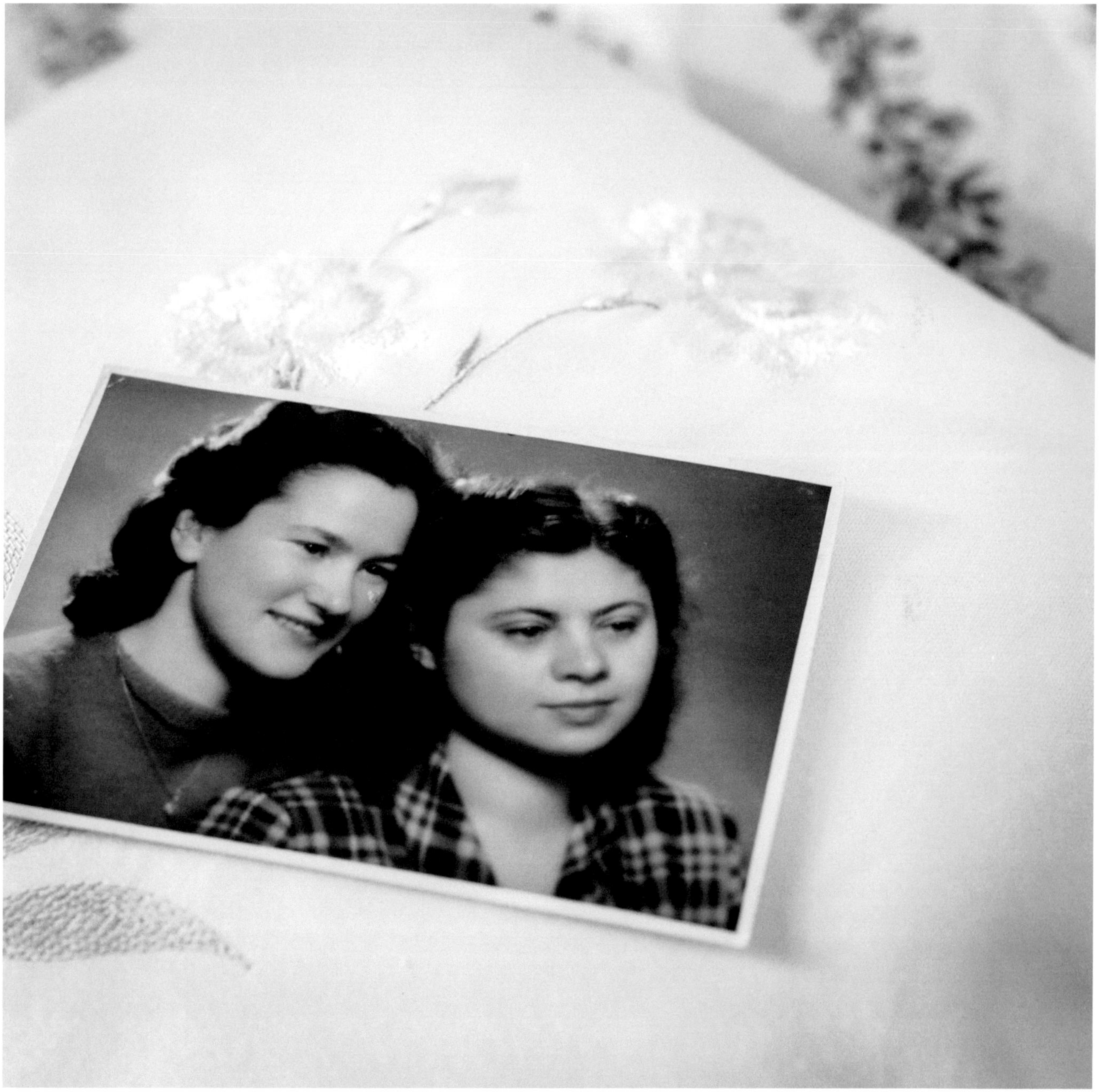

Best friends

A friendship forged in Auschwitz. Two young women who survived the horrors of the Holocaust against all odds.

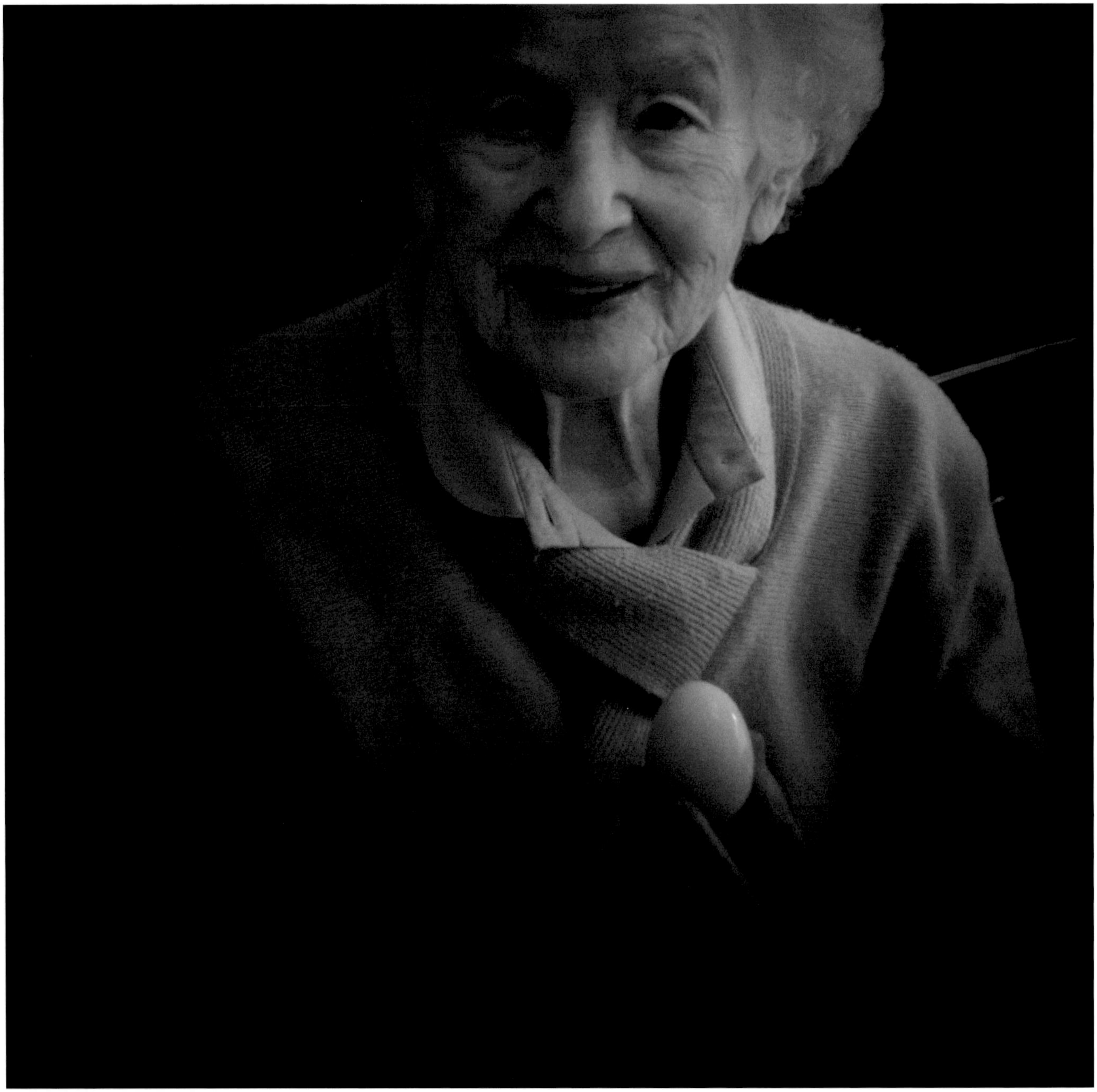

The birthday gift

"We were eight children at home. My father never remembered our birthday, but my mother did. Every birthday I got a hard boiled egg, which was a real treat for me."

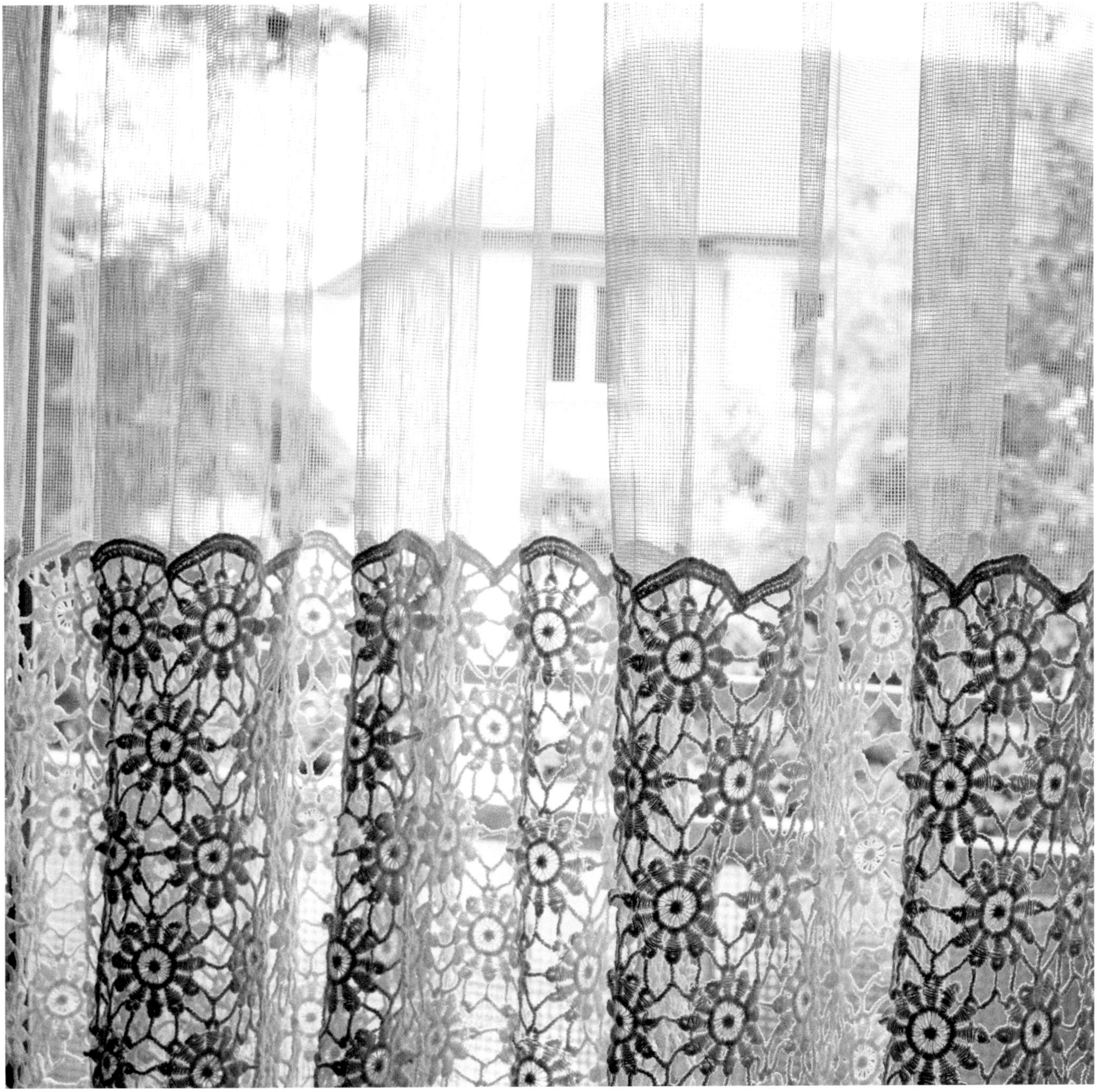

What she sees

94 years old. The eyes that saw all the brothers and sisters die rest now on a peaceful view of a quiet neighborhood in Frankfurt, Germany.

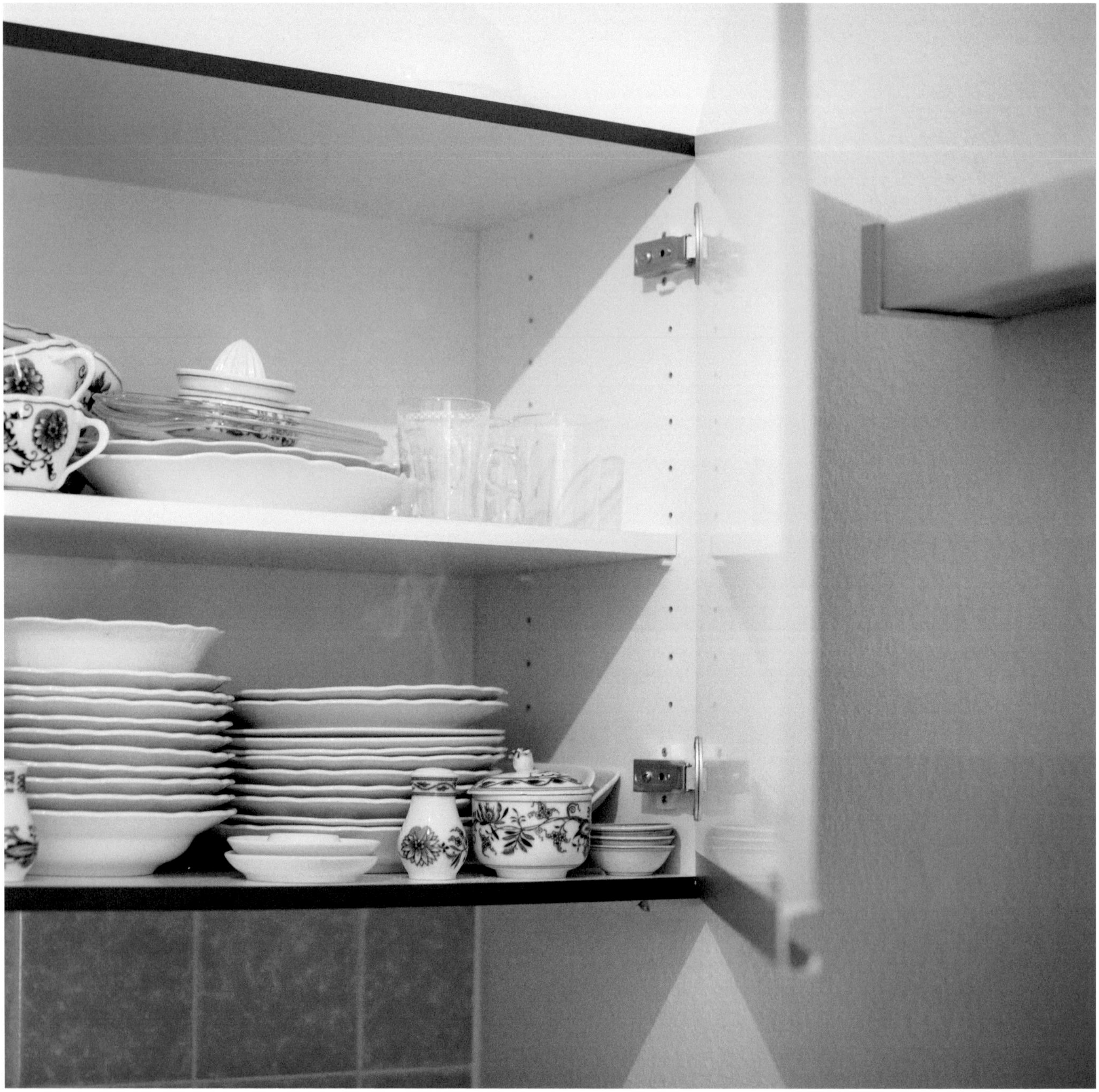

The Zwiebelmuster plates

A small one bedroom apartment, filled with books and pictures that keep her company. Once in a while the grandchildren visit and the small table is set with the blue and white Zwiebelmuster plates.

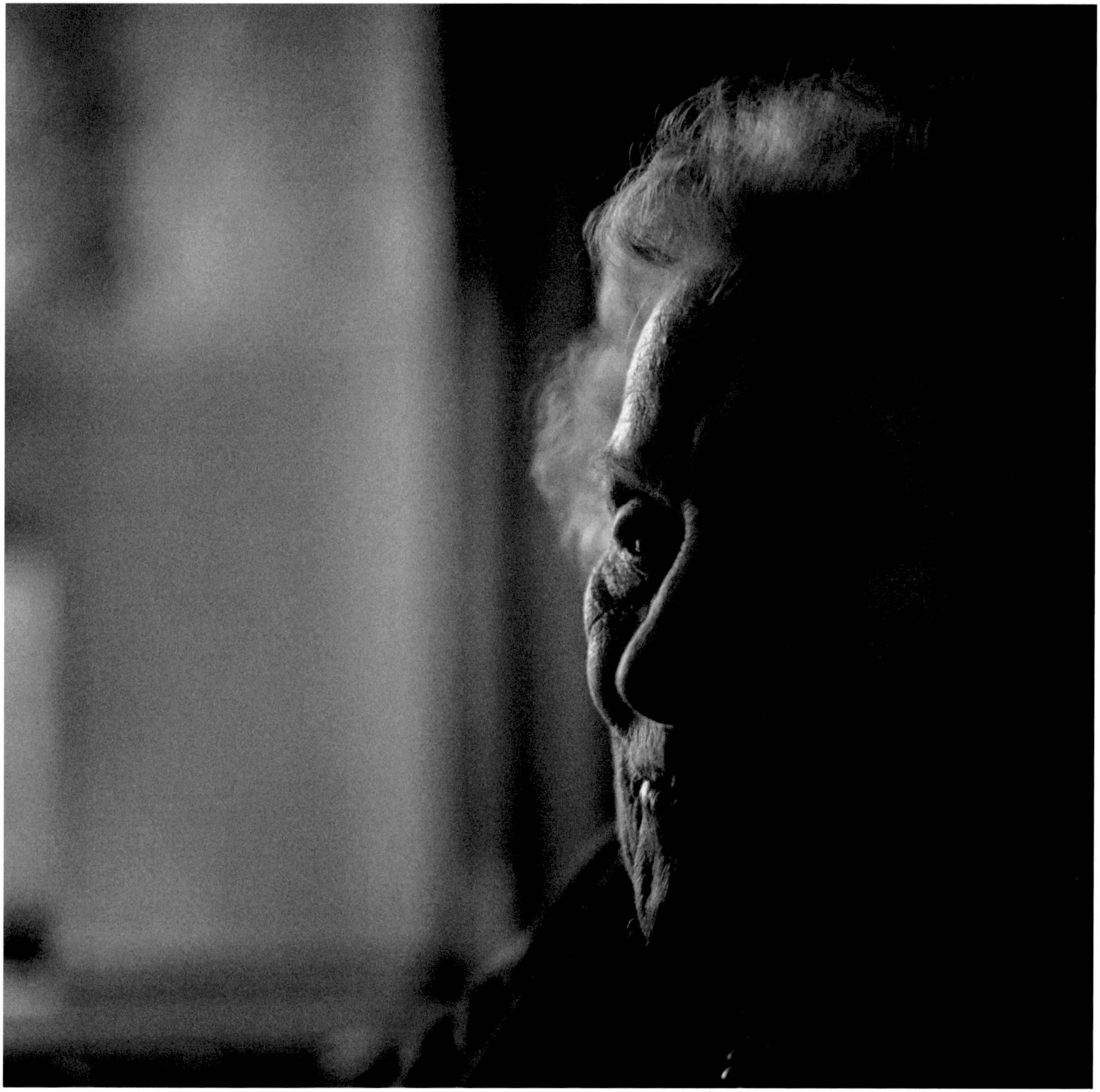

Light and shadow

She chose light. To survive, marry, and raise a son. The son became my husband. I became part of her story and she became part of mine.

Dogs and the City

by Lev Tsimring

www.levtsimring.com • lev@levtsimring.com

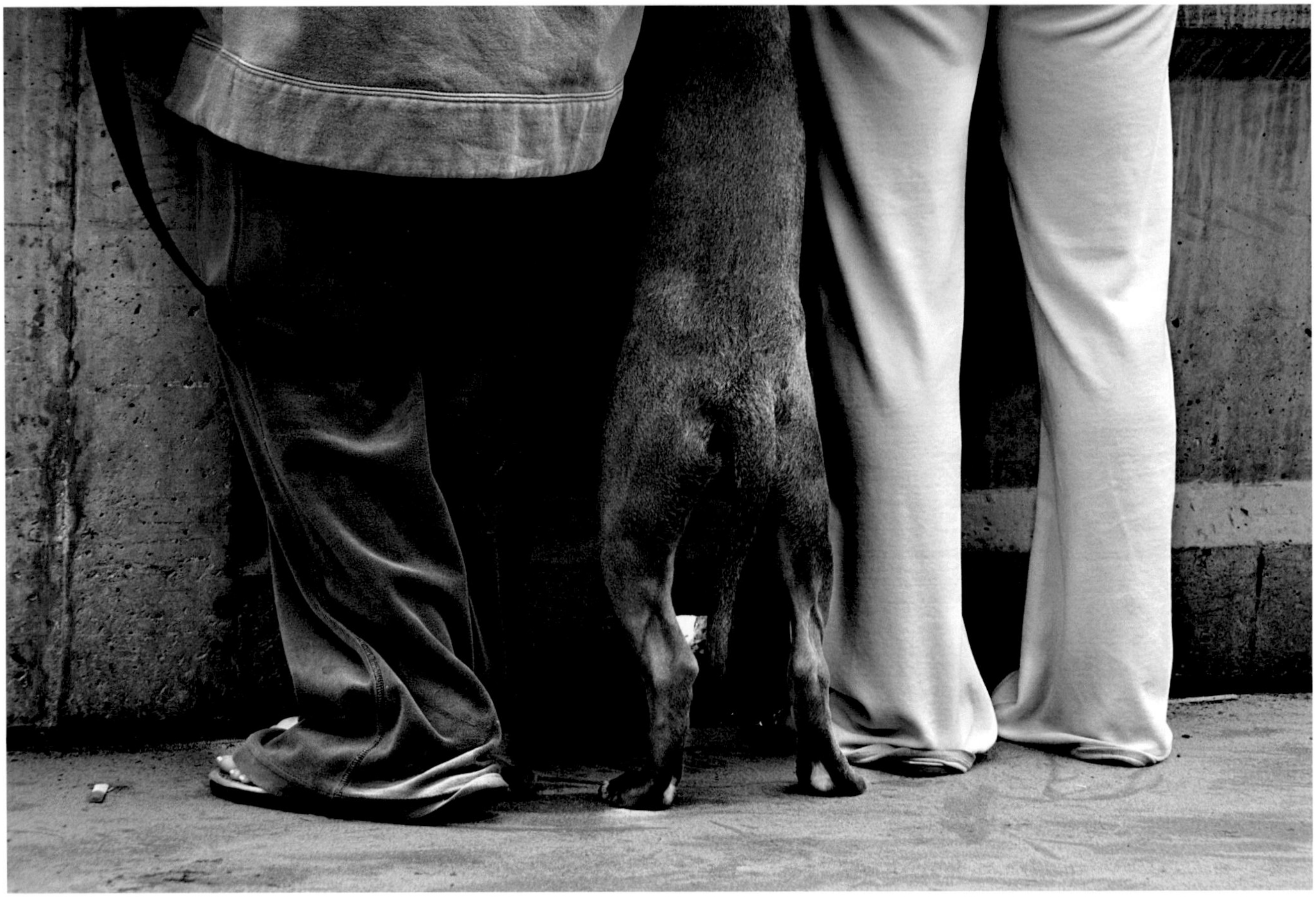

Six legs

One of my photographic heroes, Elliott Erwitt, single-handedly expanded the genre of environmental portraiture to include man's best friends. Hundreds of his wonderful and humorous images communicate the beauty, character, and a whole range of emotions of our canine companions. In a slightly different approach, I tend to focus on candid "canine street photography." In this series of photographs taken in different parts of the world, I wanted to show how well dogs adapted to living with us in our urban environment. What strikes me most is just how human-like urban dogs have become in their everyday existence, emotional responses, interactions with us humans, and with other dogs. I hope my photos will make you feel the same way.

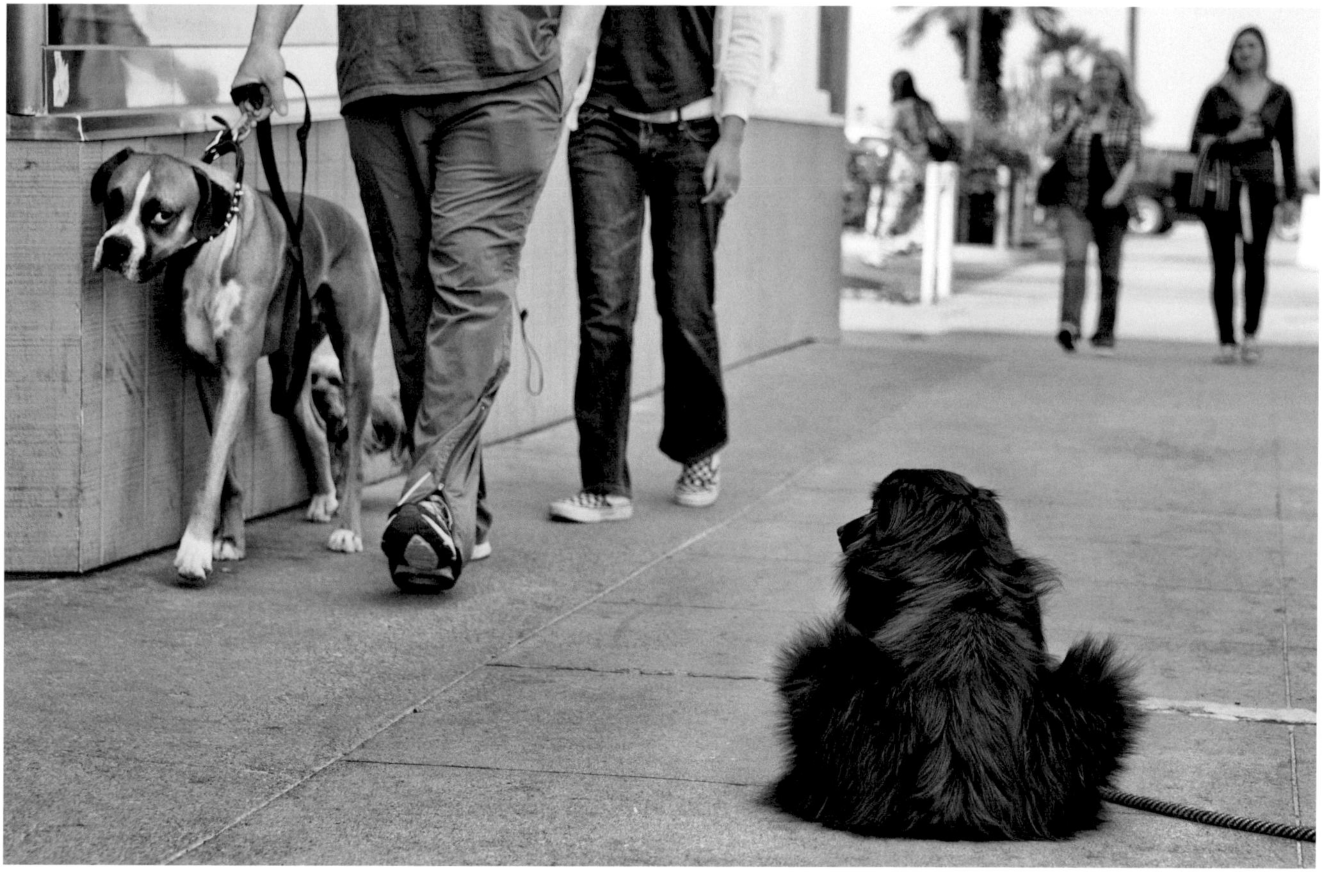

Wary eye

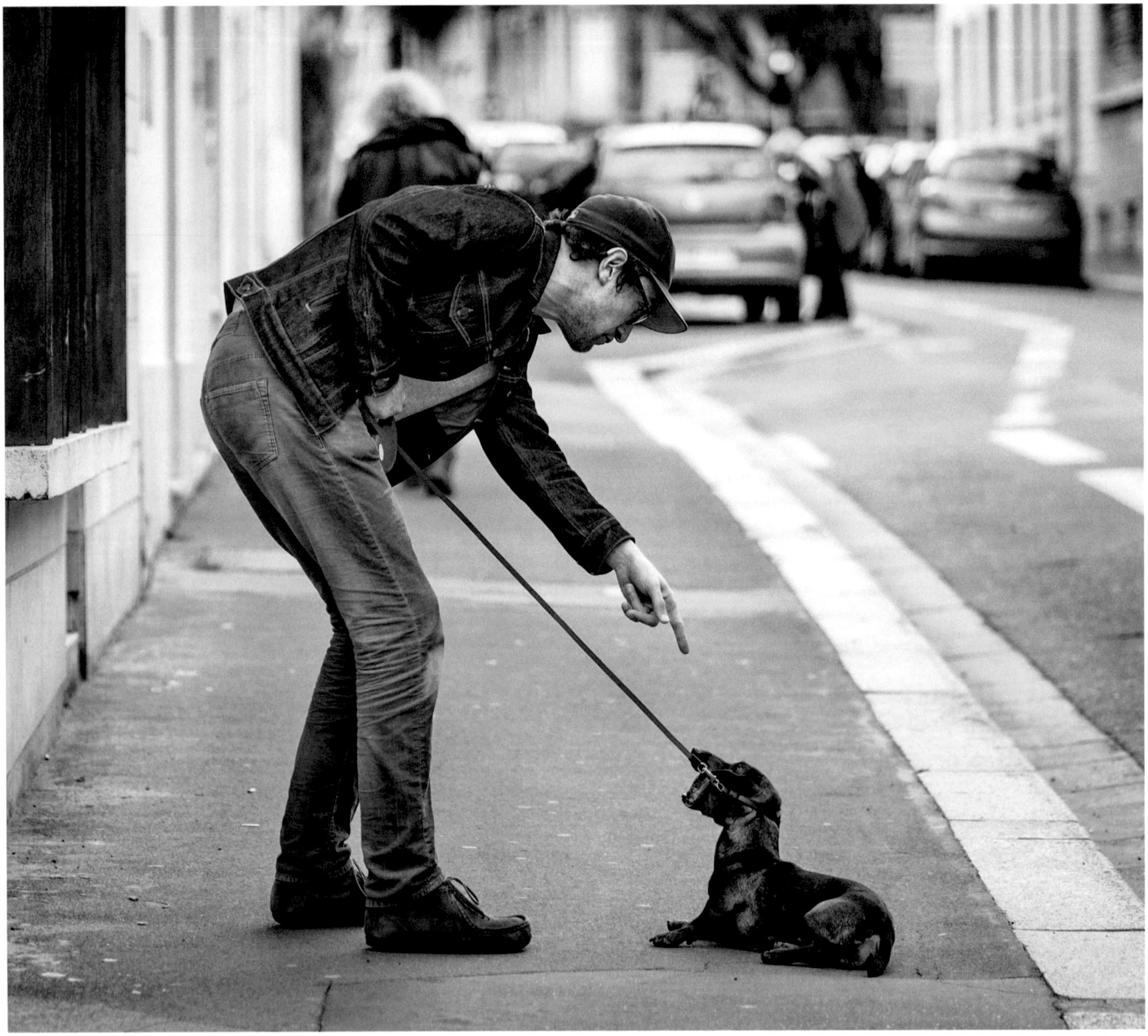

Unsentimental education

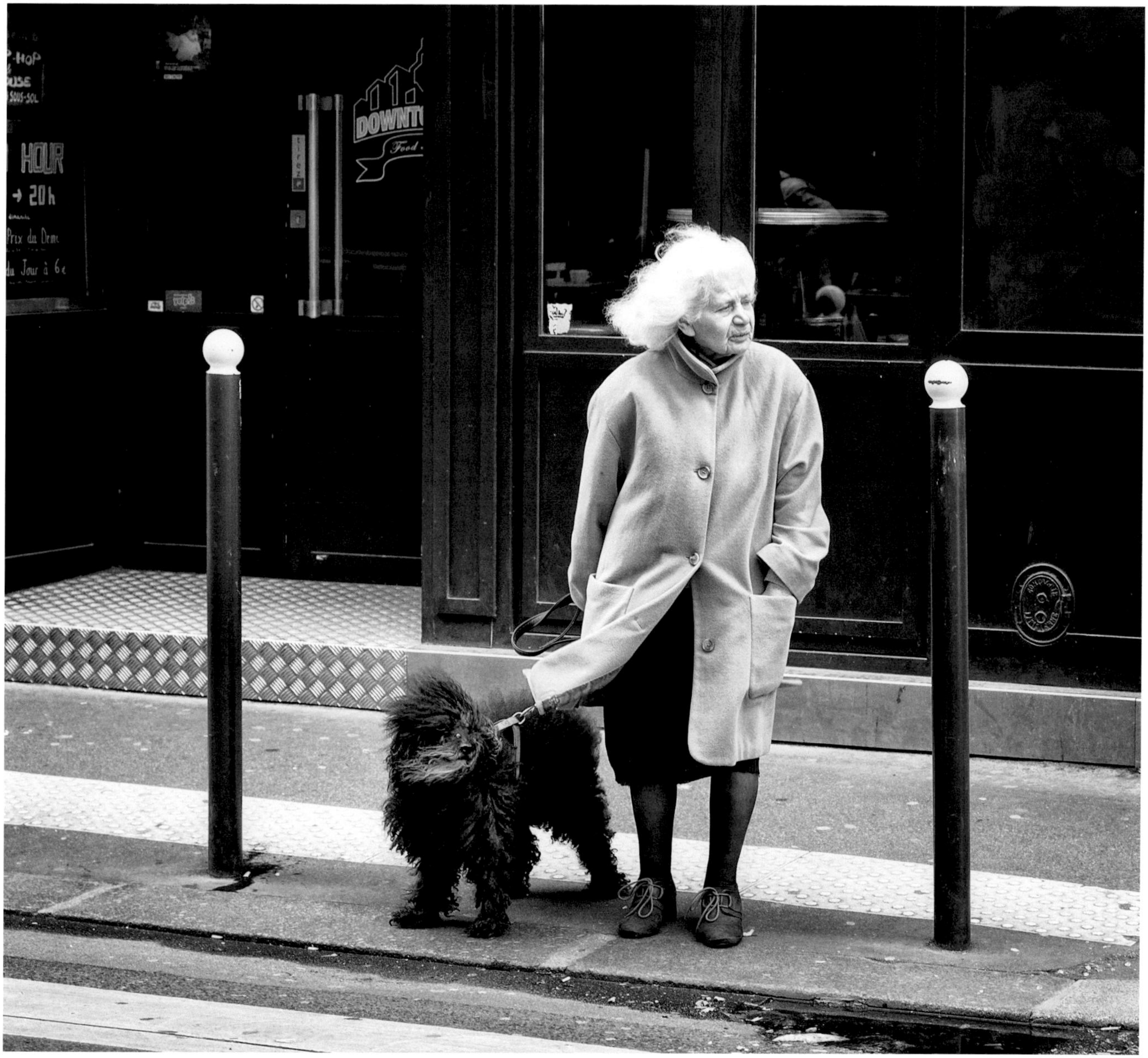

Windy day in Paris

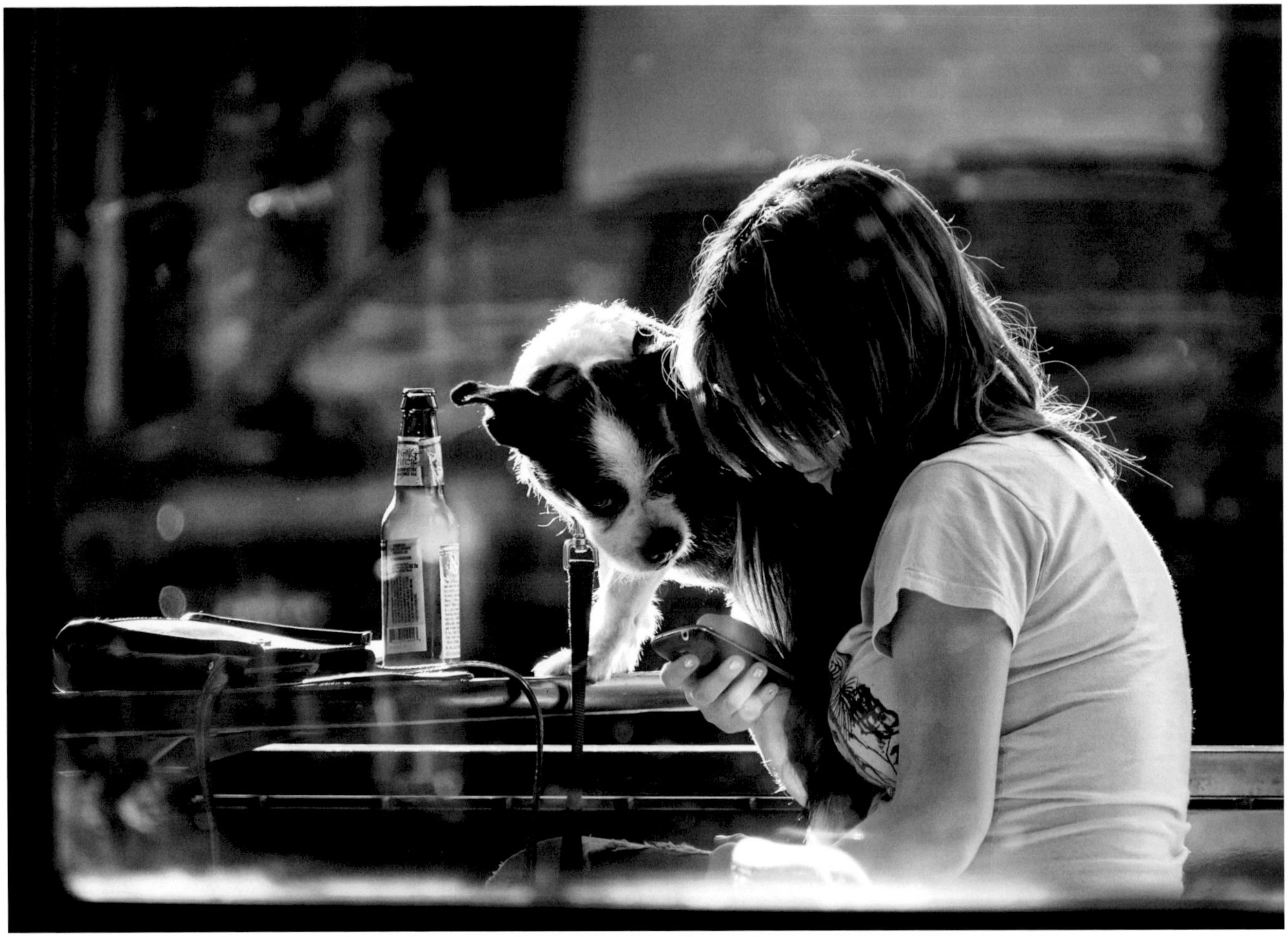

Confidants

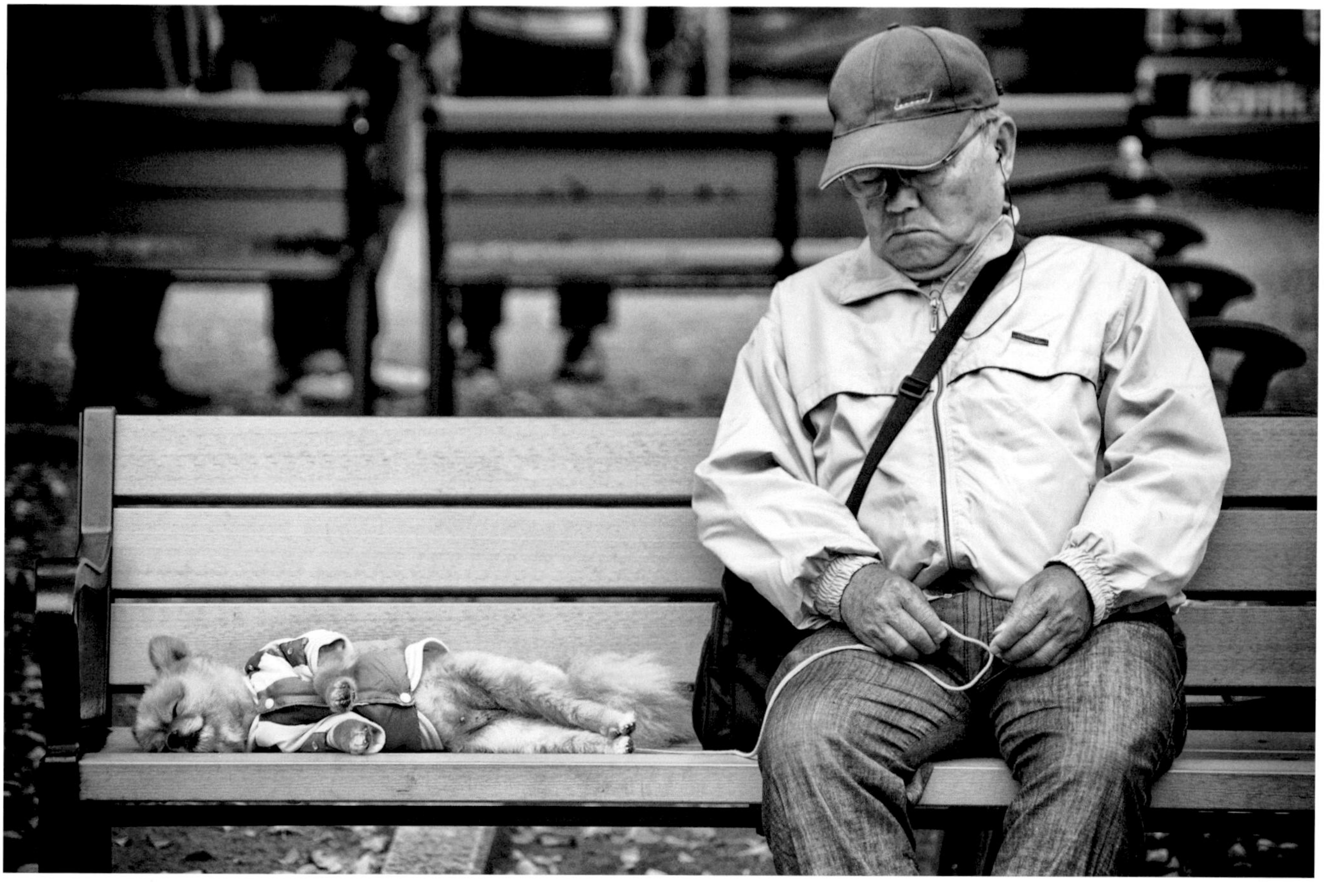

Inemuri - Japanese siesta

New York Winter

by Paul Elliott

www.paulelliottphotography.com • moviemagic1@icloud.com

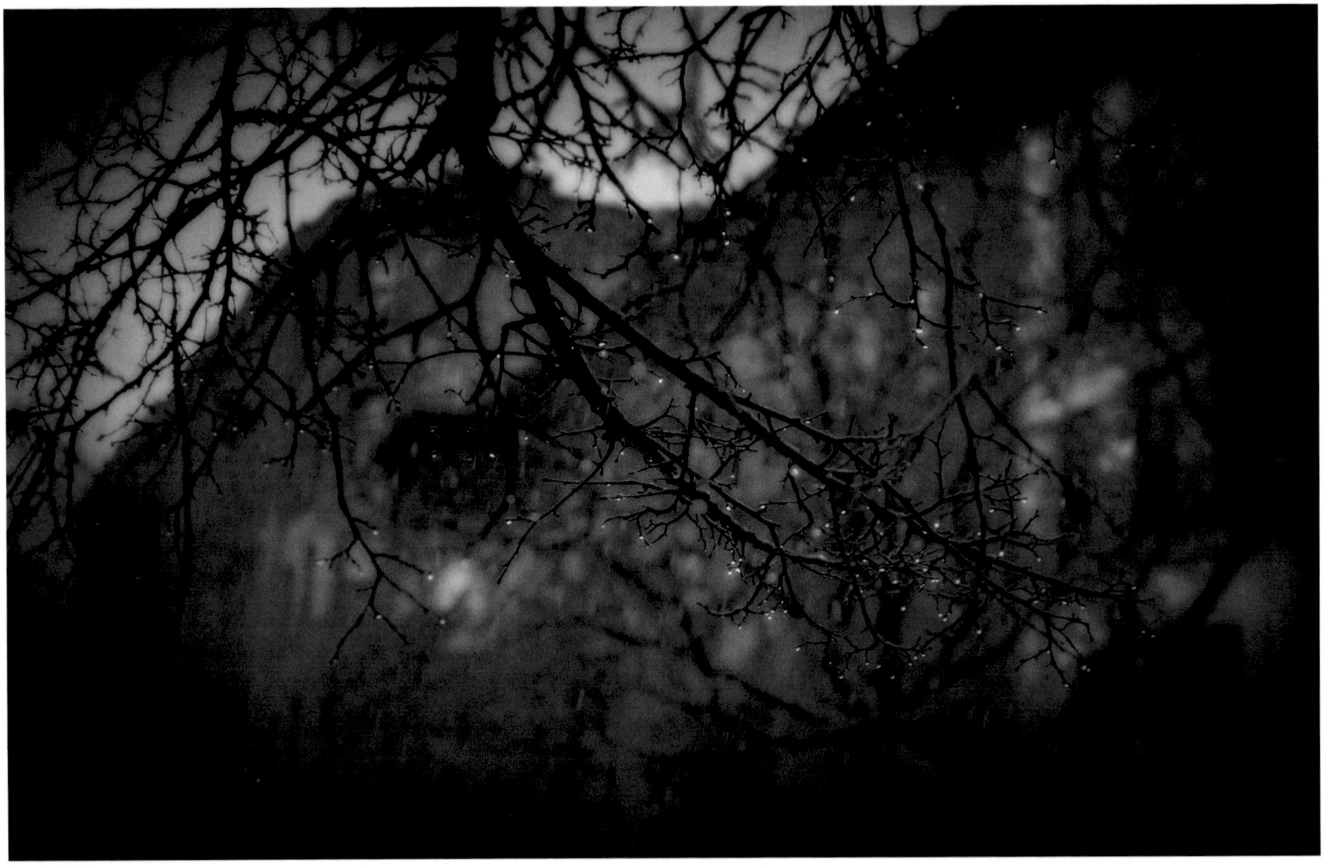

After wandering through Central Park taking these photographs after a heavy storm, I read that several large limbs had fallen from trees and had in fact killed someone waiting at a bus stop.

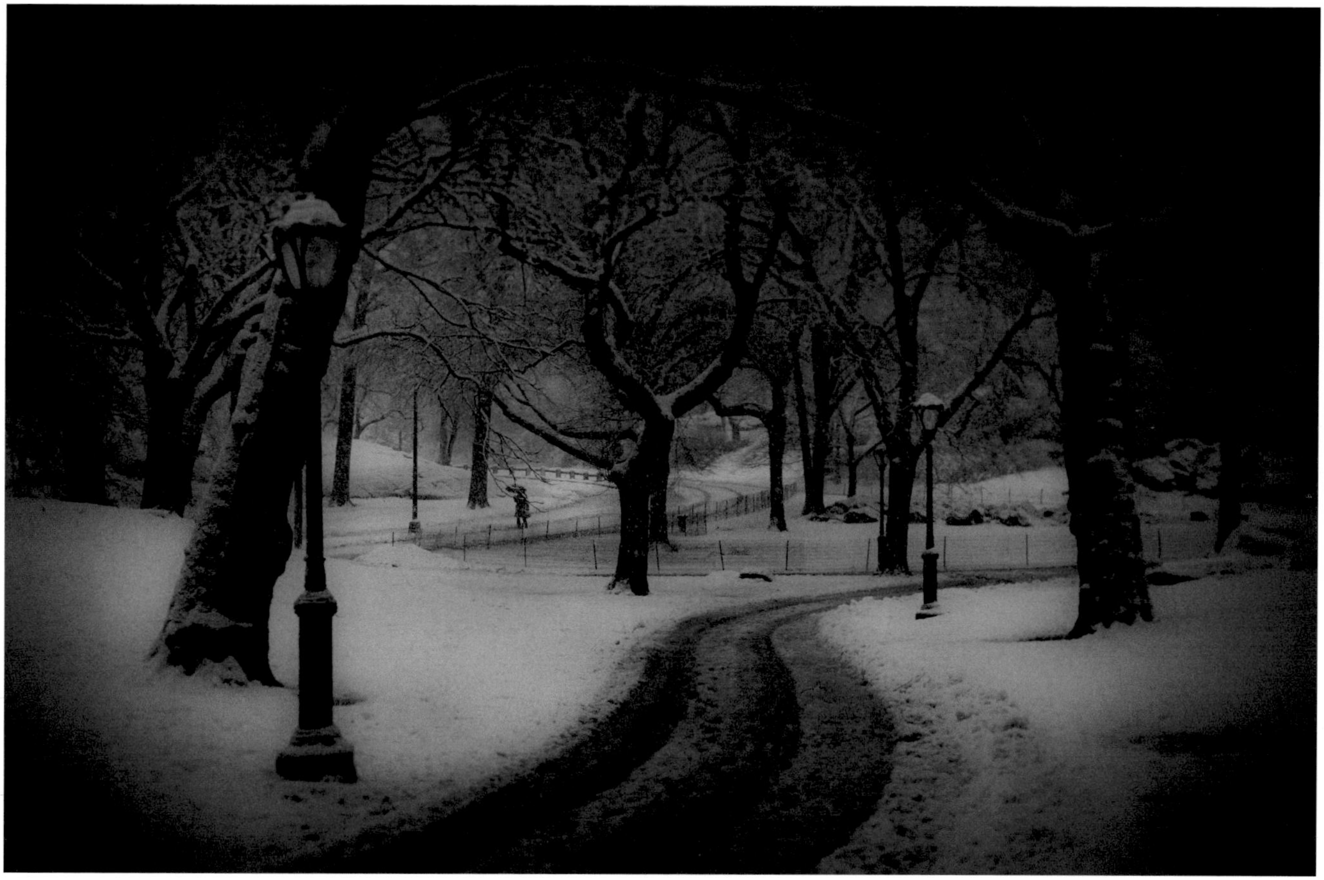

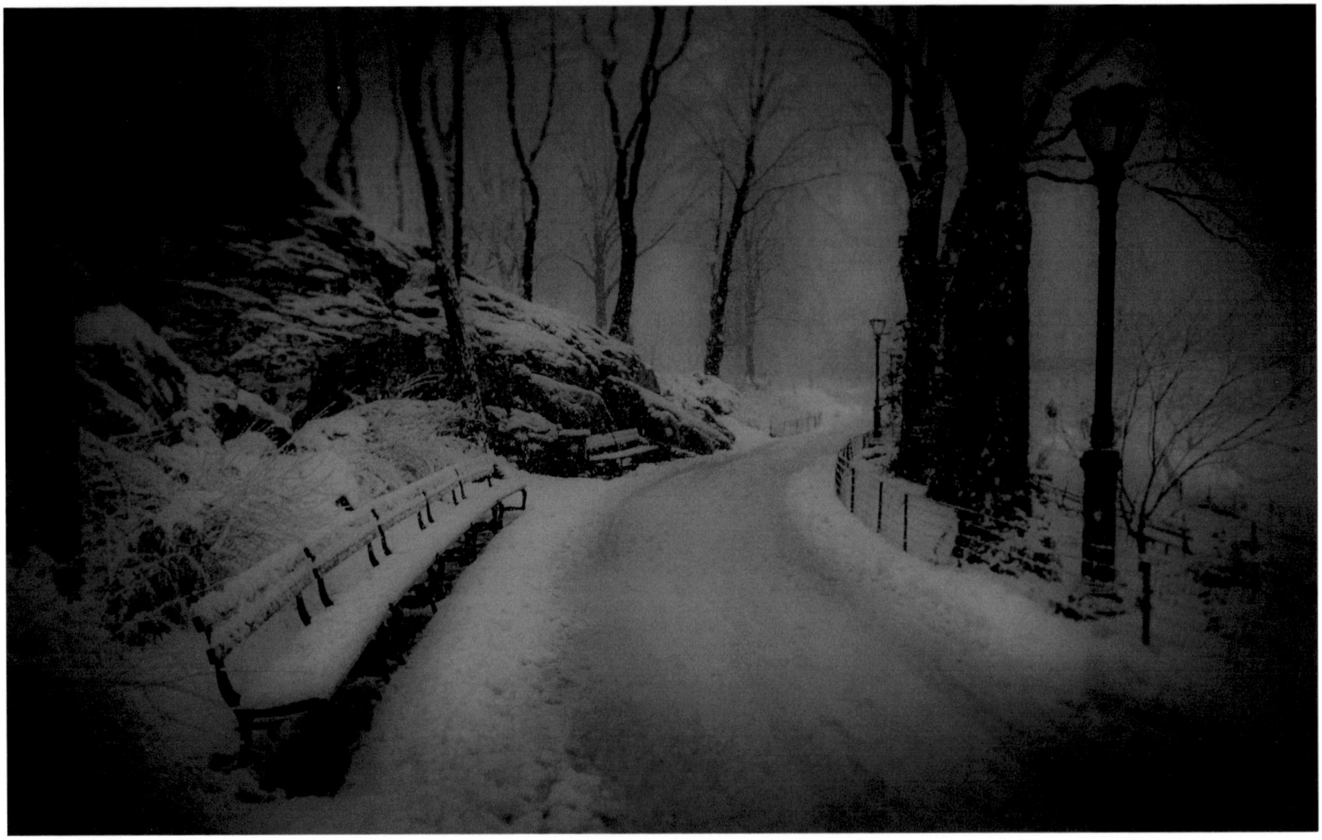

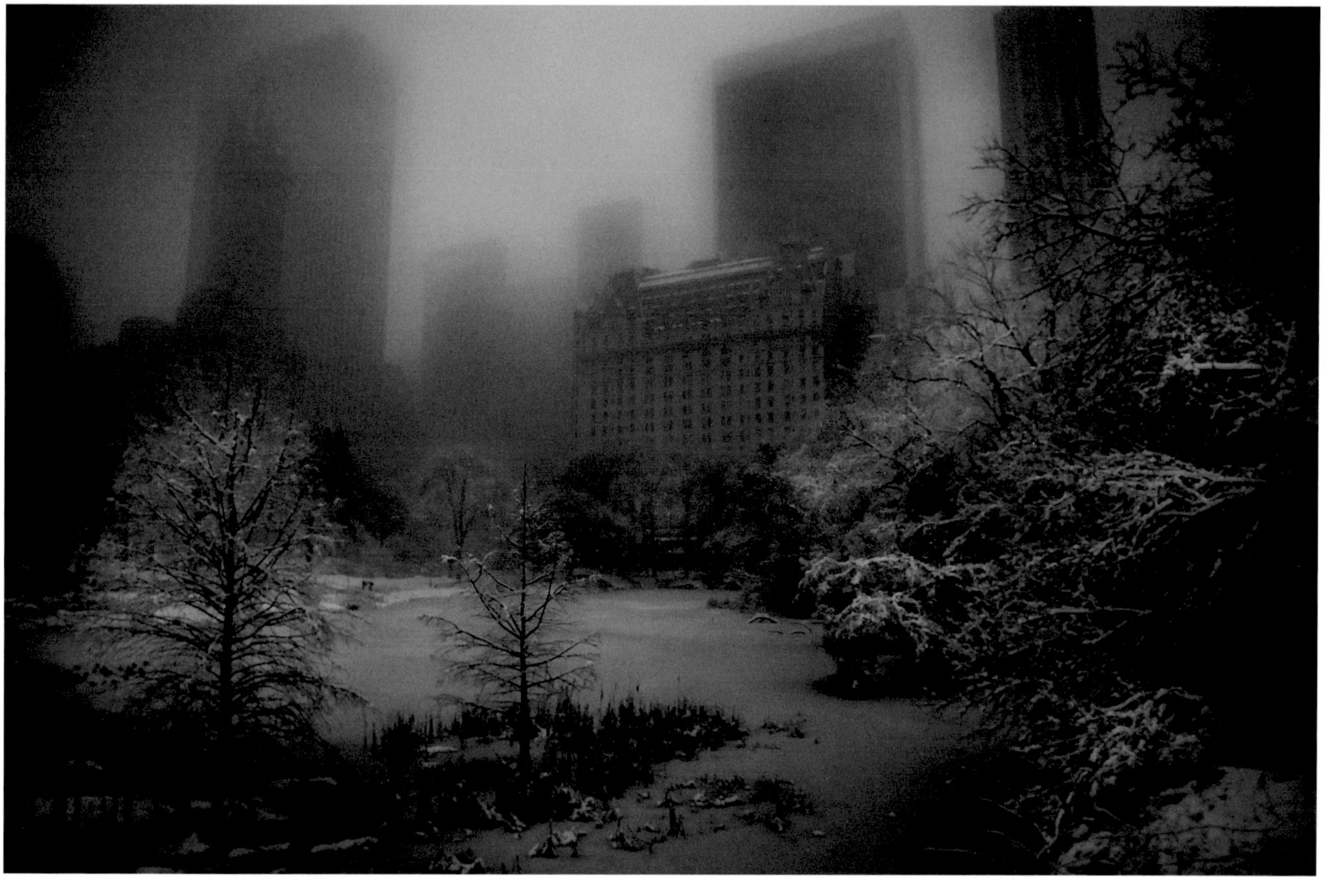

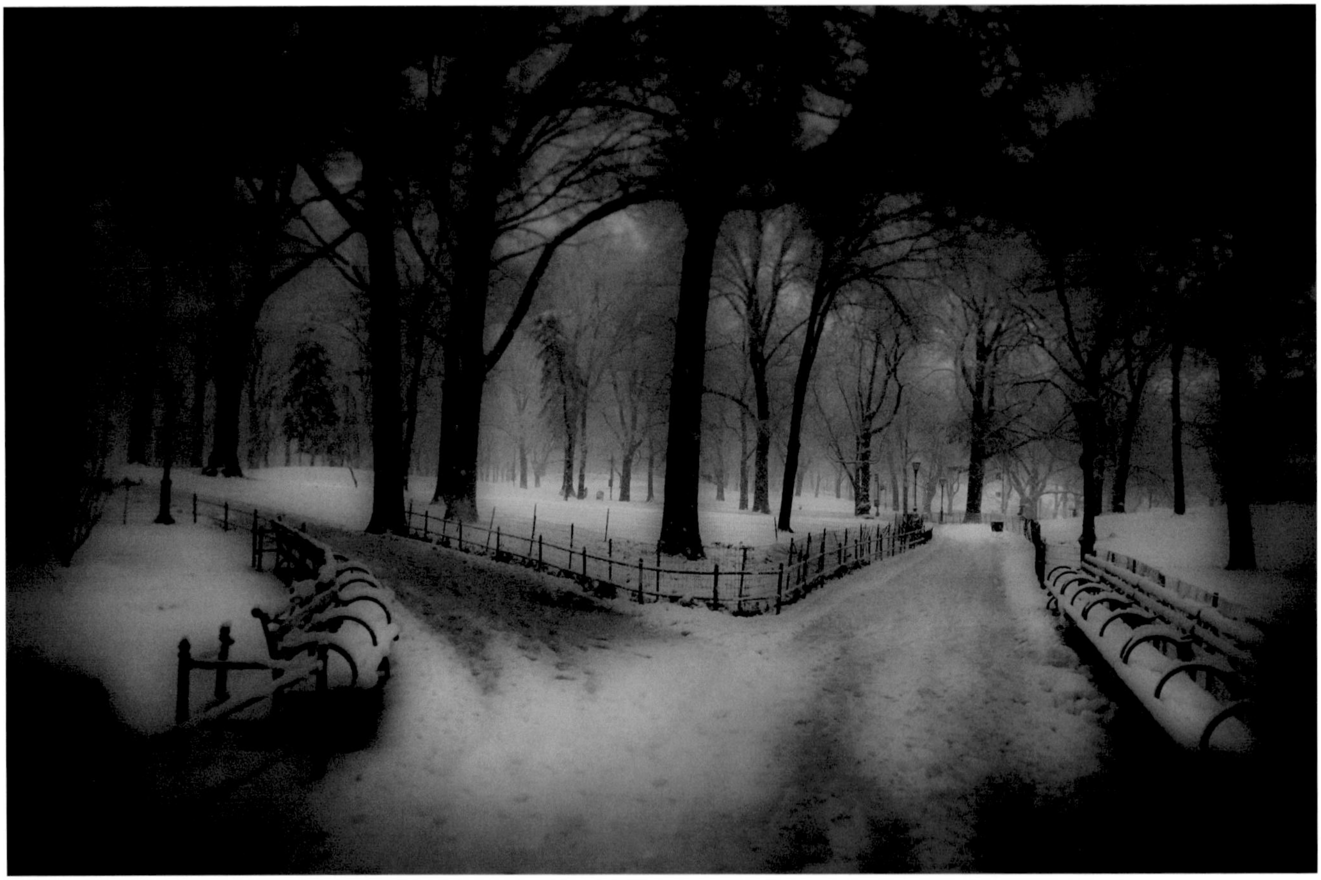

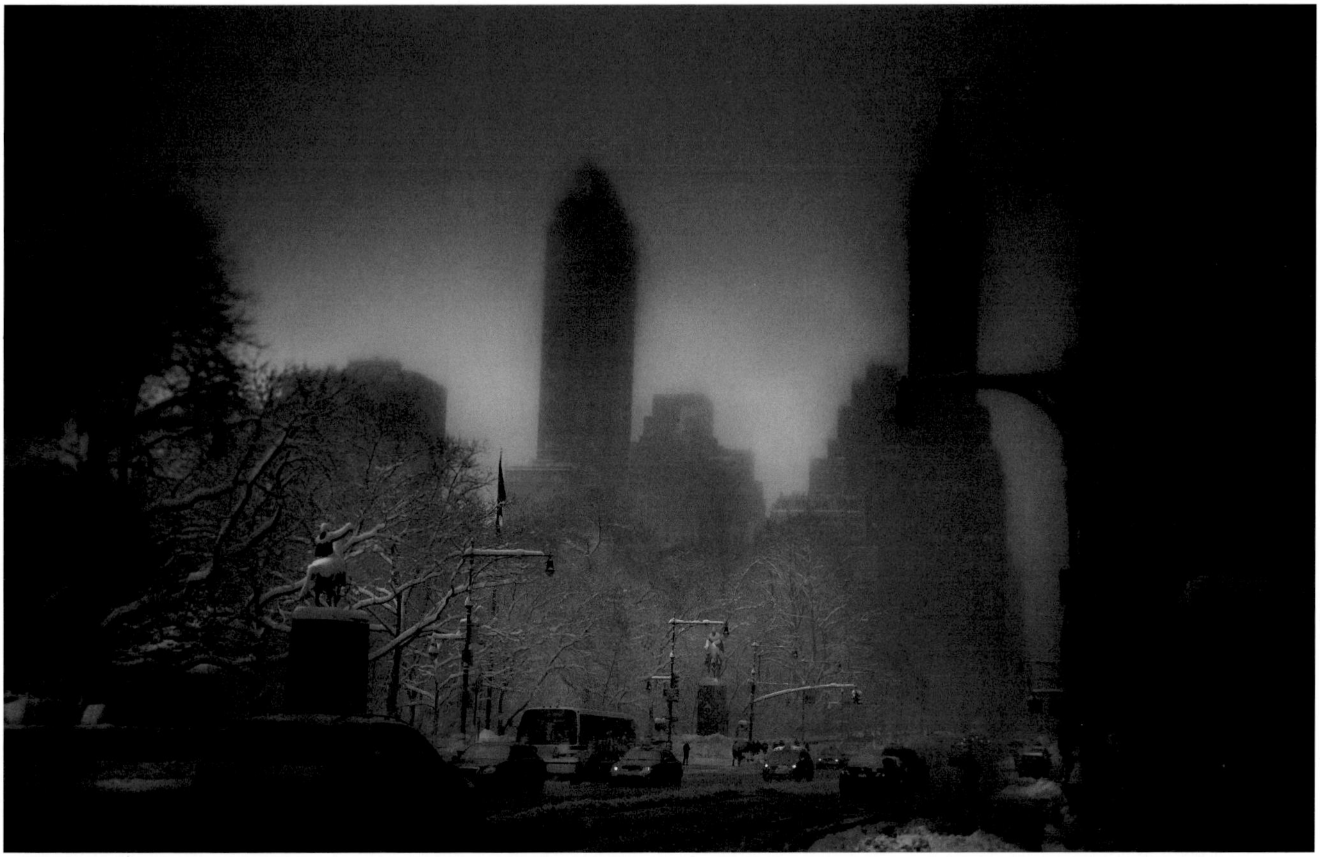

Sky Is the Limit

by Moises Levy

moiseslevy.com • moises.levy@gmail.com

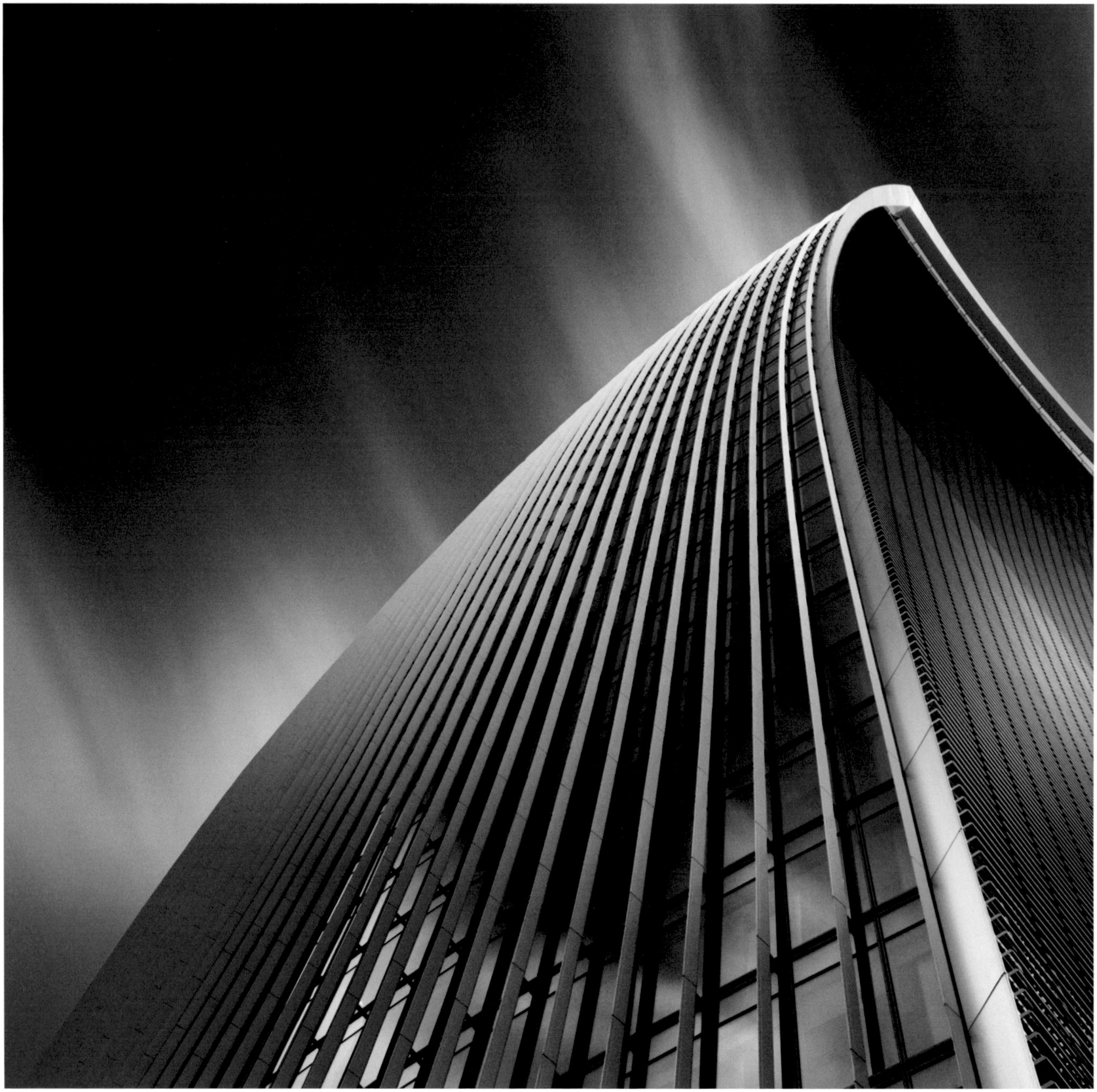

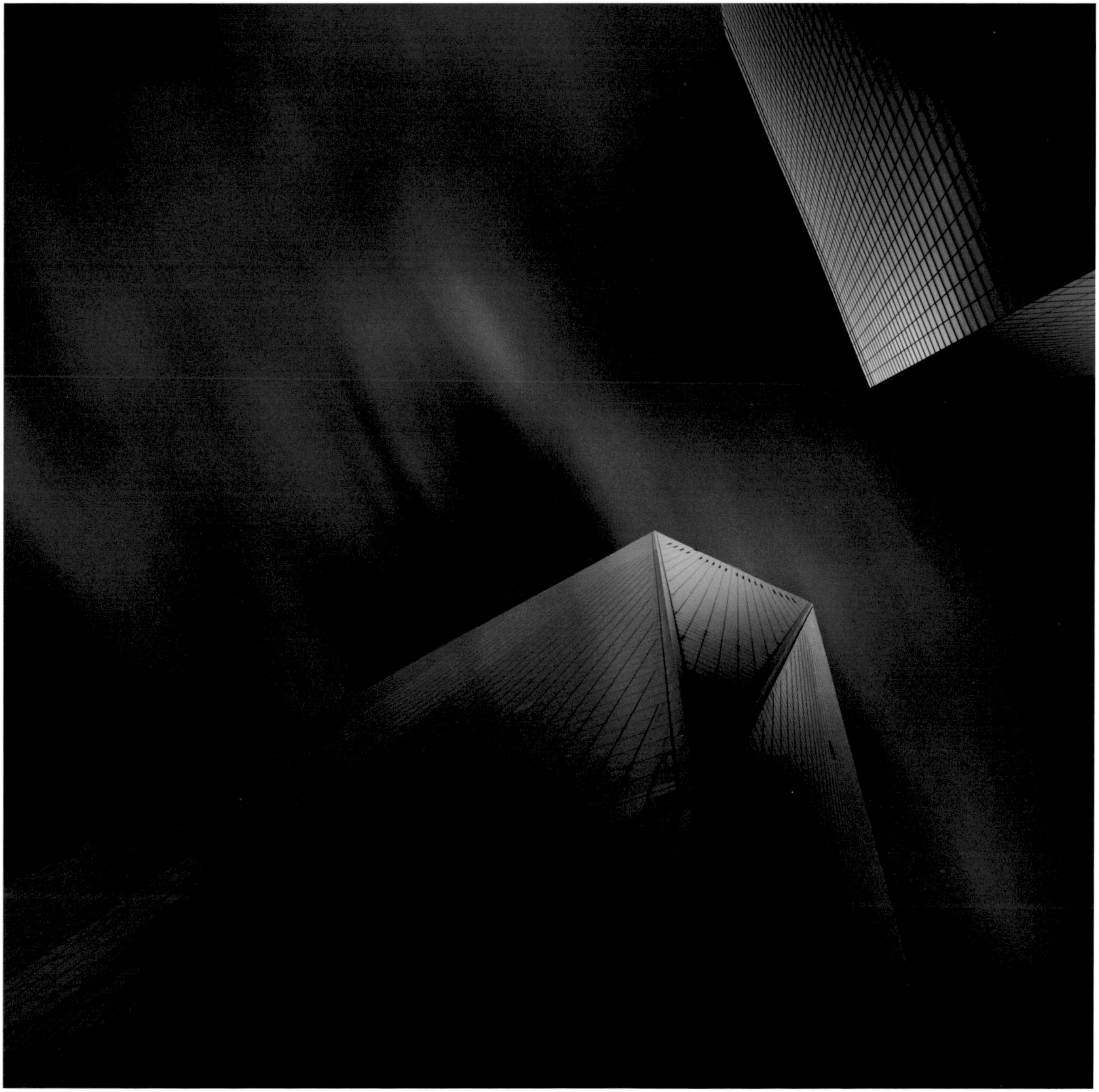

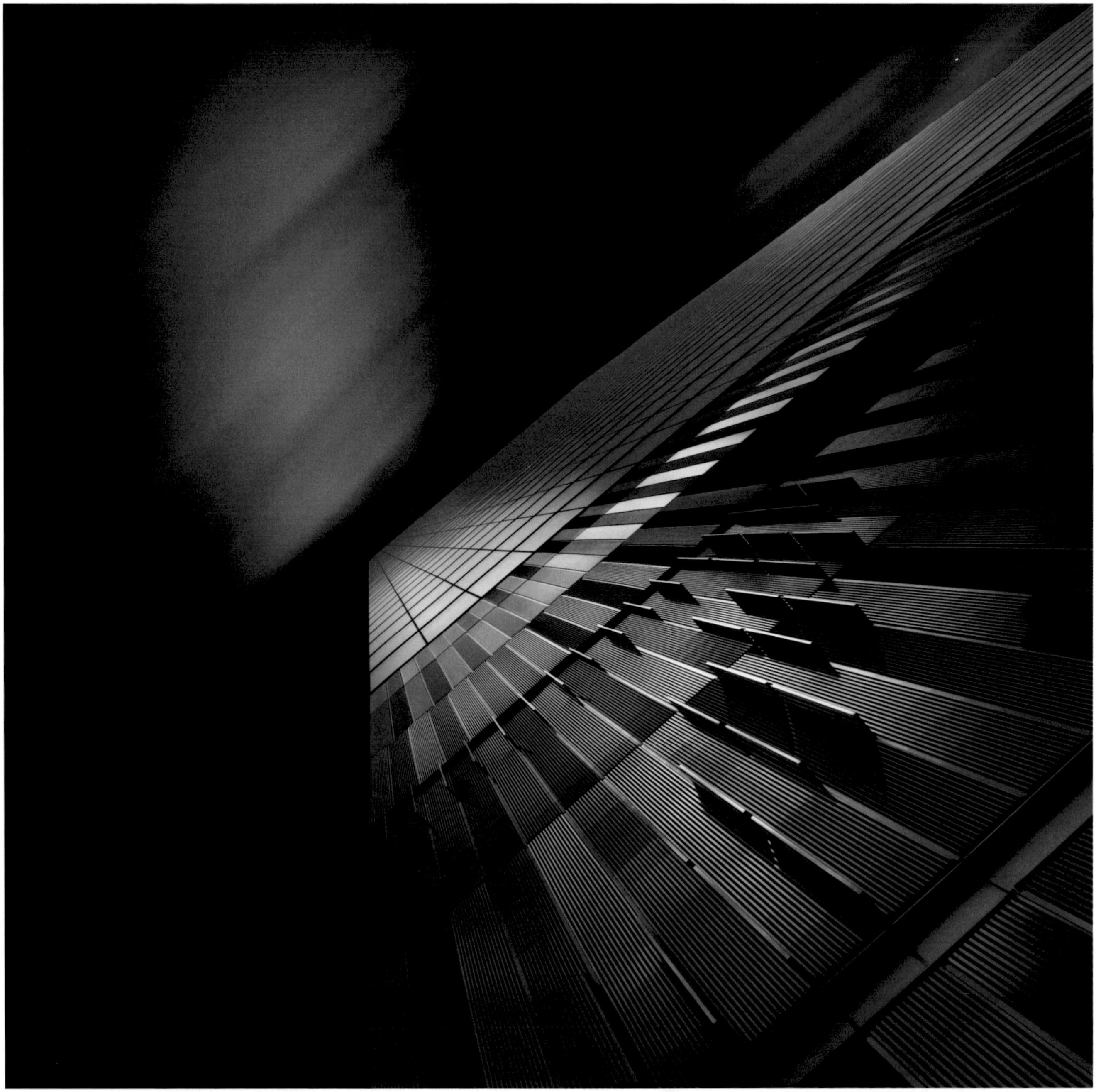

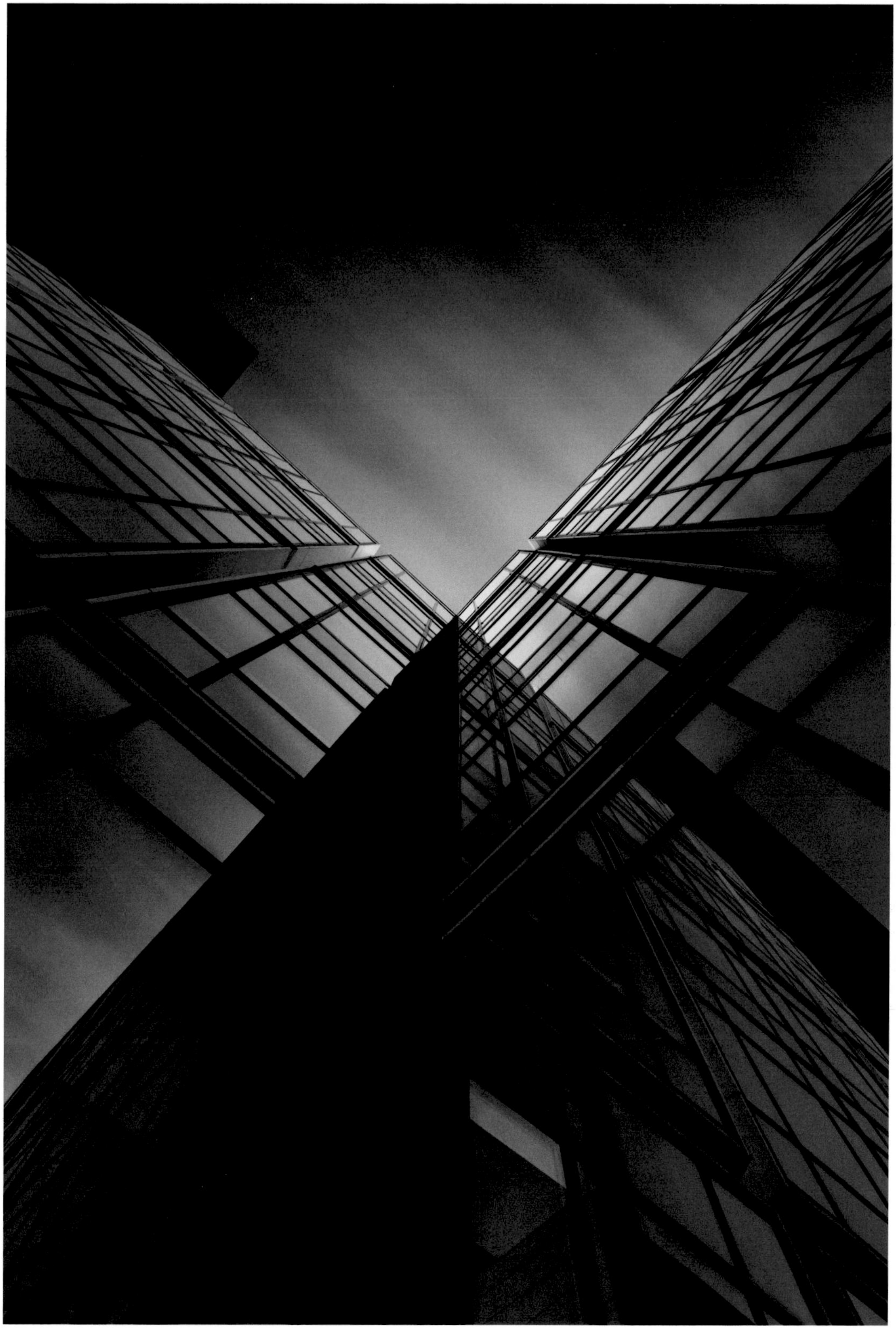

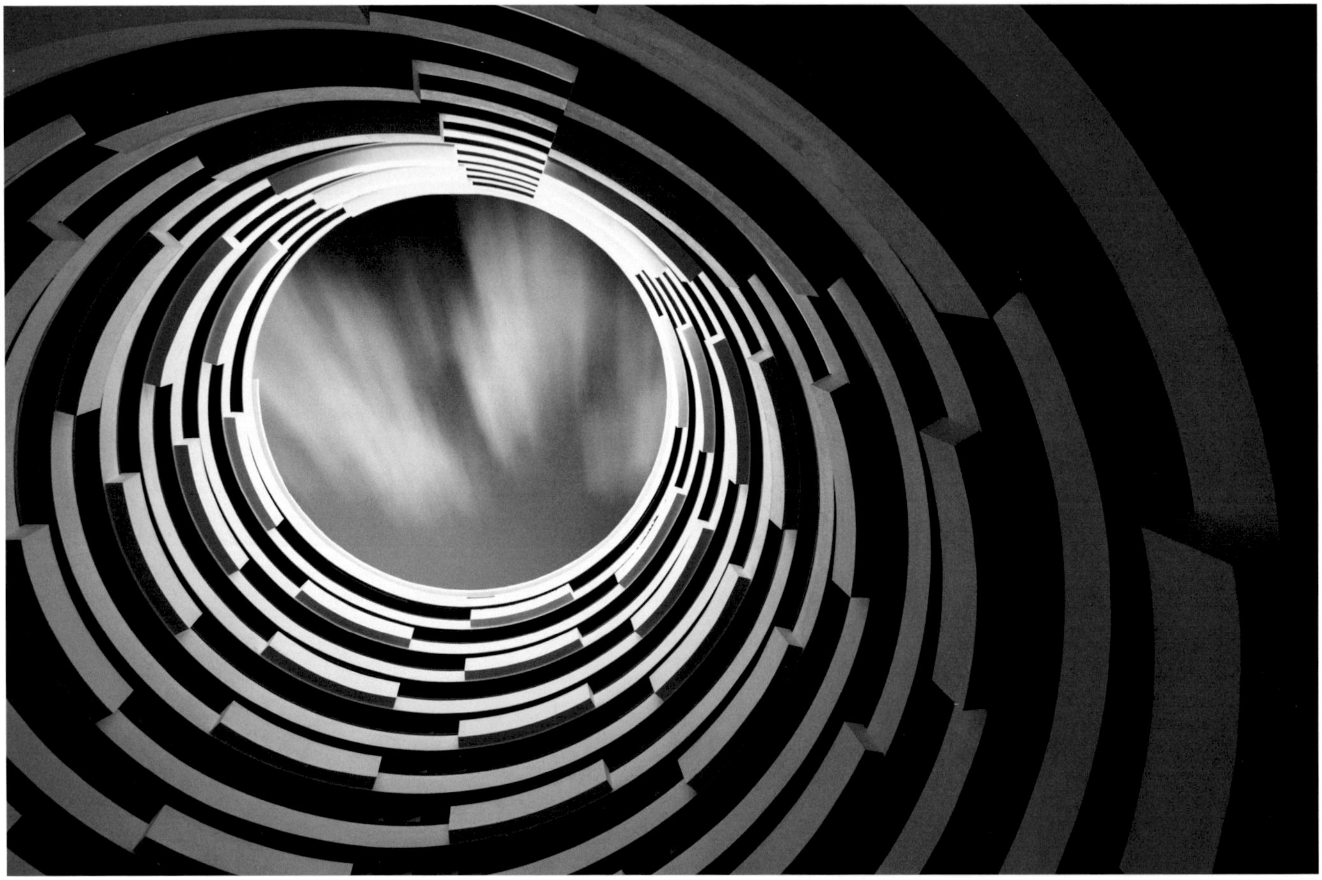

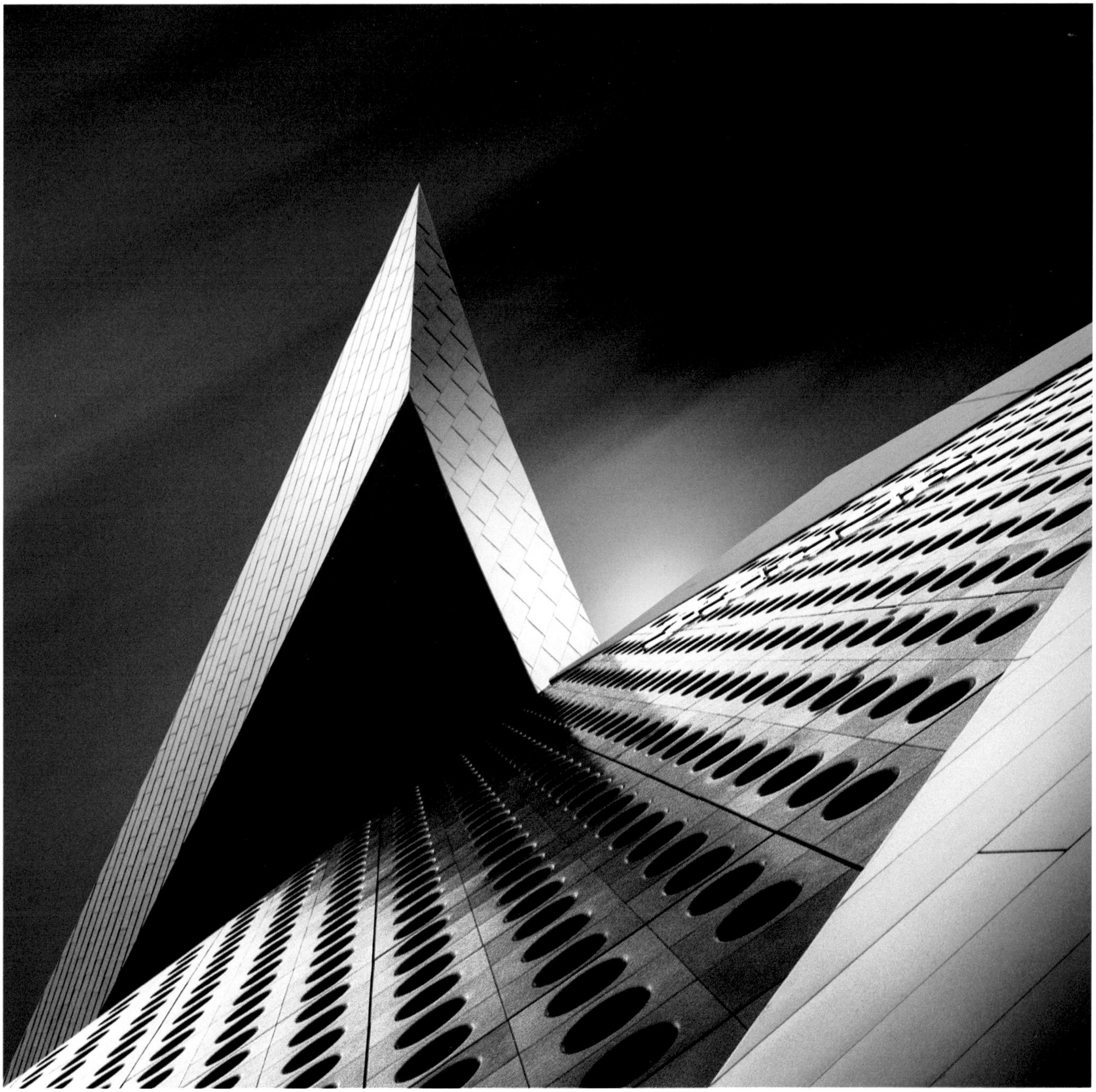

The Circle, The Sphere, The Sacred

by Richard Murai

www.richardmurai.com ♦ rmurai@sbcglobal.net

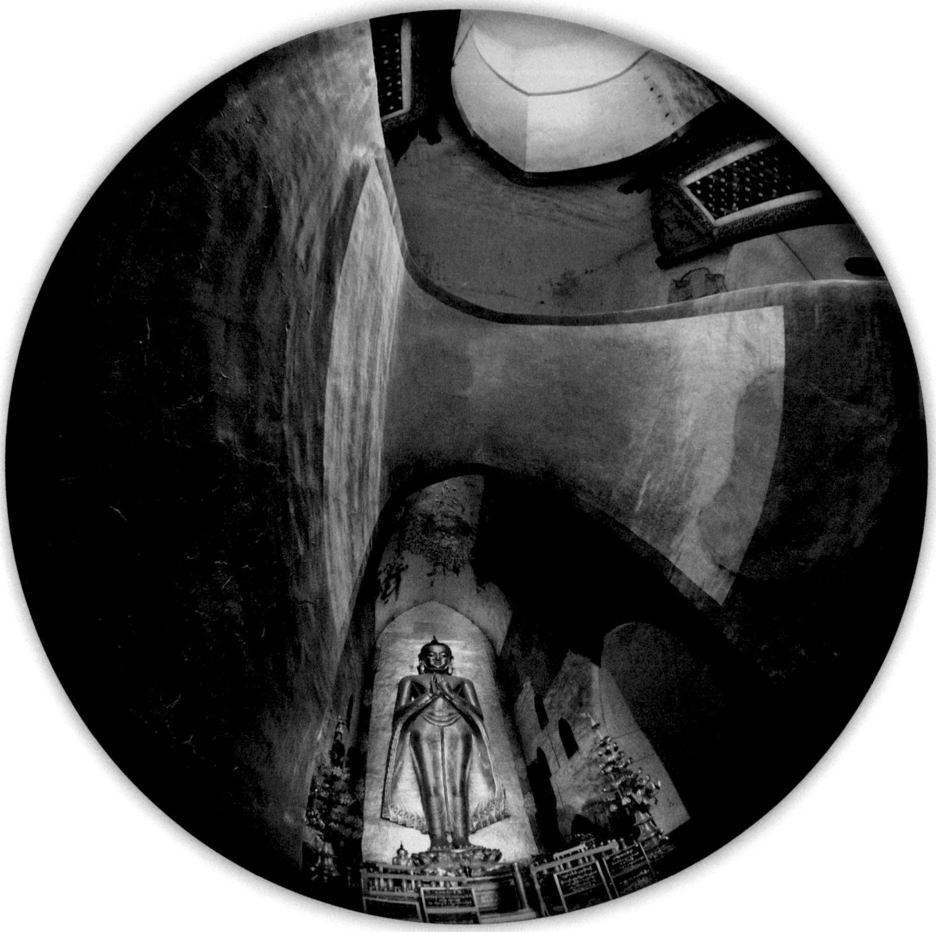

Ananda Temple, Bagan, Myanmar 2016

The sphere or circle is a symbol that transcends time and is ubiquitous to all ancient religions and cultures. Its harmonious shape has no beginning or end and can symbolize unity, protection, eternity, and harmony. The Tibetan mandala, the megalithic stone circles in Great Britain, and the Native American medicine wheels and sweat lodges are synonymous with sacred or consecrated space. The Buddhist practice of circumnambulation (the repeated clock-wise procession around a sacred shrine) bestows blessings and good fortune and affirms the meditative and healing power of the circle.

The use of circular images allows fresh inquiry into familiar locations and augments my investigation of sacred spaces. The all encompassing 220° field of view and tremendous depth of field offer voluminous information and challenges traditional compositional tenets while encouraging spontaneity.

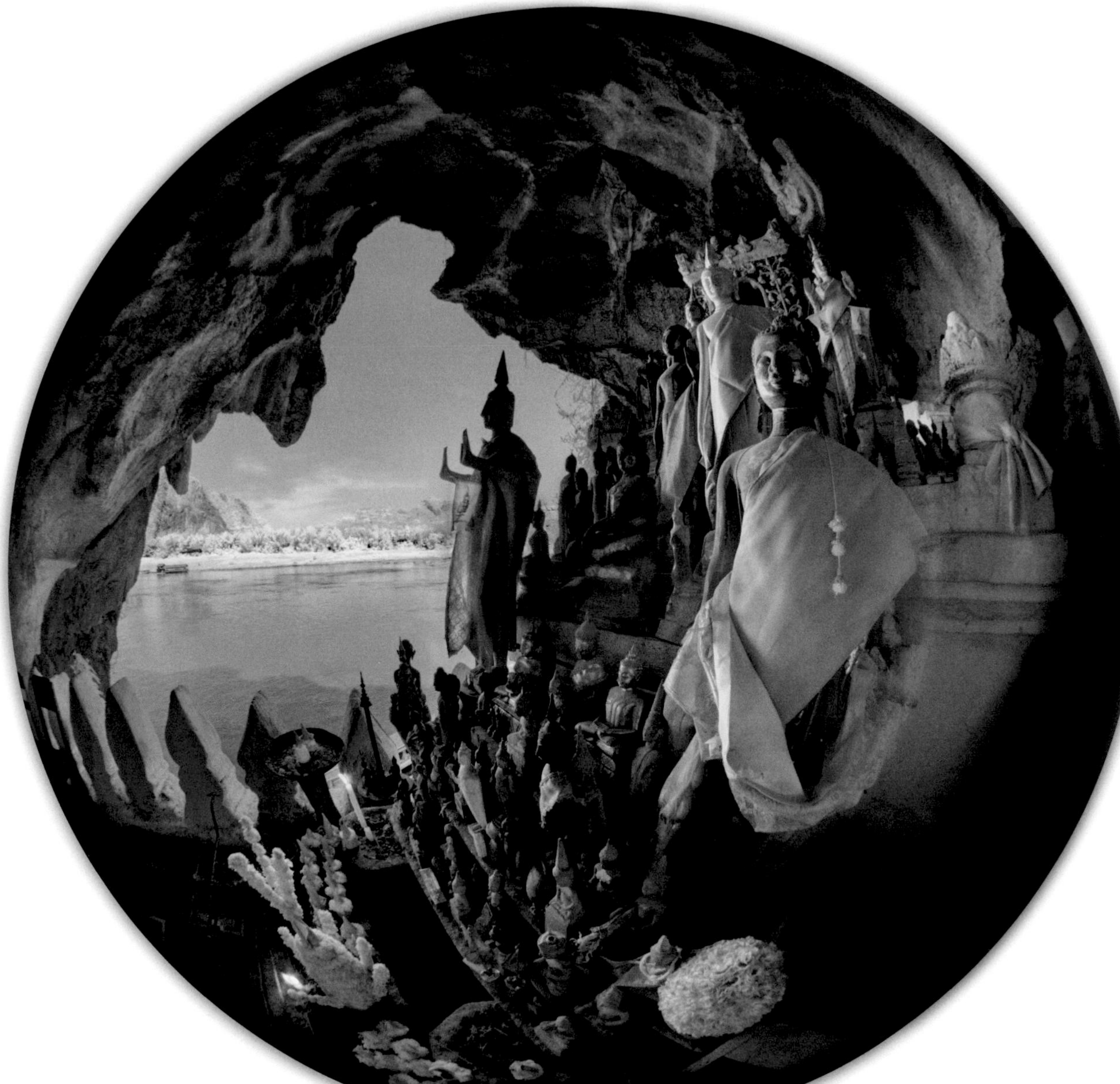

Pak Ou Caves Interior and Mekong River
Luang Prabang, Laos 2016

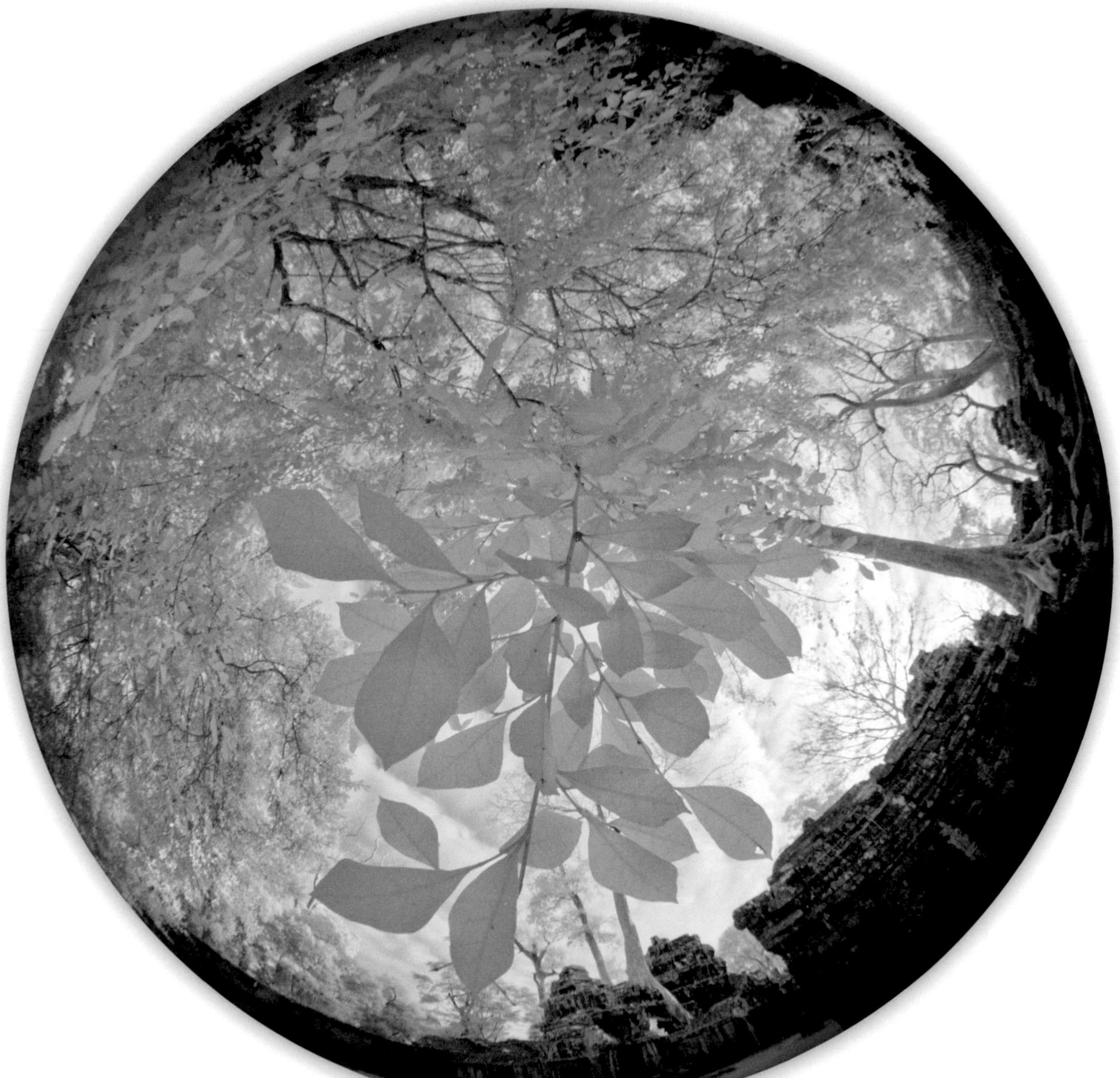

Ficus Leaves, Preah Khan
Angkor Thom, Cambodia 2016

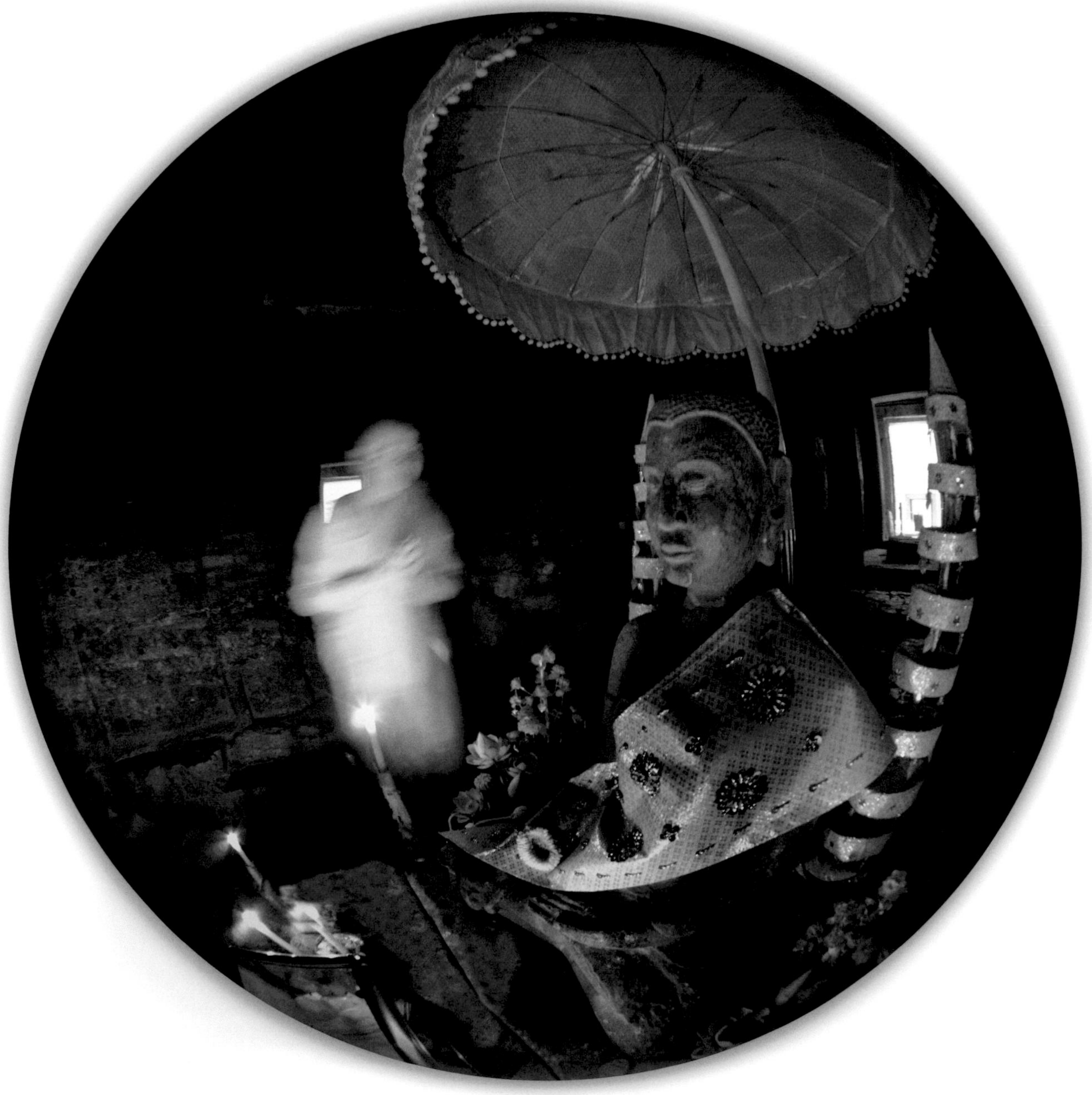

Altar Interior, The Bayon
Angkor Thom, Cambodia 2016

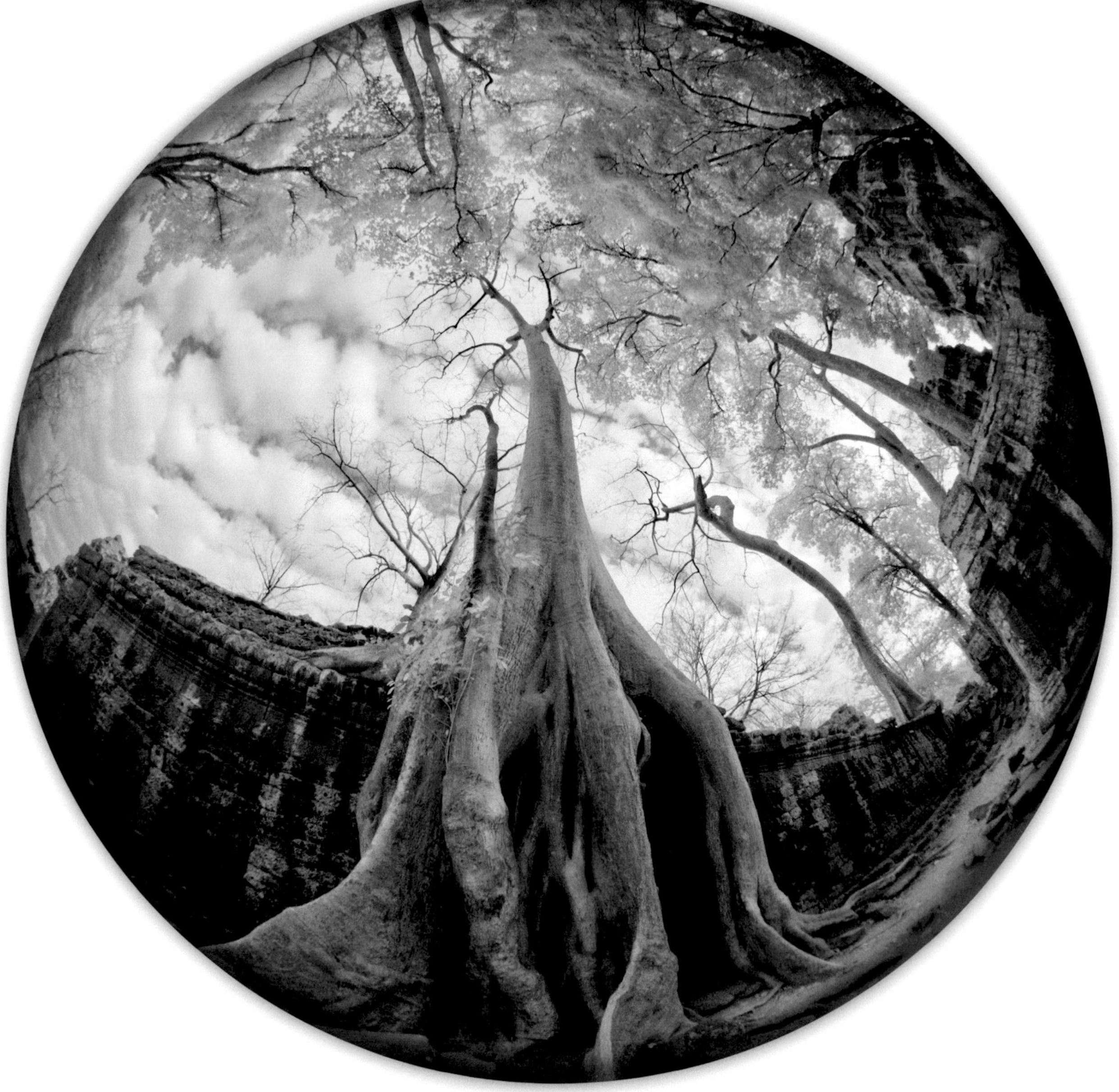

Strangler Fig, Ta Prohm
Angkor Thom, Cambodia 2016

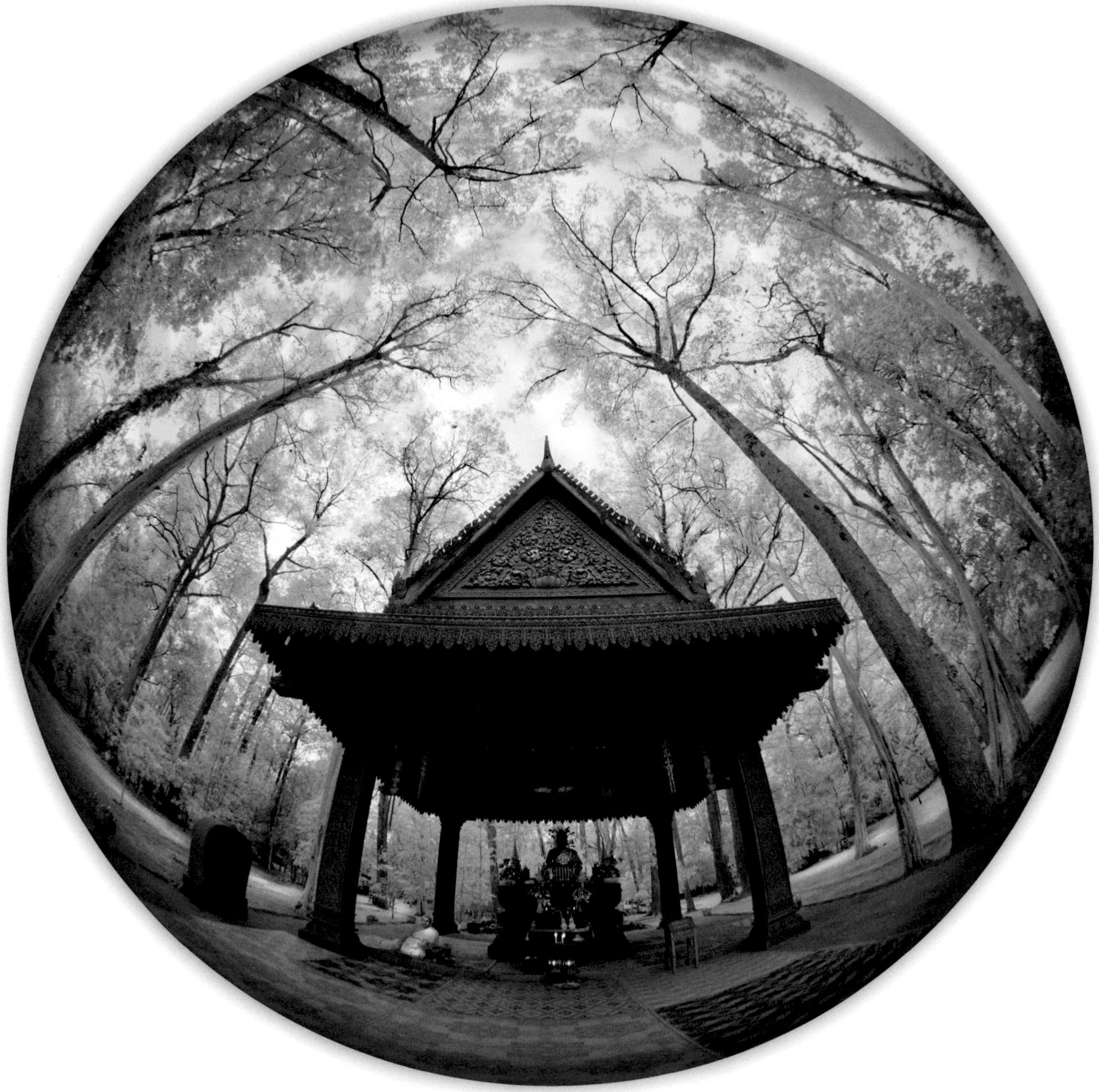

Roadside Temple
Angkor Thom, Cambodia 2016

Copyright © 2016 LensWork Publishing

All rights reserved.
No part of this book may be reproduced in any form or by any electronic or mechanical means, including information storage and retrieval systems, without written permission in writing from the author, except by a reviewer, who may quote brief passages in a review.

First Edition, First Printing August 2016

ISBN # 978-0-9904681-1-0

Published by LensWork Publishing, 1004 Commercial PMB588, Anacortes, WA, 98221 USA

www.lenswork.com

To order quantities at discount pricing, please call 1-800-659-2130

Printed in Canada